Life Studies

AN ANALYTIC READER

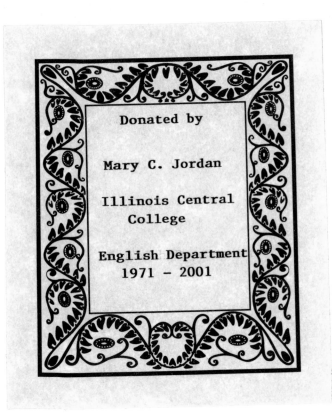

Life Studies

An Analytic Reader

SIXTH EDITION

EDITED BY

David Cavitch
Tufts University

Bedford Books ≋ BOSTON

For Bedford Books

President and Publisher: Charles H. Christensen
General Manager and Associate Publisher: Joan E. Feinberg
Managing Editor: Elizabeth M. Schaaf
Developmental Editor: Joanne Diaz
Editorial Assistant: Katherine Gilbert
Production Editor: Bridget Leahy
Copyeditor: Rosemary Winfield
Text Design: Anna Post-George
Cover Design: Hannus Design Associates
Cover Art: Christopher Brown, *November 19, 1863*, 1989, oil on canvas. Collection of the Modern Art Museum of Fort Worth, Museum Purchase, The Burnett Foundation.
Composition: Stratford Publishing Services, Inc.
Printing and Binding: Haddon Craftsmen, Inc.

For information, write: Bedford Books, 75 Arlington Street, Boston, MA 02116
(617-426-7440)

ISBN: 0–312–15714–2

Acknowledgments

Diane Ackerman, "The Chemistry of Love" (editor's title). From *The Nature of Love* by Diane Ackerman. Copyright © 1994 by Diane Ackerman. Reprinted by permission of Random House, Inc.

Kurt Andersen, "Animation Nation," *The New Yorker*, June 16, 1997. Reprinted by permission; © 1997 The New Yorker Magazine, Inc. All rights reserved.

Ian Angell, "Winners and Losers in the Information Age." From *Society*, November/December 1996. Copyright © 1996 by Transaction Publishers; all rights reserved. Reprinted by permission of Transaction Publishers.

Maya Angelou, "Graduation." From *I Know Why the Caged Bird Sings* by Maya Angelou. Copyright © 1969 and renewed 1997 by Maya Angelou. Reprinted by permission of Random House, Inc.

Acknowledgments and copyrights are continued at the back of the book on pages 523–26, which constitute an extension of the copyright page. It is a violation of the law to reproduce these selections by any means whatsoever without the written permission of the copyright holder.

TO INSTRUCTORS

A critical step in teaching composition is to find good reading. *Life Studies* has been a popular reader chiefly because students like the selections. Students using the book avidly "read around" on their own initiative. They enjoy the readings, are moved by them, and are stimulated into thinking. They then strive to attain in their writing the interesting effects of the essays. The sixth edition strengthens an analytic approach to readings that deeply engage students' attention. An expanded editorial apparatus prompts students to examine how writers validate what they say. Questions about each author's purpose and methods encourage students to think critically about the essay's voice and meaning. Writing assignments suggest further ways to explain, analyze, or take a stand on matters raised by the selection. A revised Introduction gives students additional practical advice for reading and writing analytically.

We have added two new part topics to this edition. "Word Power" and "Work Rules" examine the tricky process of acquiring language abilities and qualifications for suitable employment. In addition, "Media Images" has been revised to reflect a wider range of mixed messages from the information as well as the entertainment media. Other parts have been recast in significant ways with the addition of many selections and new topics for writing. Of the seventy-two selections, forty-four are new to this edition, and twenty-three of these new pieces have never before appeared in a composition reader.

Although the revisions are pervasive, *Life Studies* maintains its distinctive organization into topics that are truly significant to students. The organization of the book into nine thematic parts follows the progression of experience from personal to general awareness. The topics address our self-images; our family relationships; our love for people outside the family; our identification with ethnic or racial groups; our acquisition of verbal, critical intelligence; our compromising or fulfilling work roles; our connection to valued possessions; our cultural images reflected by films, magazines, and computer screens; and our dilemmas over moral issues that cannot be sidestepped. Each part opens with a number of Insights—succinct, often controversial statements by well-known writers whose colloquy of opinions offer a lively introduction to the theme. Each group of Insights includes a poem expressing a strongly personal viewpoint related to the theme. The longer works that follow include contemporary essays, memoirs, social criticism, documented essays, and reportage. Their authors provide diverse perspectives—including those of the journalist, sociologist, screenwriter, philosopher, and satirist, among others—and represent a broad range of ethnic and cultural backgrounds. In addition to the essays, each part contains one short story that develops the theme imaginatively.

Each part of *Life Studies* opens with Focusing by Writing, warm-up questions that can be used for in-class writing exercises or to generate class discussion. The Focusing topics are framed to show students that they—like the authors of the Insights—possess knowledge and opinions about the topics in the chapter. The questions raise students' awareness of the issues and underscore the significance of their own experience. Instructors may wish to use some Focusing topics for longer writing assignments as well.

Preceding each selection is a biographical and introductory headnote. Each selection is then followed by three categories of questions that promote analytic reading and writing. The Analyzing This Selection questions encourage students to consider the reading's content and meaning as well as the writer's methods and approaches. A new question in this section called The Writer's Method asks students to focus on effective writing strategies and apply what they learn to their own writing. Next, the Analyzing Connections questions ask students to connect, integrate, and analyze the reading with earlier material. (Because many instructors flexibly assign their own order of readings, other links are suggested in the instructor's manual, *Resources for Teaching Life Studies*, coauthored by Debra Spark. But as a model for students, a pattern of progressive, expansive reflectiveness is built into the book itself.) Finally, Analyzing by Writing offers a topic and suggests possible approaches to developing clear and convincing views.

To help students acquire composition techniques, the book opens with an Introduction that stresses attentive, critical reading as a means to improving writing. "Finding a Trail: An Introduction to Reading and Writing Analytically" offers guidelines and methods for improving reading comprehension. This Introduction is built around an essay that is admired by most instructors, E. B. White's "Once More to the Lake," which is annotated to suggest how a student might respond to it during a close reading. A brief discussion of White's essay shows students how to pursue their observations and develop them into insightful viewpoints. The Introduction includes advice that identifies and illustrates common writing problems.

A rhetorical index to the selections appears in the back of the book, and *Resources for Teaching Life Studies* offers suggestions for dealing with each piece in class. The instructor's manual also offers further writing suggestions.

Many instructors helped improve this book by responding to a questionnaire about the fifth edition. I am grateful for the careful consideration given by Lee Ames, Oklahoma State University; Regina Blackburn, Seton Hall University; Richard E. Cunningham, Keene State College; Paul J. de Gategno, North Carolina Wesleyan College; S. A. Eisenstein, Los Angeles

Community College; Don Foran, Centralia College; Carol A. Galbus, Winona State University; Robert A. Hagstrom, Jamestown Community College; Gloria Johnson, University of Massachusetts at Lowell; Daphne Kalotay, Portland Community College; David Levee, Broome Community College; Marjorie Maddox, Lock Haven University; Carol G. McKenzie, California State University at Los Angeles; Gretchen Papazian, University of Wisconsin at Milwaukee; Angela Peckenpaugh, University of Wisconsin at Whitewater; Margaret Pobywajlo, University of New Hampshire at Manchester; Mary Lea Pratt, Cañada College; Pamela Smith, Cañada College; Johnnie Spraggins, Madonna University; Melanie J. Springer, Oklahoma State University; Jan Swafford, Tufts University; Marion Wilson, Winthrop University; and Jean Zipke, University of New Hampshire at Manchester.

Friends and colleagues made helpful suggestions. I am grateful for contributions from Sylvan Barnet, John Fyler, and Morse Hamilton. The exceptionally capable people at Bedford Books provided much assistance. Joanne Diaz skillfully guided the development of this edition. Many new items and revised features reflect her unstinting collaboration and excellent judgment. Katherine Gilbert ably assisted with research, and Leasa Burton edited the instructor's manual, *Resources for Teaching Life Studies*, skillfully prepared by Debra Spark. Carolyn Woznick cleared permissions, and Rosemary Winfield copyedited the manuscript with a light and skillful touch. Bridget Leahy ably piloted the book through production, and Elizabeth Schaaf carefully managed the production process. Once again, Charles Christensen and Joan Feinberg gave their imaginative vision and high standards to the entire endeavor.

CONTENTS

4. GROUP PICTURES   171

5. WORD POWER   237

Joan Didion   ON KEEPING A NOTEBOOK   243

Considering "bits of the mind's string" that she finds in her journal, this writer traces what the details mean to her and how she has used them in her life and work.

Helen Vendler   KNOWING POEMS   250

A prominent literary critic credits the Psalms with giving voice to her feelings of despair and anger in adolescence.

Deborah Tannen   TALKING UP CLOSE   255

The act of arguing does not always signal disagreement, according to this well-known linguist and author.

Pico Iyer   IN PRAISE OF THE HUMBLE COMMA   260

A writer cleverly suggests that commas have a life force of their own; like the gods, they "give breath, and they take it away."

Susanne K. Langer   LANGUAGE AND THOUGHT   263

The ability to symbolize, says this influential American philosopher, frees human thought from the physical world and distinguishes us from animals.

Robert J. Sternberg   WHAT SHOULD WE ASK ABOUT
INTELLIGENCE?   269

Standard intelligence tests ask the wrong questions, according to this psychologist. Here he puts forth his own criteria for measuring intelligence.

George Steiner   BOOKS AND THE END OF LITERATURE   274

Will current technology make books obsolete? A prominent literary scholar considers the question.

7. POSSESSIONS   361

8. MEDIA IMAGES   411

9. DILEMMAS   467

Life Studies

AN ANALYTIC READER

FINDING A TRAIL

An Introduction to Reading
and Writing Analytically

Good readers become good writers. And every attentive response to good reading stimulates new possibilities of improvement in our writing.

Reading is the most important, and the most pleasurable, training for writers. From essays, fiction, and poetry we acquire a vastly increased vocabulary of knowledge and an array of models for more expressive, analytical ways of thinking about our world and ourselves. From reading we take in special verbal tools and methods that we use in writing. But we can't just swallow words and digest the meanings and uses of them. We have to become active intellectually and imaginatively in order to read with clear perception and firm emotional response. This introduction offers some practical advice on how to read and write more *analytically*, an approach explained in the next paragraph. The particular suggestions will prove effective as you practice them again and again. Like playing the piano, reading and writing are acquired abilities that no one is born with. But as we become good at what we're doing, the pleasure of doing it grows deeper and richer.

The literary meaning of *analysis* is to examine the parts and details of a piece of writing in order to explain their function and effects when all the parts work together. The basic premise of analysis is that style and form work together with ideas and emotions. The analytic reader clarifies what an author says by taking note of matters such as particular words, figures of speech, sentence structures, and links between sentences, paragraph development, the order of paragraphs, the structure of the piece as a whole, and the author's explicit and implicit attitudes — called *tone* — toward the subject and toward the reader.

That's a lot of parts and details to analyze. To keep track of them, a reader has to be systematic, and the full analysis must accumulate step by step. For instance, an observation about a writer's colloquial use of the word *colossal* may lead to another observation about her chummy tone toward the reader, and discovering that attitude may further illuminate how she controls the flow of ideas from one paragraph to the next. Good writers are always in control of their writing, even when they sound casual and spontaneous. They want readers to grasp their intended meaning. They lay out as clear a path as they can to define their exact meaning, which is often not simple or easy to arrive at. This introduction demonstrates ways to pick up and follow the trail of the author's intentions.

When you read, give an essay your undivided attention. It is probably a good idea to turn off the radio or stereo or television. You need to be able to hear how an essay sounds in your head. Read one or two paragraphs aloud to help you discover and express spoken inflections to the writing. Then return to reading silently, and listen for the tones of the written voice. "Heard melodies are sweet," wrote John Keats, "but those unheard are sweeter." The poet was not urging students to turn off the stereo, but nevertheless follow his suggestion to open your mind to the vibrations of silent things.

Approach a selection with an intention to read it word by word. Don't skim, and don't skip over details. At least once through the whole essay, take it all in, so that its full meaning will be accessible in your mind for you to consider. There is nothing in this anthology that takes very long to read. You are reading not for the broad outline or vague gist of what is said, but to grasp the full substance, both explicit and implicit, and to see how an essay is developed.

Begin with the title because the title is part of an essay. Paying attention to the title is a good first step in analytic reading. Be aware of what the title tells you or leads you to expect. For example, from the title of Nora Ephron's essay, "Shaping Up Absurd," you can foresee the author's critical attitude toward her subject, an attitude that comes across throughout the essay. The title of Raymond Carver's essay, "My Father's Life," defines the subject matter but does not hint at the author's attitude. Carver's title fittingly withholds that suggestion because the essay explores his ambivalent, hard-to-define attitudes about his father. Some titles intrigue us with their ambiguity. Wendy Lesser's title, "Conversion," cleverly suggests a weightier subject than the author presents. Susan Allen Toth's title, "Boyfriends," is deliberately general. Such titles acquire their specific meaning only after you plunge into the essay. Some titles reveal their appropriateness, or lack of it, only after you have reached the conclusion. All titles are worth reconsidering after you know where the whole essay leads.

Continue your analytic methods as you move through the essay. Give close attention to details by making observations as you read. Read with a pencil in hand, and use the pages of your anthology (only in your own copy, please!) to jot down your responses. Underline or circle whatever sounds important as you read. Words, phrases, and suggestions of meaning that seem prominent as you read are reliable indicators of what is important in the essay. Circle words you don't understand, and try to figure out what they mean from the context. The circles will remind you to look them up later. When you compare the dictionary definition with your initial sense of the word, you will discover the precise shade of meaning that the author attains in that particular word choice. Write comments in the margins. You will come back to them too. Some of your comments will refer directly to the essay's contents, and some will record your own associations or reactions.

Readers and writers learn a great deal from using a dictionary constantly. This anthology encourages you to look up words; glosses are provided only for words that do not appear in a good American dictionary. For convincing testimony about the importance of dictionaries, you might want to read Ha Jin's story about his army service in China, "Ocean of Words."

If you begin with good intentions to read analytically but find that your attention is waning and your mind wandering, perhaps the selection itself is at fault. When you are too bored to read well, ask yourself, Why is this writing so uninteresting? What is the author doing here that makes it harder to pay attention? Whether the fault is in the essay or in your reading of it, don't succumb to passivity, reading pages without noting or remembering what they are about. Like half-conscious driving, half-conscious reading can lead to no good end.

As you read, reformulate in your mind what the author is saying. Try to put the author's point into your words, even if you doubt or don't like what is said. Get the ideas up off the page and into your head. The more conscious you are of the author's thoughts, the more energized you will be to respond with thoughts of your own, in either agreement or disagreement. Be sure to record in the margin wherever you balk over an assertion or concept. Are you disagreeing? Are you puzzled? Take your mental pulse and note it. The good thing about questions is that they provoke response. Perhaps your question can be dealt with in class discussion. Sometimes you will want to answer your own question later — perhaps by writing on the topic.

Don't hesitate to include personal associations in your margin comments. Does a passage remind you of something that once happened to you? something you read or heard? something you learned in another class? Make a note of it. If the connection can be expressed briefly, your margin note will suffice. But sometimes the connections that occur as you read are worth pursuing later with a more lengthy response in a notebook or journal. The mark or note in your margin will lead you back to the thought for further development. Connections you make while reading help you to assimilate and thoroughly comprehend new material. They also frequently lead to terrific writing topics.

A good way to proceed analytically is to note how each paragraph serves the writer's purpose. Writers shape their thoughts into paragraphs in order to focus concentrated attention (theirs and yours). Identify what seems to be the main substance of important paragraphs, even when you are unsure that you grasp the point. You will later return to the paragraph to understand its purpose better. Of course, you know the usefulness of locating a topic sentence in a paragraph, when you can find one. A topic sentence states the main substance, and other sentences help make it convincing by arguing or illustrating the point. The topic often appears in the first or second sentence or in the final sentence. Note where the paragraph's strongest emphasis occurs. Does the paragraph lead off with an emphatic assertion followed by sentences supporting it, or does the paragraph progressively build up to a conclusive statement at the end? Either pattern can give effective *development* to the main point.

Identifying the substance and development of each paragraph helps you to notice also how the paragraphs fit together — that is, how the essay is organized. Look for the connecting link, or *transition*, which is usually but not always in the first sentence and which echoes or refers to the preceding paragraph. What is added to the subject as the author proceeds? Now you need to note the new paragraph's purpose.

The sequence, or order, of paragraphs establishes the author's path or direction of thought. Paragraphs cannot be jumbled into another sequence and still work effectively in an essay. They are not in random order like items on a list; they are more like chapters in a novel. They make full sense only in their intended sequence.

As you observe an author's paragraph development and organization, you will acquire a sense of the author's goal in writing the essay. You will begin to say, "I see what this is getting at." Or, if the essay is a narration of events, "I see what's shaping up here." This impression of the essay's over-all coherence may build up clearly during your first careful reading. But often it comes after repeated study. In this book the questions on Analyzing This Selection that appear at the end of each essay can help you reconsider its content and approach.

One constant guide to the author's intended meaning is his or her tone. In the margin, try to describe the writer's voice that is heard silently inside your head. Any voice includes tones that convey more than the words themselves mean — that impart the speaker's attitudes and implications. The tones of voice in written language are more subtle than in spoken language, but they are nevertheless essential to the meaning. You can begin to identify the writer's tone of voice if you first approach it as a more general quality, one of *manner*. Is the writer formal? humorous? solemn? earnest? casual? authoritative? ironic? straightforward? playful? argumentative? Come up with two or three adjectives that best describe the writer's general manner and jot them down in the margin. Then closely examine the passage that prompted your observation, and find the specific words and phrases that fit your description of the writer. Underline those words. Try to hear them as spoken words in order to check the accuracy of your description. Do they illustrate the manner you noted? Perhaps you will need to adjust your initial description of the writer's manner as you recognize the nuances of the language that express the tone of voice.

A writer's word choice expresses a particular slant, or viewpoint, toward the subject. A specialized or technical vocabulary establishes the tone of an expert authority, such as a sportswriter who addresses an audience of fans who understand the jargon of baseball or horse racing. Sportswriters also use many figures of speech to suggest the excitement of the game. The statement "Rice exploded the horsehide into the stands" doesn't make much sense to an ordinary reader or even to any too literal-minded fan.

The selections in this anthology seldom use such jargon. But even common diction and more comprehensible figures of speech indicate the writer's attitude toward the subject. Look at the first paragraph of Maya Angelou's "Graduation" (on p. 178). Words and phrases like "glorious release," "nobility," "exotic destinations," and "rites" indicate Angelou's — and the African American community's — feelings about the school graduation.

Keep noticing the tone to see where and how it changes within a selection. Sometimes it is possible to underline the sentence or circle a pivotal word or phrase where the tone shifts to express a different attitude. For example, in "Graduation" the intense, poetic language continues until the entrance of the white man who gives the speech at the ceremony. Now the language changes to officialese — boring generalities and flat clichés — revealing the white speaker's attitude toward the event. Angelou is making a point about race relations by this change in the essay's tone.

It is especially important to identify the tone at the conclusion of a selection because you want to recognize the writer's final attitude. On what note does the essay end? How does the ending affect you? Has the writer been building up to this effect all along? Or is it a slight surprise? Even a relatively short essay such as Brent Staples's "Black Men and Public Space" can achieve a shift in tone from beginning to end. Carver's essay "My Father's Life" includes several changes of tone and ends on a note that is still unexpected. The concluding paragraph of Terry Galloway's "I'm Listening as Hard as I Can" introduces a new tone to the essay that suggests another dimension of the subject.

Paying close attention to the conclusion's tone gives you a way to pull together your observations about the entire essay. Your reconsideration of the whole is the most fruitful step in making sense of your reading. It is often an exciting synthesis of the material that leads to discoveries and fresh insights. From your overview of *all* the material, you can determine what the whole essay conveys through its ideas and techniques. Reaching that kind of comprehensive viewpoint about an essay is what you want to achieve from your analytic examination.

To demonstrate these reading suggestions, we have annotated an essay as you might do when reading it on your own. Important points and connotative words are underlined, and varied comments or questions are noted in the margins. Puzzling words are circled, as are clues to vague or puzzling matters. As you read the following essay, you may find that your reactions differ from what you see in the margins. Freely add your own.

E. B. White

ONCE MORE TO THE LAKE

ELWYN BROOKS WHITE (1899–1985) was one of America's leading essayists and the author of classic books for children. He joined the staff of the *New Yorker* soon after graduating from Cornell University, and in later years he wrote also for *Harper's*. His essays are collected in *Essays of E. B. White* (1977). His children's books include *Stuart Little* (1945), *Charlotte's Web* (1952), and *The Trumpet of the Swan* (1970). In this selection he returns with his son to the lake where White's family vacationed in his boyhood.

Great stuff!

Long ago

One summer, along about 1904, my father rented a camp on a lake in Maine and took us all there for the month of August. We all got ringworm from some kittens and had to rub Pond's Extract on our arms and legs night and morning, and my father rolled over in a canoe with all his clothes on; but outside of that the vacation was a success and from then on none of us ever thought there was any place in the world like that lake in Maine. We returned summer after summer — always on August 1 for one month. I have since become a salt-water man, but sometimes in summer there are days when the restlessness of the tides and the fearful cold of the sea water and the incessant wind that blows across the afternoon and into the evening make me wish for the placidity of a lake in the woods. A few weeks ago this feeling got so strong I bought myself a couple of bass hooks and a spinner and returned to the lake where we used to go, for a week's fishing and to revisit old haunts.

Do they go anymore?

What?

Which one?

I took along my son, who had never had any fresh water up his nose and who had seen lily pads only from train windows. On the journey over to the lake I began to wonder what it would be like. I wondered how time would have marred this unique, this holy spot — the coves and streams, the hills that the sun set behind, the camps and the paths behind the camps. I was sure that the tarred road would have found it out, and I wondered in what other ways it would be desolated. It is strange how much you can remember about places like that once you allow your mind to return into the grooves that lead back. You remember one thing, and that suddenly reminds you of another thing. I guess I remembered clearest of all the early mornings, when the lake was cool and motionless, remembered how the bedroom smelled of the lumber it was made of and of the wet woods whose scent entered through the screen. The partitions in the camp were thin and did not extend clear to the top of the rooms, and as I was always the first up I would dress softly so as not to wake the others, and sneak out into the sweet outdoors and start out in the canoe, keeping close along the shore in the long shadows of the pines. I remembered being very careful never to rub my paddle against the gunwale for fear of disturbing the stillness of the cathedral.

Too much of the same word?

Why?

The lake had never been what you would call a wild lake. There were cottages sprinkled about the shores, and it was in farming country although the shores of the lake were quite heavily wooded. Some of the cottages were owned by nearby farmers, and you would live at the shore and eat your meals at the farmhouse. That's what our family did. But although it wasn't wild, it was a fairly large and undisturbed lake and there were places in it which, to a child at least, seemed infinitely remote and primeval.

Fun or boring?

1

2

3

I was right about the tar: It led to within half a mile of the shore. But when I got back there, with my boy, and we settled into a camp near a farmhouse and into the kind of summertime I had known, I could tell that it was going to be pretty much the same as it had been before — I knew it, lying in bed the first morning, smelling the bedroom and hearing the boy sneak quietly out and go off along the shore in a boat. I began to sustain the illusion that he was I, and therefore, by simple transposition, that I was my father. This sensation persisted, kept cropping up all the time we were there. It was not an entirely new feeling, but in this setting it grew much stronger. I seemed to be living a dual existence. I would be in the middle of some simple act, I would be picking up a bait box or laying down a table fork, or I would be saying something, and suddenly it would be not I but my father who was saying the words or making the gesture. It gave me a creepy sensation.

> *It comes and goes.*

> *Why?*

We went fishing the first morning. I felt the same damp moss covering the worms in the bait can, and saw the dragonfly alight on the tip of my rod as it hovered a few inches from the surface of the water. It was the arrival of this fly that convinced me beyond any doubt that everything was as it always had been, that the years were a mirage and there had been no years. The small waves were the same, chucking the rowboat under the chine as we fished at anchor, and the boat was the same boat, the same color green and the ribs broken in the same places, and under the floorboards the same fresh-water leavings and debris — the dead helgramite, the wisps of moss, the rusty discarded fishhook, the dried blood from yesterday's catch. We stared silently at the tips of our rods, at the dragonflies that came and went. I lowered the tip of mine into the water, tentatively, pensively dislodging the fly, which darted two feet away, poised, darted two feet back, and came to rest again a little farther up the rod. There had been no years between the ducking of this dragonfly and the other one — the one that was part of memory. I looked at the boy, who was silently watching his fly, and it was my hands that held his rod, my eyes watching. I felt dizzy and didn't know which rod I was at the end of.

> *What's the problem?*

We caught two bass, hauling them in briskly as though they were mackerel, pulling them over the side of the boat in a businesslike manner without any landing net, and stunning them with a blow on the back of the head. When we got back for a swim before lunch, the lake was exactly where we had left it, the same number of inches from the dock, and there was only the merest suggestion of a breeze. This seemed an utterly enchanted sea, this lake you could leave to its own devices for a few hours and come back to, and find that it had not stirred, this constant and trustworthy body of water. In the shallows, the dark, water-soaked sticks and twigs, smooth and old, were undulating in clusters on the bottom against the clean ribbed sand, and the track of the mussel was plain. A school of minnows swam by, each minnow with its small individual shadow, doubling the attendance, so clear and sharp in the sunlight. Some of the other campers were in swimming, along the shore, one of them with a cake of soap, and the water felt thin and clear and unsubstantial. Over the years there had been this person with the cake of soap, this cultist, and here he was. There had been no years.

> *Is he getting sick?*

> *Why wouldn't it be?*

Up to the farmhouse to dinner through the teeming, dusty field, the road under our sneakers was only a two-track road. The middle track was missing, the one with the marks of the hooves and splotches of dried, flaky manure. There had always been three tracks to choose from in choosing which track to walk in; now the choice was narrowed down to two. For a moment I missed terribly the middle alternative. But the way led past the tennis court, and something about the way it lay there in the sun reassured me; the tape had loosened along the backline, the alleys were green with plantains and other weeds, and the net (installed in June and removed in September) sagged in the dry noon, and the whole place steamed with midday heat and hunger and emptiness. There was a choice of pie for dessert, and one was blueberry

> *Car track/ horse track*

and one was apple, and the waitresses were the same country girls, there having been no passage of time, only the illusion of it as in a dropped curtain — the waitresses were still fifteen; their hair had been washed, that was the only difference — they had been to the movies and seen the pretty girls with the clean hair.

He's really happy in this paragraph

Summertime, oh summertime, pattern of life indelible, the fade-proof   8
lake, the woods unshatterable, the pasture with the sweetfern and the juniper forever and ever, summer without end; this was the background, and the life along the shore was the design, the cottagers with their innocent and tranquil design, their tiny docks with the flagpole and the American flag floating against the white clouds in the blue sky, the little paths over the roots of the trees leading from camp to camp and the paths leading back to the outhouses and the can of lime for sprinkling, and at the souvenir counters at the store the miniature birch-bark canoes and the postcards that showed things looking a little better than they looked. This was the American family at play, escaping the city heat, wondering whether the newcomers in the camp at the head of the cove were "common" or "nice," wondering whether it was true that the people who drove up for Sunday dinner at the farmhouse were turned away because there wasn't enough chicken.

Is he sad now?

So that's how!

It seemed to me, as I kept remembering all this, that those times and   9
those summers had been infinitely precious and worth saving. There had been jollity and peace and goodness. The arriving (at the beginning of August) had been so big a business in itself, at the railway station the farm wagon drawn up, the first smell of the pine-laden air, the first glimpse of the smiling farmer, and the great importance of the trunks and your father's enormous authority in such matters, and the feel of the wagon under you for the long ten-mile haul, and at the top of the last long hill catching the first view of the lake after eleven months of not seeing this cherished body of water. The shouts and cries of the other campers when they saw you, and the trunks to be unpacked, to give up their rich burden. (Arriving was less exciting nowadays, when you sneaked up in your car and parked it under a tree near the camp and took out the bags and in five minutes it was all over, no fuss, no loud wonderful fuss about trunks).

Again! — was it always perfect?

Peace and goodness and jollity. The only thing that was wrong now, really,   10
was the sound of the place, an unfamiliar nervous sound of the outboard motors. This was the note that jarred, the one thing that would sometimes break the illusion and set the years moving. In those other summertimes all motors were inboard; and when they were at a little distance, the noise they made was a sedative, an ingredient of summer sleep. They were one-cylinder and two-cylinder engines and some were make-and-break and some were jump-spark, but they all made a sleepy sound across the lake. The one-lungers throbbed and fluttered, and the twin-cylinder ones purred and purred, and that was a quiet sound too. But now the campers all had outboards. In the daytime, in the hot mornings, these motors made a petulant, irritable sound; at night, in the still evening when the afterglow lit the water, they whined about one's ears like mosquitoes. My boy loved our rented outboard, and his great desire was to achieve singlehanded mastery over it, and authority, and he soon learned the trick of choking it a little (but not too much), and the adjustment of the needle valve. Watching him I would remember the things you could do with the old one-cylinder engines with the heavy flywheel, how you could have it eating out of your hand if you got really close to it spiritually. Motorboats in those days didn't have clutches, and you would make a landing by shutting off the motor at the proper time and coasting in with a dead rudder. But there was a way of reversing them, if you learned the trick, by cutting the switch and putting it on again exactly on the final dying revolution of the flywheel, so that it would kick back against compression and begin reversing. Approaching a dock in a strong following

What are these?

Why all these mechanical details?

breeze, it was difficult to slow up sufficiently by the ordinary coasting method, and if a boy felt he had complete mastery over his motor, he was tempted to keep it running beyond its time and then reverse it a few feet from the dock. It took a cool nerve, because if you threw the switch a twentieth of a second too soon you could catch the flywheel when it still had speed enough to go up past center, and the boat would leap ahead, charging bull-fashion at the dock.

Less intense here

We had a good week at the camp. The bass were biting well and the sun shone endlessly, day after day. We would be tired at night and lie down in the accumulated heat of the little bedrooms after the long hot day and the breeze would stir almost imperceptibly outside and the smell of the swamp drift in through the rusty screens. Sleep would come easily and in the morning the red squirrel would be on the roof, tapping out his gay routine. I kept remembering everything, lying in bed in the mornings — the small steamboat that had a long rounded stern like the lip of a Ubangi, and how quietly she ran on the moonlight sails, when the older boys played their mandolins and the girls sang and we ate doughnuts dipped in sugar, and how sweet the music was on the water in the shining night, and what it had felt like to think about girls then. After breakfast we would go up to the store and the things were in the same place — the minnows in a bottle, the plugs and spinners disarranged and pawed over by the youngsters from the boys' camp, the Fig Newtons and the Beeman's gum. Outside, the road was tarred and cars stood in front of the store. Inside, all was just as it had always been, except there was more Coca-Cola and not so much Moxie and root beer and birch beer and sarsaparilla. We would walk out with a bottle of pop apiece and sometimes the pop would backfire up our noses and hurt. We explored the streams, quietly, where the turtles slid off the sunny logs and dug their way into the soft bottom; and we lay on the town wharf and fed worms to the tame bass. Everywhere we went I had trouble making out which was I, the one walking at my side, the one walking in my pants.

Huh?

Why doesn't he ever talk to the boy in this essay?

One afternoon while we were there at that lake a thunderstorm came up. It was like the revival of an old melodrama that I had seen long ago with childish awe. The second-act climax of the drama of the electrical disturbance over a lake in America had not changed in any important respect. This was the big scene, still the big scene. The whole thing was so familiar, the first feeling of oppression and heat and a general air around camp of not wanting to go very far away. In midafternoon (it was all the same) a curious darkening of the sky, and a lull in everything that had made life tick; and then the way the boats suddenly swung the other way at their moorings with the coming of a breeze out of the new quarter, and the premonitory rumble. Then the kettle drum, then the snare, then the bass drum and cymbals, then crackling light against the dark, and the gods grinning and licking their chops in the hills. Afterward the calm, the rain steadily rustling in the calm lake, the return of light and hope and spirits, and the campers running out in joy and relief to go swimming in the rain, their bright cries perpetuating the deathless joke about how they were getting simply drenched, and the children screaming with delight at the new sensation of bathing in the rain, and the joke about getting drenched linking the generations in a strong indestructible chain. And the comedian who waded in carrying an umbrella.

Angry?

His big theme!

When the others went swimming my son said he was going in, too. He pulled his dripping trunks from the line where they had hung all through the shower and wrung them out. Languidly, and with no thought of going in, I watched him, his hard little body, skinny and bare, saw him wince slightly as he pulled up around his vitals the small, soggy, icy garment. As he buckled the swollen belt, suddenly my groin felt the chill of death.

Why? Who is going to die?

11

12

13

Think about an essay as soon as you finish reading; don't put it aside for later. Begin to pull your thoughts together by forming simple, fundamental observations like "This essay is mainly about such and such" or "This essay asserts this and that." A matter-of-fact observation gives you a foundation on which to build other observations and connections. In thinking about "Once More to the Lake" there is no difficulty in formulating the essay's main subject — White's powerful childhood memories, which pull him back into reexperiencing his past. But it is more difficult to formulate exactly what the essay asserts about the subject. It doesn't start by making a point or appear to come to a point. There is no thesis statement in the first or the concluding paragraph; and, clearly, it is not an essay that develops a logical argument. In a personal narrative such as this, the point arises from the writer's responses to events and details.

In the sequence of events — which is the essay's narrative structure — White begins to feel that he is his son, and he temporarily loses track of himself as an adult. In responding to the boy, White's identity is shaken, and his confusion mixes three generations in his self-image. He is unsure from moment to moment whether he is the boy, or himself, or his own father. The recurring sense of being young carries him into illogical, ecstatic states of mind in which it seems that time itself has not passed. Years don't exist. Again and again he is amazed to find that so much of the past can still be present to his senses. But this joyful reexperience of the past is also sobering because each concrete memory presents something that has, in fact, disappeared from his usual adult life. White doesn't become melancholy over being old. He continues to enjoy details that bring back his youth, like the brand names of chewing gum and soft drinks. But as he spends the week in company with his son, he allows more of the boy's experiences to take precedence over his memories. The father adjusts to accompanying the boy, following the boy's initiatives and interests, watching him or helping him, but no longer enthusiastically leading him or submerging the boy entirely in his own memories. White's initial *confusion* of overlapping identities straightens out into his recognition of the *succession* of generations "in a strong indestructible chain."

The sight of the boy struggling into the cold, wet swimming trunks crystallizes the whole experience for White. By remembering the sensations, he can still feel what his son's wiry, immature little body feels. But the father also knows what the boy does not yet know — that we lose the present moment even as we experience it. Time passes and entire generations are lost. The acknowledgment of death springs fully into his mind as he winces from the imagined chill around his groin. The succession of generations that proceeds from his groin (his genitals) is also a succession of deaths. The acknowledgment of death at the end of the essay is surprising but not unprepared for. Death is not a macabre or depressing thought to White. He feels the shock of a truth rediscovered with fuller meaning.

Though the essay does not present a thesis even at the conclusion, it nevertheless comes to a point implicitly and suggestively. It is possible to formulate a thesis statement — such as, "The pleasures of reexperiencing youth intensify an adult awareness of loss and death." This is an acceptably accurate thesis statement, but to most readers it will seem to diminish or even trivialize the meaning of the essay. The thesis does not fully capture what the essay is getting at; it seems too narrow and hollow to indicate why White bothered to write "Once More to the Lake." The essay has a larger purpose, a motivation behind it, that is more important than its thesis. This purpose is embodied in White's strong emphasis on the workings of his mind as he is caught up in the excitement of reexperiencing the past. The essay reveals how memories are evoked and how memory can overwhelm our consciousness of the present. Illogically but convincingly, memory can make the past seem more real than the present. Disturbingly, memory can even change our self-image, like a mirror that reflects a face that is not ours. But even when memory is unleashed in full force, the adult mind keeps sorting out the differences between past and present. The purpose of the essay is to reveal this interplay between the immortality of memory and the mortality of actual experience.

Grasping the purpose, we understand that the essay is truly about returning to the *lake*, in the symbolic meaning of the title. Memory is that inland, interior sea where we live partly above the surface and partly deep within the water that holds all the past.

You cannot expect to make this much sense of an essay by just mulling it over in your mind. Your responses and observations have to be articulated in words in order to become coherent ideas. Writing in the margins and taking notes as you read start this process of finding what you mean. Participating in class discussions will take your understanding further. But the process of making sense is not complete until you write out your views in a fully developed essay of your own. You never really know what you think until you see what you say.

If you have been given a topic to write on, write on the assigned topic. It has probably been carefully phrased to direct your thoughts and to identify a subject that you can handle in a few pages. If you have to find your own topic after reading an essay, rely on your responses to the reading. After concentrating on "Once More to the Lake," for instance, you should have plenty of personal associations that suggest something to write about, such as a trip you took with your family or a favorite vacation spot. Perhaps you were fascinated by the relationship between White and his son. White's essay illustrates that adults are inclined to relive their past through their children. That mixing of roles between generations is something you know a lot about from your own experience. You may not have thought about this aspect of your life, but writing about it is an opportunity to examine it closely and freely. Perhaps White's essay made the power of memory itself more interesting. Why does that person dwell in the past? From writing you can discover something about yourself and others who are important to you.

Don't trap yourself into feeling blocked about writing. You can always begin to write by jotting down fleeting phrases. Don't worry about connecting up the jumble of thoughts that may cover your sheet of paper. Keep writing even if you are formulating only fragments. As you continue to energize your mind into forming phrases and sentences, you will soon begin to write longer passages and more cohesive thoughts. The important activity is to make your mind use words that you write down. The object of writing at any stage of preparation or revision is to get thoughts out of your head and onto paper. To achieve this goal you must work on the page. If you have trouble focusing your attention and getting started, push yourself to articulate one thought and then another. (It also helps to have privacy and silence where you write.)

What you get down onto paper during your first hour or two of effort will be patchy and often vague. Don't be disheartened. You can't construct the complicated network of ideas in an essay as easily and methodically as you knit a scarf or add a column of figures.

To turn your rough material into a well-formed draft, think of yourself laying out a trail that your reader must be able to follow. You are in charge of the meaning now, and you want to make yourself fully understood.

Try to establish a purpose or central idea for each paragraph. Explain your idea so that your thoughts expand into a developed paragraph with a main point and supporting discussion. Often you will have to pull together a couple of brief, fragmentary paragraphs in your rough material and synthesize them into a longer paragraph that contributes a substantive point. Do not hesitate to write paragraphs that are longer than what you find in newspapers and most magazines. You want to learn to sustain and control extended thought processes. Add concrete details and illustrations that make your writing more convincing. Paragraph by paragraph, spell out what you mean.

And emphasize what *you* mean. Don't just repeat the author. Present your ideas. Students tend to summarize what is written without adding much personal comment on it, instead of forming an idea or attitude about the selection. For example, the following sentence merely reports what happened:

> When his son learns to run the outboard, White remembers many mechanical details about early motorboat engines he tinkered with.

Turn this kind of sentence into one that includes more of your own interpretation:

> His son's fascination with an outboard renews White's obsession with early motorboat engines, adding another parallel experience to the week of memories.

The revised sentence still summarizes the event but includes an explanation of its significance. The sentence is more analytic in its purpose. The following sentence does not summarize at all. It refers to the event but does not recount it.

> The flood of remembered mechanical details about early engines draws White emotionally closer to his son because he recognizes the boy's attempts at mature independence.

That sentence is fully analytic because it explains how White achieves his purpose and effect.

You can make your sentences more analytic by revising parts that begin with *when* and *after*; use words that show causes or consequences like *because* and *since*. Such words help build supporting clauses that assert your point.

Your sentences are the very flesh and muscle of your writing. Making them strong and energetic is probably the semester goal of classroom instruction. Commonly, sentences are too inactive and do not convey specific information. Using active instead of passive verbs can galvanize lazy sentences. As you shape up your sentences, listen critically for the dull sound of flab that arises from using vague words and too many words.

Remember that your intended meaning is expressed by both what you say and how you say it. Your own tone of voice should be faintly audible in your head as you write. Is it a voice that sounds worth listening to on this particular topic? Is it a voice with a purpose?

Writers share one basic intention — that is, to be *convincing*. Whatever their subject, method, or tone, writers try to build confidence in the reader that the essay merits attention. Even humorous writing must be reliably funny. Whether it is a personal narrative, a logical argument, an explanation, or an analysis, all writing has to validate what it says. The full context gives a good essay credibility. Careful revising increases your essay's credibility.

When you think that you are finished, muster up the energy and courage to take one more critical look at your introduction and conclusion. These paragraphs have special functions that cannot be achieved until you have fully understood the point of your essay and your purpose in writing. You should make last-minute adjustments to your introduction and conclusion so that they serve your intentions. Remember from your readings that there is a rich variety of ways to begin and end an essay. Don't be humdrum in your introduction and conclusion. You owe it to yourself to win some attention to your fully developed views.

This brief bit of advice about writing should remind you that readers and writers confront much the same problems. But writing is more difficult. Writing is difficult for everyone, so you should never lose your nerve. The frustrations you face are the same frustrations that experienced writers face in their work. The standards you strive to attain are the same goals set by authors in this anthology. The work of writing is very democratic work: students, teachers, authors — we are all on this path together. If it is your turn to blaze a trail, take us to see something interesting.

PART 1

SELF-IMAGES

INSIGHTS

I conceive a man's body as a kind of flame, like a candle flame, forever upright and yet flowing: and the intellect is just the light that is shed on to the things around. And I am not so much concerned with the things around — which is really mind — but with the mystery of the flame forever flowing, coming God knows how from out of practically nowhere, and being *itself*, whatever there is around it, that it lights up. We have got so ridiculously mindful that we never know that we ourselves are anything — we think there are only the objects we shine upon. And there the poor flame goes on burning ignored, to produce this light. And instead of chasing the mystery in the fugitive, half-lighted things outside us, we ought to look at ourselves, and say "My God, I am myself!"

— D. H. LAWRENCE

We are creatures of *outside influences* — we originate *nothing* within. Whenever we take a new line of thought and drift into a new line of belief and action, the impulse is *always* suggested from the *outside*.

— MARK TWAIN

The Eagle-Feather Fan

The eagle is my power,
And my fan is an eagle.
It is strong and beautiful
In my hand. And it is real.
My fingers hold upon it
As if the beaded handle
Were the twist of bristlecone.
The bones of my hands are fine
And hollow; the fan bears them.
My hand veers in the thin air

Of the summits. All morning
It scuds on the cold currents;
All afternoon it circles
To the singing, to the drums.

          — N. SCOTT MOMADAY

The nicknames children bestow on one another can confer power. Like ancient Rome, the playground republic marks off the inner core of citizens from barbarians. Those who have no nicknames have no social existence; they are the nonpeople. . . . To be nicknamed is to be seen as having an attribute that entitles one to social attention, even if that attention is unpleasant. Thus, it may be better to be called "Sewage" than merely John.

          — ROM HARRÉ

My advice to everyone is to change their name at once if they're the least unhappy with their lives. In [my] Utopia everyone will choose a new name at seven, at eleven, at sixteen, and at twenty-four. And naturally women at forty-five, or when the last child has grown up and left home, whichever is the earliest. . . . Then life will be seen to start over, not finish. It is a perfectly legal thing to do. . . . So long as there is no intent to defraud. . . . But so many of us, either feeling our identities to be fragile, or out of misplaced loyalty to our parents, feel we must stick with the names we start out with. The given name is a dead giveaway of our parents' ambition for us — whether to diminish or enhance, ignore us as much as possible or control us forever. . . . No, it will not do. It will have to change.

          — FAY WELDON

This consciousness of self, this capacity to see one's self as though from the outside, is the distinctive characteristic of man. A friend of mine has a dog who waits at his studio door all morning and, when anybody comes to the door, he jumps up and barks, wanting to play. My friend holds that the dog is saying in his barking: "Here is a dog who has been waiting all morning for someone to come to play with him. Are you the one?" This is a nice sentiment, and all of us who like dogs enjoy projecting such cozy thoughts into their heads. But actually this is exactly what the dog cannot say. He can show that he wants to play and entice you into throwing his ball for him, but he cannot stand outside himself and see himself as a dog doing these things. He is not blessed with the consciousness of self.

— ROLLO MAY

Show me a sensible person who likes himself or herself! I know myself too well to like what I see. I know but too well that I'm not what I'd like to be.

— GOLDA MEIR

FOCUSING BY WRITING

1. People are apt to think of their personal identities as resembling either an *artichoke* or an *onion*. The outer leaves of an artichoke are inedible; they shield and nurture the vegetable but are easily peeled away. The essence of the vegetable appears closer to the innermost core, the heart of the artichoke. An onion, by contrast, has concentric layers of homogenous identity. It extends uniformly from its inner rings to its outermost. Which are you like? Explain why one metaphor reflects your sense of self better than the other.

2. If you were going to write an autobiography, where would you start — at some point in your own experience, or in someone else's experience? or with some place, such as a town, a house, or a country? Explain your reason for deciding on a particular beginning. Do not write it; merely explain why you would start your life story at that point.

3. As a child, did you ever create an imaginary name for yourself? Could you create one for yourself as you are at present? Recalling or inventing an imaginary name, explain its attractions and advantages over your given name.

4. Write about the pleasures and other possible effects of looking at old photographs, as in leafing through an album including pictures of yourself among those of other people. Do the photographic images evoke special reactions?

Nora Ephron

SHAPING UP ABSURD[1]

NORA EPHRON (b. 1941) grew up in the adult world of Hollywood screenwriters, entertainers, and celebrities. After graduating from Wellesley College she began a career as a journalist in New York by writing for *Newsweek* and contributing articles to entertainment magazines, eventually joining the staff of *New York* and *Esquire* magazines. Her essays have been collected in *Wallflower at the Orgy* (1970), *Crazy Salad* (1975), and *Nora Ephron Collected* (1991). She has also written a comic novel, *Heartburn* (1983), and several screenplays. Ephron co-wrote and directed the film *Sleepless in Seattle* (1992). "Shaping Up Absurd" considers a troubling self-image in her early life.

I have to begin with a few words about androgyny. In grammar school, in the fifth and sixth grades, we were all tyrannized by a rigid set of rules that supposedly determined whether we were boys or girls. The episode in *Huckleberry Finn* where Huck is disguised as a girl and gives himself away by the way he threads a needle and catches a ball — that kind of thing. We learned that the way you sat, crossed your legs, held a cigarette and looked at your nails, your wristwatch, the way you did these things instinctively was absolute proof of your sex. Now obviously most children did not take this literally, but I did. I thought that just one slip, just one incorrect cross of my legs or flick of an imaginary cigarette ash would turn me from whatever I was into the other thing; that would be all it took, really. Even though I was outwardly a girl and had many of the trappings generally associated with the field of girldom — a girl's name, for example, and dresses, my own telephone, an autograph book — I spent the early years of my adolescence absolutely certain that I might at any point gum it up. I did not feel at all like a girl. I was boyish. I was athletic, ambitious, outspoken, competitive, noisy, rambunctious. I had scabs on my knees and my socks slid into my loafers and I could throw a football. I wanted desperately not to be that way, not to be a mixture of both things but instead just one, a girl, a definite indisputable girl. As soft and as pink as a nursery. And nothing would do that for me, I felt, but breasts.

[1]Editor's title. [All notes are the editor's unless identified otherwise.]

I was about six months younger than everyone in my class, and so for 2
about six months after it began, for six months after my friends had begun
to develop — that was the word we used, develop — I was not particularly
worried. I would sit in the bathtub and look down at my breasts and know
that any day now, any second now, they would start growing like everyone
else's. They didn't. "I want to buy a bra," I said to my mother one night.
"What for?" she said. My mother was really hateful about bras, and by the
time my third sister had gotten to that point where she was ready to want
one, my mother had worked the whole business into a comedy routine.
"Why not use a Band-Aid instead?" she would say. It was a source of great
pride to my mother that she had never even had to wear a brassiere until
she had her fourth child, and then only because her gynecologist made
her. It was incomprehensible to me that anyone would ever be proud of
something like that. It was the 1950s, for God's sake. Jane Russell. Cash-
mere sweaters. Couldn't my mother see that? *"I am too old to wear an
undershirt."* Screaming. Weeping. Shouting. "Then don't wear an undershirt," said my mother. "But I want to buy a bra." "What for?"

I suppose that for most girls, breasts, brassieres, that entire thing, has 3
more trauma, more to do with the coming of adolescence, of becoming a
woman, than anything else. Certainly more than getting your period,
although that too was traumatic, symbolic. But you could *see* breasts; they
were there; they were visible. Whereas a girl could claim to have her
period for months before she actually got it and nobody would ever know
the difference. Which is exactly what I did. All you had to do was make a
great fuss over having enough nickels for the Kotex machine and walk
around clutching your stomach and moaning for three to five days a month
about The Curse and you could convince anybody. There is a school of
thought somewhere in the women's lib/women's mag/gynecology establishment that claims that menstrual cramps are purely psychological, and
I lean toward it. Not that I didn't have them finally. Agonizing cramps,
heating-pad cramps, go-down-to-the-school-nurse-and-lie-on-the-cot cramps.
But unlike any pain I had ever suffered, I adored the pain of cramps, welcomed it, wallowed in it, bragged about it. "I can't go. I have cramps."
"I can't do that. I have cramps." And most of all, gigglingly, blushingly: "I
can't swim. I have cramps." Nobody ever used the hard-core word. Men-
struation. God, what an awful word. Never that. "I have cramps."

The morning I first got my period, I went into my mother's bedroom to 4
tell her. And my mother, my utterly-hateful-about-bras mother, burst into
tears. It was really a lovely moment, and I remember it so clearly not just
because it was one of the two times I ever saw my mother cry on my
account (the other was when I was caught being a six-year-old kleptoma-
niac), but also because the incident did not mean to me what it meant to
her. Her little girl, her firstborn, had finally become a woman. That was
what she was crying about. My reaction to the event, however, was that I
might well be a woman in some scientific, textbook sense (and could at

least stop faking every month and stop wasting all those nickels). But in another sense — in a visible sense — I was as androgynous and as liable to tip over into boyhood as ever.

I started with a 28AA bra. I don't think they made them any smaller in those days, although I gather that now you can buy bras for five year olds that don't have any cups whatsoever in them; trainer bras they are called. My first brassiere came from Robinson's Department Store in Beverly Hills. I went there alone, shaking, positive they would look me over and smile and tell me to come back next year. An actual fitter took me into the dressing room and stood over me while I took off my blouse and tried the first one on. The little puffs stood out on my chest. "Lean over," said the fitter (to this day I am not sure what fitters in bra departments do except to tell you to lean over). I leaned over, with the fleeting hope that my breasts would miraculously fall out of my body and into the puffs. Nothing.

"Don't worry about it," said my friend Libby some months later, when things had not improved. "You'll get them after you're married."

"What are you talking about?" I said.

"When you get married," Libby explained, "your husband will touch your breasts and rub them and kiss them and they'll grow."

That was the killer. Necking I could deal with. Intercourse I could deal with. But it had never crossed my mind that a man was going to touch my breasts, that breasts had something to do with all that, petting, my God they never mentioned petting in my little sex manual about the fertilization of the ovum. I became dizzy. For I knew instantly — as naive as I had been only a moment before — that only part of what she was saying was true: the touching, rubbing, kissing part, not the growing part. And I knew that no one would ever want to marry me. I had no breasts. I would never have breasts.

My best friend in school was Diana Raskob. She lived a block from me in a house full of wonders. English muffins, for instance. The Raskobs were the first people in Beverly Hills to have English muffins for breakfast. They also had an apricot tree in the back, and a badminton court, and a subscription to *Seventeen* magazine, and hundreds of games like Sorry and Parcheesi and Treasure Hunt and Anagrams. Diana and I spent three or four afternoons a week in their den reading and playing and eating. Diana's mother's kitchen was full of the most colossal assortment of junk food I have ever been exposed to. My house was full of apples and peaches and milk and homemade chocolate-chip cookies — which were nice, and good for you, but-not-right-before-dinner-or-you'll-spoil-your-appetite. Diana's house had nothing in it that was good for you, and what's more, you could stuff it in right up until dinner and nobody cared. Bar-B-Q potato chips (they were the first in them, too), giant bottles of ginger ale, fresh popcorn with melted butter, hot fudge sauce on Baskin-Robbins jamoca ice cream, powdered-sugar doughnuts from Van de Kamps. Diana and I had been best friends since we were seven; we were about equally popular in school (which is to say, not particularly), we had about the same success with boys (extremely intermittent), and we looked much the same. Dark. Tall. Gangly.

It is September, just before school begins. I am eleven years old, about   11 to enter the seventh grade, and Diana and I have not seen each other all summer. I have been to camp and she has been somewhere like Banff with her parents. We are meeting, as we often do, on the street midway between our two houses and we will walk back to Diana's and eat junk and talk about what has happened to each of us that summer. I am walking down Walden Drive in my jeans and my father's shirt hanging out and my old red loafers with the socks falling into them and coming toward me is . . . I take a deep breath . . . a young woman. Diana. Her hair is curled and she has a waist and hips and a bust and she is wearing a straight skirt, an article of clothing I have been repeatedly told I will be unable to wear until I have the hips to hold it up. My jaw drops, and suddenly I am crying, crying hysterically, can't catch my breath sobbing. My best friend has betrayed me. She has gone ahead without me and done it. She has shaped up.

Here are some things I did to help: 12
Bought a Mark Eden Bust Developer.   13
Slept on my back for four years.   14
Splashed cold water on them every night because some French actress   15 said in *Life* magazine that that was what *she* did for her perfect bustline.

Ultimately, I resigned myself to a bad toss and began to wear padded   16 bras. I think about them now, think about all those years in high school I went around in them, my three padded bras, every single one of them with different sized breasts. Each time I changed bras I changed sizes: one week nice perky but not too obtrusive breasts, the next medium-sized slightly pointed ones, the next week knockers, true knockers; all the time, whatever size I was, carrying around this rubberized appendage on my chest that occasionally crashed into a wall and was poked inward and had to be poked outward — I think about all that and wonder how anyone kept a straight face through it. My parents, who normally had no restraints about needling me — why did they say nothing as they watched my chest go up and down? My friends, who would periodically inspect my breasts for signs of growth and reassure me — why didn't they at least counsel consistency?

And the bathing suits. I die when I think about the bathing suits. That   17 was the era when you could lay an uninhabited bathing suit on the beach and someone would make a pass at it. I would put one on, an absurd swimsuit with its enormous bust built into it, the bones from the suit stabbing me in the rib cage and leaving little red welts on my body, and there I would be, my chest plunging straight downward absolutely vertically from my collarbone to the top of my suit and then suddenly, wham, out came all that padding and material and wiring absolutely horizontally.

Buster Klepper was the first boy who ever touched them. He was my boyfriend my senior year of high school. There is a picture of him in my high-school yearbook that makes him look quite attractive in a Jewish, horn-rimmed glasses sort of way, but the picture does not show the pimples, which were air-brushed out, or the dumbness. Well, that isn't really fair. He wasn't dumb. He just wasn't terribly bright. His mother refused to accept it, refused to accept the relentlessly average report cards, refused to deal with her son's inevitable destiny in some junior college or other. "He was tested," she would say to me, apropos of nothing, "and it came out 145. That's near-genius." Had the word underachiever been coined, she probably would have lobbed that one at me, too. Anyway, Buster was really very sweet — which is, I know, damning with faint praise, but there it is. I was the editor of the front page of the high-school newspaper and he was editor of the back page; we had to work together, side by side, in the print shop, and that was how it started. On our first date, we went to see *April Love* starring Pat Boone. Then we started going together. Buster had a green coupe, a 1950 Ford with an engine he had handchromed until it shone, dazzled, reflected the image of anyone who looked into it, anyone usually being Buster polishing it or the gas-station attendants he constantly asked to check the oil in order for them to be overwhelmed by the sparkle on the valves. The car also had a boot stretched over the back seat for reasons I never understood; hanging from the rearview mirror, as was the custom, was a pair of angora dice. A previous girlfriend named Solange who was famous throughout Beverly Hills High School for having no pigment in her right eyebrow had knitted them for him. Buster and I would ride around town, the two of us seated to the left of the steering wheel. I would shift gears. It was nice. 18

There was necking. Terrific necking. First in the car, overlooking Los Angeles from what is now the Trousdale Estates. Then on the bed of his parents' cabana at Ocean House. Incredibly wonderful, frustrating necking, I loved it, really, but no further than necking, please don't, please, because there I was absolutely terrified of the general implications of going-a-step-further with a near-dummy and also terrified of his finding out there was next to nothing there (which he knew, of course; he wasn't that dumb). 19

I broke up with him at one point. I think we were apart for about two weeks. At the end of that time I drove down to see a friend at a boarding school in Palos Verdes Estates and a disc jockey played *April Love* on the radio four times during the trip. I took it as a sign. I drove straight back to Griffith Park to a golf tournament Buster was playing in (he was the sixth-seeded teenage golf player in Southern California) and presented myself back to him on the green of the 18th hole. It was all very dramatic. That night we went to a drive-in and I let him get his hand under my protuber-ances and onto my breasts. He really didn't seem to mind at all. 20

"Do you want to marry my son?" the woman asked me.   21

"Yes," I said.   22

I was nineteen years old, a virgin, going with this woman's son, this big   23
strange woman who was married to a Lutheran minister in New Hampshire
and pretended she was Gentile and had this son, by her first husband, this
total fool of a son who ran the hero-sandwich concession at Harvard Business
School and whom for one moment one December in New Hampshire I
said — as much out of politeness as anything else — that I wanted to marry.

"Fine," she said. "Now, here's what you do. Always make sure you're on   24
top of him so you won't seem so small. My bust is very large, you see, so I
always lie on my back to make it look smaller, but you'll have to be on top
most of the time."

I nodded. "Thank you," I said.   25

"I have a book for you to read," she went on. "Take it with you when you   26
leave. Keep it." She went to the bookshelf, found it, and gave it to me. It was
a book on frigidity.

"Thank you," I said.   27

That is a true story. Everything in this article is a true story, but I feel I   28
have to point out that that story in particular is true. It happened on
December 30, 1960. I think about it often. When it first happened, I naturally assumed that the woman's son, my boyfriend, was responsible. I
invented a scenario where he had had a little heart-to-heart with his mother
and confessed that his only objection to me was that my breasts were small;
his mother then took it upon herself to help out. Now I think I was wrong
about the incident. The mother was acting on her own, I think: That was
her way of being cruel and competitive under the guise of being helpful
and maternal. You have small breasts, she was saying; therefore you will
never make him as happy as I have. Or you have small breasts; therefore
you will doubtless have sexual problems. Or you have small breasts; therefore you are less woman than I am. She was, as it happens, only the first of
what seems to me to be a never-ending string of women who have made
competitive remarks to me about breast size. "I would love to wear a dress
like that," my friend Emily says to me, "but my bust is too big." Like that.
Why do women say these things to me? Do I attract these remarks the way
other women attract married men or alcoholics or homosexuals? This summer, for example, I am at a party in East Hampton and I am introduced to
a woman from Washington. She is a minor celebrity, very pretty and
Southern and blonde and outspoken and I am flattered because she has
read something I have written. We are talking animatedly, we have been
talking no more than five minutes, when a man comes up to join us. "Look
at the two of us," the woman says to the man, indicating me and her. "The
two of us together couldn't fill an A cup." Why does she say that? It isn't
even true, dammit, so why? Is she even more addled than I am on this
subject? Does she honestly believe there is something wrong with her size

breasts, which, it seems to me, now that I look hard at them, are just right? Do I unconsciously bring out competitiveness in women? In that form? What did I do to deserve it?

As for men.   29

There were men who minded and let me know they minded. There 30 were men who did not mind. In any case, I always minded.

And even now, now that I have been countlessly reassured that my figure 31 is a good one, now that I am grown up enough to understand that most of my feelings have very little to do with the reality of my shape, I am nonetheless obsessed by breasts. I cannot help it. I grew up in the terrible Fifties — with rigid stereotypical sex roles, the insistence that men be men and dress like men and women be women and dress like women, the intolerance of androgyny — and I cannot shake it, cannot shake my feelings of inadequacy. Well, that time is gone, right? All those exaggerated examples of breast worship are gone, right? Those women were freaks, right? I know all that. And yet, here I am, stuck with the psychological remains of it all, stuck with my own peculiar version of breast worship. You probably think I am crazy to go on like this: Here I have set out to write a confession that is meant to hit you with the shock of recognition and instead you are sitting there thinking I am thoroughly warped. Well, what can I tell you? If I had had them, I would have been a completely different person. I honestly believe that.

After I went into therapy, a process that made it possible for me to tell 32 total strangers at cocktail parties that breasts were the hang-up of my life, I was often told that I was insane to have been bothered by my condition. I was also frequently told, by close friends, that I was extremely boring on the subject. And my girlfriends, the ones with nice big breasts, would go on endlessly about how their lives had been far more miserable than mine. Their bra straps were snapped in class. They couldn't sleep on their stomachs. They were stared at whenever the word "mountain" cropped up in geography. And *Evangeline*, good God what they went through every time someone had to stand up and recite the Prologue to Longfellow's *Evangeline*: ". . . *stand like druids of eld . . . / With beards that rest on their bosoms.*" It was much worse for them, they tell me. They had a terrible time of it, they assure me. I don't know how lucky I was, they say.

I have thought about their remarks, tried to put myself in their place, 33 considered their point of view. I think they are full of shit.

Analyzing This Selection

1. **THE WRITER'S METHOD** Ephron establishes an informal, colloquial tone right from the start. Underline the key words and phrases in the opening paragraph that help set this tone. What is the correlation between this tone and the subject of her essay?

2. As a child, Ephron felt sure that fateful disaster lurked around every corner. In addition to her flat-chestedness, what does she worry about? How does she express these worries?

3. What is the point of the section about her friend Diana? Does her name fit the effect that she has on Ephron? Similarly, what is the point of the section about Buster Klepper? And what are the connotations of his name? Do they fit his effect on her?

Analyzing Connections

4. Two contrasting metaphors for personal identity are mentioned in the first topic of Focusing by Writing (see p. 19). Which metaphor suggests Ephron's image of herself?

Analyzing by Writing

5. Being unusually tall or short, thin or fat, red-haired, freckled, pretty, or thoroughly average can seem to be the most important fact in your existence. Write an essay explaining how one trait came to have exaggerated importance for some period of your life. Be sure to examine the reasons for their importance at that time.

Terry Galloway

I'M LISTENING AS HARD AS I CAN

Terry Galloway (b. 1950) was born in Stuttgart, Germany and grew up in Berlin and Austin, Texas. She graduated from the University of Texas. As a writer, director, and performer of one-woman performance pieces, Galloway has toured the United States, Canada, and the United Kingdom. In addition to her work in theater, Galloway has published a book of poems, *Buncha Crocs in Surch of Snac* (1980). She has written for a public television series about handicapped children. For the following essay about her own handicap, Galloway always liked the title "Huh?" — but no editor has yet agreed with her.

At the age of twelve I won the swimming award at the Lions Camp for 1 Crippled Children. When my name echoed over the PA system the girl in the wheelchair next to me grabbed the box speaker of my hearing aid and shouted, "You won!" My ear quaking, I took the cue. I stood up straight — the only physically unencumbered child in a sea of braces and canes — affixed a pained but brave grin to my face, then limped all the way to the stage.

Later, after the spotlight had dimmed, I was overcome with remorse, but 2 not because I'd played the crippled heroine. The truth was that I was ashamed of my handicap. I wanted to have something more visibly wrong with me. I wanted to be in the same league as the girl who'd lost her right leg in a car accident; her artificial leg attracted a bevy of awestruck campers. I, on the other hand, wore an unwieldy box hearing aid buckled to my body like a dog halter. It attracted no one. Deafness wasn't, in my eyes, a blue-ribbon handicap. Mixed in with my envy, though, was an overwhelming sense of guilt; at camp I was free to splash in the swimming pool, while most of the other children were stranded at the shallow end, where lifeguards floated them in lazy circles. But seventeen years of living in the "normal" world has diminished my guilt considerably, and I've learned that every handicap has its own particular hell.

I'm something of an anomaly in the deaf world. Unlike most deaf 3 people, who were either born deaf or went deaf in infancy, I lost my hearing in chunks over a period of twelve years. Fortunately I learned to speak before my loss grew too profound, and that ability freed me from the most severe problem facing the deaf — the terrible difficulty of making themselves understood. My opinion of deafness was just as biased as that of a person who can hear. I had never met a deaf child in my life, and I didn't know how to sign. I imagined deaf people to be like creatures from beyond: animal-like because their language was so physical, threatening because they were unable to express themselves with sophistication — that is, through speech. I *could* make myself understood, and because I had a talent for lipreading it was easy for me to pass in the wider world. And for most of my life that is exactly what I did — like a black woman playing white, I passed for something other than what I was. But in doing so I was avoiding some very painful facts. And for many years I was inhibited not only by my deafness but my own idea of what it meant to be deaf.

My problems all started when my mother, seven months pregnant with me, developed a serious kidney infection. Her doctors pumped her full of antibiotics. Two months later I was born, with nothing to suggest that I was anything more or less than a normal child. For years nobody knew that the antibiotics had played havoc with my fetal nervous system. I grew up bright, happy, and energetic. 4

But by the time I was ten I knew, if nobody else did, that something somewhere had gone wrong. The people around me had gradually developed fuzzy profiles, and their speech had taken on a blurred and foreign character. But I was such a secure and happy child that it didn't enter my mind to question my new perspective or mention the changes to anyone else. Finally, my behavior became noticeably erratic — I would make nonsensical replies to ordinary questions or simply fail to reply at all. My teachers, deciding that I was neither a particularly creative child nor an especially troublesome one, looked for a physical cause. They found two: I wasn't quite as blind as a bat, but I was almost as deaf as a doornail. 5

My parents took me to Wilford Hall Air Force Hospital in San Antonio, where I was examined from ear to ear. My tonsils were removed and studied, ice water was injected into my inner ear, and I underwent a series of inexplicable and at times painful exploratory tests. I would forever after associate deafness with kind attention and unusual punishment. Finally a verdict was delivered: "Congenital interference has resulted in a neural disorder for which there is no known medical or surgical treatment." My hearing loss was severe and would grow progressively worse. 6

I was fitted with my first hearing aid and sent back home to resume my childhood. I never did. I had just turned twelve, and my body was undergoing enormous changes. I had baby fat, baby breasts, hairy legs, and thick pink cat-eye glasses. My hearing aid was about the size of a small transistor radio and rode in a white linen pouch that hit exactly at breast level. It was not a welcome addition to my pubescent woe. 7

As a vain child trapped in a monster's body, I was frantic for a way to survive the next few years. Glimpsing my reflection in mirrors became such agony that I acquired a habit of brushing my teeth and hair with my eyes closed. Everything I did was geared to making my body more inhabitable, 8 but I only succeeded in making it less so. I kept my glasses in my pocket and developed an unbecoming squint; I devised a smile that hid two broken front teeth, but it looked disturbingly like the grin of a piranha; I kept my arms folded over my would-be breasts. But the hearing aid was a different story. There was no way to disguise it. I could tuck it under my blouse, but then all I could hear was the static of cotton. Besides, whenever I took a step the box bounced around like a third breast. So I resigned myself: A monster I was, a monster I would be.

I became more withdrawn, more suspicious of other people's intentions. 9 I imagined that I was being deliberately excluded from school-yard talk because the other children didn't make much of an effort to involve me — they simply didn't have the time or patience to repeat snatches of gossip ten times and slowly. Conversation always reached the point of ridiculousness before I could understand something as simple as "The movie starts at five." (The groovy shark's alive? The moving stars that thrive?) I didn't make it to many movies. I cultivated a lofty sense of superiority, and I was often brutal with people who offered the "wrong" kind of help at the "wrong" time. Right after my thirteenth birthday some well-meaning neighbors took me to a revivalist faith healing. I already had doubts about exuberant religions, and the knee-deep hysteria of the preacher simply confirmed them. He bounded to my side and put his hands on my head. "O Lord," he cried, "heal this poor little lamb!"

I leaped up as if transported and shouted, "I can walk!"   10

For the first few years my parents were as bewildered as I was. Nothing 11 had prepared them for a handicapped child on the brink of adolescence. They sensed a whole other world of problems, but in those early stages I still seemed so normal that they just couldn't see me in a school for the deaf. They felt that although such schools were there to help, they also served to isolate. I have always been grateful for their decision. Because of it, I had to contend with public schools, and in doing so I developed two methods of survival: I learned to read not just lips but the whole person, and I learned the habit of clear speech by taking every speech and drama course I could.

That is not to say my adolescent years were easygoing — they were mis- 12 ery. The lack of sound cast a pall on everything. Life seemed less fun than it had been before. I didn't associate that lack of fun with the lack of sound. I didn't begin to make the connection between the failings of my body and the failings of the world until I was well out of college. I simply did not admit to myself that deafness caused certain problems — or even that I was deaf.

From the time I was twelve until I was twenty-four, the loss of my hear- 13 ing was erratic. I would lose a decibel or two of sound and then my hearing would stabilize. A week or a year later there would be another slip and then I'd have to adjust all over again. I never knew when I would hit bottom. I remember going to bed one night still being able to make out the reassuring purr of the refrigerator and the late-night conversation of my parents, then waking the next morning to nothing — even my own voice was gone. These fits and starts continued until my hearing finally dropped to the last rung of amplifiable sound. I was a college student at the time, and whenever anyone asked about my hearing aid, I admitted to being only slightly hard of hearing.

My professors were frequently alarmed by my almost maniacal intensity 14 in class. I was petrified that I'd have to ask for special privileges just to achieve marginal understanding. My pride was in flames. I became increasingly bitter and isolated. I was terrified of being marked a deaf woman, a label that made me sound dumb and cowlike, enveloped in a protective silence that denied me my complexity. I did everything I could to hide my handicap. I wore my hair long and never wore earrings, thus keeping attention away from my ears and their riders. I monopolized conversations so that I wouldn't slip up and reveal what I was or wasn't hearing; I took on a disdainful air at large parties, hoping that no one would ask me something I couldn't instantly reply to. I lied about the extent of my deafness so I could avoid the stigma of being thought "different" in a pathetic way.

It was not surprising that in my senior year I suffered a nervous collapse 15 and spent three days in the hospital crying like a baby. When I stopped crying I knew it was time to face a few things — I had to start asking for help when I needed it because I couldn't handle my deafness alone, and I had to quit being ashamed of my handicap so I could begin to live with its consequences and discover what (if any) were its rewards.

When I began telling people that I was *really* deaf, I did so with grim 16 determination. Some were afraid to talk to me at any length, fearing perhaps that they were talking into a void; others assumed that I was somehow an unsullied innocent and always inquired in carefully enunciated sentences: "Dooooooooo youuuuuuuu driiinnk liquor?" But most people were surprisingly sympathetic — they wanted to know the best way to be understood, they took great pains to talk directly to my face, and they didn't insult me by using only words of one syllable.

It was, in part, that gentle acceptance that made me more curious about 17 my own deafness. Always before it had been an affliction to wrestle with as one would with angels, but when I finally accepted it as an inevitable part of my life, I relaxed enough to do some exploring. I would take off my hearing aid and go through a day, a night, an hour or two — as long as I could take it — in absolute silence. I felt as if I were indulging in a secret vice because I was perceiving the world in a new way — stripped of sound.

Of course I had always known that sound is vibration, but I didn't know, 18 until I stopped straining to hear, how truly sound is a refinement of feeling. Conversations at parties might elude me, but I seldom fail to pick up on moods. I enjoy watching people talk. When I am too far away to read lips I try reading postures and imagining conversations. Sometimes, to everyone's horror, I respond to things better left unsaid when I'm trying to find out what's going on around me. I want to see, touch, taste, and smell every-thing within reach; I especially have to curb a tendency to judge things by their smell — not just potato salad but people as well — a habit that seems to some people entirely too barbaric for comfort. I am not claiming that my other senses stepped up their work to compensate for the loss, but the absence of one does allow me to concentrate on the others. Deafness has left me acutely aware of both the duplicity that language is capable of and the many expressions the body cannot hide.

Nine years ago I spent the summer at the University of Texas's experi- [19] mental Shakespeare workshop at Winedale, and I went back each year for eight years, first as a student and then as a staff associate. Off and on for the last four years I have written and performed for Esther's Follies, a cabaret theater group in Austin. Some people think it's odd that, as deaf as I am, I've spent so much of my life working in the theater, but I find it to be a natural consequence of my particular circumstance. The loss of sound has enhanced my fascination with language and the way meaning is conveyed. I love to perform. Exactly the same processes occur onstage as off — except that onstage, once I've memorized the script, I know what everybody is say-ing as they say it. I am delighted to be so immediately in the know. It has provided a direct way to keep in touch with the rest of the world despite the imposed isolation.

Silence is not empty; it is simply more sobering than sound. At times I [20] prefer the sobriety. I can still "hear" with a hearing aid — that is, I can dis-cern noise, but I can't tell you where it's coming from or if it is laughter or a faulty drain. When there are many people talking together I hear a strange music, a distant rumbling in my consciousness. But when I take off my hearing aid at night and lie in bed surrounded by my fate, I wonder, "What is this — a foul subtraction or a blessing in disguise?" For despite my fears there is a kind of peace in the silence — albeit an uneasy one. There is, after all, less to distract me from my thoughts.

But I know what I've lost. The process of becoming deaf has at times [21] been frightening, akin perhaps to dying, and early in life it took away my happy confidence in the image of a world where things always work right. When I first came back from the Lions Camp that summer I cursed heaven and earth for doing such terrible wrong to me and to my friends. My grandmother tried to comfort me by promising, "Honey, God's got something special planned for you."

But I thought, "Yes. He plans to make me deaf."   [22]

Analyzing This Selection

1. How does the author's deafness differ from that of most other deaf people? In what ways has this difference made her problems both easier and more burdensome?

2. **THE WRITER'S METHOD** At the end of paragraph 5, the author uses two clichés about herself. What emotions in the twelve-year-old child do the clichés suggest? How does her use of cliché affect the reader?

3. In high school and college, why did Galloway refuse to acknowledge the serious consequences of her deafness? What other important considerations were at stake for her? Do you think that her denials were wise or immature for her age?

4. How has deafness influenced the author's adult awareness of the world? How has it influenced her self-awareness?

5. In paragraphs 21 and 22, is the interchange between the author and her grandmother an appropriate or disappointing conclusion to the essay? What attitudes and feelings does it suggest the author has found beneficial?

Analyzing Connections

6. Both Galloway and Ephron (see "Shaping Up Absurd," p. 20) suffer mortifications. Compare the kinds of humiliation they endure. What similarities and differences do you find in their self-images?

Analyzing by Writing

7. Helen Keller, who became deaf and blind when she was nineteen months old, said that deafness was the more difficult of her two misfortunes. Which deprivation would be more threatening to you? Are you primarily visually or aurally oriented? Write an essay explaining how the complete loss of sight or hearing would disconnect you from what you now value most in the world and in yourself.

Brent Staples

BLACK MEN AND PUBLIC SPACE

BRENT STAPLES (b. 1951) was born in Chester, Pennsylvania. He earned his undergraduate degree at Widener University and a Ph.D. in psychology from the University of Chicago. After working at the *Chicago Sun-Times* and several Chicago periodicals, he became an assistant metropolitan editor at the *New York Times* in 1985. He is now on the editorial board of that newspaper. Staples has published a memoir, *Parallel Time: Growing Up in Black and White* (1994). The following essay, which appeared first in *Ms.* magazine, describes his experience of "being ever the suspect" in urban America.

My first victim was a woman — white, well dressed, probably in her early 1 twenties. I came upon her late one evening on a deserted street in Hyde Park, a relatively affluent neighborhood in an otherwise mean, impoverished section of Chicago. As I swung onto the avenue behind her, there seemed to be a discreet, uninflammatory distance between us. Not so. She cast back a worried glance. To her, the youngish black man — a broad six feet two inches with a beard and billowing hair, both hands shoved into the pockets of a bulky military jacket — seemed menacingly close. After a few more quick glimpses, she picked up her pace and was soon running in earnest. Within seconds she disappeared into a cross street.

That was more than a decade ago. I was twenty-two years old, a gradu- 2 ate student newly arrived at the University of Chicago. It was in the echo of that terrified woman's footfalls that I first began to know the unwieldy inheritance I'd come into — the ability to alter public space in ugly ways. It was clear that she thought herself the quarry of a mugger, a rapist, or worse. Suffering a bout of insomnia, however, I was stalking sleep, not defenseless wayfarers. As a softy who is scarcely able to take a knife to a raw chicken — let alone hold one to a person's throat — I was surprised, embarrassed, and dismayed all at once. Her flight made me feel like an accomplice in tyranny. It also made it clear that I was indistinguishable from the muggers who occasionally seeped into the area from the surrounding ghetto. That first encounter, and those that followed, signified that a vast, unnerving gulf lay between nighttime pedestrians — particularly women — and me. And I soon gathered that being perceived as dangerous is a hazard in itself. I only needed to turn a corner into a dicey situation, or crowd some frightened, armed person in a foyer somewhere, or make an errant move after being pulled over by a policeman. Where fear and weapons meet — and they often do in urban America — there is always the possibility of death.

In that first year, my first away from my hometown, I was to become 3 thoroughly familiar with the language of fear. At dark, shadowy intersections, I could cross in front of a car stopped at a traffic light and elicit the *thunk, thunk, thunk, thunk* of the driver — black, white, male, or female — hammering down the door locks. On less traveled streets after dark, I grew accustomed to but never comfortable with people crossing to the other side of the street rather than pass me. Then there were the standard unpleasantries with policemen, doormen, bouncers, cabdrivers, and others whose business it is to screen out troublesome individuals *before* there is any nastiness.

I moved to New York nearly two years ago and I have remained an avid 4 night walker. In central Manhattan, the near-constant crowd cover minimizes tense one-on-one street encounters. Elsewhere — in SoHo, for example, where sidewalks are narrow and tightly spaced buildings shut out the sky — things can get very taut indeed.

After dark, on the warrenlike streets of Brooklyn where I live, I often see 5 women who fear the worst from me. They seem to have set their faces on neutral, and with their purse straps strung across their chests bandolier-style, they forge ahead as though bracing themselves against being tackled. I understand, of course, that the danger they perceive is not a hallucination. Women are particularly vulnerable to street violence, and young black males are drastically overrepresented among the perpetrators of that violence. Yet these truths are no solace against the kind of alienation that comes of being ever the suspect, a fearsome entity with whom pedestrians avoid making eye contact.

It is not altogether clear to me how I reached the ripe old age of twenty- 6 two without being conscious of the lethality nighttime pedestrians attributed to me. Perhaps it was because in Chester, Pennsylvania, the small, angry industrial town where I came of age in the 1960s, I was scarcely noticeable against a backdrop of gang warfare, street knifings, and murders. I grew up one of the good boys, had perhaps a half-dozen fistfights. In retrospect, my shyness of combat has clear sources.

As a boy, I saw countless tough guys locked away; I have since buried 7 several, too. They were babies, really — a teenage cousin, a brother of twenty-two, a childhood friend in his mid-twenties — all gone down in episodes of bravado played out in the streets. I came to doubt the virtues of intimidation early on. I chose, perhaps unconsciously, to remain a shadow — timid, but a survivor.

The fearsomeness mistakenly attributed to me in public places often has 8 a perilous flavor. The most frightening of these confusions occurred in the late 1970s and early 1980s, when I worked as a journalist in Chicago. One day, rushing into the office of a magazine I was writing for with a deadline story in hand, I was mistaken for a burglar. The office manager called security and, with an ad hoc posse, pursued me through the labyrinthine halls, nearly to my editor's door. I had no way of proving who I was. I could only move briskly toward the company of someone who knew me.

Another time I was on assignment for a local paper and killing time 9 before an interview. I entered a jewelry store on the city's affluent Near North Side. The proprietor excused herself and returned with an enormous red Doberman pinscher straining at the end of a leash. She stood, the dog extended toward me, silent to my questions, her eyes bulging nearly out of her head. I took a cursory look around, nodded, and bade her good night.

Relatively speaking, however, I never fared as badly as another black 10 male journalist. He went to nearby Waukegan, Illinois, a couple of summers ago to work on a story about a murderer who was born there. Mistaking the reporter for the killer, police officers hauled him from his car at gunpoint and but for his press credentials would probably have tried to book him. Such episodes are not uncommon. Black men trade tales like this all the time.

Over the years, I learned to smother the rage I felt at so often being 11 taken for a criminal. Not to do so would surely have led to madness. I now take precautions to make myself less threatening. I move about with care, particularly late in the evening. I give a wide berth to nervous people on subway platforms during the wee hours, particularly when I have exchanged business clothes for jeans. If I happen to be entering a building behind some people who appear skittish, I may walk by, letting them clear the lobby before I return, so as not to seem to be following them. I have been calm and extremely congenial on those rare occasions when I've been pulled over by the police.

And on late-evening constitutionals I employ what has proved to be an 12 excellent tension-reducing measure: I whistle melodies from Beethoven and Vivaldi and the more popular classical composers. Even steely New Yorkers hunching toward nighttime destinations seem to relax, and occasionally they even join in the tune. Virtually everybody seems to sense that a mugger wouldn't be warbling bright, sunny selections from Vivaldi's *Four Seasons*. It is my equivalent of the cowbell that hikers wear when they know they are in bear country.

Analyzing This Selection

1. **THE WRITER'S METHOD**   What is the effect of the opening paragraph?

2. How does the author's presence "alter public space in ugly ways"? Describe the difference between Staples's image of himself and how he is perceived by others.

3. Why doesn't Staples see the suspicion he elicits from being a young black man on the street as solely the result of racial attitudes?

4. How does the author defuse the explosive tensions his presence produces in other people? Do his methods compromise his own self-image and integrity?

5. What is the essay's overall purpose? Does Staples propose any remedies for the unjust assumptions he describes?

Analyzing Connections

6. Staples and Galloway (see "I'm Listening as Hard as I Can," p. 28) each relate a brief incident in their opening paragraphs. Compare the themes and tones they introduce within these anecdotal openings. Both essays conclude by echoing the opening anecdotes. What is the effect of such endings?

Analyzing by Writing

7. In what way have you been stereotyped? Perhaps as "a brain" or "a jock"; or as a black, a Jew, an Italian; or as someone who is always "good-natured" or always "responsible." In an essay, examine the stereotype that falsifies and denigrates something that is true in your nature.

John Updike

THE DISPOSABLE ROCKET

JOHN UPDIKE (b. 1932), one of America's most recognized and prolific writers, started his career on the staff of the *New Yorker* after graduating from Harvard in 1954. His contribution to this and other major magazines — of stories, poems, essays, and reviews — continues to this day. His major novels include four about Harry "Rabbit" Angstrom: *Rabbit, Run* (1960), *Rabbit Redux* (1971), *Rabbit Is Rich* (1981), which won three major literary awards, and *Rabbit at Rest* (1990). His best-known novel may well be *The Witches of Eastwick* (1984), also adapted into a movie. As an essayist Updike often writes about painting and other visual art, his secondary interest. The following essay first appeared in a special issue of the *Michigan Quarterly Review* devoted to the topic of the male body.

Inhabiting a male body is like having a bank account; as long as it's   1
healthy, you don't think much about it. Compared to the female body, it is a low-maintenance proposition: a shower now and then, trim the fingernails every ten days, a haircut once a month. Oh yes, shaving — scraping or buzzing away at your face every morning. Byron, in *Don Juan*, thought the repeated nuisance of shaving balanced out the periodic agony, for females, of childbirth. Women are, his lines tell us,

> Condemn'd to child-bed, as men for their sins
> Have shaving too entail'd upon their chins, —
>
> A daily plague, which in the aggregate
> May average on the whole with parturition.

From the standpoint of reproduction, the male body is a delivery system, as the female is a mazy device for retention. Once the delivery is made, men feel a faint but distinct falling-off of interest. Yet against the enduring female heroics of birth and nurture should be set the male's superhuman frenzy to deliver his goods: He vaults walls, skips sleep, risks wallet, health, and his political future all to ram home his seed into the gut of the chosen woman. The sense of the chase lives in him as the key to life. His body is, like a delivery rocket that falls away in space, a disposable means. Men put their bodies at risk to experience the release from gravity.

When my tenancy of a male body was fairly new — of six or so years'   2

38

duration — I used to jump and fall just for the joy of it. Falling — backwards, or down stairs — became a specialty of mine, an attention-getting stunt I was still practicing into my thirties, at suburban parties. Falling is, after all, a kind of flying, though of briefer duration than would be ideal. My impulse to hurl myself from high windows and the edges of cliffs belongs to my body, not my mind, which resists the siren call of the chasm with all its might; the interior struggle knocks the wind from my lungs and tightens my scrotum and gives any trip to Europe, with its Alps, castle parapets, and gargoyled cathedral lookouts, a flavor of nightmare. Falling, strangely, no longer figures in my dreams, as it often did when I was a boy and my subconscious was more honest with me. An airplane, that necessary evil, turns the earth into a map so quickly the brain turns aloof and calm; still, I marvel that there is no end of young men willing to become jet pilots.

Any accounting of male-female differences must include the male's 3 superior recklessness, a drive not, I think, toward death, as the darker feminist cosmogonies would have it, but to test the limits, to see what the traffic will bear — a kind of mechanic's curiosity. The number of men who do lasting damage to their young bodies is striking; war and car accidents aside, secondary-school sports, with the approval of parents and the encouragement of brutish coaches, take a fearful toll of skulls and knees. We were made for combat, back in the postsimian, East-African days, and the bumping, the whacking, the breathlessness, the pain-smothering adrenaline rush form a cumbersome and unfashionable bliss, but bliss nevertheless. Take your body to the edge, and see if it flies.

The male sense of space must differ from that of the female, who has 4 such interesting, active, and significant inner space. The space that interests men is outer. The fly ball high against the sky, the long pass spiraling overhead, the jet fighter like a scarcely visible pinpoint nozzle laying down its vapor trail at forty thousand feet, the gazelle haunch flickering just beyond arrow-reach, the uncountable stars sprinkled on their great black wheel, the horizon, the mountaintop, the quasar — these bring portents with them and awaken a sense of relation with the invisible, with the empty. The ideal male body is taut with lines of potential force, a diagram extending outward; the ideal female body curves around centers of repose. Of course, no one is ideal, and the sexes are somewhat androgynous subdivisions of a species: Diana the huntress is a more trendy body type nowadays than languid, overweight Venus, and polymorphous Dionysus poses for more underwear ads than Mars. Relatively, though, men's bodies, however elegant, are designed for covering territory, for moving on.

An erection, too, defies gravity, flirts with it precariously. It extends the 5 diagram of outward direction into downright detachability — objective in the case of the sperm, subjective in the case of the testicles and penis. Men's bodies, at this juncture, feel only partly theirs; a demon of sorts has been attached to their lower torsos, whose performance is erratic and whose errands seem, at times, ridiculous. It is like having a (much) smaller brother toward whom you feel both fond and impatient; if he is you, it is you in curiously simplified and ignoble form. This sense, of the male body being two of them, is acknowledged in verbal love play and erotic writing, where the penis is playfully given a pet name, an individuation not even the rarest rapture grants a vagina. Here, where maleness gathers to a quintessence of itself, there can be no insincerity, there can be no hiding; for sheer nakedness, there is nothing like a hopeful phallus; its aggressive shape is indivisible from its tender-skinned vulnerability. The act of intercourse, from the point of view of a consenting female, has an element of mothering, of enwrapment, of merciful concealment, even. The male body, for this interval, is tucked out of harm's way.

To inhabit a male body, then, is to feel somewhat detached from it. It is 6 not an enemy, but not entirely a friend. Our being seems to lie not in cells and muscles but in the traces that our thoughts and actions inscribe on the air. The male body skims the surface of nature's deeps wherein the blood and pain and mysterious cravings of women perpetuate the species. Participating less in nature's processes than the female body, the male body gives the impression — false — of being exempt from time. Its powers of strength and reach descend in early adolescence, along with acne and sweaty feet, and depart, in imperceptible increments, after thirty or so. It surprises me to discover, when I remove my shoes and socks, the same paper-white, hairless ankles that struck me as pathetic when I observed them on my father. I felt betrayed when, in some tumble of touch football twenty years ago, I heard my tibia snap; and when, between two reading engagements in Cleveland, my appendix tried to burst; and when, the other day, not for the first time, there arose to my nostrils out of my own body the musty attic smell my grandfather's body had.

A man's body does not betray its tenant as rapidly as a woman's. Never 7 as fine and lovely, it has less distance to fall; what rugged beauty it has is wrinkleproof. It keeps its capability of procreation indecently long. Unless intense athletic demands are made upon it, the thing serves well enough to sixty, which is my age now. From here on, it's chancy. There are no breasts or ovaries to admit cancer to the male body, but the prostate, that awkwardly located little source of seminal fluid, shows the strain of sexual function with fits of hysterical cell replication, and all that male-bonding beer and potato chips add up in the coronary arteries. A writer, whose physical equipment can be minimal as long as it gets him to the desk, the lectern, and New York City once in a while, cannot but be grateful to his body, especially to his eyes, those tender and intricate sites where the brain extrudes from the skull, and to his hands, which hold the pen or tap the keyboard. His body has been, not himself exactly, but a close pal, potbellied and balding like most of his other pals now. A man and his body are like a boy and the buddy who has a driver's license and the use of his father's car for the evening; one only goes along, gratefully, for the ride.

Analyzing This Selection

1. Does Updike oversimplify male and female self-images? Or does he accurately present basic facts? In your answer, consider the implications of the essay's emphasis on male and female biology.

2. **THE WRITER'S METHOD** How would the connotations of Updike's metaphor change if he referred to the male body as the reusable rocket? How would that metaphor change the central idea of the essay?

3. In the final two paragraphs, what is the author's attitude toward his aging body? How does it differ from his youthful attitude?

Analyzing Connections

4. Updike and Ephron (see "Shaping Up Absurd," p. 20) show that men and women can feel distinctly detached from their bodies. Do the writers have contrasting or similar explanations for this detachment in their sex?

Analyzing by Writing

5. Updike refers to "ideal" forms of men and women, but he notes that "trendy" norms may differ (paragraph 4). What is currently considered attractive in women and men? How do popular images glamorize health and sportiness, delicateness and fragility, subtlety and mystery, or something else? What are the possibly negative effects of these images?

Scott Russell Sanders

VOYAGEURS

Scott Russell Sanders (b. 1945), a fiction writer and essayist, graduated from Brown University and received a Ph.D. in English from Cambridge University in England. He teaches at Indiana University, and his writings appear in magazines such as *Harper's*, *Georgia Review*, and *Science Fiction*. His personal essays are published in *The Paradise of Bombs* (1987), *Staying Put: Making a Home in a Restless World* (1993), and *Writing from the Center* (1996), which includes the following selection.

In morning mist on a northern river, a slab of stone tumbled from a 1 boulder into the water, where it came to life and floated, turning into a sleek black head that swam in circles dragging a V of ripples behind it. A beaver, I thought, as I watched from shore. But no sooner had I named it than the creature bobbed up and then dove, exposing a long neck and humped back and pointed tail. Not a beaver, I realized, but an otter. I was pleased to find a label for this animate scrap, as though by pinning the right word on the shape-shifter I could hold it still.

Presently a second otter, then a third and fourth broke free of the boul- 2 der and slithered down into the mercury sheen of the river. They dove without a splash, their tails flipping up to gleam like wands in the early sunlight, and they surfaced so buoyantly that their forepaws and narrow shoulders lifted well out of the water. Then one after another they clambered back onto the rock and dove again, over and over, like tireless children taking turns on a playground slide.

My daughter Eva came to stand beside me, the hood of her parka drawn 3 up against the cool of this July morning here in the north woods, on the boundary between Minnesota and Ontario. We passed her binoculars back and forth, marveling at these sleek, exuberant animals.

"Wouldn't you love to swim with them?" she whispered. 4

"I'd love to sit on that boulder and let them do the swimming," I 5 answered.

"If only they'd let us!" 6

Always quick to notice the flicker of life, Eva had spent the past two 7 summers studying birds with a research team, and now, halfway through college, she had become a disciplined as well as a passionate observer. Science had complicated her vision without lessening her delight in other creatures.

"What do you suppose they're doing?" I asked.   8

"The technical term for it," she said, "is goofing around."   9

"I suppose you've got some data to back that up."   10

"I'll show you the graphs when we get home."   11

Drawn by our whispers and watchfulness, the others from our camp   12
soon joined us on the granite bluff, some bearing mugs of coffee, some with plates of steaming blueberry pancakes. We had been canoeing in the Boundary Waters Wilderness for several days, long enough for the men's faces to stubble with beards, for the women's faces to burnish from wind and sun. When all ten of us were gathered there beside the river, intently watching, suddenly the otters quit diving, swiveled their snouts in our direction, then ducked into hiding beneath some lily pads. After a couple of minutes, as though having mulled over what to do about this intrusion, they sallied out again and resumed their romping, chasing one another, bobbing and plunging, but farther and farther away, until they disappeared around the next bend.

If our scent or voices had not spooked them, then our upright silhou-   13
ettes, breaking the glacier-smoothed outline of the shore, must have signaled danger to the otters. There was no way of knowing what else, if anything, we meant to them. What did the otters mean to us? What held us there while our pancakes cooled, while acres of mist rode the current past our feet, while the sun rose above a jagged fringe of trees and poured creamy light onto the river? What did we want from these elegant swimmers?

Or, to put the question in the only form I can hope to answer, what did   14
I want? Not their hides, as the native people of this territory, the Ojibwa, or the old French voyageurs might have wanted; not their souls or meat. I did not even want their photograph, although I found them surpassingly beautiful. I wanted their company. I desired their instruction — as if, by watching them, I might learn to belong somewhere as they so thoroughly belonged here. I yearned to slip out of my skin and into theirs, to feel the world for a spell through their senses, to think otter thoughts, and then to slide back into myself, a bit wiser for the journey.

In tales of shamans the world over, men and women make just such   15
leaps, into hawks or snakes or bears, and then back into human shape, their vision enlarged, their sympathy deepened. I am a poor sort of shaman. My shape never changes, except, year by year, to wrinkle and sag. I did not become an otter, even for an instant. But the yearning to leap across the distance, the reaching out in imagination to a fellow creature, seems to me a worthy impulse, perhaps the most encouraging and distinctive one we have. It is the same impulse that moves us to reach out to one another across differences of race or gender, age or class. What I desired from the

otters was also what I most wanted from my daughter and from the friends with whom we were canoeing, and it is what I have always desired from neighbors and strangers. I wanted their blessing. I wanted to dwell alongside them with understanding and grace. I wanted them to go about their lives in my presence as though I were kin to them, no matter how much I might differ from them outwardly.

Analyzing This Selection

1. Choose two adjectives of your own that describe the mood of people watching the otters. Find details in the essay that support your choices.

2. Explain why Sanders wants temporarily to become an otter.

3. **THE WRITER'S METHOD**   The author says that an impulse such as his is "perhaps the most encouraging and distinctive one we have" (para. 15). Is Sanders exaggerating its importance? How can he make such a big claim for this wish? Explain what enlarges the significance of this impulse.

Analyzing Connections

4. What differing animal qualities are desired by Sanders and by N. Scott Momaday in the Insights on page 16? Which qualities are more attractive to you? Explain which selection you find more enjoyable reading.

Analyzing by Writing

5. Examine the lasting effects an animal had on your character. Consider either a long-term relationship with a pet or horse or a brief connection such as Sanders's encounter or a hunting trip. Be sure to give details that establish the animal's qualities. Consider both positive and negative responses that have changed your feelings and ideas.

Michael Dorris

LIFE STORIES

Michael Dorris (1945–1997) was a leading writer of fiction and essays about American Indian life and social issues. Educated at Georgetown University and Yale University, Dorris was a professor of Native American studies at Dartmouth College. In *The Broken Cord* (1990) he recounts the circumstances surrounding his adopted son's struggle with fetal alcohol syndrome. His essays, from which this selection is drawn, were collected in *Paper Trail* (1994). *Cloud Chamber* (1997) is his last novel.

In most cultures, adulthood is equated with self-reliance and responsibility, yet often Americans do not achieve this status until we are in our late twenties or early thirties — virtually the entire average lifespan of a person in a traditional non-Western society. We tend to treat prolonged adolescence as a warm-up for real life, as a wobbly suspension bridge between childhood and legal maturity. Whereas a nineteenth-century Cheyenne or Lakota teenager was expected to alter self-conception in a split-second vision, we often meander through an analogous rite of passage for more than a decade — through high school, college, graduate school.

Though he had never before traveled alone outside his village, the Plains Indian male was expected at puberty to venture solo into the wilderness. There he had to fend for and sustain himself while avoiding the menace of unknown dangers, and there he had absolutely to remain until something happened that would transform him. Every human being, these tribes believed, was entitled to at least one moment of personal, enabling insight.

Anthropology proposes feasible psychological explanations for why this flash was eventually triggered: fear, fatigue, reliance on strange foods, the anguish of loneliness, stress, and the expectation of ultimate success all contributed to a state of receptivity. Every sense was quickened, alerted to perceive deep meaning, until at last the interpretation of an unusual event — a dream, a chance encounter, or an unexpected vista — reverberated with metaphor. Through this unique prism, abstractly preserved in a vivid memory or song, a boy caught foresight of both his adult persona and of his vocation, the two inextricably entwined.

Today the best approximations that many of us get to such a heady sense   4
of eventuality come in the performance of our school vacation jobs. Summers are intermissions, and once we hit our teens it is during these breaks
in our structured regimen that we initially taste the satisfaction of remu-
neration that is earned, not merely doled. Tasks defined as *work* are not
only graded, they are compensated; they have a worth that is unarguable
because it translates into hard currency. Wage labor — and in the beginning, this generally means a confining, repetitive chore for which we are
quickly over-qualified — paradoxically brings a sense of blooming freedom.
At the outset, the complaint to a peer that business supersedes fun is oddly
liberating — no matter what drudgery requires your attention, it is by its
very required nature serious and adult.

At least that's how it seemed to me. I come from a line of people hard   5
hit by the Great Depression. My mother and her sisters went to work early
in their teens — my mother operated a kind of calculator known as a
comptometer while her sisters spent their days, respectively, at a peanut factory and at Western Union. My grandmother did piecework sewing. Their
efforts, and the Democratic Party, saw them through, and to this day they
never look back without appreciation for their later solvency. They take
nothing for granted. Accomplishments are celebrated, possessions are valuable, in direct proportion to the labor entailed to acquire them; anything
easily won or bought on credit is suspect. When I was growing up we were
far from wealthy, but what money we had was correlated to the hours some
one of us had logged. My eagerness to contribute to, or at least not diminish,
the coffer was countered by the arguments of those whose salaries kept me
in school: My higher education was a sound group investment. The whole
family was adamant that I have the opportunities they had missed and, no
matter how much I objected, they stinted themselves to provide for me.

Summer jobs were therefore a relief, an opportunity to pull a share of   6
the load. As soon as the days turned warm I began to peruse the classifieds,
and when the spring semester was done, I was ready to punch a clock. It
even felt right. Work in June, July, and August had an almost Biblical
aspect: In the hot, canicular weather your brow sweated, just as God had
ordained. Moreover, summer jobs had the luxury of being temporary. No
matter how bizarre, how onerous, how off my supposed track, employment
terminated with the falling leaves and I was back on neutral ground. So,
during each annual three-month leave from secondary school and later
from the university, I compiled an eclectic résumé: lawn cutter, hair
sweeper in a barber shop, lifeguard, delivery boy, temporary mail carrier,
file clerk, youth program coordinator on my Montana reservation, ballroom
dance instructor, theater party promoter, night-shift hospital records keeper,
human adding machine in a Paris bank, encyclopedia salesman, newspaper
stringer, recreation bus manager, salmon fisherman.

The reasonable titles disguise the madness of some of these occupations.   7
For instance, I seemed inevitably to be hired to trim the yards of the

unconventional. One woman followed beside me, step by step, as I traversed her yard in ever tighter squares, and called my attention to each missed blade of grass. Another client never had the "change" to pay me, and so reimbursed my weekly pruning with an offering culled from his library. I could have done without the *Guide to Artificial Respiration* (1942) or the many well-worn copies of Reader's Digest Condensed Books, but sometimes the selection merited the wait. Like a rat lured repeatedly back to the danger of mild electric shock by the mystique of intermittent reenforcement, I kept mowing by day in hopes of turning pages all night.

The summer I was eighteen a possibility arose for a rotation at the post 8 office, and I grabbed it. There was something casually sophisticated about work that required a uniform, about having a federal ranking, even if it was GS-1 (Temp/Sub), and it was flattering to be entrusted with a leather bag containing who knew what important correspondence. Every day I was assigned a new beat, usually in a rough neighborhood avoided whenever possible by regular carriers, and I proved quite capable of complicating what would normally be fairly routine missions. The low point came on the first of August when I diligently delivered four blocks' worth of welfare checks to the right numbers on the wrong streets. It is no fun to snatch unexpected wealth from the hands of those who have but moments previously opened their mailboxes and received a bonus.

After my first year of college, I lived with relatives on an Indian reserva- 9 tion in eastern Montana and filled the only post available: Coordinator of Tribal Youth Programs. I was seduced by the language of the announcement into assuming that there existed Youth Programs to be coordinated. In fact, the Youth consisted of a dozen bored, disgruntled kids — most of them my cousins — who had nothing better to do each day than to show up at what was euphemistically called "the gym" and hate whatever Program I had planned for them. The Youth ranged in age from fifteen to five and seemed to have as their sole common ambition the determination to smoke cigarettes. This put them at immediate and on-going odds with the Coordinator, who on his first day naively encouraged them to sing the "Doe, a deer, a female deer" song from *The Sound of Music*. They looked at me, that bleak morning, and I looked at them, each boy and girl equipped with a Pall Mall behind an ear, and we all knew it would be a long, struggle-charged battle. It was to be a contest of wills, the hearty and wholesome vs. prohibited vice. I stood for dodge ball, for collecting bugs in glass jars, for arts and crafts; they had pledged a preternatural allegiance to sloth. The odds were not in my favor and each waking dawn I experienced the lightheadedness of anticipated exhaustion, that thrill of giddy dissociation in which nothing seems real or of great significance. I went with the flow and learned to inhale.

The next summer, I decided to find work in an urban setting for a 10 change, and was hired as a general office assistant in the Elsa Hoppenfeld Theatre Party Agency, located above Sardi's restaurant in New York City.

The Agency consisted of Elsa Hoppenfeld herself, Rita Frank, her regular deputy, and me. Elsa was a gregarious Viennese woman who established contacts through personal charm, and she spent much of the time courting trade away from the building. Rita was therefore both my immediate supervisor and constant companion; she had the most incredible fingernails I had ever seen — long, carefully shaped pegs lacquered in cruel primary colors and hard as stone — and an attitude about her that could only be described as zeal.

The goal of a theater party agent is to sell blocks of tickets to imminent 11 Broadway productions, and the likely buyers are charities, B'nai Briths, Hadassahs, and assorted other fund-raising organizations. We received commissions on volume, and so it was necessary to convince a prospect that a play — preferably an expensive musical — for which we had reserved the rights to seats would be a boffo smash hit.

The object of our greatest expectation that season was an extravaganza 12 called *Chu Chem*, a saga that aspired to ride the coattails of *Fiddler on the Roof* into entertainment history. It starred the estimable Molly Picon and told the story of a family who had centuries ago gone from Israel to China during the disapora, yet had, despite isolation in an alien environment, retained orthodox culture and habits. The crux of the plot revolved around a man with several marriageable daughters and nary a kosher suitor within 5,000 miles. For three months Rita and I waxed eloquent in singing the show's praises. We sat in our little office, behind facing desks, and every noon while she redid her nails I ordered out from a deli that offered such exotic (to me) delicacies as fried egg sandwiches, lox and cream cheese, pastrami, *tongue*. I developed of necessity and habit a telephone voice laced with a distinctly Yiddish accent. It could have been a great career. However, come November, *Chu Chem* bombed. Its closing was such a financial catastrophe for all concerned that when the following January one Monsieur Dupont advertised on the Placement Board at my college, I decided to put an ocean between me and my former trusting clientele.

M. Dupont came to campus with the stated purpose of interviewing 13 candidates for teller positions in a French bank. Successful applicants, required to be fluent in *français*, would be rewarded with three well-paid months and a rent-free apartment in Paris. I headed for the language lab and registered for an appointment.

The only French in the interview was *Bonjour, ça va?*, after which M. 14 Dupont switched into English and described the wonderful deal on charter air flights that would be available to those who got the nod. Round-trip to Amsterdam, via Reykjavik, leaving the day after exams and returning in mid-September, no changes or substitutions. I signed up on the spot. I was to be a *banquier*, with *pied-à-terre* in Montparnasse!

Unfortunately, when I arrived with only $50 in travelers checks in my 15 pocket — the flight had cleaned me out, but who needed money since my paycheck started right away — no one in Paris had ever heard of M. Dupont.

Alors.   16

I stood in the Gare du Nord and considered my options. There weren't   17
any. I scanned a listing of Paris hotels and headed for the cheapest one: the
Hotel Villedo, $10 a night. The place had an ambiance that I persuaded
myself was antique, despite the red light above the sign. The only accommodation available was "the bridal suite," a steal at $20. The glass door to
my room didn't lock and there was a rather continual floor show, but at
some point I must have dozed off. When I awoke the church bells were
ringing, the sky was pink, and I felt renewed. No little setback was going to
spoil my adventure. I stood and stretched, then walked to a mirror that
hung above the sink next to the bed. I leaned forward to punctuate my
resolve with a confident look in the eye.

The sink disengaged and fell to the floor. Water gushed. In panic I rum-   18
maged through my open suitcase, stuffed two pair of underwear into the
pipe to quell the flow, and before the dam broke, I was out the door. I barreled through the lobby of the first bank I passed, asked to see the director,
and told the startled man my sad story. For some reason, whether from
shock or pity, he hired me at $1.27 an hour to be a cross-checker of foreign
currency transactions, and with two phone calls found me lodgings at a
commercial school's dormitory.

From eight to five each weekday my duty was to sit in a windowless   19
room with six impeccably dressed people, all of whom were totaling identical additions and subtractions. We were highly dignified with each other,
very professional, no *tutoyer*ing. Monsieur Saint presided, but the formidable Mademoiselle was the true power; she oversaw each of our columns
and shook her head sadly at my American-shaped numbers.

My legacy from that summer, however, was more than an enduring pen-   20
chant for crossed 7s. After I had worked for six weeks, M. Saint asked me
during a coffee break why I didn't follow the example of other foreign students he had known and depart the office at noon in order to spend the
afternoon touring the sights of Paris with the *Alliance Française.*

"Because," I replied in my halting French, "that costs money. I depend   21
upon my full salary the same as any of you." M. Saint nodded gravely and
said no more, but then on the next Friday he presented me with a white
envelope along with my check.

"Do not open this until you have left the Société Générale," he said   22
ominously. I thought I was fired for the time I had mixed up krøners and
guilders, and, once on the sidewalk, I steeled myself to read the worst. I felt
the quiet panic of blankness.

"Dear Sir," I translated the perfectly formed script. "You are a person of   23
value. It is not correct that you should be in our beautiful city and not see
it. Therefore we have amassed a modest sum to pay the tuition for a two-
week afternoon program for you at the *Alliance Française.* Your wages will
not suffer, for it is your assignment to appear each morning in this bureau
and reacquaint us with the places you have visited. We shall see them

afresh through your eyes." The letter had thirty signatures, from the Director to the janitor, and stuffed inside the envelope was a sheaf of franc notes in various denominations.

I rushed back to the tiny office. M. Saint and Mademoiselle had waited, 24 and accepted my gratitude with their usual controlled smiles and precise handshakes. But they had blown their Gallic cover, and for the next ten days and then through all the days until I went home in September, our branch was awash with sightseeing paraphernalia. Everyone had advice, favorite haunts, criticisms of the *Alliance*'s choices or explanations. Paris passed through the bank's granite walls as sweetly as a June breeze through a window screen, and ever afterward the lilt of overheard French, a photograph of *Sacré Coeur* or the Louvre, even a monthly bank statement, recalls to me that best of all summers.

I didn't wind up in an occupation with any obvious connection to the 25 careers I sampled during my school breaks, but I never altogether abandoned those brief professions either. They were jobs not so much to be held as to be weighed, absorbed, and incorporated, and, collectively, they carried me forward into adult life like overlapping stairs, unfolding a particular pattern at once haphazard and inevitable.

Analyzing This Section

1. **THE WRITER'S METHOD** Dorris begins by contrasting how Native American and white culture recognize maturity. What positive and negative effects does the author see in each approach? Do you see additional pros and cons?

2. Dorris recounts some summer jobs that were futile or absurd. Are they effective rites of passage? What did Dorris gain from them? Can you find evidence of these gains in the essay's tone?

3. Explain why the dignified formality of the French bank contributed to the job's ultimate value to Dorris. Why was it "the best of all summers"?

Analyzing Connections

4. Compare Dorris's view of identity with Fay Weldon's suggestion in the Insights on page 17 that we change our names as a frequent rite of passage. What do both writers imply about self-image and identity?

Analyzing by Writing

5. Examine the task that made you aware of doing something "serious and adult," as Dorris felt about summer jobs. What responsibilities and challenges stirred this sense of maturity? Consider how this task differed from your other activities at that time. What effects of that experience continue in your personality?

Jamaica Kincaid

GIRL

Jamaica Kincaid (b. 1949) was born in Antigua in the West Indies, and much of her work draws on her early life on the island. She came to the United States at seventeen and soon began writing fiction and essays. From 1974 to 1995 Kincaid was a staff writer at the *New Yorker* and wrote fiction at the same time, producing a collection of stories, *At the Bottom of the River* (1983), and three novels, *Annie John* (1985), *Lucy* (1990), and *The Autobiography of My Mother* (1996). Kincaid writes about the destructive effects of colonial rule in Antigua in *A Small Place* (1988). The very short story "Girl" is her first published piece of fiction.

Wash the white clothes on Monday and put them on the stone heap; wash the color clothes on Tuesday and put them on the clothesline to dry; don't walk barehead in the hot sun; cook pumpkin fritters in very hot sweet oil; soak your little cloths right after you take them off; when buying cotton to make yourself a nice blouse, be sure that it doesn't have gum on it, because that way it won't hold up well after a wash; soak salt fish overnight before you cook it; is it true that you sing benna[1] in Sunday school?; always eat your food in such a way that it won't turn someone else's stomach; on Sundays try to walk like a lady and not like the slut you are so bent on becoming; don't sing benna in Sunday school; you mustn't speak to wharf-rat boys, not even to give directions; don't eat fruits on the street — flies will follow you; *but I don't sing benna on Sundays at all and never in Sunday school*; this is how to sew on a button; this is how to make a buttonhole for the button you have just sewed on; this is how to hem a dress when you see the hem coming down and so to prevent yourself from looking like the slut I know you are so bent on becoming; this is how you iron your father's khaki shirt so that it doesn't have a crease; this is how you iron your father's khaki pants so that they don't have a crease; this is how you grow okra — far from the house, because okra tree harbors red ants; when you are growing dasheen,[2] make sure it gets plenty of water or else it makes your throat itch when you are eating it; this is how you sweep a corner; this is how you sweep a whole house; this is how you sweep a yard; this is how you smile to someone you don't like

---

[1] *benna* Calypso music.
[2] *dasheen* Tropical plant with an edible root.

too much; this is how you smile to someone you don't like at all; this is how you smile to someone you like completely; this is how you set a table for tea; this is how you set a table for dinner; this is how you set a table for dinner with an important guest; this is how you set a table for lunch; this is how you set a table for breakfast; this is how to behave in the presence of men who don't know you very well, and this way they won't recognize immediately the slut I have warned you against becoming; be sure to wash every day, even if it is with your own spit; don't squat down to play marbles — you are not a boy, you know; don't pick people's flowers — you might catch something; don't throw stones at blackbirds, because it might not be a blackbird at all; this is how to make a bread pudding; this is how to make doukona;[3] this is how to make pepper pot; this is how to make a good medicine for a cold; this is how to make a good medicine to throw away a child before it even becomes a child; this is how to catch a fish; this is how to throw back a fish you don't like, and that way something bad won't fall on you; this is how to bully a man; this is how a man bullies you; this is how to love a man, and if this doesn't work there are other ways, and if they don't work don't feel too bad about giving up; this is how to spit up in the air if you feel like it, and this is how to move quick so that it doesn't fall on you; this is how to make ends meet; always squeeze bread to make sure it's fresh; *but what if the baker won't let me feel the bread?*; you mean to say that after all you are really going to be the kind of woman who the baker won't let near the bread?

[3]*doukona* Spicy pudding made from plantains.

Analyzing This Selection

1. **THE WRITER'S METHOD**   "Girl" is a running monologue with no interrupting explanations. Explain who the speakers are and their relationship. How do you know?

2. What kind of warnings and instructions are repeated? What do they tell you about the other speaker? How does the girl answer? Find specific instances of her responses.

3. What sort of adult do you think this girl will become? Support your answer by referring to details in the story that indicate her probable, or possible, future.

Analyzing Connections

4. This girl and Galloway (see "I'm Listening as Hard as I Can," p. 28) react to humiliating situations. How does each adolescent try to protect her self-image?

Analyzing by Writing

5. Write a brief script of voices inside your head this semester — parents, professors, friends. Include your own voice and responses. Try to vary the voices and attitudes without breaking the monologue.

Andrew Sullivan

WHAT IS A HOMOSEXUAL?

ANDREW SULLIVAN (b. 1963) graduated from Oxford University and received a Ph.D. in political science from Harvard University. His writing about American politics and social issues has appeared in the *New York Times*, the *Wall Street Journal*, *Esquire*, and the *New Republic*, where he became the editor. This selection is excerpted from his book about gay identity, *Virtually Normal* (1995).

Gay adolescents are offered what every heterosexual teenager longs for: 1
to be invisible in the girls' locker room. But you are invisible in the boys'
locker room, your desire as unavoidable as its object. In that moment, you
learn the first homosexual lesson: that your survival depends upon self-
concealment. I remember specifically coming back to high school after a
long summer when I was fifteen and getting changed in the locker room
for the first time again with a guy I had long had a crush on. But since the
vacation, he had developed enormously: suddenly he had hair on his chest,
his body had grown and strengthened, he was — clearly — no longer a boy.
In front of me, he took off his shirt, and unknowingly, slowly, erotically
stripped. I became literally breathless, overcome by the proximity of my
desire. The gay teenager learns in that kind of event a form of control and
sublimation, of deception and self-contempt, that never leaves his consciousness. He learns that that which would most give him meaning is most
likely to destroy him in the eyes of others; that the condition of his friendships is the subjugation of himself.

In the development of any human being, these are powerful emotions. 2
They form a person. The homosexual learns to make distinctions between
his sexual desire and his emotional longings — not because he is particularly prone to objectification of the flesh, but because he needs to survive
as a social and sexual being. The society separates these two entities, and
for a long time the homosexual has no option but to keep them separate.
He learns certain rules; and, as with a child learning grammar, they are
hard, later on in life, to unlearn.

It's possible, I think, that whatever society teaches or doesn't teach about 3
homosexuality, this fact will always be the case. No homosexual child, surrounded overwhelmingly by heterosexuals, will feel at home in his sexual

and emotional world, even in the most tolerant of cultures. And every homosexual child will learn the rituals of deceit, impersonation, and appearance. Anyone who believes political, social, or even cultural revolution will change this fundamentally is denying reality. This isolation will always hold. It is definitional of homosexual development. And children are particularly cruel. At the age of eleven, no one wants to be the odd one out; and in the arena of dating and hormones, the exclusion is inevitably a traumatic one.

It's also likely to be forlorn. Most people are liable to meet emotional rejection by sheer force of circumstance; but for a homosexual, the odds are simply far, far higher. My own experience suggests that somewhere between two and five percent of the population have involuntarily strong emotional and sexual attractions to the same sex. Which means that the pool of possible partners *starts* at one in twenty to one in fifty. It's no wonder, perhaps, that male homosexual culture has developed an ethic more of anonymous or promiscuous sex than of committed relationships. It's as if the hard lessons of adolescence lower permanently — by the sheer dint of the odds — the aspiration for anything more.

Did I know what I was? Somewhere, maybe. But it was much easier to know what I wasn't. I wasn't going to be able to enter into the world of dating girls; I wasn't going to be able to feel fully comfortable among the heterosexual climate of the male teenager. So I decided, consciously or subconsciously, to construct a trajectory of my life that would remove me from their company; give me an excuse, provide a dignified way out. In Anglo-Saxon culture, the wonk has such an option: he's too nerdy or intellectual to be absorbed by girls. And there is something masculine and respected in the discipline of the arts and especially the sciences. You can gain respect and still be different.

So I threw myself into my schoolwork, into (more dubiously) plays, into creative writing, into science fiction. Other homosexuals I have subsequently met pursued other strategies: some paradoxically threw themselves into sports, outjocking the jocks, gaining ever greater proximity, seeking respect, while knowing all the time that they were doomed to rejection. Others withdrew into isolation and despair. Others still, sensing their difference, flaunted it. At my high school, an older boy insisted on wearing full makeup to class; and he was accepted in a patronizing kind of way, his brazen otherness putting others at ease. They knew where they were with him; and he felt at least comfortable with their stable contempt. The rest of us who lived in a netherworld of sexual insecurity were not so lucky.

Most by then had a far more acute sense of appearances than those who did not need to hide anything; and our sense of irony, and of aesthetics, assumed a precociously arch form, and drew us subtly together. Looking back, I realize that many of my best friends in my teen years were probably homosexual; and that somewhere in our coded, embarrassed dialogue we admitted it. Many of us also embraced those ideologies that seemed most alien to what we feared we might be: of the sports jock, of the altar boy, of the young conservative. They were the ultimate disguises. And our recognition of ourselves in the other only confirmed our desire to keep it quiet.

I should add that many young lesbians and homosexuals seem to have 8 had a much easier time of it. For many, the question of sexual identity was not a critical factor in their life choices or vocation, or even a factor at all. Perhaps because of a less repressive upbringing or because of some natural ease in the world, they affected a simple comfort with their fate, and a desire to embrace it. These people alarmed me: their very ease was the sternest rebuke to my own anxiety, because it rendered it irrelevant. But later in life, I came to marvel at the naturalness of their self-confidence, in the face of such concerted communal pressure, and to envy it. I had the more common self-dramatizing urge of the tortured homosexual, trapped between feeling wicked and feeling ridiculous. It's shameful to admit it, but I was more traumatized by the latter than by the former: my pride was more formidable a force than my guilt.

When people ask the simple question, *What is a homosexual?* I can only 9 answer with stories like these. I could go on, but too many stories have already been told. Ask any lesbian or homosexual, and they will often provide a similar account. I was once asked at a conservative think tank what evidence I had that homosexuality was far more of an orientation than a choice, and I was forced to reply quite simply: my life. It's true that I have met a handful of lesbians and gay men over the years who have honestly told me that they genuinely had a choice in the matter (and a few heterosexuals who claim they too chose their orientation). I believe them; but they are the exception and not the rule. As homosexual lives go, my own was somewhat banal and typical.

This is not, of course, the end of the matter. Human experience begins 10 with such facts, it doesn't end with them. There's a lamentable tendency to try to find some definitive solution to permanent human predicaments — in a string of DNA, in a conclusive psychological survey, in an analysis of hypothalami, in a verse of the Bible — in order to cut the argument short. Or to insist on the emotional veracity of a certain experience and expect it to trump any other argument on the table. But none of these things can replace the political and moral argument about how a society should deal with the presence of homosexuals in its midst. I relate my experience here not to impress or to shock or to gain sympathy, but merely to convey what the homosexual experience is actually like. You cannot discuss something until you know roughly what it is. . . .

In a society more and more aware of its manifold cultures and subcul- 11 tures, we have been educated to be familiar and comfortable with what has been called "diversity": the diversity of perspective, culture, meaning. And this diversity is usually associated with what are described as cultural constructs: race, gender, sexuality, and so on. But as the obsession with diversity intensifies, the possibility of real difference alarms and terrifies all the more. The notion of collective characteristics — of attributes more associated with blacks than with whites, with Asians than with Latinos, with gay men than with straight men, with men than with women — has become anathema. They are marginalized as "stereotypes." The acceptance of diversity has come to mean the acceptance of the essential sameness of all types of people, and the danger of generalizing among them at all. In fact, it has become virtually a definition of "racist" to make any substantive generalizations about a particular ethnicity, and a definition of "homophobic" to make any generalizations about homosexuals.

What follows, then, is likely to be understood as "homophobic." But I   12
think it's true that certain necessary features of homosexual life lead to certain unavoidable features of homosexual character. This is not to say that they define any random homosexual: they do not. As with any group or way of life, there are many, many exceptions. Nor is it to say that they define the homosexual life: it should be clear by now that I believe that the needs and feelings of homosexual children and adolescents are largely interchangeable with those of their heterosexual peers. But there are certain generalizations that can be made about adult homosexuals and lesbians that have the ring of truth.

Of course, in a culture where homosexuals remain hidden and wrapped   13
in self-contempt, in which their emotional development is often stunted and late, in which the closet protects all sorts of self-destructive behavior that a more open society would not, it is still very hard to tell what is inherent in a homosexual life that makes it different, and what is simply imposed upon it. Nevertheless, it seems to me that even in the most tolerant societies, some of the differences that I have just described would inhere.

The experience of growing up profoundly different in emotional and   14
psychological makeup inevitably alters a person's self-perception, tends to make him or her more wary and distant, more attuned to appearance and its foibles, more self-conscious and perhaps more reflective. The presence of homosexuals in the arts, in literature, in architecture, in design, in fashion could be understood, as some have, as a simple response to oppression. Homosexuals have created safe professions within which to hide and protect each other. But why these professions? Maybe it's also that these are professions of appearance. Many homosexual children, feeling distant from their peers become experts at trying to figure out how to disguise their inner feelings, to "pass." They notice the signs and signals of social interaction, because they do not come instinctively. They develop skills early on that help them notice the inflections of a voice, the quirks of a particular movement, and the ways in which meaning can be conveyed in code. They have an ear for irony and for double meanings. Sometimes, by virtue

of having to suppress their natural emotions, they find formal outlets to express themselves: music, theater, art. And so their lives become set on a trajectory which reinforces these trends.

As a child, I remember, as I suppressed the natural emotions of an ado- 15 lescent, how I naturally turned in on myself — writing, painting, and participating in amateur drama. Or I devised fantasies of future exploits — war leader, parliamentarian, famous actor — that could absorb those emotions that were being diverted from meeting other boys and developing natural emotional relationships with them. And I developed mannerisms, small ways in which I could express myself, tiny revolts of personal space — a speech affectation, a ridiculous piece of clothing — that were, in retrospect, attempts to communicate something in code which could not be communicated in language. In this homosexual archness there was, of course, much pain. And it came as no surprise that once I had become more open about my homosexuality, these mannerisms declined. Once I found the strength to be myself, I had no need to act myself. So my clothes became progressively more regular and slovenly; I lost interest in drama; my writing moved from fiction to journalism; my speech actually became less affected.

This of course, is not a universal homosexual experience. Many homo- 16 sexuals never become more open, and the skills required to survive the closet remain skills by which to earn a living. And many homosexuals, even once they no longer need those skills, retain them. My point is simply that the universal experience of self-conscious difference in childhood and adolescence — common, but not exclusive, to homosexuals — develops identifiable skills. They are the skills of mimesis; and one of the goods that homosexuals bring to society is undoubtedly a more highly developed sense of form, of style. Even in the most open of societies, I think, this will continue to be the case. It is not something genetically homosexual; it is something environmentally homosexual. And it begins young.

Analyzing This Selection

1. **THE WRITER'S METHOD**   In paragraphs 1 to 3 the author argues that a gay adolescent learns a lesson true only for gays and lesbians. How does Sullivan use personal experience to support that generalization?

2. What protective strategies did Sullivan adopt as a teenager? Which did he reject?

3. According to Sullivan, what is flawed about current attitudes supporting "diversity"? In view of the risks involved in stereotyping, how do you deal with this dilemma? Does Sullivan solve the problem?

4. What are the positive adult traits that usually develop in homosexuals? Since there is no way to validate or challenge Sullivan's assertion, what makes it convincing in the essay?

Analyzing Connections

5. Did Sullivan and Staples (see "Black Men and Public Space," p. 34) become similar in their "collective characteristics," or do their adult types contrast? Does considering race weaken or strengthen Sullivan's point about his development?

Analyzing by Writing

6. This essay defines *homosexuality*, while carefully avoiding the pitfalls of either reductiveness or overgeneralization. Write an essay that defines your dominant self-image. Are you primarily an intellectual? an explorer? a competitor? an outsider? an organizer? Write concretely about the abstraction, giving examples from your experience and analyzing their formative influences.

PART 2

FAMILY TIES

INSIGHTS

The family, not the individual, is the real molecule of society, the key link in the social chain of being.

— ROBERT NISBET

The family is a subversive organization. In fact, it is the ultimate and only consistently subversive organization. Only the family has continued throughout history and still continues to undermine the State. The family is the enduring permanent enemy of all hierarchies, churches, and ideologies. Not only dictators, bishops, and commissars, but also humble parish priests and café intellectuals find themselves repeatedly coming up against the stony hostility of the family and its determination to resist interference to the last.

— FERDINAND MOUNT

No people are ever as divided as those of the same blood.

— MAVIS GALLANT

But what we think of as a social crisis of this generation — the rapid growth of divorce, the emancipation of women and adolescents, the sexual and educational revolutions, even the revolution in eating which is undermining the family as the basis of nourishment, for over a hundred years ago the majority of Europeans never ate in public in their lives — all of these things, which are steadily making the family weaker and weaker, are the inexorable result of the changes in society itself. The family as a unit of social organization was remarkably appropriate for a less complex world of agriculture and craftsmanship, a world which stretches back some seven thousand years, but ever since industry and highly urbanized societies began to take its place, the social functions of the family have steadily weakened — and this is a process that is unlikely to be halted. And there is no historical reason to believe that human beings could be less or more happy, less or more stable.

— J. H. PLUMB

The family is the basic cell of government: it is where we are trained to believe that we are human beings or that we are chattel, it is where we are trained to see the sex and race divisions and become callous to injustice even if it is done to ourselves, to accept as biological a full system of authoritarian government.

— GLORIA STEINEM

Those Winter Sundays

Sundays too my father got up early
and put his clothes on in the blueblack cold,
then with cracked hands that ached
from labor in the weekday weather made
banked fires blaze. No one ever thanked him.

I'd wake and hear the cold splintering, breaking.
When the rooms were warm, he'd call,
and slowly I would rise and dress,
fearing the chronic angers of that house,

Speaking indifferently to him,
who had driven out the cold
and polished my good shoes as well.
What did I know, what did I know
of love's austere and lonely offices?

— ROBERT HAYDEN

Children become attached to parents whatever the parents' characteristics, so long as the parents are adequately accessible and attentive. It does not matter to the intensity of the children's attachment, though it may matter greatly in the development of their personalities, whether their parents are reliable, consistently loving, or considerate of the children's health and welfare. Nor does it matter whether the children admire their parents or even whether they feel friendly toward them. Children who are battered and bruised by parents will continue to feel attached to them. Attachment, like walking or talking, is an intrinsic capacity that is developed under appropriate circumstances; it is not willed into being after a calculation of its advantages.

— ROBERT WEISS

FOCUSING BY WRITING

1. Do you have too many brothers and sisters or too few? Almost everyone sometimes wishes for a few changes in that area of fate. Explain one way your life might have been improved by changing the number, sex, or ages of your siblings.

2. It usually requires more than one person's adverse behavior to produce a black sheep in any family. A child or adult who is consistently a maverick or a delinquent may be relegated to that role by other family members who maintain stereotypical attitudes and expectations. Examine an example of family stereotyping that contributed to the formation of a black sheep you know.

3. Does family life encourage independence or dependence? Does it promote liberty or authority? Present at least two good reasons why in your view the effects of family life support mainly a free individual or mainly a cohesive society.

4. Adolescents and their parents customarily go through a period of sustained bickering, which may last a few years, over simple issues such as household cleanliness, going out, studying, or spending money. In your family, what were the recurrent themes or persistent issues during this period of mutual irritation? Were the differences ever resolved? In a brief essay, clarify both sides of the key issue in your own passage through the valley of family harassment.

Thomas Simmons

MOTORCYCLE TALK

THOMAS SIMMONS (b. 1956) lived his first thirteen years in West Chester, Pennsylvania, where he developed an enduring passion for motorcycles. Simmons graduated from Stanford University and received a Ph.D. in English at the University of California at Berkeley. He has taught writing at the Massachusetts Institute of Technology and at the University of Iowa. "Motorcycle Talk" is taken from *The Unseen Shore: Memories of a Christian Science Childhood* (1991), his memoir about struggling with his religious upbringing. His autobiography continues in his book about learning how to fly, *A Season in the Air* (1993). Simmons's most recent book is *Erotic Reckonings: Mastery and Apprenticeship in the Works of Poets and Lovers* (1994).

My father, who suffered from so many private griefs, was not an easy 1 man to get along with, but in one respect he was magnificent: he was unfailing in his devotion to machines of almost any variety. When he chose to, he could talk to me at length on the virtues of, say, the 1966 Chevrolet four-barrel carburetor or the drawbacks of the Wankel rotary engine. Talking, however, was not his strongest suit: he was a man of action. As he liked to point out, talking would never make an engine run more smoothly.

On weekends sometimes, or on his rare summer days of vacation, he 2 would encourage me in my first and last steps toward automotive literacy. He would allow me to stand beside him as he worked on the car, and when he needed a simple tool — a crescent wrench or needlenose pliers — I would be allowed to hand them to him. And when I was 12, he and my daring mother bought me a motorcycle.

It was a 50cc Benelli motocross bike — neither new, nor large, nor pow- 3 erful, nor expensive. But it gave form and life to my imaginings. No longer did I have to confine myself wistfully to magazine photos of high-speed turns and hair-raising rides through rough country. I had the thing itself — the device that would make these experiences possible, at least to some degree.

And, although I did not know it at the time, I also had a new kind of lex- 4 icon. The motorcycle was a compendium of gears and springs and sprockets and cylinder heads and piston rings, which between my father and me acquired the force of more affectionate words that we could never seem to use in each other's presence.

Almost immediately the Benelli became a meeting ground, a magnet for the two of us. We would come down to look at it — even if it was too late in the day for a good ride — and my father would check the tension of the chain, or examine the spark plug for carbon, or simply bounce the shock absorbers a few times as he talked. He'd tell me about compression ratios and ways of down-shifting smoothly through a turn; I'd tell him about my latest ride, when I leaped two small hummocks or took a spill on a tight curve.

More rarely, he'd tell the stories of his youth. His favorite, which he recounted in slightly different versions about four times a year, had to do with the go-kart he built from scrap parts in his father's basement during the Depression. It was by any account a masterful performance: he managed to pick up a small, broken gasoline engine for free, and tinkered with it until it came back to life. The wheels, steering gear, axles, chassis — all were scrounged for a few cents, or for free, from junkyards and vacant lots in and around Philadelphia.

Winter was in full swing when my father had his go-kart ready for a test-drive; snow lay thick on the ground. But he'd built the go-kart in his father's large basement, and given the weather he felt it made sense to make the trial run indoors. His engineering skills were topnotch. Assembled from orphaned parts, the go-kart performed like a well-tuned race car. My father did what any good 13-year-old would have done: he got carried away. He laid on the power coming around the corner of the basement, lost control, and smashed head-on into the furnace. It was a great loss for him. The jagged wood and metal cut and bruised him; he had destroyed his brand-new car. Far worse was the damage to the furnace. In 1933 such damage was almost more than the family finances could sustain. Furious, my father's father called him names, upbraided him for his stupidity and irresponsibility, and made him feel worthless. Years later, as he would tell this story to me, my father would linger over those words — "stupid," "irresponsible" — as if the pain had never gone away.

In these moments he and I had a common stake in something. Though he might not know whether I was reading at the eighth-grade level or the twelfth-grade level — or whether my math scores lagged behind those of the rest of the class — he was delighted to see that I knew how to adjust a clutch cable or stop after a low-speed, controlled skid. These skills were a source of genuine adventure for me, and I came to life when he observed my progress.

But this was only part of our rapport with the motorcycle. My father found few occasions to be overtly tender with the family, but he could be tender with a machine. I began to notice this in the countless small adjustments he regularly made. His touch on the cranky carburetor settings for gas and air was gentle, even soothing; at least it seemed to soothe the motorcycle, which ran smoothly under his touch but not under mine.

I found that, from time to time, this tenderness buoyed me up in its wake. If my father was, in his dreams, a flat-track mechanic, then I was his driver: he owed me the best he could give me; that was his job. This dream of his bound us in a metaphor which, at its heart, was not so different from the kind of straightforward love another child might have received from a more accessible father. I did not know this then, not exactly. But I knew, when we both hovered over the Benelli's cylinder head or gearbox, adjusting a cam or replacing a gasket, that he would not have worked on this machine for himself alone.

Yet there was a secret to our new language, a secret that only slowly 11 revealed itself. What we shared through the motorcycle contradicted most of our other encounters in the family. It was almost as if we lived in another world when we came together over this machine, and for a time I hoped that that world might be the new one, the ideal on the horizon. I was wrong. The bands of our words were strong, but too narrow to encompass the worlds rising before me.

Almost without knowing it I began to acquire other vocabularies — the 12 tough, subtle speech of girls, the staccato syllables of independence, the wrenching words of love and emptiness. In this I began to leave him behind. He could not talk of these things with me. He remained with his engines; and long after I had ceased to ride it, he would occasionally open the gas jets, prime the carburetor, and take my motorcycle for a spin around the block.

But as it seems that nothing is ever wholly lost, this vocabulary of the 13 garage and the flat-track speed-way has a kind of potency, a place in the scheme of things. When, recently, I had dinner with my father, after not having seen him for nearly a year, we greeted each other with the awkwardness of child cousins: we hardly knew what to say. I had almost given up on the possibility of a prolonged conversation until I happened to mention that my car needed a new clutch. Suddenly we were safe again, as we moved from the clutch to the valves on his souped-up VW and the four-barrel carburetor on the '66 Chevrolet Malibu, still pouring on the power after all these years. We had moved back to the language of our old country. And though one of us had journeyed far and had almost forgotten the idioms, the rusty speech still held, for a time, the words of love.

Analyzing This Selection

1. **THE WRITER'S METHOD**   The first sentence carries many implications about the author and his family. Which suggestions are fully considered in the rest of the essay? Which remain implied?

2. How does the motorcycle change the son's and father's perceptions of each other?

3. How does the father appear different from the adult writer? What resemblances are visible?

Analyzing Connections

4. In the Insights on page 61, psychologist Robert Weiss theorizes about the development of a child's attachment to his or her parents. Test out the strengths and weaknesses of the theory by applying it to Simmons's relationship with his father.

Analyzing by Writing

5. In many families, a sport or hobby provides the vocabulary for talk between the generations. Baseball, basketball, tennis, hockey, skiing, photography, camping: each can become the medium for relationships that do not flow as smoothly without this shared interest. Examine a shared interest that bridges the generation gap in your family (or in another family you know well). As if you were examining the dialect of another tribe, clarify the vocabulary that the family uses to discuss the interest. For instance, does custom allow for praise and criticism from young to old and not just from old to young? Explain the forms and limits of expressiveness in this family idiom.

Raymond Carver

MY FATHER'S LIFE

RAYMOND CARVER (1938–1988), acclaimed for his poetry and for his short stories about hardscrabble contemporary lives, was born in a logging town in Oregon. He graduated from California State University at Humboldt and spent a year at the Writers' Workshop at the University of Iowa. He taught writing at the University of California at Santa Cruz and at Syracuse University. His poetry and short stories appeared in magazines such as *Esquire, Harper's,* the *Atlantic,* and the *New Yorker.* His fiction has been collected in *What We Talk About When We Talk About Love* (1981) (see the story on page 160), *Cathedral* (1984), and *Where I'm Calling From* (1988). His verse is collected in three books — *Where Water Comes Together with Other Water* (1985), *Ultramarine* (1986), and the posthumously published *A New Path to the Waterfall* (1989). In this memoir of his father, which first appeared in *Esquire* in 1984, Carver emphasizes the hardships that his father faced as a laborer during the Great Depression of the 1930s and later during the years of his psychological depression.

My dad's name was Clevie Raymond Carver. His family called him Raymond and friends called him C.R. I was named Raymond Clevie Carver, Jr. I hated the "Junior" part. When I was little my dad called me Frog, which was okay. But later, like everybody else in the family, he began calling me Junior. He went on calling me this until I was thirteen or fourteen and announced that I wouldn't answer to that name any longer. So he began calling me Doc. From then until his death, on June 17, 1967, he called me Doc, or else Son.

When he died, my mother telephoned my wife with the news. I was away from my family at the time, between lives, trying to enroll in the School of Library Science at the University of Iowa. When my wife answered the phone, my mother blurted out, "Raymond's dead!" For a moment, my wife thought my mother was telling her that I was dead. Then my mother made it clear *which* Raymond she was talking about and my wife said, "Thank God. I thought you meant *my* Raymond."

My dad walked, hitched rides, and rode in empty boxcars when he went from Arkansas to Washington State in 1934, looking for work. I don't know whether he was pursuing a dream when he went out to Washington. I doubt it. I don't think he dreamed much. I believe he was simply looking for steady work at decent pay. Steady work was meaningful work. He picked apples for a time and then landed a construction laborer's job on the Grand Coulee Dam. After he'd put aside a little money, he bought a car and drove back to Arkansas to help his folks, my grandparents, pack up for the move west. He said later that they were about to starve down there, and this wasn't meant as a figure of speech. It was during that short while in Arkansas, in a town called Leola, that my mother met my dad on the side-walk as he came out of a tavern.

"He was drunk," she said. "I don't know why I let him talk to me. His eyes were glittery. I wish I'd had a crystal ball." They'd met once, a year or so before, at a dance. He'd had girlfriends before her, my mother told me. "Your dad always had a girlfriend, even after we married. He was my first and last. I never had another man. But I didn't miss anything."

They were married by a justice of the peace on the day they left for Washington, this big, tall country girl and a farmhand-turned-construction worker. My mother spent her wedding night with my dad and his folks, all of them camped beside the road in Arkansas.

In Omak, Washington, my dad and mother lived in a little place not much bigger than a cabin. My grandparents lived next door. My dad was still working on the dam, and later, with the huge turbines producing elec-tricity and the water backed up for a hundred miles into Canada, he stood in the crowd and heard Franklin D. Roosevelt when he spoke at the con-struction site. "He never mentioned those guys who died building that dam," my dad said. Some of his friends had died there, men from Arkansas, Oklahoma, and Missouri.

He then took a job in a sawmill in Clatskanie, Oregon, a little town alongside the Columbia River. I was born there, and my mother has a pic-ture of my dad standing in front of the gate to the mill, proudly holding me up to face the camera. My bonnet is on crooked and about to come untied. His hat is pushed back on his forehead, and he's wearing a big grin. Was he going in to work or just finishing his shift? It doesn't matter. In either case, he had a job and a family. These were his salad days.

In 1941 we moved to Yakima, Washington, where my dad went to work as a saw filer, a skilled trade he'd learned in Clatskanie. When war broke out, he was given a deferment because his work was considered necessary to the war effort. Finished lumber was in demand by the armed services, and he kept his saws so sharp they could shave the hair off your arm.

After my dad had moved us to Yakima, he moved his folks into the same neighborhood. By the mid-1940s the rest of my dad's family — his brother, his sister, and her husband, as well as uncles, cousins, nephews, and most of their extended family and friends — had come out from Arkansas. All because my dad came out first. The men went to work at Boise Cascade, where my dad worked, and the women packed apples in the canneries. And in just a little while, it seemed — according to my mother — every-body was better off than my dad. "Your dad couldn't keep money," my mother said. "Money burned a hole in his pocket. He was always doing for others."

The first house I clearly remember living in, at 1515 South Fifteenth Street, in Yakima, had an outdoor toilet. On Halloween night, or just any night, for the hell of it, neighbor kids, kids in their early teens, would carry our toilet away and leave it next to the road. My dad would have to get somebody to help him bring it home. Or these kids would take the toilet and stand it in somebody else's backyard. Once they actually set it on fire. But ours wasn't the only house that had an outdoor toilet. When I was old enough to know what I was doing, I threw rocks at the other toilets when I'd see someone go inside. This was called bombing the toilets. After a while, though, everyone went to indoor plumbing until, suddenly, our toilet was the last outdoor one in the neighborhood. I remember the shame I felt when my third-grade teacher, Mr. Wise, drove me home from school one day. I asked him to stop at the house just before ours, claiming I lived there.

I can recall what happened one night when my dad came home late to find that my mother had locked all the doors on him from the inside. He was drunk, and we could feel the house shudder as he rattled the door. When he'd managed to force open a window, she hit him between the eyes with a colander and knocked him out. We could see him down there on the grass. For years afterward, I used to pick up this colander — it was as heavy as a rolling pin — and imagine what it would feel like to be hit in the head with something like that.

It was during this period that I remember my dad taking me into the bedroom, sitting me down on the bed, and telling me that I might have to go live with my Aunt LaVon for a while. I couldn't understand what I'd done that meant I'd have to go away from home to live. But this, too — whatever prompted it — must have blown over, more or less, anyway, because we stayed together, and I didn't have to go live with her or anyone else.

I remember my mother pouring his whiskey down the sink. Sometimes she'd pour it all out and sometimes, if she was afraid of getting caught, she'd only pour half of it out and then add water to the rest. I tasted some of his whiskey once myself. It was terrible stuff, and I don't see how anybody could drink it.

After a long time without one, we finally got a car, in 1949 or 1950, a 1938 Ford. But it threw a rod the first week we had it, and my dad had to have the motor rebuilt.

"We drove the oldest car in town," my mother said. "We could have had a Cadillac for all he spent on car repairs." One time she found someone else's tube of lipstick on the floorboard, along with a lacy handkerchief. "See this?" she said to me. "Some floozy left this in the car."

Once I saw her take a pan of warm water into the bedroom where my dad was sleeping. She took his hand from under the covers and held it in the water. I stood in the doorway and watched. I wanted to know what was going on. This would make him talk in his sleep, she told me. There were things she needed to know, things she was sure he was keeping from her.

Every year or so, when I was little, we would take the North Coast Lim- 17 ited across the Cascade Range from Yakima to Seattle and stay in the Vance Hotel and eat, I remember, at a place called the Dinner Bell Cafe. Once we went to Ivar's Acres of Clams and drank glasses of warm clam broth.

In 1956, the year I was to graduate from high school, my dad quit his 18 job at the mill in Yakima and took a job in Chester, a little sawmill town in northern California. The reasons given at the time for his taking the job had to do with a higher hourly wage and the vague promise that he might, in a few years' time, succeed to the job of head filer in this new mill. But I think, in the main, that my dad had grown restless and simply wanted to try his luck elsewhere. Things had gotten a little too predictable for him in Yakima. Also, the year before, there had been the deaths, within six months of each other, of both his parents.

But just a few days after graduation, when my mother and I were packed 19 to move to Chester, my dad penciled a letter to say he'd been sick for a while. He didn't want us to worry, he said, but he'd cut himself on a saw. Maybe he'd got a tiny sliver of steel in his blood. Anyway, something had happened and he'd had to miss work, he said. In the same mail was an unsigned postcard from somebody down there telling my mother that my dad was about to die and that he was drinking "raw whiskey."

When we arrived in Chester, my dad was living in a trailer that 20 belonged to the company. I didn't recognize him immediately. I guess for a moment I didn't want to recognize him. He was skinny and pale and looked bewildered. His pants wouldn't stay up. He didn't look like my dad. My mother began to cry. My dad put his arm around her and patted her shoulder vaguely, like he didn't know what this was all about, either. The three of us took up life together in the trailer, and we looked after him as best we could. But my dad was sick, and he couldn't get any better. I worked with him in the mill that summer and part of the fall. We'd get up in the mornings and eat eggs and toast while we listened to the radio, and then go out the door with our lunch pails. We'd pass through the gate together at eight in the morning, and I wouldn't see him again until quitting time. In November I went back to Yakima to be closer to my girlfriend, the girl I'd made up my mind I was going to marry.

He worked at the mill in Chester until the following February, when he 21 collapsed on the job and was taken to the hospital. My mother asked if I would come down there and help. I caught a bus from Yakima to Chester, intending to drive them back to Yakima. But now, in addition to being physically sick, my dad was in the midst of a nervous breakdown, though none of us knew to call it that at the time. During the entire trip back to Yakima, he didn't speak, not even when asked a direct question. ("How do you feel, Raymond?" "You okay, Dad?") He'd communicate, if he communicated at all, by moving his head or by turning his palms up as if to say he didn't know or care. The only time he said anything on the trip, and for nearly a month afterward, was when I was speeding down a gravel road in Oregon and the car muffler came loose. "You were going too fast," he said.

Back in Yakima a doctor saw to it that my dad went to a psychiatrist. My mother and dad had to go on relief, as it was called, and the county paid for the psychiatrist. The psychiatrist asked my dad, "Who is the President?" He'd had a question put to him that he could answer. "Ike," my dad said. Nevertheless, they put him on the fifth floor of Valley Memorial Hospital and began giving him electroshock treatments. I was married by then and about to start my own family. My dad was still locked up when my wife went into this same hospital, just one floor down, to have our first baby. After she had delivered, I went upstairs to give my dad the news. They let me in through a steel door and showed me where I could find him. He was sitting on a couch with a blanket over his lap. *Hey*, I thought. *What in hell is happening to my dad?* I sat down next to him and told him he was a grandfather. He waited a minute and then he said, "I feel like a grandfather." That's all he said. He didn't smile or move. He was in a big room with a lot of other people. Then I hugged him, and he began to cry.

Somehow he got out of there. But now came the years when he couldn't work and just sat around the house trying to figure what next and what he'd done wrong in his life that he'd wound up like this. My mother went from job to crummy job. Much later she referred to that time he was in the hospital, and those years just afterward, as "when Raymond was sick." The word *sick* was never the same for me again.

In 1964, through the help of a friend, he was lucky enough to be hired on at a mill in Klamath, California. He moved down there by himself to see if he could hack it. He lived not far from the mill, in a one-room cabin not much different from the place he and my mother had started out living in when they went west. He scrawled letters to my mother, and if I called she'd read them aloud to me over the phone. In the letters, he said it was touch and go. Every day that he went to work, he felt like it was the most important day of his life. But every day, he told her, made the next day that much easier. He said for her to tell me he said hello. If he couldn't sleep at night, he said, he thought about me and the good times we used to have. Finally, after a couple of months, he regained some of his confidence. He could do the work and didn't think he had to worry that he'd let anybody down ever again. When he was sure, he sent for my mother.

He'd been off from work for six years and had lost everything in that time — home, car, furniture, and appliances, including the big freezer that had been my mother's pride and joy. He'd lost his good name too — Raymond Carver was someone who couldn't pay his bills — and his self-respect was gone. He'd even lost his virility. My mother told my wife, "All during that time Raymond was sick we slept together in the same bed, but we didn't have relations. He wanted to a few times, but nothing happened. I didn't miss it, but I think he wanted to, you know."

During those years I was trying to raise my own family and earn a living. But, one thing and another, we found ourselves having to move a lot. I couldn't keep track of what was going down in my dad's life. But I did have a chance one Christmas to tell him I wanted to be a writer. I might as well have told him I wanted to become a plastic surgeon. "What are you going to write about?" he wanted to know. Then, as if to help me out, he said, "Write about stuff you know about. Write about some of those fishing trips we took." I said I would, but I knew I wouldn't. "Send me what you write," he said. I said I'd do that, but then I didn't. I wasn't writing anything about fishing, and I didn't think he'd particularly care about, or even necessarily understand, what I was writing in those days. Besides, he wasn't a reader. Not the sort, anyway, I imagined I was writing for. 26

Then he died. I was a long way off, in Iowa City, with things still to say to him. I didn't have the chance to tell him goodbye, or that I thought he was doing great at his new job. That I was proud of him for making a comeback. 27

My mother said he came in from work that night and ate a big supper. Then he sat at the table by himself and finished what was left of a bottle of whiskey, a bottle she found hidden in the bottom of the garbage under some coffee grounds a day or so later. Then he got up and went to bed, where my mother joined him a little later. But in the night she had to get up and make a bed for herself on the couch. "He was snoring so loud I couldn't sleep," she said. The next morning when she looked in on him, he was on his back with his mouth open, his cheeks caved in. *Graylooking,* she said. She knew he was dead — she didn't need a doctor to tell her that. But she called one anyway, and then she called my wife. 28

Among the pictures my mother kept of my dad and herself during those early days in Washington was a photograph of him standing in front of a car, holding a beer and a stringer of fish. In the photograph he is wearing his hat back on his forehead and has this awkward grin on his face. I asked her for it and she gave it to me, along with some others. I put it up on my wall, and each time we moved, I took the picture along and put it up on another wall. I looked at it carefully from time to time, trying to figure out some things about my dad, and maybe myself in the process. But I couldn't. My dad just kept moving further and further away from me and back into time. Finally, in the course of another move, I lost the photograph. It was then that I tried to recall it, and at the same time make an attempt to say something about my dad, and how I thought that in some important ways we might be alike. I wrote the poem when I was living in an apartment house in an urban area south of San Francisco, at a time when I found myself, like my dad, having trouble with alcohol. The poem was a way of trying to connect up with him. 29

Photograph of My Father in His Twenty-Second Year

October. Here in this dank, unfamiliar kitchen
I study my father's embarrassed young man's face.
Sheepish grin, he holds in one hand a string
of spiny yellow perch, in the other
a bottle of Carlsberg beer.

In jeans and flannel shirt, he leans
against the front fender of a 1934 Ford.
He would like to pose brave and hearty for his posterity,
wear his old hat cocked over his ear.
All his life my father wanted to be bold.

But the eyes gave him away, and the hands
that limply offer the string of dead perch
and the bottle of beer. Father, I love you,
yet how can I say thank you, I who can't hold my liquor either
and don't even know the places to fish.

The poem is true in its particulars, except that my dad died in June and 30
not October, as the first word of the poem says. I wanted a word with more
than one syllable to it to make it linger a little. But more than that, I wanted
a month appropriate to what I felt at the time I wrote the poem — a month
of short days and failing light, smoke in the air, things perishing. June was
summer nights and days, graduations, my wedding anniversary, the birthday
of one of my children. June wasn't a month your father died in.

After the service at the funeral home, after we had moved outside, a 31
woman I didn't know came over to me and said, "He's happier where he is
now." I stared at this woman until she moved away. I still remember the
little knob of a hat she was wearing. Then one of my dad's cousins — I
didn't know the man's name — reached out and took my hand, "We all
miss him," he said, and I knew he wasn't saying it just to be polite.

I began to weep for the first time since receiving the news. I hadn't been 32
able to before. I hadn't had the time, for one thing. Now, suddenly, I
couldn't stop. I held my wife and wept while she said and did what she
could do to comfort me there in the middle of that summer afternoon.

I listened to people say consoling things to my mother, and I was glad 33
that my dad's family had turned up, had come to where he was. I thought
I'd remember everything that was said and done that day and maybe find
a way to tell it sometime. But I didn't. I forgot it all, or nearly. What I
do remember is that I heard our name used a lot that afternoon, my dad's
name and mine. But I knew they were talking about my dad. *Raymond,*
these people kept saying in their beautiful voices out of my childhood.
Raymond.

Analyzing This Selection

1. In paragraphs 1 and 2, the author implicitly suggests some of the effects of having a name similar to his father's. What were these effects? Define his reaction explicitly.

2. **THE WRITER'S METHOD** Carver includes his mother's remarks and her other direct views about his father. How do we know whether the author's attitude differs from the mother's? Why does Carver merely imply agreement and disagreement?

3. What episodes and details in Carver's early life indicate that he and his father felt closely connected?

4. In Carver's poem about his father he writes, "All his life my father wanted to be bold." Do you think that line sums up the father fairly accurately? Does the essay indicate other things that the father also wanted to be? Was he more successful or less successful in those other aspirations?

5. In the final paragraph, Carver again notes the similarity of their names. How has his attitude toward this similarity changed from his attitude at the beginning of the essay?

Analyzing Connections

6. Both Carver and Simmons (see "Motorcycle Talk," p. 63) express mixed attitudes toward their difficult fathers. Compare their mixture of admiration and blame. Compare Carver and Robert Hayden in the Insights on page 61. Which writer identifies more closely with his father?

Analyzing by Writing

7. Write an extended description of the person in your family whom you most closely resemble in physical appearance. Be precise and detailed about his or her features that are like your own. If it is useful, include matters such as the person's tone of voice, way of walking, gestures and mannerisms, or other physical characteristics. Be sure to differentiate yourself at some point or at various points in your essay. In what ways do the similarities please or disturb you?

Calvin Trillin

IT'S JUST TOO LATE

CALVIN TRILLIN (b. 1935) grew up in Kansas City, Missouri, and attended Yale University. He worked as a reporter for *Time* magazine, and from 1963 to 1982 he was a staff writer for the *New Yorker*. His regular reports of his travels around the United States focused on daily life, including where and how Americans eat. His widely syndicated humorous columns are collected in *If You Can't Say Something Nice* (1987) and *Enough's Enough* (1990). On the darker side, Trillin wrote a memoir of a Yale classmate who committed suicide, *Remembering Denny* (1993). Believing that the way people die can illuminate the way they lived, Trillin reported about deadly crimes and accidents in *Killings* (1984), which included the following account of the death of a teenage girl. Much fonder accounts of family life appear in his memoir, *Messages from My Father* (1996).

Knoxville, Tennessee
March 1979

Until she was sixteen, FaNee Cooper was what her parents sometimes called an ideal child. "You'd never have to correct her," FaNee's mother has said. In sixth grade, FaNee won a spelling contest. She played the piano and the flute. She seemed to believe what she heard every Sunday at the Beaver Dam Baptist Church about good and evil and the hereafter. FaNee was not an outgoing child. Even as a baby, she was uncomfortable when she was held and cuddled. She found it easy to tell her parents she loved them but difficult to confide in them. Particularly compared to her sister, Kristy, a cheerful, open little girl two and a half years younger, she was reserved and introspective. The thoughts she kept to herself, though, were apparently happy thoughts. Her eighth-grade essay on Christmas — written in a remarkably neat hand — talked of the joys of helping put together toys for her little brother, Leo, Jr., and the importance of her parents' reminder that Christmas is the birthday of Jesus. Her parents were the sort of people who might have been expected to have an ideal child. As a boy, Leo Cooper had been called "one of the greatest high-school basketball players ever developed in Knox County." He went on to play basketball at East Tennessee State, and he married the homecoming queen, JoAnn Henson. After college, Cooper became a high-school basketball coach and

75

teacher and, eventually, an administrator. By the time FaNee turned thirteen, in 1973, he was in his third year as the principal of Gresham Junior High School, in Fountain City — a small Knox County town that had been swallowed up by Knoxville when the suburbs began to move north. A tall man, with curly black hair going on gray, Leo Cooper has an elaborate way of talking ("Unless I'm very badly mistaken, he has never related to me totally the content of his conversation") and a manner that may come from years of trying to leave errant junior-high-school students with the impression that a responsible adult is magnanimous, even humble, about invariably being in the right. His wife, a high-school art teacher, paints and does batik, and created the name FaNee because she liked the way it looked and sounded — it sounds like "Fawn*ee*" when the Coopers say it — but the impression she gives is not of artiness but of soft-spoken small-town gentility. When she found, in the course of cleaning up FaNee's room, that her ideal thirteen-year-old had been smoking cigarettes, she was, in her words, crushed. "FaNee was such a perfect child before that," JoAnn Cooper said some time later. "She was angry that we found out. She knew we knew that she had done something we didn't approve of, and then the rebellion started. I was hurt. I was very hurt. I guess it came through as disappointment."

Several months later, FaNee's grandmother died. FaNee had been   2 devoted to her grandmother. She wrote a poem in her memory — an almost joyous poem, filled with Christian faith in the afterlife ("Please don't grieve over my happiness / Rejoice with me in the presence of the Angels of Heaven"). She also took some keepsakes from her grandmother's house, and was apparently mortified when her parents found them and explained that they would have to be returned. By then, the Coopers were aware that FaNee was going to have a difficult time as a teenager. They thought she might be self-conscious about the double affliction of glasses and braces. They thought she might be uncomfortable in the role of the principal's daughter at Gresham. In ninth grade, she entered Halls High School, where JoAnn Cooper was teaching art. FaNee was a loner at first. Then she fell in with what could only be considered a bad crowd.

Halls, a few miles to the north of Fountain City, used to be known as   3 Halls Crossroads. It is what Knoxville people call "over the ridge" — on the side of Black Oak Ridge that has always been thought of as rural. When FaNee entered Halls High, the Coopers were already in the process of building a house on several acres of land they had bought in Halls, in a sparsely settled area along Brown Gap Road. Like two or three other houses along the road, it was to be constructed basically of huge logs taken from old buildings — a house that Leo Cooper describes as being, like the name FaNee, "just a little bit different." Ten years ago, Halls Crossroads was literally a crossroads. Then some of the Knoxville expansion that had swollen Fountain City spilled over the ridge, planting subdivisions here and there on roads that still went for long stretches with nothing but an occasional house with a cow or two next to it. The increase in population did not create a town. Halls has no center. Its commercial area is a series of two or three shopping centers strung together on the Maynardville Highway, the four-lane that leads north into Union County — a place almost synonymous in east Tennessee with mountain poverty. Its restaurant is the Halls Freezo Drive-In. The gathering place for the group FaNee Cooper eventually found herself in was the Maynardville Highway Exxon station.

At Halls High School, the social poles were represented by the Jocks and the Freaks. FaNee found her friends among the Freaks. "I am truly enlighted upon irregular trains of thought aimed at strange depots of mental wards," she wrote when she was fifteen. "Yes! Crazed farms for the mental off — Oh! I walked through the halls screams & loud laughter fill my ears — Orderlys try to reason with me — but I am unreasonable! The joys of being a FREAK in a circus of imagination." The little crowd of eight or ten young people that FaNee joined has been referred to by her mother as "the Union County group." A couple of the girls were from backgrounds similar to FaNee's, but all the boys had the characteristics, if not the precise address, that Knoxville people associate with the poor whites of Union County. They were the sort of boys who didn't bother to finish high school, or finished it in a special program for slow learners, or got ejected from it for taking a swing at the principal.

"I guess you can say they more or less dragged us down to their level with the drugs," a girl who was in the group — a girl who can be called Marcia — said recently. "And somehow we settled for it. It seems like we had to get ourselves in the pit before we could look out." People in the group used marijuana and Valium and LSD. They sneered at the Jocks and the "prim and proper little ladies" who went with Jocks. "We set ourselves aside," Marcia now says. "We put ourselves above everyone. How we did that I don't know." In a Knox County high school, teenagers who want to get themselves in the pit need not mainline heroin. The Jocks they mean to be compared to do not merely show up regularly for classes and practice football and wear clean clothes; they watch their language and preach temperance and go to prayer meetings on Wednesday nights and talk about having a real good Christian witness. Around Knoxville, people who speak of well-behaved high-school kids often seem to use words like "perfect," or even "angels." For FaNee's group, the opposite was not difficult to figure out. "We were into wicked things, strange things," Marcia says. "It was like we were on some kind of devil trip." FaNee wrote about demons and vultures and rats. "Slithering serpents eat my sanity and bite my ass," she wrote in an essay called "The Lovely Road of Life," just after she turned sixteen, "while tornadoes derail and ever so swiftly destroy every car in my train of thought." She wrote a lot about death.

FaNee's girlfriends spoke of her as "super-intelligent." Her English teacher found some of her writing profound — and disturbing. She was thought to be not just super-intelligent but super-mysterious, and even, at times, super-weird — an introverted girl who stared straight ahead with

4

5

6

deep-brown, nearly black eyes and seemed to have thoughts she couldn't share. Nobody really knew why she had chosen to run with the Freaks — whether it was loneliness or rebellion or simple boredom. Marcia thought it might have had something to do with a feeling that her parents had settled on Kristy as their perfect child. "I guess she figured she couldn't be the best," Marcia said recently. "So she decided she might as well be the worst."

Toward the spring of FaNee's junior year at Halls, her problems seemed 7 to deepen. Despite her intelligence, her grades were sliding. She was what her mother called "a mental dropout." Leo Cooper had to visit Halls twice because of minor suspensions. Once, FaNee had been caught smoking. Once, having ducked out of a required assembly, she was spotted by a favorite teacher, who turned her in. At home, she exchanged little more than short, strained formalities with Kristy, who shared their parents' opinion of FaNee's choice of friends. The Coopers had finished their house — a large house, its size accentuated by the huge old logs and a great stone fireplace and outsize "Paul Bunyan"–style furniture — but FaNee spent most of her time there in her own room, sleeping or listening to rock music through earphones. One night, there was a terrible scene when FaNee returned from a concert in a condition that Leo Cooper knew had to be the result of marijuana. JoAnn Cooper, who ordinarily strikes people as too gentle to raise her voice, found herself losing her temper regularly. Finally, Leo Cooper asked a counselor he knew, Jim Griffin, to stop in at Halls High School and have a talk with FaNee — unofficially.

Griffin — a young man with a warm, informal manner — worked for 8 the Juvenile Court of Knox County. He had a reputation for being able to reach teenagers who wouldn't talk to their parents or to school administrators. One Friday in March of 1977, he spent an hour and a half talking to FaNee Cooper. As Griffin recalls the interview, FaNee didn't seem alarmed by his presence. She seemed to him calm and controlled — Griffin thought it was something like talking to another adult — and, unlike most of the teenagers he dealt with, she looked him in the eye the entire time. Griffin, like some of FaNee's friends, found her eyes unsettling — "the coldest, most distant, but, at the same time, the most knowing eyes I'd ever seen." She expressed affection for her parents, but she didn't seem interested in exploring ways of getting along better with them. The impression she gave Griffin was that they were who they were, and she was who she was, and there didn't happen to be any connection. Several times, she made the same response to Griffin's suggestions: "It's too late."

That weekend, neither FaNee nor her parents brought up the subject of 9 Griffin's visit. Leo Cooper has spoken of the weekend as being particularly happy; a friend of FaNee's who stayed over remembers it as particularly strained. FaNee stayed home from school on Monday because of a bad headache — she often had bad headaches — but felt well enough on Monday evening to drive to the library. She was to be home at nine. When she wasn't, Mrs. Cooper began to phone her friends. Finally, around ten, Leo Cooper got into his other car and took a swing around Halls — past the teenage hangouts like the Exxon station and the Pizza Hut and the Smoky Mountain Market. Then he took a second swing. At eleven, FaNee was still not home.

She hadn't gone to the library. She had picked up two girlfriends and 10 driven to the home of a third, where everyone took five Valium tablets. Then the four girls drove over to the Exxon station, where they met four boys from their crowd. After a while, the group bought some beer and some marijuana and reassembled at Charlie Stevens's trailer. Charlie Stevens was five or six years older than everyone else in the group — a skinny, slow-thinking young man with long black hair and a sparse beard. He was married and had a child, but he and his wife had separated; she was back in Union County with the baby. Stevens had remained in their trailer — parked in the yard near his mother's house, in a back-road area of Knox County dominated by decrepit, unpainted sheds and run-down trailers and rusted-out automobiles. Stevens had picked up FaNee at home once or twice — apparently, more as a driver for the group than as a date — and the Coopers, having learned that his unsuitability extended to being married, had asked her not to see him.

In Charlie's trailer, which had no heat or electricity, the group drank 11 beer and passed around joints, keeping warm with blankets. By eleven or so, FaNee was what one of her friends has called "super-messed-up." Her speech was slurred. She was having trouble keeping her balance. She had decided not to go home. She had apparently persuaded herself that her parents intended to send her away to some sort of home for incorrigibles. "It's too late," she said to one of her friends. "It's just too late." It was decided that one of the boys, David Munsey, who was more or less the leader of the group, would drive the Coopers' car to FaNee's house, where FaNee and Charlie Stevens would pick him up in Steven's car — a worn Pinto with four bald tires, one light, and a dragging muffler. FaNee wrote a note to her parents, and then, perhaps because her handwriting was suffering the effects of beer and marijuana and Valium, asked Stevens to rewrite it on a large piece of paper, which would be left on the seat of the Coopers' car. The Stevens version was just about the same as FaNee's, except that Stevens left out a couple of sentences about trying to work things out ("I'm willing to try") and, not having won any spelling championship himself, he misspelled a few words, like "tomorrow." The note said, "Dear Mom and Dad. Sorry I'm late. Very late. I left your car because I thought you might need it tomorrow. I love you all, but this is something I just had to do. The man talked to me privately for one and a half hours and I was really scared, so this is something I just had to do, but don't worry. I'm with a very good friend. Love you all. FaNee. P.S. Please try to understand I love you all very much, really I do. Love me if you have a chance."

At eleven-thirty or so, Leo Cooper was sitting in his living room, looking 12 out the window at his driveway — a long gravel road that runs almost four hundred feet from the house to Brown Gap Road. He saw the car that FaNee had been driving pull into the driveway. "She's home," he called to his wife, who had just left the room. Cooper walked out on the deck over the garage. The car had stopped at the end of the driveway, and the lights had gone out. He got into his other car and drove to the end of the driveway. David Munsey had already joined Charlie Stevens and FaNee, and the Pinto was just leaving, traveling at a normal rate of speed. Leo Cooper pulled out on the road behind them.

Stevens turned left on Crippen Road, a road that has a field on one side   13 and two or three small houses on the other, and there Cooper pulled his car in front of the Pinto and stopped, blocking the way. He got out and walked toward the Pinto. Suddenly, Stevens put the car in reverse, backed into a driveway a hundred yards behind him, and sped off. Cooper jumped in his car and gave chase. Stevens raced back to Brown Gap Road, ran a stop sign there, ran another stop sign at Maynardville Highway, turned north, veered off onto the old Andersonville Pike, a nearly abandoned road that runs parallel to the highway, and then crossed back over the highway to the narrow, dark country roads on the other side. Stevens sometimes drove with his lights out. He took some of the corners by suddenly applying his hand brake to make the car swerve around in a ninety-degree turn. He was in familiar territory — he actually passed his trailer — and Cooper had difficulty keeping up. Past the trailer, Stevens swept down a hill into a sharp left turn that took him onto Foust Hollow Road, a winding, hilly road not much wider than one car.

At a fork, Cooper thought he had lost the Pinto. He started to go right   14 and then saw what seemed to be a spark from Stevens's dragging muffler off to the left, in the darkness. Cooper took the left fork, down Salem Church Road. He went down a hill and then up a long, curving hill to a crest, where he saw the Stevens car ahead. "I saw the car airborne. Up in the air," he later testified. "It was up in the air. And then it completely rolled over one more time. It started to make another flip forward, and just as it started to flip to the other side it flipped back this way, and my daughter's body came out."

Cooper slammed on his brakes and skidded to a stop up against the   15 Pinto. "Book!" Stevens shouted — the group's equivalent of "Scram!" Stevens and Munsey disappeared into the darkness. "It was dark, no one around, and so I started yelling for FaNee," Cooper had testified. "I thought it was an eternity before I could find her body, wedged under the back end of that car. . . . I tried everything I could, and saw that I couldn't get her loose. So I ran to a trailer back up to the top of the hill back up there to try to get that lady to call to get me some help, and then apparently she didn't think that I was serious. . . . I took the jack out of my car and got under, and it was dark, still couldn't see too much what was going on . . . and started prying and got her loose, and I don't know how. And then I dragged her over to the side, and, of course, at the time I felt reasonably assured that she was gone, because her head was completely — on one side just as if you had taken a sledgehammer and just hit it and bashed it in. And I did have the pleasure of one thing. I had the pleasure of listening to her breathe about the last three times she ever breathed in her life."

David Munsey did not return to the wreck that night, but Charlie Stevens did. Leo Cooper was kneeling next to his daughter's body. Cooper insisted that Stevens come close enough to see FaNee. "He was kneeling down next to her," Stevens later testified. "And he said, 'Do you know what you've done? Do you really know what you've done?' Like that. And I just looked at her, and I said, 'Yes,' and just stood there. Because I couldn't say nothing." There was, of course, a legal decision to be made about who was responsible for FaNee Cooper's death. In a deposition, Stevens said he had been fleeing for his life. He testified that when Leo Cooper blocked Crippen Road, FaNee had said that her father had a gun and intended to hurt them. Stevens was bound over and eventually indicted for involuntary manslaughter. Leo Cooper testified that when he approached the Pinto on Crippen Road, FaNee had a strange expression that he had never seen before. "It wasn't like FaNee, and I knew something was wrong," he said. "My concern was to get FaNee out of the car." The district attorney's office asked that Cooper be bound over for reckless driving, but the judge declined to do so. "Any father would have done what he did," the judge said. "I can see no criminal act on the part of Mr. Cooper." 16

Almost two years passed before Charlie Stevens was brought to trial. Part of the problem was assuring the presence of David Munsey, who had joined the Navy but seemed inclined to assign his own leaves. In the meantime, the Coopers went to court with a civil suit — they had "uninsured-motorist coverage," which requires their insurance company to cover any defendant who has no insurance of his own — and they won a judgment. There were ways of assigning responsibility, of course, which had nothing to do with the law, civil or criminal. A lot of people in Knoxville thought that Leo Cooper had, in the words of his lawyer, "done what any daddy worth his salt would have done." There were others who believed that FaNee Cooper had lost her life because Leo Cooper had lost his temper. Leo Cooper was not among those who expressed any doubts about his actions. Unlike his wife, whose eyes filled with tears at almost any mention of FaNee, Cooper seemed able, even eager to go over the details of the accident again and again. With the help of a school-board security man, he conducted his own investigation. He drove over the route dozens of times. "I've thought about it every day, and I guess I will the rest of my life," he said as he and his lawyer and the prosecuting attorney went over the route again the day before Charlie Stevens's trial finally began. "But I can't tell any alternative for a father. I simply wanted her out of that car. I'd have done the same thing again, even at the risk of losing her." 17

Tennessee law permits the family of a victim to hire a special prosecutor 18
to assist the district attorney. The lawyer who acted for the Coopers in the
civil case helped prosecute Charlie Stevens. Both he and the district attorney assured the jurors that the presence of a special prosecutor was not to
be construed to mean that the Coopers were vindictive. Outside the courtroom, Leo Cooper said that the verdict was of no importance to him —
that he felt sorry, in a way, for Charlie Stevens. But there were people in
Knoxville who thought Cooper had a lot riding on the prosecution of Charlie Stevens. If Stevens was not guilty of FaNee Cooper's death — found so
by twelve of his peers — who was?

At the trial, Cooper testified emotionally and remarkably graphically 19
about pulling FaNee out from under the car and watching her die in his
arms. Charlie Stevens had shaved his beard and cut his hair, but the effort
did not transform him into an impressive witness. His lawyer — trying to
argue that it would have been impossible for Stevens to concoct the story
about FaNee's having mentioned a gun, as the prosecution strongly
implied — said, "His mind is such that if you ask him a question you can
hear his mind go around, like an old mill creaking." Stevens did not deny
the recklessness of his driving or the sorry condition of his car. It happened
to be the only car he had available to flee in, he said, and he had fled in
fear for his life.

The prosecution said that Stevens could have let FaNee out of the car 20
when her father stopped them, or could have gone to the commercial strip
on the Maynardville Highway for protection. The prosecution said that Leo
Cooper had done what he might have been expected to do under the circumstances — alone, late at night, his daughter in danger. The defense
said precisely the same about Stevens: He had done what he might have
been expected to do when being pursued by a man he had reason to be
afraid of. "I don't fault Mr. Cooper for what he did, but I'm sorry he did it,"
the defense attorney said. "I'm sorry the girl said what she said." The jury
deliberated for eighteen minutes. Charlie Stevens was found guilty. The
jury recommended a sentence of from two to five years in the state peni-
tentiary. At the announcement, Leo Cooper broke down and cried, JoAnn
Cooper's eyes filled with tears; she blinked them back and continued to
stare straight ahead.

In a way, the Coopers might still strike a casual visitor as an ideal 21
family — handsome parents, a bright and bubbly teenage daughter, a little
boy learning the hook shot from his father, a warm house with some land
around it. FaNee's presence is there, of course. A picture of her, with a small
bouquet of flowers over it, hangs in the living room. One of her poems is displayed in a frame on a table. Even if Leo Cooper continues to think about
that night for the rest of his life, there are questions he can never answer.
Was there a way that Leo and JoAnn Cooper could have prevented FaNee

from choosing the path she chose? Would she still be alive if Leo Cooper had not jumped into his car and driven to the end of the driveway to investigate? Did she in fact tell Charlie Stevens that her father would hurt them — or even that her father had a gun? Did she want to get away from her family even at the risk of tearing around dark country roads in Charlie Stevens's dismal Pinto? Or did she welcome the risk? The poem of FaNee's that the Coopers have displayed is one she wrote a week before her death:

> I think I'm going to die
> And I really don't know why.
> But look in my eye
> When I tell you good-bye.
> I think I'm going to die.

Analyzing This Selection

1. **THE WRITER'S METHOD**　What is the author's purpose in giving detailed descriptions, as in paragraph 3 and other places, of the setting and the local conditions of life?

2. What is the effect of the two full paragraphs that recount the car chase? What would be lost by condensing paragraphs 13 and 14 into a short statement that reports what happened?

3. FaNee's own writings, including her farewell note, show sharp contrasts between her different outlooks on life. Does this contrast make her any more sympathetic as a person? Or does it turn her into more of a freak?

4. If Mr. Cooper had been able to stop Charlie Stevens's car (immediately after paragraph 12), what might have happened? Use your insight into the characters and your sense of the situation to explain the most likely reactions of each of the main characters.

Analyzing Connections

5. In Focusing by Writing (see p. 62), the second topic suggests that families sometimes play an unwitting role in the formation of a "black sheep." Considering FaNee as a "black sheep," do you think this role was partly created by her family? Why or why not?

Analyzing by Writing

6. The essay presents the difficulties of assigning legal and moral blame for the death of FaNee. Do you think the author is too harsh or too soft in his judgment of who is guilty? who is responsible? who is victimized? In a short essay, explain the author's implied judgment in this accidental death. Include at least one point on which your judgment differs from the author's viewpoint.

7. The only viewpoint missing from Trillin's account is, of course, FaNee's. Offer some possible explanations for FaNee's withdrawal from her family. You might want to draw on insights from the other daughters and sons described in this chapter.

Leo Rosten

HOME IS WHERE TO LEARN
HOW TO HATE

Leo Rosten (1908–1997) was born in Poland and emigrated to the
United States, where he was educated at the University of Chicago, earning a doctorate in political science. During the depression years, he took
a part-time job teaching English to immigrant adults in night school, an
experience that provided the material for his widely enjoyed collection of
humorous short stories, *The Education of H*Y*M*A*N K*A*P*L*A*N*
(1937), which he published under a pseudonym that he continued to use
for his humorous pieces, Leonard Q. Ross. His interest in popular entertainment is evident in his collection of Jewish wit, *The Joys of Yiddish*
(1968). As a political observer, Rosten reported on current events in his
column "Dateline Europe"; he also lectured on politics at Columbia
University and served in the federal government under several adminis-
trations. In this article, Rosten argues that we need to acknowledge and
train our capacity to hate or else our hatreds acquire ungovernable force.

I once committed a lecture, to an entirely innocent group of women, on 1
"Pacifism and Its Problems." My theme was simple: The human race is
plagued by powerful, irrational, intransigent passions; men could not kill
each other unless they possessed the *capacity* to hate and the will to slaughter. During a war, each side even invests its killing with the highest moral
purpose. Theologians of every faith, philosophers and psychologists of every
bent, know that our tormented species is caught in a ceaseless struggle
between good and evil, generosity and greed, love and hate. Men inflict
unspeakable horrors upon each other because they hate what they fear, and
kill what they hate.

So pacifism, I ruefully concluded, confronts an ancient, tragic, almost 2
insurmountable task: to mobilize reason and compassion against the terrible trio of insecurity, irrationality, and aggression. War, the most hideous
of man's acts, has its roots not only in malevolent leaders or ambitious generals, megalomaniacal statesmen or deluded patriots — but in ordinary,
decent men and women, who carry within themselves rages that can be
aroused, passions that can be manipulated, emotions that can become so
exacerbated that they become unbearable and cry for release — against an
enemy.

After my lecture, the usual number of survivors came up to pay the 3 usual compliments and ask the usual questions. One pink-cheeked, beaming little dowager, who looked as if she had stepped right off the cover of a Mother's Day candy box, addressed me, with the utmost kindliness: "Any man who goes around saying God's children are capable of the horrid things you described should be stood up against a blank wall and shot dead!" Off she marched, trailing clouds of sweetness and light and love for her fellow men. (She never even let me ask why the wall had to be blank.)

I think what was wrong with that dear little old lady (as with so many of 4 our young rebels) is that she had never been taught how to hate properly. By "properly" I mean: (a) relevantly; (b) in proportion, fitting the thing or person hated; (c) without blind rage; (d) without guilt. Her love of "mankind" blinded her to her hatred of those who made her uneasy.

Where does hate begin? In the womb? During "the trauma of birth"? In 5 the crib? Because of spanking? Frustration? In "bad" homes or overly permissive kindergartens?

I do not know. Nor does anyone else; one or another authority pinpoints 6 one or another source. But the fact that we do not know why and where hate originates in no way invalidates the fact that hate exists, and that it is deep, virulent, and dangerous. (We don't know what electricity is, either, but we use it.)

No one who has seen a baby scream until its face turns blue would deny 7 that the baby is convulsed by — call it fury. Anyone who has watched tots playing together would be foolish to deny their propensity to violence. For where does anger erupt more swiftly than among the very young? Where are impulses more nakedly displayed and more selfishly gratified? Where are baubles more fiercely guarded or seized? Where are blows, kicks, bites, spits, pinches, and punches delivered with less hesitation?

The maudlin may praise childhood's "innocence," uttering sugary 8 prattle about the little angels in our midst. But if you will reflect upon your own experience you will, I think, agree that it is not heaven but hell that "lies about us in our infancy."

When hate flares up in a little darling (I say "when," not "if"), what 9 should one do? The question is like the one a thousand parents ask a thousand times a day: "Should you spank a child?"

Now, no one would approve of parents who are so vicious as to say, 10 "Dear, let's have some fun: Let's beat up the kids." But "*should* one spank . . ." is better asked: "What should you do *if you are angry enough, for whatever reason, to want to spank a child?*" The real problem is: How do you handle that anger?

Consider what you do if you do *not* spank, when you are angry enough 11 to want to. The child, of course, sees that you are angry. What can it think?

(1) "Oh, he's mad. He's *real* mad. If *I* were that mad, I'd wallop, I'd hit, 12

I'd bite, I'd kick, I'd throw things, I'd knock him down, I'd beat him. But he doesn't hit me. Oh, how much better he is than I. *Will I ever be that good?"* (This is an awful burden to place on a child.)

(2) "He's *mad*. He's really busting to hit me. Why doesn't he? Because   13
he's afraid to! Because he knows that if he ever let go, he'd kill me — which is what I've suspected all along he's wanted to do." (How unwise to fortify this common childhood fantasy.)

(3) "He's mad, so mad he'd like to swat me. Why *doesn't* he? Why   14
doesn't he act like all the fathers of my friends? Why must I be the only one who has never been spanked?" (How unwise to make your child a pariah in his group.)

(4) "I made him mad, and I could understand his punishing me because   15
it's what I would do if I were in his place. When will he show his anger? What do I have to *do* to make him hit me the way I deserve, and expect — and want?!" (How can you prolong a child's tortured waiting? How can you refuse to mete out the justice he may secretly crave? Children *want* restraints put upon their freedom, which delivers them into the hands of their passion.)

Conclusion: If you are angry enough to want to spank a child, *it is cruel*   16
not to. A slap on the hand or a swat on the butt is clear, simple, comprehensible. It releases the anger of the parent, resolves the child's confusions, and clears the emotional air. I think Bernard Shaw put it best: "Never strike a child in cold blood."

It grieves me to say that, to the best of our knowledge, hate is as much a   17
part of man as hunger. You can no more stop a child from hating than you can stop him from dreaming. So we must each learn how to manage hate, how to channel it, how to use it where hate is justified — and how to teach our children to do these things, too.

To raise children by drumming into their minds that they do not "really"   18
hate is to tell them a fearful lie. To moon benignly to the child who cries, "I *hate* you!" that (at that moment) he does not — not *really* — is to confuse a child about an emotion he really feels, knows he possesses, and cannot avoid harboring.

The opposite of hate, in this context, is not love; it is hypocrisy. And   19
children loathe the mealymouthed.

To ask a child to *repress* hate is to play with fire. Modern psychiatry and   20
medicine agree that people who cannot voice their hostilities express them in other ways: eczema, ulcers, migraine, hypertension, constipation, insomnia, impotence, hallucinations, nightmares, suicide. (Look around you.)

For hate concealed is far more dangerous than hate revealed. To try to   21
"bury" hate is to intensify it. Hate is more virulent, in the long run, when it is closeted rather than confronted. (Those of you who are shuddering at this point, or who recoil from the unpleasant thought of "animal hate," might remember that animals do not hate the way men and women do:

Animals attack out of instinct or fear; and they kill for food or safety —
without the vindictive satisfactions that human hate can obtain.)

You may retort that we should teach a child to *understand,* and argue   22
that understanding will defuse his hatreds. But is it not true that the more
we understand some people or acts, the more we detest them — and
should? Ought we to alter our horror and hatred of a Torquemada, a Hitler,
a Charles Manson?

Do you protest, "But they had an unhappy childhood!" Or do you cry,   23
"They're *sick,* not bad!" All childhood is full of unhappiness, yet few of us
become murderers; and, though most sick people are not "bad," *some* sick
people are so evil, so monstrous, that they pass the limits of compassion or
defense.

You tell me "Love thy neighbor"? What if your neighbor happens to be   24
Jack the Ripper?

You say "turn the other cheek"? Turn it, if you will, if only *your* life or   25
nightmares are at stake; but would you turn the cheek of a little girl (or
boy) about to be gagged, abused, and irreparably damaged by a pervert or a
rapist?

Please notice: In a psychology seminar, I would try to analyze the rea-   26
sons for A's cruelty, or B's greed; in a sociology class, I would place C's
delusions or D's hostilities in the larger context of political-social-economic
pressures; in a psychiatric clinic, I would seek enlightenment on the
unconscious drives, the thwarted hungers, the symbolic function served by
X's madness or Y's paranoia. But in my capacity as a human being, as a living, responsible, hurtable mortal, as a member of the human community
that must live together in this neighborhood-village-city-country-continent-
world — in *that* capacity, can I react to evil except with the most profound
moral outrage?

I see no reason to hate sadists less because we understand sadism more.   27
(You may remember the couple in England who tape-recorded the screams
of the children they tortured, then murdered. They were psychopaths, to be
sure; and, to be equally sure, they committed unspeakable horrors — which
they enjoyed.)

There is a subtler point here: Not *ever* to hate is to surrender a just scale   28
of decent values. Not ever to hate is to drain *love* of its meaning. Not to
hate *anyone* is as crazy as to hate everyone.

Besides, a world of automatic, indiscriminate loving is suicidal — for the   29
good and the loving are enslaved or exterminated by those who gratify their
cruelty and their lust. A world that so recently wept over the bloodshed in
Russia, Germany, China, Hungary, Poland, Czechoslovakia, Cuba, Paki-
stan, and Ireland has reason to know that neither truth nor justice nor compassion can possibly survive unprepared and unarmed.

Blind hatred is, of course, horrid and indefensible. But hate need not be   30
blind. Hate can be clear-eyed — and moral. Hate need not be our master

but our servant, for it can be enlisted in the service of decency (hating those who hate decency), of kindness (hating those who choose to be cruel), of love itself (hating those who hate love and seek to destroy or corrupt it).

Are you thinking that this violates "our better selves," or betrays our 31 Judeo-Christian precepts? But the Bible tells us: "The bloodthirsty hate the upright" (Proverbs). I am not about to parade my uprightness, but I hate the bloodthirsty; and I think the upright *should* hate them. Shall we allow the bloodthirsty to prevail?

There is indeed a time to love and a time to hate, and the Eighty-ninth 32 Psalm uses a phrase of transcendent morality: "I hate them with perfect hatred."

I, for one, hate fanatics (regardless of race, color, or creed) who are 33 ready to kill me or you or our children in the detestable certainty that they are absolutely right.

I hate injustice, therefore I hate those who treat others unjustly (because 34 of their color, or creed, or simply because they are powerless).

I hate those who teach others to hate those who disagree with them: I 35 loathe demagogues.

I hate anyone who hates indiscriminately — without hard thought, for 36 irrational reasons, or out of false principles. I think my hatreds are the result of careful thought, reason, and moral principle.

All these things I would teach our children. 37

I would not offend their good sense, or nauseate their sensibilities, by 38 glutinous yammerings about indiscriminate love — love that does not brand evil for what it is, that does not respond with moral passion to those who inflict agony or indignities on others. Such love Emerson dismissed with contempt as the love that "pules and whines."

I hope our children will learn how and whom and when to hate, no less 39 than how and whom and when to help, forgive, or love.

Home is where hate can and should first express itself, and be taught to 40 contain itself, in proper dosages and proportions. Home is where children should be allowed to practice and test and begin to conquer this powerful, terrible human passion.

Home is where it is *safe* to hate — first. 41

Analyzing This Selection

1. Do you agree with Rosten that hitting a child is usually better than restraining the impulse? What consideration, pro or con, would you add that he overlooks?

2. Rosten says that the principle of general loving is "suicidal." How does he support that point? What could be added to make his argument more convincing?

3. **THE WRITER'S METHOD**   In this short essay, eleven of the paragraphs end with parenthetical statements. What are the effects of this device? Does Rosten overdo it, or do you like the recurrence of the comments?

Analyzing Connections

4. Challenge Rosten's argument with Gloria Steinem's warning against authoritarian practices in families in the Insights on page 61. How might the two writers debate the point?

Analyzing by Writing

5. Argue for or against Rosten's thesis that children at home need to be taught how to hate. Why does he emphasize *home*? What would be made better or worse by instruction outside the home? Would home instruction be effective without some reinforcement by society? What forms of reinforcement are acceptable?

Tillie Olsen

I STAND HERE IRONING

Tillie Olsen (b. 1913) dropped out of high school in Nebraska at fifteen in order to help support her family during the Depression. She held jobs as a factory worker or secretary while she organized labor unions, married, raised four children, and continued to read prodigiously. "Public libraries were my college," she has said. When she was forty, she resumed her early efforts to write fiction. Her volume of stories, *Tell Me a Riddle* (1961), established her as a champion of the poor and overburdened. In *Silences* (1978), a collection of essays, Olsen examines the injustices of social class, racism, and sexism that hinder creativity, particularly in women. The cruelty of harmful social conditions is a theme in all her work, including the following story.

I stand here ironing, and what you asked me moves tormented back and 1 forth with the iron.

"I wish you would manage the time to come in and talk with me about 2 your daughter. I'm sure you can help me understand her. She's a youngster who needs help and whom I'm deeply interested in helping."

"Who needs help." . . . Even if I came, what good would it do? You 3 think because I am her mother I have a key, or that in some way you could use me as a key? She has lived for nineteen years. There is all that life that has happened outside of me, beyond me.

And when is there time to remember, to sift, to weigh, to estimate, to 4 total? I will start and there will be an interruption and I will have to gather it all together again. Or I will become engulfed with all I did or did not do, with what should have been and what cannot be helped.

She was a beautiful baby. The first and only one of our five that was 5 beautiful at birth. You do not guess how new and uneasy her tenancy in her now-loveliness. You did not know her all those years she was thought homely, or see her poring over her baby pictures, making me tell her over and over how beautiful she had been — and would be, I would tell her — and was now, to the seeing eye. But the seeing eyes were few or nonexistent. Including mine.

I nursed her. They feel that's important nowadays. I nursed all the chil- 6 dren, but with her, with all the fierce rigidity of first motherhood, I did like the books then said. Though her cries battered me to trembling and my breasts ached with swollenness, I waited till the clock decreed.

Why do I put that first? I do not even know if it matters, or if it explains 7 anything.

She was a beautiful baby. She blew shining bubbles of sound. She loved 8 motion, loved light, loved color and music and textures. She would lie on the floor in her blue overalls patting the surface so hard in ecstasy her hands and feet would blur. She was a miracle to me, but when she was eight months old I had to leave her daytimes with the woman downstairs to whom she was no miracle at all, for I worked or looked for work and for Emily's father, who "could no longer endure" (he wrote in his good-bye note) "sharing want with us."

I was nineteen, it was the pre-relief, pre-WPA world of the Depression. I 9 would start running as soon as I got off the streetcar, running up the stairs, the place smelling sour, and awake or asleep to startle awake, when she saw me she would break into a clogged weeping that could not be comforted, a weeping I can hear yet.

After a while I found a job hashing at night so I could be with her days, 10 and it was better. But it came to where I had to bring her to his family and leave her.

It took a long time to raise the money for her fare back. Then she got 11 chicken pox and I had to wait longer. When she finally came, I hardly knew her, walking quick and nervous like her father, looking like her father, thin, and dressed in a shoddy red that yellowed her skin and glared at the pockmarks. All the baby loveliness gone.

She was two. Old enough for nursery school they said, and I did not 12 know then what I know now — the fatigue of the long day, and the lacerations of group life in the kinds of nurseries that are only parking places for children.

Except that it would have made no difference if I had known. It was the 13 only place there was. It was the only way we could be together, the only way I could hold a job.

And even without knowing, I knew. I knew the teacher that was evil 14 because all these years it has curdled into my memory, the little boy hunched in the corner, her rasp, "why aren't you outside, because Alvin hits you? that's no reason, go out, scaredy." I knew Emily hated it even if she did not clutch and implore "don't go Mommy" like the other children, mornings.

She always had a reason why we should stay home. Momma, you look 15 sick. Momma, I feel sick. Momma, the teachers aren't there today, they're sick. Momma, we can't go, there was a fire there last night. Momma, it's a holiday today, no school, they told me.

But never a direct protest, never rebellion. I think of our others in their 16 three-, four-year-oldness — the explosions, the tempers, the denunciations, the demands — and I feel suddenly ill. I put the iron down. What in me demanded that goodness in her? And what was the cost, the cost to her of such goodness?

The old man living in the back once said in his gentle way: "You should   17
smile at Emily more when you look at her." What *was* in my face when I looked at her? I loved her. There were all the acts of love.

It was only with the others I remembered what he said, and it was the   18
face of joy, and not of care or tightness or worry I turned to them — too late for Emily. She does not smile easily, let alone almost always as her brothers and sisters do. Her face is closed and somber, but when she wants, how fluid. You must have seen it in her pantomimes, you spoke of her rare gift for comedy on the stage that rouses a laughter out of the audience so dear they applaud and applaud and do not want to let her go.

Where does it come from, that comedy? There was none of it in her   19
when she came back to me that second time, after I had had to send her away again. She had a new daddy now to learn to love, and I think perhaps it was a better time.

Except when we left her alone nights, telling ourselves she was old   20
enough.

"Can't you go some other time, Mommy, like tomorrow?" she would   21
ask. "Will it be just a little while you'll be gone? Do you promise?"

The time we came back, the front door open, the clock on the floor in   22
the hall. She rigid awake. "It wasn't just a little while. I didn't cry. Three times I called you, just three times, and then I ran downstairs to open the door so you could come faster. The clock talked loud. I threw it away, it scared me what it talked."

She said the clock talked loud again that night I went to the hospital to   23
have Susan. She was delirious with the fever that comes before red measles, but she was fully conscious all the week I was gone and the week after we were home when she could not come near the new baby or me.

She did not get well. She stayed skeleton thin, not wanting to eat, and   24
night after night she had nightmares. She would call for me, and I would rouse from exhaustion to sleepily call back: "You're all right, darling, go to sleep, it's just a dream," and if she still called, in a sterner voice, "now go to sleep, Emily, there's nothing to hurt you." Twice, only twice, when I had to get up for Susan anyhow, I went in to sit with her.

Now when it is too late (as if she would let me hold and comfort her like   25
I do the others) I get up and go to her at once at her moan or restless stirring. "Are you awake, Emily? Can I get you something?" And the answer is always the same. "No, I'm all right, go back to sleep, Mother."

They persuaded me at the clinic to send her away to a convalescent   26
home in the country where "she can have the kind of food and care you can't manage for her, and you'll be free to concentrate on the new baby." They still send children to that place. I see pictures on the society page of sleek young women planning affairs to raise money for it, or dancing at

the affairs, or decorating Easter eggs or filling Christmas stockings for the children.

They never have a picture of the children so I do not know if the girls   27
still wear those gigantic red bows and the ravaged looks on the every other Sunday when parents can come to visit "unless otherwise notified" — as we were notified the first six weeks.

Oh it is a handsome place, green lawns and tall trees and fluted flower   28
beds. High up on the balconies of each cottage the children stand, the girls in their red bows and white dresses, the boys in white suits and gigantic red ties. The parents stand below shrieking up to be heard and the children shriek down to be heard, and between them the invisible wall "Not To Be Contaminated by Parental Germs or Physical Affection."

There was a tiny girl who always stood hand in hand with Emily. Her   29
parents never came. One visit she was gone. "They moved her to Rose Cottage," Emily shouted in explanation. "They don't like you to love anybody here."

She wrote once a week, the labored writings of a seven-year-old. "I am   30
fine. How is the baby. If I write my leter nicly I will have a star. Love." There never was a star. We wrote every other day, letters she could never hold or keep but only hear read — once. "We simply do not have room for children to keep any personal possessions," they patiently explained when we pieced one Sunday's shrieking together to plead how much it would mean to Emily, who loved so to keep things, to be allowed to keep her letters and cards.

Each visit she looked frailer. "She isn't eating," they told us.   31

(They had runny eggs for breakfast or mush with lumps, Emily said   32
later, I'd hold it in my mouth and not swallow. Nothing ever tasted good, just when they had chicken.)

It took us eight months to get her released home, and only the fact that   33
she gained back so little of her seven lost pounds convinced the social worker.

I used to try to hold and love her after she came back, but her body   34
would stay stiff, and after a while she'd push away. She ate little. Food sickened her, and I think much of life too. Oh she had physical lightness and brightness, twinkling by on skates, bouncing like a ball up and down up and down over the jump rope, skimming over the hill; but these were momentary.

She fretted about her appearance, thin and dark and foreign-looking at a   35
time when every little girl was supposed to look or thought she should look like a chubby blonde replica of Shirley Temple. The doorbell sometimes rang for her, but no one seemed to come and play in the house or be a best friend. Maybe because we moved so much.

There was a boy she loved painfully through two school semesters.   36
Months later she told me how she had taken pennies from my purse to buy him candy. "Licorice was his favorite and I brought him some every day,

but he still liked Jennifer better'n me. Why, Mommy?" The kind of question for which there is no answer.

School was a worry to her. She was not glib or quick in a world where 37
glibness and quickness were easily confused with ability to learn. To her
overworked and exasperated teachers she was an over-conscientious "slow
learner" who kept trying to catch up and was absent entirely too often.

I let her be absent, though sometimes the illness was imaginary. How 38
different from my now-strictness about attendance with the others. I wasn't
working. We had a new baby, I was home anyhow. Sometimes, after Susan
grew old enough, I would keep her home from school, too, to have them
all together.

Mostly Emily had asthma, and her breathing, harsh and labored, would 39
fill the house with a curiously tranquil sound. I would bring the two old
dresser mirrors and her boxes of collections to her bed. She would select
beads and single earrings, bottle tops and shells, dried flowers and pebbles,
old postcards and scraps, all sorts of oddments; then she and Susan would
play Kingdom, setting up landscapes and furniture, peopling them with
action.

Those were the only times of peaceful companionship between her and 40
Susan. I have edged away from it, that poisonous feeling between them,
that terrible balancing of hurts and needs I had to do between the two, and
did so badly, those earlier years.

Oh there are conflicts between the others too, each one human, need- 41
ing, demanding, hurting, taking — but only between Emily and Susan, no,
Emily toward Susan that corroding resentment. It seems so obvious on the
surface, yet it is not obvious. Susan, the second child, Susan, golden- and
curly-haired and chubby, quick and articulate and assured, everything in
appearance and manner Emily was not; Susan, not able to resist Emily's
precious things, losing or sometimes clumsily breaking them; Susan telling
jokes and riddles to company for applause while Emily sat silent (to say to
me later: That was *my* riddle, Mother, I told it to Susan); Susan, who for
all the five years' difference in age was just a year behind Emily in developing physically.

I am glad for that slow physical development that widened the differ- 42
ence between her and her contemporaries, though she suffered over it. She
was too vulnerable for that terrible world of youthful competition, of preen-
ing and parading, of constant measuring of yourself against every other, of
envy, "If I had that copper hair," "If I had that skin. . . ." She tormented
herself enough about not looking like the others, there was enough of the
unsureness, the having to be conscious of words before you speak, the constant caring — what are they thinking of me? without having it all magnified by the merciless physical drives.

Ronnie is calling. He is wet and I change him. It is rare there is such a 43
cry now. That time of motherhood is almost behind me when the ear is not
one's own but must always be racked and listening for the child cry, the

child call. We sit for a while and I hold him, looking out over the city spread in charcoal with its soft aisles of light. "*Shoogily*," he breathes and curls closer. I carry him back to bed, asleep. *Shoogily*. A funny word, a family word, inherited from Emily, invented by her to say: *comfort*.

In this and other ways she leaves her seal, I say aloud. And startle at me 44 saying it. What do I mean? What did I start to gather together, to try and make coherent? I was at the terrible, growing years. War years. I do not remember them well. I was working, there were four smaller ones now, there was not time for her. She had to help be a mother, and housekeeper, and shopper. She had to set her seal. Mornings of crisis and near hysteria trying to get lunches packed, hair combed, coats and shoes found, everyone to school or Child Care on time, the baby ready for transportation. And always the paper scribbled on by a smaller one, the book looked at by Susan then mislaid, the homework not done. Running out to that huge school where she was one, she was lost, she was a drop; suffering over her unpreparedness, stammering and unsure in her classes.

There was so little time left at night after the kids were bedded down. 45 She would struggle over books, always eating (it was in those years she developed her enormous appetite that is legendary in our family) and I would be ironing, or preparing food for the next day, or writing V-mail to Bill, or tending the baby. Sometimes, to make me laugh, or out of her despair, she would imitate happenings or types at school.

I think I said once: "Why don't you do something like this in the school 46 amateur show?" One morning she phoned me at work, hardly understandable through the weeping: "Mother, I did it. I won, I won; they gave me first prize; they clapped and clapped and wouldn't let me go."

Now suddenly she was Somebody, and as imprisoned in her difference 47 as she had been in anonymity.

She began to be asked to perform at other high schools, even in col- 48 leges, then at city and statewide affairs. The first one we went to, I only recognized her that first moment when thin, shy, she almost drowned herself into the curtains. Then: Was this Emily? The control, the command, the convulsing and deadly drowning, the spell, then the roaring, stamping audience, unwilling to let this rare and precious laughter out of their lives.

Afterwards: You ought to do something about her with a gift like that — 49 but without money or knowing how, what does one do? We have left it all to her, and the gift has as often eddied inside, clogged and clotted, as been used and growing.

She is coming. She runs up the stairs two at a time with her light grace- 50 ful step, and I know she is happy tonight. Whatever it was that occasioned your call did not happen today.

"Aren't you ever going to finish the ironing, Mother? Whistler painted 51 his mother in a rocker. I'd have to paint mine standing over an ironing board." This is one of her communicative nights and she tells me everything and nothing as she fixes herself a plate of food out of the icebox.

She is so lovely. Why did you want me to come in at all? Why were you 52 concerned? She will find her way.

She starts up the stairs to bed. "Don't get me up with the rest in the 53 morning." "But I thought you were having midterms." "Oh, those," she comes back in, kisses me, and says quite lightly, "in a couple of years when we'll be all atom-dead they won't matter a bit."

She has said it before. She *believes* it. But because I have been dredging 54 the past, and all that compounds a human being is so heavy and meaningful in me, I cannot endure it tonight.

I will never total it all. I will never come in to say: She was a child sel- 55 dom smiled at. Her father left me before she was a year old. I had to work her first six years when there was work, or I sent her home and to his relatives. There were years she had care she hated. She was dark and thin and foreign-looking in a world where the prestige went to blondeness and curly hair and dimples, she was slow where glibness was prized. She was a child of anxious, not proud, love. We were poor and could not afford for her the soil of easy growth. I was a younger mother, I was a distracted mother. There were the other children pushing up, demanding. Her younger sister seemed all that she was not. There were years she did not want me to touch her. She kept too much in herself, her life was such she had to keep too much in herself. My wisdom came too late. She has much to her and probably little will come of it. She is a child of her age, of depression, of war, of fear.

Let her be. So all that is in her will not bloom — but in how many does 56 it? There is still enough left to live by. Only help her to know — help make it so there is cause for her to know — that she is more than this dress on the ironing board, helpless before the iron.

Analyzing This Selection

1. **THE WRITER'S METHOD**   Who has phoned Emily's mother? How has the caller's request affected the mother?

2. Does the mother blame herself too much or too little for causing Emily's hardships? At which points do you disagree with the mother's judgment of her own actions?

3. How did Emily differ from her brothers and sisters? What explanations does the mother have for Emily's difference? Which of her explanations do you think are most valid and important?

4. In the final two paragraphs, why does the mother refuse to consult about Emily?

5. Does the story reflect specific political views toward particular social conditions and historical events? What attitudes toward government assistance does the story stimulate in the reader?

6. To what extent do the mother's aspirations for Emily reflect her own?

Analyzing Connections

7. Emily and FaNee (see "It's Just Too Late," p. 75) cause problems for their parents. What lessons have the parents learned?

Analyzing by Writing

8. How would a child like Emily perceive her mother's conflict of responsibilities? What problems do you think the child faced? Adopt Emily's viewpoint in a monologue (like this story) that explores Emily's thoughts during any one incident or situation suggested in the fiction.

Anndee Hochman

EXTENDING FAMILY

ANNDEE HOCHMAN (b. 1962) graduated from Yale University. She writes about feminist and lesbian issues in establishing unconventional, women-centered families. This selection is excerpted from her first book, *Everyday Acts and Small Subversions: Women Reinventing Family, Community, and Home* (1994).

Popular culture always depicts estranged couples as opposing forces in a 1 permanent war of vengeance. It's the flip side of the romantic myth: either live happily ever after or become lifelong foes.

Clearly there are other possibilities. It's long been a custom — practi- 2 cally a cliché — for lesbian couples to remain friends after a breakup. That phenomenon might stem partly from a sense of scarcity: people in small, oppressed communities can't afford to make enemies with each other. It may also be an effort to counter the invisibility lesbians face; perhaps remaining close with ex-partners helps to affirm, in the face of a hostile, doubting world, that the relationship did exist.

I think there's more. A habit of keeping former lovers in the family stems 3 from an important vision, with impact far beyond the lesbian community — a recognition that relationships rarely evolve or dissolve in clear-cut ways, that it is possible to love a person deeply yet no longer wish to make a life with her.

These efforts challenge the myth of eternal love and replace it with 4 something more complicated and more pragmatic. Today, one out of every two marriages does not last. For both heterosexual and lesbian women, the ideal of a single lifetime partner is ceding to the reality of serial commitments that last for two, ten, or twenty years, but not necessarily forever.

Still, we have no words, let alone models, for maintaining relationships 5 as they shift course. Existing terms always use the past as a reference — "ex-lover," "former partner" — while failing to articulate what the relationship means now. Sustaining such bonds requires not only semantic ingenuity but emotional endurance, two partners willing to paddle through jealousy, possessiveness, grief, guilt, and anger in order to reach friendship on the other shore. . . .

I had tried it myself, and found the trip a challenging one. From the 6
time I was in high school, the pattern of my friends' breakups made no
sense to me. On Tuesday you could be sweethearts, leaving flirty notes in
each other's lockers, celebrating your seven-month anniversary with pepper-
oni pizza. Then — crash! — by Friday you were enemies, cold-shouldering
each other in the hallway, divvying up your friends, returning the ID
bracelet and the borrowed sweatshirt. Through high school and college I
felt determined to at least make peace, if not family, with my former
boyfriends. Anything else seemed both painful and absurd.

In college, I dated Barry for nine months and ended the relationship 7
shortly before we both graduated. In that time, he'd become close to my
family, spending Thanksgiving with us, holding vigil by my grandmother's
hospital bed, dancing the hora at my cousin's Bar Mitzvah.

When we broke up, Barry and my family stayed in touch. He and my 8
parents exchanged notes. He visited them if business took him to Philadelphia. My mother occasionally met him for lunch in New York. At first,
those continuing ties made me angry and edgy; they seemed to undermine
my desire to put some distance between us.

And yet, we hadn't parted in anger. I simply felt sure the relationship 9
wasn't right for me. No one else in the family had reason to cancel their
affection. "I have a relationship with Barry that's independent of you," my
mother explained.

Now, nearly ten years later, postcards in Barry's deliberate squarish print 10
arrive in my mailbox several times a year. On the phone, we catch up on
each other's families, commiserate about jobs. I think of Barry not as my
"ex-anything," but as a friend of the family, a man who was, for a time,
important to all of us. We appear and retreat from each other's lives like
cousins who, no matter how their lives evolve, will always hold a piece of
each other's past.

At one time, you could diagram the *mishpokhe* — Yiddish for "extended 11
family" — with clear lines of blood, marriage, and legal adoption. But
changing life patterns have built a new family, with connections scribbled
out and drawn in again, in convoluted links.

This new family confounds us sometimes. Do we continue sending 12
Christmas presents to the former-partner-now-good-friend, as we always
have? Invite her to holiday celebrations? What is the relationship of children, say, to a single parent's former lover? How does it change if a new
lover enters the picture? If we don't oust the "ex" from our midst, how do
friends and family acknowledge the relationship's shift and respect the
changes in both partners' lives?

Instead of a pattern that rips each time a couple end their relationship, 13
the new *mishpokhe* demands a more expansive vision. It refuses to choose
sides, to split loyalties. Instead, it insists that there is enough: enough love,
enough time, enough space for kinship to evolve in unpredictable directions.

I think about the notion of "extended" family, what that word means.   14
When I extend myself, I go beyond an old limit, stretch in unexpected
ways. I leave behind my assumptions about who I can include, who I must
shut out.

Perhaps the exact junctures of family extension were once easier to find.   15
They were the second-cousins-twice-removed, the aunts-by-marriage, the
kin acquired automatically each time a couple wed. The links are less obvious, more complicated, now. But they are there, these points of necessity
and affection, entrances to one another's lives.

Analyzing This Selection

1. According to Hochman, new patterns have altered the traditional family.
   Which changes are fully considered in the essay? Which are not considered?

2. The author redefines the term *extended family*. Would her definition or
   model apply to your present extended family? Which model do you prefer?

Analyzing Connections

3. Hochman considers the deterioration of traditional family life that J. H.
   Plumb assesses in the Insights on page 60. Whose suggested changes are
   more radical and why?

Analyzing by Writing

4. If you were designing a utopian society, how would you change the family's
   role in bearing, nurturing, socializing, and educating children? What would
   you eliminate, preserve, or strengthen in the family? Explain the reasons for
   your position about one or two current features of family life. Don't get
   caught up in working out the details of an alternative plan.

Barbara Dafoe Whitehead

WOMEN AND THE FUTURE
OF FATHERHOOD

BARBARA DAFOE WHITEHEAD (b. 1944), a social historian, earned her
B.A. at the University of Wisconsin and a Ph.D. in American social history from the University of Chicago. Her essays on parenting and family
life have appeared in magazines such as the *Atlantic Monthly, Common-
weal,* and the *Wilson Quarterly,* where "Women and the Future of Fatherhood" first appeared. Her book, *The Divorce Culture,* was published in
1997.

Much of our contemporary debate over fatherhood is governed by the 1
assumption that men can solve the fatherhood problem on their own.
Organizers of the Million Man March asked women to stay home, and the
leaders of Promise Keepers and other grass-roots fatherhood movements
whose members gather with considerably less fanfare simply do not admit
women.

There is a cultural rationale for the exclusion of women. The father- 2
hood movement sees the task of reinstating responsible fatherhood as an
effort to alter today's norms of masculinity and correctly believes that such
an effort cannot succeed unless it is voluntarily undertaken and supported
by men. There is also a political rationale in defining fatherlessness as a
men's issue. In the debate about marriage and parenthood, which women
have dominated for at least thirty years, the fatherhood movement gives
men a powerful collective voice and presence.

Yet however effective the grass-roots movement is at stirring men's con- 3
sciences and raising their consciousness, the fatherhood problem will not
be solved by men alone. To be sure, by signaling their commitment to
accepting responsibility for the rearing of their children, men have taken
the essential first step. But what has not yet been acknowledged is that the
success of any effort to renew fatherhood as a social fact and a cultural
norm also hinges on the attitudes and behavior of women. Men can't be
fathers unless the mothers of their children allow it.

Merely to say this is to point to how thoroughly marital disruption has 4
weakened the bond between fathers and children. More than half of
all American children are likely to spend at least part of their lives in

one-parent homes. Since the vast majority of children in disrupted families live with their mothers, fathers do not share a home or a daily life with their children. It is much more difficult for men to make the kinds of small, routine, instrumental investments in their children that help forge a good relationship. It is hard to fix a flat bike tire or run a bath when you live in another neighborhood or another town. Many a father's instrumental contribution is reduced to the postal or electronic transmission of money, or, all too commonly, to nothing at all. Without regular contact with their children, men often make reduced emotional contributions as well. Fathers must struggle to sustain close emotional ties across time and space, to "be there" emotionally without being there physically. Some may pick up the phone, send a birthday card, or buy a present, but for many fathers, physical absence also becomes emotional absence.

Without marriage, men also lose access to the social and emotional 5
intelligence of women in building relationships. Wives teach men how to care for young children, and they also encourage children to love their fathers. Mothers who do not live with the father of their children are not as likely as married mothers to represent him in positive ways to the children; nor are the relatives who are most likely to have greatest contact with the children — the mother's parents, brothers, and sisters — likely to have a high opinion of the children's father. Many men are able to overcome such obstacles, but only with difficulty. In general, men need marriage in order to be good fathers.

If the future of fatherhood depends on marriage, however, its future is 6
uncertain. Marriage depends on women as well as men, and women are less committed to marriage than ever before in the nation's history. In the past, women were economically dependent on marriage and assumed a disproportionately heavy responsibility for maintaining the bond, even if the underlying relationship was seriously or irretrievably damaged. In the last third of the twentieth century, however, as women have gained more opportunities for paid work and the availability of child care has increased, they have become less dependent on marriage as an economic arrangement. Though it is not easy, it is possible for women to raise children on their own. This has made divorce far more attractive as a remedy for an unsatisfying marriage, and a growing number of women have availed themselves of the option.

Today, marriage and motherhood are coming apart. Remarriage and 7
marriage rates are declining even as the rates of divorce remain stuck at historic highs and childbearing outside marriage becomes more common. Many women see single motherhood as a choice and a right to be exercised if a suitable husband does not come along in time.

The vision of the "first stage" feminism of the 1960s and '70s, which 8
held out the model of the career woman unfettered by husband or children, has been accepted by women only in part. Women want to be fet-

tered by children, even to the point of going through grueling infertility treatments or artificial insemination to achieve motherhood. But they are increasingly ambivalent about the ties that bind them to a husband and about the necessity of marriage as a condition of parenthood. In 1994, a National Opinion Research survey asked a group of Americans, "Do you agree or disagree: One parent can bring up a child as well as two parents together." Women split 50/50 on the question; men disagreed by more than two to one.

And indeed, women enjoy certain advantages over men in a society 9 marked by high and sustained levels of family breakup. Women do not need marriage to maintain a close bond to their children, and thus to experience the larger sense of social and moral purpose that comes with raising children. As the bearers and nurturers of children and (increasingly) as the sole breadwinners for families, women continue to be engaged in personally rewarding and socially valuable pursuits. They are able to demonstrate their feminine virtues outside marriage.

Men, by contrast, have no positive identity as fathers outside marriage. 10 Indeed, the emblematic absent father today is the infamous "deadbeat dad." In part, this is the result of efforts to stigmatize irresponsible fathers who fail to pay alimony and child support. But this image also reflects the fact that men are heavily dependent on the marriage partnership to fulfill their role as fathers. Even those who keep up their child support payments are deprived of the social importance and sense of larger purpose that comes from providing for children and raising a family. And it is the rare father who can develop the qualities needed to meet the new cultural ideal of the involved and "nurturing" father without the help of a spouse.

These differences are reflected in a growing virtue gap. American popu- 11 lar culture today routinely recognizes and praises the achievements of single motherhood, while the widespread failure of men as fathers has resulted in a growing sense of cynicism and despair about men's capacity for virtuous conduct in family life. The enormously popular movie *Waiting to Exhale* captures the essence of this virtue gap with its portrait of steadfast mothers and deadbeat fathers, morally sleazy men and morally unassailable women. And women feel free to vent their anger and frustration with men in ways that would seem outrageous to women if the shoe were on the other foot. In *Operating Instructions* (1993), her memoir of single motherhood, Ann LaMott mordantly observes, "On bad days, I think straight white men are so poorly wired, so emotionally unenlightened and unconscious that you must approach each one as if he were some weird cross between a white supremacist and an incredibly depressing T. S. Eliot poem."

Women's weakening attachment to marriage should not be taken as a 12 lack of interest in marriage or in a husband-wife partnership in child rearing. Rather, it is a sign of women's more exacting emotional standards for husbands and their growing insistence that men play a bigger part in caring for children and the household. Given their double responsibilities as breadwinners and mothers, many working wives find men's need for ego reinforcement and other forms of emotional and physical upkeep irksome and their failure to share housework and child care absolutely infuriating. (Surveys show that husbands perform only one-third of all household tasks even if their wives are working full-time). Why should men be treated like babies? women complain. If men fail to meet their standards, many women are willing to do without them. Poet and polemicist Katha Pollitt captures the prevailing sentiment: "If single women can have sex, their own homes, the respect of friends, and interesting work, they don't need to tell themselves that any marriage is better than none. Why not have a child on one's own? Children are a joy. Many men are not."

For all these reasons, it is important to see the fatherhood problem as   13 part of the larger cultural problem of the decline of marriage as a lasting relationship between men and women. The traditional bargain between men and women has broken down, and a new bargain has not yet been struck. It is impossible to predict what that bargain will look like — or whether there will even be one. However, it is possible to speculate about the talking points that might bring women to the bargaining table. First, a crucial proviso: There must be recognition of the changed social and economic status of women. Rightly or wrongly, many women fear that the fatherhood movement represents an effort to reinstate the status quo ante, to repeal the gains and achievements women have made over the past thirty years and return to the "separate spheres" domestic ideology that put men in the workplace and women in the home. Any effort to rethink marriage must accept the fact that women will continue to work outside the home.

Therefore, a new bargain must be struck over the division of paid work   14 and family work. This does not necessarily mean a 50/50 split in the work load every single day, but it does mean that men must make a more determined and conscientious effort to do more than one-third of the household chores. How each couple arrives at a sense of what is fair will vary, of course, but the goal is to establish some mutual understanding and commitment to an equitable division of tasks.

Another talking point may focus on the differences in the expectations   15 men and women have for marriage and intimacy. Americans have a "best friends" ideal for marriage that includes some desires that might in fact be more easily met by a best friend — someone who doesn't come with all the complicated entanglements of sharing a bed, a bank account, and a bathroom. Nonetheless, high expectations for emotional intimacy in marriage often are confounded by the very different understandings men and women have of intimacy. Much more than men, women seek intimacy and affection through talking and emotional disclosure. Men often prefer sex to talking, and physical disrobing to emotional disclosing. They tend to be less than fully committed to (their own) sexual fidelity, while women view fidelity as a crucial sign of commitment. These are differences that the sexes need to engage with mutual recognition and tolerance.

In renegotiating the marital bargain, it may also be useful to acknowl- 16
edge the biosocial differences between mothers and fathers rather than to assume an androgynous model for the parental partnership. There can be a high degree of flexibility in parental roles, but men and women are not interchangeable "parental units," particularly in their children's early years. Rather than struggle to establish identical tracks in career and family lives, it may be more realistic to consider how children's needs and well-being might require patterns of paid work and child rearing that are different for mothers and fathers but are nevertheless equitable over the course of a life-time.

Finally, it may be important to think and talk about marriage in another 17
kind of language than the one that suffuses our current discourse on rela-tionships. The secular language of "intimate relationships" is the language of politics and psychotherapy, and it focuses on individual rights and indi-vidual needs. It can be heard most clearly in the personal-ad columns, a kind of masked ball where optimists go in search of partners who respect their rights and meet their emotional needs. These are not unimportant in the achievement of the contemporary ideal of marriage, which emphasizes egalitarianism and emotional fulfillment. But this notion of marriage as a union of two sovereign selves may be inadequate to define a relationship that carries with it the obligations, duties, and sacrifices of parenthood. There has always been tension between marriage as an intimate relation-ship between a man and a woman and marriage as an institutional arrange-ment for raising children, and though the language of individual rights plays a part in defining the former, it cannot fully describe the latter. The parental partnership requires some language that acknowledges differences, mutuality, complementarity, and, more than anything else, altruism.

There is a potentially powerful incentive for women to respond to an 18
effort to renegotiate the marriage bargain, and that has to do with their children. Women can be good mothers without being married. But espe-cially with weakened communities that provide little support, children need levels of parental investment that cannot be supplied solely by a good mother, even if she has the best resources at her disposal. These needs are more likely to be met if the child has a father as well as a mother under the same roof. Simply put, even the best mothers cannot be good fathers.

Analyzing This Selection

1. **THE WRITER'S METHOD**   According to Whitehead, why were women more committed to marriage in the past than they are today? Does she rec-ommend that families return to that situation?

2. What is the "growing virtue gap" that Whitehead observes in contemporary culture?

3. In what ways have women raised the standards for husbands? Do you think there has been a comparable change in men's standards for wives?

Analyzing Connections

4. What do *men* learn at home? Do Whitehead's observations strengthen or weaken Rosten's views about family life (see "Home Is Where to Learn How to Hate," p. 84)?

Analyzing by Writing

5. Whitehead cites some writers who question whether men are even desirable in a family. Hochman (see "Extending Family," p. 98) believes they are not necessary. Do you think fathers provide advantages that financially self-reliant, emotionally responsive women do not? Explain your views on this issue.

Amitai Etzioni

THE VALUE OF FAMILIES[1]

AMITAI ETZIONI (b. 1929) is a noted social policy advisor and a leader of
the Communitarian movement to improve society. He emigrated from
Germany and fought in the Israeli army before graduating from Hebrew
University in Jerusalem. He received a Ph.D. in sociology from the University of California at Berkeley. Formerly a professor at Columbia University, Etzioni currently teaches at George Washington University. His
books include *The Spirit of Community: The Reinvention of American
Society* (1993), from which the following selection is excerpted. His most
recent book is *The New Golden Rule: Community and Morality in a
Democratic Society* (1997).

Consider for a moment parenting as an industry. As farming declined, 1
most fathers left to work away from home. Over the past twenty years millions of American mothers have sharply curtailed their work in the "parenting industry" by moving to work outside the home. By 1991 two-thirds
(66.7 percent) of all mothers with children under eighteen were in the
labor force and more than half (55.4 percent) of women with children
under the age of three. At the same time a much smaller number of child
care personnel moved into the parenting industry.[2]

If this were any other business, say, shoemaking, and more than half of 2
the labor force had been lost and replaced with fewer, less-qualified hands
and still we asked the shoemakers to produce the same number of shoes of
the same quality (with basically no changes in technology), we would be
considered crazy. But this is what happened to parenting. As first men and
then women left to work outside the home, they were replaced by some
child care services, a relatively small increase in baby-sitters and nannies,
and some additional service by grandparents — leaving parenting woefully
shorthanded. The millions of latchkey children, who are left alone for long
stretches of time, are but the most visible result of the parenting deficit.

---

[1]Editor's title.

[2]Two-thirds of mothers with children under eighteen are in the labor force: *Current Population Survey*, Bureau of Labor Statistics, unpublished tabulations, 1991. [This and subsequent notes in the selection are the author's.]

Is this the "fault" of the women's movement, feminism, or mothers per   3
se? Obviously not. All women did was demand for themselves what men
had long possessed, working outside the home not only for their own personal satisfaction, but because of what they often perceived as the economic necessity. Whatever the cause, the result is an empty nest. Only it
isn't the small fry who grew up and took off: it is the parents who flew the
coop. Those who did not leave altogether increased their investment of
time, energy, involvement, and commitment outside the home.

Although parenting is the responsibility of both parents — and may well   4
be discharged most effectively in two-parent families immersed in a community context of kin and neighbors — *most important is the scope of commitment.* Single parents may do better than two-career absentee parents.
Children require attention, as Robert Beliah and the other authors of *The
Good Society* declared. Kids also require a commitment of time, energy,
and, above all, of self.

The prevalent situation is well captured by a public service commercial   5
in which a mother calls her child and reassures him that she has left
money for him next to the phone. "Honey, have some dinner," she mutters
as the child takes the twenty-dollar bill she left behind, rolls it up, and
snorts cocaine. One might add that the father didn't even call.

The fact is that parenting cannot be carried out over the phone, however   6
well meaning and loving the calls may be. It requires physical presence. The
notion of "quality time" (not to mention "quality phone calls") is a lame
excuse for parental absence; it presupposes that bonding and education can
take place in brief time bursts, on the run. *Quality time occurs within quantity time.* As you spend time with one's children — fishing, gardening, camping, or "just" eating a meal — there are unpredictable moments when an
opening occurs and education takes hold. As family expert Barbara Dafoe
Whitehead puts it: "Maybe there is indeed such a thing as a one-minute
manager, but there is no such thing as a one-minute parent."[3] . . .

Is the answer to the parenting deficit building more child care centers?   7
After all, other societies have delegated the upbringing of their children,
from black nannies in the antebellum South to Greek slaves in ancient
Rome. True enough. But in these historical situations the person who
attended to the children was an adjunct to the parents rather than a
replacement for them and an accessory reserved mostly for upper-class families with leisure. A caregiver remained with the family throughout the children's formative years and often beyond; she was, to varying degrees,
integrated into the family. The caregiver, in turn, reflected, at least in part,
the family's values and educational posture. Some children may have been

[3]Barbara Dafoe Whitehead says there's no such thing as a one-minute parent: Barbara
Whitehead, "The New Politics in Action — Fortifying the Family," presentation at the conference "Left and Right: The Emergence of a New Politics in the 1990s?" sponsored by the
Heritage Foundation and the Progressive Foundation, October 30, 1991, Washington, D.C.
(see transcript, 25).

isolated from their parents, but as a rule there was a warm, committed figure dedicated to them, one who bonded and stayed with them.

Today most child care centers are woefully understaffed with poorly paid   8
and underqualified personnel. Child care workers are in the lowest tenth of all wage earners (with an average salary of $5.35 per hour in 1988), well below janitors.[4] They frequently receive no health insurance or other benefits, which makes child care an even less attractive job. As Edward Zigler, a professor of child development at Yale, put it: "We pay these people less than we do zoo keepers — and then we expect them to do wonders."[5] The personnel come and go, at a rate of 41 percent per year at an average day care center.

Bonding between children and caregivers under these circumstances is   9
very difficult to achieve. Moreover, children suffer a loss every time their surrogate parents leave. It would be far from inaccurate to call the worst of these facilities "kennels for kids." Sure, there are exceptions. There are a few fine, high-quality child care centers, but they are as rare and almost as expensive as the nannies that some truly affluent households can command. These exceptions should not distract us from the basically dismal picture: substandard care and all-too-frequent warehousing of children, with overworked parents trying frantically to make up the deficit in their free time.

Government or social supervision of the numerous small institutions and   10
home facilities in which child care takes place to ensure proper sanitation and care, even to screen out child abusers, is difficult and is often completely neglected or only nominally carried out. We should not be surprised to encounter abuses such as the case of the child care home in which fifty-four children were left in the care of a sixteen-year-old and were found strapped into child car seats for the entire day.[6]

Certainly many low-income couples and single parents have little or no   11
choice except to use the minimum that such centers provide. All we can offer here is to urge that before parents put their children in such institutions, they should check them out as extensively as possible (including surprise visits in the middle of the day). Moreover, we should all support these parents' quest for additional support from corporations and government if they cannot themselves spend more on child care.

Particularly effective are cooperative arrangements that require each parent to contribute some time — four hours a week? — to serve at his or her   12
child's center. Not only do such arrangements reduce the center's costs,

---

[4]Child care workers in the lowest tenth percentile for income: Richard T. Gill, Nathan Glazer, Stephen A. Thernstrom, *Our Changing Population* (Englewood Cliffs, NJ: Prentice-Hall, 1992), 278. Child care workers' average salary: *Who Cares? Child Care and the Quality of Care in America* (Oakland, CA: Child Care Employee Project, 1989), 49.

[5]Zigler says child care workers are treated like zoo keepers: Kenneth Labich, "Can Your Career Hurt Your Kids?" *Fortune*, May 20, 1991, 49.

[6]Children strapped into car seats all day: ibid., 49.

they also allow parents to see firsthand what actually goes on, ensuring some measure of *built-in accountability*. It provides for continuity — while staff come and go, parents stay. (Even if they divorce, they may still participate in their child care center.) And as parents get to know other parents of children in the same stage of development, they form social bonds, which can be drawn upon to work together to make these centers more responsive to children's needs.

Above all, age matters. Infants under two years old are particularly vul-   13
nerable to separation anxiety. Several bodies of data strongly indicate that infants who are institutionalized at a young age will not mature into well-adjusted adults.[7] As Edward Zigler puts it: "We are cannibalizing children. Children are dying in the system, never mind achieving optimum development."[8] A study of third-graders by two University of Texas researchers compared children who returned home after school to their mothers with children who remained in day care centers:

> children who stayed at the day care centers after school were having problems. They received more negative peer nominations, and their negative nominations outweighed their positive nominations. In addition, the day care third-graders made lower academic grades on their report card and scored lower on standardized tests. There was some evidence of poor conduct grades.[9]

[7]Several bodies of data showing that institutionalized children become maladjusted adults: N. Baydar and Jeanne Brooks-Gunn, "Effects of Maternal Employment and Child Care Arrangements on Preschoolers' Cognitive and Behavioral Outcomes: Evidence from the Children of the National Longitudinal Survey of Youth," *Developmental Psychology* 27 (November 1991): 932–46; J. Belsky and Michael J. Rovine, "Nonmaternal Care in the First Year of Life and the Security of Infant-Parent Attachment," *Child Development* 59 (February 1988): 157–67; T. B. Brazelton, "Issues for Working Parents," *American Journal of Orthopsychiatry* 56 (1986): 14–25; J. Belsky and D. Eggebeen, "Early and Extensive Maternal Employment in Young Children's Socioemotional Development: Children of the National Longitudinal Survey of Youth," *Journal of Marriage and Family* 53 (November 1991): 1083–1110; B. E. Vaughn, K. E. Deane, and E. Waters, "The Impact of Out-of-Home Care on Child-Mother Attachment Quality: Another Look at Some Enduring Questions," 1–2, in I. Bretherton and E. Water, eds., *Growing Points of Attachment Theory and Research. Monographs for the Society for Research in Child Development*, 50 (1985): 1–2, serial no. 209.

Some studies have found that the effects of child care are not different from parental care. For example, see K. A. Clarke-Stewart and G. G. Fein, "Early Childhood Programs," 917–99, in P. H. Mussen, ed., *Handbook of Child Psychology*, Vol. 2 (New York: Wiley, 1983). And a few studies show that child care rather than parental care is more effective for the intellectual development of poor children. For example, see Jay Belsky, "Two Waves of Day Care Research: Development Effects and Conditions of Quality," 1–34, in R. C. Ainslie, ed., *The Child and the Day Care Setting: Qualitative Variations and Development* (New York: Praeger, 1984).

[8]Zigler says we are cannibalizing children: Kenneth Labich, "Can Your Career Hurt Your Kids?" *Fortune*, May 20, 1991, 38.

[9]University of Texas study: Deborah Lowe Vandell and Mary Anne Corasaniti, "The Relationship Between Third-Graders' After-School Care and Social, Academic, and Emotional Functioning," *Child Development* 59 (August 1988): 874.

Unless the parents are absent or abusive, infants are better off at home. 14
Older children, between two and four, may be able to handle some measure of institutionalization in child care centers, but their personalities often seem too unformed to be able to cope well with a nine-to-five separation from a parent.

As a person who grew up in Israel, I am sometimes asked whether it is 15
true that kibbutzim succeed in bringing up toddlers in child care centers. I need to note first that unlike the personnel in most American child care centers, the people who care for children in kibbutzim are some of the most dedicated members of the work force because these communities consider child care to be a very high priority. As a result, child care positions are highly sought after and there is little turnover, which allows for essential bonding to take place. In addition, both parents are intimately involved in bringing up their children, and they frequently visit the child care centers, which are placed very close to where they live and work. Even so, Israeli kibbutzim are rapidly dismantling their collective child care centers and returning children to live with their families — because both the families and the community established that even a limited disassociation of children from their parents at a tender age is unacceptable.

There is no sense looking back and beating our breasts over how we got 16
ourselves into the present situation. But we must acknowledge that as a matter of social policy (as distinct from some individual situations) we have made a mistake in assuming that strangers can be entrusted with the effective personality formation of infants and toddlers. Over the last twenty-five years we have seen the future, and it is not a wholesome one. With poor and ineffective community child care, and with ever more harried parents, it will not suffice to tell their graduates to "just say no" and expect them to resist all temptations, to forgo illegal drugs and alcohol, and to postpone sexual activity. If we fervently wish them to grow up in a civilized society, and if we seek to live in one, let's face facts: it will not happen unless we dedicate more of ourselves to our children and their care and education. . . .

Nobody likes to admit it, but between 1960 and 1990 American society 17
allowed children to be devalued, while the golden call of "making it" was put on a high pedestal. Recently, college freshmen listed "being well off financially" as more important than "raising a family." (In 1990 the figures were 74 percent versus 70 percent, respectively, and in 1991 they were 74 percent versus 68 percent.)[10] . . .

Some blame this development on the women's rights movement, others 18
on the elevation of materialism and greed to new historical heights. These and other factors may have all combined to devalue children. However, women are obviously entitled to all the same rights men are, including the pursuit of greed.

---

[10]Poll on college freshmen's views on being well off, raising a family: American Enterprise Institute, 1990.

But few people who advocated equal rights for women favored a society in which sexual equality would mean a society in which all adults would act like men, who in the past were relatively inattentive to children. The new gender-equalized world was supposed to be a combination of all that was sound and ennobling in the traditional roles of women and men. Women were to be free to work any place they wanted, and men would be free to show emotion, care, and domestic commitment. For children this was not supposed to mean, as it too often has, that they would be bereft of dedicated parenting. Now that we have seen the result of decades of widespread neglect of children, the time has come for both parents to revalue children and for the community to support and recognize their efforts. . . .   19

We return then to the value we as a community put on having and bringing up children. In a society that places more value on Armani suits, winter skiing, and summer houses than on education, parents are under pressure to earn more, whatever their income. They feel that it is important to work overtime and to dedicate themselves to enhancing their incomes and advancing their careers. We must recognize now, after two decades of celebrating greed and in the face of a generation of neglected children, the importance of educating one's children.   20

Analyzing This Selection

1. **THE WRITER'S METHOD**   The essay begins with a comparison between parenting and another "industry." What point does the analogy illustrate? Is the analogy fully valid, or do you see ways it doesn't solidly hold?

2. What does the author recommend for short-term improvement of day care centers? for their permanent remedy?

3. According to Etzioni, what reasons explain our neglect of child raising? Do you think his explanation faults men and women equally?

Analyzing Connections

4. Etzioni and Whitehead (see "Women and the Future of Fatherhood," p. 101) find family life currently failing its purpose. How do they agree or disagree in their suggestions for strengthening its purpose?

Analyzing by Writing

5. Examine one practical way in which society can raise the perceived value of child raising. Explain how your measure would affect fathers and mothers.

PART 3

SIGNIFICANT OTHERS

INSIGHTS

All love is self-love.

— FRANÇOIS DE LA ROCHEFOUCAULD

The word love has by no means the same sense for both sexes, and this is one of the serious misunderstandings that divide them.

— SIMONE DE BEAUVOIR

Christ here's my discovery. You have got hold of the wrong absolutes and infinities. God as absolute? God as infinity? I don't even understand the words. I'll tell you what's absolute and infinite. Loving a woman. But how would you know? You see, your church knows what it's doing: Rule out one absolute so you have to look for another.

Do you know what it's like to be a self-centered not unhappy man who leads a tolerable finite life, works, eats, drinks, hunts, sleeps, then one fine day discovers that the great starry heavens have opened to him and that his heart is bursting with it. It? She. Her. Woman. Not a category, not a sex, not one of two sexes, a human female creature, but an infinity. $\female = \infty$. What else is infinity but a woman become meat and drink to you, life and your heart's own music, the air you breathe? Just to be near her is to live and have your soul's own self. Just to open your mouth on the skin of her back. What joy just to wake up with her beside you in the morning. I didn't know there was such happiness.

But there is the dark converse: Not having her is not breathing. I'm not kidding: I couldn't get my breath without her.

What else is man made for but this? I can see you agree about love but you look somewhat ironic. Are we talking about two different things? In any case, there's a catch. Love is infinite happiness. Losing it is infinite unhappiness.

— WALKER PERCY

During the first six months, the baby has the rudiments of a love language available to him. There is the language of the embrace, the language of the eyes, the language of the smile, vocal communications of pleasure and distress. It is the essential vocabulary of love before we can speak of love. Eighteen years later, when this baby is full grown and "falls in love" for the first time, he will woo his partner through the language of the eyes, the language of the smile, through the utterance of endearments, and the joy of the embrace. In his declarations of love he will use such phrases as "When I first looked into your eyes," "When you smiled at me," "When I held you in my arms." And naturally, in his exalted state, he will believe that he invented this love song.

— SELMA FRAIBERG

No one can fall in love if he is even partially satisfied with what he has or who he is. The experience of falling in love originates in an extreme depression, an inability to find something that has value in everyday life. The "symptom" of the predisposition to fall in love is not the conscious desire to do so, the intense desire to enrich our lives; it is the profound sense of being worthless and of having nothing that is valuable and the shame of not having it. This is the first sign that we are prepared for the experience — the feeling of nothingness and shame over our own nothingness. For this reason, falling in love occurs more frequently among young people, since they are profoundly uncertain, unsure of their worth, and often ashamed of themselves. The same thing applies to people of other ages when they lose something in their lives — when their youth ends or when they start to grow old. There is an irreparable loss of something in the self, a feeling that we will inevitably become devoid of value or degraded, compared with what we have been. It isn't the longing for an affair that makes us fall in love, but the conviction that we have nothing to lose by becoming whatever we will become; it is the prospect of nothingness stretching before us. Only then do we develop the inclination for the different and the risky, that propensity to hurl ourselves into all or nothing which those who are in any way satisfied with their lives cannot feel.

— FRANCESCO ALBERONI

Sex Without Love

How do they do it, the ones who make love
without love? Beautiful as dancers,

gliding over each other like ice skaters
over the ice, fingers hooked
inside each other's bodies, faces
red as steak, wine, wet as the
children at birth whose mothers are going to
give them away. How do they come to the
come to the   come to the   God   come to the
still waters, and not love
the one who came there with them, light
rising slowly as steam off their joined
skin? These are the true religious,
the purists, the pros, the ones who will not
accept a false Messiah, love the
priest instead of the God. They do not
mistake the lover for their own pleasure,
they are like great runners: they know they are alone
with the road surface, the cold, the wind,
the fit of their shoes, their over-all cardiovascular health — just factors, like the partner
in the bed, and not the truth, which is the
single body alone in the universe
against its own best time.

— SHARON OLDS

We are too ego-centered. The ego-shell in which we live is the hardest thing to outgrow. We seem to carry it all the time from childhood up to the time we finally pass away. We are, however, given many chances to break through this shell, and the first and greatest of them is when we reach adolescence. This is the first time the ego really comes to recognize the "other." I mean the awakening of sexual love. An ego, entire and undivided, now begins to feel a sort of split in itself. Love hitherto dormant deep in his heart lifts its head and causes a great commotion in it. For the love now stirred demands at once the assertion of the ego and its annihilation. Love makes the ego lose itself in the object it loves, and yet at the same time it wants to have the object as its own. This is a contradiction, and a great tragedy of life.

— D. T. SUZUKI

FOCUSING BY WRITING

1. Is your campus preparing you for equality or for war between the sexes? How were sex roles and sexual expectations discussed by college officials during your freshman orientation program? What possible positive or negative results do you foresee from the presentation of the issues?

2. Children of early elementary school age often develop a crush on somebody — frequently a teacher, sometimes another child two or three years older. Characterize the person you had a crush on. How did the object of your crush resemble or differ from your family members? Examine the wishes and ideas that your crush expressed to you.

3. A fan is usually involved in an imaginary romantic relationship. A fan cherishes the star's face and image, delights in knowing details of the star's life, identifies with the star's successes and tribulations, and often fantasizes reciprocated attention and affection. Define one specific imaginary relationship that you have had as a fan. Do not just reminisce; keep your attention on examining the behavior and responses of a fan.

4. What is your favorite song that deals with love? Write down the lyrics you can remember, and examine the attitude about love that the song expresses both explicitly and implicitly.

Susan Allen Toth

BOYFRIENDS

SUSAN ALLEN TOTH (b. 1940) grew up in Ames, Iowa, and was graduated from Smith College before she returned to the Midwest for a Ph.D. in English and a college teaching career. She describes her college years in *Ivy Days: Making My Way Out East* (1984). Toth writes for magazines such as *Redbook* and *Harper's*, and her scholarly articles have appeared in professional journals. She recounts her precollege years in *Blooming: A Small Town Girlhood* (1981), from which this excerpt is taken. In regard to boyfriends generally, she writes, "I can't remember when I didn't want one."

Just when I was approaching sixteen, I found Peter Stone. Or did he find 1 me? Perhaps I magicked him into existence out of sheer need. I was spooked by the boys who teased us nice girls about being sweet-sixteen-and-never-been-kissed. I felt that next to being an old maid forever, it probably was most demeaning to reach sixteen and not to have experienced the kind of ardent embrace Gordon MacRae periodically bestowed on Kathryn Grayson between choruses of "Desert Song." I was afraid I would never have a real boyfriend, never go parking, never know true love. So when Peter Stone asked his friend Ted to ask Ted's girlfriend Emily who asked me if I would ever neck with anyone, I held my breath until Emily told me she had said to Ted to tell Peter that maybe I would.

Not that Peter Stone had ever necked with anyone either. But I didn't 2 realize that for a long time. High-school courtship usually was meticulously slow, progressing through inquiry, phone calls, planned encounters in public places, double or triple dates, single dates, handholding, and finally a goodnight kiss. I assumed it probably stopped there, but I didn't know. I had never gotten that far. I had lots of time to learn about Peter Stone. What I knew at the beginning already attracted me. He was a year ahead of me, vice-president of Hi-Y, a shot-putter who had just managed to earn a letter sweater. An older man, *and* an athlete. Tall, heavy, and broad-shouldered, Peter had a sweet slow smile. Even at a distance there was something endearing about the way he would blink nearsightedly through his glasses and light up with pleased recognition when he saw me coming toward him down the hall.

For a long while I didn't come too close. Whenever I saw Peter he was 3 in the midst of his gang, a group of five boys as close and as self-protective as any clique we girls had. They were an odd mixture: Jim, an introspective son of a lawyer; Brad, a sullen hot-rodder; Ted, an unambitious and gentle boy from a poor family; Andy, a chubby comedian; and Peter. I was a little afraid of all of them, and they scrutinized me carefully before opening their circle to admit me, tentatively, as I held tight to Peter's hand. The lawyer's son had a steady girl, a fast number who was only in eighth grade but looked eighteen; the hot-rodder was reputed to have "gone all the way" with his adoring girl, a coarse brunette with plucked eyebrows; gentle Ted pursued my friend Emily with hangdog tenacity; but Peter had never shown real interest in a girlfriend before.

Although I had decided to go after Peter, I was hesitant about how to 4 plot my way into the interior of his world. It was a thicket of strange shrubs and tangled branches. Perhaps I see it that way because I remember the day Peter took me to a wild ravine to shoot his gun. Girls who went with one of "the guys" commiserated with each other that their boyfriends all preferred two other things to them: their cars and their guns. Although Peter didn't hunt and seldom went to practice at the target range, still he valued his gun. Without permits, "the guys" drove outside of town to fire their guns illegally. I had read enough in my *Seventeen* about how to attract boys to know I needed to show enthusiasm about Peter's hobbies, so I asked him if someday he would take me someplace and teach me how to shoot.

One sunny fall afternoon he did. I remember rattling over gravel roads 5 into a rambling countryside that had surprising valleys and woods around cultivated farmland. Eventually we stopped before a barred gate that led to an abandoned bridge, once a railroad trestle, now a splintering wreck. We had to push our way through knee-high weeds to get past the gate. I was afraid of snakes. Peter took my hand; it was the first time he had ever held it, and my knees weakened a little. I was also scared of walking onto the bridge, which had broken boards and sudden gaps that let you look some fifty feet down into the golden and rust-colored brush below. But I didn't mind being a little scared as long as Peter was there to take care of me.

I don't think I had ever held a gun until Peter handed me his pistol, a 6 heavy metal weapon that looked something like the ones movie sheriffs carried in their holsters. I was impressed by its weight and power. Peter fired it twice to show me how and then stood close to me, watching carefully, while I aimed at an empty beer can he tossed into the air. I didn't hit it. The noise of the gun going off was terrifying. I hoped nobody was walking in the woods where I had aimed. Peter said nobody was, nobody ever came here. When I put the gun down, he put his arm around me, very carefully. He had never done that before, either. We both just stood there, looking off into the distance, staring at the glowing maples and elms, dark red patches of sumac, brown heaps of leaves. The late afternoon sun beat down on us.

It was hot, and after a few minutes Peter shifted uncomfortably. I moved away, laughing nervously, and we walked back to the car, watching the gaping boards at our feet.

What Peter and I did with our time together is a mystery. I try to picture 7 us at movies or parties or somebody's house, but all I can see is the two of us in Peter's car. "Going for a drive!" I'd fling at my mother as I rushed out of the house; "rinking" was our high-school term for it, drawn from someone's contempt for the greasy "hoods" who hung out around the roller-skating rink and skidded around corners on two wheels of their souped-up cars. Peter's car barely made it around a corner on all four wheels. Though he had learned something about how to keep his huge square Ford running, he wasn't much of a mechanic. He could make jokes about the Ford, but he didn't like anyone else, including me, to say it looked like an old black hearse or remind him it could scarcely do forty miles an hour on an open stretch of highway. Highways were not where we drove, anyway, nor was speed a necessity unless you were trying to catch up with someone who hadn't seen you. "Rinking" meant cruising aimlessly around town, looking for friends in *their* cars, stopping for conversations shouted out of windows, maybe parking somewhere for a while, ending up at the A&W Root Beer Stand or the pizza parlor or the Rainbow Cafe.

Our parents were often puzzled about why we didn't spend time in each 8 other's homes. "Why don't you invite Peter in?" my mother would ask a little wistfully, as I grabbed my billfold and cardigan and headed toward the door. Sometimes Peter would just pause in front of the house and honk; if I didn't come out quickly, he assumed I wasn't home and drove away. Mother finally made me tell him at least to come to the door and knock. I couldn't explain to her why we didn't want to sit in the living room, or go down to the pine-paneled basement at the Harbingers', or swing on the Harrises' front porch. We might not have been bothered at any of those places, but we really wouldn't have been alone. Cars were our private space, a rolling parlor, the only place we could relax and be ourselves. We could talk, fiddle with the radio if we didn't have much to say, look out the window, watch for friends passing by. Driving gave us a feeling of freedom.

Most of my memories of important moments with Peter center in that 9 old black Ford. One balmy summer evening I remember particularly because my friend Emily said I would. Emily and Ted were out cruising in his rusty two-tone Chevy, the lawyer's son Jim and his girl had his father's shiny Buick, and Peter and I were out driving in the Ford. As we rumbled slowly down the Main Street, quiet and dark at night, Peter saw Ted's car approaching. We stopped in the middle of the street so the boys could exchange a few laconic grunts while Emily and I smiled confidentially at each other. We were all in a holiday mood, lazy and happy in the warm breezes that swept through the open windows. One of us suggested that we all meet later at Camp Canwita, a wooded park a few miles north of town. Whoever saw Jim would tell him to join us too. We weren't sure what we would do there, but it sounded like an adventure. An hour or so later, Peter and I bumped over the potholes in the road that twisted through the woods to the parking lot. We were the first ones there. When Peter turned off the motor, we could hear grasshoppers thrumming on all sides of us and leaves rustling in the dark. It was so quiet, so remote, I was a little frightened, remembering one of my mother's unnerving warnings about the dangerous men who sometimes preyed upon couples who parked in secluded places. We didn't have long to wait, though, before Ted's car coughed and sputtered down the drive. Soon Jim arrived too, and then we all pulled our cars close together in a kind of circle so we could talk easily out the windows. Someone's radio was turned on, and Frank Sinatra's mournful voice began to sing softly of passing days and lost love. Someone suggested that we get out of the cars and dance. It wouldn't have been Peter, who was seldom romantic. Ted opened his door so the overhead light cast a dim glow over the tiny area between the cars. Solemnly, a little self-consciously, we began the shuffling steps that were all we knew of what we called "slow dancing." Peter was not a good dancer, nor was I, though I liked putting my head on his bulky shoulder. But he moved me around the small lighted area as best he could, trying not to bump into Ted and Emily or Jim and his girl. I tried not to step on his toes. While Sinatra, Patti Page, and the Four Freshmen sang to us about moments to remember and Cape Cod, we all danced, one-two back, one-two back. Finally Emily, who was passing by my elbow, looked significantly at me and said, "This is something we'll be able to tell our grandchildren." Yes, I nodded, but I wasn't so sure. The mosquitoes were biting my legs and arms, my toes hurt, and I was getting a little bored. I think the others were too, because before long we all got into our cars and drove away.

Not all the time we spent in Peter's car was in motion. After several 10 months, we did begin parking on deserted country roads, side streets, even sometimes my driveway, if my mother had heeded my fierce instructions to leave the light turned off. For a while we simply sat and talked with Peter's arm draped casually on the back of the seat. Gradually I moved a little closer. Soon he had his arm around me, but even then it was a long time before he managed to kiss me good-night. Boys must have been as scared as we girls were, though we always thought of them as having much more experience. We all compared notes, shyly, about how far our boyfriends had gone; was he holding your hand yet, or taking you parking, or . . . ? When a girl finally got kissed, telephone lines burned with the news next day. I was getting a little embarrassed about how long it was taking Peter to get around to it. My sixteenth birthday was only a few weeks away, and so far I had nothing substantial to report. I was increasingly nervous too because I still didn't know quite how I was going to behave. We girls joked about wondering where your teeth went and did glasses get in the way, but no one could give a convincing description. For many years I never told anyone about what *did* happen to me that first time. I was too ashamed.

Peter and I were parked down the street from my house, talking, snuggling, listening to the radio. During a silence I turned my face toward him, and then he kissed me, tentatively and quickly. I was exhilarated but frightened. I wanted to respond in an adequate way but my instincts did not entirely cooperate. I leaned towards Peter, but at the last moment I panicked. Instead of kissing him, I gave him a sudden lick on the cheek. He didn't know what to say. Neither did I.

Next morning I was relieved that it was all over. I dutifully reported my news to a few key girlfriends who could pass it on to others. I left out the part about the lick. That was my last bulletin. After a first kiss, we girls also respected each other's privacy. What more was there to know? We assumed that couples sat in their cars and necked, but nice girls, we also assumed, went no farther. We knew the girls who did. Their names got around. We marveled at them, uncomprehending as much as disapproving. Usually they talked about getting married to their boyfriends, and eventually some of them did. A lot of "nice" girls suffered under this distinction. One of them told me years later how she and her steady boyfriend had yearned and held back, stopped just short, petted and clutched and gritted their teeth. "When we went together to see the movie *Splendor in the Grass*, we had to leave the theater," she said ruefully. "The part about how Natalie Wood and Warren Beatty wanted to make love so desperately and couldn't. . . . Well, that was just how we felt." 11

My mother worried about what was going on in the car during those long evenings when Peter and I went "out driving." She needn't have. Amazing as it seems now, when courting has speeded up to a freeway pace, when I wonder if a man who doesn't try to get me to bed immediately might possibly be gay, Peter and I gave each other hours of affection without ever crossing the invisible line. We sat in his car and necked, a word that was anatomically correct. We hugged and kissed, nuzzling ears and noses and hairlines. But Peter never put a hand on my breast, and I wouldn't have known whether Peter had an erection if it had risen up and thwapped me in the face. I never got that close. Although we probably should have perished from frustration, in fact I reveled in all that holding and touching. Peter seemed pleased too, and he never demanded more. Later, I suppose, he learned quickly with someone else about what he had been missing. But I remember with gratitude Peter's awkward tenderness and the absolute faith I had in his inability to hurt me. 12

After Peter graduated and entered the university, our relationship changed. Few high-school girls I knew went out with college men; it was considered risky, like dating someone not quite in your social set or from another town. You were cut off. At the few fraternity functions Peter took me to, I didn't know anyone there. I had no idea what to talk about or how to act. So I refused to go, and I stopped asking Peter to come with me to parties or dances at the high school. I thought he didn't fit in there either. When I was honest with myself, I admitted that romance had gone. Already 13 planning to go away to college, I could sense new vistas opening before me, glowing horizons whose light completely eclipsed a boyfriend like Peter. When I got on the Chicago & Northwestern train to go east to Smith, I felt with relief that the train trip was erasing one problem for me. I simply rode away from Peter.

On my sixteenth birthday, Peter gave me a small cross on a chain. All the guys had decided that year to give their girlfriends crosses on chains, even though none of them was especially religious. It was a perfect gift, they thought, intimate without being soppy. Everyone's cross cost ten dollars, a lot of money, because it was real sterling silver. Long after Peter and I stopped seeing each other, I kept my cross around my neck, not taking it off even when I was in the bathtub. Like my two wooden dolls from years before, I clung to that cross as a superstitious token. It meant that someone I had once cared for had cared for me in return. Once I had had a boyfriend.   14

Analyzing This Selection

1. What moved Toth into her first romance? What was apparently *not* part of the impetus?

2. Where did Toth learn the appropriate way for her to interest Peter? What indicates her present attitude toward the episode with the gun?

3. **THE WRITER'S METHOD** Is there any part of this account that strikes you as probably oversimplified or idealized? What additions might make it more true to life without changing the main points of her memoir?

4. What was the lasting effect of this romance after it ended? Was it different from what she sought or expected?

Analyzing Connections

5. Toth, born in 1940, and Nora Ephron, born in 1941, grew up during the same period, the 1950s (see "Shaping Up Absurd," p. 20). What are some similarities in their adolescent experiences? What differences arise in the authors' tones and attitudes toward their adolescence?

Analyzing by Writing

6. Many high schools distribute condoms in order to reduce the likelihood of teenage pregnancies and sexually transmitted diseases. How would, or did, this sort of prevention program affect student attitudes in the school you attended? Explain the impact on high school attitudes toward romance and sexuality.

Stephen Dunn

LOCKER ROOM TALK

STEPHEN DUNN (b. 1939), a poet and essayist, graduated from Hofstra University. His ten collections of poetry include *New and Selected Poems* (1994) and *Loosestrife* (1996). Dunn has received a Guggenheim Fellowship and other major awards. His essays are collected in *Walking Light: Essays and Memoirs* (1993).

Having been athletic most of my life, I've spent a fair amount of time in locker rooms and have overheard my share of "locker room talk." For reasons I couldn't understand for many years, I rarely participated in it and certainly never felt smug or superior about my lack of participation. In fact, I felt quite the opposite; I thought something was wrong with me. As a teenager and well into my twenties I'd hear someone recount his latest real or wishful conquest, there'd be a kind of general congratulatory laughter, tacit envy, but what I remember feeling most was wonderment and then embarrassment.

There was of course little or no public information about sex when I was growing up in the forties and fifties. The first time I heard someone talk about having sex was in the school yard (the locker room without walls) when I was twelve or thirteen. Frankie Salvo, a big boy of sixteen. Frankie made it sound dirty, something great you do with a bad girl. It was my first real experience with pornography and it was thrilling, a little terrifying too. My mind conjured its pictures. Wonderment. Not wonderful.

Some years later, after experience, wonderment gave way to embarrassment. I wasn't sure for whom I was embarrassed, the girl spoken about, the story teller, or myself. Nevertheless, I understood the need to tell. I, too, wanted to tell my good friend, Alan, but for some reason I never told him very much. In retrospect, it was my first test with what Robert Frost calls knowing "the delicacy of when to stop short," a delicacy I took no pride in. I felt excessively private, cut off.

I began thinking about all of this recently because in the locker room at college a young man was telling his friend — loud enough for all of us to hear — what he did to this particular young woman the night before, and what she did to him. It was clear how important it was for him to impress his friend, far more important than the intimacy itself, as if the sexual act weren't complete until he had completed it among other men.

This time I knew something about the nature of my embarrassment. It wasn't just that he had cheapened himself in the telling, but like all things which embarrass us it had struck some part of me that was complicitous, to a degree guilty, the kind of guilt you feel every time there's a discrepancy between what you know you're supposed to feel (correct feelings) and what in fact you've thought of, if not done. But more than that, I was embarrassed by the young man's assumption — culturally correct for the most part — that we other men in the locker room were his natural audience. There were five or six of us, and we certainly didn't boo or hiss. Those of us who were silent (all of us except his friend) had given our quiet sanctions.

What did it all mean? That men, more often than not, in a very fundamental way prefer other men? Or was it all about power, an old story, success with women as a kind of badge, an accoutrement of power? Was the young man saying to the rest of us, "I'm powerful"? I thought so for a while, but then I thought that he seemed to be saying something different. He was saying out loud to himself and to the rest of us that he hadn't succumbed to the greatest loss of power, yielding to the attractiveness and power of women, which could mean admitting he felt something or, at the furthest extreme, had fallen in love.

From Samson, to the knight in Keats' poem "La Belle Dame Sans Merci," to countless examples in world literature, the warning is clear: women take away your power. To fall in love with one is to be distracted from the world of accomplishment and acquisitiveness. But to have sex and then to talk about it publicly is a kind of final protection, the ultimate prophylactic against the dangers of feeling.

"Love means always having to say you're sorry," a friend once said to me. The joke had its truth, and it implied — among other things — a mature love, a presumption of mutual respect and equality. On some level the young man in the locker room sensed and feared such a relationship. He had ventured into the dark and strange world of women and had come out unscathed, literally untouched. He was back with us, in the locker room which was the country he understood and lived in, with immunity. He thought we'd be happy for him.

Analyzing This Selection

1. **THE WRITER'S METHOD**   The author makes a strong point in a very brief essay. What makes his presentation convincing? Find details that illustrate Dunn's method.

2. Dunn acquired an older man's understanding of his lifelong embarrassment. Why is he still embarrassed by locker room talk? How does his analysis of embarrassment hold up when applied to nonsexual topics?

Analyzing Connections

3. Updike (see "The Disposable Rocket," p. 38) suggests a contrasting explanation for the prevalence of locker room talk. Does his biological view modify, or entirely refute, Dunn's psychological explanation?

Analyzing by Writing

4. What might have happened in this locker room situation if one or more men had reacted differently to the storyteller? Would the embarrassment have persisted or even increased? Explain your views about how to deal with conversations about sex that overstep the limits of some but not all members of the group. Use Dunn's methods to help make your point.

Diane Ackerman

THE CHEMISTRY OF LOVE

DIANE ACKERMAN (b. 1948), a poet and natural history writer, earned a doctorate in English from Cornell University. Her collections of verse include *Jaguar of Sweet Laughter* (1991). As a staff contributor to the *New Yorker*, Ackerman writes about various roles of nature in human experience. Her *Natural History of the Senses* (1990) examines each of the five senses. The following essay is excerpted from *A Natural History of Love* (1994). Recently, Ackerman wrote about her telephone duty at a suicide crisis center in *Slender Thread* (1997).

Oxytocin, a hormone that encourages labor and the contractions during childbirth, seems to play an important role in mother love. The sound of a crying baby makes its mother's body secrete more oxytocin, which in turn erects her nipples and helps the milk to flow. As the baby nurses, even more oxytocin is released, making the mother want to nuzzle and hug it. It's been called the "cuddle chemical" by zoologists who have artificially raised the oxytocin level in goats and other animals and produced similar behavior. Oxytocin has many functions, some of them beneficial for the mother. The baby feels warm and safe as it nurses, and its digestive and respiratory systems run smoothly. The baby's nursing, which also coaxes the oxytocin level to rise in the mother, results, too, in contractions of the uterus that stop bleeding and detach the placenta. So mother and baby find themselves swept away in a chemical dance of love, interdependency, and survival.

Later in life, oxytocin seems to play an equally important role in romantic love, as a hormone that encourages cuddling between lovers and increases pleasure during lovemaking. The hormone stimulates the smooth muscles and sensitizes the nerves, and snowballs during sexual arousal — the more intense the arousal, the more oxytocin is produced. As arousal builds, oxytocin is thought to cause the nerves in the genitals to fire spontaneously, bringing on orgasm. Unlike other hormones, oxytocin arousal can be generated both by physical and emotional cues — a certain look, voice, or gesture is enough — and can become conditioned to one's personal love history. The lover's smell or touch may trigger the production of oxytocin. So might a richly woven and redolent sexual fantasy. Women are more

127

responsive to oxytocin's emotional effects, probably because of the important role it plays in mothering. Indeed, women who have gone through natural childbirth sometimes report that they felt an orgasmic sense of pleasure during delivery. Some nonorgasmic women have found it easier to achieve orgasm after they've been through childbirth; the secretion of oxytocin during delivery and nursing melts their sexual blockage. This hormonal outpouring may help explain why women more than men prefer to continue embracing after sex. A woman may yearn to feel close and connected, tightly coiled around the mainspring of the man's heart. In evolutionary terms, she hopes the man will be staying around for a while, long enough to protect her and the child he just fathered.

Men's oxytocin levels quintuple during orgasm. But a Stanford University study showed that women have even higher levels of oxytocin than men do during sex, and that it takes more oxytocin for women to achieve orgasm. Drenched in this spa of the chemical, women are able to have more multiple orgasms than men, as well as full body orgasms. Mothers have told me during their baby's first year or so they were surprised to find themselves "in love" with it, "turned on" by it, involved with it in "the best romance ever." Because the same hormone controls a woman's pleasure during orgasm, childbirth, cuddling, and nursing her baby, it makes perfect sense that she should feel this way. The brain may have an excess of gray matter, but in some things it's economical. It likes to reuse convenient pathways and chemicals for many purposes. Why plow fresh paths through the snow of existence when old paths already lead part of the way there?

"The meeting of two personalities is like the contact of two chemical substances," Carl Jung wrote, "if there is any reaction, both are transformed." When two people find each other attractive, their bodies quiver with a gush of PEA (phenylethylamine), a molecule that speeds up the flow of information between nerve cells. An amphetaminelike chemical, PEA whips the brain into a frenzy of excitement, which is why lovers feel euphoric, rejuvenated, optimistic, and energized, happy to sit up talking all night or making love for hours on end. Because "speed" is addictive, even the body's naturally made speed, some people become what Michael Liebowitz and Donald Klein of the New York State Psychiatric Institute refer to as "attraction junkies," needing a romantic relationship to feel excited by life. The craving catapults them from high to low in an exhilarating, exhausting cycle of thrill and depression. Driven by a chemical hunger, they choose unsuitable partners, or quickly misconstrue a potential partner's feelings. Sliding down the slippery chute of their longing, they fall head over heels into a sea of all-consuming, passionate love. Soon the relationship crumbles, or they find themselves rejected. In either case, tortured by lovesick despair, they plummet into a savage depression, which they try to cure by falling in love again. Liebowitz and Klein think that this roller coaster is fueled by a chemical imbalance in the brain, a craving for PEA.

When they gave some attraction junkies MAO inhibitors — antidepressants that work by disabling certain enzymes that can subdue PEA and other neurotransmitters — they were amazed to find how quickly the therapy worked. No longer craving PEA, the patients were able to choose partners more calmly and realistically. Other studies with humans seem to confirm these findings. Researchers have also found that injecting mice, rhesus monkeys, and other animals with PEA produces noises of pleasure, courting behavior, and addiction (they keep pressing a lever to get more PEA). All this strongly suggests that when we fall in love the brain drenches itself in PEA, a chemical that makes us feel pleasure, rampant excitement, and well-being. A sweet fix, love.

The body uses PEA for more than infatuation. The same chemical soars in thrill-seeking of any kind, because it keeps one alert, confident, and ready to try something new. That may help explain a fascinating phenomenon: People are more likely to fall in love when they're in danger. Wartime romances are legendary. I am part of a "baby boom" produced by such an event. Love thrives especially well in exotic locales. When the senses are heightened because of stress, novelty, or fear, it's much easier to become a mystic or feel ecstasy or fall in love. Danger makes one receptive to romance. Danger is an aphrodisiac. To test this, researchers asked single men to cross a suspension bridge. The bridge was safe, but frightening. Some men met women on the bridge. Other men encountered the same women — but not on the bridge — in a safer setting such as a campus or an office.

The men who met the women on the trembling bridge were much more likely to ask them out on dates.

While the chemical sleigh ride of infatuation carries one at a fast clip over uneven terrain, lives become blended, people mate and genes mix, and babies are born. Then the infatuation subsides and a new group of chemicals takes over, the morphinelike opiates of the mind, which calm and reassure. The sweet blistering rage of infatuation gives way to a narcotic peacefulness, a sense of security and belonging. Being in love is a state of chaotic equilibrium. Its rewards of intimacy, warmth, empathy, dependability, and shared experiences trigger the production of that mental comfort food, the endorphins. The feeling is less steep than falling in love, but it's steadier and more addictive. The longer two people have been married, the more likely it is they'll stay married. And couples who have three or more children tend to be lifelong spouses. Stability, friendship, familiarity, and affection are rewards the body clings to. As much as we love being happily unsettled, not to mention dizzied by infatuation, such a state is stressful. On the other hand, it also feels magnificent to rest, to be free of anxiety or fretting, and to enjoy one's life with a devoted companion who is as comfortable as a childhood playmate, as predictable if at times irksome as a sibling, as attentive as a parent, and also affectionate and loving: a longtime spouse. This is a tonic that is hard to give up, even if the relationship isn't perfect, and one is tempted by rejuvenating affairs. Shared events, including shared stresses and crises, are rivets that draw couples closer together. Soon they are fastened by so many it becomes difficult to pull free. It takes a vast amount of courage to leap off a slowly moving ship and grab a lifebuoy drifting past, not knowing exactly where it's headed or if it will keep one afloat. As the "other women" embroiled with long-married men discover, the men are unlikely to divorce, no matter how mundane their marriages, what they may promise, or how passionately in love they genuinely feel.

Analyzing This Selection

1. Ackerman lists several functions researchers have noted for oxytocin. How does she explain its many unrelated or contradictory functions?

2. Ackerman says, "When the senses are heightened . . . it is much easier . . . to fall in love" (para. 5). Do you agree? Some might argue that novelty, fear, and danger can also deaden the senses — that fear, for example, retards love. Explain where you stand on this question and whether Ackerman's arguments about PEA ring true.

3. **THE WRITER'S METHOD**   Find phrases and sentences that help you recognize Ackerman's purpose in identifying love chemicals. Does she achieve this purpose?

Analyzing Connections

4. Ackerman and Francesco Alberoni in the Insights on page 115 explain chemical or psychological mechanisms to account for love. Does either scientific view allow for free choice? Do you think a free choice can occur?

Analyzing by Writing

5. Since the love chemicals affect our good feelings, should we sometimes use supplemental doses? For instance, in recent years the hormone melatonin has been widely sold to help people fall asleep. How do the love chemicals differ, if at all, from taking vitamins or antidepressants, which also supply the body's natural chemicals? Explain what you would consider and decide if given the choice.

Eugene Goodheart

FAST FRIENDS

EUGENE GOODHEART (b. 1931) studied literature and received B.A. and Ph.D. degrees from Columbia University. A prominent scholar, Goodheart has taught at Boston University and Brandeis University. He has received a Guggenheim Fellowship and other major awards. His many books of literary and cultural criticism include *Desire and Its Discontents* (1991) and *The Reign of Ideology* (1996). Goodheart's critical articles have appeared in the *Partisan Review, Daedalus,* and *New Literary History.* Most recently Goodheart has written personal essays such as the following selection, which appeared in the *Sewanee Review.*

I tell a friend of mine that I am writing an essay on friendship. He has a dark vision of the world. He figures that the essay will be a page and a half. I think I know what he means. Most essays on friendship, including the ones by the great essayists Montaigne and Emerson, don't usually get beyond the idealizing of it. In that vein there isn't much more to say. And what they say doesn't much square with my sense of its reality. It may be the difference in the way we live now (or, to be less presumptuous, the way I live) that keeps me from understanding their idealism.

Montaigne writes about friendship with Etienne de la Boétie as if it were a love that excluded the whole world. "For this perfect friendship I speak of is indivisible. Each one gives himself so wholly to his friend that he has nothing left to distribute elsewhere." We might call it homoerotic nowadays (maybe even homosexual), but there is no suggestion of this in Montaigne's sense of his friendship. He was married, perhaps happily married; but marriage in his time was a "bargain ordinarily made for other ends." If you want real intimacy, find a friend; the spouse knows her place and won't give trouble. Montaigne betrays no anxiety about what his wife thinks of him and La Boétie. For a contrast consider D. H. Lawrence's *Women in Love,* in which Birkin's desire for a big friendship, "another kind of love," with Gerald tears at his marriage with Ursula. But the difference in time still doesn't explain to me Montaigne's friendship with La Boétie: it seems more like utopia than reality. I'd like to know what La Boétie thought of Montaigne. I have too much mistrust of my own feelings, too much uncertainty about what my friends feel, to believe in the perfection of friendship or of anything else.

In his essay on friendship Emerson rides in all directions. He can be   3
sappy. "Sometimes he sits down to write, and all his years of meditation do
not furnish him with one good thought or happy expression, [but with the
thought of a friend] forthwith troops of gentle thoughts invest themselves,
on every hand, with chosen words." Who wants to read on? But then he
writes an imaginary letter to a friend in which he speaks of mismatched
moods, of not being able to fathom "thy genius" (one must read past the
thy), of not being able to "presume" that his friend knows him and the tor-
ment of it all. Then I find him congenial to my own feelings. Later he
speaks of the "rough courage" of friendship, of resisting "a mush of concession," of letting a friend have it when he deserves it. I always let my friends
have it. "It's part of your charm," a disspirited friend of mine ruefully
remarked.

In thoughts about friendship, the other subject — marriage — inevitably   4
rears its head. Marriage is the defined subject, friendship ill-defined and
elusive. Most novels have marriage plots, how many have friendship plots?
The traditional marriage plot begins with courtship and ends with the
happy marriage. The modern narrative is grimmer: it ends in divorce or in
a breakup in the middle with the feeling of liberation perhaps, but more
often misery. But marriage is what life is all about. The tipsy Tom Brang-
wen in Lawrence's *The Rainbow* blurts out at a wedding feast: "Man is born
for marriage." The Talmud says "an unmarried person isn't human." Marriage encompasses the couple, parents, aunts, uncles, cousins. It is the family. But friendship has no contracts, no "for better or worse," no promises
that the law enforces, no rules of conduct, no center.

A woman says "He's my husband" — we know what she means. A boy   5
says, "She's my aunt." But what is friend? What are the agreements, the
tokens, the understandings of friendship? When you are late in coming
home, you call your wife. When do you call your friend? The lover passionately pursues his beloved: the person who passionately seeks friendship
risks being ridiculous because he has the inappropriate look of a lover. A
lover says to his beloved, "I miss you"; you may say it to a friend. Can he
say, "I love you"? Can you love a friend without being a lover? Can you be
a friend without loving him? Is sex the only difference between love and
friendship?

Freud believed that friendship is a diversion from sexual love: "aim-   6
inhibited" homoeroticism, he called it. That makes love primary and friendship secondary. Why should we want a mere friendship if sexual love is the
real thing? The real thing has the more explosive charge: it is danger as
well as fulfillment. I don't only have in mind same-sex relationships in
which the inhibitions reflect anxiety about homosexuality or homophobia.
Friendship between men and women is fraught with sexual danger. To say
this is to turn things around. If the aim of the relationship is friendship, sex
becomes the diversion or the interference. In which case the possibility of
a friendship between a man and woman is in inverse relation to their phys-

ical attractiveness to each other. A sad state of affairs. Here's a conundrum: if friendship and sex don't go together, then heterosexuals must seek friends of the same sex, homosexuals friends among women, lesbians among men, and bisexuals among extraterrestrials. The solution: we are not sexually attracted to everyone in the group to which we are attracted. But can there be friendship without attraction?

The hierarchy that places love above friendship ignores friendship's dis- 7 tinct advantage of longevity. Love dies more easily than friendship, because it is like a burning match that consumes itself; in marriage, if it is to sustain itself, it must become an ember — low burning. What is the metaphor for friendship? Neither too hot nor too cold, more like a temperate climate: California without earthquakes.

Friendship and marriage are rivals. The strongest friendship is one in 8 which you are free to confess your most intimate feelings. Intimacy with a friend after marriage is potentially, if not actually, a betrayal of one's spouse. Marriage is the great inhibitor of friendship. The Catholic poet Coventry Patmore cautioned the husband "to keep your mistress in your wife." If you want an intimate friend and a happy marriage, keep your friend in your wife.

Friendship like marriage can grow stale. It has an advantage, however. A 9 polygamous "institution," it allows you to seek its pleasures with others without being accused of infidelity. Is this true? Have you ever been in a group of three close friends? Triangular jealousy, the bane of lovers, is also the bane of friendship. So Max will arrange to see Sam for lunch; Sam, Morris; Morris, Max: the three together are a cauldron of rivalrous feelings. One evening three of us, all friends, went out to dinner. I drove both friends back to their respective homes. After driving one friend back, the other friend and I stood next to my car, and we spoke to each other for some time. My friend had something to tell me: a problem in his family that troubled him. I was the sympathetic ear. We noticed that the other friend whom I had just let off stood at the window of his apartment, and though his features were not discernible in the dark, I could almost feel his jealousy for having been excluded from the intimacy of the conversation down below as something palpable. What was he thinking? Were we talking about him? Or were we displaying a connection between us in which he had no place? We had in effect disburdened ourselves of his presence. We should have been considerate enough to drive away, but my friend, fully conscious of what was occurring, smiled with a faint sadistic delight and continued talking, and I was complicit.

Friends may quarrel, experience rivalry and envy, but the ultimate test of 10 a friendship, a venerable old friend of mine reminds me (reminds me because he assumes that it is fundamental knowledge), is that you defend him when he is attacked by someone else (not a friend of his) and not in his presence. You say, "Stop, I don't want to hear this: he is my friend." Not to do this is betrayal. Have I been faithful? We complain about friends to other friends all the time, but that doesn't count. There must be implicit in the complaint an underlying affection. It is a venting of frustration rather than disloyalty. On one occasion I protested to a person, who spoke seemingly about a friend, not knowing that he was my friend, but not strongly enough.

Friends, like lovers, may experience unrequited friendship. A recent writer   11
on love and friendship remarks that "you can love without being loved in return, but you cannot be the friend of one who is not your friend." True enough. But this eloquent and incisive writer treats ideal types. He doesn't inquire into the dynamics of friendship once it has been established. In every one of us, there is the ebb and flow of feeling, so that on one occasion Sam's feeling for me is stronger than mine for him and on another occasion the opposite is the case. He is in my mind, when I am out of his. When we don't recognize in our feelings in friendship what the lover feels when his love is unrequited, we fool ourselves.

The telephone test: why doesn't he call me; I called him. My friend   12
Stanley once said after a quarrel about mutual expectations: "Tenderness is no transaction." Tenderness should be a gift, gratuitous, without the expectation of reciprocity. . . .

The psychology of friendship doesn't square with its ideal. It is ideally   13
the relationship of democracy: its collective form carried in the word *comradeship*. Every other relationship is unequal: parent-child, husband-wife, employer-employee, sovereign-subject. Even brother or sister is marked by the invidiousness of age (except in the case of twins: do a few minutes make a difference?). The younger sibling knows his place. But friendship has no rules of deference. Yet equality is impossible. In every friendship there is the smarter one, the more beautiful, the more successful, the more generous, the more venerable. Friendship with celebrities is impossible. The aura they cultivate or is thrust upon them becomes a barrier to intimacy. Celebrities cultivate discipleship. They want to see themselves reflected in the admiration of others, and disciples are too apprehensive of their effect to be candid. Nietzsche and Emerson deplored discipleship as an affront to the individual integrity of both the master and the disciple. Nietzsche's view may have been motivated by a monumental vanity that didn't want his uniqueness to be diminished by the imitation of a disciple. I imagine celebrities to be lonely, wanting friendship as a holiday from their fame. The resentments in friendship are a protest against inequality, against the imperfections in the transactions or the gift-giving. Why do your phone calls go unrequited, why the inattention, the failure to listen, the tendency to dominate in conversation, the envy, the mistrust?

Friendship has its phases or stages of development. There is the uncon-   14
scious friendship of childhood play in the sandbox. At some point in childhood, the child speaks the word and refers to a playmate as a friend. But our strongest memories of friendship probably are of adolescence. Among males its site is the sports field. The unfortunate ones are those without athletic ability or inclination. They become the loners, friendless and intro-

spective; if they have the gift, artists and scholars. Adolescent friendship is in the swagger, sometimes in sympathy with the swagger of others, sometimes in confrontation. What matters is who is taller, stronger, more agile, more skillful in hitting, throwing, passing, catching, dunking. Friends wrestle, box — mostly wrestle. Lawrence's instinct was perfect in having Gerald and Birkin wrestle. When I was fourteen or fifteen I wrestled my best friend to the floor in the hallway of our apartment house, and we beat each other's head against the floor. Yes, he was my best friend.

Early adolescent friendship is friendship of the bodies, later of the emotions. Both the bodies and the emotions change, and friends grow apart as they age. I broke with my childhood friends for reasons that may be different from what I remember. I remember a quarrel with my best friend at the age of seventeen that made me feel that there was more rivalry than affection between us. (He was great with girls, I was the better student.) Another friend came to seem cardboard stiff, a habit foisted on me by my mother's friendship with his mother. The friendship with still another "best friend" eroded because of a discovery he made that our friendship excluded a host of friends of mine that he had never met and didn't know that I had. He found this out at a going-away party my parents gave me before my departure to France on a Fulbright. (In retrospect it was a humiliating affair: my parents didn't know how to give parties for young people, and neither did I know at the age of twenty-five. We were seated around the living room on couches and chairs in conversation — no music, no dancing, no flirting. But this is beside the point.) My friend arrived and found himself among people he had never met. It was as if he discovered me to be someone he did not know. In my behavior to others he saw me in a light different from anything he had experienced with me. And he was deeply jealous. Months later he wrote to tell me this (pushed I supposed by his therapist); the friendship never recovered.

Early friendships like early marriages have a low survival rate, because friends outgrow each other. But who hasn't felt the pathos of the loss of a friend of one's youth? It's as if the experience of that period in one's life has been canceled. I am a sucker for the Lowenbrau commercial in which a group of young men are seated around a campfire, drinking beer while a voice-over speaks or sings: "Here's to good friends." (Whether or not the voice sings, I remember it as a song.) Lowenbrau's brew is pure nostalgia. Call it bathos, but I find the commercial irresistible.

The loner who survives early adolescence may find his soulmate in college, which has a large quota of loners. My own athletic inclinations concealed the fact that I belonged with the loners: what only child doesn't? I had a friend in college who was the saint of loners. He called me Jean-Jacques. I was a confessor, in the Rousseau tradition, a speaker of intimacies. I wore my heart on my sleeve. He was called Alyosha, after the character in *The Brothers Karamazov*. For all of us who knew him, he was the light toward which we all came to confess ourselves, not of sins (because we were all secularists to the core), but of our anxieties. Alyosha reassured us, but never sought reassurance from us. He invited our confidences, but his reserve was absolute. Seated at a table in a diner or cafe, he would bend his giant frame toward us in an attitude of reception, smoking an endless cigarette, and invite our confidences with the most sympathetic and intelligent eyes.

It is hard to describe Alyosha's gift, the special aura he emanated. I was 18 not alone in feeling that I was in the presence of someone extraordinary. He and his family had emigrated from Vienna in the early days of the Nazi takeover of the city where his father was a distinguished member of the Socialist party. His most vivid memory was the visit from the Gestapo to his home; his father had escaped shortly before the arrival of the Germans, and he and his mother had remained behind, expecting to follow him in a few months. The memory of the grim-faced Gestapo officers was indelible. He was the only person of my generation whom I knew who had encountered Evil, and it seemed to have given him an intelligence, a wisdom and compassion, unavailable to his contemporaries. He was old before his time without the slightest trace of childhood in his bearing.

We met in public spaces. I can't recall a time either during my college 19 days or after when I visited him where he lived. He made no invitations, and when others uninvited knocked on his door, he would not let them in, suggesting instead that they go out to a cafe — as if there was something shameful behind the door or some vast disarray that he wanted no one to see. But its effect was strangely to enhance him in my eyes. He possessed and projected a mystery to which I would never have access, whereas I had emptied myself out to him, and there was nothing more to be known.

He was the only saint we knew. After graduation he and I briefly main- 20 tained our connection but drifted apart as I formed other relationships and married. Alyosha remained single and virtually disappeared. I could never learn anything about him, except for the external facts of his life. I had heard that he had become a teacher in a small college, a great teacher much loved by his students. One of them, whom I had met at a party long after she had been graduated, spoke adoringly of him. She said his great gift was to elicit something of value from the garbled expression of his students. I thought to myself: he had found a profession for his gift. Years later I encountered him by chance in the city. He was aging rapidly, and those remarkable eyes of his had undergone a change: they seemed inward looking, furtive and defensive — as if he were about to be put in the unaccustomed role of confessor. In a moment of rare candor he once told a mutual friend that he had grown to hate his Alyosha role. He eluded every effort I made to get in touch with him. I think he detested Jean-Jacques as much as he detested his Alyosha role. Jean-Jacques must have been like a torrent of water engulfing Alyosha. Here was a case of giving and receiving, not mutual and reciprocal, but a division of labor: one the giver, the other the receiver. But who was the giver and who the receiver? I poured myself out so that he did not have to show himself. I cherished him for his generosity in hearing me out and worried about my selfishness in not giving him a chance; but I know now that he didn't want the chance; indeed dreaded it, because of God only knows what he harbored. He must have feared the Jean-Jacques in himself.

We were more alike than different. He and I were only children. Think 21 of all the possibilities in the phrase: children but nothing else, a rhyme for lonely children, a partial pun: owned by our parents. The only child, more than most, knows the need for friends. They are the brothers and sisters others grow up with. Without a brother or sister one has *only* one's parents. But what of the friendship between two only children where the need is illimitable — like two imperial powers confronting each other? . . .

In adulthood we grow into the rituals of marriage, adult responsibility, 22 professional duties. The need for the intimacy of friendship gets buried or absorbed by the spouse. The dinner parties, the collective outings with other couples are exercises in sheer gregariousness: they have little to do with friendship. Who are friends in the relationships of couples: the men, the women, the men and women? Rarely all together. Scales fall from the eyes of anyone who has lived through a divorce (I have). In the divorce, friendship becomes a matter of loyalty — at least for those going through the divorce. The friends would rather not be forced to choose. "How can you remain a friend after the way he (or she) has behaved?" The discrimination of friendship means support, and those who refuse to make the discrimination are seen as traitors. But the divorce may have an effect apart from the demands made by the warring couple. It can demystify the friendship. The husband or the wife discovers how little liked either one was by the "close" friends. It was one or the other, not both, who carried the friendship. Divorce betrays the hidden failures in all the relationships of the couple.

Remarriage creates new problems: each of the spouses late in life has to 23 plug into relationships with people he or she would not care to know by themselves. My second and present wife resisted what seemed to her any demand that she reenact the patterns of my former life with friends. (Young couples have the advantage of forming new friendships together.) It took me a long time to see the justice of her view. If friendship becomes an obligation like family or a necessitous passion like love, it compromises its very principle — which is the freedom to choose. We don't inherit our friends: we choose them.

We have all met people with a "talent for friendship." They turn out to 24 be smiling Jacks or Jills who bathe in the water of geniality. For the time you're with them you feel singled out; they have discerned your unique charm, your intelligence, your capacity for friendship, but then their attention slides to others; and if you are present, you observe that others receive exactly the same response. There is no alteration in their smile, or rapt attention. The talent for friendship is friendship without discrimination. You begin to suspect — or at least I do — that they lack the capacity for friendship. Like fish in an aquarium, they slide against other fish for the momentary pleasure of contact. Neither adolescents nor the very old have this talent, which comes with maturity. All politicians must have it.

As I grow older, friendship becomes harder. Boredom? An acquaintance, 25 not a friend, once told me that his pleasure in old friends has diminished. They have become so predictable to him, he to them. That is part of the explanation, but the reasons may go deeper and may have not yet been remarked: changes in the cells. Why do we change as we grow older, why do we become more difficult with ourselves and each other? We become more what we are and as a consequence less available to one another. We lose our eagerness for the reciprocal modifications of friendship. (There may be a partial remedy for this in cross-generational friendship. Older persons have younger friends to keep young, younger ones older to become wise.) Eternal friendship, the utopia of the classic friendship essay, is an oxymoron, for it assumes that we are cast in marble or that we change in relation to each other like the harmonies of a string quartet. In relationships people are always pulling against each other. Without the guarantees of a contract (and even those guarantees are breakable), there is no permanence. Friendship lives in the pathos of contingency and uncertainty: the contingency and uncertainty of just being alive.

What is friendship in very old age? I observe my elders and imagine 26 their lives. Their lives become retrospective. Beyond ambition, rivalries diminish, or the emptier days (of retirement) get filled with memories (none without pain): the pleasant ones move them to nostalgia, the unhappy ones revive the rivalries and resentments, the sense of regret over missed opportunities. The bodies age, become increasingly painful, the will apathetic. It may no longer be necessary for friends to see one another: they can communicate by phone. In *Back to Methuselah* George Bernard Shaw imagines a utopia of disembodied spirits, living a thousand years freed of the travails of the flesh. But the disembodied voices of the old are charged with those travails.

My ninety-year-old widowed mother speaks to surviving widowed friends 27 her age several times a week. She has not seen them for years, many years. My wife and I offer to take her to see them, to invite them home, but she refuses. She wants the protection of distance, of disembodiment.

I take my mother to her ophthalmologist and on entering the waiting 28 room notice a familiar face. It is the face of a ninety-year-old woman, a friend of my mother's whom I have not seen since the funeral of my father fifteen years ago. This woman has managed to retain features of younger days; and, what is surprising to me, they have remained etched in my consciousness. My mother has been speaking to her several times a week, but hasn't seen her for many years. I tell Mother, who is hard of seeing, that her friend is in the room and she seems to straighten with anxiety. I say, "Why don't you go up to her?"

She hesitates, then approaches her friend and speaks her name. But 29 there is no sign of recognition. She repeats her name and still no response.

Mother retreats to the bench where I am sitting and observing. She is in distress. "How I must have changed?" First thought: her own appearance. Vanity — the last emotion to disappear.

Actually both Mother and her friend have changed remarkably little in their facial features during the past fifteen years. But this is the waiting room of the near blind. Mother wonders whether she should try again. Meanwhile the doctor calls the friend in. Mother decides she will wait for her to reappear; and when she does, Mother approaches her and this time speaks her own name: recognition, delight, tears, animated discussion. From a distance I can hear the familiar sound of complaint, this time coming from the friend. My mother holds her hand with a quiet dignity, uncomplaining about herself. (Complaints seemed to be reserved for intimacies with her son.) I don't think that Mother and this friend were particularly fond of each other when they were younger. But the wear and tear of aging seems to have purified the relationship. They could now concentrate on essentials. The friend looks up and now recognizes me: "How well you look! How you have filled out!" She remembers me as a skinny kid of twelve. Several months later my mother calls to tell me that her friend is no more: "She was tired and just gave out." And I hear her own mounting fatigue — as if the end of her friend is an omen of her own end. Friendship is her last link to life, stronger perhaps than her bond with her son with whom there is the disaffinity of generations. The friend is that other voice not always in tune with yours, but striving for a life-sustaining connection.

Analyzing This Selection

1. **THE WRITER'S METHOD**   How does the author contrast his approach with other, well-known essays on friendship? Find details that indicate whether Goodheart follows his approach throughout the essay.

2. How does love enrich or threaten friendship between the sexes? Within the same sex? Do you think Goodheart overstates or understates these issues?

3. Goodheart identifies types of friendship by considering the phases of an entire life. Does this approach create a positive or negative bias toward some types?

Analyzing Connections

4. Apply François de La Rouchefoucauld's maxim in the Insights on page 114 to Goodheart's analysis of friendship. Does the remark about love fit Goodheart's view of friendship? Does it fit your view?

Analyzing by Writing

5. Analyze a situation in which your friendship came into conflict with change or growth. Do not merely tell the story but examine its test on friendship, as Goodheart does with Jean-Jacques and Alyosha. In what way, if at all, did friendship continue?

Patricia J. Williams

MY BEST WHITE FRIEND

PATRICIA J. WILLIAMS (b. 1951) graduated from Wellesley College and received her law degree from Harvard University. As a professor of law at Columbia University she teaches and writes about social issues, particularly the rights of women and minorities. Her essays are published in *The Alchemy of Race and Rights* (1992) and *The Rooster's Egg* (1995). The following account of a friendship appeared first in the *New Yorker* in 1996.

Cinderella Revisited

My best white friend is giving me advice on how to get myself up like a trophy-wife-in-waiting. We are obliged to attend a gala fund-raiser for an organization on whose board we both sit. I'm not a wife of any sort at all, and she says she knows why: I'm prickly as all getout, I dress down instead of up, and my hair is "a complete disaster." My best white friend, who is already a trophy wife of considerable social and philanthropic standing, is pressing me to borrow one of her Real Designer gowns and a couple of those heavy gold bracelets that are definitely not something you can buy on the street.

I tell her she's missing the point. Cinderella wasn't an over-thirty black professional with an attitude. What sort of Master of the Universe is going to go for that?

"You're not a *racist*, are you?" she asks.

"How could I be?" I reply, with wounded indignation. "What, being the American Dream personified and all."

"Then let's get busy and make you *up*," she says soothingly, breaking out the little pots of powder, paint, and polish.

From the first exfoliant to the last of the cucumber rinse, we fight about my man troubles. From powder base through lip varnish, we fight about hers.

You see, part of the problem is that white knights just don't play the same part in my mythical landscape of desire. If poor Cinderella had been black, it would have been a whole different story. I tell my best white friend the kind of stories my mother raised me on: about slave girls who worked their fingers to the bone for their evil half sisters, the "legitimate" daughters of their mutual father, the master of the manse, the owner of them all; about scullery maids whose oil-and-ashes complexions would not wash clean even after multiple waves of the wand. These were the ones who harbored impossible dreams of love for lost mates who had been sold down rivers of tears into oblivion. These were the ones who became runaways.

"Just think about it," I say. "The human drama is compact enough so 8 that when my mother was little she knew women who had been slaves, including a couple of runaways. Cinderellas who had burned their masters' beds and then fled for their lives. It doesn't take too much, even across the ages, to read between those lines. Women who invented their own endings, even when they didn't get to live happily or very long thereafter."

My best white friend says, "Get a grip. It's just a party." 9

I've called my best white friend my best white friend ever since she 10 started calling me her best black friend. I am her only black friend, as far as I know, a circumstance for which she blames "the class thing." At her end of the social ladder, I am *my* only black friend — a circumstance for which I blame "the race thing."

"People should stop putting so much emphasis on color — it doesn't mat- 11 ter whether you're black or white or blue or green," she says from beneath an avocado mask.

Lucky for you, I think, even as my own pores are expanding or contract- 12 ing — I forget which — beneath a cool neon-green sheath.

In fact, I have been looking forward to the makeover. M.B.W.F. has a 13 masseuse and a manicurist and colors in her palette like Après Sun and Burnt Straw, which she swears will match my skin tones more or less.

"Why don't they just call it Racial Envy?" I ask, holding up a tube of 14 Deep Copper Kiss.

"Now, now, we're all sisters under the makeup," she says cheerfully. 15

"When ever will we be sisters without?" I grumble. 16

I've come this far because she's convinced me that my usual slapdash 17 routine is the equivalent of being "unmade"; and being unmade, she under- scores, is a most exclamatory form of unsophistication. "Even Strom Thur- mond wears a little pancake when he's in public."

M.B.W.F. is somewhat given to hyperbole, but it *is* awfully hard to bear, 18 the thought of making less of a fashion statement than old Strom. I do draw the line, though. She has a long history of nips, tucks, and liposuction. Once, I tried to suggest how appalled I was, but I'm not good at being graceful when I have a really strong opinion roiling up inside. She dismissed me sweetly: "You can afford to disapprove. You are aging *so* very nicely."

There was the slightest pause as I tried to suppress the anxious rise in my 19 voice: "You think I'm aging?"

Very gently, she proceeded to point out the flawed and falling features 20 that give me away to the carefully trained eye, the insistent voyeur. There were the pores. And those puffs beneath my eyes. No, not there — those are the bags under my eyes. The bags aren't so bad, according to her — no deep wrinkling just yet. But keep going — the puffs are just below the bags. Therein lies the facial decay that gives my age away.

I had never noticed them before, but for a while after that those puffs 21 just dominated my face. I couldn't look at myself for their explosive insolence — the body's betrayal, obscuring every other feature.

I got over it the day we were standing in line by a news rack at the Food 22 Emporium. Gazing at a photo of Princess Diana looking radiantly, elegantly melancholic on the cover of some women's magazine, M.B.W.F. snapped, "God! Bulimia must work!"

This is not the first time M.B.W.F. has shepherded me to social doom. 23 The last time, it was a very glitzy cocktail party where husband material supposedly abounded. I had a long, businesslike conversation with a man she introduced me to, who, I realized as we talked, grew more and more fascinated by me. At first, I was only conscious of winning him over; then I remember becoming aware that there was something funny about his fierce infatuation. I was *surprising* him, I slowly realized. Finally, he came clean: He said that he had never before had a conversation like this with a black person. "I think I'm in love," he blurted in a voice bubbling with fear.

"I think not," I consoled him. "It's just the power of your undone expec- 24 tations, in combination with my being a basically likable person. It's throwing you for a loop. That and the Scotch, which, as you ought to know, is inherently depoliticizing."

I remember telling M.B.W.F. about him afterward. She had always 25 thought of him as "that perfect Southern gentleman." The flip side of the Southern gentleman is the kind master, I pointed out. "Bad luck," she said. "It's true, though — he's the one man I wouldn't want to be owned by, if I were you."

My best white friend doesn't believe that race is a big social problem 26 anymore. "It's all economics," she insists. "It's how you came to be my *friend*" — for once, she does not qualify me as black — "the fact that we were both in college together." I feel compelled to remind her that affirmative action is how both of us ended up in the formerly all-male bastion we attended.

The odd thing is, we took most of the same classes. She ended up musi- 27 cally proficient, gifted in the art of interior design, fluent in the mother tongue, whatever it might be, of the honored visiting diplomat of the moment. She actively aspired, she says, to be "a cunning little meringue of a male prize."

"You," she says to me, "were always more like Gladys Knight."   28

"Come again?" I say.   29

"Ethnic woman warrior, always on that midnight train to someplace else,   30
intent on becoming the highest-paid Aunt Jemima in history."

"Ackh," I cough, a sudden strangulation of unmade thoughts fluttering   31
in my windpipe.

The night after the cocktail party, I dreamed that I was in a bedroom   32
with a tall, faceless man. I was his breeding slave. I was trying to be very,
very good, so that I might one day earn my freedom. He did not trust me.
I was always trying to hide some essential part of myself from him, which I
would preserve and take with me on that promised day when I was permitted to leave; he felt it as an innate wickedness in me, a darkness that he
could not penetrate, a dangerous secret that must be wrested from me. I
tried everything I knew to please him; I walked a tightrope of anxious servitude and survivalist withholding. But it was not good enough. One morning, he just reached for a sword and sliced me in half, to see for himself
what was inside. A casual flick, and I lay dead on the floor in two dark,
unyielding halves; in exasperated disgust, he stepped over my remains and
rushed from the room, already late for other business, leaving the cleanup
for another slave.

"You didn't dream that!" M.B.W.F. says in disbelief.   33
"I did so."   34
"You're making it up," she says. "People don't really have dreams like   35
that."
"*I* do. Aren't I a people, too?"   36
"That's amazing! Tell me another."   37
"O.K., here's a fairy tale for you," I say, and tell her I dreamed I was   38
being held by Sam Malone, the silly, womanizing bartender on *Cheers*. He
was tall, broad-chested, good-looking, unbelievably strong. My head, my
face were pressed against his chest. We were whispering our love for each
other. I was moved deeply, my heart was banging, he held me tight and
told me that he loved me. I told him that I loved him, too. We kissed so
that heaven and earth moved in my heart; I wanted to make love to him
fiercely. He put a simple thick gold band on my finger. I turned and, my
voice cracking with emotion and barely audible, said, "What's this?" He
asked me to marry him. I told him yes, I loved him, yes, yes, I loved him.
He told me he loved me, too. I held out my hand and admired the ring in
awe. I was the luckiest woman on earth.

Suddenly Diane Chambers, Sam's paramour on *Cheers*, burst through   39
the door. She was her perky, petulant self, bouncing blond hair and black-
green eyes like tarnished copper beads, like lumps of melted metal — eyes
that looked carved yet soft, almost brimming. She turned those soft-hard
eyes on me and said, "Oh no, Sam, not tonight — you promised!"

And with that I realized that I was to be consigned to a small room on   40 the other side of the house. Diane followed me as I left, profusely apologetic with explanations: She was sorry, and she didn't mind him being with me once or twice a month, but this was getting ridiculous. I realized that I was Sam's part-time mistress — a member of the household somehow, but having no rights.

Then Diane went back into the master bedroom and Sam came in to apologize, to say that there had been a mixup, that it was just this once, that he'd make it up to me, that he was sorry. And, of course, I forgave him, for there was nothing I wanted more than to relive the moment when he held me tightly and our love was a miracle and I was the only woman he wanted in the world, forever.   41

"Have you thought of going into therapy?" she jokes.   42

"As a matter of fact, I have," I say, sighing and rubbing my temples. "On average, we black women have bigger, better problems than any other women alive. We bear the burden of being seen as pretenders to the thrones of both femininity and masculinity, endlessly mocked by the ambiguously gendered crown-of-thorns imagery of 'queen' — Madame Queen, snap queen, welfare queen, quota queen, Queenie Queen, *Queen* Queen Queen. We black women are figured more as stand-ins for men, sort of like reverse drag queens: women pretending to be women but more male than men — bare-breasted, sweat-glistened, plow-pulling, sole supporters of their families. Arnold Schwarzenegger and Sylvester Stallone meet Sojourner Truth, the *Real* Real Thing, the Ace-of-Spades Gender Card Herself, Thelma and Louise knocked up by Wesley Snipes, the ultimate hard-drinking, tobacco-growing-and-aspitting, nut-crushing ball-buster of all time. . . . I mean, think about it — how'd you like to go to the ball dressed like a walking cultural pathology? Wouldn't it make you just a wee bit tense?"   43

"But," she sputters, "but — you always seem so *strong!*"   44

We have just about completed our toilette. She looks at my hair as though it were a rude construction of mud and twigs, bright glass beads, and flashy bits of tinfoil. I look at hers for what it is — the high-tech product of many hours of steam rollers, shine enhancers, body spritzers, perms, and about eighteen hundred watts of blow-dried effort. We gaze at each other with the deep disapproval of one gazing into a mirror. It is inconceivable to both of us that we have been friends for as long as we have. We shake our heads in sympathetic unison and sigh.   45

One last thing: It seems we have forgotten about shoes. It turns out that my feet are much too big to fit into any of her sequined little evening slippers, so I wear my own sensible square-soled pumps. My prosaic feet, like overgrown roots, peek out from beneath the satiny folds of the perfect dress. She looks radiant; I feel dubious. Our chariot and her husband await. As we climb into the limousine, her husband lights up a cigar and holds forth on the reemerging popularity of same. My friend responds charmingly with a remarkably detailed production history of the Biedermeier humidor.   46

I do not envy her. I do not resent her. I do not hold my breath.   47

Analyzing This Selection

1. **THE WRITER'S METHOD**   Williams describes herself as a person "with an attitude." What is the author's tone or attitude in this essay? Choose three adjectives that fit, and explain your choice.

2. How do Williams's romantic dreams compare to the classic Cinderella fantasy?

3. What do you think are the strengths of this friendship? What might change if the friends were of the same color?

4. Do you think Williams is one of the "women who invented their own endings" (para. 8)? Using specific details from the essay to support your view, try to account for the differences between her romantic fantasies and the person she seems to be.

Analyzing Connections

5. Does friendship have different traits and meaning for men and women? Compare Williams and Goodheart (see "Fast Friends," p. 131) for views about long-standing friendships. Which differences are more of personality or gender?

Analyzing by Writing

6. Parents often maintain fairy-tale expectations for their sons' and daughters' romantic lives, thinking that they will be magically awakened to adult life like Sleeping Beauty. Have you had to struggle against this or another fairy tale imposed by parents? Analyze the main features of the active myth, and explain how it is imposed on your life.

Lindsy Van Gelder

MARRIAGE AS A RESTRICTED CLUB

LINDSY VAN GELDER (b. 1944) was born in New Jersey and earned her B.A. at Sarah Lawrence College. After graduating, she worked as a reporter for United Press International and then for the *New York Post*. She has been a staff writer for *Ms.* and contributes articles to periodicals including *Esquire, New York, Redbook, Rolling Stone,* and the *Village Voice.* The following article originally appeared in *Ms.* Van Gelder has described one of her major concerns as a writer this way: "I constantly worry about how to convey seemingly radical ideas to an unconvinced audience."

Several years ago, I stopped going to weddings. In fact, I no longer cele- 1
brate the wedding anniversaries or engagements of friends, relatives, or any-one else, although I might wish them lifelong joy in their relationships. My explanation is that the next wedding I attend will be my own — to the woman I've loved and lived with for nearly six years.

Although I've been legally married to a man myself (and come close to 2
marrying two others), I've come, in these last six years with Pamela, to see heterosexual marriage as very much a restricted club. (Nor is this likely to change in the near future, if one can judge by the recent clobbering of what was actually a rather tame proposal to recognize "domestic partner-ships" in San Francisco.) Regardless of the *reason* people marry — whether to save on real estate taxes or qualify for married student housing or simply to express love — lesbians and gay men can't obtain the same results should they desire to do so. It seems apparent to me that few friends of Pamela's and mine would even join a club that excluded blacks, Jews, or women, much less assume that they could expect their black, Jewish, or female friends to toast their new status with champagne. But probably no other stand of principle we've ever made in our lives has been so misunderstood, or caused so much bad feeling on both sides.

Several people have reacted with surprise to our views, it never having 3
occurred to them that gay people *can't* legally marry. (Why on earth did they think that none of us had bothered?) The most common reaction, however, is acute embarrassment, followed by a denial of our main point — that the about-to-be-wed person is embarking on a privileged status. (One friend of Pamela's insisted that lesbians are "lucky" not to have to agonize

146

over whether or not to get married.) So wrapped in gauze is the institution of marriage, so ingrained the expectation that brides and grooms can enjoy the world's delighted approval, that it's hard for me not to feel put on the defensive for being so mean-spirited, eccentric, and/or politically rigid as to boycott such a happy event.

Another question we've fielded more than once (usually from our most radical friends, both gay and straight) is why we'd want to get married in the first place. In fact, I have mixed feelings about registering my personal life with the state, but — and this seems to me to be the essence of radical politics — I'd prefer to be the one making the choice. And while feminists in recent years have rightly focused on puncturing the Schlaflyite[1] myth of the legally protected homemaker, it's also true that marriage does confer some very real dollars-and-cents benefits. One example of inequity is our inability to file joint tax returns, although many couples, both gay and straight, go through periods when one partner in the relationship is unemployed or makes considerably less money than the other. At one time in our relationship, Pamela — who is a musician — was between bands and earning next to nothing. I was making a little over $37,000 a year as a newspaper reporter, a salary that put me in the 42 percent tax bracket — about $300 a week taken out of my paycheck. If we had been married, we could have filed a joint tax return and each paid taxes on half my salary, in the 25 or 30 percent bracket. The difference would have been nearly $100-a-week in our pockets.

Around the same time, Pamela suffered a months'-long illness which would have been covered by my health insurance if she were my spouse. We were luckier than many; we could afford it. But on top of the worry and expense involved (and despite the fact that intellectually we believe in the ideal of free medical care for everyone), we found it almost impossible to avoid internalizing a sense of personal failure — the knowledge that *because of who we are, we can't take care of each other.* I've heard of other gay people whose lovers were deported because they couldn't marry them and enable them to become citizens; still others who were barred from intensive-care units where their lovers lay stricken because they weren't "immediate family."

I would never begrudge a straight friend who got married to save a lover from deportation or staggering medical bills, but the truth is that I no longer sympathize with most of the less tangible justifications. This includes the oft-heard "for the sake of the children" argument, since (like many gay people, especially women) I *have* children, and I resent the implication that some families are more "legitimate" than others. (It's important to safeguard one's children's rights to their father's property, but a legal contract will do the same thing as marriage.)

---

[1]Phyllis Schlafly, a political activist, opposed the Equal Rights Amendment.

But the single most painful and infuriating rationale for marriage, as far   7
as I'm concerned, is the one that goes: "We wanted to stand up and show
the world that we've made a *genuine* commitment." When one is gay, such
sentiments are labeled "flaunting." My lover and I almost never find ourselves in public settings outside the gay ghetto where we are (a) perceived
to be a couple at all (people constantly ask us if we're sisters, although we
look nothing like each other), and (b) valued as such. Usually we're forced
to choose between being invisible and being despised. "Making a genuine
commitment" in this milieu is like walking a highwire without a net —
with most of the audience not even watching and a fair segment rooting for
you to fall. A disproportionate number of gay couples do.

I think it's difficult for even my closest, most feminist straight women   8
friends to empathize with the intensity of my desire to be recognized as
Pamela's partner. (In fact, it may be harder for feminists to understand than
for others; I know that when I was straight, I often resented being viewed as
one half of a couple. My struggle was for an independent identity, not the
cojoined one I now crave.) But we are simply not considered *authentic*,
and the reminders are constant. Recently at a party, a man I'd known for
years spied me across the room and came over to me, arms outstretched,
big happy-to-see-you grin on his face. Pamela had a gig that night and
wasn't at the party; my friend's wife was there but in another room, and I
hadn't seen her yet. "How's M—— ?" I asked the man. "Oh, she's fine," he
replied, continuing to smile pleasantly. "Are you and Pam still together?"

Our sex life itself is against the law in many states, of course, and like all   9
lesbians and gay men, we are without many other rights, both large and
small. (In Virginia, for instance, it's technically against the law for us to buy
liquor.) But as a gay couple, we are also most likely to be labeled and dis-
criminated against in those very settings that, for most heterosexual Americans, constitute the most relaxed and personal parts of life. Virtually every
tiny public act of togetherness — from holding hands on the street to rent-
ing a hotel room to dancing — requires us constantly to risk humiliation (I
think, for example, of the two California women who were recently thrown
out of a restaurant that had special romantic tables for couples), sexual
harassment (it's astonishing how many men can't resist coming on to a lesbian couple), and even physical assault. A great deal of energy goes into
just expecting possible trouble. It's a process which, after six years, has
become second nature for me — but occasionally, when I'm in Province-
town or someplace else with a large lesbian population, I experience the
absence of it as a feeling of virtual weightlessness.

What does all this have to do with my friends' weddings? Obviously, I   10
can't expect my friends to live my life. But I do think that lines are being
drawn . . . , and I have no choice about what side I'm placed on. My
straight friends do, and at the very least, I expect them to acknowledge that.
I certainly expect them to understand why I don't want to be among the

rice-throwers and well-wishers at their weddings; beyond that, I would hope that they would commit themselves to fighting for my rights — preferably in personally visible ways, like marching in gay pride parades. But I also wish they wouldn't get married, period. And if that sounds hard-nosed, I hope I'm only proving my point — that not being able to marry isn't a minor issue.

Not that my life would likely be changed as the result of any individual   11 straight person's symbolic refusal to marry. (Nor, for that matter, do all gay couples want to be wed.) But it's a political reality that heterosexual live-together couples are among our best tactical allies. The movement to repeal state sodomy laws has profited from the desire of straight people to keep the government out of *their* bedrooms. Similarly, it was a heterosexual New York woman who went to court several years ago to fight her land-lord's demand that she either marry her live-in boyfriend or face eviction for violating a lease clause prohibiting "unrelated" tenants — and whose struggle led to the recent passage of a state rent law that had ramifications for thousands of gay couples, including Pamela and me.

The right wing has seized on "homosexual marriage" as its bottom-line   12 scare phrase in much the same way that "Would you want your sister to marry one?" was brandished twenty-five years ago. *They* see marriage as their turf. And so when I see feminists crossing into that territory of respectabil-ity and "sinlessness," I feel my buffer zone slipping away. I feel as though my friends are taking off their armbands, leaving me exposed.

Analyzing This Selection

1. Explain whether you think Van Gelder is "mean-spirited, eccentric, and/or politically rigid" for boycotting engagements, weddings, and anniversaries and for not wanting her friends to marry.

2. **THE WRITER'S METHOD**   What reasons does the author give for wanting to marry her gay lover? Which is the most important reason to her?

3. Van Gelder sees herself as an outsider, one who does not share equal privi-leges with the rest of society. How does she cope with the problems of her minority status?

Analyzing Connections

4. Society has no words or recognition for lesbian couples or for established, straight friendships as Goodheart observes (see "Fast Friends," p. 131). What new terminology and customs might acknowledge these bonds? What risks does each author see in increased public visibility?

Analyzing by Writing

5. Do anniversaries sometimes create myths? Consider the meaning and validity of wedding anniversaries as they are celebrated in your family. Do children or grandparents have a role? Do the observances emphasize romance?
   Do the celebrations include and preserve family history, or do they emphasize the present and future? Explain the customs, symbolism, and other
   kinds of significance that you have witnessed in these events.

Jonathan Rauch

FOR BETTER OR WORSE?

Jonathan Rauch (b. 1960) graduated from Yale University. His articles about economics and politics have appeared in the *Atlantic Monthly, Fortune, Harper's,* and the *National Journal,* where he is presently a contributing editor. He recounts his visiting-scholar's impressions of contemporary Japan in his first book, *The Outnation: A Search for the Soul of Japan* (1992). Rauch examines American economic and ideological threats to democracy in *Kindly Inquisitors: The New Attacks on Free Thought* (1993) and *Demosclerosis: The Silent Killer of American Government* (1994). The following tightly argued selection supporting gay marriage appeared in the *New Republic.*

Whatever else marriage may or may not be, it is certainly falling apart. 1 Half of today's marriages end in divorce, and, far more costly, many never begin — leaving mothers poor, children fatherless and neighborhoods chaotic. With timing worthy of Neville Chamberlain, homosexuals have chosen this moment to press for the right to marry. What's more, Hawaii's courts are moving toward letting them do so. I'll believe in gay marriage in America when I see it, but if Hawaii legalizes it, even temporarily, the uproar over this final insult to a besieged institution will be deafening.

Whether gay marriage makes sense — and whether straight marriage 2 makes sense — depends on what marriage is actually for. Current secular thinking on this question is shockingly sketchy. Gay activists say: marriage is for love, and we love each other, therefore we should be able to marry. Traditionalists say: marriage is for children, and homosexuals do not (or should not) have children, therefore you should not be able to marry. That, unfortunately, pretty well covers the spectrum. I say "unfortunately" because both views are wrong. They misunderstand and impoverish the social meaning of marriage.

So what is marriage for? Modern marriage is, of course, based upon tra- 3 ditions that religion helped to codify and enforce. But religious doctrine has no special standing in the world of secular law and policy (the "Christian nation" crowd notwithstanding). If we want to know what and whom marriage is for in modern America, we need a sensible secular doctrine.

At one point, marriage in secular society was largely a matter of busi- 4 ness: cementing family ties, providing social status for men and economic support for women, conferring dowries, and so on. Marriages were typically arranged, and "love" in the modern sense was no prerequisite. In Japan, remnants of this system remain, and it works surprisingly well. Couples stay together because they view their marriage as a partnership: an investment in social stability for themselves and their children. Because Japanese couples don't expect as much emotional fulfillment as we do, they are less inclined to break up. They also take a somewhat more relaxed attitude toward adultery. What's a little extracurricular love provided that each partner is fulfilling his or her many other marital duties?

In the West, of course, love is a defining element. The notion of lifelong love is charming, if ambitious, and certainly love is a desirable element of marriage. In society's eyes, however, it cannot be the defining element. You may or may not love your husband, but the two of you are just as married either way. You may love your mistress, but that certainly doesn't make her your spouse. Love helps make sense of marriage emotionally, but it is not terribly important in making sense of marriage from the point of view of social policy.

If love does not define the purpose of secular marriage, what does? Neither the law nor secular thinking provides a clear answer. Today marriage is almost entirely a voluntary arrangement whose contents are up to the people making the deal. There are few if any behaviors that automatically end a marriage. If a man beats his wife, which is about the worst thing he can do to her, he may be convicted of assault, but his marriage is not automatically dissolved. Couples can be adulterous ("open") yet remain married. They can be celibate, too; consummation is not required. All in all, it is an impressive and also rather astonishing victory for modern individualism that so important an institution should be so bereft of formal social instruction as to what should go on inside of it.

Secular society tells us only a few things about marriage. First, marriage depends on the consent of the parties. Second, the parties are not children. Third, the number of parties is two. Fourth, one is a man and the other a woman. Within those rules a marriage is whatever anyone says it is.

Perhaps it is enough simply to say that marriage is as it is and should not be tampered with. This sounds like a crudely reactionary position. In fact, however, of all the arguments against reforming marriage, it is probably the most powerful.

Call it a Hayekian argument, after the great libertarian economist F. A. Hayek, who developed this line of thinking in his book *The Fatal Conceit*. In a market system, the prices generated by impersonal forces may not make sense from any one person's point of view, but they encode far more information than even the cleverest person could ever gather. In a similar fashion, human societies evolve rich and complicated webs of nonlegal rules in the form of customs, traditions and institutions. Like prices, they may seem irrational or arbitrary. But the very fact that they are the customs that have evolved implies that they embody a practical logic that may not be apparent to even a sophisticated analyst. And the web of custom cannot be torn apart and reordered at will because once its internal logic is violated it falls apart. Intellectuals, such as Marxists or feminists, who seek to deconstruct and rationally rebuild social traditions, will produce not better order but chaos.

So the Hayekian view argues strongly against gay marriage. It says that 10 the current rules may not be best and may even be unfair. But they are all we have, and, once you say that marriage need not be male-female, soon marriage will stop being anything at all. You can't mess with the formula without causing unforeseen consequences, possibly including the implosion of the institution of marriage itself.

However, there are problems with the Hayekian position. It is untenable 11 in its extreme form and unhelpful in its milder version. In its extreme form, it implies that no social reforms should ever be undertaken. Indeed, no laws should be passed, because they interfere with the natural evolution of social mores. How could Hayekians abolish slavery? They would probably note that slavery violates fundamental moral principles. But in so doing they would establish a moral platform from which to judge social rules, and thus acknowledge that abstracting social debate from moral concerns is not possible.

If the ban on gay marriage were only mildly unfair, and if the costs of 12 changing it were certain to be enormous, then the ban could stand on Hayekian grounds. But, if there is any social policy today that has a fair claim to be scaldingly inhumane, it is the ban on gay marriage. As conservatives tirelessly and rightly point out, marriage is society's most fundamental institution. To bar any class of people from marrying as they choose is an extraordinary deprivation. When not so long ago it was illegal in parts of America for blacks to marry whites, no one could claim that this was a trivial disenfranchisement. Granted, gay marriage raises issues that interracial marriage does not; but no one can argue that the deprivation is a minor one.

To outweigh such a serious claim it is not enough to say that gay mar- 13 riage might lead to bad things. Bad things happened as a result of legalizing contraception, but that did not make it the wrong thing to do. Besides, it seems doubtful that extending marriage to, say, another 3 or 5 percent of the population would have anything like the effects that no-fault divorce has had, to say nothing of contraception. By now, the "traditional" understanding of marriage has been sullied in all kinds of ways. It is hard to think of a bigger affront to tradition, for instance, than allowing married women to own property independently of their husbands or allowing them to charge their husbands with rape. Surely it is unfair to say that marriage may be reformed for the sake of anyone and everyone except homosexuals, who must respect the dictates of tradition.

Faced with these problems, the milder version of the Hayekian argu- 14 ment says not that social traditions shouldn't be tampered with at all, but that they shouldn't be tampered with lightly. Fine. In this case, no one is talking about casual messing around; both sides have marshaled their arguments with deadly seriousness. Hayekians surely have to recognize that appeals to blind tradition and to the risks inherent in social change do not, a priori, settle anything in this instance. They merely warn against frivolous change.

So we turn to what has become the standard view of marriage's purpose. 15 Its proponents would probably like to call it a child-centered view, but it is actually an anti-gay view, as will become clear. Whatever you call it, it is the view of marriage that is heard most often, and in the context of the debate over gay marriage it is heard almost exclusively. In its most straightforward form it goes as follows (I quote from James Q. Wilson's fine book *The Moral Sense*):

> A family is not an association of independent people; it is a human commitment designed to make possible the rearing of moral and healthy children. Governments care — or ought to care — about families for this reason, and scarcely for any other.

Wilson speaks about "family" rather than "marriage" as such, but one 16 may, I think, read him as speaking of marriage without doing any injustice to his meaning. The resulting proposition — government ought to care about marriage almost entirely because of children — seems reasonable. But there are problems. The first, obviously, is that gay couples may have children, whether through adoption, prior marriage or (for lesbians) artificial insemination. Leaving aside the thorny issue of gay adoption, the point is that if the mere presence of children is the test, then homosexual relationships can certainly pass it.

You might note, correctly, that heterosexual marriages are more likely to 17 produce children than homosexual ones. When granting marriage licenses to heterosexuals, however, we do not ask how likely the couple is to have children. We assume that they are entitled to get married whether or not they end up with children. Understanding this, conservatives often make an interesting move. In seeking to justify the state's interest in marriage, they shift from the actual presence of children to the anatomical possibility of making them. Hadley Arkes, a political science professor and prominent opponent of homosexual marriage, makes the case this way:

> The traditional understanding of marriage is grounded in the "natural teleology of the body" — in the inescapable fact that only a man and a woman, and only two people, not three, can generate a child. Once marriage is detached from that natural teleology of the body, what ground of principle would thereafter confine marriage to two people rather than some larger grouping? That is, on what ground of principle would the law reject the claim of a gay couple that their love is not confined to a coupling of two, but that they are woven into a larger ensemble with yet another person or two?

What he seems to be saying is that, where the possibility of natural chil- 18 dren is nil, the meaning of marriage is nil. If marriage is allowed between members of the same sex, then the concept of marriage has been emptied of content except to ask whether the parties love each other. Then anything goes, including polygamy. This reasoning presumably is what those opposed to gay marriage have in mind when they claim that, once gay marriage is legal, marriage to pets will follow close behind.

But Arkes and his sympathizers make two mistakes. To see them, break   19 down the claim into two components: (1) Two-person marriage derives its special status from the anatomical possibility that the partners can create natural children; and (2) Apart from (1), two-person marriage has no purpose sufficiently strong to justify its special status. That is, absent justification (1), anything goes.

The first proposition is wholly at odds with the way society actually views   20 marriage. Leave aside the insistence that natural, as opposed to adopted, children define the importance of marriage. The deeper problem, apparent right away, is the issue of sterile heterosexual couples. Here the "anatomical possibility" crowd has a problem, for a homosexual union is, anatomically speaking, nothing but one variety of sterile union and no different even in principle: a woman without a uterus has no more potential for giving birth than a man without a vagina.

It may sound like carping to stress the case of barren heterosexual mar-   21 riage: the vast majority of newlywed heterosexual couples, after all, can have children and probably will. But the point here is fundamental. There are far more sterile heterosexual unions in America than homosexual ones. The "anatomical possibility" crowd cannot have it both ways. If the possibility of children is what gives meaning to marriage, then a postmenopausal woman who applies for a marriage license should be turned away at the courthouse door. What's more, she should be hooted at and condemned for stretching the meaning of marriage beyond its natural basis and so reducing the institution to frivolity. People at the Family Research Council or Concerned Women for America should point at her and say, "If she can marry, why not polygamy?"

Obviously, the "anatomical" conservatives do not say this, because they   22 are sane. They instead flail around, saying that sterile men and women were at least born with the right-shaped parts for making children, and so on. Their position is really a nonposition. It says that the "natural children" rationale defines marriage when homosexuals are involved but not when heterosexuals are involved. When the parties to union are sterile heterosexuals, the justification for marriage must be something else. But what?

Now arises the oddest part of the "anatomical" argument. Look at propo-   23 sition (2) above. It says that, absent the anatomical justification for marriage, anything goes. In other words, it dismisses the idea that there might be other good reasons for society to sanctify marriage above other kinds of relationships. Why would anybody make this move? I'll hazard a guess: to exclude homosexuals. Any rationale that justifies sterile heterosexual marriages can also apply to homosexual ones. For instance, marriage makes women more financially secure. Very nice, say the conservatives. But that rationale could be applied to lesbians, so it's definitely out.

The end result of this stratagem is perverse to the point of being funny.   24
The attempt to ground marriage in children (or the anatomical possibility thereof) falls flat. But, having lost that reason for marriage, the antigay people can offer no other. In their fixation on excluding homosexuals, they leave themselves no consistent justification for the privileged status of *heterosexual* marriage. They thus tear away any coherent foundation that secular marriage might have, which is precisely the opposite of what they claim they want to do. If they have to undercut marriage to save it from homosexuals, so be it!

For the record, I would be the last to deny that children are one central   25
reason for the privileged status of marriage. When men and women get together, children are a likely outcome; and, as we are learning in ever more unpleasant ways, when children grow up without two parents, trouble ensues. Children are not a trivial reason for marriage; they just cannot be the only reason.

What are the others? It seems to me that the two strongest candidates are   26
these: domesticating men and providing reliable caregivers. Both purposes are critical to the functioning of a humane and stable society, and both are much better served by marriage — that is, by one-to-one lifelong commitment — than by any other institution.

Civilizing young males is one of any society's biggest problems. Wher-   27
ever unattached males gather in packs, you see no end of trouble: wildings in Central Park, gangs in Los Angeles, soccer hooligans in Britain, skinheads in Germany, fraternity hazings in universities, grope-lines in the military and, in a different but ultimately no less tragic way, the bathhouses and wanton sex of gay San Francisco or New York in the 1970s.

For taming men, marriage is unmatched. "Of all the institutions through   28
which men may pass — schools, factories, the military — marriage has the largest effect," Wilson writes in *The Moral Sense*. (A token of the casualness of current thinking about marriage is that the man who wrote those words could, later in the very same book, say that government should care about fostering families for "scarcely any other" reason than children.) If marriage — that is, the binding of men into couples — did nothing else, its power to settle men, to keep them at home and out of trouble, would be ample justification for its special status.

Of course, women and older men don't generally travel in marauding or   29
orgiastic packs. But in their case the second rationale comes into play. A second enormous problem for society is what to do when someone is beset by some sort of burdensome contingency. It could be cancer, a broken back, unemployment or depression; it could be exhaustion from work or stress under pressure. If marriage has any meaning at all, it is that, when

you collapse from a stroke, there will be at least one other person whose "job" is to drop everything and come to your aid; or that when you come home after being fired by the postal service there will be someone to persuade you not to kill the supervisor.

Obviously, both rationales — the need to settle males and the need to have people looked after — apply to sterile people as well as fertile ones, and apply to childless couples as well as to ones with children. The first explains why everybody feels relieved when the town delinquent gets married, and the second explains why everybody feels happy when an aging widow takes a second husband. From a social point of view, it seems to me, both rationales are far more compelling as justifications of marriage's special status than, say, love. And both of them apply to homosexuals as well as to heterosexuals. 30

Take the matter of settling men. It is probably true that women and children, more than just the fact of marriage, help civilize men. But that hardly means that the settling effect of marriage on homosexual men is negligible. To the contrary, being tied to a committed relationship plainly helps stabilize gay men. Even without marriage, coupled gay men have steady sex partners and relationships that they value and therefore tend to be less wanton. Add marriage, and you bring a further array of stabilizing influences. One of the main benefits of publicly recognized marriage is that it binds couples together not only in their own eyes but also in the eyes of society at large. Around the partners is woven a web of expectations that they will spend nights together, go to parties together, take out inortgages together, buy furniture at Ikea together, and so on — all of which helps tie them together and keep them off the streets and at home. Surely that is a very good thing, especially as compared to the closet-gay culture of furtive sex with innumerable partners in parks and bathhouses. 31

The other benefit of marriage — caretaking — clearly applies to homosexuals. One of the first things many people worry about when coming to terms with their homosexuality is: Who will take care of me when I'm ailing or old? Society needs to care about this, too, as the AIDS crisis has made horribly clear. If that crisis has shown anything, it is that homosexuals can and will take care of each other, sometimes with breathtaking devotion — and that no institution can begin to match the care of a devoted partner. Legally speaking, marriage creates kin. Surely society's interest in kin-creation is strongest of all for people who are unlikely to be supported by children in old age and who may well be rejected by their own parents in youth. 32

Gay marriage, then, is far from being a mere exercise in political point-making or rights-mongering. On the contrary, it serves two of the three social purposes that make marriage so indispensable and irreplaceable for heterosexuals. Two out of three may not be the whole ball of wax, but it is more than enough to give society a compelling interest in marrying off homosexuals. 33

There is no substitute. Marriage is the *only* institution that adequately 34
serves these purposes. The power of marriage is not just legal but social. It
seals its promise with the smiles and tears of family, friends and neighbors.
It shrewdly exploits ceremony (big, public weddings) and money (expensive
gifts, dowries) to deter casual commitment and to make bailing out embarrassing. Stag parties and bridal showers signal that what is beginning is not
just a legal arrangement but a whole new stage of life. "Domestic partner"
laws do none of these things.

I'll go further: far from being a substitute for the real thing, marriage-lite 35
may undermine it. Marriage is a deal between a couple and society, not
just between two people: society recognizes the sanctity and autonomy of
the pair-bond, and in exchange each spouse commits to being the other's
nurse, social worker and policeman of first resort. Each marriage is its own
little society within society. Any step that weakens the deal by granting the
legal benefits of marriage without also requiring the public commitment is
begging for trouble.

So gay marriage makes sense for several of the same reasons that straight 36
marriage makes sense. That would seem a natural place to stop. But the
logic of the argument compels one to go a twist further. If it is good for
society to have people attached, then it is not enough just to make marriage available. Marriage should also be *expected*. This, too, is just as true
for homosexuals as for heterosexuals. So, if homosexuals are justified in
expecting access to marriage, society is equally justified in expecting them
to use it. I'm not saying that out-of-wedlock sex should be scandalous or
that people should be coerced into marrying. The mechanisms of expectation are more subtle. When grandma cluck-clucks over a still-unmarried
young man, or when mom says she wishes her little girl would settle down,
she is expressing a strong and well-justified preference: one that is quietly
echoed in a thousand ways throughout society and that produces subtle but
important pressure to form and sustain unions. This is a good and necessary thing, and it will be as necessary for homosexuals as heterosexuals. If
gay marriage is recognized, single gay people over a certain age should not
be surprised when they are disapproved of or pitied. That is a vital part of
what makes marriage work. It's stigma as social policy.

If marriage is to work it cannot be merely a "lifestyle option." It must be 37
privileged. That is, it must be understood to be better, on average, than
other ways of living. Not mandatory, not good where everything else is bad,
but better: a general norm, rather than a personal taste. The biggest worry
about gay marriage, I think, is that homosexuals might get it but then
mostly not use it. Gay neglect of marriage wouldn't greatly erode the bonding power of heterosexual marriage (remember, homosexuals are only a
tiny fraction of the population) — but it would certainly not help. And heterosexual society would rightly feel betrayed if, after legalization, homosexuals treated marriage as a minority taste rather than as a core institution of
life. It is not enough, I think, for gay people to say we want the right to
marry. If we do not use it, shame on us.

Analyzing This Selection

1. In paragraphs 1 to 6 Rauch assesses traditional social meanings of marriage. Does he value what marriage means to you? Is he accurate about what marriage currently means to society?

2. **THE WRITER'S METHOD**　By acknowledging at least two major arguments against gay marriage, does Rauch strengthen or weaken his position favoring change? Which parts of the opposing arguments does he easily refute, and which points of the opposition remain persuasive to you?

3. Rauch adds two new validations for marriage. Are both reasons compelling? That is, do they motivate marriage?

4. What new social pressures would encourage gays and lesbians to marry? How and by whom do you think these pressures would be exercised?

Analyzing Connections

5. Rauch and Whitehead (see "Women and the Future of Fatherhood," p. 101) see a function marriage performs especially for men. Whose recommendations better serve that function?

Analyzing by Writing

6. Rauch examines the social meaning of marriage. Its meaning probably changes in different phases of life and probably differs for men and for women. Noting these fluctuations from a social norm, examine the meaning of marriage that is evident in television situation comedies.

Raymond Carver

WHAT WE TALK ABOUT
WHEN WE TALK ABOUT LOVE

See the earlier headnote about Raymond Carver on page 67. This selection is the title story of his volume *What We Talk About When We Talk About Love* (1981). The story is a contemporary symposium (Plato's *Symposium*, an after-dinner conversation about love, seems to loom in the background) in which four people half-drunkenly discuss the peculiarities of loves they have known and witnessed.

My friend Mel McGinnis was talking. Mel McGinnis is a cardiologist, 1 and sometimes that gives him the right.

The four of us were sitting around his kitchen table drinking gin. Sun- 2 light filled the kitchen from the big windows behind the sink. There were Mel and me and his second wife, Teresa — Terri, we called her — and my wife, Laura. We lived in Albuquerque then. But we were all from somewhere else.

There was an ice bucket on the table. The gin and the tonic water kept 3 going around, and we somehow got on the subject of love. Mel thought real love was nothing less than spiritual love. He said he'd spent five years in a seminary before quitting to go to medical school. He said he still looked back on those years in the seminary as the most important years in his life.

Terri said the man she lived with before she lived with Mel loved her so 4 much he tried to kill her. Then Terri said, "He beat me up one night. He dragged me around the living room by my ankles. He kept saying, 'I love you, I love you, you bitch.' He went on dragging me around the living room. My head kept knocking on things." Terri looked around the table. "What do you do with love like that?"

She was a bone-thin woman with a pretty face, dark eyes, and brown 5 hair that hung down her back. She liked necklaces made of turquoise, and long pendant earrings.

"My God, don't be silly. That's not love, and you know it," Mel said. "I 6 don't know what you'd call it, but I sure know you wouldn't call it love."

"Say what you want to, but I know it was," Terri said. "It may sound 7 crazy to you, but it's true just the same. People are different, Mel. Sure, sometimes he may have acted crazy. Okay. But he loved me. In his own way maybe, but he loved me. There was love there, Mel. Don't say there wasn't."

Mel let out his breath. He held his glass and turned to Laura and me. "The man threatened to kill me," Mel said. He finished his drink and reached for the gin bottle. "Terri's a romantic. Terri's of the kick-me-so-I'll-know-you-love-me school. Terri, hon, don't look that way." Mel reached across the table and touched Terri's cheek with his fingers. He grinned at her.

"Now he wants to make up," Terri said.

"Make up what?" Mel said. "What is there to make up? I know what I know. That's all."

"How'd we get started on this subject, anyway?" Terri said. She raised her glass and drank from it. "Mel always has love on his mind," she said. "Don't you, honey?" She smiled, and I thought that was the last of it.

"I just wouldn't call Ed's behavior love. That's all I'm saying, honey," Mel said. "What about you guys?" Mel said to Laura and me. "Does that sound like love to you?"

"I'm the wrong person to ask," I said. "I didn't even know the man. I've only heard his name mentioned in passing. I wouldn't know. You'd have to know the particulars. But I think what you're saying is that love is an absolute."

Mel said, "The kind of love I'm talking about is. The kind of love I'm talking about, you don't try to kill people."

Laura said, "I don't know anything about Ed, or anything about the situation. But who can judge anyone else's situation?"

I touched the back of Laura's hand. She gave me a quick smile. I picked up Laura's hand. It was warm, the nails polished, perfectly manicured. I encircled the broad wrist with my fingers, and I held her.

"When I left, he drank rat poison," Terri said. She clasped her arms with her hands. "They took him to the hospital in Santa Fe. That's where we lived then, about ten miles out. They saved his life. But his gums went crazy from it. I mean they pulled away from his teeth. After that, his teeth stood out like fangs. My God," Terri said. She waited a minute, then let go of her arms and picked up her glass.

"What people won't do!" Laura said.

"He's out of the action now," Mel said. "He's dead."

Mel handed me the saucer of limes. I took a section, squeezed it over my drink, and stirred the ice cubes with my finger.

"It gets worse," Terri said. "He shot himself in the mouth. But he bungled that too. Poor Ed," she said. Terri shook her head.

"Poor Ed nothing," Mel said. "He was dangerous."

Mel was forty-five years old. He was tall and rangy with curly soft hair. His face and arms were brown from the tennis he played. When he was sober, his gestures, all his movements, were precise, very careful.

"He did love me though, Mel. Grant me that," Terri said. "That's all I'm   24
asking. He didn't love me the way you love me. I'm not saying that. But he
loved me. You can grant me that, can't you?"

"What do you mean, he bungled it?" I said.   25

Laura leaned forward with her glass. She put her elbows on the table   26
and held her glass in both hands. She glanced from Mel to Terri and
waited with a look of bewilderment on her open face, as if amazed that
such things happened to people you were friendly with.

"How'd he bungle it when he killed himself?" I said.   27

"I'll tell you what happened," Mel said. "He took his twenty-two pistol   28
he'd bought to threaten Terri and me with. Oh, I'm serious, the man was
always threatening. You should have seen the way we lived in those days.
Like fugitives. I even bought a gun myself. Can you believe it? A guy like
me? But I did. I bought one for self-defense and carried it in the glove
compartment. Sometimes I'd have to leave the apartment in the middle of
the night. To go to the hospital, you know? Terri and I weren't married
then, and my first wife had the house and kids, the dog, everything, and
Terri and I were living in this apartment here. Sometimes, as I say, I'd get
a call in the middle of the night and have to go into the hospital at two or
three in the morning. It'd be dark out there in the parking lot, and I'd break
into a sweat before I could even get to my car. I never knew if he was going
to come up out of the shrubbery or from behind a car and start shooting. I
mean, the man was crazy. He was capable of wiring a bomb, anything. He
used to call my service at all hours and say he needed to talk to the doctor,
and when I'd return the call, he'd say, 'Son of a bitch, your days are numbered.' Little things like that. It was scary, I'm telling you."

"I still feel sorry for him," Terri said.   29

"It sounds like a nightmare," Laura said. "But what exactly happened   30
after he shot himself?"

Laura is a legal secretary. We'd met in a professional capacity. Before we   31
knew it, it was a courtship. She's thirty-five, three years younger than I am.
In addition to being in love, we like each other and enjoy one another's
company. She's easy to be with.

"What happened?" Laura said.   32

Mel said, "He shot himself in the mouth in his room. Someone heard   33
the shot and told the manager. They came in with a passkey, saw what had
happened, and called an ambulance. I happened to be there when they
brought him in, alive but past recall. The man lived for three days. His
head swelled up to twice the size of a normal head. I'd never seen anything
like it, and I hope I never do again. Terri wanted to go in and sit with him
when she found out about it. We had a fight over it. I didn't think she
should see him like that. I didn't think she should see him, and I still
don't."

"Who won the fight?" Laura said.   34

"I was in the room with him when he died," Terri said. "He never came 35
up out of it. But I sat with him. He didn't have anyone else."

"He was dangerous," Mel said. "If you call that love, you can have it." 36

"It was love," Terri said. "Sure, it's abnormal in most people's eyes. But 37
he was willing to die for it. He did die for it."

"I sure as hell wouldn't call it love," Mel said. "I mean, no one knows 38
what he did it for. I've seen a lot of suicides, and I couldn't say anyone ever
knew what they did it for."

Mel put his hands behind his neck and tilted his chair back. "I'm not 39
interested in that kind of love," he said. "If that's love, you can have it."

Terri said, "We were afraid. Mel even made a will out and wrote to his 40
brother in California who used to be a Green Beret. Mel told him who to
look for if something happened to him."

Terri drank from her glass. She said, "But Mel's right — we lived like 41
fugitives. We were afraid. Mel was, weren't you, honey? I even called the
police at one point, but they were no help. They said they couldn't do anything until Ed actually did something. Isn't that a laugh?" Terri said.

She poured the last of the gin into her glass and waggled the bottle. Mel 42
got up from the table and went to the cupboard. He took down another
bottle.

"Well, Nick and I know what love is," Laura said. "For us, I mean," 43
Laura said. She bumped my knee with her knee. "You're supposed to say
something now," Laura said, and turned her smile on me.

For an answer, I took Laura's hand and raised it to my lips. I made a big 44
production out of kissing her hand. Everyone was amused.

"We're lucky," I said. 45

"You guys," Terri said. "Stop that now. You're making me sick. You're 46
still on the honeymoon, for God's sake. You're still gaga, for crying out
loud. Just wait. How long have you been together now? How long has it
been? A year? Longer than a year?"

"Going on a year and a half," Laura said, flushed and smiling. 47

"Oh, now," Terri said. "Wait awhile." 48

She held her drink and gazed at Laura. 49

"I'm only kidding," Terri said. 50

Mel opened the gin and went around the table with the bottle. 51

"Here, you guys," he said. "Let's have a toast. I want to propose a toast. 52
A toast to love. To true love," Mel said.

We touched glasses. 53

"To love," we said. 54

Outside in the backyard, one of the dogs began to bark. The leaves of 55
the aspen that leaned past the window ticked against the glass. The afternoon sun was like a presence in this room, the spacious light of ease and
generosity. We could have been anywhere, somewhere enchanted. We raised

our glasses again and grinned at each other like children who had agreed on something forbidden.

"I'll tell you what real love is," Mel said. "I mean, I'll give you a good example. And then you can draw your own conclusions." He poured more gin into his glass. He added an ice cube and a sliver of lime. We waited and sipped our drinks. Laura and I touched knees again. I put a hand on her warm thigh and left it there.   56

"What do any of us really know about love?" Mel said. "It seems to me we're just beginners at love. We say we love each other and we do, I don't doubt it. I love Terri and Terri loves me, and you guys love each other too. You know the kind of love I'm talking about now. Physical love, that impulse that drives you to someone special, as well as love of the other person's being, his or her essence, as it were. Carnal love and, well, call it sentimental love, the day-to-day caring about the other person. But sometimes I have a hard time accounting for the fact that I must have loved my first wife too. But I did, I know I did. So I suppose I am like Terri in that regard. Terri and Ed." He thought about it and then he went on. "There was a time when I thought I loved my first wife more than life itself. But now I hate her guts. I do. How do you explain that? What happened to that love? What happened to it, is what I'd like to know. I wish someone could tell me. Then there's Ed. Okay, we're back to Ed. He loves Terri so much he tries to kill her and he winds up killing himself." Mel stopped talking and swallowed from his glass. "You guys have been together eighteen months and you love each other. It shows all over you. You glow with it. But you both loved other people before you met each other. You've both been married before, just like us. And you probably loved other people before that too, even. Terri and I have been together five years, been married for four. And the terrible thing, the terrible thing is, but the good thing too, the saving grace, you might say, is that if something happened to one of us — excuse me for saying this — but if something happened to one of us tomorrow, I think the other one, the other person, would grieve for a while, you know, but then the surviving party would go out and love again, have someone else soon enough. All this, all of this love we're talking about, it would just be a memory. Maybe not even a memory. Am I wrong? Am I way off base? Because I want you to set me straight if you think I'm wrong. I want to know. I mean, I don't know anything, and I'm the first one to admit it."   57

"Mel, for God's sake," Terri said. She reached out and took hold of his wrist. "Are you getting drunk? Honey? Are you drunk?"   58

"Honey, I'm just talking," Mel said. "All right? I don't have to be drunk to say what I think. I mean, we're all just talking, right?" Mel said. He fixed his eyes on her.   59

"Sweetie, I'm not criticizing," Terri said.   60

She picked up her glass.   61

"I'm not on call today," Mel said. "Let me remind you of that. I am not on call," he said.   62

"Mel, we love you," Laura said.   63

Mel looked at Laura. He looked at her as if he could not place her, as if   64
she was not the woman she was.

"Love you too, Laura," Mel said. "And you, Nick, love you too. You   65
know something?" Mel said. "You guys are our pals," Mel said.

He picked up his glass.   66

Mel said, "I was going to tell you about something. I mean, I was going   67
to prove a point. You see, this happened a few months ago, but it's still
going on right now, and it ought to make us feel ashamed when we talk
like we know what we're talking about when we talk about love."

"Come on now," Terri said. "Don't talk like you're drunk if you're not   68
drunk."

"Just shut up for once in your life," Mel said very quietly. "Will you do me   69
a favor and do that for a minute? So as I was saying, there's this old couple
who had this car wreck out on the interstate. A kid hit them and they were
all torn to shit and nobody was giving them much chance to pull through."

Terri looked at us and then back at Mel. She seemed anxious, or maybe   70
that's too strong a word.

Mel was handing the bottle around the table.   71

"I was on call that night," Mel said. "It was May or maybe it was June.   72
Terri and I had just sat down to dinner when the hospital called. There'd
been this thing out on the interstate. Drunk kid, teenager, plowed his dad's
pickup into this camper with this old couple in it. They were up in their
mid-seventies, that couple. The kid — eighteen, nineteen, something — he
was DOA. Taken the steering wheel through his sternum. The old couple,
they were alive, you understand. I mean, just barely. But they had everything. Multiple fractures, internal injuries, hemorrhaging, contusions, lacerations, the works, and they each of them had themselves concussions.
They were in a bad way, believe me. And, of course, their age was two
strikes against them. I'd say she was worse off than he was. Ruptured spleen
along with everything else. Both kneecaps broken. But they'd been wearing
their seatbelts and, God knows, that's what saved them for the time being."

"Folks, this is an advertisement for the National Safety Council," Terri   73
said. "This is your spokesman, Dr. Melvin R. McGinnis, talking." Terri
laughed. "Mel," she said, "sometimes you're just too much. But I love you,
hon," she said.

"Honey, I love you," Mel said.   74

He leaned across the table. Terri met him halfway. They kissed.   75

"Terri's right," Mel said as he settled himself again. "Get those seatbelts   76
on. But seriously, they were in some shape, those oldsters. By the time I got
down there, the kid was dead, as I said. He was off in a corner, laid out on
a gurney. I took one look at the old couple and told the ER nurse to get me
a neurologist and an orthopedic man and a couple of surgeons down there
right away."

He drank from his glass. "I'll try to keep this short," he said. "So we took   77
the two of them up to the OR and worked like fuck on them most of the
night. They had these incredible reserves, those two. You see that once in
a while. So we did everything that could be done, and toward morning
we're giving them a fifty-fifty chance, maybe less than that for her. So here
they are, still alive the next morning. So, okay, we move them into the
ICU, which is where they both kept plugging away at it for two weeks, hitting it better and better on all the scopes. So we transfer them out to their
own room."

Mel stopped talking. "Here," he said, "let's drink this cheapo gin the hell   78
up. Then we're going to dinner, right? Terri and I know a new place. That's
where we'll go, to this new place we know about. But we're not going until
we finish up this cut-rate, lousy gin."

Terri said, "We haven't actually eaten there yet. But it looks good. From   79
the outside, you know."

"I like food," Mel said. "If I had it to do all over again, I'd be a chef, you   80
know? Right? Terri?" Mel said.

He laughed. He fingered the ice in his glass.   81

"Terri knows," he said. "Terri can tell you. But let me say this. If I could   82
come back again in a different life, a different time and all, you know
what? I'd like to come back as a knight. You were pretty safe wearing all
that armor. It was all right being a knight until gunpowder and muskets and
pistols came along."

"Mel would like to ride a horse and carry a lance," Terri said.   83

"Carry a woman's scarf with you everywhere," Laura said.   84

"Or just a woman," Mel said.   85

"Shame on you," Laura said.   86

Terri said, "Suppose you came back as a serf. The serfs didn't have it so   87
good in those days," Terri said.

"The serfs never had it good," Mel said. "But I guess even the knights   88
were vessels to someone. Isn't that the way it worked? But then everyone is
always a vessel to someone. Isn't that right? Terri? But what I liked about
knights, besides their ladies, was that they had that suit of armor, you know,
and they couldn't get hurt very easy. No cars in those days, you know? No
drunk teenagers to tear into your ass."

"Vassals," Terri said.   89

"What?" Mel said.   90

"Vassals," Terri said. "They were called vassals, not vessels."   91

"Vassals, vessels," Mel said, "what the fuck's the difference? You knew   92
what I meant anyway. All right," Mel said. "So I'm not educated. I learned
my stuff. I'm a heart surgeon, sure, but I'm just a mechanic. I go in and
fuck around and fix things. Shit," Mel said.

"Modesty doesn't become you," Terri said.   93

"He's just a humble sawbones," I said. "But sometimes they suffocated in   94 all that armor, Mel. They'd even have heart attacks if it got too hot and they were too tired and worn out. I read somewhere that they'd fall off their horses and not be able to get up because they were too tired to stand with all that armor on them. They got trampled by their own horses sometimes."

"That's terrible," Mel said. "That's a terrible thing, Nicky. I guess they'd 95 just lay there and wait until somebody came along and made a shish kebab out of them."

"Some other vessel," Terri said. 96

"That's right," Mel said. "Some vassal would come along and spear the 97 bastard in the name of love. Or whatever the fuck it was they fought over in those days."

"Same things we fight over these days," Terri said. 98

Laura said, "Nothing's changed." 99

The color was still high in Laura's cheeks. Her eyes were bright. She 100 brought her glass to her lips.

Mel poured himself another drink. He looked at the label closely as if 101 studying a long row of numbers. Then he slowly put the bottle down on the table and slowly reached for the tonic water.

"What about the old couple?" Laura said. "You didn't finish that story 102 you started."

Laura was having a hard time lighting her cigarette. Her matches kept 103 going out.

The sunshine inside the room was different now, changing, getting thin- 104 ner. But the leaves outside the window were still shimmering, and I stared at the pattern they made on the panes and on the Formica counter. They weren't the same patterns, of course.

"What about the old couple?" I said. 105

"Older but wiser," Terri said. 106

Mel stared at her. 107

Terri said, "Go on with your story, hon. I was only kidding. Then what 108 happened?"

"Terri, sometimes," Mel said. 109

"Please, Mel," Terri said. "Don't always be so serious, sweetie. Can't you 110 take a joke?"

"Where's the joke?" Mel said. 111

He held his glass and gazed steadily at his wife. 112

"What happened?" Laura said. 113

Mel fastened his eyes on Laura. He said, "Laura, if I didn't have Terri 114 and if I didn't love her so much, and if Nick wasn't my best friend, I'd fall in love with you. I'd carry you off, honey," he said.

"Tell your story," Terri said. "Then we'll go to that new place, okay?" 115

"Okay?" Mel said. "Where was I?" he said. He stared at the table and 116 then he began again.

"I dropped in to see each of them every day, sometimes twice a day if I 117 was up doing other calls anyway. Casts and bandages, head to foot, the both of them. You know, you've seen it in the movies. That's just the way they looked, just like in the movies. Little eye-holes and nose-holes and mouth-holes. And she had to have her legs slung up on top of it. Well, the husband was very depressed for the longest while. Even after he found out that his wife was going to pull through, he was still very depressed. Not about the accident, though. I mean, the accident was one thing, but it wasn't everything. I'd get up to his mouth-hole, you know, and he'd say no, it wasn't the accident exactly but it was because he couldn't see her through his eye-holes. He said that was what was making him feel so bad. Can you imagine? I'm telling you, the man's heart was breaking because he couldn't turn his goddamn head and *see* his goddamn wife."

Mel looked around the table and shook his head at what he was going to say.   118

"I mean, it was killing the old fart just because he couldn't *look* at the fucking woman."   119

We all looked at Mel.   120

"Do you see what I'm saying?" he said.   121

Maybe we were a little drunk by then. I know it was hard keeping things in focus. The light was draining out of the room, going back through the window where it had come from. Yet nobody made a move to get up from the table to turn on the overhead light.   122

"Listen," Mel said. "Let's finish this fucking gin. There's about enough left here for one shooter all around. Then let's go eat. Let's go to the new place."   123

"He's depressed," Terri said. "Mel, why don't you take a pill?"   124

Mel shook his head. "I've taken everything there is."   125

"We all need a pill now and then," I said.   126

"Some people are born needing them," Terri said.   127

She was using her finger to rub at something on the table. Then she stopped rubbing.   128

"I think I want to call my kids," Mel said. "Is that all right with everybody? I'll call my kids," he said.   129

Terri said, "What if Marjorie answers the phone? You guys, you've heard us on the subject of Marjorie? Honey, you know you don't want to talk to Marjorie. It'll make you feel even worse."   130

"I don't want to talk to Marjorie," Mel said. "But I want to talk to my kids."   131

"There isn't a day goes by that Mel doesn't say he wishes she'd get married again. Or else die," Terri said. "For one thing," Terri said, "She's bankrupting us. Mel says it's just to spite him that she won't get married again. She has a boyfriend who lives with her and the kids, so Mel is supporting the boyfriend too."   132

"She's allergic to bees," Mel said. "If I'm not praying she'll get married   133 again, I'm praying she'll get herself stung to death by a swarm of fucking bees."

"Shame on you," Laura said.   134

"Bzzzzzzz," Mel said, turning his fingers into bees and buzzing them at   135
Terri's throat. Then he let his hands drop all the way to his sides.

"She's vicious," Mel said. "Sometimes I think I'll go up there dressed   136
like a beekeeper. You know, that hat that's like a helmet with the plate that
comes down over your face, the big gloves, and the padded coat? I'll knock
on the door and let a loose hive of bees in the house. But first I'd make
sure the kids were out, of course."

He crossed one leg over the other. It seemed to take him a lot of time to   137
do it. Then he put both feet on the floor and leaned forward, elbows on the
table, his chin cupped in his hands.

"Maybe I won't call the kids, after all. Maybe it isn't such a hot idea.   138
Maybe we'll just go eat. How does that sound?"

"Sounds fine to me," I said. "Eat or not eat. Or keep drinking. I could   139
head right on out into the sunset."

"What does that mean, honey?" Laura said.   140

"It just means what I said," I said. "It means I could just keep going.   141
That's all it means."

"I could eat something myself," Laura said. "I don't think I've ever been   142
so hungry in my life. Is there something to nibble on?"

"I'll put out some cheese and crackers," Terri said.   143

But Terri just sat there. She did not get up to get anything.   144

Mel turned his glass over. He spilled it out on the table.   145

"Gin's gone," Mel said.   146

Terri said, "Now what?"   147

I could hear my heart beating. I could hear everyone's heart. I could   148
hear the human noise we sat there making, not one of us moving, not even
when the room went dark.

Analyzing This Selection

1. **THE WRITER'S METHOD**   Think of three adjectives that together summarize Mel's character in the first half of the story. Would you change the
   adjectives to fit his character at the end of the story?

2. At what times and how do the characters express their love for their partners
   and for their friends during the conversation? What motives or satisfactions
   enter into their expressions of love? Examine the details closely.

3. What aspect of love is especially troubling to Mel? What bearing does it
   have on his earlier intention to become a priest and his present vocation as
   a cardiologist?

4. Why does Mel's language become more vulgar as he tells his story about the
   old people? What is agitating him?

5. What do Nick and Laura find disturbing about Mel's story? How do we know?

6. Mel divides love into "carnal" and "sentimental." Does his example of true love fit either category? How would you define it?

Analyzing Connections

7. Add another participant to this conversation around the kitchen table: If Simone de Beauvoir contributed her viewpoint in the Insights on page 114, how would the other characters respond?

Analyzing by Writing

8. Our commonly used expressions about love indicate that love is not just an emotion: it is also a whole set of ideas and beliefs about that emotion. Is love something to "work on"? Is it something to "share"? Is it "communication"? or a "commitment"? Is it a "feeling"? or a "trip"? Consider the assumptions and implications surrounding the concept of love that is current among a group of people you know. Examine the specific words, gestures, and reactions that indicate their assumed view of love.

PART 4

GROUP PICTURES

INSIGHTS

No man is an island, entire of itself; every man is a piece of the continent, a part of the main; if a clod be washed away by the sea, Europe is less, as well as if a promontory were, as well as if a manor of thy friends or of thine own were; any man's death diminishes me, because I am involved in mankind; and therefore never send to know for whom the bell tolls: it tolls for thee.

— JOHN DONNE

Hell is other people.

— JEAN-PAUL SARTRE

Society everywhere is in conspiracy against the manhood of every one of its members. Society is a joint-stock company, in which the members agree, for the better securing of his bread to each shareholder, to surrender the liberty and culture of the eater. The virtue in most request is conformity. Self-reliance is its aversion. It loves not realities and creators, but names and customs. Whoso would be a man must be a nonconformist.

— RALPH WALDO EMERSON

Being ashamed of one's parents is, psychologically, not identical with being ashamed of one's people. I believe every one of us will, if he but digs deeply enough into the realm of unconscious memories, remember having been ashamed of his parents. Being ashamed of our people must have another psychological meaning. It must be the expression of a tendency to disavow the most essential part of ourself. To be ashamed of being Jewish means not only to be a coward and insincere in disavowing the proud inheritance of an old people who have made an eternal contribution to the civilization of mankind. It also means to disavow the best and the most pre-

172

cious part we get from our parents, their parents, and their ancestors, who continue to live in us. It means, furthermore, to renounce oneself. When the Jewish proverb proclaims that he who is ashamed of his family will have no luck in life, it must mean just that: he cannot have that self-confidence which makes life worth living. Strange that the folklore of an oriental people coincides here with the viewpoint of Goethe; any life can be lived if one does not miss oneself, if one but remains oneself.

The thought that my children are sometimes ashamed of the human faults and failings of their father does not sadden me; but, for their own sake, I wish that they will never be ashamed that their father was Jewish. The one feeling concerns only the personal shortcomings of an individual who was striving, sometimes succeeding and often failing. The other shame concerns something superpersonal, something beyond the narrow realm of the individual. It concerns the community of fate, it touches the bond that ties one generation to those preceding it and those following it.

— THEODOR REIK

It is difficult to let others see the full psychological meaning of caste segregation. It is as though one, looking out from a dark cave in a side of an impending mountain, sees the world passing and speaks to it; speaks courteously and persuasively, showing them how these entombed souls are hindered in their natural movement, expression, and development; and how their loosening from prison would be a matter not simply of courtesy, sympathy, and help to them, but aid to all the world. One talks on evenly and logically in this way, but notices that the passing throng does not even turn its head, or if it does, glances curiously and walks on. It gradually penetrates the minds of the prisoners that the people passing do not hear; that some thick sheet of invisible but horribly tangible plate glass is between them and the world. They get excited; they talk louder; they gesticulate. Some of the passing world stop in curiosity; these gesticulations seem so pointless; they laugh and pass on. They still either do not hear at all, or hear but dimly, and even what they hear, they do not understand. Then the people within may become hysterical. They may scream and hurl themselves against the barriers, hardly realizing in their bewilderment that they are screaming in a vacuum unheard and that their antics may actually seem funny to those outside looking in. They may even, here and there, break through in blood and disfigurement, and find themselves faced by a horrified, implacable, and quite overwhelming mob of people frightened for their own very existence.

— W. E. B. DU BOIS

The New Colossus

Not like the brazen giant of Greek fame,
With conquering limbs astride from land to land;
Here at our sea-washed, sunset gates shall stand
A mighty woman with a torch, whose flame
Is the imprisoned lightning, and her name
Mother of Exiles. From her beacon-hand
Glows world-wide welcome; her mild eyes command
The air-bridged harbor that twin cities frame.
"Keep, ancient lands, your storied pomp!" cries she
With silent lips. "Give me your tired, your poor,
Your huddled masses yearning to breathe free,
The wretched refuse of your teeming shore.
Send these, the homeless, tempest-tost to me,
I lift my lamp beside the golden door!"

         — EMMA LAZARUS

The brotherhood of man is not a mere poet's dream; it is a most depressing and humiliating reality.

         — OSCAR WILDE

Among aristocratic nations families maintain the same station for centuries and often live in the same place. So there is a sense in which all the generations are contemporaneous. A man almost always knows about his ancestors and respects them; his imagination extends to his great-grandchildren, and he loves them. He freely does his duty by both ancestors and descendants and often sacrifices personal pleasures for the sake of beings who are no longer alive or are not yet born.

Moreover, aristocratic institutions have the effect of linking each man closely with several of his fellows.

Each class is an aristocratic society, being clearly and permanently limited, forms, in a sense, a little fatherland for all its members, to which they are attached by more obvious and more precious ties than those linking them to the fatherland itself.

Each citizen of an aristocratic society has his fixed station, one above another, so that there is always someone above him whose protection he needs and someone below him whose help he may require.

So people living in an aristocratic age are almost always closely involved with something outside themselves, and they are often inclined to forget about themselves. It is true that in these ages the general conception of *human fellowship* is dim and that men hardly ever think of devoting themselves to the cause of humanity, but men do often make sacrifices for the sake of certain other men.

In democratic ages, on the contrary, the duties of each to all are much clearer but devoted service to any individual much rarer. The bonds of human affection are wider but more relaxed.

Among democratic peoples new families continually rise from nothing while others fall, and nobody's position is quite stable. The woof of time is ever being broken and the track of past generations lost. Those who have gone before are easily forgotten, and no one gives a thought to those who will follow. All a man's interests are limited to those near himself.

As each class catches up with the next and gets mixed with it, its members do not care about one another and treat one another as strangers. Aristocracy links everybody, from peasant to king, in one long chain. Democracy breaks the chain and frees each link.

As social equality spreads there are more and more people who, though neither rich nor powerful enough to have much hold over others, have gained or kept enough wealth and enough understanding to look after their own needs. Such folk owe no man anything and hardly expect anything from anybody. They form the habit of thinking of themselves in isolation and imagine that their whole destiny is in their own hands.

Thus, not only does democracy make men forget their ancestors, but also clouds their view of their descendants and isolates them from their contemporaries. Each man is forever thrown back on himself alone, and there is danger that he may be shut up in the solitude of his own heart.

— ALEXIS DE TOCQUEVILLE

The "natural" approach to human relations presumes to know any person well enough is to love him, that the only human problem is a communication problem. This denies that people might be separated by basic, genuinely irreconcilable differences — philosophical, political, or religious — and assumes that all such differences are no more than misunderstandings.

Many forms of etiquette are employed precisely to disguise those antipathies that arise from irreconcilable differences, in order to prevent mayhem. The reason that diplomacy, for example, is so stilted is that its purpose is to head off the most natural social relation between countries in conflict, namely war.

The idea that people can behave "naturally" without resorting to an artificial code tacitly agreed upon by their society is as silly as the idea that they can communicate by using a language without commonly accepted semantic and grammatical rules. Like language, a code of manners can be used with more or less skill, for laudable or evil purposes, to express a great variety of ideas and emotions. Like language, manners continually undergo slow changes and adaptations, but these changes have to be global, not atomic. For if everyone improvises his own manners, no one will understand the meaning of anyone else's behavior, and the result will be social chaos and the end of civilization, or about what we have now.

– JUDITH MARTIN ("Miss Manners")

FOCUSING BY WRITING

1. If you had to choose among the natural dwelling places of animals, what fantasy home would be suitable for you? You might prefer to live in a robin's nest, a beaver lodge, a rabbit warren, a bear's cave, an ant colony, a beehive, an eagle's aerie, a wasp's nest, a fox's lair, a lion's den. (Do not pick manmade places such as a doghouse or fishbowl.) Describe some concrete details of your primal dwelling place. Why would it feel good to live there?

2. You must know someone you could call a "total jerk" — that is, someone who never knows the right way to act. Explain the code of behavior that this person does not follow. Do not just relate an anecdote that ridicules someone. Focus on explaining the accepted standard of behavior that this person consistently violates.

3. What particular place has made you aware of your entire country? It might be a historical site, a busy city street, or a wilderness area, a schoolyard, a game, a mall, or any place that at a specific moment epitomized America — for better or worse. Describe the place, giving the concrete details that affected you with their national symbolism.

4. As a tourist in a foreign country, as a visitor to a large city, or as a pre-freshman interviewee on a college campus, were you self-conscious about being an outsider? Were you embarrassed to be seen as distinguishable from the local people? What kind of exposure did you wish to cover up? Conversely, what did you try to emphasize or exaggerate about yourself?

Maya Angelou

GRADUATION

MAYA ANGELOU (b. 1928) was raised by her grandmother, who ran a small store for African Americans in the town of Stamps, Arkansas. She survived a childhood that seemed certain to defeat her, and as she once told an interviewer: "One would say of my life — born loser — had to be; from a broken family, raped at eight, unwed mother at sixteen." During her adult life, she became a dancer, an actress, a poet, a television writer and producer, and a coordinator in Martin Luther King, Jr.'s Southern Christian Leadership Conference. She is most widely known for her autobiographical books, beginning with *I Know Why the Caged Bird Sings* (1970), from which this selection is taken. Her most recent memoir is *Even the Stars Look Lonesome* (1997). Angelou's latest collection of essays is *Wouldn't Take Nothing for My Journey Now* (1993).

The children in Stamps trembled visibly with anticipation. Some adults 1
were excited too, but to be certain the whole young population had come
down with graduation epidemic. Large classes were graduating from both
the grammar school and the high school. Even those who were years removed from their own day of glorious release were anxious to help with
preparations as a kind of dry run. The junior students who were moving
into the vacating classes' chairs were tradition-bound to show their talents
for leadership and management. They strutted through the school and
around the campus exerting pressure on the lower grades. Their authority
was so new that occasionally if they pressed a little too hard it had to be
overlooked. After all, next term was coming, and it never hurt a sixth grader
to have a play sister in the eighth grade, or a tenth-year student to be able
to call a twelfth grader Bubba. So all was endured in a spirit of shared
understanding. But the graduating classes themselves were the nobility. Like
travelers with exotic destinations on their minds, the graduates were remarkably forgetful. They came to school without their books, or tablets, or even
pencils. Volunteers fell over themselves to secure replacements for the
missing equipment. When accepted, the willing workers might or might
not be thanked, and it was of no importance to the pregraduation rites. Even
teachers were respectful of the now quiet and aging seniors, and tended to
speak to them, if not as equals, as beings only slightly lower than themselves. After tests were returned and grades given, the student body, which

acted like an extended family, knew who did well, who excelled, and what piteous ones had failed.

Unlike the white school, Lafayette County Training School distin-   2
guished itself by having neither lawn, nor hedges, nor tennis court, nor climbing ivy. Its two buildings (main classrooms, the grade school, and home economics) were set on a dirt hill with no fence to limit either its boundaries or those of bordering farms. There was a large expanse to the left of the school which was used alternately as a baseball diamond or a basketball court. Rusty hoops on the swaying poles represented the perma-nent recreational equipment, although bats and balls could be borrowed from the P.E. teacher if the borrower was qualified and if the diamond wasn't occupied.

Over this rocky area relieved by a few shady tall persimmon trees the   3
graduating class walked. The girls often held hands and no longer bothered to speak to the lower students. There was a sadness about them, as if this old world was not their home and they were bound for higher ground. The boys, on the other hand, had become more friendly, more outgoing. A decided change from the closed attitude they projected while studying for finals. Now they seemed not ready to give up the old school, the familiar paths and classrooms. Only a small percentage would be continuing on to college — one of the South's A & M (agricultural and mechanical) schools, which trained Negro youths to be carpenters, farmers, handymen, masons, maids, cooks, and baby nurses. Their future rode heavily on their shoul-ders, and blinded them to the collective joy that had pervaded the lives of the boys and girls in the grammar school graduating class.

Parents who could afford it had ordered new shoes and ready-made   4
clothes for themselves from Sears and Roebuck or Montgomery Ward. They also engaged the best seamstresses to make the floating graduating dresses and to cut down secondhand pants which would be pressed to a military slickness for the important event.

Oh, it was important, all right. Whitefolks would attend the ceremony,   5
and two or three would speak of God and home, and the Southern way of life, and Mrs. Parsons, the principal's wife, would play the graduation march while the lower-grade graduates paraded down the aisles and took their seats below the platform. The high school seniors would wait in empty classrooms to make their dramatic entrance.

In the Store I was the person of the moment. The birthday girl. The   6
center. Bailey[1] had graduated the year before, although to do so he had had to forfeit all pleasures to make up for his time lost in Baton Rouge.

My class was wearing butter-yellow piqué dresses, and Momma launched   7
out on mine. She smocked the yoke into tiny crisscrossing puckers, then shirred the rest of the bodice. Her dark fingers ducked in and out of the

[1]The author's brother. The children help out in their grandmother's store.

lemony cloth as she embroidered raised daisies around the hem. Before she considered herself finished she had added a crocheted cuff on the puff sleeves, and a pointy crocheted collar.

I was going to be lovely. A walking model of all the various styles of fine   8 hand sewing and it didn't worry me that I was only twelve years old and merely graduating from the eighth grade. Besides, many teachers in Arkansas Negro schools had only that diploma and were licensed to impart wisdom.

The days had become longer and more noticeable. The faded beige of   9 former times had been replaced with strong and sure colors. I began to see my classmates' clothes, their skin tones, and the dust that waved off pussy willows. Clouds that lazed across the sky were objects of great concern to me. Their shiftier shapes might have held a message that in my new happiness and with a little bit of time I'd soon decipher. During that period I looked at the arch of heaven so religiously my neck kept a steady ache. I had taken to smiling more often, and my jaws hurt from the unaccustomed activity. Between the two physical sore spots, I suppose I could have been uncomfortable, but that was not the case. As a member of the winning team (the graduating class of 1940) I had outdistanced unpleasant sensations by miles. I was headed for the freedom of open fields.

Youth and social approval allied themselves with me and we trammeled   10 memories of slights and insults. The wind of our swift passage remodeled my features. Lost tears were pounded to mud and then to dust. Years of withdrawal were brushed aside and left behind, as hanging ropes of parasitic moss.

My work alone had awarded me a top place and I was going to be one   11 of the first called in the graduating ceremonies. On the classroom blackboard, as well as on the bulletin board in the auditorium, there were blue stars and white stars and red stars. No absences, no tardinesses, and my academic work was among the best of the year. I could say the preamble to the Constitution even faster than Bailey. We timed ourselves often: "Wethe-peopleoftheUnitedStatesinordertoformamoreperfectunion . . ." I had memorized the Presidents of the United States from Washington to Roosevelt in chronological as well as alphabetical order.

My hair pleased me too. Gradually the black mass had lengthened and   12 thickened, so that it kept at last to its braided pattern, and I didn't have to yank my scalp off when I tried to comb it.

Louise and I had rehearsed the exercises until we tired out ourselves.   13 Henry Reed was class valedictorian. He was a small, very black boy with hooded eyes, a long, broad nose, and an oddly shaped head. I had admired him for years because each term he and I vied for the best grades in our class. Most often he bested me, but instead of being disappointed I was pleased that we shared top places between us. Like many Southern Black children, he lived with his grandmother, who was as strict as Momma and as kind as she knew how to be. He was courteous, respectful, and soft-spoken to elders, but on the playground he chose to play the roughest games. I admired him. Anyone, I reckoned, sufficiently afraid or sufficiently dull could be polite. But to be able to operate at a top level with both adults and children was admirable.

His valedictory speech was entitled "To Be or Not to Be." The rigid 14 tenth-grade teacher had helped him to write it. He'd been working on the dramatic stresses for months.

The weeks until graduation were filled with heady activities. A group of 15 small children were to be presented in a play about buttercups and daisies and bunny rabbits. They could be heard throughout the building practicing their hops and their little songs that sounded like silver bells. The older girls (nongraduates, of course) were assigned the task of making refreshments for the night's festivities. A tangy scent of ginger, cinnamon, nutmeg, and chocolate wafted around the home economics building as the budding cooks made samples for themselves and their teachers.

In every corner of the workshop, axes and saws split fresh timber as the 16 woodshop boys made sets and stage scenery. Only the graduates were left out of the general bustle. We were free to sit in the library at the back of the building or look in quite detachedly, naturally, on the measures being taken for our event.

Even the minister preached on graduation the Sunday before. His sub- 17 ject was, "Let your light so shine that men will see your good works and praise your Father, Who is in Heaven." Although the sermon was purported to be addressed to us, he used the occasion to speak to backsliders, gamblers, and general ne'er-do-wells. But since he had called our names at the beginning of the service we were mollified.

Among Negroes the tradition was to give presents to children going only 18 from one grade to another. How much more important this was when the person was graduating at the top of the class. Uncle Willie and Momma had sent away for a Mickey Mouse watch like Bailey's. Louise gave me four embroidered handkerchiefs. (I gave her three crocheted doilies.) Mrs. Sneed, the minister's wife, made me an underskirt to wear for graduation, and nearly every customer gave me a nickel or maybe even a dime with the instruction "Keep on moving to higher ground," or some such encouragement.

Amazingly the great day finally dawned and I was out of bed before I 19 knew it. I threw open the back door to see it more clearly, but Momma said, "Sister, come away from that door and put your robe on."

I hoped the memory of that morning would never leave me. Sunlight 20 was itself still young, and the day had none of the insistence maturity would bring it in a few hours. In my robe and barefoot in the backyard, under cover of going to see about my new beans, I gave myself up to the gentle warmth and thanked God that no matter what evil I had done in my life He had allowed me to live to see this day. Somewhere in my fatalism I had expected to die, accidentally, and never have the chance to walk up the stairs in the auditorium and gracefully receive my hard-earned diploma. Out of God's merciful bosom I had won reprieve.

Bailey came out in his robe and gave me a box wrapped in Christmas   21
paper. He said he had saved his money for months to pay for it. It felt like
a box of chocolates, but I knew Bailey wouldn't save money to buy candy
when we had all we could want under our noses.

He was as proud of the gift as I. It was a soft-leather-bound copy of a col-   22
lection of poems by Edgar Allan Poe, or, as Bailey and I called him, "Eap."
I turned to "Annabel Lee" and we walked up and down the garden rows,
the cool dirt between our toes, reciting the beautifully sad lines.

Momma made a Sunday breakfast although it was only Friday. After we   23
finished the blessing, I opened my eyes to find the watch on my plate. It
was a dream of a day. Everything went smoothly and to my credit. I didn't
have to be reminded or scolded for anything. Near evening I was too jittery
to attend to chores, so Bailey volunteered to do all before his bath.

Days before, we had made a sign for the Store and as we turned out   24
the lights Momma hung the cardboard over the doorknob. It read clearly:
CLOSED. GRADUATION.

My dress fitted perfectly and everyone said that I looked like a sunbeam   25
in it. On the hill, going toward the school, Bailey walked behind with
Uncle Willie, who muttered, "Go on, Ju." He wanted him to walk ahead
with us because it embarrassed him to have to walk so slowly. Bailey said
he'd let the ladies walk together, and the men would bring up the rear. We
all laughed, nicely.

Little children dashed by out of the dark like fireflies. Their crepepaper   26
dresses and butterfly wings were not made for running and we heard more
than one rip, dryly, and the regretful "uh uh" that followed.

The school blazed without gaiety. The windows seemed cold and un-   27
friendly from the lower hill. A sense of ill-fated timing crept over me, and
if Momma hadn't reached for my hand I would have drifted back to Bailey
and Uncle Willie, and possibly beyond. She made a few slow jokes about
my feet getting cold, and tugged me along to the now-strange building.

Around the front steps, assurance came back. There were my fellow   28
"greats," the graduating class. Hair brushed back, legs oiled, new dresses
and pressed pleats, fresh pocket handkerchiefs and little handbags, all
homesewn. Oh, we were up to snuff, all right. I joined my comrades and
didn't even see my family go in to find seats in the crowded auditorium.

The school band struck up a march and all classes filed in as had been   29
rehearsed. We stood in front of our seats, as assigned, and on a signal from
the choir director, we sat. No sooner had this been accomplished than the
band started to play the national anthem. We rose again and sang the song,
after which we recited the pledge of allegiance. We remained standing for
a brief minute before the choir director and the principal signaled to us,
rather desperately I thought, to take our seats. The command was so unusual
that our carefully rehearsed and smooth-running machine was thrown off.
For a full minute we fumbled for our chairs and bumped into each other
awkwardly. Habits change or solidify under pressure, so in our state of ner-

vous tension we had been ready to follow our usual assembly pattern: the American National Anthem, then the pledge of allegiance, then the song every Black person I knew called the Negro National Anthem. All done in the same key, with the same passion and most often standing on the same foot.

Finding my seat at last, I was overcome with a presentiment of worse 30 things to come. Something unrehearsed, unplanned, was going to happen, and we were going to be made to look bad. I distinctly remember being explicit in the choice of pronoun. It was "we," the graduating class, the unit, that concerned me then.

The principal welcomed "parents and friends" and asked the Baptist 31 minister to lead us in prayer. His invocation was brief and punchy, and for a second I thought we were getting back on the high road to right action. When the principal came back to the dais, however, his voice had changed. Sounds always affected me profoundly and the principal's voice was one of my favorites. During assembly it melted and lowed weakly into the audience. It had not been in my plan to listen to him, but my curiosity was piqued and I straightened up to give him my attention.

He was talking about Booker T. Washington, our "late great leader," 32 who said we can be as close as the fingers on the hand, etc. . . . Then he said a few vague things about friendship and the friendship of kindly people to those less fortunate than themselves. With that his voice nearly faded, thin, away. Like a river diminishing to a stream and then to a trickle. But he cleared his throat and said, "Our speaker tonight, who is also our friend, came from Texarkana to deliver the commencement address, but due to the irregularity of the train schedule, he's going to, as they say, 'speak and run.'" He said that we understood and wanted the man to know that we were most grateful for the time he was able to give us and then something about how we were willing always to adjust to another's program, and without more ado — "I give you Mr. Edward Donleavy."

Not one but two white men came through the door offstage. The shorter 33 one walked to the speaker's platform, and the tall one moved over to the center seat and sat down. But that was our principal's seat, and already occupied. The dislodged gentleman bounced around for a long breath or two before the Baptist minister gave him his chair, then with more dignity than the situation deserved, the minister walked off the stage.

Donleavy looked at the audience once (on reflection, I'm sure that he 34 wanted only to reassure himself that we were really there), adjusted his glasses, and began to read from a sheaf of papers.

He was glad "to be here and to see the work going on just as it was in 35 the other schools."

At the first "Amen" from the audience I willed the offender to immedi- 36 ate death by choking on the word. But Amens and Yes, sir's began to fall around the room like rain through a ragged umbrella.

He told us of the wonderful changes we children in Stamps had in store. 37

The Central School (naturally, the white school was Central) had already been granted improvements that would be in use in the fall. A well-known artist was coming from Little Rock to teach art to them. They were going to have the newest microscopes and chemistry equipment for their laboratory. Mr. Donleavy didn't leave us long in the dark over who made these improvements available to Central High. Nor were we to be ignored in the general betterment scheme he had in mind.

He said that he had pointed out to people at a very high level that one   38
of the first-line football tacklers at Arkansas Agricultural and Mechanical College had graduated from good old Lafayette County Training School. Here fewer Amen's were heard. Those few that did break through lay dully in the air with the heaviness of habit.

He went on to praise us. He went on to say how he had bragged that   39
"one of the best basketball players at Fisk sank his first ball right here at Lafayette County Training School."

The white kids were going to have a chance to become Galileos and   40
Madame Curies and Edisons and Gauguins, and our boys (the girls weren't even in on it) would try to be Jessie Owenses and Joe Louises.

Owens and the Brown Bomber were great heroes in our world, but what   41
school official in the white-goddom of Little Rock had the right to decide that those two men must be our only heroes? Who decided that for Henry Reed to become a scientist he had to work like George Washington Carver, as a bootblack, to buy a lousy microscope? Bailey was obviously always going to be too small to be an athlete, so which concrete angel glued to what country seat had decided that if my brother wanted to become a lawyer he had to first pay penance for his skin by picking cotton and hoeing corn and studying correspondence books at night for twenty years?

The man's dead words fell like bricks around the auditorium and too   42
many settled in my belly. Constrained by hard-learned manners I couldn't look behind me, but to my left and right the proud graduating class of 1940 had dropped their heads. Every girl in my row had found something new to do with her handkerchief. Some folded the tiny squares into love knots, some into triangles, but most were wadding them, then pressing them flat on their yellow laps.

On the dais, the ancient tragedy was being replayed. Professor Parsons   43
sat, a sculptor's reject, rigid. His large, heavy body seemed devoid of will or willingness, and his eyes said he was no longer with us. The other teachers examined the flag (which was draped stage right) or their notes, or the windows which opened on our now-famous playing diamond.

Graduation, the hush-hush magic time of frills and gifts and congratula-   44
tions and diplomas, was finished for me before my name was called. The accomplishment was nothing. The meticulous maps, drawn in three colors of ink, learning and spelling decasyllabic words, memorizing the whole of *The Rape of Lucrece* — it was nothing. Donleavy had exposed us.

We were maids and farmers, handymen and washerwomen, and any- 45
thing higher that we aspired to was farcical and presumptuous. Then I
wished that Gabriel Prosser and Nat Turner had killed all whitefolks in
their beds and that Abraham Lincoln had been assassinated before the sign-
ing of the Emancipation Proclamation, and that Harriet Tubman had been
killed by that blow on her head and Christopher Columbus had drowned
in the *Santa Maria.*

It was awful to be Negro and have no control over my life. It was brutal 46
to be young and already trained to sit quietly and listen to charges brought
against my color with no chance of defense. We should all be dead. I
thought I should like to see us all dead, one on top of the other. A pyramid
of flesh with the whitefolks on the bottom, as the broad base, then the Indians with their silly tomahawks and teepees and wigwams and treaties, the
Negroes with their mops and recipes and cotton sacks and spirituals sticking out of their mouths. The Dutch children should all stumble in their
wooden shoes and break their necks. The French should choke to death on
the Louisiana Purchase (1803) while silkworms ate all the Chinese with
their stupid pigtails. As a species, we were an abomination. All of us.

Donleavy was running for election, and assured our parents that if he 47
won we could count on having the only colored paved playing field in that
part of Arkansas. Also — he never looked up to acknowledge the grunts of
acceptance — also, we were bound to get some new equipment for the
home economics building and the workshop.

He finished, and since there was no need to give any more than the 48
most perfunctory thank-you's, he nodded to the men on the stage, and the
tall white man who was never introduced joined him at the door. They left
with the attitude that now they were off to something really important.
(The graduation ceremonies at Lafayette County Training School had been
a mere preliminary.)

The ugliness they left was palpable. An uninvited guest who wouldn't 49
leave. The choir was summoned and sang a modern arrangement of "On-
ward, Christian Soldiers," with new words pertaining to graduates seeking
their place in the world. But it didn't work. Elouise, the daughter of the
Baptist minister, recited "Invictus," and I could have cried at the imperti-
nence of "I am the master of my fate, I am the captain of my soul."

My name had lost its ring of familiarity and I had to be nudged to go 50
and receive my diploma. All my preparations had fled. I neither marched
up to the stage like a conquering Amazon, nor did I look in the audience
for Bailey's nod of approval. Marguerite Johnson, I heard the name again,
my honors were read, there were noises in the audience of appreciation,
and I took my place on the stage as rehearsed.

I thought about colors I hated: ecru, puce, lavender, beige, and black. 51

There was shuffling and rustling around me, then Henry Reed was giv- 52
ing his valedictory address, "To Be or Not to Be." Hadn't he heard the

whitefolks? We couldn't *be*, so the question was a waste of time. Henry's voice came out clear and strong. I feared to look at him. Hadn't he got the message? There was no "nobler in the mind" for Negroes because the world didn't think we had minds, and they let us know it. "Outrageous fortune"? Now, that was a joke. When the ceremony was over I had to tell Henry Reed some things. That is, if I still cared. Not "rub," Henry, "erase." "Ah, there's the erase." Us.

Henry had been a good student in elocution. His voice rose on tides of promise and fell on waves of warnings. The English teacher had helped him to create a sermon winging through Hamlet's soliloquy. To be a man, a doer, a builder, a leader, or to be a tool, an unfunny joke, a crusher of funky toadstools. I marveled that Henry could go through the speech as if we had a choice.

I had been listening and silently rebutting each sentence with my eyes closed; then there was a hush, which in an audience warns that something unplanned is happening. I looked up and saw Henry Reed, the conservative, the proper, the A student, turn his back to the audience and turn to us (the proud graduating class of 1940) and sing, nearly speaking,

> Lift ev'ry voice and sing
> Till earth and heaven ring
> Ring with the harmonies of Liberty . . .

It was the poem written by James Weldon Johnson. It was the music composed by J. Rosamond Johnson. It was the Negro National Anthem. Out of habit we were singing it.

Our mothers and fathers stood in the dark hall and joined the hymn of encouragement. A kindergarten teacher led the small children onto the stage and the buttercups and daisies and bunny rabbits marked time and tried to follow:

> Stony the road we trod
> Bitter the chastening rod
> Felt in the days when hope, unborn, had died.
> Yet with a steady beat
> Have not our weary feet
> Come to the place for which our fathers sighed?

Every child I knew had learned that song with his ABCs and along with "Jesus Loves Me This I Know." But I personally had never heard it before. Never heard the words, despite the thousands of times I had sung them. Never thought they had anything to do with me.

On the other hand, the words of Patrick Henry had made such an impression on me that I had been able to stretch myself tall and trembling and say, "I know not what course others may take, but as for me, give me liberty or give me death."

And now I heard, really for the first time: 58

> We have come over a way that with tears has been watered,
> We have come, treading our path through the blood
>   of the slaughtered.

While echoes of the song shivered in the air, Henry Reed bowed his   59
head, said "Thank you," and returned to his place in the line. The tears
that slipped down many faces were not wiped away in shame.

We were on top again. As always, again. We survived. The depths had   60
been icy and dark, but now a bright sun spoke to our souls. I was no longer
simply a member of the proud graduating class of 1940; I was a proud
member of the wonderful, beautiful Negro race.

Oh, Black known and unknown poets, how often have your auctioned   61
pains sustained us? Who will compute the lonely nights made less lonely
by your songs, or by the empty pots made less tragic by your tales?

If we were a people much given to revealing secrets, we might raise   62
monuments and sacrifice to the memories of our poets, but slavery cured
us of that weakness. It may be enough, however, to have it said that we survive in exact relationship to the dedication of our poets (include preachers,
musicians, and blues singers).

Analyzing This Selection

1. What changes come over the student body as the time for graduation approaches? What phrases convey a special atmosphere? What changes come
   over Angelou in particular?

2. What details indicate the involvement of the entire African American community in the student graduations? Does the selection seem to exaggerate
   the public importance of the event, or is the account entirely believable?
   Does Angelou as an eighth-grader appear too impressionable to be storing
   up accurate memories?

3. **THE WRITER'S METHOD**   What details in the narrative contribute to the
   suspense and the worry that something might go wrong? What kind of a
   calamity are we led to anticipate?

4. How do you explain Angelou's immediate response to Donleavy's speech?
   Does it seem excessive?

5. In what sense is this graduation truly a "commencement" for Angelou?
   Make your answer detailed and explicit.

Analyzing Connections

6. Angelou and Nora Ephron (see "Shaping Up Absurd," p. 20) recapture the
   style of adolescent impulsiveness and exaggeration. Compare their uses of
   humor in dealing with serious subjects.

Analyzing by Writing

7. Traditional ceremonies are formal initiations to a new status, as in a graduation, confirmation, bar or bat mitzvah, or wedding. Analyze the customs associated with one such passage you experienced or witnessed. What meanings and ideals are suggested by the details of the ritual? If you could, what parts of the ceremony would you change? Which parts do you think are most important?

Amy Tan

MOTHER TONGUE

AMY TAN (b. 1952), the daughter of Chinese immigrants, grew up in California and graduated from San Jose State University. She began a business career writing speeches and reports for corporate executives. She turned to fiction writing as part of her remedy for workaholism. Tan's first novel, *The Joy Luck Club* (1989), recounts interconnected stories of conflict and loyalty between Chinese mothers and their American-born daughters. The novel was made into a popular movie. The Chinese heroine in her second novel, *The Kitchen God's Wife* (1991), resembles Tan's mother as she is represented in "Mother Tongue," which first appeared in *Threepenny Review* (1990). Tan's third novel is *The Hundred Secret Senses* (1995).

I am not a scholar of English or literature. I cannot give you much more than personal opinions on the English language and its variations in this country or others.

I am a writer. And by that definition, I am someone who has always loved language. I am fascinated by language in daily life. I spend a great deal of my time thinking about the power of language — the way it can evoke an emotion, a visual image, a complex idea, or a simple truth. Language is the tool of my trade. And I use them all — all the Englishes I grew up with.

Recently, I was made keenly aware of the different Englishes I do use. I was giving a talk to a large group of people, the same talk I had already given to half a dozen other groups. The nature of the talk was about my writing, my life, and my book, *The Joy Luck Club.* The talk was going along well enough, until I remembered one major difference that made the whole talk sound wrong. My mother was in the room. And it was perhaps the first time she had heard me give a lengthy speech, using the kind of English I have never used with her. I was saying things like, "The intersection of memory upon imagination" and "There is an aspect of my fiction that relates to thus-and-thus" — a speech filled with carefully wrought grammatical phrases, burdened, it suddenly seemed to me, with nominalized forms, past perfect tenses, conditional phrases, all the forms of standard English that I had learned in school and through books, the forms of English I did not use at home with my mother.

Just last week, I was walking down the street with my mother, and I again found myself conscious of the English I was using, the English I do use with her. We were talking about the price of new and used furniture and I heard myself saying this: "Not waste money that way." My husband was with us as well, and he didn't notice any switch in my English. And then I realized why. It's because over the twenty years we've been together I've often used that same kind of English with him, and sometimes he even uses it with me. It has become our language of intimacy, a different sort of English that relates to family talk, the language I grew up with.

So you'll have some idea of what this family talk I heard sounds like, I'll 5
quote what my mother said during a recent conversation which I video-taped and then transcribed. During this conversation, my mother was talking about a political gangster in Shanghai who had the same last name as her family's, Du, and how the gangster in his early years wanted to be adopted by her family, which was rich by comparison. Later, the gangster became more powerful, far richer than my mother's family, and one day showed up at my mother's wedding to pay his respects. Here's what she said in part:

"Du Yusong having business like fruit stand. Like off the street kind. He 6
is Du like Du Zong — but not Tsung-ming Island people. The local people call putong, the river east side, he belong to that side local people. That man want to ask Du Zong father take him in like become own family. Du Zong father wasn't look down on him, but didn't take seriously, until that man big like become a mafia. Now important person, very hard to inviting him. Chinese way, came only to show respect, don't stay for dinner. Respect for making big celebration, he shows up. Mean gives lots of respect. Chinese custom. Chinese social life that way. If too important won't have to stay too long. He come to my wedding. I didn't see, I heard it. I gone to boy's side, they have YMCA dinner. Chinese age I was nineteen."

You should know that my mother's expressive command of English belies 7
how much she actually understands. She reads the *Forbes* report, listens to *Wall Street Week*, converses daily with her stockbroker, reads all of Shirley MacLaine's books with ease — all kinds of things I can't begin to understand. Yet some of my friends tell me they understand 50 percent of what my mother says. Some say they understand 80 to 90 percent. Some say they understand none of it, as if she were speaking pure Chinese. But to me, my mother's English is perfectly clear, perfectly natural. It's my mother tongue. Her language, as I hear it, is vivid, direct, full of observation and imagery. That was the language that helped shape the way I saw things, expressed things, made sense of the world.

Lately, I've been giving more thought to the kind of English my mother 8
speaks. Like others, I have described it to people as "broken" or "fractured" English. But I wince when I say that. It has always bothered me that I can think of no way to describe it other than "broken," as if it were damaged and needed to be fixed, as if it lacked a certain wholeness and soundness.

I've heard other terms used, "limited English," for example. But they seem just as bad, as if everything is limited, including people's perceptions of the limited English speaker.

I know this for a fact, because when I was growing up, my mother's "lim- 9 ited" English limited *my* perception of her. I was ashamed of her English. I believed that her English reflected the quality of what she had to say. That is, because she expressed them imperfectly her thoughts were imperfect. And I had plenty of empirical evidence to support me: the fact that people in department stores, at banks, and at restaurants did not take her seriously, did not give her good service, pretended not to understand her, or even acted as if they did not hear her.

My mother has long realized the limitations of her English as well. When 10 I was fifteen, she used to have me call people on the phone to pretend I was she. In this guise, I was forced to ask for information or even to complain and yell at people who had been rude to her. One time it was a call to her stockbroker in New York. She had cashed out her small portfolio and it just so happened we were going to go to New York the next week, our very first trip outside California. I had to get on the phone and say in an adolescent voice that was not very convincing, "This is Mrs. Tan."

And my mother was standing in the back whispering loudly, "Why he 11 don't send me check, already two weeks late. So mad he lie to me, losing me money."

And then I said in perfect English, "Yes, I'm getting rather concerned. 12 You had agreed to send the check two weeks ago, but it hasn't arrived."

Then she began to talk more loudly. "What he want, I come to New 13 York tell him front of his boss, you cheating me?" And I was trying to calm her down, make her be quiet, while telling the stockbroker, "I can't tolerate any more excuses. If I don't receive the check immediately, I am going to have to speak to your manager when I'm in New York next week." And sure enough, the following week there we were in front of this astonished stockbroker, and I was sitting there red-faced and quiet, and my mother, the real Mrs. Tan, was shouting at his boss in her impeccable broken English.

We used a similar routine just five days ago, for a situation that was far 14 less humorous. My mother had gone to the hospital for an appointment, to find out about a benign brain tumor a CAT scan had revealed a month ago. She said she had spoken very good English, her best English, no mistakes. Still, she said, the hospital did not apologize when they said they had lost the CAT scan and she had come for nothing. She said they did not seem to have any sympathy when she told them she was anxious to know the exact diagnosis, since her husband and son had both died of brain tumors. She said they would not give her any more information until the next time and she would have to make another appointment for that. So she said she would not leave until the doctor called her daughter. She wouldn't budge. And when the doctor finally called her daughter, me, who spoke in perfect English — lo and behold — we had assurances the CAT scan would be found, promises that a conference call on Monday would be held, and apologies for any suffering my mother had gone through for a most regrettable mistake.

I think my mother's English almost had an effect on limiting my possi-   15
bilities in life as well. Sociologists and linguists probably will tell you that a person's developing language skills are more influenced by peers. But I do think that the language spoken in the family, especially in immigrant families which are more insular, plays a large role in shaping the language of the child. And I believe that it affected my results on achievement tests, IQ tests, and the SAT. While my English skills were never judged as poor, compared to math, English could not be considered my strong suit. In grade school I did moderately well, getting perhaps B's, sometimes B-pluses, in English and scoring perhaps in the sixtieth or seventieth per-centile on achievement tests. But those scores were not good enough to override the opinion that my true abilities lay in math and science, because in those areas I achieved A's and scored in the ninetieth percentile or higher.

This was understandable. Math is precise; there is only one correct   16
answer. Whereas, for me at least, the answers on English tests were always a judgment call, a matter of opinion and personal experience. Those tests were constructed around items like fill-in-the-blank sentence completion, such as, "Even though Tom was _____, Mary thought he was _____."
And the correct answer always seemed to be the most bland combinations of thoughts, for example, "Even though Tom was shy, Mary thought he was charming," with the grammatical structure "even though" limiting the cor-rect answer to some sort of semantic opposites, so you wouldn't get answers like, "Even though Tom was foolish, Mary thought he was ridiculous." Well, according to my mother, there were very few limitations as to what Tom could have been and what Mary might have thought of him. So I never did well on tests like that.

The same was true with word analogies, pairs of words in which you   17
were supposed to find some sort of logical, semantic relationship — for example, "*Sunset* is to *nightfall* as _____ is to _____." And here you would be presented with a list of four possible pairs, one of which showed the same kind of relationship: *red* is to *stoplight, bus* is to *arrival, chills* is to *fever, yawn* is to *boring*. Well, I could never think that way. I knew what the tests were asking, but I could not block out of my mind the images already created by the first pair, "*sunset* is to *nightfall*" — and I would see a burst of colors against a darkening sky, the moon rising, the lowering of a curtain of stars. And all the other pairs of words — red, bus, stoplight, boring — just threw up a mass of confusing images, making it impossible for me to sort out something as logical as saying: "A sunset precedes nightfall" is the same as "a chill precedes a fever." The only way I would have gotten that answer right would have been to imagine an associative situation, for ex-

ample, my being disobedient and staying out past sunset, catching a chill at night, which turns into feverish pneumonia as punishment, which indeed did happen to me.

I have been thinking about all this lately, about my mother's English, 18 about achievement tests. Because lately I've been asked, as a writer, why there are not more Asian Americans represented in American literature. Why are there few Asian Americans enrolled in creative writing programs? Why do so many Chinese students go into engineering? Well, these are broad sociological questions I can't begin to answer. But I have noticed in surveys — in fact, just last week — that Asian students, as a whole, always do significantly better on math achievement tests than in English. And this makes me think that there are other Asian-American students whose English spoken in the home might also be described as "broken" or "limited." And perhaps they also have teachers who are steering them away from writing and into math and science, which is what happened to me.

Fortunately, I happen to be rebellious in nature and enjoy the challenge 19 of disproving assumptions made about me. I became an English major my first year in college, after being enrolled as pre-med. I started writing non-fiction as a freelancer the week after I was told by my former boss that writing was my worst skill and I should hone my talents toward account management.

But it wasn't until 1985 that I finally began to write fiction. And at first 20 I wrote using what I thought to be wittily crafted sentences, sentences that would finally prove I had mastery over the English language. Here's an example from the first draft of a story that later made its way into *The Joy Luck Club*, but without this line: "That was my mental quandary in its nascent state." A terrible line, which I can barely pronounce.

Fortunately, for reasons I won't get into today, I later decided I should 21 envision a reader for the stories I would write. And the reader I decided upon was my mother, because these were stories about mothers. So with this reader in mind — and in fact she did read my early drafts — I began to write stories using all the Englishes I grew up with: the English I spoke to my mother, which for lack of a better term might be described as "simple"; the English she used with me, which for lack of a better term might be described as "broken"; my translation of her Chinese, which could certainly be described as "watered down"; and what I imagined to be her translation of her Chinese if she could speak in perfect English, her internal language, and for that I sought to preserve the essence, but neither an English nor a Chinese structure. I wanted to capture what language ability tests can never reveal: her intent, her passion, her imagery, the rhythms of her speech and the nature of her thoughts.

Apart from what any critic had to say about my writing, I knew I had 22 succeeded where it counted when my mother finished reading my book and gave me her verdict: "So easy to read."

Analyzing This Selection

1. The author starts by emphasizing her professional viewpoint. What focus and freedoms does she claim by virtue of her profession?

2. **THE WRITER'S METHOD**   What is Tan's tone toward her mother? Find details that indicate her feelings and attitudes in their relationship. How have they changed through the years?

3. According to Tan, what is the public attitude toward people with limited English? As a child, how did she respond to this attitude?

Analyzing Connections

4. Tan says that as a writer she uses "all the Englishes I grew up with." Compare the differing styles that she and Angelou (see "Graduation," p. 178) had to deal with. Which kind of discourse is most burdensome to either child?

Analyzing by Writing

5. The sense of inhabiting double spheres, or parallel worlds, can arise for young people in religious, ethnic, and socioeconomic groups — or in any strongly defined cultural grouping such as military families or Americans employed abroad. Analyze your own experience of participating in two groups. Explain the differing dimensions, expectations, styles, and manners of the two realms. How did you bridge them? Were you a full citizen in both groups or partly an outsider in one or both?

Maxine Hong Kingston

THE MISERY OF SILENCE[1]

MAXINE HONG KINGSTON (b. 1940) grew up in a Chinese immigrant community in Stockton, California, where her parents ran a laundry. Kingston graduated from the University of California at Berkeley. As a first-generation American, Kingston had to learn how to live in two distinctly contrasting societies. This was confusing and difficult for a five- to seven-year-old child, as she recalls in this selection from her autobiography, *The Woman Warrior: Memoirs of a Girlhood Among Ghosts* (1976). The immigrants regarded all non-Chinese as "ghosts"— pale, insubstantial, and threatening. *China Men* (1980) extends her story of Chinese-American girlhood by describing the lives of the fathers and sons in China and America. Kingston published her first novel, *Tripmaster Monkey: His Fake Book*, in 1989.

When I went to kindergarten and had to speak English for the first time, 1 I became silent. A dumbness — a shame — still cracks my voice in two, even when I want to say "hello" casually, or ask an easy question in front of the check-out counter, or ask directions of a bus driver. I stand frozen, or I hold up the line with the complete, grammatical sentence that comes squeaking out at impossible length. "What did you say?" says the cab driver, or "Speak up," so I have to perform again, only weaker the second time. A telephone call makes my throat bleed and takes up that day's courage. It spoils my day with self-disgust when I hear my broken voice come skittering out into the open. It makes people wince to hear it. I'm getting better, though. Recently I asked the postman for special-issue stamps; I've waited since childhood for postmen to give me some of their own accord. I am making progress, a little every day.

My silence was thickest — total — during the three years that I covered 2 my school paintings with black paint. I painted layers of black over houses and flowers and suns, and when I drew on the blackboard, I put a layer of chalk on top. I was making a stage curtain, and it was the moment before the curtain parted or rose. The teachers called my parents to school, and I saw they had been saving my pictures, curling and cracking, all alike and black. The teachers pointed to the pictures and looked serious, talked seri-

[1]Editor's title.

ously too, but my parents did not understand English. ("The parents and teachers of criminals were executed," said my father.) My parents took the pictures home. I spread them out (so black and full of possibilities) and pretended the curtains were swinging open, flying up, one after another, sunlight underneath, mighty operas.

During the first silent year I spoke to no one at school, did not ask 3 before going to the lavatory, and flunked kindergarten. My sister also said nothing for three years, silent in the playground and silent at lunch. There were other quiet Chinese girls not of our family, but most of them got over it sooner than we did. I enjoyed the silence. At first it did not occur to me I was supposed to talk or to pass kindergarten. I talked at home and to one or two of the Chinese kids in class. I made motions and even made some jokes. I drank out of a toy saucer when the water spilled out of the cup, and everybody laughed, pointing at me, so I did it some more. I didn't know that Americans don't drink out of saucers.

I liked the Negro students (Black Ghosts) best because they laughed the 4 loudest and talked to me as if I were a daring talker too. One of the Negro girls had her mother coil braids over her ears Shanghai-style like mine; we were Shanghai twins except that she was covered with black like my paintings. Two Negro kids enrolled in Chinese school, and the teachers gave them Chinese names. Some Negro kids walked me to school and home, protecting me from the Japanese kids, who hit me and chased me and stuck gum in my ears. The Japanese kids were noisy and tough. They appeared one day in kindergarten, released from concentration camp, which was a tic-tac-toe mark, like barbed wire, on the map.

It was when I found out I had to talk that school became a misery, that 5 the silence became a misery. I did not speak and felt bad each time that I did not speak. I read aloud in first grade, though, and heard the barest whisper with little squeaks come out of my throat. "Louder," said the teacher, who scared the voice away again. The other Chinese girls did not talk either, so I knew the silence had to do with being a Chinese girl.

Reading out loud was easier than speaking because we did not have to 6 make up what to say, but I stopped often, and the teacher would think I'd gone quiet again. I could not understand "I." The Chinese "I" has seven strokes, intricacies. How could the American "I," assuredly wearing a hat like the Chinese, have only three strokes, the middle so straight? Was it out of politeness that this writer left off the strokes the way a Chinese has to write her own name small and crooked? No, it was not politeness; "I" is a capital and "you" is lower-case. I stared at that middle line and waited so long for its black center to resolve into tight strokes and dots that I forgot to pronounce it. The other troublesome word was "here," no strong consonant to hang on to, and so flat, when "here" is two mountainous ideographs. The teacher, who had already told me every day how to read "I" and "here," put me in the low corner under the stairs again, where the noisy boys usually sat.

When my second grade class did a play, the whole class went to the 7
auditorium except the Chinese girls. The teacher, lovely and Hawaiian,
should have understood about us, but instead left us behind in the classroom. Our voices were too soft or nonexistent, and our parents never signed
the permission slips anyway. They never signed anything unnecessary. We
opened the door a crack and peeked out, but closed it again quickly. One
of us (not me) won every spelling bee, though.

I remember telling the Hawaiian teacher, "We Chinese can't sing 'land 8
where our fathers died.'" She argued with me about politics, while I meant
because of curses. But how can I have that memory when I couldn't talk?
My mother says that we, like the ghosts, have no memories.

After American school, we picked up our cigar boxes, in which we had 9
arranged books, brushes, and an inkbox neatly, and went to Chinese school,
from 5:00 to 7:30 P.M. There we chanted together, voices rising and falling,
loud and soft, some boys shouting, everybody reading together, reciting
together and not alone with one voice. When we had a memorization test,
the teacher let each of us come to his desk and say the lesson to him privately, while the rest of the class practiced copying or tracing. Most of the
teachers were men. The boys who were so well behaved in the American
school played tricks on them and talked back to them. The girls were not
mute. They screamed and yelled during recess, when there were no rules;
they had fistfights. Nobody was afraid of children hurting themselves or of
children hurting school property. The glass doors to the red and green balconies with the gold joy symbols were left wide open so that we could run
out and climb the fire escapes. We played capture-the-flag in the auditorium, where Sun Yat-sen and Chiang Kai-shek's pictures hung at the back
of the stage, the Chinese flag on their left and the American flag on their
right. We climbed the teak ceremonial chairs and made flying leaps off
the stage. One flag headquarters was behind the glass door and the other
on stage right. Our feet drummed on the hollow stage. During recess the
teachers locked themselves up in their office with the shelves of books,
copybooks, inks from China. They drank tea and warmed their hands at a
stove. There was no play supervision. At recess we had the school to ourselves, and also we could roam as far as we could go — downtown, China-
town stores, home — as long as we returned before the bell rang.

At exactly 7:30 the teacher again picked up the brass bell that sat on his 10
desk and swung it over our heads, while we charged down the stairs, our
cheering magnified in the stairwell. Nobody had to line up.

Not all of the children who were silent at American school found voice 11
at Chinese school. One new teacher said each of us had to get up and
recite in front of the class, who was to listen. My sister and I had memorized the lesson perfectly. We said it to each other at home, one chanting,
one listening. The teacher called on my sister to recite first. It was the first
time a teacher had called on the second-born to go first. My sister was
scared. She glanced at me and looked away; I looked down at my desk. I

hoped that she could do it because if she could, then I would have to. She opened her mouth and a voice came out that wasn't a whisper, but it wasn't a proper voice either. I hoped that she would not cry, fear breaking up her voice like twigs underfoot. She sounded as if she were trying to sing through weeping and strangling. She did not pause or stop to end the embarrassment. She kept going until she said the last word, and then she sat down. When it was my turn, the same voice came out, a crippled animal running on broken legs. You could hear splinters in my voice, bones rubbing jagged against one another. I was loud, though. I was glad I didn't whisper.

How strange that the emigrant villagers are shouters, hollering face to   12
face. My father asks, "Why is it I can hear Chinese from blocks away? Is it that I understand the language? Or is it they talk loud?" They turn the radio up full blast to hear the operas, which do not seem to hurt their ears. And they yell over the singers that wail over the drums, everybody talking at once, big arm gestures, spit flying. You can see the disgust on American faces looking at women like that. It isn't just the loudness. It is the way Chinese sounds, ching-chong ugly, to American ears, not beautiful like Japanese sayonara words with the consonants and vowels as regular as Italian. We make guttural peasant noise and have Ton Duc Thang names you can't remember. And the Chinese can't hear Americans at all; the language is too soft and western music unhearable. I've watched a Chinese audience laugh, visit, talk-story, and holler during a piano recital, as if the musician could not hear them. A Chinese-American, somebody's son, was playing Chopin, which has no punctuation, no cymbals, no gongs. Chinese piano music is five black keys. Normal Chinese women's voices are strong and bossy. We American-Chinese girls had to whisper to make ourselves American-feminine. Apparently we whispered even more softly than the Americans. Once a year the teachers referred my sister and me to speech therapy, but our voices would straighten out, unpredictably normal, for the therapists. Some of us gave up, shook our heads, and said nothing, not one word. Some of us could not even shake our heads. At times shaking my head no is more self-assertion than I can manage. Most of us eventually found some voice, however faltering. We invented an American-feminine speaking personality.

Analyzing This Selection

1. What was the connection between Kingston's silence and her paintings? What did the paintings signify to *her*?

2. Why did the English pronouns "I" and "you" strike Kingston as unnatural? How do they differ from their Chinese equivalents? What looks wrong about the word "here"?

3. Does this account reinforce a stereotype of the Asian woman? What does Kingston suggest that Chinese women are like when they are among Chinese?

4. In the concluding sentence Kingston refers to "an American-feminine speaking personality." What would that be? Can you describe or imitate the tone and manner she suggests?

Analyzing Connections

5. W. E. B. Du Bois says in the Insights on page 173 that segregation makes people inaudible but not silent. Does Kingston's silence fit Du Bois's description of inaudibility, or was she merely shy?

Analyzing by Writing

6. **THE WRITER'S METHOD**   At the beginning of this selection, Kingston says that even today she has trouble speaking up in public situations. Does her style of writing indicate any hesitation or absence of assertiveness in using English for writing to the public? Is her language easy or hard to read? What is the tone of her voice? Write about Kingston's style in relation to her childhood experience.

Richard Rodriguez

PUBLIC AND PRIVATE LANGUAGE

RICHARD RODRIGUEZ (b. 1944) grew up in San Francisco, where as the child of Spanish-speaking Mexican Americans he received his education in a language that was not spoken at home. His attraction to English and to English-speaking culture became his avenue to a promising future. Rodriguez graduated from Stanford University. He pursued graduate study in English at other universities until he decided to write about the conflicting aspirations that divided him between two cultures. This selection from his autobiography, *Hunger of Memory* (1982), recounts the origin of his adult views about bilingualism. Rodriguez has continued his memoir in *Days of Obligation: An Argument with My Mexican Father* (1992).

Supporters of bilingual education today imply that students like me miss 1 a great deal by not being taught in their family's language. What they seem not to recognize is that, as a socially disadvantaged child, I considered Spanish to be a private language. What I needed to learn in school was that I had the right — and the obligation — to speak the public language of *los gringos*.[1] The odd truth is that my first-grade classmates could have become bilingual, in the conventional sense of that word, more easily than I. Had they been taught (as upper-middle-class children are often taught early) a second language like Spanish or French, they could have regarded it simply as that: another public language. In my case such bilingualism could not have been so quickly achieved. What I did not believe was that I could speak a single public language.

Without question, it would have pleased me to hear my teachers address 2 me in Spanish when I entered the classroom. I would have felt much less afraid. I would have trusted them and responded with ease. But I would have delayed — for how long postponed? — having to learn the language of public society. I would have evaded — and for how long could I have afforded to delay? — learning the great lesson of school, that I had a public identity.

Fortunately, my teachers were unsentimental about their responsibility. 3 What they understood was that I needed to speak a public language. So their voices would search me out, asking me questions. Each time I'd hear

[1] *los gringos* Foreigners.

them, I'd look up in surprise to see a nun's face frowning at me. I'd mumble, not really meaning to answer. The nun would persist, "Richard, stand up. Don't look at the floor. Speak up. Speak to the entire class, not just to me!" but I couldn't believe that the English language was mine to use. (In part, I did not want to believe it.) I continued to mumble. I resisted the teacher's demands. (Did I somehow suspect that once I learned public language my pleasing family life would be changed?) Silent, waiting for the bell to sound, I remained dazed, diffident, afraid.

Because I wrongly imagined that English was intrinsically a public language and Spanish an intrinsically private one, I easily noted the difference between classroom language and the language of home. At school, words were directed to a general audience of listeners. ("Boys and girls.") Words were meaningfully ordered. And the point was not self-expression alone but to make oneself understood by many others. The teacher quizzed: "Boys and girls, why do we use that word in this sentence? Could we think of a better word to use there? Would the sentence change its meaning if the words were differently arranged? And wasn't there a better way of saying much the same thing?" (I couldn't say. I wouldn't try to say.)

Three months. Five. Half a year passed. Unsmiling, ever watchful, my teachers noted my silence. They began to connect my behavior with the difficult progress my older sister and brother were making. Until one Saturday morning three nuns arrived at the house to talk to our parents. Stiffly, they sat on the blue living room sofa. From the doorway of another room, spying the visitors, I noted the incongruity — the clash of two worlds, the faces and voices of school intruding upon the familiar setting of home. I overheard one voice gently wondering, "Do your children speak only Spanish at home, Mrs. Rodriguez?" While another voice added, "That Richard especially seems so timid and shy."

That Rich-heard!

With great tact the visitors continued, "Is it possible for you and your husband to encourage your children to practice their English when they are home?" Of course, my parents complied. What would they not do for their children's well-being? And how could they have questioned the Church's authority which those women represented? In an instant, they agreed to give up the language (the sounds) that had revealed and accentuated our family's closeness. The moment after the visitors left, the change was observed. "*Ahora*, speak to us *en inglés*,"[2] my father and mother united to tell us.

At first, it seemed a kind of game. After dinner each night, the family gathered to practice "our" English. (It was still then *inglés*, a language foreign to us, so we felt drawn as strangers to it.) Laughing, we would try to define words we could not pronounce. We played with strange English sounds, often overanglicizing our pronunciations. And we filled the smiling

---

[2]"*Now*, speak to us *in English*."

gaps of our sentences with familiar Spanish sounds. But that was cheating, somebody shouted. Everyone laughed. In school, meanwhile, like my brother and sister, I was required to attend a daily tutoring session. I needed a full year of special attention. I also needed my teachers to keep my attention from straying in class by calling out, *Rich-heard* — their English voices slowly prying loose my ties to my other name, its three notes, *Ri-car-do.* Most of all I needed to hear my mother and father speak to me in a moment of seriousness in broken — suddenly heartbreaking — English. The scene was inevitable: One Saturday morning I entered the kitchen where my parents were talking in Spanish. I did not realize that they were talking in Spanish however until, at the moment they saw me, I heard their voices change to speak English. Those *gringo* sounds they uttered startled me. Pushed me away. In that moment of trivial misunderstanding and profound insight, I felt my throat twisted by unsounded grief. I turned quickly and left the room. But I had no place to escape to with Spanish. (The spell was broken.) My brother and sisters were speaking English in another part of the house.

Again and again in the days following, increasingly angry, I was obliged   9
to hear my mother and father: "Speak to us *en inglés.*" (*Speak.*) Only then did I determine to learn classroom English. Weeks after, it happened: One day in school I had my hand raised to volunteer an answer. I spoke out in a loud voice. And I did not think it remarkable when the entire class understood. That day, I moved very far from the disadvantaged child I had been only days earlier. The belief, that calming assurance that I belonged in public, had at last taken hold.

Shortly after, I stopped hearing the high and loud sounds of *los gringos.*   10
A more and more confident speaker of English, I didn't trouble to listen to *how* strangers sounded, speaking to me. And there simply were too many English-speaking people in my day for me to hear American accents anymore. Conversations quickened. Listening to persons whose voices sounded eccentrically pitched, I usually noted their sounds for an initial few seconds before I concentrated on *what* they were saying. Conversations became content-full. Transparent. Hearing someone's *tone* of voice — angry or questioning or sarcastic or happy or sad — I didn't distinguish it from the words it expressed. Sound and word were thus tightly wedded. At the end of a day, I was often bemused, always relieved, to realize how "silent," though crowded with words, my day in public had been. (This public silence measured and quickened the change in my life.)

At last, seven years old, I came to believe what had been technically true   11
since my birth: I was an American citizen.

But the special feeling of closeness at home was diminished by then.   12
Gone was the desperate, urgent, intense feeling of being at home; rare was the experience of feeling myself individualized by family intimates. We remained a loving family, but one greatly changed. No longer so close; no longer bound tight by the pleasing and troubling knowledge of our public

separateness. Neither my older brother nor sister rushed home after school anymore. Nor did I. When I arrived home there would often be neighborhood kids in the house. Or the house would be empty of sounds.

Following the dramatic Americanization of their children, even my parents grew more publicly confident. Especially my mother. She learned the names of all the people on our block. And she decided we needed to have a telephone installed in the house. My father continued to use the word *gringo*. But it was no longer charged with the old bitterness or distrust. (Stripped of any emotional content, the word simply became a name for those Americans not of Hispanic descent.) Hearing him, sometimes, I wasn't sure if he was pronouncing the Spanish word *gringo* or saying gringo in English.   13

Matching the silence I started hearing in public was a new quiet at home. The family's quiet was partly due to the fact that, as we children learned more and more English, we shared fewer and fewer words with our parents. Sentences needed to be spoken slowly when a child addressed his mother or father. (Often the parent wouldn't understand.) The child would need to repeat himself. (Still the parent misunderstood.) The young voice, frustrated, would end up saying, "Never mind" — the subject was closed. Dinners would be noisy with the clinking of knives and forks against dishes. My mother would smile softly between her remarks; my father at the other end of the table would chew and chew at his food, while he stared over the heads of his children.   14

My *mother*! My *father*! After English became my primary language, I no longer knew what words to use in addressing my parents. The old Spanish words (those tender accents of sound) I had used earlier — *mamá* and *papá* — I couldn't use anymore. They would have been too painful reminders of how much had changed in my life. On the other hand, the words I heard neighborhood kids call *their* parents seemed equally unsatisfactory. *Mother* and *Father*; *Ma, Papa, Pa, Dad, Pop* (how I hated the all-American sound of that last word especially) — all these terms I felt were unsuitable, not really terms of address for *my* parents. As a result, I never used them at home. Whenever I'd speak to my parents, I would try to get their attention with eye contact alone. In public conversations, I'd refer to "my parents" or "my mother and father."   15

My mother and father, for their part, responded differently, as their children spoke to them less and less. She grew restless, seemed troubled and anxious at the scarcity of words exchanged in the house. It was she who would question me about my day when I came home from school. She smiled at the small talk. She pried at the edges of my sentences to get me to say something more. (What?) She'd join conversations she overheard, but her intrusions often stopped her children's talking. By contrast, my father seemed reconciled to the new quiet. Though his English improved somewhat, he retired into silence. At dinner he spoke very little. One night his children and even his wife helplessly giggled at his garbled English   16 pronunciation of the Catholic Grace before Meals. Thereafter he made his wife recite the prayer at the start of each meal, even on formal occasions, when there were guests in the house. Hers became the public voice of the family. On official business, it was she, not my father, one would usually hear on the phone or in stores, talking to strangers. His children grew so accustomed to his silence that, years later, they would speak routinely of his shyness. (My mother would often try to explain: Both his parents died when he was eight. He was raised by an uncle who treated him like little more than a menial servant. He was never encouraged to speak. He grew up alone. A man of few words.) But my father was not shy, I realized, when I'd watch him speaking Spanish with relatives. Using Spanish, he was quickly effusive. Especially when talking with other men, his voice would spark, flicker, flare alive with sounds. In Spanish, he expressed ideas and feelings he rarely revealed in English. With firm Spanish sounds, he conveyed confidence and authority English would never allow him.

The silence at home, however, was finally more than a literal silence.   17 Fewer words passed between parent and child, but more profound was the silence that resulted from my inattention to sounds. At about the time I no longer bothered to listen with care to the sounds of English in public, I grew careless about listening to the sounds family members made when they spoke. Most of the time I heard someone speaking at home and didn't distinguish his sounds from the words people uttered in public. I didn't even pay much attention to my parents' accented and ungrammatical speech. At least not at home. Only when I was with them in public would I grow alert to their accents. Though, even then, their sounds caused me less and less concern. For I was increasingly confident of my own public identity.

Today I hear bilingual educators say that children lose a degree of "indi-   18 viduality" by becoming assimilated into public society. (Bilingual schooling was popularized in the seventies, that decade when middle-class ethnics began to resist the process of assimilation — the American melting pot.) But the bilingualists simplistically scorn the value and necessity of assimilation. They do not seem to realize that there are *two* ways a person is individualized. So they do not realize that while one suffers a diminished sense of *private* individuality by becoming assimilated into public society, such assimilation makes possible the achievement of *public* individuality.

Analyzing This Selection

1. How does Rodriguez regard his childhood teachers? Distinguish between his childhood and his adult perspectives.
2. How does the English language change his parents' lives? How does Rodriguez respond to those changes?

3. **THE WRITER'S METHOD**   Rodriguez differentiates between private and public individuality, but he does not explicitly define either concept. Has he defined them implicitly? Explain his terms, adding your understanding of what they mean.

Analyzing Connections

4. Rodriguez and Kingston (see "The Misery of Silence," p. 195) were isolated by increased silences when the English language entered their lives. In your opinion, which writer's silences caused longer lasting solitude?

Analyzing by Writing

5. Should schools offer bilingual education to children of minority groups? Or perhaps to all children? (For instance, in Canada, all children learn both English and French.) Consider positive and negative effects of having a single public language in a multicultural society.

Arthur Ashe and Arnold Rampersad

THE BURDEN OF RACE

ARTHUR ASHE (1943–1993) broke the color barrier in professional tennis. Born in Richmond, Virginia, he lived under segregation. He ascended to top world rank by winning the U.S. Open in 1968 and Wimbledon in 1975. Illness requiring heart bypass surgery forced his retirement and led to his contracting AIDS through blood transfusions. By publicizing his illness, Ashe increased public awareness of AIDS and raised funds for research. The following selection is excerpted from his memoir *Days of Grace* (1993), which was written with assistance from Arnold Rampersad.

I had spent more than an hour talking in my office at home with a reporter for *People* magazine. Her editor had sent her to do a story about me and how I was coping with AIDS. The reporter's questions had been probing and yet respectful of my right to privacy. Now, our interview over, I was escorting her to the door. As she slipped on her coat, she fell silent. I could see that she was groping for the right words to express her sympathy for me before she left. 1

"Mr. Ashe, I guess this must be the heaviest burden you have ever had to bear, isn't it?" she asked finally. 2

I thought for a moment, but only a moment. "No, it isn't. It's a burden, all right. But AIDS isn't the heaviest burden I have had to bear." 3

"Is there something worse? Your heart attack?" 4

I didn't want to detain her, but I let the door close with both of us still inside. "You're not going to believe this," I said to her, "but being black is the greatest burden I've had to bear." 5

"You can't mean that." 6

"No question about it. Race has always been my biggest burden. Having to live as a minority in America. Even now it continues to feel like an extra weight tied around me." 7

I can still recall the surprise and perhaps even the hurt on her face. I may even have surprised myself, because I simply had never thought of comparing the two conditions before. However, I stand by my remark. Race is for me a more onerous burden than AIDS. My disease is the result of biological factors over which we, thus far, have had no control. Racism, however, is entirely made by people, and therefore it hurts and inconveniences infinitely more. 8

206

Since our interview (skillfully presented as a first-person account by me) 9
appeared in *People* in June 1992, many people have commented on my
remark. A radio station in Chicago aimed primarily at blacks conducted a
lively debate on its merits on the air. Most African Americans have little
trouble understanding and accepting my statement, but other people have
been baffled by it. Even Donald Dell, my close friend of more than thirty
years, was puzzled. In fact, he was so troubled that he telephoned me in
the middle of the night from Hamburg, Germany, to ask if I had been mis-
quoted. No, I told him, I had been quoted correctly. Some people have
asked me flatly, what could *you*, Arthur Ashe, possibly have to complain
about? Do you want more money or fame than you already have? Isn't
AIDS inevitably fatal? What can be worse than death?

The novelist Henry James suggested somewhere that it is a complex fate 10
being an American. I think it is a far more complex fate being an African
American. I also sometimes think that this indeed may be one of those fates
that are worse than death.

I do not want to be misunderstood. I do not mean to appear fatalistic, 11
self-pitying, cynical, or maudlin. Proud to be an American, I am also proud
to be an African American. I delight in the accomplishments of fellow citizens of my color. When one considers the odds against which we have
labored, we have achieved much. I believe in life and hope and love, and
I turn my back on death until I must face my end in all its finality. I am an
optimist, not a pessimist. Still, a pall of sadness hangs over my life and the
lives of almost all African Americans because of what we as a people have
experienced historically in America, and what we as individuals experience
each and every day. Whether one is a welfare recipient trapped in some
blighted "housing project" in the inner city or a former Wimbledon champion who is easily recognized on the streets and whose home is a luxurious
apartment in one of the wealthiest districts of Manhattan, the sadness is
still there.

In some respects, I am a prisoner of the past. A long time ago, I made 12
peace with the state of Virginia and the South. While I, like other blacks,
was once barred from free association with whites, I returned time and time
again, under the new rule of desegregation, to work with whites in my
hometown and across the South. But segregation had achieved by that time
what it was intended to achieve: It left me a marked man, forever aware of
a shadow of contempt that lays across my identity and my sense of self-
esteem. Subtly the shadow falls on my reputation, the way I know I am perceived; the mere memory of it darkens my most sunny days. I believe that
the same is true for almost every African American of the slightest sensitivity
and intelligence. Again, I don't want to overstate the case. I think of myself,
and others think of me, as supremely self-confident. I know objectively that
it is almost impossible for someone to be as successful as I have been as an
athlete and to lack self-assurance. Still, I also know that the shadow is
always there; only death will free me, and blacks like me, from its pall.

The shadow fell across me recently on one of the brightest days, literally   13
and metaphorically, of my life. On August 30, 1992, the day before the
U.S. Open, the USTA and I together hosted an afternoon of tennis at the
National Tennis Center in Flushing Meadows, New York. The event was a
benefit for the Arthur Ashe Foundation for the Defeat of AIDS. Before the
start, I was nervous. Would the invited stars (McEnroe, Graf, Navratilova,
et al.) show up? Would they cooperate with us, or be difficult to manage?
And, on the eve of a Grand Slam tournament, would fans pay to see light-
hearted tennis? The answers were all a resounding yes (just over ten thousand fans turned out). With CBS televising the event live and Aetna having
provided the air time, a profit was assured. The sun shone brightly, the
humidity was mild, and the temperature hovered in the low 80s.

What could mar such a day? The shadow of race, and the sensitivity, or   14
perhaps hypersensitivity, to its nuances. Sharing the main stadium box with
Jeanne, Camera, and me, at my invitation, were Stan Smith, his wife Mar-
jory, and their daughter Austin. The two little girls were happy to see one
another. During Wimbledon in June, they had renewed their friendship
when we all stayed near each other in London. Now Austin, seven years
old, had brought Camera a present. She had come with twin dolls, one for
herself, one for Camera. A thoughtful gesture on Austin's part, and on her
parents' part, no doubt. The Smiths are fine, religious people. Then I noticed
that Camera was playing with her doll above the railing of the box, in full
view of the attentive network television cameras. The doll was the problem;
or rather, the fact that the doll was conspicuously a blond. Camera owns
dolls of all colors, nationalities, and ethnic varieties. But she was now on
national television playing with a blond doll. Suddenly I heard voices in
my head, the voices of irate listeners to a call-in show on some "black format" radio station. I imagined insistent, clamorous callers attacking Camera, Jeanne, and me:

"Can you believe the doll Arthur Ashe's daughter was holding up at the   15
AIDS benefit? Wasn't that a shame?"

"Is that brother sick or what? Somebody ought to teach that poor child   16
about her true black self!"

"What kind of role model is Arthur Ashe if he allows his daughter to be   17
brainwashed that way?"

"Doesn't the brother understand *that he is corrupting his child's mind*   18
with notions about the superiority of the white woman? I tell you, I thought
we were long past that!"

The voices became louder in my head. Despite the low humidity, I   19
began to squirm in my seat. What should I do? Should I say, To hell with
what some people might think? I know that Camera likes her blond dolls,
black dolls, brown dolls, Asian dolls, Indian dolls just about equally; I know
that for a fact, because I have watched her closely. I have searched for signs
of racial partiality in her, indications that she may be dissatisfied with herself, with her own color. I have seen none. But I cannot dismiss the voices.

I try always to live practically, and I do not wish to hear such comments on the radio. On the other hand, I do not want Austin's gift to be sullied by an ungracious response. Finally, I act.

"Jeanne," I whisper, "we have to do something." 20

"About what?" she whispers back. 21

"That doll. We have to get Camera to put that doll down." 22

Jeanne takes one look at Camera and the doll and she understands 23 immediately. Quietly, cleverly, she makes the dolls disappear. Neither Camera nor Austin is aware of anything unusual happening. Smoothly, Jeanne has moved them on to some other distraction.

I am unaware if Margie Smith has noticed us, but I believe I owe her an 24 explanation. I get up and go around to her seat. Softly I tell her why the dolls have disappeared. Margie is startled, dumbfounded.

"Gosh, Arthur, I never thought about that. I never *ever* thought about 25 anything like that!"

"*You* don't have to think about it," I explain. "But it happens to us, in 26 similar situations, all the time."

"All the time?" She is pensive now. 27

"All the time. It's perfectly understandable. And it certainly is not your 28 fault. You were doing what comes naturally. But for us, the dolls make for a bit of a problem. All for the wrong reasons. It shouldn't be this way, but it is."

I return to my seat, but not to the elation I had felt before I saw that 29 blond doll in Camera's hand. I feel myself becoming more and more angry. I am angry at the force that made me act, the force of racism in all its complexity, as it spreads into the world and creates defensiveness and intolerance among the very people harmed by racism. I am also angry with myself. I am angry with myself because I have just acted out of pure practicality, not out of morality. The moral act would have been to let Camera have her fun, because she was innocent of any wrongdoing. Instead, I had tampered with her innocence, her basic human right to act impulsively, to accept a gift from a friend in the same beautiful spirit in which it was given.

Deeply embarrassed now, I am ashamed at what I have done. I have 30 made Camera adjust her behavior merely because of the likelihood that some people in the African American community would react to her innocence foolishly and perhaps even maliciously. I know I am not misreading the situation. I would have had telephone calls that very evening about the unsuitability of Camera's doll. Am I being a hypocrite? Yes, definitely, up to a point. I have allowed myself to give in to those people who say we must avoid even the slightest semblance of "Eurocentric" influence. But I also know what stands behind the entire situation. Racism ultimately created the state in which defensiveness and hypocrisy are our almost instinctive responses, and innocence and generosity are invitations to trouble.

This incident almost ruined the day for me. That night, when Jeanne 31 and I talked about the excitement of the afternoon, and the money that would go to AIDS research and education because of the event, we never-theless ended up talking mostly about the incident of the dolls. We also talked about perhaps its most ironic aspect. In 1954, when the Supreme Court ruled against school segregation in *Brown v. Board of Education,* some of the most persuasive testimony came from the psychologist Dr. Kenneth Clark concerning his research on black children and their pathetic prefer-ence for white dolls over black. In 1992, the dolls are still a problem.

Once again, the shadow of race had fallen on me.   32

Analyzing This Selection

1. **THE WRITER'S METHOD**   Clarify Ashe's statement that he is proud to be an African American, though it is a fate worse than death. Is this a contra-diction?

2. How did earlier segregation affect Ashe's later character?

3. In your opinion, did Ashe act appropriately with the doll? Was the alterna-tive truly better? Explain the dilemma and its effects.

Analyzing Connections

4. Read the interview in *People* magazine (June 1992), and compare both ver-sions of the incident. What aspects are developed differently? In your opin-ion, why did Ashe reconsider it in this memoir?

Analyzing by Writing

5. Ashe examines the fate of being an African American, and Theodor Reik defines group identity as "the community of fate" in the Insights on page 173. What sense of *fate* connects you to other people? Examine how, if at all, your identity includes a destiny in common with others.

Shelby Steele

ON BEING BLACK AND MIDDLE CLASS

SHELBY STEELE (b. 1946), grew up in an African American community in Chicago. He earned his Ph.D. in history from the University of Utah. His essays on race relations have appeared in magazines such as *Harper's*, the *New York Times Magazine, Commentary, Black World,* and the *New Republic.* His criticisms of both white and black social policies on affirmative action and other issues are collected in *The Content of Our Character: A New Vision of Race in America* (1990), which won a National Book Critics Circle Award.

Not long ago a friend of mine, black like myself, said to me that the term "black middle class" was actually a contradiction in terms. Race, he insisted, blurred class distinctions among blacks. If you were black, you were just black and that was that. When I argued, he let his eyes roll at my naivete. Then he went on. For us, as black professionals, it was an exercise in self-flattery, a pathetic pretention, to give meaning to such a distinction. Worse, the very idea of class threatened the unity that was vital to the black community as a whole. After all, since when had white America taken note of anything but color when it came to blacks? He then reminded me of an old Malcolm X line that had been popular in the sixties. Question: What is a black man with a Ph.D.? Answer: A nigger.

For many years I had been on my friend's side of this argument. Much of my conscious thinking on the old conundrum of race and class was shaped during my high school and college years in the race-charged sixties, when the fact of my race took on an almost religious significance. Progressively, from the mid-sixties on, more and more aspects of my life found their explanation, their justification, and their motivation in race. My youthful concerns about career, romance, money, values, and even styles of dress became a subject [of] consultation with various oracular sources of racial wisdom. And these ranged from a figure as ennobling as Martin Luther King, Jr., to the underworld elegance of dress I found in jazz clubs on the South Side of Chicago. Everywhere there were signals, and in those days I considered myself so blessed with clarity and direction that I pitied my white classmates who found more embarrassment than guidance in the face of *their* race. In 1968, inflated by my new power, I took a mischievous delight in calling them culturally disadvantaged.

But now, hearing my friend's comment was like hearing a priest from a church I'd grown disenchanted with. I understood him, but my faith was weak. What had sustained me in the sixties sounded monotonous and off the mark in the eighties. For me, race had lost much of its juju, its singular capacity to conjure meaning. And today, when I honestly look at my life and the lives of many other middle-class blacks I know, I can see that race never fully explained our situation in American society. Black though I may be, it is impossible for me to sit in my single-family house with two cars in the driveway and a swing set in the back yard and *not* see the role class has played in my life. And how can my friend, similarly raised and similarly situated, not see it?

Yet despite my certainty I felt a sharp tug of guilt as I tried to explain myself over my friend's skepticism. He is a man of many comedic facial expressions and, as I spoke, his brow lifted in extreme moral alarm as if I were uttering the unspeakable. His clear implication was that I was being elitist and possibly (dare he suggest?) antiblack — crimes for which there might well be no redemption. He pretended to fear for me. I chuckled along with him, but inwardly I did wonder at myself. Though I never doubted the validity of what I was saying, I felt guilty saying it. Why?

After he left (to retrieve his daughter from a dance lesson) I realized that the trap I felt myself in had a tiresome familiarity and, in a sort of slow-motion epiphany, I began to see its outline. It was like the suddenly sharp vision one has at the end of a burdensome marriage when all the long-repressed incompatibilities come undeniably to light.

What became clear to me is that people like myself, my friend, and middle-class blacks generally are caught in a very specific double bind that keeps two equally powerful elements of our identity at odds with each other. The middle-class values by which we were raised — the work ethic, the importance of education, the value of property ownership, of respectability, of "getting ahead," of stable family life, of initiative, of self-reliance, etc. — are, in themselves, raceless and even assimilationist. They urge us toward participation in the American mainstream, toward integration, toward a strong identification with the society — and toward the entire constellation of qualities that are implied in the word "individualism." These values are almost rules for how to prosper in a democratic, free-enterprise society that admires and rewards individual effort. They tell us to work hard for ourselves and our families and to seek our opportunities whenever they appear, inside or outside the confines of whatever ethnic group we may belong to.

But the particular pattern of racial identification that emerged in the sixties and that still prevails today urges middle-class blacks (and all blacks) in the opposite direction. This pattern asks us to see ourselves as an embattled minority, and it urges an adversarial stance toward the mainstream, an emphasis on ethnic consciousness over individualism. It is organized around an implied separatism.

The opposing thrust of these two parts of our identity results in the double bind of middle-class blacks. There is no forward movement on either plane that does not constitute backward movement on the other. This was the familiar trap I felt myself in while talking with my friend. As I spoke about class, his eyes reminded me that I was betraying race. Clearly, the two indispensable parts of my identity were a threat to each other.

Of course when you think about it, class and race are both similar in   9 some ways and also naturally opposed. They are two forms of collective identity with boundaries that intersect. But whether they clash or peacefully coexist has much to do with how they are defined. Being both black and middle class becomes a double bind when class and race are defined in sharply antagonistic terms, so that one must be repressed to appease the other.

But what is the "substance" of these two identities, and how does each   10 establish itself in an individual's overall identity? It seems to me that when we identify with any collective we are basically identifying with images that tell us what it means to be a member of that collective. Identity is not the same thing as the fact of membership in a collective; it is, rather, a form of self-definition, facilitated by images of what we wish our membership in the collective to mean. In this sense, the images we identify with may reflect the aspirations of the collective more than they reflect reality, and their content can vary with shifts in those aspirations.

But the process of identification is usually dialectical. It is just as neces-   11 sary to say what we are *not* as it is to say what we are — so that finally identification comes about by embracing a polarity of positive and negative images. To identify as middle class, for example, I must have both positive and negative images of what being middle class entails; then I will know what I should and should not be doing in order to be middle class. The same goes for racial identity.

In the racially turbulent sixties the polarity of images that came to define   12 racial identification was very antagonistic to the polarity that defined middle-class identification. One might say that the positive images of one lined up with the negative images of the other, so that to identify with both required either a contortionist's flexibility or a dangerous splitting of the self. The double bind of the black middle class was in place.

The black middle class has always defined its class identity by means of   13 positive images gleaned from middle- and upper-class white society, and by means of negative images of lower-class blacks. This habit goes back to the institution of slavery itself, when "house" slaves both mimicked the whites they served and held themselves above the "field" slaves. But in the sixties the old bourgeois impulse to dissociate from the lower classes (the "we-they" distinction) backfired when racial identity suddenly called for the celebration of this same black lower class. One of the qualities of a double bind is that one feels it more than sees it, and I distinctly remember the tension and strange sense of dishonesty I felt in those days as I moved back and forth like a bigamist between the demands of class and race.

Though my father was born poor, he achieved middle-class standing   14
through much hard work and sacrifice (one of his favorite words) and by
identifying fully with solid middle-class values — mainly hard work, family
life, property ownership, and education for his children (all four of whom
have advanced degrees). In his mind these were not so much values as laws
of nature. People who embodied them made up the positive images in his
class polarity. The negative images came largely from the blacks he had left
behind because they were "going nowhere."

No one in my family remembers how it happened, but as time went on,   15
the negative images congealed into an imaginary character named Sam,
who, from the extensive service we put him to, quickly grew to mythic proportions. In our family lore he was sometimes a trickster, sometimes a
boob, but always possessed a catalogue of sly faults that gave up graphic
images of everything we should not be. On sacrifice: "Sam never thinks
about tomorrow. He wants it now or he doesn't care about it." On work:
"Sam doesn't favor it too much." On children: "Sam likes to have them but
not to raise them." On money: "Sam drinks it up and pisses it out." On
fidelity: "Sam has to have two or three women." On clothes: "Sam features
loud clothes. He likes to see and be seen." And so on. Sam's persona
amounted to a negative instruction manual in class identity.

I don't think that any of us believed Sam's faults were accurate repre-   16
sentations of lower-class black life. He was an instrument of self-definition,
not of sociological accuracy. It never occurred to us that he looked very
much like the white racist stereotype of blacks, or that he might have been
a manifestation of our own racial self-hatred. He simply gave us a counter-
point against which to express our aspirations. If self-hatred was a factor, it
was not, for us, a matter of hating lower-class blacks but of hating what we
did not want to be.

Still, hate or love aside, it is fundamentally true that my middle-class   17
identity involved a dissociation from images of lower-class black life and a
corresponding identification with values and patterns of responsibility that
are common to the middle class everywhere. These values sent me a clear
message: Be both an individual and a responsible citizen; understand that
the quality of your life will approximately reflect the quality of effort you
put into it; know that individual responsibility is the basis of freedom and
that the limitations imposed by fate (whether fair or unfair) are no excuse
for passivity.

Whether I live up to these values or not, I know that my acceptance of   18
them is the result of lifelong conditioning. I know also that I share this conditioning with middle-class people of all races and that I can no more easily be free of it than I can be free of my race. Whether all this got started
because the black middle class modeled itself on the white middle class is
no longer relevant. For the middle-class black, conditioned by these values
from birth, the sense of meaning they provide is as immutable as the color
of his skin.

In my junior year in college I rode to a debate tournament with three   19
white students and our faculty coach, an elderly English professor. The
experience of being the lone black in a group of whites was so familiar to
me that I thought nothing of it as our trip began. But then, halfway
through the trip, the professor casually turned to me and, in an isn't-the-
world-funny sort of tone, said that he had just refused to rent an apartment
in a house he owned to a "very nice" black couple because their color
would "offend" the white couple who lived downstairs. His eyebrows lifted
helplessly over his hawkish nose, suggesting that he too, like me, was a victim of America's racial farce. His look assumed a kind of comradeship: He
and I were above this grimy business of race, though for expediency we had
occasionally to concede the world its madness.

My vulnerability in this situation came not so much from the professor's   20
blindness to his own racism as from his assumption that I would participate
in it, that I would conspire with him against my own race so that he might
remain comfortably blind. Why did he think I would be amenable to this?
I can only guess that he assumed my middle-class identity was so complete
and all-encompassing that I would see his action as nothing more than a
trifling concession to the folkways of our land, that I would in fact applaud
his decision not to disturb propriety. Blind to both his own racism and to
me — one blindness serving the other — he could not recognize that he
was asking me to betray my race in the name of my class.

His blindness made me feel vulnerable because it threatened to expose   21
my own repressed ambivalence. His comment pressured me to choose between my class identification, which had contributed to my being a college
student and a member of the debating team, and my desperate desire to be
"black." I could have one but not both; I was double-bound.

Because double binds are repressed there is always an element of terror   22
in them: the terror of bringing to the conscious mind the buried duplicity,
self-deception, and pretense involved in serving two masters. This terror is
the stuff of vulnerability, and since vulnerability is one of the least tolerable
of all human feelings, we usually transform it into an emotion that seems
to restore the control of which it has robbed us; most often, that emotion is
anger. And so, before the professor had even finished his little story, I had
become a furnace of rage. The year was 1967, and I had been primed by
endless hours of nap-matching[1] to feel, at least consciously, completely at
one with the victim-focused black identity. This identity gave me the
license, and the impunity, to unleash upon this professor one of those
volcanic eruptions of racial indignation familiar to us from the novels of
Richard Wright. Like Cross Damon in *Outsider*, who kills in perfectly
righteous anger, I tried to annihilate the man. I punished him not according to the measure of his crime but according to the measure of my vulnerability, a measure set by the cumulative tension of years of repressed

---

[1]**Nap-matching** Slang for measuring one's black identification.

terror. Soon I saw that terror in *his* face, as he stared hollow-eyed at the road ahead. My white friends in the back seat, knowing no conflict between their own class and race, were astonished that someone they had taken to be so much like themselves could harbor a rage that for all the world looked murderous.

Though my rage was triggered by the professor's comment, it was deep- 23 ened and sustained by a complex of need, conflict, and repression in myself of which I had been wholly unaware. Out of my racial vulnerability I had developed the strong need of an identity with which to defend myself. The only such identity available was that of me as victim, him as victimizer. Once in the grip of this paradigm, I began to do far more damage to myself than he had done.

Seeing myself as a victim meant that I clung all the harder to my racial 24 identity, which, in turn, meant that I suppressed my class identity. This cut me off from all the resources my class values might have offered me. In those values, for instance, I might have found the means to a more dispassionate response, the response less of a victim attacked by a victimizer than of an individual offended by a foolish old man. As an individual I might have reported this professor to the college dean. Or I might have calmly tried to reveal his blindness to him, and possibly won a convert. (The flagrancy of his remark suggested a hidden guilt and even self-recognition on which I might have capitalized. Doesn't confession usually signal a willingness to face oneself?) Or I might have simply chuckled and then let my silence serve as an answer to his provocation. Would not my composure, in any form it might take, deflect into his own heart the arrow he'd shot at me?

Instead, my anger, itself the hair-trigger expression of a long-repressed 25 double bind, not only cut me off from the best of my own resources, it also distorted the nature of my true racial problem. The righteousness of this anger and the easy catharsis it brought buoyed the delusion of my victimization and left me as blind as the professor himself.

Analyzing This Selection

1. In paragraph 6, Steele lists specific values that define the middle class. Would you add to or challenge any items on his list? What items would define a lower class? An upper class?

2. **THE WRITER'S METHOD** How, if at all, did the imaginary Sam differ from a racist image? From an advertising image?

3. Steele criticizes his younger reaction to an insult from his college debate coach. How do you regard his response? Do you think the alternatives he names are preferable?

4. Do you think Steele was most powerfully influenced by race, class, or family? Choose one and support your choice.

Analyzing Connections

5. Steele and Ashe (see "The Burden of Race," p. 206) differ about the effects of race. Does Steele consider all the circumstances that Ashe discusses?

Analyzing by Writing

6. In your family or social group, what circumstances put you in conflict with another good part of yourself? What two identities or allegiances can turn into a double bind? Perhaps your religious or ethnic upbringing, your athletic ability, your family's expectations for you, or your desire to travel aimlessly for a while threatens some other value or goal you uphold. Explain the double bind that can operate in your situation.

Barbara Ehrenreich

CULTURAL BAGGAGE

BARBARA EHRENREICH (b. 1941) graduated from Reed College and received her Ph.D. from Rockefeller University. Her commentaries on social history, popular culture, and contemporary issues have been published in magazines such as *Mother Jones*, the *Nation*, the *New Republic*, and *Ms.* Ehrenreich's book-length critiques of American society include *The Worst Years of Our Lives* (1981) and *The Hearts of Men: American Dreams and Flight from Commitment* (1983). Her collection of essays *The Snarling Citizen* (1995) includes this article.

An acquaintance was telling me about the joys of rediscovering her ethnic and religious heritage. "I know exactly what my ancestors were doing 2,000 years ago," she said, eyes gleaming with enthusiasm, "and I can *do the same things now.*" Then she leaned forward and inquired politely, "And what is your ethnic background, if I may ask?"

"None," I said, that being the first word in line to get out of my mouth. Well, not "none," I backtracked. Scottish, English, Irish — that was something, I supposed. Too much Irish to qualify as a WASP, too much of the hated English to warrant a "Kiss Me, I'm Irish" button; plus there are a number of dead ends in the family tree due to adoptions, missing records, failing memories, and the like. I was blushing by this time. Did "none" mean I was rejecting my heritage out of Anglo-Celtic self-hatred? Or was I revealing a hidden chauvinism in which the Britannically-derived serve as a kind of neutral standard compared to the ethnic "others"?

Throughout the sixties and seventies I watched one group after another — African Americans, Latinos, Native Americans — stand up and proudly reclaim their roots while I just sank back ever deeper into my seat. All this excitement over ethnicity stemmed, I realized, from a past in which *their* ancestors had been trampled upon by *my* ancestors, or at least by people who looked very much like them. In addition, it had begun to seem almost un-American not to have some sort of hyphen in hand, linking one to more venerable times and locales.

But the truth is I was raised with "none." We'd eaten ethnic foods in my childhood home, but these were all borrowed, like the pasties, or Cornish meat pies, my father had picked up from his fellow miners in Butte. If my mother had one rule, it was militant ecumenicism in all matters of food

218

and experience: "Try new things," she would say, meaning anything from sweetbreads to clams, with an emphasis on the "new."

As a child, I briefly nourished a craving for roots. I immersed myself in the works of Sir Walter Scott. I pretended to believe the bagpipe was a musical instrument. I was fascinated to learn from a grandmother that we were descended from certain Highland clans, and I longed for a pleated skirt in one of their distinctive tartans.

But in *Ivanhoe* it was the dark-eyed "Jewess" Rebecca I identified with, not the flaxen-haired bimbo Rowena. As for clans: why not call them "tribes," those bands of half-clad peasants and warriors whose idea of cuisine was stuffed sheep gut washed down with whiskey? And then there was the sting of Disraeli's remark, which I came across in my teens, to the effect that his ancestors had been leading orderly, literate lives when my ancestors were still daubing themselves with blue paint.

Motherhood put the screws on me, ethnicity-wise. I had hoped that by marrying a man of Eastern European–Jewish descent I would acquire for my descendants the ethnic genes that my own forebears so sadly lacked. At one point I even subjected the children to a seder of my own design, including a little talk about the flight from Egypt and its relevance to modern social issues. But the kids insisted on buttering their matzohs and snickering through the sermon. "Give us a break, Mom," they said. "You don't even believe in God."

After the tiny pagans had been put to bed, I lit a cigarette and sat down to brood over Elijah's wine. What had I been thinking? The kids knew that their Jewish grandparents were secular folks who didn't do seders themselves. And if ethnicity eluded me, how could I expect it to take root in my children, who are not only Scottish-English-Irish but Hungarian-Polish-Russian to boot?

But then, on the fumes of Manischewitz, a great insight took form in my mind. It was true, as the kids said, that I didn't "believe in God." But this could be taken as something very different from an accusation — a reminder of a genuine heritage. My parents had not believed in God either, nor had my grandparents or any other progenitors going back to the great-great level. They had become disillusioned with Christianity generations ago — just as, on the in-law side, my children's other ancestors had shaken off their Orthodox Judaism. This insight did not exactly furnish me with an "identity," but it was something at least to work with: we are the kind of people, I realized — whatever our distant ancestors' religions — who do *not* believe, who do not carry on traditions, who do not do things just because someone has done them before.

The epiphany went on: I recalled that my mother never introduced a domestic procedure by telling me, "Grandma did it this way." What did Grandma know, living in the days before vacuum cleaners and disposable toilet mops? In my parents' general view, new things were better than old, and the very fact that some ritual had been performed in the past was a

good reason for abandoning it now. Because what was the past, as our forebears knew it? Nothing but poverty, superstition, and grief. "Think for yourself," Dad used to say. "Always ask why."

In fact, this may have been the ideal cultural heritage for an ethnic strain   11
like my own — bounced as it was from the Highlands of Scotland across
the sea, then across the plains to the Rockies, down into the mines, and
finally spewed out into high-tech, suburban America. What better philosophy, for a race of migrants, than "Think for yourself"? What better maxim,
for a people whose whole world was rudely inverted every thirty years or so,
than "Try new things"?

The more tradition-minded, the newly enthusiastic celebrants of Purim   12
and Kwanzaa and Solstice, will be clucking sadly as they read this. They
will see little point to survival if the survivors carry no cultural freight —
religion, for example, or ethnic tradition. To which I would say that skepticism, curiosity, and wide-eyed ecumenical tolerance are also part of the
human tradition, and are at least as old as such notions as "Serbian" or
"Croatian," "Scottish" or "Jewish." I make no claims for my personal line of
progenitors except that they remained steadfastly loyal to the values that
induced all of our ancestors, long, long ago, to climb down from the trees
and make their way into the open savanna.

A few weeks ago, I cleared my throat and asked the children, now mostly   13
grown and fearsomely smart, whether they felt any stirrings of ethnic identity, etc., which might have been, ahem, insufficiently nourished at home.
"None," they said, adding firmly, "and the world would be a better place if
nobody else did either." My chest swelled with pride, as my mother's would
have, to know that the race of "none" marches on.

Analyzing This Selection

1. **THE WRITER'S METHOD**   Ehrenreich repeats many clichés either to dismiss or reassess them. Find a few instances of each, and explain how she
indicates her positive or negative attitude toward the phrases. Why does she
use them at all?

Analyzing Connections

2. Ehrenreich and Ralph Waldo Emerson in the Insights on page 172 encourage nonconformity. Which author is more radical about nonconformism?

Analyzing by Writing

3. The author says the past was "Nothing but poverty, superstition, and grief."
If that is true, then why do we study history? What is the point of preserving
knowledge of things we would never want to return to? Explain your views
for or against studying history, including cultural traditions.

Alice Walker

EVERYDAY USE

ALICE WALKER (b. 1944), one of America's leading contemporary writers, was raised in a Georgia sharecropper's family as the youngest of eight children. After graduating from Sarah Lawrence College, she became active in the civil rights and feminist movements. Her work as a poet, essayist, and fiction writer includes five novels, among them *The Color Purple* (1982), winner of both the Pulitzer Prize and the American Book Award. Walker's most recent collection of essays is *The Same River Twice: Honoring the Difficult* (1996). The following short story was collected in *In Love and Trouble: Stories of Black Women* (1973).

for your grandmama

I will wait for her in the yard that Maggie and I made so clean and wavy 1
yesterday afternoon. A yard like this is more comfortable than most people
know. It is not just a yard. It is like an extended living room. When the
hard clay is swept clean as a floor and the fine sand around the edges lined
with tiny, irregular grooves, anyone can come and sit and look up into the
elm tree and wait for the breezes that never come inside the house.

Maggie will be nervous until after her sister goes: She will stand hope- 2
lessly in corners, homely and ashamed of the burn scars down her arms
and legs, eying her sister with a mixture of envy and awe. She thinks her
sister has held life always in the palm of one hand, that "no" is a word the
world never learned to say to her.

You've no doubt seen those TV shows where the child who has "made 3
it" is confronted, as a surprise, by her own mother and father, tottering in
weakly from backstage. (A pleasant surprise, of course: What would they do
if parent and child came on the show only to curse out and insult each
other?) On TV mother and child embrace and smile into each other's faces.
Sometimes the mother and father weep, the child wraps them in her arms
and leans across the table to tell how she would not have made it without
their help. I have seen these programs.

Sometimes I dream a dream in which Dee and I are suddenly brought 4
together on a TV program of this sort. Out of a dark and soft-seated limousine I am ushered into a bright room filled with many people. There I

221

meet a smiling, gray, sporty man like Johnny Carson who shakes my hand and tells me what a fine girl I have. Then we are on the stage and Dee is embracing me with tears in her eyes. She pins on my dress a large orchid, even though she has told me once that she thinks orchids are tacky flowers.

In real life I am a large, big-boned woman with rough, man-working   5
hands. In the winter I wear flannel nightgowns to bed and overalls during the day. I can kill and clean a hog as mercilessly as a man. My fat keeps me hot in zero weather. I can work outside all day, breaking ice to get water for washing; I can eat pork liver cooked over the open fire minutes after it comes steaming from the hog. One winter I knocked a bull calf straight in the brain between the eyes with a sledge hammer and had the meat hung up to chill before nightfall. But of course all this does not show on television. I am the way my daughter would want me to be: a hundred pounds lighter, my skin like an uncooked barley pancake. My hair glistens in the hot bright lights. Johnny Carson has much to do to keep up with my quick and witty tongue.

But that is a mistake. I know even before I wake up. Who ever knew a   6
Johnson with a quick tongue? Who can even imagine me looking a strange white man in the eye? It seems to me I have talked to them always with one foot raised in flight, with my head turned in whichever way is farthest from them. Dee, though. She would always look anyone in the eye. Hesitation was no part of her nature.

"How do I look, Mama?" Maggie says, showing just enough of her thin   7
body enveloped in pink skirt and red blouse for me to know she's there, almost hidden by the door.

"Come out into the yard," I say.   8

Have you ever seen a lame animal, perhaps a dog run over by some   9
careless person rich enough to own a car, sidle up to someone who is ignorant enough to be kind to him? That is the way my Maggie walks. She has been like this, chin on chest, eyes on ground, feet in shuffle, ever since the fire that burned the other house to the ground.

Dee is lighter than Maggie, with nicer hair and a fuller figure. She's a   10
woman now, though sometimes I forget. How long ago was it that the other house burned? Ten, twelve years? Sometimes I can still hear the flames and feel Maggie's arms sticking to me, her hair smoking and her dress falling off her in little black papery flakes. Her eyes seemed stretched open, blazed open by the flames reflected in them. And Dee. I see her standing off under the sweet gum tree she used to dig gum out of; a look of concentration on her face as she watched the last dingy gray board of the house fall in toward the red-hot brick chimney. Why don't you do a dance around the ashes? I'd wanted to ask her. She had hated the house that much.

I used to think she hated Maggie, too. But that was before we raised the   11
money, the church and me, to send her to Augusta to school. She used to read to us without pity; forcing words, lies, other folks' habits, whole lives

upon us two, sitting trapped and ignorant underneath her voice. She washed us in a river of make-believe, burned us with a lot of knowledge we didn't necessarily need to know. Pressed us to her with the serious way she read, to shove us away at just the moment, like dimwits, we seemed about to understand.

Dee wanted nice things. A yellow organdy dress to wear to her gradua- 12 tion from high school; black pumps to match a green suit she'd made from an old suit somebody gave me. She was determined to stare down any disaster in her efforts. Her eyelids would not flicker for minutes at a time. Often I fought off the temptation to shake her. At sixteen she had a style of her own: and knew what style was.

I never had an education myself. After second grade the school was 13 closed down. Don't ask me why: In 1927 colored asked fewer questions than they do now. Sometimes Maggie reads to me. She stumbles along good-naturedly but can't see well. She knows she is not bright. Like good looks and money, quickness passed her by. She will marry John Thomas (who has mossy teeth in an earnest face) and then I'll be free to sit here and I guess just sing church songs to myself. Although I never was a good singer. Never could carry a tune. I was always better at a man's job. I used to love to milk till I was hooked in the side in '49. Cows are soothing and slow and don't bother you, unless you try to milk them the wrong way.

I have deliberately turned my back on the house. It is three rooms, just 14 like the one that burned, except the roof is tin; they don't make shingle roofs any more. There are no real windows, just some holes cut in the sides, like the portholes in a ship, but not round and not square, with rawhide holding the shutters up on the outside. This house is in a pasture, too, like the other one. No doubt when Dee sees it she will want to tear it down. She wrote me once that no matter where we "choose" to live, she will manage to come see us. But she will never bring her friends. Maggie and I thought about this and Maggie asked me, "Mama, when did Dee ever *have* any friends?"

She had a few. Furtive boys in pink shirts hanging about on washday 15 after school. Nervous girls who never laughed. Impressed with her they worshiped the well-turned phrase, the cute shape, the scalding humor that erupted like bubbles in lye. She read to them.

When she was courting Jimmy T she didn't have much time to pay to 16 us, but turned all her faultfinding power on him. He *flew* to marry a cheap city girl from a family of ignorant flashy people. She hardly had time to recompose herself.

When she comes I will meet — but there they are! 17

Maggie attempts to make a dash for the house, in her shuffling way, but 18 I stay her with my hand. "Come back here," I say. And she stops and tries to dig a well in the sand with her toe.

It is hard to see them clearly through the strong sun. But even the first 19
glimpse of leg out of the car tells me it is Dee. Her feet were always neat-
looking, as if God himself had shaped them with a certain style. From the
other side of the car comes a short, stocky man. Hair is all over his head a
foot long and hanging from his chin like a kinky mule tail. I hear Maggie
suck in her breath. "Uhnnnh," is what it sounds like. Like when you see
the wriggling end of a snake just in front of your foot on the road. "Uhnnnh."

Dee next. A dress down to the ground, in this hot weather. A dress so 20
loud it hurts my eyes. There are yellows and oranges enough to throw back
the light of the sun. I feel my whole face warming from the heat waves
it throws out. Earrings gold, too, and hanging down to her shoulders.
Bracelets dangling and making noises when she moves her arm up to shake
the folds of the dress out of her armpits. The dress is loose and flows, and
as she walks closer, I like it. I hear Maggie go "Uhnnnh" again. It is her sister's hair. It stands straight up like the wool on a sheep. It is black as night
and around the edges are two long pigtails that rope about like small
lizards disappearing behind her ears.

"Wa-su-zo-Tean-o!" she says, coming on in that gliding way the dress 21
makes her move. The short stocky fellow with the hair to his navel is all
grinning and he follows up with "Asalamalakim, my mother and sister!" He
moves to hug Maggie but she falls back, right up against the back of my
chair. I feel her trembling there and when I look up I see the perspiration
falling off her chin.

"Don't get up," says Dee. Since I am stout it takes something of a push. 22
You can see me trying to move a second or two before I make it. She turns,
showing white heels through her sandals, and goes back to the car. Out she
peeks next with a Polaroid. She stoops down quickly and lines up picture
after picture of me sitting there in front of the house with Maggie cowering
behind me. She never takes a shot without making sure the house is included. When a cow comes nibbling around the edge of the yard she snaps
it and me and Maggie *and* the house. Then she puts the Polaroid in the
back seat of the car, and comes up and kisses me on the forehead.

Meanwhile Asalamalakim is going through motions with Maggie's hand. 23
Maggie's hand is as limp as a fish, and probably as cold, despite the sweat,
and she keeps trying to pull it back. It looks like Asalamalakim wants to
shake hands but wants to do it fancy. Or maybe he don't know how people
shake hands. Anyhow, he soon gives up on Maggie.

"Well," I say. "Dee." 24

"No, Mama," she says. "Not 'Dee,' Wangero Leewanika Kemanjo!" 25

"What happened to 'Dee'?" I wanted to know. 26

"She's dead," Wangero said. "I couldn't bear it any longer, being named 27
after the people who oppress me."

"You know as well as me you was named after your aunt Dicie," I said. 28
Dicie is my sister. She named Dee. We called her "Big Dee" after Dee was
born.

"But who was *she* named after?" asked Wangero. 29

"I guess after Grandma Dee," I said. 30

"And who was she named after?" asked Wangero. 31

"Her mother," I said, and saw Wangero was getting tired. "That's about 32
as far back as I can trace it," I said. Though, in fact, I probably could have
carried it back beyond the Civil War through the branches.

"Well," said Asalamalakim, "there you are." 33

"Uhnnnh," I heard Maggie say. 34

"There I was not," I said, "before 'Dicie' cropped up in our family, so 35
why should I try to trace it that far back?"

He just stood there grinning, looking down on me like somebody inspect- 36
ing a Model A car. Every once in a while he and Wangero sent eye signals
over my head.

"How do you pronounce this name?" I asked. 37

"You don't have to call me by it if you don't want to," said Wangero. 38

"Why shouldn't I?" I asked. "If that's what you want us to call you, we'll 39
call you."

"I know it might sound awkward at first," said Wangero. 40

"I'll get used to it," I said. "Ream it out again." 41

Well, soon we got the name out of the way. Asalamalakim had a name 42
twice as long and three times as hard. After I tripped over it two or three
times he told me to just call him Hakim-a-barber. I wanted to ask him was
he a barber, but I didn't really think he was, so I didn't ask.

"You must belong to those beef-cattle peoples down the road," I said. 43
They said "Asalamalakim" when they met you, too, but they didn't shake
hands. Always too busy: feeding the cattle, fixing the fences, putting up salt-
lick shelters, throwing down hay. When the white folks poisoned some of
the herd the men stayed up all night with rifles in their hands. I walked a
mile and a half just to see the sight.

Hakim-a-barber said, "I accept some of their doctrines, but farming 44
and raising cattle is not my style." (They didn't tell me, and I didn't ask,
whether Wangero (Dee) had really gone and married him.)

We sat down to eat and right away he said he didn't eat collards and pork 45
was unclean. Wangero, though, went on through the chitlins and corn bread,
the greens and everything else. She talked a blue streak over the sweet potatoes. Everything delighted her. Even the fact that we still used the benches
her daddy made for the table when we couldn't afford to buy chairs.

"Oh, Mama!" she cried. Then turned to Hakim-a-barber. "I never knew 46
how lovely these benches are. You can feel the rump prints," she said, running her hands underneath her and along the bench. Then she gave a sigh
and her hand closed over Grandma Dee's butter dish. "That's it!" she said.
"I knew there was something I wanted to ask you if I could have." She
jumped up from the table and went over in the corner where the churn
stood, the milk in it clabber by now. She looked at the churn and looked
at it.

"This churn top is what I need," she said. "Didn't Uncle Buddy whittle 47
it out of a tree you all used to have?"

"Yes," I said. 48

"Uh huh," she said happily. "And I want the dasher, too." 49

"Uncle Buddy whittle that, too?" asked the barber. 50

Dee (Wangero) looked up at me. 51

"Aunt Dee's first husband whittled the dash," said Maggie so low you 52
almost couldn't hear her. "His name was Henry, but they called him Stash."

"Maggie's brain is like an elephant's," Wangero said, laughing. "I can 53
use the churn top as a centerpiece for the alcove table," she said, sliding a
plate over the churn, "and I'll think of something artistic to do with the
dasher."

When she finished wrapping the dasher the handle stuck out. I took it 54
for a moment in my hands. You didn't even have to look close to see where
hands pushing the dasher up and down to make butter had left a kind of
sink in the wood. In fact, there were a lot of small sinks; you could see
where thumbs and fingers had sunk into the wood. It was beautiful light
yellow wood, from a tree that grew in the yard where Big Dee and Stash
had lived.

After dinner Dee (Wangero) went to the trunk at the foot of my bed 55
and started rifling through it. Maggie hung back in the kitchen over the
dishpan. Out came Wangero with two quilts. They had been pieced by
Grandma Dee and then Big Dee and me had hung them on the quilt
frames on the front porch and quilted them. One was in the Lone Star pattern. The other was Walk Around the Mountain. In both of them were
scraps of dresses Grandma Dee had worn fifty and more years ago. Bits and
pieces of Grandpa Jarrell's Paisley shirts. And one teeny faded blue piece,
about the size of a penny matchbox, that was from Great Grandpa Ezra's
uniform that he wore in the Civil War.

"Mama," Wangero said sweet as a bird. "Can I have these old quilts?" 56

I heard something fall in the kitchen, and a minute later the kitchen 57
door slammed.

"Why don't you take one or two of the others?" I asked. "These old 58
things was just done by me and Big Dee from some tops your grandma
pieced before she died."

"No," said Wangero. "I don't want those. They are stitched around the 59
borders by machine."

"That'll make them last better," I said. 60

"That's not the point," said Wangero. "These are all pieces of dresses 61
Grandma used to wear. She did all this stitching by hand. Imagine!" She
held the quilts securely in her arms, stroking them.

"Some of the pieces, like those lavender ones, come from old clothes 62
her mother handed down to her," I said, moving up to touch the quilts.
Dee (Wangero) moved back just enough so that I couldn't reach the quilts.
They already belonged to her.

"Imagine!" she breathed again, clutching them closely to her bosom. 63

"The truth is," I said, "I promised to give them quilts to Maggie, for 64 when she marries John Thomas."

She gasped like a bee had stung her. 65

"Maggie can't appreciate these quilts!" she said. "She'd probably be back- 66 ward enough to put them to everyday use."

"I reckon she would," I said. "God knows I been saving 'em for long 67 enough with nobody using 'em. I hope she will!" I didn't want to bring up how I had offered Dee (Wangero) a quilt when she went away to college. Then she had told me they were old-fashioned, out of style.

"But they're *priceless!*" she was saying now, furiously; for she has a tem- 68 per. "Maggie would put them on the bed and in five years they'd be in rags. Less than that!"

"She can always make some more," I said. "Maggie knows how to quilt." 69

Dee (Wangero) looked at me with hatred. "You just will not understand. 70 The point is these quilts, *these* quilts!"

"Well," I said, stumped. "What would *you* do with them?" 71

"Hang them," she said. As if that was the only thing you *could* do with 72 quilts.

Maggie by now was standing in the door. I could almost hear the sound 73 her feet made as they scraped over each other.

"She can have them, Mama," she said, like somebody used to never win- 74 ning anything, or having anything reserved for her. "I can 'member Grandma Dee without the quilts."

I looked at her hard. She had filled her bottom lip with checkerberry 75 snuff and it gave her face a kind of dopey, hangdog look. It was Grandma Dee and Big Dee who taught her how to quilt herself. She stood there with her scarred hands hidden in the folds of her skirt. She looked at her sister with something like fear but she wasn't mad at her. This was Maggie's por- tion. This was the way she knew God to work.

When I looked at her like that something hit me in the top of my head 76 and ran down to the soles of my feet. Just like when I'm in church and the spirit of God touches me and I get happy and shout. I did something I never had done before: hugged Maggie to me, then dragged her on into the room, snatched the quilts out of Miss Wangero's hands and dumped them into Maggie's lap. Maggie just sat there on my bed with her mouth open.

"Take one or two of the others," I said to Dee. 77

But she turned without a word and went out to Hakim-a-barber. 78

"You just don't understand," she said, as Maggie and I came out to 79 the car.

"What don't I understand?" I wanted to know. 80

"Your heritage," she said. And then she turned to Maggie, kissed her, 81 and said, "You ought to try to make something of yourself, too, Maggie. It's really a new day for us. But from the way you and Mama still live you'd never know it."

She put on some sunglasses that hid everything above the tip of her nose 82
and her chin.

Maggie smiled; maybe at the sunglasses. But a real smile, not scared. 83
After we watched the car dust settle I asked Maggie to bring me a dip of
snuff. And then the two of us sat there just enjoying, until it was time to go
in the house and go to bed.

Analyzing This Selection

1. **THE WRITER'S METHOD**   Mama says, "I was always better at a man's
   job." How does her mannishness affect our sympathy with or detachment
   from her as the narrator?

2. How does Mama's decision about the quilts add to the meaning of the story's
   title?

3. Analyze the conflict of generations between Mama and Dee. How does
   each generation appear in the eyes of the other?

Analyzing Connections

4. Do Mama and Ehrenreich (see "Cultural Baggage," p. 218) have similar or
   differing opinions about Dee's allegiance? Do Mama and Ehrenreich have
   similar or differing views of themselves as mothers?

Analyzing by Writing

5. Do young people (adolescents through twenty-somethings) need to identify
   with or be liberated from their group identities? What strengths and vulnerabilities draw you close to your heritage — or pull you farther away? Discuss
   one connection to your ethnic, racial, or religious heritage that you have
   embraced or rejected. Explain why you made the choice you did.

Henry Louis Gates, Jr.

IN THE KITCHEN

HENRY LOUIS GATES, JR. (b. 1950) was born and raised in West Virginia. He graduated from Yale University. After serving as a London correspondent for *Time* magazine, Gates earned a Ph.D. in English from Cambridge University. He has taught at Duke University and Harvard University, where he is now the chairman of Afro-American Studies. His *The Signifying Monkey: A Theory of African-American Literary Criticism* won a National Book Award in 1989. Gates writes on issues of popular culture and race relations, contributing to magazines such as *Harper's*, the *Village Voice*, and the *New Yorker*. The following essay is part of his memoir *Colored People* (1994).

We always had a gas stove in the kitchen, in our house in Piedmont, West Virginia, where I grew up. Never electric, though using electric became fashionable in Piedmont in the sixties, like using Crest toothpaste rather than Colgate, or watching Huntley and Brinkley rather than Walter Cronkite. But not us: gas, Colgate, and good ole Walter Cronkite, come what may. We used gas partly out of loyalty to Big Mom, Mama's Mama, because she was mostly blind and still loved to cook, and could feel her way more easily with gas than with electric. But the most important thing about our gas-equipped kitchen was that Mama used to do hair there. The "hot comb" was a fine-toothed iron instrument with a long wooden handle and a pair of iron curlers that opened and closed like scissors. Mama would put it in the gas fire until it glowed. You could smell those prongs heating up.

I liked that smell. Not the smell so much, I guess, as what the smell meant for the shape of my day. There was an intimate warmth in the women's tones as they talked with my Mama, doing their hair. I knew what the women had been through to get their hair ready to be "done," because I would watch Mama do it to herself. How that kink could be transformed through grease and fire into that magnificent head of wavy hair was a miracle to me, and still is.

Mama would wash her hair over the sink, a towel wrapped around her shoulders, wearing just her slip and her white bra. (We had no shower — just a galvanized tub that we stored in the kitchen — until we moved down Rat Tail Road into Doc Wolverton's house, in 1954.) After she dried it, she would grease her scalp thoroughly with blue Bergamot hair grease, which came in a short, fat jar with a picture of a beautiful colored lady on it. It's important to grease your scalp real good, my Mama would explain, to keep from burning yourself. Of course, her hair would return to its natural kink almost as soon as the hot water and shampoo hit it. To me, it was another miracle how hair so "straight" would so quickly become kinky again the second it even approached some water.

My Mama had only a few "clients" whose heads she "did" — did, I think,   4
because she enjoyed it, rather than for the few pennies it brought in. They would sit on one of our red plastic kitchen chairs, the kind with the shiny metal legs, and brace themselves for the process. Mama would stroke that red-hot iron — which by this time had been in the gas fire for half an hour or more — slowly but firmly through their hair, from scalp to strand's end. It made a scorching, crinkly sound, the hot iron did, as it burned its way through kink, leaving in its wake straight strands of hair, standing long and tall but drooping over at the ends, their shape like the top of a heavy willow tree. Slowly, steadily, Mama's hands would transform a round mound of Odetta kink into a darkened swamp of everglades. The Bergamot made the hair shiny; the heat of the hot iron gave it a brownish-red cast. Once all the hair was as straight as God allows kink to get, Mama would take the well-heated curling iron and twirl the straightened strands into more or less loosely wrapped curls. She claimed that she owed her skill as a hairdresser to the strength in her wrists, and as she worked her little finger would poke out, the way it did when she sipped tea. Mama was a southpaw, and wrote upside down and backward to produce the cleanest, roundest letters you've ever seen.

The "kitchen" she would all but remove from sight with a handheld pair   5
of shears, bought just for this purpose. Now, the kitchen was the room in which we were sitting — the room where Mama did her hair and washed clothes, and where we all took a bath in that galvanized tub. But the word has another meaning, and the kitchen that I'm speaking of is the very kinky bit of hair at the back of your head, where your neck meets your shirt collar. If there was ever a part of our African past that resisted assimilation, it was the kitchen. No matter how hot the iron, no matter how powerful the chemical, no matter how stringent the mashed-potatoes-and-lye formula of a man's "process," neither God nor woman nor Sammy Davis, Jr., could straighten the kitchen. The kitchen was permanent, irredeemable, irresistible kink. Unassimilably African. No matter what you did, no matter how hard you tried, you couldn't de-kink a person's kitchen. So you trimmed it off as best you could.

When hair had begun to "turn," as they'd say — to return to its natural   6
kinky glory — it was the kitchen that turned first (the kitchen around the back, and nappy edges at the temples). When the kitchen started creeping up the back of the neck, it was time to get your hair done again.

———————

Sometimes, after dark, a man would come to have his hair done. It was 7
Mr. Charlie Carroll. He was very light-complected and had a ruddy nose —
it made me think of Edmund Gwenn, who played Kris Kringle in "Miracle
on 34th Street." At first, Mama did him after my brother, Rocky, and I had
gone to sleep. It was only later that we found out that he had come to our
house so Mama could iron his hair — not with a hot comb or a curling
iron but with our very own Proctor-Silex steam iron. For some reason I
never understood, Mr. Charlie could conceal his Frederick Douglass-like
mane under a big white Stetson hat. I never saw him take it off except
when he came to our house, at night, to have his hair pressed. (Later,
Daddy would tell us about Mr. Charlie's most prized piece of knowledge,
something that the man would only confide after his hair had been pressed,
as a token of intimacy. "Not many people know this," he'd say, in a tone of
circumspection, "but George Washington was Abraham Lincoln's daddy."
Nodding solemnly, he'd add the clincher: "A white man told me." Though
he was in dead earnest, this became a humorous refrain around our house —
"a white man told me" — which we used to punctuate especially preposter-
ous assertions.)

My mother examined my daughters' kitchens whenever we went home 8
to visit, in the early eighties. It became a game between us. I had told her
not to do it, because I didn't like the politics it suggested — the notion of
"good" and "bad" hair. "Good" hair was "straight," "bad" hair kinky. Even
in the late sixties, at the height of Black Power, almost nobody could bring
themselves to say "bad" for good and "good" for bad. People still said that
hair like white people's hair was "good," even if they encapsulated it in a
disclaimer, like "what we used to call 'good.'"

Maggie would be seated in her high chair, throwing food this way and 9
that, and Mama would be coming about how cute it all was, how I used to
do just like Maggie was doing, and wondering whether her flinging her
food with her left hand meant that she was going to be left-handed like
Mama. When my daughter was just about covered with Chef Boyardee
Spaghetti-O's, Mama would seize the opportunity: wiping her clean, she
would tilt Maggie's head to one side and reach down the back of her neck.
Sometimes Mama would even rub a curl between her fingers, just to make
sure that her bifocals had not deceived her. Then she'd sigh with satisfaction and relief: No kink . . . yet. Mama! I'd shout, pretending to be angry.
Every once in a while, if no one was looking, I'd peek, too.

I say "yet" because most black babies are born with soft, silken hair. But 10
after a few months it begins to turn, as inevitably as do the seasons or the
leaves on a tree. People once thought baby oil would stop it. They were
wrong.

Everybody I knew as a child wanted to have good hair. You could be as 11
ugly as homemade sin dipped in misery and still be thought attractive if
you had good hair. "Jesus moss," the girls at Camp Lee, Virginia, had
called Daddy's naturally "good" hair during the war. I know that he played

that thick head of hair for all it was worth, too. My own hair was "not a bad grade," as barbers would tell me when they cut it for the first time. It was like a doctor reporting the results of the first full physical he has given you. Like "You're in good shape" or "Blood pressure's kind of high — better cut down on salt."

I spent most of my childhood and adolescence messing with my hair. I 12 definitely wanted straight hair. Like Pop's. When I was about three, I tried to stick a wad of Bazooka bubble gum to that straight hair of his. I suppose what fixed that memory for me is the spanking I got for doing so: he turned me upside down, holding me by my feet, the better to paddle my behind. Little *nigger*, he had shouted, walloping away. I started to laugh about it two days later, when my behind stopped hurting.

When black people say "straight," of course, they don't usually mean 13 literally straight — they're not describing hair like, say, Peggy Lipton's (she was the white girl on "The Mod Squad"), or like Mary's of Peter, Paul & Mary fame; black people call that "stringy" hair. No, "straight" just means not kinky, no matter what contours the curl may take. I would have done *anything* to have straight hair — and I used to try everything, short of getting a process.

Of the wide variety of techniques and methods I came to master in the 14 challenging prestidigitation of the follicle, almost all had two things in common: a heavy grease and the application of pressure. It's not an accident that some of the biggest black-owned companies in the fifties and sixties made hair products. And I tried them all, in search of that certain silken touch, the one that would leave neither the hand nor the pillow sullied by grease.

I always wondered what Frederick Douglass put on *his* hair, or what 15 Phillis Wheatley put on hers. Or why Wheatley has that rag on her head in the little engraving in the frontispiece of her book. One thing is for sure: you can bet that when Phillis Wheatley went to England and saw the Countess of Huntingdon she did not stop by the Queen's coiffeur on her way there. So many black people still get their hair straightened that it's a wonder we don't have a national holiday for Madame C. J. Walker, the woman who invented the process of straightening kinky hair. Call it Jheri-Kurled or call it "relaxed," it's still fried hair.

I used all the greases, from sea-blue Bergamot and creamy vanilla Duke 16 (in its clear jar with the orange-white-and-green label) to the godfather of grease, the formidable Murray's. Now, Murray's was some *serious* grease. Whereas Bergamot was like oily jello, and Duke was viscous and sickly sweet, Murray's was light brown and *hard*. Hard as lard and twice as greasy, Daddy used to say. Murray's came in an orange can with a press-on top. It was so hard that some people would put a match to the can, just to soften the stuff and make it more manageable. Then, in the late sixties, when Afros came into style, I used Afro Sheen. From Murray's to Duke to Afro Sheen: that was my progression in black consciousness.

We used to put hot towels or wash rags over our Murray-coated heads, in   17
order to melt the wax into the scalp and the follicles. Unfortunately, the
wax also had the habit of running down your neck, ears, and forehead. Not
to mention your pillowcase. Another problem was that if you put two palm-
fuls of Murray's on your head your hair turned white. (Duke did the same
thing.) The challenge was to get rid of that white color. Because if you got
rid of the white stuff you had a magnificent head of wavy hair. That was the
beauty of it: Murray's was so hard that it froze your hair into the wavy style
you brushed it into. It looked really good if you wore a part. A lot of guys
had parts *cut* into their hair by a barber, either with the clippers or with a
straightedge razor. Especially if you had kinky hair — then you'd generally
wear a short razor cut, or what we called a Quo Vadis.

We tried to be as innovative as possible. Everyone knew about using a   18
stocking cap, because your father or your uncle wore one whenever something really big was about to happen, whether sacred or secular: a funeral
or a dance, a wedding or a trip in which you confronted official white
people. Any time you were trying to look really sharp, you wore a stocking
cap in preparation. And if the event was really a big one, you made a new
cap. You asked your mother for a pair of her hose, and cut it with scissors
about six inches or so from the open end — the end with the elastic that goes
up to the top of the thigh. Then you knotted the cut end, and it became a
beehive-shaped hat, with an elastic band that you pulled down low on your
forehead and down around your neck in the back. To work well, the cap
had to fit tightly and snugly, like a press. And it had to fit that tightly
because it *was* a press: it pressed your hair with the force of the hose's elastic. If you greased your hair down real good, and left the stocking cap on
long enough, voilà: you got a head of pressed-against-the-scalp waves. (You
also got a ring around your forehead when you woke up, but it went away.)
And then you could enjoy your concrete do. Swore we were bad, too, with
all that grease and those flat heads. My brother and I would brush it out a
bit in the mornings, so that it looked — well, "natural." Grown men still
wear stocking caps — especially older men, who generally keep their stocking caps in their top drawers, along with their cufflinks and their see-through
silk socks, their "Maverick" ties, their silk handkerchiefs, and whatever else
they prize the most.

A Murrayed-down stocking cap was the respectable version of the pro-   19
cess, which, by contrast, was most definitely not a cool thing to have unless
you were an entertainer by trade. Zeke and Keith and Poochie and a few
other stars of the high-school basketball team all used to get a process once
or twice a year. It was expensive, and you had to go somewhere like Pittsburgh or D.C. or Uniontown — somewhere where there were enough colored people to support a trade. The guys would disappear, then reappear a
day or two later, strutting like peacocks, their hair burned slightly red from
the lye base. They'd also wear "rags" — cloths or handkerchiefs — around
their heads when they slept or played basketball. Do-rags, they were called.

But the result was straight hair, with just a hint of wave. No curl. Do-it-yourselfers took their chances at home with a concoction of mashed potatoes and lye.

The most famous process of all, however, outside of the process Malcolm X describes in his "Autobiography," and maybe the process of Sammy Davis, Jr., was Nat King Cole's process. Nat King Cole had patent-leather hair. That man's got the finest process money can buy, or so Daddy said the night we saw Cole's TV show on NBC. It was November 5, 1956. I remember the date because everyone came to our house to watch it and to celebrate one of Daddy's buddies' birthdays. Yeah, Uncle Joe chimed in, they can do shit to his hair that the average Negro can't even *think* about — secret shit.

Nat King Cole was *clean.* I've had an ongoing argument with a Nigerian friend about Nat King Cole for twenty years now. Not about whether he could sing — any fool knows that he could — but about whether or not he was a handkerchief head for wearing that patent-leather process.

Sammy Davis, Jr.'s, process was the one I detested. It didn't look good on him. Worse still, he liked to have a fried strand dangling down the middle of his forehead, so he could shake it out from the crown when he sang. But Nat King Cole's hair was a thing unto itself, a beautifully sculpted work of art that he and he alone had the right to wear. The only difference between a process and a stocking cap, really, was taste; but Nat King Cole, unlike, say, Michael Jackson, looked *good* in his. His head looked like Valentino's head in the twenties, and some say it was Valentino the process was imitating. But Nat King Cole wore a process because it suited his face, his demeanor, his name, his style. He was as clean as he wanted to be.

I had forgotten all about that patent-leather look until one day in 1971, when I was sitting in an Arab restaurant on the island of Zanzibar surrounded by men in fezzes and white caftans, trying to learn how to eat curried goat and rice with the fingers of my right hand and feeling two million miles from home. All of a sudden, an old transistor radio sitting on top of a china cupboard stopped blaring out its Swahili music and started playing "Fly Me to the Moon," by Nat King Cole. The restaurant's din was not affected at all, but in my mind's eye I saw it: the King's magnificent sleek black tiara. I managed, barely, to blink back the tears.

Analyzing This Selection

1. **THE WRITER'S METHOD**   What were Gates's boyhood attitudes toward his mother's hairstyling business? Find words and phrases that suggest the sort of child he was.

2. How does the other meaning of "kitchen" affect the essay's title?

3. Why couldn't African Americans easily switch their definitions of "good" and "bad" hair? What were the complications in using these terms?

4. When and why did Gates first accept the natural style of his hair? Why doesn't the author give more emphasis to his change in attitude?

5. What seemed so great about Nat King Cole's hair? Why does the author nearly weep when reminded of it?

Analyzing Connections

6. As children, Gates and Ashe (see "The Burden of Race," p. 206) were raised in neighboring states, Ashe only seven years older. What different forms of segregation did they encounter? Which effects did they overcome?

Analyzing by Writing

7. Men and women send messages about themselves through hairstyles. There are messages visible in the crewcut, the bouffant, the lacquered spike, the metallic dyes, shaved heads, mohawks, men's ponytails, women's butch cuts, and other styles, whether modest or outlandish. Hair can convey political, racial, ethnic, or religious meanings. Analyze the meaning of the hairstyle of your alter ego — that is, either your ideal self, a suppressed self, or some identity you would like to try out. Explain your similarities to and differences from this alter ego's appearance.

PART 5

WORD POWER

INSIGHTS

Language conveys a certain power. It is one of the instruments of domination. It is carefully guarded by the superior people because it is one of the means through which they conserve their supremacy.

— SHEILA ROWBOTHAM

Education! Which of the various me's do you propose to educate, and which do you propose to suppress?

Anyhow I defy you. I defy you, oh society, to educate me or to suppress me, according to your dummy standards. . . .

There are other men in me, besides this patient ass who sits here in a tweed jacket. What am I doing, playing the patient ass in a tweed jacket? Who am I talking to? Who are you, at the other end of this patience?

Who are you? How many selves have you? And which of these selves do you want to be?

Is Yale College going to educate the self that is in the dark of you, or Harvard College?

— D. H. LAWRENCE

You go to a great school not for knowledge so much as for arts and habits; for the habit of attention, for the art of expression, for the art of assuming at a moment's notice a new intellectual posture, for the art of entering quickly into another person's thought, for the habit of submitting to censure and refutation, for the art of indicating assent or dissent in graduated terms, for the habit of regarding minute points of accuracy, for the habit of working out what is possible in a given time, for taste, for discrimination, for mental courage and mental soberness. Above all, you go to a great school for self-knowledge.

— WILLIAM CORY

Books are the best of things, well used; abused, among the worst. What is the right use? What is the one end which all means go to effect? They are for nothing but to inspire. I had better never see a book than to be warped by its attraction clean out of my own orbit, and made a satellite instead of a system. The one thing in the world, of value, is the active soul. This every man is entitled to; this every man contains within him, although in almost all men obstructed and as yet unborn. The soul active sees absolute truth and utters truth, or creates. In this action it is genius; not the privilege of here and there a favorite, but the sound estate of every man. In its essence it is progressive. The book, the college, the school of art, the institution of any kind, stop with some past utterance of genius. This is good, say they, — let us hold by this. They pin me down. They look backward and not forward. But genius looks forward: the eyes of man are set in his forehead, not in his hindhead: man hopes: genius creates. Whatever talents may be, if the man create not, the pure efflux of the Deity is not his; — cinders and smoke there may be, but not yet flame. There are creative manners, there are creative actions, and creative words; manners, actions, words, that is, indicative of no custom or authority, but springing spontaneous from the mind's own sense of good and fair.

— RALPH WALDO EMERSON

But it is not hard work which is dreary; it is superficial work. That is always boring in the long run, and it has always seemed strange to me that in our endless discussions about education so little stress is ever laid on the pleasure of becoming an educated person, the enormous interest it adds to life. To be able to be caught up into the world of thought — that is to be educated.

— EDITH HAMILTON

A change of heart is the essence of all other change and it is brought about by a re-education of the mind.

— EMMELINE PETHICK-LAWRENCE

M. Degas Teaches Art & Science at Durfee Intermediate School

Detroit, 1942

He made a line on the blackboard,
one bold stroke from right to left
diagonally downward and stood back
to ask, looking as always at no one
in particular, "What have I done?"
From the back of the room Freddie
shouted, "You've broken a piece
of chalk." M. Degas did not smile.
"What have I done?" he repeated.
The most intellectual students
looked down to study their desks
except for Gertrude Bimmler, who raised
her hand before she spoke. "M. Degas,
you have created the hypotenuse
of an isosceles triangle." Degas mused.
Everyone knew that Gertrude could not
be incorrect. "It is possible,"
Louis Warshowsky added precisely,
"that you have begun to represent
the roof of a barn." I remember
that it was exactly twenty minutes
past eleven, and I thought at worst
this would go on another forty
minutes. It was early April,
the snow had all but melted on
the playgrounds, the elms and maples
bordering the cracked walks shivered
in the new winds, and I believed
that before I knew it I'd be
swaggering to the candy store
for a Milky Way. M. Degas
pursed his lips, and the room
stilled until the long hand
of the clock moved to twenty one
as though in complicity with Gertrude,
who added confidently, "You've begun
to separate the dark from the dark."
I looked back for help, but now
the trees bucked and quaked, and I
knew this could go on forever.

— PHILIP LEVINE

The plots and stories in the novels did not interest me so much as the point of view revealed. I gave myself over to each novel without reserve, without trying to criticize it; it was enough for me to see and feel something different. And for me, everything was something different. Reading was like a drug, a dope. The novels created moods in which I lived for days. But I could not conquer my sense of guilt, my feeling that the white men around me knew that I was changing, that I had begun to regard them differently.

— RICHARD WRIGHT

FOCUSING BY WRITING

1. Certain vague words become popular for suggestive precision when spoken with the right tone. The meaning of *whatever* or *like* or *bad* can be varied or mishandled by slight intonations. Clarify the range of implications for one such word. With other students you may want to dramatize the interactive uses and ask the class to interpret the exact meanings.

2. Write a newspaper report of your recent disappearance or death. Treat this imaginary event as real; maintain detachment and thoroughness in reporting.

3. Some people enjoy word games such as "Scrabble" and "Definitions," and some love crossword puzzles, but many avoid word games or are agitated by playing them. The differing responses are unrelated to their vocabulary or intelligence. Examine your disposition toward word games, and clarify differences among family and friends. What do you think accounts for these varied responses?

4. Examine a few differences between *knowing about* and *believing in* a religious text such as the Book of Exodus, the Gospels, or the Koran. Consider *knowing* and *believing* as distinct activities of mind, and try to identify their similarities and differences.

Joan Didion

ON KEEPING A NOTEBOOK

JOAN DIDION (b. 1934) was raised in California and graduated from the University of California at Berkeley. Her career in journalism has included work as an editor and columnist for magazines such as *Vogue* and the *Saturday Evening Post*. Her essays are collected in *Slouching Towards Bethlehem* (1968), *The White Album* (1979), and *After Henry* (1992). Didion has reported on international issues in *Salvador* (1983) and *Miami* (1987), and with her husband she has coauthored several screenplays. Her most recent novel is *The Last Thing He Wanted* (1996). A prolific and versatile author, Didion examines her earliest, most fundamental reasons for writing in the following essay.

"'That woman Estelle,'" the note reads, "'is partly the reason why 1 George Sharp and I are separated today.' *Dirty crepe-de-Chine wrapper, hotel bar, Wilmington RR, 9:45 A.M. August Monday morning.*"

Since the note is in my notebook, it presumably has some meaning to 2 me. I study it for a long while. At first I have only the most general notion of what I was doing on an August Monday morning in the bar of the hotel across from the Pennsylvania Railroad station in Wilmington, Delaware (waiting for a train? missing one? 1960? 1961? why Wilmington?), but I do remember being there. The woman in the dirty crepe-de-Chine wrapper had come down from her room for a beer, and the bartender had heard before the reason why George Sharp and she were separated today. "Sure," he said, and went on mopping the floor. "You told me." At the other end of the bar is a girl. She is talking, pointedly, not to the man beside her but to a cat lying in the triangle of sunlight cast through the open door. She is wearing a plaid silk dress from Peck & Peck, and the hem is coming down.

Here is what it is: The girl has been on the Eastern Shore, and now she 3 is going back to the city, leaving the man beside her, and all she can see ahead are the viscous summer sidewalks and the 3 A.M. long-distance calls that will make her lie awake and then sleep drugged through all the steaming mornings left in August (1960? 1961?). Because she must go directly from the train to lunch in New York, she wishes that she had a safety pin for the hem of the plaid silk dress, and she also wishes that she could forget about the hem and the lunch and stay in the cool bar that smells of disinfectant and malt and make friends with the woman in the crepe-de-Chine wrapper. She is afflicted by a little self-pity, and she wants to compare Estelles. That is what that was all about.

Why did I write it down? In order to remember, of course, but exactly 4 what was it I wanted to remember? How much of it actually happened? Did any of it? Why do I keep a notebook at all? It is easy to deceive oneself on all those scores. The impulse to write things down is a peculiarly compulsive one, inexplicable to those who do not share it, useful only accidentally, only secondarily, in the way that any compulsion tries to justify itself. I suppose that it begins or does not begin in the cradle. Although I have felt compelled to write things down since I was five years old, I doubt that my daughter ever will, for she is a singularly blessed and accepting child, delighted with life exactly as life presents itself to her, unafraid to go to sleep and unafraid to wake up. Keepers of private notebooks are a different breed altogether, lonely and resistant rearrangers of things, anxious malcontents, children afflicted apparently at birth with some presentiment of loss.

My first notebook was a Big Five tablet, given to me by my mother with 5 the sensible suggestion that I stop whining and learn to amuse myself by writing down my thoughts. She returned the tablet to me a few years ago; the first entry is an account of a woman who believed herself to be freezing to death in the Arctic night, only to find, when day broke, that she had stumbled onto the Sahara Desert, where she would die of the heat before lunch. I have no idea what turn of a five-year-old's mind could have prompted so insistently "ironic" and exotic a story, but it does reveal a certain predilection for the extreme which has dogged me into adult life; perhaps if I were analytically inclined I would find it a truer story than any I might have told about Donald Johnson's birthday party or the day my cousin Brenda put Kitty Litter in the aquarium.

So the point of my keeping a notebook has never been, nor is it now, to 6 have an accurate factual record of what I have been doing or thinking. That would be a different impulse entirely, an instinct for reality which I sometimes envy but do not possess. At no point have I ever been able successfully to keep a diary; my approach to daily life ranges from the grossly negligent to the merely absent, and on those few occasions when I have tried dutifully to record a day's events, boredom has so overcome me that the results are mysterious at best. What is this business about "shopping, typing piece, dinner with E, depressed"? Shopping for what? Typing what piece? Who is E? Was this "E" depressed, or was I depressed? Who cares?

In fact I have abandoned altogether that kind of pointless entry; instead 7 I tell what some would call lies. "That's simply not true," the members of my family frequently tell me when they come up against my memory of a shared event. "The party was *not* for you, the spider was *not* a black widow, *it wasn't that way at all.*" Very likely they are right, for not only have I always had trouble distinguishing between what happened and what merely might have happened, but I remain unconvinced that the distinction, for my purposes, matters. The cracked crab that I recall having for lunch the day my father came home from Detroit in 1945 must certainly be embroidery, worked into the day's pattern to lend verisimilitude; I was ten years old and would not now remember the cracked crab. The day's events did not turn on cracked crab. And yet it is precisely that fictitious crab that makes me see the afternoon all over again, a home movie run all too often, the father bearing gifts, the child weeping, an exercise in family love and guilt. Or that is what it was to me. Similarly, perhaps it never did snow that August in Vermont; perhaps there never were flurries in the night wind, and maybe no one else felt the ground hardening and summer already dead even as we pretended to bask in it, but that was how it felt to me, and it might as well have snowed, could have snowed, did snow.

How it felt to me: That is getting closer to the truth about a notebook. I 8 sometimes delude myself about why I keep a notebook, imagine that some thrifty virtue derives from preserving everything observed. See enough and write it down, I tell myself, and then some morning when the world seems drained of wonder, some day when I am only going through the motions of doing what I am supposed to do, which is write — on that bankrupt morning I will simply open my notebook and there it will all be, a forgotten account with accumulated interest, paid passage back to the world out there: dialogue overheard in hotels and elevators and at the hatcheck counter in Pavillon (one middle-aged man shows his hat check to another and says, "That's my old football number"); impressions of Bettina Aptheker and Benjamin Sonnenberg and Teddy ("Mr. Acapulco") Stauffer; careful *aperçus* about tennis bums and failed fashion models and Greek shipping heiresses, one of whom taught me a significant lesson (a lesson I could have learned from F. Scott Fitzgerald, but perhaps we all must meet the very rich for ourselves) by asking, when I arrived to interview her in her orchid-filled sitting room on the second day of a paralyzing New York blizzard, whether it was snowing outside.

I imagine, in other words, that the notebook is about other people. But 9 of course it is not. I have no real business with what one stranger said to another at the hatcheck counter in Pavillon; in fact I suspect that the line "That's my old football number" touched not my own imagination at all, but merely some memory of something once read, probably "The Eighty-Yard Run." Nor is my concern with a woman in a dirty crepe-de-Chine wrapper in a Wilmington bar. My stake is always, of course, in the unmentioned girl in the plaid silk dress. *Remember what it was to be me:* That is always the point.

It is a difficult point to admit. We are brought up in the ethic that oth- 10 ers, any others, all others, are by definition more interesting than ourselves; taught to be diffident, just this side of self-effacing. ("You're the least important person in the room and don't forget it," Jessica Mitford's governess would hiss in her ear on the advent of any social occasion; I copied that into my notebook because it is only recently that I have been able to enter a room without hearing some such phrase in my inner ear.) Only the very young and the very old may recount their dreams at breakfast, dwell upon self, interrupt with memories of beach picnics and favorite Liberty lawn dresses and the rainbow trout in a creek near Colorado Springs. The rest of us are expected, rightly, to affect absorption in other people's favorite dresses, other people's trout.

And so we do. But our notebooks give us away, for however dutifully we   11
record what we see around us, the common denominator of all we see is always, transparently, shamelessly, the implacable "I." We are not talking here about the kind of notebook that is patently for public consumption, a structural conceit for binding together a series of graceful *pensées*;[1] we are talking about something private, about bits of the mind's string too short to use, an indiscriminate and erratic assemblage with meaning only for its maker.

And sometimes even the maker has difficulty with the meaning. There   12
does not seem to be, for example, any point in my knowing for the rest of my life that, during 1964, 720 tons of soot fell on every square mile of New York City, yet there it is in my notebook, labeled "FACT." Nor do I really need to remember that Ambrose Bierce liked to spell Leland Stanford's name "£eland $tanford" or that "smart women almost always wear black in Cuba," a fashion hint without much potential for practical application. And does not the relevance of these notes seem marginal at best?:

> In the basement museum of the Inyo County Courthouse in Independence, California, sign pinned to a mandarin coat: "This MANDARIN COAT was often worn by Mrs. Minnie S. Brooks when giving lectures on her TEAPOT COLLECTION."

> Redhead getting out of car in front of Beverly Wilshire Hotel, chinchilla stole, Vuitton bags with tags reading:

> MRS LOU FOX
> HOTEL SAHARA
> VEGAS

Well, perhaps not entirely marginal. As a matter of fact, Mrs. Minnie S.   13
Brooks and her MANDARIN COAT pull me back into my own childhood, for although I never knew Mrs. Brooks and did not visit Inyo County until I was thirty, I grew up in just such a world, in houses cluttered with Indian relics and bits of gold ore and ambergris and the souvenirs my Aunt Mercy Farnsworth brought back from the Orient. It is a long way from that world to Mrs. Lou Fox's world, where we all live now, and is it not just as well to

---

[1] *pensées* In French, connected thoughts or philosophical reflections.

remember that? Might not Mrs. Minnie S. Brooks help me to remember what I am? Might not Mrs. Lou Fox help me to remember what I am not?

But sometimes the point is harder to discern. What exactly did I have in 14 mind when I noted down that it cost the father of someone I know $650 a month to light the place on the Hudson in which he lived before the Crash? What use was I planning to make of this line by Jimmy Hoffa: "I may have my faults, but being wrong ain't one of them"? And although I think it interesting to know where the girls who travel with the Syndicate have their hair done when they find themselves on the West Coast, will I ever make suitable use of it? Might I not be better off just passing it on to John O'Hara? What is a recipe for sauerkraut doing in my notebook? What kind of magpie keeps this notebook? "*He was born the night the Titanic went down.*" That seems a nice enough line, and I even recall who said it, but is it not really a better line in life than it could ever be in fiction?

But of course that is exactly it: not that I should ever use the line, but 15 that I should remember the woman who said it and the afternoon I heard it. We were on her terrace by the sea, and we were finishing the wine left from lunch, trying to get what sun there was, a California winter sun. The woman whose husband was born the night the *Titanic* went down wanted to rent her house, wanted to go back to her children in Paris. I remember wishing that I could afford the house, which cost $1,000 a month. "Someday you will," she said lazily. "Someday it all comes." There in the sun on her terrace it seemed easy to believe in someday, but later I had a low-grade afternoon hangover and ran over a black snake on the way to the supermarket and was flooded with inexplicable fear when I heard the checkout clerk explaining to the man ahead of me why she was finally divorcing her husband. "He left me no choice," she said over and over as she punched the register. "He has a little seven-month-old baby by her, he left me no choice." I would like to believe that my dread then was for the human condition, but of course it was for me, because I wanted a baby and did not then have one and because I wanted to own the house that cost $1,000 a month to rent and because I had a hangover.

It all comes back. Perhaps it is difficult to see the value in having one's 16 self back in that kind of mood, but I do see it; I think we are well advised to keep on nodding terms with the people we used to be whether we find them attractive company or not. Otherwise they turn up unannounced and surprise us, come hammering on the mind's door at 4 A.M. of a bad night and demand to know who deserted them, who betrayed them, who is going to make amends. We forget all too soon the things we thought we could never forget. We forget the loves and the betrayals alike, forget what we whispered and what we screamed, forget who we were. I have already lost touch with a couple of people I used to be; one of them, a seventeen-year-old, presents little threat, although it would be of some interest to me to know again what it feels like to sit on a river levee drinking vodka-and-orange-juice and listening to Les Paul and Mary Ford and their echoes sing "How High the Moon" on the car radio. (You see I still have the scenes, but I no longer perceive myself among those present, no longer could even improvise the dialogue.) The other one, a twenty-three-year-old, bothers me more. She was always a good deal of trouble, and I suspect she will reappear when I least want to see her, skirts too long, shy to the point of aggravation, always the injured party, full of recriminations and little hurts and stories I do not want to hear again, at once saddening me and angering me with her vulnerability and ignorance, an apparition all the more insistent for being so long banished.

It is a good idea, then, to keep in touch, and I suppose that keeping in   17
touch is what notebooks are all about. And we are all on our own when it comes to keeping those lines open to ourselves: Your notebook will never help me, nor mine you. "*So what's new in the whiskey business?*" What could that possibly mean to you? To me it means a blonde in a Pucci bathing suit sitting with a couple of fat men by the pool at the Beverly Hills Hotel. Another man approaches, and they all regard one another in silence for a while. "So what's new in the whiskey business?" one of the fat men finally says by way of welcome, and the blonde stands up, arches one foot and dips it in the pool, looking all the while at the cabaña where Baby Pignatari is talking on the telephone. That is all there is to that, except that several years later I saw the blonde coming out of Saks Fifth Avenue in New York with her California complexion and a voluminous mink coat. In the harsh wind that day she looked old and irrevocably tired to me, and even the skins in the mink coat were not worked the way they were doing them that year, not the way she would have wanted them done, and there is the point of the story. For a while after that I did not like to look in the mirror, and my eyes would skim the newspapers and pick out only the deaths, the cancer victims, the premature coronaries, the suicides, and I stopped riding the Lexington Avenue IRT because I noticed for the first time that all the strangers I had seen for years — the man with the seeing-eye dog, the spinster who read the classified pages every day, the fat girl who always got off with me at Grand Central — looked older than they once had.

It all comes back. Even that recipe for sauerkraut: Even that brings it   18
back. I was on Fire Island when I first made that sauerkraut, and it was raining, and we drank a lot of bourbon and ate the sauerkraut and went to bed at ten, and I listened to the rain and the Atlantic and felt safe. I made the sauerkraut again last night and it did not make me feel any safer, but that is, as they say, another story.

Analyzing This Selection

1. How does Didion contrast the purposes of a diary and of a notebook? Why does she consider herself unsuited to diary-keeping?

2. **THE WRITER'S METHOD** How does Didion's style illustrate her statement of purpose for writing?

3. Didion says, "I have already lost touch with a couple of people I used to be" (paragraph 16) and names two such people. Has she really lost touch with them?

Analyzing Connections

4. Autobiographical essayists such as Ephron (p. 20), Angelou (p. 178), and Tan (p. 189) also write about people they "used to be." What similar or differing methods enrich notebook-writing and writing about oneself for an audience?

Analyzing by Writing

5. Explain the reasons you once had for starting a diary, notebook, or journal. Include enough details to illustrate your motives and interests at that time. If you have never kept one, try to imagine why you might want to now.

Helen Vendler

KNOWING POEMS[1]

HELEN VENDLER (b. 1933), a distinguished literary critic, went to parochial school in Boston, Massachusetts, as the following selection discusses. She graduated from Emmanuel College and received a Ph.D. from Harvard University, where she now teaches. She has received numerous fellowships, such as a Guggenheim Fellowship, and awards, including the Lowell Prize for *On Extended Wings: Wallace Stevens' Longer Poems* (1969) and the National Book Critics Award for *Part of Nature, Part of Us: Modern American Poets* (1980). "Knowing Poems" is excerpted from a longer personal essay commissioned for *Communion: Contemporary Writers Reveal the Bible in Their Lives* (1996).

My days as a child invariably began with the morning Mass to which my 1
mother took us. It was almost always a requiem Mass, sung in Latin, since deaths were commemorated a month afterward and a year afterward, and, in a sizable parish, such memorials crowded the calendar. My earliest memories are of the *Dies Irae* and, for some reason, of the long mournful strophes of the preface: "*Tuis enim fidelibus, Domine, vita mutatur, non tollitur; et dissoluta huius terrestris incolatus domo, aeterna in coelo habitatio comparatur,*"[2] all sung to the plangent lifts and falls of Gregorian chant. At nine, teaching my seven-year-old brother the Latin responses to the Mass so that he could be an altar boy, I learned the Latin of the Mass more or less by heart, and this gave me the wish to learn Latin (I already knew Spanish, French, and Italian, which my father had taught us). It was in the text of the Mass that I first met the antiphonal rhythms of the Psalms: "*Introibo ad altare Dei, ad Deum qui laetificat juventutem meam.*"[3] At the same time, I was hearing the Psalms (the more amiable ones, naturally) read to us, in the King James Version, in my public school, one a day, before we pledged

---

[1]Editor's title.

[2]*Tuis . . . comparatur* For those who are faithful to thee, Lord, life is changed, not ended; and when their earthly dwelling place decays, an everlasting mansion stands prepared for them in heaven (from the Missal).

[3]*Introibo . . . meam* I will go in to the altar of God: to God who giveth joy to my youth (from the Douay Bible).

allegiance to the flag. Miss Fallon's low, harmonious voice is still in my ear, reading the obscurely satisfying cadences: "I will lift up mine eyes unto the hills, from whence cometh my help." But the Psalms were then no more than ravishing turns of phrase, whether in Latin or in English. I did not yet *need* the Psalms, or didn't know I needed them.

At ten, old enough for the streetcar, I was sent to the parochial school in the next parish (our parish had not yet acquired a school). Among many ungifted teachers, there was one uncannily inspired one, a young Lebanese nun who was (in spite of my having had two piano teachers) the first musical person I had encountered. She believed that a random group of mostly lower-class children could be taught to sing the Latin liturgy in Gregorian chant, and with her expressive eyes and her even more expressive conducting hand, she took us into the Psalms, notably during the long Holy Week service (now discontinued in the Roman Catholic Church) called *Tenebrae*. The nine Psalms of Matins and the four of Lauds for the appropriate day were sung: for Good Friday, for instance, this meant (in the Douay Bible numbering), Psalms 2, 21, 26, 37, 39, 53, 58, 87, 93, 50, 142, 84, and 147. I took to spending my spare time in the seventh and eighth grade learning Latin so I could follow the texts at least approximately; and since I was steeped in friendless adolescent misery at school, and the beginnings of appalled recognition of the life at home, the Psalms became my poems of reference.

I had had poetry read to me since birth by my melancholy mother (a primary-school teacher who, by marrying, had lost her fourteen-year career, since married women were not permitted to continue to work in the Boston school system); and I had read a fair amount of verse here and there on my own; but the Psalms were, I think, the first sublime poetry I consciously took on as my own. I didn't, even then, read them as the word of God. I don't believe I read them, or sang them, chiefly in an inner atmosphere of belief. I had already begun the rude questioning of the dogma and discipline of Roman Catholicism that led to my abandoning the Church forever as soon as I left my parents' house; and I was always of a skeptical temperament, impatient of all nonevidential talk of Virgin Birth and Resurrection (taught by the church as facts, not symbols).

When I try, now, to recapture my feelings at eleven and twelve, singing the verses of the Psalms, what I recall is the fierceness with which I appropriated the Psalmist's voice as mine. *I* cried out of the depths; *I* asked my soul, "Why art thou sad, O my soul? and why doest thou trouble me? Why go *I* mourning, whilst my enemy afflicteth me?" I was as likely to say it to myself in the language of the Mass — "*Quare tristis es, anima mea, et quare conturbas me?*" — as I was to read it in the Bible.

What did I gain, between ten and thirteen, from the Voice of the Psalmist? Equivalents for all my stifled and inarticulate feelings. I didn't often turn to those kinder psalms that had been read to me in public school. What I found were the wild psalms:

> I am poured out like water; and all my bones are scattered.
> My heart is become like wax melting in the midst of my bowels.
> My strength is dried up like a potsherd, and my tongue hath cleaved
>   to my jaws: and thou hast brought me down into the dust of death.

If anyone doubts that these are the emotions of adolescence, he has forgotten his youth. The insanity of stifled feeling, in my case, could only be stemmed by adequacy of expression, and since I had absolutely no adequate words myself for my own despair, I was abjectly grateful to the Psalmist.

The Psalms gave me, too, my first intuition of intertextuality.[4] As I came   6 on Psalm 21 for the first time, I remember being shocked, because I had had no idea, when I had heard the Passion read in church, that Jesus was *quoting* when he cried out, "My God, my God, why hast thou forsaken me" — the phrase that opens Psalm 21. If *he* could borrow the Psalmist's words and say them *in propria persona*,[5] so could I. The psalm that best expressed my feeling of being sentenced to indefinite punishment merely by living as and where I did, in an atmosphere that permitted no personal freedom of thought or action, was 128:

> Often have they fought against me from my youth, let Israel now say.
> Often have they fought against me from my youth; but they could not
>   prevail over me.
> The wicked have wrought upon my back: they have lengthened their
>   iniquity . . .
> And they that passed by have not said: The blessing of the Lord be
>   upon you: we have blessed you in the name of the Lord.

Lest it be thought that I exaggerate my feelings, let me add the fact that a poem I wrote at fifteen began, "Pitiless with repression, / They told me I must dwell / Within the narrow prison / They lived in." I was enraged, and helpless, and in prison; and I knew, in my twelfth year, no words but the Psalmist's to say my feelings for me. The Psalmist had satisfying curses, a form not much encouraged in books for the young; the Psalms thus became my first clandestine literature:

> May his children be fatherless, and his wife a widow.
> Let his children be carried about vagabonds, and beg; and let them be
>   cast out of their dwellings . . .
> May the iniquity of his fathers be remembered in the sight of the Lord:
>   and let not the sin of his mother be blotted out . . .
> And he put on cursing, like a garment: and it went in like water into
>   his entrails, and like oil in his bones. (108)

---

[4]*intertextuality* Allusion to another work.
[5]*in propria persona* Jesus quoted this familiar line as if it were his own.

These words were for me like plasters applied to nameless wounds. 7
Almost everything I felt the Psalmist had words for. (The other feelings
found solace three years later, when I was fifteen, in Shakespeare's sonnets.) I don't know what I would have done with the grinding and self-
abasing and furious and lacerating feelings of my twelfth year without the
Psalms. They drew off the worst of the poison (by allowing me, among
other things, to put on cursing like a garment), and they filled my mouth
with language. A choking sensation in the heart, a smothering in the lungs,
a frenzy in the brain, an anger in the blood, tormented me every day, all
day, in those years. I had no one to confide in and no one to explain my
feelings to me. Only the Psalmist knew my soul, and I his. . . .

Because the speech of the Psalms is often choral, and because it was 8
adapted to liturgical use, it never seemed to me language written with
respect to gender. Rather, like most lyric speech, it was voiceable by anyone. I believe that poetry became for me the most natural of the genres
because of the Psalms; and later, when I came to study poetry and write
about it, I found that the web composed of biblical texts, the liturgy, and
the hymnal extended its threads deep into the English lyric. Most readers
are drawn to narrative, to the line that prolongs itself to an end; but I was
drawn to meditation, to the ripples of intensification extending out from a
center of thought. It is that concentric structure of the meditative lyric,
from the Psalms to Wallace Stevens, that still seems to me the most compelling form of writing ever invented. . . .

The Psalms were not the sort of reading given to young girls by schools 9
and public libraries in my day — nor would they be recommended to twelve-
year-old girls these days, either. Without disparaging the release of inchoate
feeling offered adolescents by the Judy Blumes of the Young Adult shelves,
I wish that our culture dealt out the wild verities of the Psalmist (and, to
supplement him, the Shakespeare of the *Sonnets*) instead. Imagine a school
system where every day a psalm and a Shakespeare sonnet were chorally
recited by every class. When the end of the Psalter was reached, Psalm I
would come round again; when the end of the *Sonnets* was reached, the
cycle would rebegin. From, say, the third grade on, the whole Psalter, every
year, and the 154 sonnets, every year: why, by Grade 12 the students would
be literate. And, as a dividend, liberated in their hearts' passions.

Analyzing This Selection

1. **THE WRITER'S METHOD**   The author's upbringing was unusual, but
   Vendler says her feelings were "the emotions of adolescence." Do you think
   they expressed what most adolescents feel? What details help generalize her
   feelings?

2. When Vendler was twelve, how did the Psalms affect her? When she was fifteen, why did she prefer other poems?

3. What is your view of Vendler's proposal for schools? How would such a requirement have affected your schooling? affected your feelings?

Analyzing Connections

4. Vendler and Angelou (see "Graduation," p. 178) were sustained in adolescence by poems. What similar and differing circumstances and feelings did they experience? Consider whether Angelou's essay supports or contradicts Vendler's statement that her feelings were "the emotions of adolescence."

Analyzing by Writing

5. Examine your reasons for reading a novel or collection of poems over and over. What satisfactions did you find in that particular book and not another? Take into account the range of relevant circumstances that may have included reading aloud, reading in solitude, imagining yourself participating, getting away, or other repetitions.

Deborah Tannen

TALKING UP CLOSE

DEBORAH TANNEN (b. 1945) received a Ph.D. in linguistics from the University of California at Berkeley. She teaches at Georgetown University. Her scholarly research in sociolinguistics led to her writing also for a general audience. *You Just Don't Understand: Women and Men in Conversation* (1990) raised public awareness of gender differences in communication style. The following selection is excerpted from *Talking 9 to 5* (1994).

It is frequently observed that male speakers are more likely to be confrontational by arguing, issuing commands, and taking opposing stands for the sake of argument, whereas females are more likely to avoid confrontation by agreeing, supporting, and making suggestions rather than commands.[1] . . . Cultural linguist Walter Ong argues that "adversativeness" — a tendency to fight — is universal, but "conspicuous or expressed adversativeness is a larger element in the lives of males than of females."[2] In other words, females may well fight, but males are more likely to fight often, openly, and for the fun of it.

But what does it mean to say that males fight more than females? One thing it does not mean is that females therefore are more connected to each other. Because status and connection are mutually evocative, both fighting with each other and banding together to fight others can create strong connections among males, for example by affiliation within a team. In this regard, a man recalled that when he was young, he and his friends amused themselves after school by organizing fights among themselves. When school let out, the word would go out about who was going to fight whom in whose backyard. Yet these fights were part of the boys' friendship and did not evidence mutual animosity. (Contrast this with a group of girls

---

[1]The research on male and female styles of conflict is summarized by Maltz and Borker and by Maccoby. Many researchers who study children at play have documented that boys of all ages engage in conflict that is physically rougher and takes up more of their time than girls' conflicts. In her article "Pickle Fights: Gendered Talk in Preschool Disputes," Amy Sheldon both presents evidence from her own research to support this and summarizes other research. [Au.]

[2]"*Adversativeness is a larger element in the lives of males than of females.*" Ong, p. 51. [Au.]

banding together to pick on a low-status girl, without anyone landing a physical blow.)

I think, as well, of my eighty-five-year-old uncle who still meets yearly   3
with his buddies from World War II, even though the members of his battalion are from vastly different cultural and geographic backgrounds. It is difficult to imagine anything other than war that could have bonded men from such different backgrounds into a group whose members feel such lasting devotion. Indeed, a man who was sent to Vietnam because of an error gave this as the reason he did not try to set the record straight and go home: "I found out I belonged in Vietnam," he said. "The bonding of men at war was the strongest thing I'd felt in my life."[3]

Folklore provides numerous stories in which fighting precipitates friend-   4
ship among men. Robert Bly recounts one such story which he identifies as Joseph Campbell's account of the Sumerian epic *Gilgamesh*. In Bly's rendition, Gilgamesh, a young king, wants to befriend a wild man named Enkidu. When Enkidu is told of Gilgamesh,

> . . . his heart grew light. He yearned for a friend. "Very well!" he said. "And I shall challenge him."

Bly paraphrases the continuation: "Enkidu then travels to the city and meets Gilgamesh; the two wrestle, Enkidu wins, and the two become inseparable friends."[4]

A modern-day equivalent of the bonding that results from ritual opposi-   5
tion can be found in business, where individuals may compete, argue, or even fight for their view without feeling personal enmity. Opposition as a ritualized format for inquiry is institutionalized most formally in the legal profession, and it is expected that each side will do its best to attack the other and yet retain friendly relations when the case is closed.

These examples show that aggression can be a way of establishing   6
connection to others. Many cultures see arguing as a pleasurable sign of intimacy. Linguist Deborah Schiffrin examined conversations among lower-middle-class men *and women* of East European Jewish background in Philadelphia and found that friendly banter was one of the fundamental ways they enjoyed and reinforced their friendship. A similar ethic obtains among Germans, who like to engage in combative intellectual debate about such controversial topics as politics and religion, according to linguist Heidi Byrnes, who was born and raised in Germany. Byrnes points out that this has rather negative consequences in cross-cultural contact. German

---

[3]*"The bonding of men at war was the strongest thing I'd felt in my life." People* magazine, March 21, 1994, p. 110. The man is Paul Mahar. He showed up to be shipped to Vietnam in his best friend's place because he was sure they would send him home when they discovered a metal plate in his arm. They didn't. They sent him to Vietnam. [Au.]

[4]*". . . and the two become inseparable friends."* Bly recounts this story in *Iron John: A Book About Men* (Reading, MA: Addison-Wesley, 1990), pp. 243–44. He cites as his source Joseph Campbell's *The Masks of God: Occidental Mythology* (New York: Viking, 1964). [Au.]

students try to show their friendliness to American students by provoking heated arguments about American foreign policy. But the Americans, who consider it inappropriate to argue with someone they have just met, refuse to take part. The German students conclude that Americans are uninformed and uncommitted, while the Americans go away convinced that Germans are belligerent and rude.

Linguist Christina Kakava shows that modern Greek conversation is also   7
characterized by friendly argument. She found, by taping dinner-table conversation, that members of a Greek family enjoyed opposing each other. In a study we conducted together, Kakava and I showed that modern Greek speakers routinely disagree when they actually agree, a practice that explains my own experience — and discomfort — when I lived in Greece.[5]

I was in a suburb of Athens, talking to an older woman whom I call Ms.   8
Stella, who had just told me about complaining to the police because a construction crew working on the house beside hers illegally continued drilling and pounding through the siesta hours, disturbing her midafternoon nap. I tried to be nice by telling her she was right, but she would not accept my agreement. She managed to maintain her independence by restating her position in different terms. Our conversation (which I taped), translated into English, went like this:

Deborah: You're right.

Stella: I *am* right. My dear girl, I don't know if I'm right or I'm not right. But I am watching out for my interests and my rights.

Clearly, Ms. Stella thought she was right, but she did not want the lively conversation to dissipate in so dull a way as her accepting my statement, "You're right," so she managed to disagree: "I don't know if I'm right or I'm not right." Disagreeing allowed her to amplify her position as well.

This was typical of conversations I found myself in when I lived in   9
Greece. I vividly recall my frustration when I uttered what to me were fairly automatic expressions of agreement and support and found myself on the receiving end of what seemed like hostile refusal to accept my agreement. I frequently felt distanced and put down when my attempts to agree were met with contentious responses. In an effort to make things right, I would try harder to be agreeable, so that my conversations became veritable litanies of agreement: Exactly!, Absolutely!, Without a doubt! But my Greek interlocutors probably were puzzled, irritated, and bored by my relentless agreement, and stepped up their contentiousness in their efforts to liven up the interactions.

As evidence that contentious argument helps create connection among   10
Greek friends, I offer an example taken from the study by Kakava, who was also a participant. The other two speakers were her friends, two brothers

---

[5]My paper, written with Christina Kakava, is "Power and Solidarity in Modern Greek Conversation." [Au.]

she calls George and Alkis. George was showing off a belt he had received as a gift, and the three friends argued animatedly about its color:

George: I've got burgundy shoes, but the belt's got black in it too.

Kakava: Does it have black in it? Let me see.

George: It has a stripe in it that's kind of black.

Alkis: Dark brown.

George: It's kind of dark.

Alkis: It's tobacco-colored, dummy! It goes with everything.

George: Tobacco-colored? What are you talking about?! Are you color-blind?!

Conversations in this spirit often give Americans the impression that Greeks are fighting when they are just having an animated conversation.

The discussion of fighting, silence, and interrupting is intended to show   11
that it is impossible to determine what a way of speaking "really means" because the same way of speaking can create either status differences or connection, or both at the same time.

"Is It You or Me?"

Again and again, when I have explained two different ways of saying or   12
doing the same thing, I am asked, "Which way is best?" or "Which way is right?" We are all in pursuit of the right way of speaking, like the holy grail. But there is no one right way, any more than there is a holy grail — at least not one we can hope to find. Most important, and most frustrating, the "true" intention or motive of any utterance cannot be determined merely by considering the linguistic strategy used.

Intentions and effects are not identical. When people have differing con-   13
versational styles, the effect of what they say may be very different from their intention. And anything that happens between two people is the result of both their actions. Sociolinguists talk about this by saying that all inter-action is "a joint production." The double meaning of status and connection makes every utterance potentially ambiguous and even polysemous (meaning many things at once).

When we think we have made ourselves clear, or think we understand   14
what someone else has said, we feel safe in the conviction that we know what words mean. When someone insists those words meant something else, we can feel like Alice trying to talk to Humpty-Dumpty, who isn't fazed by her protest that "glory doesn't mean a nice knock-down argument" but claims with aplomb, "When I use a word it means what I want it to mean, neither more nor less." If others get to make up their own rules for what words mean, the earth starts slipping beneath our feet. One of the

sources of that slippage is the ambiguity and polysemy of status and connection — the fact that the same linguistic means can reflect and create one or the other or both. Understanding this makes it easier to understand the logic behind others' apparently willful misinterpretations and makes the earth feel a little more firm beneath our feet.

References

Maccoby, Eleanor E., and Carol Jacklin. 1974. *The Psychology of Sex Differences*. Stanford, CA: Stanford University Press.

Maltz, Daniel N., and Ruth A. Borker. 1982. "A Cultural Approach to Male-Female Miscommunication." *Language and Social Identity*, ed. by John J. Gumperz, 196–216. Cambridge: Cambridge University Press.

Ong, Walter J. 1981. *Fighting for Life: Contest, Sexuality, and Consciousness*. Ithaca: Cornell University Press.

Tannen, Deborah, and Christina Kakava. 1992. "Power and Solidarity in Modern Greek Conversation: Disagreeing to Agree." *Journal of Modern Greek Studies* 10:1.11–34.

Analyzing This Selection

1. According to Tannen and other sociolinguists, what are the two purposes of conversations?

2. This selection includes examples of typically male speech, even from the Greek woman. Provide your examples of female conversational style. Do you think styles truly differ for men and women?

3. **THE WRITER'S METHOD**   What evidence in the essay gives the most convincing support to Tannen's generalizations?

Analyzing Connections

4. From a linguistic viewpoint, analyze the conversational styles in Carver's story ("What We Talk About When We Talk About Love," p. 160). How and for what purposes do the speakers interact?

Analyzing by Writing

5. Collect and examine examples of conversational styles among your acquaintances. Give details of their vocabulary, explaining the uses and tones of three or four key words or phrases. Illustrate your points with bits of dialogue, if helpful. Try to analyze the purposes of making conversations.

Pico Iyer

IN PRAISE OF THE HUMBLE COMMA

PICO IYER (b. 1957) was born in England to Indian parents. Educated at Eton and Oxford University, he became a travel writer by taking notes on vacation trips and "just writing about my holidays," he said in a recent interview. In graduate school at Harvard University, Iyer held summer jobs doing field work for *Let's Go*, a series of guidebooks for students. His travel book, *Video Night in Kathmandu: And Other Reports from the Not-So-Far East* (1988), observes the effects of consumer culture on traditional societies. His most recent book is *Tropic Classical: Essays from Several Directions* (1997). Iyer contributes articles to *Harper's*, the *New York Times*, and *Time* magazine, where this essay appeared.

The gods, they say, give breath, and they take it away. But the same 1 could be said — could it not? — of the humble comma. Add it to the present clause, and, of a sudden, the mind is, quite literally, given pause to think; take it out if you wish or forget it and the mind is deprived of a resting place. Yet still the comma gets no respect. It seems just a slip of a thing, a pedant's tick, a blip on the edge of our consciousness, a kind of printer's smudge almost. Small, we claim, is beautiful (especially in the age of the microchip). Yet what is so often used, and so rarely recalled, as the comma — unless it be breath itself?

Punctuation, one is taught, has a point: to keep up law and order. Punc- 2 tuation marks are the road signs placed along the highway of our communications — to control speeds, provide directions and prevent head-on collisions. A period has the unblinking finality of a red light; the comma is a flashing yellow light that asks us only to slow down; and the semicolon is a stop sign that tells us to ease gradually to a halt, before gradually starting up again. By establishing the relations between words, punctuation establishes the relations between the people using words. That may be one reason why schoolteachers exalt it and lovers defy it ("We love each other and belong to each other let's don't ever hurt each other Nicole let's don't ever hurt each other," wrote Gary Gilmore[1] to his girlfriend). A comma, he must have known, "separates inseparables," in the clinching words of H. W. Fowler, King of English Usage.

[1]*Gary Gilmore* A serial killer executed in 1977.

Punctuation, then, is a civic prop, a pillar that holds society upright. (A 3
run-on sentence, its phrases piling up without division, is as unsightly as a
sink piled high with dirty dishes.) Small wonder, then, that punctuation
was one of the first proprieties of the Victorian age, the age of the corset,
that the modernists threw off: the sexual revolution might be said to have
begun when Joyce's Molly Bloom spilled out all her private thoughts in 36
pages of unbridled, almost unperioded and officially censored prose; and
another rebellion was surely marked when E. E. Cummings first felt free to
commit "God" to the lower case.

Punctuation thus becomes the signature of cultures. The hot-blooded 4
Spaniard seems to be revealed in the passion and urgency of his doubled
exclamation points and question marks ("*¡Caramba! ¿Quien sabe?*"), while
the impassive Chinese traditionally added to his so-called inscrutability by
omitting directions from his ideograms. The anarchy and commotion of
the '60s were given voice in the exploding exclamation marks, riotous capital letters and Day-Glo italics of Tom Wolfe's spray-paint prose; and in
Communist societies, where the State is absolute, the dignity — and divinity — of capital letters is reserved for Ministries, Sub-Committees and Sec-
retariats.

Yet punctuation is something more than a culture's birthmark; it scores 5
the music in our minds, gets our thoughts moving to the rhythm of our
hearts. Punctuation is the notation in the sheet music of our words, telling
us where to rest, or when to raise our voices; it acknowledges that the
meaning of our discourse, as of any symphonic composition, lies not in
the units but in the pauses, the pacing and the phrasing. Punctuation is the
way one bats one's eyes, lowers one's voice or blushes demurely. Punctuation adjusts the tone and color and volume till the feeling comes into perfect focus, not disgust exactly, but distaste; not lust, or like, but love.

Punctuation, in short, gives us the human voice, and all the meanings 6
that lie between the words. "You aren't young, are you?" loses its innocence
when it loses the question mark. Every child knows the menace of a
dropped apostrophe (the parent's "Don't do that" shifting into the more
slowly enunciated "Do not do that"), and every believer, the ignominy of
having his faith reduced to "faith." Add an exclamation point to "To be or
not to be . . ." and the gloomy Dane has all the resolve he needs; add a
comma, and the noble sobriety of "God save the Queen" becomes a cry of
desperation bordering on double sacrilege.

Sometimes, of course, our markings may be simply a matter of aesthet- 7
ics. Popping in a comma can be like slipping on the necklace that gives an
outfit quiet elegance, or like catching the sound of running water that com-
plements, as it completes, the silence of a Japanese landscape. When V. S.
Naipaul, in his latest novel, writes, "He was a middle-aged man, with
glasses," the first comma can seem a little precious. Yet it gives the description a spin, as well as a subtlety, that it otherwise lacks, and it shows that
the glasses are not part of the middle-agedness, but something else.

Thus all these tiny scratches give us breadth and heft and depth. A world ⁸ that has only periods is a world without inflections. It is a world without shade. It has a music without sharps and flats. It is a martial music. It has a jackboot rhythm. Words cannot bend and curve. A comma, by comparison, catches the gentle drift of the mind in thought, turning in on itself and back on itself, reversing, redoubling and returning along the course of its own sweet river music; while the semicolon brings clauses and thoughts together with all the silent discretion of a hostess arranging guests around her dinner table.

Punctuation, then, is a matter of care. Care for words, yes, but also, and ⁹ more important, for what the words imply. Only a lover notices the small things: the way the afternoon light catches the nape of a neck, or how a strand of hair slips out from behind an ear, or the way a finger curls around a cup. And no one scans a letter so closely as a lover, searching for its small print, straining to hear its nuances, its gasps, its sighs and hesitations, poring over the secret messages that lie in every cadence. The difference between "Jane (whom I adore)" and "Jane, whom I adore," and the difference between them both and "Jane — whom I adore —" marks all the distance between ecstasy and heartache. "No iron can pierce the heart with such force as a period put at just the right place," in Isaac Babel's lovely words: a comma can let us hear a voice break, or a heart. Punctuation, in fact, is a labor of love. Which brings us back, in a way, to gods.

Analyzing This Selection

1. **THE WRITER'S METHOD**   In paragraph 1, how does the author make the topic humorous? What details and methods start it off?

2. What is the effect of the selection's abundant metaphors and analogies? Are there too many, overcrowding and cluttering the explanations?

Analyzing Connections

3. Examine the punctuation in paragraphs 1 to 3 of Didion's essay ("On Keeping a Notebook," p. 243), and explain how the marks express her "care . . . for what the words imply." How do changes in punctuation alter the meaning?

Analyzing by Writing

4. Write two paragraphs using no commas but including other punctuation marks. Write fully developed sentences, and try to find varied, equivalent punctuation for nuances of meaning.

Susanne K. Langer

LANGUAGE AND THOUGHT

Susanne K. Langer (1895–1985) was an influential American philosopher. Educated at Radcliffe College and Harvard University, where she first taught, Langer continued a distinguished academic career at Columbia University and Connecticut College. Her books include *Philosophy in a New Key: A Study in the Symbolism of Reason, Rite, and Art* (1942), *Feeling and Form* (1953), and *Mind: An Essay in Human Feeling* (1967). The following essay appeared in *Ms.* magazine.

A symbol is not the same thing as a sign; that is a fact that psychologists 1 and philosophers often overlook. All intelligent animals use signs; so do we. To them as well as to us sounds and smells and motions are signs of food, danger, the presence of other beings, or of rain or storm. Furthermore, some animals not only attend to signs but produce them for the benefit of others. Dogs bark at the door to be let in; rabbits thump to call each other; the cooing of doves and the growl of a wolf defending his kill are unequivocal signs of feelings and intentions to be reckoned with by other creatures.

We use signs just as animals do, though with considerably more elabo- 2 ration. We stop at red lights and go on green; we answer calls and bells, watch the sky for coming storms, read trouble or promise or anger in each other's eyes. That is animal intelligence raised to the human level. Those of us who are dog lovers can probably all tell wonderful stories of how high our dogs have sometimes risen in the scale of clever sign interpretation and sign using.

A sign is anything that announces the existence or the imminence of 3 some event, the presence of a thing or a person, or a change in the state of affairs. There are signs of the weather, signs of danger, signs of future good or evil, signs of what the past has been. In every case a sign is closely bound up with something to be noted or expected in experience. It is always a part of the situation to which it refers, though the reference may be remote in space and time. In so far as we are led to note or expect the signified event we are making correct use of a sign. This is the essence of rational behavior, which animals show in varying degrees. It is entirely realistic, being closely bound up with the actual objective course of history — learned by experience, and cashed in or voided by further experience.

If man had kept to the straight and narrow path of sign using, he would   4
be like the other animals, though perhaps a little brighter. He would not
talk, but grunt and gesticulate the point. He would make his wishes known,
give warnings, perhaps develop a social system like that of bees and ants,
with such a wonderful efficiency of communal enterprise that all men
would have plenty to eat, warm apartments — all exactly alike and perfectly convenient — to live in, and everybody could and would sit in the
sun or by the fire, as the climate demanded, not talking but just basking,
with every want satisfied, most of his life. The young would romp and
make love, the old would sleep, the middle-aged would do the routine
work almost unconsciously and eat a great deal. But that would be the life
of a social, superintelligent, purely sign-using animal.

To us who are human, it does not sound very glorious. We want to go   5
places and do things, own all sorts of gadgets that we do not absolutely
need, and when we sit down to take it easy we want to talk. Rights and
property, social position, special talents and virtues, and above all our ideas,
are what we live for. We have gone off on a tangent that takes us far away
from the mere biological cycle that animal generations accomplish; and
that is because we can use not only signs but symbols.

A symbol differs from a sign in that it does not announce the presence   6
of the object, the being, condition, or whatnot, which is its meaning, but
merely *brings this thing to mind*. It is not a mere "substitute sign" to which
we react as though it were the object itself. The fact is that our reaction to
hearing a person's name is quite different from our reaction to the person
himself. There are certain rare cases where a symbol stands directly for its
meaning: in religious experience, for instance, the Host is not only a symbol but a Presence. But symbols in the ordinary sense are not mystic. They
are the same sort of thing that ordinary signs are; only they do not call our
attention to something necessarily present or to be physically dealt with —
they call up merely a conception of the thing they "mean."

The difference between a sign and a symbol is, in brief, that a sign   7
causes us to think or act *in face* of the thing signified, whereas a symbol
causes us to think *about* the thing symbolized. Therein lies the great
importance of symbolism for human life, its power to make this life so different from any other animal biography that generations of men have
found it incredible to suppose that they were of purely zoological origin. A
sign is always embedded in reality, in a present that emerges from the
actual past and stretches to the future; but a symbol may be divorced from
reality altogether. It may refer to what is not the case, to a mere idea, a fig-
ment, a dream. It serves, therefore, to liberate thought from the immediate
stimuli of a physically present world; and that liberation marks the essential
difference between human and nonhuman mentality. Animals think, but
they think *of* and *at* things; men think primarily *about* things. Words, pictures, and memory images are symbols that may be combined and varied
in a thousand ways. The result is a symbolic structure whose meaning is

a complex of all their respective meanings, and this kaleidoscope of *ideas* is the typical product of the human brain that we call the "stream of thought."

The process of transforming all direct experience into imagery or into   8 that supreme mode of symbolic expression, language, has so completely taken possession of the human mind that it is not only a special talent but a dominant, organic need. All our sense impressions leave their traces in our memory not only as signs disposing our practical reactions in the future but also as symbols, images representing our *ideas* of things; and the tendency to manipulate ideas, to combine and abstract, mix and extend them by playing with symbols, is man's outstanding characteristic. It seems to be what his brain most naturally and spontaneously does. Therefore his primitive mental function is not judging reality, but *dreaming his desires.*

Dreaming is apparently a basic function of human brains, for it is free   9 and unexhausting like our metabolism, heartbeat, and breath. It is easier to dream than not to dream, as it is easier to breathe than to refrain from breathing. The symbolic character of dreams is fairly well established. Symbol mongering, on this ineffectual, uncritical level, seems to be instinctive, the fulfillment of an elementary need rather than the purposeful exercise of a high and difficult talent.

The special power of man's mind rests on the evolution of this special   10 activity, not on any transcendently high development of animal intelligence. We are not immeasurably higher than other animals; we are different. We have a biological need and with it a biological gift that they do not share.

Because man has not only the ability but the constant need of *conceiving* what has happened to him, what surrounds him, what is demanded of   11 him — in short, of symbolizing nature, himself, and his hopes and fears — he has a constant and crying need of *expression.* What he cannot express, he cannot conceive; what he cannot conceive is chaos, and fills him with terror.

If we bear in mind this all-important craving for expression we get a new   12 picture of man's behavior; for from this trait spring his powers and his weaknesses. The process of symbolic transformation that all our experiences undergo is nothing more nor less than the process of *conception,* underlying the human faculties of abstraction and imagination.

When we are faced with a strange or difficult situation, we cannot react   13 directly, as other creatures do, with flight, aggression, or any such simple instinctive pattern. Our whole reaction depends on how we manage to conceive the situation — whether we cast it in a definite dramatic form, whether we see it as a disaster, a challenge, a fulfillment of doom, or a fiat of the Divine Will. In words or dreamlike images, in artistic or religious or even in cynical form, we must *construe* the events of life. There is great virtue in the figure of speech, "I can *make* nothing of it," to express a failure to understand something. Thought and memory are processes of *making* the thought content and the memory image; the pattern of our ideas is given by the symbols through which we express them. And in the course of manipulating those symbols we inevitably distort the original experience, as we abstract certain features of it, embroider and reinforce those features with other ideas, until the conception we project on the screen of memory is quite different from anything in our real history.

Conception is a necessary and elementary process; what we do with our conceptions is another story. That is the entire history of human culture — of intelligence and morality, folly and superstition, ritual, language, and the arts — all the phenomena that set man apart from, and above, the rest of the animal kingdom. As the religious mind has to make all human history a drama of sin and salvation in order to define its own moral attitudes, so a scientist wrestles with the mere presentation of "the facts" before he can reason about them. The process of *envisaging* facts, values, hopes, and fears underlies our whole behavior pattern; and this process is reflected in the evolution of an extraordinary phenomenon found always, and only, in human societies — the phenomenon of language. 14

Language is the highest and most amazing achievement of the symbolistic human mind. The power it bestows is almost inestimable, for without it anything properly called "thought" is impossible. The birth of language is the dawn of humanity. The line between man and beast — between the highest ape and the lowest savage — is the language line. Whether the primitive Neanderthal man was anthropoid or human depends less on his cranial capacity, his upright posture, or even his use of tools and fire, than on one issue we shall probably never be able to settle — whether or not he spoke. 15

In all physical traits and practical responses, such as skills and visual judgments, we can find a certain continuity between animal and human mentality. Sign using is an ever evolving, ever improving function throughout the whole animal kingdom, from the lowly worm that shrinks into his hole at the sound of an approaching foot, to the dog obeying his master's command, and even to the learned scientist who watches the movements of an index needle. 16

This continuity of the sign-using talent has led psychologists to the belief that language is evolved from the vocal expressions, grunts and coos and cries, whereby animals vent their feelings or signal their fellows; that man has elaborated this sort of communion to the point where it makes a perfect exchange of ideas possible. 17

I do not believe that this doctrine of the origin of language is correct. The essence of language is symbolic, not signific; we use it first and most vitally to formulate and hold ideas in our own minds. Conception, not social control, is its first and foremost benefit. 18

Watch a young child that is just learning to speak play with a toy; he says the name of the object, e.g.: "Horsey! horsey! horsey!" over and over again, looks at the object, moves it, always saying the name to himself or to the 19 world at large. It's quite a time before he talks to anyone in particular; he talks first of all to himself. This is his way of forming and fixing the *conception* of the object in his mind, and around this conception all his knowledge of it grows. *Names* are the essence of language; for the *name* is what abstracts the conception of the horse from the horse itself, and lets the mere idea recur at the speaking of the name. This permits the conception gathered from one horse experience to be exemplified again by another instance of a horse, so that the notion embodied in the name is a general notion.

To this end, the baby uses a word long before he *asks* for the object; 20 when he wants his horsey he is likely to cry and fret, because he is reacting to an actual environment, not forming ideas. He uses the animal language of *signs* for his wants; talking is still a purely symbolic process — its practical value has not really impressed him yet.

Language need not be vocal; it may be purely visual, like written lan- 21 guage, or even tactual, like the deaf-mute system of speech; but it *must be denotative*. The sounds, intended or unintended, whereby animals communicate do not constitute a language because they are signs, not names. They never fall into an organic pattern, a meaningful syntax of even the most rudimentary sort, as all language seems to do with a sort of driving necessity. That is because signs refer to actual situations, in which things have obvious relations to each other that require only to be noted; but symbols refer to ideas, which are not physically there for inspection, so their connections and features have to be represented. This gives all true language a natural tendency toward growth and development, which seems almost like a life of its own. Languages are not invented; they grow with our need for expression.

In contrast, animal "speech" never has a structure. It is merely an emo- 22 tional response. Apes may greet their ration of yams with a shout of "Nga!" But they do not say "Nga" between meals. If they could *talk about* their yams instead of just saluting them, they would be the most primitive men instead of the most anthropoid of beasts. They would have ideas, and tell each other things true or false, rational or irrational; they would make plans and invent laws and sing their own praises, as men do.

Analyzing This Selection

1. Animals think and communicate but not in language, according to Langer. How do they do this? Does her explanation fit your experience with animal responses? If you know about recent experiments with dolphins or gorillas, explain whether that research studied language.

2. **THE WRITER'S METHOD**   The author says in paragraph 5 that ideas are among the things "we live for." How is this generalization supported in the essay? What evidence, concepts, or arguments does she use?

3. As a philosopher Langer defines the essential human traits. What are they? That is, how do human minds *and* bodies differ from other animals'?

4. Langer rejects one scientific theory about the origin of language (para. 17–18). Do you think the essay encourages scientific research in another direction? Given Langer's views, what direction of research would you take to find how and why language starts?

Analyzing Connections

5. Does Langer agree or disagree with Tannen, a sociolinguist (see "Talking Up Close," p. 255), about the purposes of making conversations? Do animals communicate for these purposes?

Analyzing by Writing

6. Langer says, "*Names* are the essence of language." Learning names for kinds of birds, plants, rocks, scenic places, and people changes how we experience them. Examine how being able to name something affected your feelings and ideas about it.

7. If you know (or wish to research) recent studies of animal communication, discuss how a particular study relates to Langer's separation of human and animal capacities.

Robert J. Sternberg

WHAT SHOULD WE ASK
ABOUT INTELLIGENCE?

ROBERT J. STERNBERG (b. 1949) is a research psychologist best known for his innovative theory of intelligence. He graduated from Yale University, where he currently teaches, having received his Ph.D. in psychology from Stanford University. His books include the influential *Beyond IQ: A Triarchic Theory of Human Intelligence* (1987). In the following selection, excerpted from a longer essay in the *American Scholar* in 1996, Sternberg explains the controversy between "traditionalists" and "revolutionaries" in the field of intelligence measurement.

Many psychologists, myself among them, . . . [maintain] that conven- 1 tional notions of intelligence may be correct as far as they go but that they do not go far enough. These psychologists have suggested that conventional notions of intelligence (a) define intelligence too restrictively and (b) often provide reasonable answers, but to narrow questions. The problem is that the answers may be fine, but the questions are not.

Today, the field of intelligence is going through a heated, no-holds- 2 barred battle between adherents to a conventional paradigm that has its roots at the turn of the century and adherents to new paradigms that are attempting to turn the old paradigm on its head. The adherents to the old paradigm have reacted in various ways to the revolutionaries, all of these ways predicted in spirit by Thomas Kuhn in *The Structure of Scientific Revolutions*. The traditionalists' reactions are similar to those of any entrenched power structure: they ignore the revolutionaries, hoping they will go away or not be noticed; or they give them a glancing notice but try not to take them seriously; or they fight them head-on.

Some traditionalists choose to ignore the revolutionaries altogether. 3 Other traditionalists, such as Richard Herrnstein and Charles Murray in *The Bell Curve*, briefly acknowledge the existence of the revolutionaries and then move on. But the revolutionaries are becoming harder to ignore. For example, every major college-level textbook in introductory psychology now prominently features two of the revolutionary theories, my own theory and that of Howard Gardner, a kindred spirit. Moreover, research as well as theory in the field of intelligence more and more is reflecting the revolutionary paradigms. . . .

But what is the battle about, anyway? On what grounds is it being 4 fought?

The grounds of the intellectual battle ought to be over "What should we 5 ask about intelligence?" Consider a concrete example. The traditionalists take a battery of conventional tasks used to measure intelligence, such as the tasks on an IQ test, and ask: "What is the latent structure of intelligence underlying observable scores on conventional tasks used to measure intelligence?"

This is the question that Charles Spearman sought to answer in his 1904 6 analysis of intelligence-test performance, and it is the question that traditionalists have sought to answer ever since. Practically speaking, traditionalists are intellectual descendants of Edwin Boring, who in 1923 espoused the operationist dictum that intelligence is what intelligence tests test. . . .

The revolutionaries do not accept the answers of any of the traditional-7 ists, because they do not accept their question. They believe that the kinds of tasks used in conventional tests of intelligence are largely arbitrary and lacking in any theoretical basis. The revolutionaries do not believe that conventional tests adequately sample the universe of tasks needed to assess intelligence. These researchers believe that the general factor [of intelligence (called g)] is in part an artifact of the method used to analyze test scores — factor analysis. This method is mathematically designed to maximize the amount of variation that occurs in the first factor, thus yielding a general factor as a result of mathematical rather than psychological necessity. But more important, they believe that g is an artifact of the narrow range of kinds of tests conventionally used to measure intelligence. In their view, the general factor would disappear if the tests were more widely conceived and based on a broad, well-specified theory of intelligence.

Thus, these researchers believe that what traditionalists believe they 8 know is a result of the traditionalists' asking too narrow a question. The revolutionaries see the so-called intelligence quotient — the IQ — as neither a quotient nor an indicator of intelligence, broadly defined. Indeed, IQs today are virtually never computed as quotients, but rather as scores derived from properties of normal statistical distributions. And they are based on a notion of intelligence that the revolutionaries believe the field should recognize as outdated.

The revolutionaries are uncomfortable with the fact that the two major 9 tests used to measure intelligence, the Stanford-Binet and the Wechsler, are very old in their conception. The Binet tests date back to the first decade of the twentieth century; the Wechsler tests to the fourth. Successive editions of the Binet and the Wechsler tests differ largely in cosmetic ways from the original versions. Although the statistics are more sophisticated and the printing of the test booklets is better, the technology of intelligence testing has changed little in almost a century.

What kinds of abilities do the revolutionary theories. of intelligence 10
encompass? One such theory, Howard Gardner's theory of multiple intelligences, comprises seven abilities, which Gardner believes are distinct and
relatively independent intelligences: (a) *linguistic intelligence,* used in reading a novel, writing a poem or an article such as this one, or generating an
extemporaneous talk; (b) *logical-mathematical intelligence,* used in solving
mathematical problems, proving logical theorems, or completing categorical or other forms of syllogisms; (c) *spatial intelligence,* used in finding
one's way in unfamiliar terrain, figuring out how to fit suitcases into the
trunk of a car, or figuring out where in a playing field a baseball batter's fly
ball will land; (d) *musical intelligence,* used in remembering a tune,
singing a song, or composing a sonata; (e) *bodily-kinesthetic. intelligence,*
used in dancing ballet, performing gymnastics, or playing tennis; (f) *interpersonal intelligence,* used in figuring out what other people mean from
what they say, decoding what their facial expressions communicate, or
deciding what is appropriate to say in an interaction with a superior; and
(g) *intrapersonal intelligence,* used in understanding why one takes rejection so poorly, why one tends to be overconfident in certain instances, or
why one has failed in achieving an important personal goal.

Gardner points out that conventional tests of intelligence measure only 11
the first two, and sometimes the third, of the multiple intelligences. Moreover, their form of measurement is quite limited, often encompassing solely
multiple-choice test items or test items that require only very restricted
kinds of performances. Gardner has offered evidence from diverse sources
to support his theory, including studies of brain damage, psychometric and
experimental studies, and studies of psychological development, among
other kinds of evidence.

Another such theory, my own triarchic theory of human intelligence, . . . 12
holds that intelligence has three major aspects: analytical, creative, and
practical. Conventional good test takers and good students tend to excel in
analytical intelligence but not necessarily in the creative and practical aspects
of intelligence. Underlying each of these aspects are various kinds of mental operations used to process information — for example, some operations
that define what should be asked and other operations that then seek to
answer what has been asked.

An implication of this theory is that the reason conventional intelligence 13
tests predict school achievement as well as they do is that schools, like conventional tests, tend to emphasize analytical skills far more than they
emphasize creative and practical skills. Indeed, the latter kinds of skills may
even be punished, as when students who depart from a teacher's expectations or point of view find themselves graded down for having done so.

It is scarcely surprising that conventional intelligence tests should so 14
well reflect the abilities required for conventional schooling. The first
major intelligence test — that of Alfred Binet and Théodore Simon in
turn-of-the-century France — was designed to distinguish students who were

genuinely lacking in academic abilities from those who were behavior problems but not lacking in these abilities. Throughout their development, there has always been a close association between tests and academic performance, which is what the tests have been designed primarily to predict.

If tests predict academic performance fairly well, why do we need revo- 15 lutionary conceptions of intelligence, or, indeed, any new conceptions at all? After all, the tests are doing fairly well what they were designed to do. Why not leave well enough alone? . . .

Suppose it is indeed the case that courses are taught in ways that pri- 16 marily benefit analytical students, especially those with good memories. What follows is that students who are high in these abilities will look "smart" in the classroom, while those who are equally high in other abilities, such as creative or practical ones, may look quite ordinary, or even undesirable. . . .

The failure to recognize these students' abilities may have quite serious 17 implications for their careers. We have created a system of tests that values certain kinds of abilities, but not others. It is scarcely surprising that our society has formed what Herrnstein and Murray and others refer to as a "cognitive elite": in order to gain access to competitive colleges, as well as to competitive graduate programs, one has to test well. Students with lower test scores are often, and in many institutions, routinely, rejected. They are denied entrance to the access routes that would allow them to become distinguished doctors, lawyers, academics, executives, and so forth. The so-called cognitive elite is no fact of nature: it is something we have created, much as other societies (and our own in the past) have created elites based on the social class of one's birth. Moreover, it is based on a very limited kind of cognitive ability. The divine right of kings was neither divine nor a right: it was a creation, much like the cognitive elite. Were we to admit students to competitive colleges and graduate programs on the basis of their height, eventually we would find that individuals who are in highly regarded occupations are tall. We should never confuse something we have invented with something we have discovered.

Analyzing This Selection

1. **THE WRITER'S METHOD**   This excerpt begins with the author's summary of his controversy with other psychologists. Is he reasonably fair in stating his opponents' views?

2. Gardner's theory includes seven "relatively independent" intelligences. Do you think they all are separable? Which, if any, would you combine? Does Sternberg's theory synthesize all or omit some?

3. In paragraph 15 Sternberg questions his purpose. How does he answer his question? Do you think his changes are important enough to pursue?

Analyzing Connections

4. Do Tan's troubles with tests (see "Mother Tongue," p. 189) add another argument against them or merely additional support for Sternberg's point? What kinds of intelligence interfered with Tan's test achievements?

Analyzing by Writing

5. What is your idea of intelligence? Do you give high or low value to analytical skills with words? with math? Are creative people smart? Do athletes function mentally in their athletic abilities? Analyze your attitudes, and explain what you think intelligence really is. (Keep focused on intelligence. Don't drift into what you like or dislike about personalities.)

George Steiner

BOOKS AND THE END
OF LITERATURE[1]

GEORGE STEINER (b. 1929) grew up in Paris and was brought by his family to the United States in 1940. He graduated from the University of Chicago and received a Ph.D. from Oxford University, where he now teaches comparative literature. He contributes articles and reviews to the *New Yorker,* the *Times Literary Supplement,* and *Salmagundi.* Steiner's numerous books include *In Bluebeard's Castle: Some Notes Towards the Redefinition of Culture* (1974) and *The Death of Tragedy* (1961). The following selection, first delivered as a public lecture at Oxford, was printed in *New Perspectives Quarterly* in 1996.

I imagine many of you will already have seen it, so I apologize. The current issue of that key journal of comparative papyrology of the Romanian Academy has an enormously interesting fragment, recently deciphered. It appears to be a conversation from 5th century B.C. Corinth about the first public readings of the *Iliad* and the *Odyssey.* It is quite clear from the conversation that these are judged to have no future whatsoever. The issue is whether to waste expensive sheep skin — and a great many sheep — on transcription when the story is so manifestly too long, too repetitive, full of endless formulas, with that rosy-fingered dawn every 10 lines, so full of dull patches and with such a messy ending. Is Odysseus going to stay at home, or is he leaving? No one can really make it out. It was a very brave effort, but destined for oblivion.

The point is obvious. When did literature have a future? Probably never. What we know as literature has had a very, very short run. Scholars say we can start with St. Augustine's famous observation of his master and teacher, St. Ambrose, in the courtyard in Milan. Augustine says: "This is the first man in the West who could read without moving his lips." A man reading in silence, having a relationship to a text which is more or less that of a modern act of reading. This sense of a private and personal relationship to the text, of remembrance and return, and of text engendering text, breaks down around 1914 — the beginning of the catastrophe of our culture in the West.

---

[1]Editor's title.

Today, we need to address these themes again for two reasons: technol- 3
ogy and talent. Gutenberg was not a fundamental revolution. It extended
the life of the written word. In the 80 years following Gutenberg, there
were more illuminated manuscripts produced and commissioned than in
the previous century. It was not a revolution of the kind we may now be
experiencing. What will virtual reality mean for the imagination, for the
habits of narrative and imagining of its practitioners? It is not only virtual
reality. My colleagues in the Cambridge engineering department tell me
that they are very close to a "small-scale, portable, total display" computer —
meaning that you will carry with you or have on your desk or by your bed,
for bedtime reading, this small and versatile screen. It will be online to the
libraries of the world; the 14 million books of the Library of Congress will
be at your fingertips and it will be clearer, easier to carry, infinitely more
responsive to your interests and needs than any book. Then, we are truly in
a new world.

But it takes two. There can be no literature without readers. Readers 4
shape literature. Literature shapes readers and has done so since the beginning of the notion of literacy. So if readers change altogether, as they will
with the new possibilities, what they are reading will change also, however
ancient it is. A CD-ROM presentation of *Homer*, now available, is completely different from the papyrus version, the print version, the comic book
version. They all have a metaphysic of their own in terms of narrative,
pace, excitement, stimulus.

From my boyhood I remember the smell of books, immensely different, 5
the different kinds of savor, the paper, the print. Books are complex phenomena. The way we hold them. Where we store them. The way we can
return to them. The paperback is a revolution of its own, as was the folio,
the quarto, the duodecimo. Books, and the libraries in which they were
kept, shaped much of what we think of as literature, history and philosophy. If the book is to be replaced by electronic means, many of them as yet
unimagined, if it is to become an archive of remembrance, an archaeology
of dead love, then literature itself will change very profoundly.

Marxism taught us a brilliant, simple observation (the big thoughts are 6
so simple and yet one does not have them!): that there is no chamber
music before chambers. That is to say, what you and I know as chamber
music — particularly the quartet, the dominant form of high music —
could only occur under very specific spatial, economic and sociological
conditions. If there are no more private spaces for chamber music, no new
chamber music will be commissioned or written; and that vast musical literature will have to find, as it does now, an essentially museum character.
It will be the historical reproduction of conditions which are no longer
immediate or natural to performer and listener. This will also become true
of literature and the book.

Let me move from technology to talent. We do not know why it is, but   7
in any given historical moment, the amount of creative talent is not infinite. There are phenomena here which we do not understand. Thank God
there is something for us not to understand! Why should certain periods
produce a floreat of great writers and others be barren for long periods?
Why should great literatures — Portuguese, Spanish, Italian are cases in
point — know two or three high moments of concentrated force? What
determines, on a distribution curve, the cluster of talent in a given moment
and what that talent wants to do? Very roughly — and these figures, of
course, are always open to challenge — the latest evidence we have on IQ
curves or any comparable measure (to be treated with care, of course) is
that over 80 percent of the top of the curve today are in the sciences. Less
than 20 percent are doing anything we could identify as the humanities at
the top end of the curve — top in intelligence, will, energy, ambition. If I
had lived in Florence in the *quattrocento* I would, from time to time, have
begged breakfast off a painter. Instead, I have tried all my life to be among
scientists because today that is where the joy is, that is where the hope is,
the energy, the sense of world upon world opening up.

There are fewer and fewer prerequisites to studying the humanities.   8
But in today's Cambridge, in today's MIT, in today's Princeton or, until
recently still, in Moscow, the entrance exams in mathematics and physics
for the first-year student now include what was classified as post-doctoral
research only 15 years ago. That is your *accelerando*. That is the measure of
what is being asked of the young and what they are able to supply.

There is no law which says that great literature gets produced in any   9
given time or that a language will renew its poetic and creative energies.
There are periods of tiredness and exhaustion in certain great literatures.
Probably fewer people are at the top end of excellence today in the production of literary artistic works. Does this mean that less is being produced? No. We have a paradox of prodigality and plethora. More books are
being published and remaindered and pulped very rapidly. There is a huge
amount being produced; very little of it seems to be of commanding
stature. Talent is going into the competing media of television, film and
their allied arts. Again and again there will crackle off our screen a piece of
dialogue, a confrontation, a scene, where you say — "My God, that is better than any novel I have read in a long time." It is more insightful, it is
better written, it is sharper.

Film is already in a condition where it can proudly speak of its classics,   10
of classics which have changed perception, which have changed imagining, which have altered our sense of what a narrative is — of how you tell
a story. It is not the same thing as in the novel. It can resemble the novel,
and it is fascinating to watch the interaction between classic fiction and
television.

The commissioning of a book is now often done with a view to its pro-   11
duction in other media. The calculation of the print run is almost unim-

portant compared to the hope of its acquisition for television or film rights which, in turn, presses on the structure of the written text. There are masters of this form who write knowing that if the television or cinema production is a great success, people will return to the book. It is a creative boomerang of the most interesting kind. There are even cases where the book has been commissioned after the film or the television version. The book is no longer the pretext, it is the post-text of its distribution.

None of us can measure the quantum of intelligence, of imagining going into the media. It is prodigious — even the quantum of intelligence that can go into a great advertising campaign. The difference between poetry and jingles is difficult to distinguish. There are advertising people who can write one-liners of which Restoration comedy would have been proud — you can compare the skill, the caricature skill of a human situation exploding into an unforgettable *bon mot* or *repartee*. Imagination, fun, energy, even serious political and social comment often see in the book a form that is too slow, when in other media they can get through immediately on a vast scale to a great public and to the shapers of political opinion. 12

But can "literature" be preserved? A very, very difficult question. Some years ago, you remember, a number of young publishers began publishing film scripts. It did not work out well. That does not mean it will not. Certain great television artists, Dennis Potter and others, have hoped that their works would be preserved in some literary form so that people could read with the play or film. 13

There is an oral dimension as well. This became clear to me on a recent visit to Harvard University. *Casablanca* was being shown for the millionth time. There was a queue outside of students who had seen it 10 or 15 times. At a certain point, about 10 minutes from the end, hands shot up and they switched off the sound and the students got up, crossed their arms, and recited in chorus the last 10 minutes, which are quite complex. I was yelling with them: "Arrest the usual suspects." These are students who, if you said to them, "Would you please learn a poem by heart," would blench with dismay; but they see no difficulty whatsoever in learning the polyphonic, six or eight voices of those last 10 minutes. 14

This suggests a tenacity in the oral form. Poetry has an immense future — limitless, I think. Russian poetry survived orally and then in readings to 10 and 20 thousand — Yevgeny Yevtushenko, Andre Voznesensky. Also Allen Ginsberg. Poetry always has behind it the probability of the oral, of being spoken together and learnt by heart if you love it. We are in a period of great poets and many, many are to come; they will work with music and drama, with choreography, forms as yet unimagined, which go back to the origins of poetry in ancient Greece so far as we can make them out. 15

Poetry means every form of drama, and I would like to be around for it. Television drama, amateur drama, audience participation. The world of 16 drama for children seems, at the moment, almost boundless. The theater in the largest sense — the art of the human body — is opening up. The elimination of the human body from so much of high literature is a brief phenomenon which took place roughly between Christianity's triumph in late Hellenism and the academic, mandarin, high bourgeois cultures at the beginning of this century. It is no longer so. The body is reasserting its presence at every range of the culture. Language is, after all, a bodily function, deeply and intensely.

Hegel said it so clearly. The novel is inseparable from the triumph of the   17 middle classes, their habits of leisure, of privacy, the space for reading, the time for reading; the novel philosophically is a narrative in a large, rich, stable, social context, even if its own particular narrative is one of chaos, revolution or disorder. The way George Lukacs, the greatest of Marxist critics, put it was: "No novel ends unhappily." That is not a stupid statement. What he referred to was the fact that after you have read a novel, you can go back to it; there is always a window on the future, on the story continuing, and it is in essence a middle-class story.

It is no accident that the industrial revolution, the French revolution,   18 occurred in the great age of the novel. It is almost axiomatic that today the great novels are coming from the far rim, from India, from the Caribbean, from Latin America — from countries which are in an earlier stage of bourgeois culture, in a rougher, more problematic form.

We are getting very tired in our novel writing; that makes perfect sense,   19 there is nothing apocalyptic about it. Genres rise, genres fall, the epic, the verse epic, the formal verse tragedy, all have great moments, then they ebb. Novels will continue to be written for some time, but increasingly the search is on for hybrid forms, what we call fact/fiction. This alerts us to something important. What novel can today compete with the best of reportage, the best of immediate narrative? Not only the media, but also journalism in the high and legitimate sense, the masters of the immediate whom we can read every day.

James Joyce was certain that *Finnegans Wake* would be the end of the   20 novel. It is a very deliberate attempt, marvelously arrogant, to say: "Not after this, that is it. In *Ulysses* I had once more done the totality, once more held the world in one grasp, now *Finnegans Wake* is the chaos of the night," and when told it was unreadable he said, "Of course, that is the point, then you have understood. This is meant to be the epilogue." There are still excellent novels after *Finnegans Wake*. But my guess is that nothing at the moment is more artificial, in some ways more a gamble against reality, than a first novel, and I think many publishers know this.

We have a very exciting time ahead, when literature itself will have to re-   21 examine what literacy is. Who is literate today? There are children who are finding "beautiful" solutions to problems on their computers, on their holographic screens.

I meet one of these children; I am told he can neither read nor write, or   22 barely; he resents any attempt to pull him away from the screen and make him read. I lose my temper and shout, "You are illiterate?" and the child says, "You are illiterate" because, indeed, I cannot follow what he is doing. If you have watched some of these children, their fingers are like those of a great piano virtuoso. I cannot put this intelligently — their fingers are thinking and creating. The way the fingers move is the way a musician with a motif, or the sketch of a motif or a bar relation, comes back to it through his fingers to re-examine its possibilities, to correct it. And the child says I am illiterate. *Dialogue de sourds.*[2] We stare at each other.

And what next? Who is going to be literate? Who will define basic liter- 23
acy? It is a very frightening period. That is what makes it so exciting and rewarding. Underlying it may be a slow, glacial shift in Western culture's attitude toward death. The way we think of death, the way we experience it, imagine it; the way we turn our consciousness toward it. Literature, as we have known it, springs out of a wild and magnificent piece of arrogance, old as Pindar, Horace and Ovid. *Exegi aere perennius* — what I have writ-ten will outlive time. Stronger than bronze, less breakable than marble, this poem. Pindar was the first man on record to say that his poem will be sung when the city which commissioned it has ceased to exist. Literature's immense boast against death. Even the greatest poet, I dare venture, would be profoundly embarrassed to be quoted saying such a thing today.

Something enormous is happening, due in part to the barbarism of this 24
century, perhaps due to DNA, perhaps due to fundamental changes in longevity, in cellular biology, in the conception of what it is to have chil-dren. We cannot phrase it with any confidence, but it will profoundly affect the great classical vainglory of literature — I am stronger than death! I can speak about death in poetry, drama, the novel, because I have overcome it; I am more or less permanent.

That is no longer available. A quite different order of imagining is begin- 25
ning to arise, and it may be that when we look back on this time we will suddenly see that the very great artists, in the sense of changing our views — of what is art, what is human identity — are not the ones we usu-ally name but rather exasperating, surrealist, jokers. Marcel Duchamp.[3] If I call this *pisoir* a great work of art and sign it, who are you to disprove that? Or, even more so, the artist Jean Tinguely, who built immense structures which he then set on fire, saying: "I want this to be ephemeral. I want it to have happened only once."

That is the contrary of literature as we have known it, literature which 26
always says: "I want to be returned to over and over and over." This does not mean that the new work will be any less exciting. It does not mean that it will be any less inventive. It just means that to be a publisher in the next century is going to be a very chancy enterprise.

[2]**Dialogue de sourds** A conversation in which neither hears the other.
[3]**Marcel Duchamp** French artist (1887–1968) who exhibited a urinal in a Dada art show.

Analyzing This Selection

1. What indications suggest to Steiner that literature may not continue? What suggests it will? If it continues, what specific kinds of literature are most likely to change?

2. Do you agree with Steiner that technology may influence basic attitudes toward death? Form an opinion about connections, if any, between literature, technology, and permanence.

3. **THE WRITER'S METHOD**   Steiner makes speculative observations about our past, present, and future. Is his manner pompous? What tone does he maintain in the essay as a whole? How does it differ or develop from the tone in paragraph 1?

4. What are Steiner's goals in this lecture? How do you rate him as a lecturer?

Analyzing Connections

5. Steiner says language is "a bodily function." From Langer's viewpoint about language (see "Language and Thought," p. 263), does this make sense or nonsense?

Analyzing by Writing

6. Steiner suggests that films based on books create a world of their own in terms of story, viewpoint, and stimulus. Examine the differences between a book and its film version. Are the same things possible or meaningful in each?

Ha Jin

OCEAN OF WORDS

HA JIN (b. 1956) lived his first twenty-eight years in mainland China. He served in the army from age fourteen to nineteen. For his college education the subject of English was selected by the government. When Ha Jin came to Brandeis University for a Ph.D., he began writing fiction and poetry. His work has appeared in the *Paris Review*, the *Kenyon Review*, *Ploughshares*, and the *Atlantic Monthly*. He has published a volume of poems, *Between Silences* (1990), and his fiction collection *Ocean of Words* (1996) includes the following title story.

Zhou Wen's last year in the People's Army was not easy. All his comrades pestered him, because in their eyes he was a bookworm, a scholar of sorts. Whenever they played poker, or chatted, or cracked jokes, he would sneak out to a place where he could read alone. This habit annoyed not only his fellow soldiers but also the chief of the Radio-telegram Station, Huang Peng, whose rank was equal to a platoon commander's. Chief Huang would say to his men, "This is not college. If you want to be a college student, you'd better go home first." Everybody knew he referred to Zhou.

The only thing they liked about Zhou was that he would work the shift they hated most, from 1:00 A.M. to 8:00 A.M. During the small hours Zhou read novels and middle school textbooks instead of the writings by Chairman Mao, Marx, Lenin, and Stalin. Often in the early morning he watched the eastern sky turn gray, pale, pink, and bright. The dawn was driving the night away from Longmen City bit by bit until, all of a sudden, a fresh daybreak descended, shining upon thousands of red roofs.

If not for the help of Director Liang Ming of the Divisional Logistics Department, Zhou's last year in the army would have been disastrous. Liang and his family lived in a grand church built by nineteenth-century Russian missionaries, which was at the southern corner of the Divisional Headquarters compound. A large red star stood atop the steeple. Within the church many walls had been knocked down to create a large auditorium, which served as the division's conference hall, movie house, and theater. All the fancy bourgeois pews had been pulled out and replaced by long proletarian benches, and Chairman Mao's majestic portrait had driven off the superstitious altarpiece.

The Liangs lived in the back of the church, as did the soldiers of the 4
Radio-telegram Station. Because the antennas needed height, the radiomen
occupied the attic, while the director's family had for themselves the three
floors underneath. Whenever there was a movie on, the men at the station
would steal into the auditorium through the rear door and sit against the
wall, watching the screen from the back stage. They never bothered to get
tickets. But except for those evenings when there were movies shown or
plays performed, the back door would be locked. Very often Zhou dreamed
of studying alone in the spacious front hall. Unable to enter it, he had to
go outside to read in the open air.

One evening in October he was reading under a road lamp near the 5
church. It was cloudy and a snow was gathering, just as the loudspeaker
had announced that morning. Zhou was so engrossed he didn't notice
somebody approaching until a deep voice startled him. "What are you
doing here, little comrade?" Director Liang stood in front of Zhou, smiling
kindly. His left sleeve, without an arm inside, hung listlessly from his shoulder, the cuff lodged in his pocket. His baggy eyes were fixed on Zhou's
face.

"Reading," Zhou managed to say, closing the book and reluctantly show- 6
ing him the title. He tried to smile but only twitched his lips, his eyes dim
with fear.

"*The Three Kingdoms!*"[1] Liang cried. He pointed at the other book under 7
Zhou's arm. "How about this one?"

"*Ocean of Words*, a dictionary." Zhou regretted having taken the big 8
book out with him.

"Can I have a look?" 9

Zhou handed it to the old man, who began flicking through the pages 10
between the green covers. "It looks like a good book," Liang said and gave
it back to Zhou. "Tell me, what's your name?"

"Zhou Wen." 11

"You're in the Radio Station upstairs, aren't you?" 12

"Yes." 13

"Do you often read old books?" 14

"Yes." Zhou was afraid the officer would confiscate the novel, which he 15
had borrowed from a friend in the Telephone Company.

"Why don't you read inside?" Liang asked. 16

"It's noisy upstairs. They won't let me read in peace." 17

"Tickle their grandmothers!" Liang shook his gray head. "Follow me." 18

Unsure what was going on, Zhou didn't follow him. Instead he watched 19
Liang's stout back moving away.

"I order you to come in," the director said loudly, opening the door to 20
his home.

[1]*The Three Kingdoms* A historical novel by Lo Kuan-Chung, popular writer of the four-
teenth century. It is comparable to *Ivanhoe* for British readers.

Zhou followed Liang to the second floor. The home was so spacious that 21 the first floor alone had five or six rooms. Down the hall the red floor was shiny under the chandelier; the brown windowsill at the stairway was large enough to be a bed. Liang opened a door and said, "You use this room. Whenever you want to study, come here and study inside."

"This, this —" 22

"I order you to use it. We have lots of rooms. From now on, if I see you 23 reading outside again, I will kick all of you out of this building."

"No, no, they may want me at any time. What should I say if they can't 24 find me?"

"Tell them I want you. I want you to study and work for me here." Liang 25 closed the door, and his leather boots thumped away downstairs.

Outside, snowflakes suddenly began fluttering to the ground. Through 26 the window Zhou saw the backyard of the small grocery that was run by some officers' wives. A few naked branches were tossing, almost touching the panes. Inside, green curtains covered the corners of the large window. Though bright and clean, the room seemed to be used as a repository for old furniture. On the floor was a large desk, a stool, a chair, a wooden bed standing on its head against the wall, and a rickety sofa. But for Zhou this was heaven. Full of joy, he read three chapters that evening.

Soon the downstairs room became Zhou's haven. In the Radio Com- 27 pany he could hardly get along with anybody; there was a lot of ill feeling between him and his leaders and comrades. He tried forgetting all the unhappy things by making himself study hard downstairs, but that didn't always help. His biggest headache was his imminent discharge from the army: not the demobilization itself so much as his non-Party status. It was obvious that without Communist Party membership he wouldn't be assigned a good job once he returned home. Thinking him bookish, the Party members in the Radio Company were reluctant to consider his application seriously. Chief Huang would never help him; neither would Party Secretary Si Ma Lin. Zhou had once been on good terms with the secretary; he had from time to time helped Si Ma write articles on current political topics and chalked up slogans and short poems on the large blackboard in front of the Company Headquarters. That broad piece of wood was the company's face, because it was the first thing a visitor would see and what was on it displayed the men's sincere political attitudes and lofty aspirations. The secretary had praised Zhou three times for the poems and calligraphy on the blackboard, but things had gone bad between Zhou and Si Ma because of *Ocean of Words*.

The dictionary was a rare book, which Zhou's father had bought in the 28 early 1950s. It was compiled in 1929, was seven by thirteen inches in size and over three thousand pages thick, and had Chinese, Latin, and English indexes. Its original price was eighty silver dollars, but Zhou's father had paid a mere one *yuan* for it at a salvage station, where all things were sold by weight. The book weighed almost three *jin*. Having grown up with the small *New China Dictionary,* which had only a few thousand entries, Secretary Si Ma had never imagined there was such a big book in the world. When he saw it for the first time, he browsed through the pages for two hours, pacing up and down in his office with the book in his arms as if cradling a baby. He told Zhou, "I love this book. What a treasure. It's a gold mine, an armory!"

One day at the Company Headquarters the secretary asked Zhou, "Can   29
I have that great book, Young Zhou?"

"It's my family's heirloom. I can't give it to anybody." Zhou regretted   30
having shown him the dictionary and having even told him that his father had spent only one *yuan* for it.

"I won't take it for free. Give me a price. I'll pay you a good sum."   31

"Secretary Si Ma, I can't sell it. It's my father's book."   32

"How about fifty *yuan?*"   33

"If it were mine I would give it to you free."   34

"A hundred?"   35

"No, I won't sell."   36

"Two hundred?"   37

"No."   38

"You are a stubborn, Young Zhou, you know." The secretary looked at   39
Zhou with a meaningful smile.

From that moment on, Zhou knew that as long as Si Ma was the Party   40
secretary in the company, there would be no hope of his joining the Party. Sometimes he did think of giving him the dictionary, but he could not bear to part with it. After he had refused Si Ma's request for the second time, his mind could no longer remain at ease; he was afraid somebody would steal the book the moment he didn't have it with him. There was no safe place to hide it at the station; his comrades might make off with it if they knew the secretary would pay a quarter of his yearly salary for it. Fortunately, Zhou had his own room now, so he kept the dictionary downstairs in a drawer of the desk.

One evening as Zhou was reading in the room, Director Liang came in,   41
followed by his wife carrying two cups. "Have some tea, Little Zhou?" Liang said. He took a cup and sat down on the sofa, which began squeaking under him.

Zhou stood up, receiving the cup with both hands from Mrs. Liang.   42
"Please don't do this for me."

"Have some tea, Little Zhou," she said with a smile. She looked very   43
kind, her face covered with wrinkles. "We are neighbors, aren't we?"

"Yes, we are."   44

"Sit down, and you two talk. I have things to do downstairs." She turned   45
and walked away.

"Don't be so polite. If you want tea, just take it," Liang said, blowing   46
away the tea leaves in his cup. Zhou took a sip.

"Little Zhou," Liang said again, "you know I like young people who 47
study hard."

"Yes, I know." 48

"Tell me, why do you want to study?" 49

"I don't know for sure. My grandfather was a scholar, but my father 50
didn't finish middle school. He joined the Communist Army to fight the
Japanese. He always wants me to study hard and says we are a family of
scholars and must carry on the tradition. Besides, I like reading and writing."

"Your father is a good father," Liang announced, as if they were at a 51
meeting. "I'm from a poor peasant's family. If a carrying pole stood up on
the ground, my father couldn't tell it means 'one.' But I always say the
same thing to my kids like your father says. You see, nowadays schools are
closed. Young people don't study but make revolution outside school. They
don't know a fart about the revolution. For the revolutionary cause I lost
my arm and these fingers." He raised his only hand, whose little and ring
fingers were missing. The stumps quivered in the fluorescent light.

Zhou nerved himself for the question. "Can I ask how you lost your arm?" 52

"All right, I'm going to tell you the story, so that you will study harder." 53
Liang lifted the cup and took a gulp. The tea gargled in his mouth for
a few seconds and then went down. "In the fall of 1938, I was a commander of a machine-gun company in the Red Army, and we fought
against Chiang Kai-shek's troops in a mountain area in Gansu. My company's task was to hold a hilltop. From there you could control two roads
with machine guns. We took the hill and held it to protect our retreating
army. The first day we fought a battle with two enemy battalions that
attempted to take the hill from us. They left about three hundred bodies on
the slopes, but our Party secretary and sixteen other men were killed.
Another twenty were badly wounded. Night came, and we had no idea if
all of our army had passed and how long we had to stay on the hill. At
about ten o'clock, an orderly came from the Regimental Staff and delivered a message. It had only two words penciled on a scrap of paper. I could
tell it was Regimental Commander Hsiao Hsiong's bold handwriting.

"I turned the paper up and down, left and right, but couldn't figure out 54
the meaning. I shouted to the whole company, 'Who can read?' Nobody
answered. In fact, only the Party secretary could read, but we had lost him.
You can imagine how outraged I was. We were all blind with good eyes! I
beat my head with my fists and couldn't stop cursing. Grabbing the messenger's throat, I yelled, 'If you don't tell me what the message is, I'll shoot
you in the eye!'

"The platoon leaders saved the boy's life. They told me it wasn't his 55
fault; he couldn't read either. And a messenger never knew the contents of
a message, because if he was caught by the enemy they could make him
tell them what he knew. Usually, he was ordered to swallow the message
before it fell into the enemy's hands.

"What should we do now? We had no idea where our army was, 56 although we had been told that if we retreated we should go to Maliang Village. That was twenty *li* away in the north. Racking our brains together, we figured there could be only two meanings in the message; one was to stay and the other to retreat, but we couldn't decide which was the one. If the message said to stay but we retreated, then the next day, when our troops passed the mountain without covering fire, there would be heavy casualties and I would be shot by the higher-ups. If the message said to retreat but we stayed, we merely took a risk. That meant to fight more battles or perhaps lose contact with our army for some time afterwards. After weighing the advantages and disadvantages, I decided to stay and told my men to sleep so we could fight the next day. Tired out, we all slept like dead pigs."

Zhou almost laughed, but he restrained himself. Liang went on, "At 57 about five in the morning, the enemy began shelling us. We hadn't expected they would use heavy artillery. The day before they had only launched some mortar shells. Within a minute, rocks, machine guns, arms and legs, branches and trunks of trees were flying everywhere. I heard bugles buzzing on all sides below. I knew the enemy had surrounded us and was charging. At least two thirds of my men were already wiped out by the artillery — there was no way to fight such a battle. I shouted, 'Run for your lives, brothers!' and led my orderly and a dozen men running away from the hilltop. The enemy was climbing all around. Machine guns were cracking. We had only a few pistols with us — no way to fight back. We were just scrambling for our lives. A shell exploded at our rear and killed seven of the men following me. My left arm was smashed. These two fingers were cut off by a piece of shrapnel from that shell." Liang raised his crippled hand to the level of his collarbone. "Our regiment was at Maliang Village when we arrived. Regimental Commander Hsiao came and slapped my face while the medical staff were preparing to saw my arm off. I didn't feel anything; I almost blacked out. Later I was told that the words in the message were 'Retreat immediately.' If I hadn't lost this arm, Commander Hsiao would've finished me off on the spot. The whole company and twenty-two heavy machine guns, half the machine guns our regiment had, were all gone. Commander Hsiao punished me by making me a groom for the Regimental Staff. I took care of horses for six years. You see, Little Zhou, just two small words, each of them cost sixty lives. Sixty lives! It's a bloody lesson, a bloody lesson!" Liang shook his gray head and drank up the tea.

"Director Liang, I will always remember this lesson. " Zhou was moved. 58 "I understand now why you want us to study hard."

"Yes, you're a good young man, and you know the value of books and 59 knowledge. To carry out the revolution we must have literacy and knowledge first."

"Yes, we must." 60

"All right, it's getting late. I must go. Stay as long as you want. Remember, come and study every day. Never give up. A young man must have a high aspiration and then pursue it."   61

From then on, Zhou spent more time studying in the room. In the morning, when he was supposed to sleep, he would doze for only an hour and then read for three hours downstairs. His comrades wondered why his bed was empty every morning. When they asked where he had been, he said that Director Liang had work for him to do and that if they needed him, just give the Liangs a ring. Of course, none of them dared go down to check or call the director's home.   62

Now the "study" was clean and more furnished. The floor was mopped every day. On the desk sat a cup and a thermos bottle always filled with boiled water. Liang's orderly took care of that. Occasionally, the director would come and join Zhou in the evenings. He wanted Zhou to tell him the stories in *The Three Kingdoms*, which in fact Liang knew quite well, for he had heard them time and again for decades. Among the five generals in the classic, he adored Guan Yu, because Guan had both bravery and strategy. After *The Three Kingdoms*, they talked of *All Men Are Brothers*.[2] Liang had Zhou tell him the stories of those outlaw heroes, which Liang actually knew by heart; he was just fond of listening to them. Whenever a battle took a sudden turn, he would give a hearty laugh. Somehow Zhou felt the old man looked younger during these evenings — pink patches would appear on his sallow cheeks after they had sat together for an hour.   63

Naturally Zhou became an enigma to his comrades, who were eager to figure out what he did downstairs. One afternoon Chief Huang had a talk with Zhou. He asked, "Why do you go to Director Liang's home so often, Young Zhou?"   64

"I work for him." Zhou would never reveal that he studied downstairs, because the chief could easily find a way to keep him busy at the station.   65

"What work exactly?"   66

"Sometimes little chores, and sometimes he wants me to read out Chairman Mao's works and newspaper to him."   67

"Really? He studies every day?"   68

"Yes, he studies hard."   69

"How can you make me believe you?"   70

"Chief Huang, if you don't believe me, go ask him yourself." Zhou knew the chief dared not make a peep before the director. Huang had better keep himself away from Liang, or the old man would curse his ancestors of eight generations.   71

"No, it's unnecessary. Zhou Wen, you know I'm not interested in what you do downstairs. It's Secretary Si Ma Lin who asked me about what's going on. I have no idea how he came to know you often stay in Director Liang's home."   72

[2]***All Men Are Brothers*** Another novel by Lo.

"Thanks for telling me that, Chief Huang. Please tell Secretary Si Ma   73
that Director Liang wants me to work for him."

After that, the chief never bothered Zhou again, but Zhou's fellow com-   74
rades didn't stop showing their curiosity. They even searched through his
suitcase and turned up his mattress to see what he had hidden from them.
Zhou realized how lucky it was that he had put his *Ocean of Words* downstairs beforehand. They kept asking him questions. One would ask, "How
did you get so close to Director Liang?" Another, "Does he pay you as his
secretary?" Another would sigh and say, "What a pity Old Liang doesn't
have a daughter!"

It was true Director Liang had only three sons. The eldest son was an   75
officer in Nanjing Military Region; the second worked as an engineer at an
ordnance factory in Harbin; his youngest son, Liang Bin, was a middle
school student at home. The boy, tall and burly, was a wonderful soccer
player. One afternoon during their break from the telegraphic training,
Zhou Wen, Zhang Jun, and Gu Wan were playing soccer in the yard
behind the church when Liang Bin came by. Bin put down his satchel,
hooked up the ball with his instep, and began juggling it on his feet, then
on his head, on his shoulders, on his knees — every part of his body
seemed to have a spring. He went on doing this for a good three minutes
without letting the ball touch the ground. The soldiers were all impressed
and asked the boy why he didn't play for the Provincial Juvenile Team.

"They've asked me many times," Bin said, "but I never dare play for them."   76
"Why?" Gu asked.   77
"If I did, my dad would break my legs. He wants me to study." He   78
picked up his satchel and hurried home.

Both Zhang and Gu said Director Liang was a fool and shouldn't ruin   79
his son's future that way. Zhou understood why, but he didn't tell them,
uncertain if Director Liang would like other soldiers to know his story,
which was profound indeed but not very glorious.

Every day the boy had to return home immediately after school, to   80
study. One evening Zhou overheard Director Liang criticizing his son.
"Zhou Wen read *The Three Kingdoms* under the road lamp. You have
everything here, your own lamp, your own books, your own desk, and your
own room. What you lack is your own strong will. Your mother has spoiled
you. Come on, work on the geometry problems. I'll give you a big gift at
the Spring Festival if you study hard."

"Will you allow me to join the soccer team?"   81
"No, you study."   82
A few days later, Director Liang asked Zhou to teach his son, saying that   83
Zhou was the most knowledgeable man he had ever met and that he
trusted him as a young scholar. Zhou agreed to try his best. Then Liang
pulled a dog-eared book out of his pocket. "Teach him this," he said. It was
a copy of *The Three-Character Scripture*.[3]

---

[3]***The Three-Character Scripture*** A selection of Confucian texts simplified for readers.

Zhou was surprised, not having expected the officer wanted him to teach his son classical Chinese, which Zhou had merely taught himself a little. Where did Liang get this small book? Zhou had heard of the scripture but never seen a copy. Why did a revolutionary officer like Liang want his son to study such a feudal book? Zhou dared not ask and kept the question to himself. Neither did he ever mention the scripture to his comrades. Instead he told them that Director Liang ordered him to teach his son Chairman Mao's *On Practice*, a booklet Zhou knew well enough to talk about in their political studies. Since none of his comrades understood the Chairman's theory, they believed what Zhou told them, and they were impressed by his comments when they studied together. 84

As his demobilization drew near, Zhou worried desperately and kept asking himself, What will you do now? Without the Party membership you won't get a good job at home, but how can you join the Party before leaving the army? There are only five weeks left. If you can't make it by the New Year, you'll never be able to in the future. Even if you give the dictionary to Secretary Si Ma now, it's already too late. Too late to do anything. But you can't simply sit back waiting for the end; you must do something. There must be a way to bring him around. How? 85

After thinking of the matter for three days, he decided to talk to Director Liang. One evening, as soon as Zhou sat down in the room, the old man rushed in with snowflakes on his felt hat. "Little Zhou," he said in a thick voice, "I came to you for help." 86

"How can I help?" Zhou stood up. 87

"Here, here is Marx's book." Liang put his fur mitten on the desk and pulled a copy of *Manifesto of the Communist Party* out of it. "This winter we divisional leaders are studying this little book. Vice Commissar Hou gave the first lecture this afternoon. I don't understand what he said at all. It wasn't a good lecture. Maybe he doesn't understand Marx either." 88

"I hope I can help." 89

"For example," Liang said, putting the book on the desk and turning a few pages, "here, listen: 'An apparition — an apparition of Communism — has wandered throughout Europe.'[4] Old Hou said an apparition is a 'spook.' Europe was full of spooks. I wonder if it's true. What's an 'apparition,' do you know?" 90

"Let's see what it means exactly." Zhou took his *Ocean of Words* out of the drawer and began to turn the pages. 91

"This must be a treasure book, having all the rare characters in it," Liang said, standing closer to watch Zhou searching for the word. 92

"Here it is." Zhou lifted the dictionary and read out the definition: " 'Apparition — specter, ghost, spiritual appearance.' " 93

"See, no 'spook' at all." 94

[4] ***An apparition . . . Europe*** "A specter is haunting Europe — the specter of Communism."

"'Spook' may not be completely wrong for 'apparition,' but it's too low a   95
word."

"You're right. Good. Tomorrow I'll tell Old Hou to drop his 'spook.' By   96
the way, I still don't understand why Marx calls Communism 'an operation.' Isn't Communism a good ideal?"

Zhou almost laughed out loud at Liang's mispronunciation, but con-   97
trolled himself and said, "Marx must be ironic here, because the bour-
geoisie takes the Communists as poisonous snakes and wild beasts —
something like an apparition."

"That's right." Liang slapped his paunch, smiling and shaking his head.   98
"You see, Little Zhou, my mind always goes straight and never makes turns.
You're a smart young man. I regret I didn't meet you earlier."

Here came Zhou's chance. He said, "But we can't be together for long,   99
because I'll leave for home soon. I'm sure I will miss you and this room."

"What? You mean you'll be discharged?"   100

"Yes."   101

"Why do they want a good soldier like you to go?"   102

Zhou told the truth. "I want to leave the army myself, because my old   103
father is in poor health."

"Oh, I'm sorry you can't stay longer."   104

"I will always be grateful to you."   105

"Anything I can do for you before you leave?"   106

"One thing, though I don't know if it's right to mention."   107

"Just say it. I hate men who mince words. Speak up. Let's see if this old   108
man can be helpful." Liang sat down on the sofa.

Zhou pulled over the chair and sat on it. "I'm not a Party member yet.   109
It's shameful."

"Why? Do you know why they haven't taken you into the Party?"   110

"Yes, because my comrades think I have read too much and I am differ-   111
ent from them."

"What?" The thick eyebrows stood up on Liang's forehead. "Does Sec-   112
retary Si Ma Lin have the same opinion?"

"Yes, he said I had some stinking airs of a petty intellectual. You know I   113
didn't even finish middle school."

"The bastard, I'll talk to him right now. Come with me." Liang went out   114
to the corridor, where a telephone hung on the wall. Zhou was scared but
had to follow him. He regretted having blurted out what the secretary had
said and was afraid Director Liang would ask Si Ma what he meant by
"stinking airs of a petty intellectual."

"Give me Radio Company," Liang grunted into the phone.   115

"Hello, who's this? . . . I want to speak to Si Ma Lin." Liang turned to   116
Zhou. "I must teach this ass a lesson."

"Hello," he said into the phone again. "Is that you, Little Si Ma? . . .   117
Sure, you can tell my voice. Listen, I have a serious matter to discuss with
you. . . . It's about Zhou Wen's Party membership. He is a young friend of

mine. I have known him for a while and he is a good soldier, a brilliant young man. For what reason haven't you accepted him as a Party member? Isn't he going to leave soon?"

He listened to the receiver. Then he said out loud, "What? The devil take you! That's exactly why he can be a good Party member. What time are we in now? — the seventies of the twentieth century — and you are still so hostile to a knowledgeable man. You still have a peasant's mind. Why does he have to stand the test longer than others? Only because he's learned more? You have a problem in your brain, you know. Tell me, how did we Communists defeat Chiang Kai-shek? With guns? Didn't he have American airplanes and tanks? How come our army, with only rifles plus millet, beat his eight million troops equipped with modern weapons?" 118

The smart secretary was babbling his answer at the other end. Zhou felt a little relieved, because the director hadn't mentioned what he had told him. 119

"That's rubbish!" Liang said. "We defeated him by having the Pen. Old Chiang only had the Gun, but we had both the Gun and the Pen. As Chairman Mao has taught us: The Gun and the Pen, we depend on both of them to make revolution and cannot afford to lose either. Are you not a Party secretary? Can't you understand this simple truth? You have a problem here, don't you?" 120

The clever secretary seemed to be admitting his fault, because the old man sounded less scathing now. "Listen, I don't mean to give you a hard time. I'm an older soldier, and my Party membership is longer than your age, so I know what kind of people our Party really needs. We can recruit men who carry guns by the millions, easily. What we want badly is those who carry pens. My friend Zhou Wen is one of them, don't you think? . . . Comrade Si Ma Lin, don't limit your field of vision to your own yard. Our revolutionary cause is a matter of the entire world. Zhou Wen may not be good in your eyes, but to our revolutionary cause, he is good and needed. Therefore, I suggest you consider his application seriously. . . . Good, I'm pleased you understood it so quickly. . . . Good-bye now." Liang hung up and said to Zhou, "The ass, he's so dense." Zhou was sweating, his heart thumping. 121

Director Liang's call cleared away all obstacles. Within two weeks Zhou joined the Party. Neither Secretary Si Ma nor Chief Huang said a word alluding to the call. It seemed the secretary had not divulged to anybody the lesson he had received on the telephone. Certainly Zhou's comrades were amazed by the sudden breakthrough, and he became more mysterious in their eyes. It was rumored that Zhou wouldn't be discharged and instead would be promoted to officer's rank and do propaganda work in the Divisional Political Department. But that never materialized. 122

The day before he left the army, Zhou went downstairs to fetch his things and say good-bye to Director Liang. No sooner had he entered the room than the old man came in holding something in his hand. It was a 123 small rectangular box covered with purple satin. Liang placed it on the desk and said, "Take this as a keepsake."

Zhou picked it up and opened the lid — a brown Hero pen perched in   124 the white cotton groove. On its chunky body was a vigorous inscription carved in golden color: "For Comrade Zhou Wen — May You Forever Hold Tight the Revolutionary Pen, Liang Ming Present."

"I appreciate your helping my son," the old man said.   125

Too touched to say a word, Zhou put the pen into his pocket. Though   126 he had taught the boy *The Three-Character Scripture*, Liang had helped him join the Party, which was an important event in anyone's life, like marriage or rebirth. Even without this gift, Zhou was the one who was indebted, so now he had to give something in return. But he didn't have any valuables with him. At this moment it dawned on him that his *Ocean of Words* was in the drawer. He took it out and presented it to Liang with both hands. "You may find this useful, Director Liang."

"Oh, I don't want to rob you of your inheritance. You told me it's your   127 father's book." Liang was rubbing his hand on his leg.

"Please keep it. My father will be glad if he knows it's in your hands."   128

"All right, it's a priceless treasure." Liang's three fingers were caressing   129 the solid spine of the tome. "I'll cherish it and make my son read ten pages of this good book every day."

Zhou was ready to leave. Liang held out his hand; for the first time   130 Zhou shook that crippled hand, which was ice cold.

"Good-bye," Liang said, looking him in the eye. "May you have a bright   131 future, Little Zhou. Study hard and never give up. You will be a great man, a tremendous scholar. I just know that in my heart."

"I will study hard. Take good care of yourself, Director Liang. I'll write   132 to you. Good-bye."

The old man heaved a feeble sigh and waved his hand. Zhou walked   133 out, overwhelmed by the confidence and resolution surging up in his chest. Outside, the air seemed to be gleaming, and the sky was blue and high. Up there, in the distance, two Chinese jet fighters were soaring noiselessly, ready to knock down any intruder. It was at this moment that Zhou made up his mind to become a socialist man of letters, fighting with the Revolutionary Pen for the rest of his life.

Analyzing This Selection

1. **THE WRITER'S METHOD** In addition to Chinese names, what details indicate that the society described in this selection is different from ours? How is the story addressed to readers in China or in the United States?

2. What mistreatment and risks increase for Zhou by following his bookish interests? Does he deal with the problem as you would?

3. In the final paragraph Zhou confidently foresees "the rest of his life." Do you think his life will turn out that way? Explain reasons in the story to share or not to share his confidence.

Analyzing Connections

4. The story's political perspective raises issues about books that Steiner doesn't consider in "Books and the End of Literature" (p. 274). What possible gains or losses of freedom would result from producing literature using high technology without books? In "Ocean of Words" which is the political instrument — pen or book?

Analyzing by Writing

5. Should a book be banned? Assuming that censorship is designed to protect the interests of society, consider reasons for and against banning hate literature, hard-core pornography, or other deeply offensive material. Examine difficulties and risks in the problem; do not rush into a glib solution.

PART 6

WORK RULES

INSIGHTS

Winning is not the most important thing. It's the only thing.

— VINCE LOMBARDI

The school that pays its students to play games for it not only loses some of its integrity as a school (i.e. as a self-sufficient exchange center for academic goods and services, ideas, and values), it is also saying some very peculiar things about the nature of games themselves and their relationship to other college activities across the board.

It is saying, for instance, that playing in the band at half time is still fun (no one has ever suggested paying the band), but that throwing and catching a ball is work — and that even this depends on what kind of ball you're using. A football equals work, a volleyball is only play. Appearing on television is obviously work, but even here distinctions are made: players work, cheerleaders have fun. Shooting baskets is work, helping to clean up afterward is its own reward.

The greatest chasm of all would open up between sports and the whole outside world of student activity, including such strenuous matters as staying up all night for a month to put the yearbook to bed, rehearsing the class play till your eyes cross, or working overtime in the lab. All of these tortures are considered so much part of the college experience that you actually pay the place to let you undergo them. But basketball is different. For basketball, the college pays *you*.

— WILFRID SHEED

In sheer quantity, household labor, including child care, constitutes a huge amount of socially necessary production. Nevertheless, in a society based on commodity production, it is not usually considered as "real work" since it is outside of trade and the marketplace. . . . In a society in which money determines value, women are a group who work outside the money economy.

— MARGARET LOWE BENSTON

The ability to take pride in your own work is one of the hallmarks of sanity. Take away the ability to both work and be proud of it and you can drive anyone insane.

— NIKKI GIOVANNI

You cannot hope to build a better world without improving the individuals. To that end each of us must work for his own improvement, and at the same time share a general responsibility for all humanity, our particular duty being to aid those to whom we think we can be most useful.

— MARIE CURIE

If you hear a voice within you saying, "You are not a painter," *then by all means paint,* boy, and that voice will be silenced, but only by working. He who goes to friends and tells his troubles when he feels like that loses part of his manliness, part of the best that's in him; your friends can only be those who themselves struggle against it, who raise your activity by their own example of action. One must undertake it with confidence, with a certain assurance that one is doing a reasonable thing, like the farmer drives his plow, or like our friend in the scratch below, who is harrowing, and even drags the harrow himself. If one hasn't a horse, one is one's own horse — many people do so here.

— VINCENT VAN GOGH

To a Friend Whose Work Has Come to Nothing

Now all the truth is out,
Be secret and take defeat
From any brazen throat,
For how can you compete,
Being honour bred, with one
Who, were it proved he lies,
Were neither shamed in his own
Nor in his neighbours' eyes?
Bred to a harder thing
Than Triumph, turn away
And like a laughing string

Whereon mad fingers play
Amid a place of stone,
Be secret and exult,
Because of all things known
That is most difficult.

— W. B. YEATS

FOCUSING BY WRITING

1. The word *professional* is widely and often carelessly used to signify someone's attitudes and special skills. What does the concept mean to you? Clarify the standards, values, and occupations that define it for you. Include at least one illustration of a careless or misleading use of the term.

2. At Montessori schools and other progressive schools, children ages five to nine are not told that what they are doing is either work or play, as *work* can sound stimulating or discouraging. Should the word be used or avoided in school? If you think it doesn't matter, explain your reasons.

3. In the first semester of college should freshmen *strive* or *survive*? Write a guide to the work situation of starting college. Be informative about serious stresses, and offer an insider's knowledge of customs, expectations, and other practical lore.

4. Military personnel are not supposed to follow orders that violate their conscience, but what if regulations prohibit what their own conscience condones? Consider one of many recent situations involving consensual sex relations between military men and women. Examine issues of authority and freedom in this complicated matter. Should people obey rules they don't believe are valid?

Abigail Witherspoon (Pseud.)

THIS PEN FOR HIRE

ABIGAIL WITHERSPOON is a pseudonym adopted to protect the writer and her co-workers. This essay is excerpted from a longer article that appeared in *Harper's* magazine in 1995.

I am an academic call girl. I write college kids' papers for a living. Term 1
papers, book reports, senior theses, take-home exams. My "specialties": art history and sociology, international relations and comparative literature, English, psychology, "communications," Western philosophy (ancient and contemporary), structural anthropology, film history, evolutionary biology, waste management and disposal, media studies, and pre-Confederation Canadian history. I throw around allusions to Caspar Weinberger and Alger Hiss, Sacco and Vanzetti, Haldeman and Ehrlichman, Joel Steinberg and Baby M. The teaching assistants eat it up. I can do simple English or advanced jargon. Like other types of prostitutes, I am, professionally, very accommodating.

I used to tell myself I'd do this work only for a month or two, until I 2
found something else. But the official unemployment rate in this large Canadian city where I live is almost 10 percent, and even if it were easy to find a job, I'm American, and therefore legally prohibited from receiving a paycheck. So each day I walk up the stairs of a rotting old industrial build-ing to an office with a sign on the window: TAILORMADE ESSAYS, WRITING AND RESEARCH. The owner, whom I'll call Matthew, claims that he started the business for ghostwriters, speechwriters, and closet biographers, and only gradually moved into academic work as a sideline. But even Grace, the oldest surviving writer on Tailormade's staff, can't remember anybody ever writing much other than homework for students at one university or another.

This is a good city for Tailormade. Next door is the city's university and 3
its tens of thousands of students, a school that was once somewhat better when not all of its computer-registered classes numbered in the hundreds. Orders come in from Vancouver, Calgary, Winnipeg. There are plenty of essay services in the States, of course; they advertise in campus newspapers and the back pages of music magazines. Some of the big ones have toll-free

phone numbers. They're sprinkled all over: California, Florida, New Jersey. But we still get American business too. Orders come in here from Michigan, Vermont, Pennsylvania; from Illinois, Wisconsin, upstate New York, sometimes California; from Harvard, Cornell, and Brown. They come in from teachers' colleges, from people calling themselves "gifted students" (usually teenagers at boarding schools), and, once in a while, from the snazzy places some of our customers apparently vacation with their divorced dads, like Paris.

Matthew runs the business with his wife, Sylvia. Or maybe she is his ex-   4 wife, nobody's exactly sure. When you call Tailormade — it's now in the phone book — you hear Sylvia say that Tailormade is Canada's foremost essay service; that our very qualified writers handle most academic subjects; and that we are fast, efficient, and completely confidential. Sylvia speaks loudly and slowly and clearly, especially to Asian customers. She is convinced that everyone who phones the office will be Asian, just as she's convinced that all Asians drive white Mercedes or black BMWs with cellular phones in them. From my personal experience, I find the Asian customers at least more likely to have done the assigned reading. . . .

This afternoon, October 10, I'm here to hand in a paper and fight it out   5 with the other writers for more assignments. Some of us are legal, some aren't. Some have mortgages and cars, some don't. All of us are hungry. The office is jammed, since it's almost time for midterms. Tailormade does a brisk business from October to May, except for January. The chairs are full of customers studiously filling out order forms. You can always tell who is a student and who is a writer. The students are dressed elegantly and with precision; the writers wear ripped concert T-shirts or stained denim jackets with white undershirts peeking out. The students wear mousse and hair gel and nail polish and Tony Lama western boots and Tourneau watches and just the right amount of makeup. They smell of Escape, Polo for men, and gum. The writers smell of sweat, house pets, and crushed cigarettes. Four of the other writers are lolling in their chairs and fidgeting; work usually isn't assigned until all the order forms have been filled out, unless somebody requests a topic difficult to fill. Then Matthew will call out like an auctioneer: "Root Causes of the Ukrainian Famine? Second year? Anyone? Grace?" or "J. S. Mill's Brand of Humane Utilitarianism? Third year? Henry, that for you?" as some customer hovers in front of the desk, eyes straight ahead. Someone else in the room might idly remark that he or she took that course back in freshman year and it was a "gut" or a "real bird."

I suspect that each of us in the Tailormade stable of hacks sorts out the   6 customers differently: into liberal-arts students and business students; into those that at least do the reading and those that don't bother; into those that have trouble writing academic English and those that just don't care about school; into those that do their assignments in other subjects and those that farm every last one of them out to us; into the struggling and inept versus the rich, lazy, and stupid. But for Matthew and Sylvia, the clientele are divisible, even before cash versus credit card, or paid-up versus owing, into Asian customers and non-Asian ones. There's been an influx of wealthy immigrants from Hong Kong in recent years, fleeing annexation. Matthew and Sylvia seem to resent their presence and, particularly, their money. Yet they know that it's precisely this pool of customers — who have limited written English language skills but possess education, sophistication, ambition, cash, and parents leaning hard on them for good grades — that keeps the business going. . . .

I'm still waiting for an assignment. In fact, all the writers are still wait- 7 ing. We often wait at the bar around the corner; Tailormade has its own table there, permanently reserved. But we all have to get ourselves to the office eventually to pick up assignments. Grace, the oldest writer and by now, probably, the best, sits sorrowfully by the window, her long gray hair falling into her lap and her head jammed into her turtleneck, on her thin face a look of permanent tragedy. Grace gets up at three in the morning to work; she never forgets a name, a fact, or an assignment; she has a deep, strange love for Japanese history and in ten years here has probably hatched enough pages and research for several doctoral dissertations in that field. Elliott, another writer, reclines near the door, his little dog asleep under his chair. He uses the dog as an icebreaker with the clients, especially young women. He is six and a half feet tall and from somewhere far up in the lunar landscape of northern Ontario. He has a huge head of blond hair down to his eyes and pants as tight as a rock star's. Elliott is the business writer. He specializes in finance, investment, management, and economics. He lives out of a suitcase; he and the little dog, perhaps practicing fiscal restraint, seem to stay with one of a series of girlfriends. When the relationship comes to an end, Elliott and the little dog wind up back in the office, where they sleep in the fax room and Elliott cranks out essays on his laptop. Henry and Russell, two other writers, twist around, changing position, the way travelers do when they're trying to nap on airport lounge chairs. They both look a little like El Greco saints, although perhaps it just seems that way to me because lately I've been doing a lot of art history papers. They both have long skinny legs, long thin white nervous twiddling hands, long thin faces with two weeks' worth of unintentional beard. Henry points out how good Russell looks, and we all agree. Russell is forty. He has a new girlfriend half his age who has, he says, provided a spiritual reawakening. Before he met her, Russell drank so much and held it so badly that he had the distinction of being the only staff member to be banned from the bar around the corner for life. Henry, by contrast, looks terrible. He's always sick, emaciated, coughing, but he invariably manages to meet his deadlines, to make his page quotas, and to show up on time. We used to have another writer on staff, older even than Russell or Grace, who smoked a pipe, nodded a lot, and never said anything. He was a professor who'd been fired from some school, we were never really sure where. Eventually, he went AWOL and started an essay-writing service of his own. He's now Tailormade's main competition. The only other competitors, apparently, worked out of a hot-dog stand parked next to a campus bookstore. Nobody knows whether they're open anymore.

In general, there is a furtiveness about the way we writers talk to one 8 another, the way we socialize. In the office, we're a little like people who know each other from A.A. meetings or rough trade bars encountering each other on a Monday morning at the photocopy machine. It's not because we're competing for work. It's not even because some of us are illegal and everyone else knows it. It is, if anything, collective embarrassment. We know a lot more than Matthew and Sylvia do. They sit dumbly as we bullshit with the clients about their subjects and assignments ("Ah, introductory psychology! The evolution of psychotherapy is a fascinating topic . . . ever read a guy called Russell Jacoby?") in order to impress them and get them to ask for us. This must be the equivalent of the harlots' competitive bordello promenade. But we work for Matthew and Sylvia. They have the sense to pit us against each other, and it works. We can correct their pronunciation of "Goethe" and they don't care. They know it makes no difference. I suspect they have never been farther away than Niagara Falls; neither of them may have even finished high school. It doesn't matter. The laugh's on us, of course: they own the business.

OCTOBER 12, 1994. A tall gangly kid comes in for a twenty-page senior 9 history essay about the ancient local jail. It involves research among primary sources in the provincial archives, and I spend a week there, going page by page through the faded brown script of the warden's prison logbooks of the 1830s. Agitators are being executed for "high treason" or "banished from the realm," which, I assume, means being deported. Once in a while there's a seductive joy to a project. You forget that you've undertaken it for money, that it isn't yours.

Most of the time, though, all I think about is the number of pages done, 10 the number to go. Tailormade charges twenty dollars Canadian a page for first- and second-year course assignments, twenty-two a page for third- and fourth-year assignments, twenty-four for "technical, scientific, and advanced" topics. "Technical, scientific, and advanced" can mean nuclear physics, as it does in September when there is no business. Or it can mean anything Matthew and Sylvia want it to, as it does in March. Most major spring-term essays are due when final exams begin, in April, and so in March kids are practically lined up in the office taking numbers and spilling out into the hall. The writers get half, in cash: ten and eleven bucks a page; twelve for the technical, scientific, and advanced.

There's one other charge: if the client doesn't bring in her or his own 11 books, except in September and January, she or he is "dinged," charged an extra two dollars a page for research. When the writers get an assignment, we ask if there are books. If there are, it saves us time, but we have to lug them home, and often they're the wrong books. If there are no books, we have to go to the libraries and research the paper ourselves. "Client wants twelve pages on clinical social work intervention," Matthew and Sylvia might tell us. "She has a reading list but no books. I think we can ding her." "He wants a book report on something called *Gravity's Rainbow?* Doesn't have the book, though. I'm gonna ding him." . . .

OCTOBER 13. . . . It was different, though, when I was a university student   12
in the early 1980s. I wasn't aware of anyone who bought his or her home-work anywhere, although it must have happened. It was about that time that Tailormade was putting up signs on the telephone poles outside the university's main classroom buildings. It advertised just outside the huge central library as well as outside the libraries of three or four smaller schools a few minutes' drive away. This burst of entrepreneurial confidence almost led to the service's undoing. In a spectacular cooperative sting oper-ation among the security departments of the various schools, the office was raided. This event has become a sort of fearsome myth at Tailormade, dis-cussed not unlike the way Syrians might occasionally mention the Israeli raid on Entebbe. Matthew and Sylvia were hauled off to court and a dozen or so clients were thrown out of their respective universities. Matthew and Sylvia, however, must have hired the right lawyer: they were allowed to reopen, provided that they stayed away from campuses and that they stamped every page of every essay TAILORMADE ESSAY SERVICE: FOR RE-SEARCH PURPOSES ONLY. Now the clients take the stamped essays home, retype them, and print them out on high-end laser printers much better than ours. If the client is obnoxious, complains, or is considered a whiner, each typewritten page will be stamped in the middle. If the client is steady and has good credit, each page will be stamped in the margin so that the stamp can be whited out and the pages photocopied.

By the time Tailormade reopened, I had moved back to this country   13
after some years at home in the States. I had no money and no prospects of a legal job. I came in, handed Matthew a résumé, spent a couple of weeks on probationary trial, and then began a serious career as a hack. "What are your specialties?" Matthew had asked me. I told him I'd majored in history and political science as an undergraduate. Over time, as my financial situ-ation grew worse, my "specialties" grew to include everything except math, accounting, economics, and the hard sciences.

OCTOBER 23. Three weeks ago I was assigned an essay on the establish-   14
ment and growth of political action committees among the Christian right. I am earnest about this one; I actually overprepare. I want to document, with carefully muted horror, the world of Paul Laxalt and direct mail, the

arm-twisting of members of Congress on the school prayer issue. My contempt for the client was mixed with pity: he knew not how much he was missing. Only afterward do I realize that after doing an essay I take seriously, I still expect, as in college, to get something back with a mark on it, as a reward or at least as an acknowledgment. I hear nothing, of course. I feel oddly let down. I'm certain it got the client an A. Today, the same client stops in to order something else and helpfully points out what he thinks I could have done to improve the essay I'd written for him. . . .

NOVEMBER 8. I will not go into any of the university's libraries. I will not 15 risk running into anyone I know, anyone who might think I'm one of those perpetual graduate students who never finished their dissertations and drift pathetically around university libraries like the undead, frightening the undergraduates. It would be as bad to be thought one of these lifelong grad students as to be suspected of being what I am. So I use the public libraries, usually the one closest to my apartment, on my street corner. It's a community library, with three wonderful librarians, three daily newspapers, and remarkably few books. If I haven't been given the books already, if the client has been dinged and I have to do research on my own, I come here. I have my favorite chair. The librarians assume I am a "mature" and "continuing" community college student, and make kind chitchat with me.

Sometimes, when I can't find any of the sources listed in the library's 16 computer and don't have time to go to a real library, I use books barely appropriate for the essay: books for "young adults," which means twelve-year-olds, or books I have lying around my apartment. . . . Books somewhere between the classic and the old chestnut; terrific books, yet with no relation to the topic at hand. But they're good for the odd quote and name-drop, and they can pad a bibliography. Sometimes I can't get away with this, though, and then I have no choice but to go back to an actual place of research, like the archives. . . .

NOVEMBER 18. Things are picking up for Christmas vacation; everything, 17 it seems, is due December 5 or December 15. The essay order form asks, "Subject & Level," "Topic," "No. of Pages," "Footnotes," "Bibliography," and then a couple of lines marked "Additional Information," by far the most common of which is "Simple English." As the year rolls on, we hacks will all, out of annoyance, laziness, or just boredom, start unsimplifying this simple English; by April it will approach the mega-watt vocabulary and tortured syntax of the Frankfurt School. But people hand these papers in and don't get caught, people who have difficulty speaking complete sentences in English; perhaps this is because classes and even tutorials are so big they never have to speak. But in December we're all still on pretty good behavior, simple instead of spiteful. I've just handed in an assignment in "Simple English," a paper titled "Mozart's Friendship with Joseph and

Johann Michael Haydn and Its Impact on Mozart's Chamber Music." It reads, in part:

> Mozart was undeniably original. He was never derivative. That was part of his genius. So were the Haydn brothers. All of them were totally unique.

The little library on my corner didn't have much on Mozart or the 18 Haydn brothers. As a result, one of the items in my bibliography is a child's book with a cardboard pop-up of a doughy-looking little Mozart, in a funky pigtail and knee breeches, standing proudly beside a harpsichord. . . .

DECEMBER 2. Occasionally there is an assignment the writers fight for. 19 This week somebody — not me — gets to take home *Fanny Hill* and *Lady Chatterley's Lover*, and get paid for it. I guess some kids really, *really* hate to read.

DECEMBER 5. A bad assignment: unnecessarily obscure, pedantic, point- 20 less. Certain courses seem to consist of teaching kids the use of jargon as though it were a substitute for writing or thinking well. Often there is an implied pressure to agree with the assigned book. And many are simply impossible to understand; I often take home a textbook or a sheaf of pho- tocopies for an assignment and see, next to a phrase such as "responsible acceptance of the control dimension," long strings of tiny Chinese charac- ters in ballpoint pen. No wonder the students find the assignments incom- prehensible; they are incomprehensible to me.

DECEMBER 8. I hand in a paper on Machiavelli. "How'd it go?" asked the 21 client, a boy in a leather bomber jacket reading John Grisham. I begin to go on about how great one of the books was, a revisionist biography called *Machiavelli in Hell*. I am hoping, with my scholarly enthusiasm, to make the client feel particularly stupid. "It's an amazing book," I tell him. "It makes a case for Machiavelli actually being kind of a liberal humanist instead of the cynical guy everybody always thinks he was — amazing." "That's good," the kid says. "I'm glad you're enjoying yourself on my tab. Did you answer the essay question the way you were supposed to?"

DECEMBER 16. Every so often clients come in with an opinion they want 22 us to replicate. The freshman sociology and political science essays are already starting to rain in: a deluge of "Show why immigrants are a dead weight on the economy and take jobs away from us"; "Show why most social programs will become too expensive for an aging population"; "Show why gun control can be interpreted as an infringement on civil rights"; "Show the Pacific Rim's single-handed assault on North American economies." I ignore them. I write, depending on my mood, about the INS's unequal criteria for refugee status, or the movie *Roger and Me*, or the

NRA's political clout. For instance, there is today's assignment: to describe Locke's influence, as an Enlightenment figure, on our own time. I think this is baloney. I talk about how the postwar military-industrial complex proves that God really did give the world, whatever Locke thought, to the covetous and contentious instead of to the industrious and the rational. No one's ever complained about finding my opinion in a paper instead of their own. Now I realize this isn't because I've persuaded anybody of anything. It's just laziness: there are some customers who actually retype their stamped essays without bothering to read them. . . .

JANUARY 10, 1995. School has been back in session for a week now. The   23 only work that is in are essays from the education students. I hate these assignments. I have trouble manipulating the self-encapsulated second language in which teaching students seem compelled to write. But it's after Christmas, and I'm broke. Education assignments all involve writing up our customers' encounters in their "practicum." Teaching students work several times a week as assistant teachers in grade school classrooms; instead of getting paid for this work, they pay tuition for it. Unfortunately, these expensive practice sessions don't seem to go well. My first such assignment was to write "reflections" on a "lesson plan" for a seventh-grade English class. The teaching student had given me some notes, and I had to translate these into the pedagogical jargon used in her textbooks. The idea seems to be that you have to say, as obscurely as possible, what you did with your seventh-grade kids and what you think about what you did:

> Preliminary Lesson Formulations: My objectives were to integrate lesson content with methodology to expand students' receptiveness and responsiveness to the material and to one another by teaching them how to disagree with one another in a constructive way. The class will draw up a T-chart covering "Disagreeing in an Agreeable Way," roughly in the manner of Bennett et al. Check for understanding. When the students discuss this, they are encouraged to listen to one another's language carefully and "correct" it if the wording is unhelpful, negative, or destructive. I shared my objectives with the class by asking them to read a fable and then divide into pairs and decide together what the moral was. Clearly, this is the "Think-Pair-Share" technique, as detailed in Bennett et al. The three strategies in use, then, are: 1) pair and sharing; 2) group discussion of the fable with mind-mapping; 3) group discussion of ways of disagreement. The teacher, modeling, divides the board in two with a line.

"Pair and share" seemed to mean "find a partner." I had no idea what   24 "mind-mapping" or a "T-chart" was supposed to be. And come to think of it, after reading the fable, I had no idea what the moral was.

JANUARY 18. Somebody is applying to the graduate program in family   25 therapy at some university somewhere and wants us to write the application. "She's my friend," said the young woman sitting across from Matthew at the desk. "She wants to start her own private practice as a therapist, right? So she can buy a house, right? And if you're a psychiatrist you have to go all the way through med school, right? So she's given me some notes for you about her here — she only needs one credit for her B.A. in psychology, and she volunteered at a shelter one summer. She wants you to tell them all that. Maybe make up some other things."

"See," Matthew tells me after she leaves. "If you ever go to one of those therapists, that's something you should think about."   26

JANUARY 20. When I first started this work, friends of mine would try to comfort me by telling me it would teach me to write better. Actually, academic prostitution, just like any other kind, seems to bring with it diseases, afflictions, vices, and bad habits. There is, for instance, the art of pretending you've read a book you haven't. It's just like every speed-reading course ever offered by the Learning Annex: read the introduction, where the writer outlines what he's going to say, and the conclusion, where he repeats what he's said.   27

> In his book *The Technological Society,* Jacques Ellul begins by defining the technical simply as the search for efficiency. He claims, however, that technique itself is subdivided into three categories: the social, the organizational, and the economic.

This is all on the book's *first four pages.* Sometimes — often — I find myself eating up as much space as possible. There are several ways to do this. One is to reproduce lengthy, paragraph-long quotes in full; another is to ramble on about your own apparently passionate opinion on something. Or you start talking about the United States and what a handbasket it's going to hell in. This is equally useful, for different reasons, on either side of the border. You can ask rhetorical questions to obsessive excess. ("Can Ellul present the technical in such a reductionist way? Can he really define technique in such a way? And is it really valid to distinguish between the social and the organizational?" etc.) And there's always the art of name-dropping as a way to fill pages and convince the teaching assistant that your client has read *something,* even if it wasn't what was on the syllabus.   28

> Certainly, as writers from Eduardo Galeano to Andre Gunder Frank to Noam Chomsky to Philip Agee to Allan Frankovich to Ernesto Laclau document, the CIA has long propped up the United Fruit Company.

At least you can make the client feel stupid. It's the third week of January, my apartment is cold, and I am bitter.

FEBRUARY 8. I'm learning, as the environmentalists tell us, to reuse and recycle. It's easier when I adapt a paper, with minor changes, on the same topic for different classes, or when I use the same paper for the same class again the following year. I've never worried much about a recycled essay   29 being recognized: the pay for teaching assistants is low enough, and the burnout rate high enough, that the odds are substantially against the same person reading and grading papers for the same course two years in a row. Some topics just seem to beg for recycling: freshmen are forever being asked to mull over the roles of determinism, hubris, and moral responsibility in the Oedipus cycle; sociology and philosophy majors, the ethics of abortion. There are essays on shantytowns in developing countries, export-oriented economies in developing countries, structural adjustment in developing countries, and one only has to make the obvious case that the three are interrelated to be able to extend the possibilities for parts of essays in any of those three categories to resurface magically within another. Other essays can be recycled with just a little tinkering to surmount minor differences in topic or in emphasis: for instance, "Italian Fascists in North America," to which "The Italian-Canadian Family" lends itself nicely; "Taboo-Breaking in Racine and Ford," which re-emerges, after minor cosmetic surgery, as "Master-Slave Relationships in Ford and Racine: What They Tell Us About Lust, Fate, and Obligation." And so on. . . .

MARCH 16. There's a regular customer whose course load would be 30 appropriate for the résumé of a U.N. secretary general. She's taking several courses on developing economies, including one referred to by other clients in the same class as "Third World Women." And one on the history of black Americans from Reconstruction to the present. I wrote her a twenty-five-page history of the early years of the civil-rights movement. She was sitting in the office when I handed it in. "Interesting course, isn't it?" she asked. She requested me again. I wrote her a paper on Costa Rica, one on dowry murders in India, one on the black leader W. E. B. Du Bois. "It's a great course isn't it?" she asked me when she got the paper on dowry murders. "He seems like a fascinating guy," she said the day she collected W. E. B. Du Bois. "Somebody told me he wound up in *Ghana*." Today I take a shortcut across the university campus on my way to the essay service and see her with a group of other students. I make a direct beeline for her and I smile. I watch her blanch, look around, try to decide whether to pretend not to know me, decide that maybe that isn't a good idea. She gives me a stricken look and a big toothy grin.

MARCH 26. One day I'm given five pages on the Treaty of Versailles. Last 31 year at the same time, I was assigned a paper on the same topic. A memorable paper. Two days after I turned it in, there was a camera crew outside. It turned out to be the local cable station for kids, doing an "exposé" on cheating. We taped it when it came on. It featured kids sitting in shadow, faces obscured, *60 Minutes* style.

"There she is, the little rat," Sylvia glowered at the time. The pretty 32 young fake client handed my paper to some professor sitting behind a desk and asked, "What do you think about this? Is it better or worse than what you would normally get? Would you assume that it was a real paper or one that had been bought?"

"Well . . . it's a *credible* paper," said the professor. "I mean, one wouldn't 33 think it was . . . *synthetic* unless one had reason to."

"What kind of grade would you give it?"   34

"Oh, I'd give it . . . a B minus."   35

"*Please.*" I was really offended. Elliott comforted me. "Well, he has to 36 say that. Now that he knows it's ours, he can't admit it's an A paper even if he wants to."

We all sat tight and waited for every professor within fifty miles to call 37 us, threatening death. But professors don't watch cable shows for teenagers; neither do ambitious young teaching assistants. Instead, the show turned out to be a free advertising bonanza. Soon the phone rang off the hook with kids calling up and asking, "You mean, like, you can write my term paper for me if I pay you?"

APRIL 16. Today, working on a paper, I was reminded that there *are* good 38 professors. They're the ones who either convince the kids the course content is inherently interesting and get them to work hard on the assignments or who figure out ways to make the assignments, at least, creative events to enjoy. But students with shaky language skills falter at surprises, even good ones; lazy students farm the assignments out no matter what they are. Such assignments are oddly comforting for me: I can almost pretend the two of us are talking over the clients' heads. When I'm alone in my room, in front of the computer and between the headphones, it's hard not to want to write something good for myself and maybe even for the imaginary absentee professor or appreciative T.A., something that will last. But when I'm standing in the crowded Tailormade office, next to someone elegant and young and in eight hundred bucks' worth of calfskin leather, someone who not only has never heard of John Stuart Mill and never read *Othello* but doesn't even know he hasn't, doesn't even mind that he hasn't, and doesn't even care that he hasn't, the urge to make something that will last somehow vanishes.

APRIL 28. The semester is almost at an end. Exams have started; the 39 essays have all been handed in. Elliott and Russell begin their summer jobs as bike couriers. Henry, like me, is illegal; but he confides to me that he's had enough. "You can only do so much of this," he says. I know, I tell him. I know.

Analyzing This Selection

1. What details indicate the atmosphere around the office? When Abigail is there, how is she affected?

2. **THE WRITER'S METHOD** From paragraph 9 the essay continues in the form of a diary. Are Abigail's entries for herself or readers? What does the diary form contribute to her account?

3. In addition to her attitudes about students using the service, what does Abigail criticize in the educational system? Do you observe similar conditions in your college?

Analyzing Connections

4. This job and the summer jobs held by Michael Dorris (see "Life Stories," p. 45) required dishonest efforts. How did the jobs change the writers' outlook?

Analyzing by Writing

5. Examine attitudes among college students and their families toward earning high grades. How strenuously are grades pursued? How are academic achievements acknowledged? What hypocrisies are accepted by students or parents? What dishonesties are tolerated? What happens when loyalty, ambition, or sympathy comes into conflict with academic honesty? Examine attitudes closely, and suggest a remedy for problems you find.

Greta Foff Paules

HUMBLE PIE[1]

GRETA FOFF PAULES (b. 1962) graduated from the University of California at Berkeley and received her Ph.D. in cultural anthropology from
Princeton University. She examines the workplace situation of waitresses
in her book *Dishing It Out: Power and Resistance among Waitresses in a
New Jersey Restaurant* (1991). In the following excerpt, the restaurant
referred to as Route belongs to a large chain of roadside restaurants,
employing three shifts of servers. Paules writes, "In many respects, the
waitress epitomizes the position of women in low-reward, traditionally
female occupations."

Employees of service industries are encouraged to treat customers with 1
unflinching reverence and solicitude; to regard their concerns and needs as
paramount; to look upon them as masters and kings. But to accept this
image of the other requires that one adopt a particular image of self. If the
customer is king (or queen), the employee by extension is subject, or servant. In the restaurant, a complex system of symbolism encourages customer and worker alike to approach service as an encounter between
beings of vastly different social standing, with unequal claims to courtesy,
consideration, and respect. Though the customer accepts the imagery of
servitude and adopts an interactive posture appropriate to the role of master, the waitress rejects the role of servant in favor of images of self in which
she is an active and controlling force in the service encounter. Perhaps
because of this, she is able to control the feelings she experiences and
expresses toward her customers, and she is neither disoriented nor self-
alienated by the emotional demands of her work.

Conventions of Interaction

The image of waitress as servant is fostered above all by the conventions 2
that govern interaction between server and served. Much as domestic servants in the nineteenth century did not dine with or in the presence of

[1]Editor's title.

masters, so today waitresses are forbidden to take breaks, sit, smoke, eat, or drink in the presence of customers.[2] At Route, employees are not allowed to consume so much as a glass of water on the floor, though they are welcome to imbibe unlimited quantities of soda and coffee out of sight of customers. The prohibition against engaging in such physically necessary acts as eating, drinking, and resting in the customer's presence functions to limit contact between server and served and fortify status lines. It is, in addition, a means of concealing the humanness of those whom one would like to deny the courtesies of personhood. When indications of the server's personhood inadvertently obtrude into the service encounter, customers may be forced to modify their interactive stance. One Route waitress commented that when her parents ate at the restaurant her customers treated her with greater respect.

> They look at me like, "Oh my God. They have *parents?*" It's sometimes like we're not human. It's like they become more friendly when my parents are there and I get better tips off them. And I've never gotten stiffed when my parents have been sitting there. . . . They see that outside of this place I am a person and I have relationships with other people.

. . . The waitress is discouraged from adorning herself in a way that might appear cheap. She is also discouraged from dressing above her station. The common interdiction in service dress codes against conspicuous jewelry may serve the same purpose as medieval decrees forbidding low-ranking persons to wear gold (Simmel 1950:343). In each case those of subordinate status are prohibited from assuming symbols of wealth or status that might obscure their position and blur class lines. The aggressively plain uniform of the waitress underscores status distinctions between those who render and those who receive service in the same way that the black dress and white cap of the nineteenth-century domestic acted as a "public announcement of subservience" (Rothman 1987:169; Sutherland 1981: 29–30). Today the standard uniform of the waitress (plain dress and apron or pinafore) and that of a maid are similar enough that it is difficult to determine whether certain drawings in school textbooks represent waitresses or maids (Federbush 1974:181). In the modern service encounter, the need to underscore the server's inferiority may be especially strong as the status differential between server and served is intrinsically tenuous. The superiority of customer to waitress is limited temporally to the duration of the encounter and spatially to the boundaries of the restaurant. Rigidly defined dress codes, which eliminate all clues of the server's nonwork status, may serve to put the customer at ease in issuing orders to one whose subordination is so narrowly defined.

---

[2]Though servants are still employed in some households, domestic service is referred to here in the past tense because it is no longer a commonplace of middle- and upper-middle-class life, as it was in the last century. [Au.]

It is in their implications for the worker's status that the dress codes of   4
direct services differ from those of other categories of work. As the titles
suggest, blue- and white-collar workers are also subject to dress codes, but
the primary function of these codes is not to proclaim the worker's low
social standing or control her projected personality. The appearance regulations of factory workers are designed at least partly with the security of
the company and the safety of the worker in mind.[3] The appearance codes
of service workers are concerned primarily with image and status delin-
eation and may actually interfere with the worker's ability to perform her
job safely or effectively. Some flight attendants are required to wear heels,
which decrease their stability and increase their fatigue (Hochschild
1983). And in some restaurants, waitresses who carry plates on their arms
rather than on trays are required to wear short-sleeved, and hence less
authoritative uniforms.[4] Because plates are heated (by heat lamps or in the
oven) to keep the food warm, waitresses must allow the plates (and the
food) to cool, or pad their arms with napkins before delivering orders. Both
strategies waste time and produce lukewarm food, and the latter can lead
to burned arms, as napkins tend to absorb heat or fly away en route to
the table.

The businesswoman who would "dress for success" is, like the waitress,   5
subject to dress regulations of remarkable specificity. She is advised by a
bestselling dress manual to wear a wool skirt with ample hem, reinforced
waist, and zipper the same color as the fabric. She is counseled to wear
dark pumps, closed at the heel and toe, with one-and-a-half-inch heels, and
she is urged to carry an umbrella with at least ten spokes, preferably solid
(Molloy 1977). While the waitress's maidlike uniform functions to diminish
her status, however, the executive's "uniform" is designed for status
enhancement. A basic dress-for-success guideline is "always wear upper-
middle-class clothing" (Molloy 1977:186).[5] The uniform of the executive
also differs from that of the service worker in that it is at least ostensibly voluntary, indicating that however strictly the businessperson's appearance is
controlled by her work, this control is not recognized as a right.

---

[3]Factory dress codes may also serve to diminish the employee's status, but hard hats and
protective goggles are more easily justified on practical grounds than chef's hats or blue eye
shadow for female flight attendants. [Au.]

[4]Hochschild (1983:178) reports that the management of one airline "objected to a union
request that men be allowed to wear short-sleeved shirts on warm days, arguing that such
shirts 'lacked authority.'" John Molloy (1977:50) contends that long sleeves are essential to
the standard "success suit." [Au.]

[5]The uniform of the female executive serves additionally to conceal her femininity. Molloy (1977:50) recommends that women wear "man-tailored" jackets, cut to "cover the contours of the bust," and man-tailored shirts as well as carry attaché cases. A full-blown
"imitation man look" (complete with pinstriped suit and tie) is discouraged on the grounds
that "when a woman wears certain clothes with male colors or patterns, her femaleness is
accentuated" (1977:28). [Au.]

Linguistic Conventions of Service

The linguistic conventions of the restaurant and, in particular, the uni- 6
lateral use of first names, further emphasize status differences between customer and waitress. Like the nonreciprocal use of terms of endearment
(Wolfson and Manes 1980), the unilateral use of first names signals the subordinate status of the addressee; thus, African Americans, children, and
household domestics have traditionally been addressed by first names by
those whom they in turn address as *sir, ma'am, Mr.* or *Mrs.* Restaurants perpetuate this practice by requiring servers to wear name tags which, regardless of the worker's age, bear only her first name, and by requiring servers to
introduce themselves by first name to each party they wait on. Waitresses
generally have no access to the customer's first or last name (the customer's
larger "information preserve" prohibits inquiry) and are constrained to resort
to the polite address forms *sir* and *ma'am* when addressing their parties.[6]

The etymological nearness of the terms *service worker* and *server/servant* 7
to *servile* (Hollander 1985:56) contributes to the imagery of servitude by
providing linguistic continuity between historically stigmatized and modern
forms of service. Throughout the nineteenth century domestic workers
rebelled against the label *servant*, which carried connotations of serfdom,
indentured servitude, and slavery. As a result of this rebellion, euphemisms
such as *help* were gradually substituted for the implicitly demeaning *servant*
(Sutherland 1981:125). The term *server*, a relatively new innovation in the
restaurant industry (Jerome n.d.), is thus anachronistic rather than conservative and suggests a desire to resurrect more traditional forms of service.

The symbolism of service is not a creation of Route, or of other service 8
industries in which it is found. The symbolic similarities between direct-
service work and domestic servitude are the product of actual historical
connections between past and present forms of service. The proliferation of
restaurants in the early twentieth century coincided with the appearance of
smaller, mechanized houses and the corresponding disappearance of the
domestic servant as an essential fixture in middle- and upper-middle-class
homes (Sutherland 1981:182–99). It seems likely that the symbolism of
service was simply transported along with the physical and social functions
of the domestic from private home to private enterprise.

Even so, modern service organizations must be charged with actively per- 9
petuating the conventions of servitude and, in some cases, inventing new
conventions that restate ties with the past. The restaurant requires the waitress to dress as a maid and introduce herself by first name; the restaurant

---

[6]Goffman's (1971:38–40) "information preserve" roughly corresponds to Georg Simmel's
(1950:322–24) notion of "intellectual private-property." Both encompass biographical facts
about the individual, in which category first names may be included. As in the case of dress
codes, the server's formal lack of control over the borders of this territory of self reflects her
low status. [Au.]

commissions the building of separate bathrooms for employee and customer; and the restaurant promotes the degrading term *server*. In preserving the conventions of servitude the company encourages the waitress to internalize an image of self as servant and to adopt an interactive stance consistent with this image. In promoting an image of server as servant to the public, the restaurant encourages customers to treat, or mistreat, the waitress as they would a member of a historically degraded class.

Public Perceptions of Service as Servitude

That customers embrace the service-as-servitude metaphor is evidenced   10
by the way they speak to and about service workers. Virtually every rule of etiquette is violated by customers in their interaction with the waitress: the waitress can be interrupted; she can be addressed with the mouth full; she can be ignored and stared at; and she can be subjected to unrestrained anger. Lacking the status of a person she, like the servant, is refused the most basic considerations of polite interaction. She is, in addition, the subject of chronic criticism. Just as in the nineteenth century servants were perceived as ignorant, slow, lazy, indifferent, and immoral (Sutherland 1981), so in the twentieth century service workers are condemned for their stupidity, apathy, slowness, incompetence, and questionable moral character. The full range of criticism commonly directed toward service workers is captured in a 1987 *Time* cover story entitled "Pul-eeze! Will Somebody Help Me?" (Koepp 1987). The article and its accompanying cartoons portray service workers as ignorant: cabdrivers do not know where Main Street is, and bookstore cashiers have never heard of Dickens; incompetent: a clerk in an appliance store "does not know how to turn on the tape recorder he is trying to sell"; lazy: men at work play cards and smoke, while painters snooze; and immoral: cabin attendants "stand by unconcerned, aloof and bored, while old folks and children struggle with their bags." The *Time* story is not unique. Television commercials regularly caricature the ineptitude of service workers, and newspapers and magazines are inundated with articles bemoaning the service problem, as newspapers and magazines in the last decades of the last century were flooded with articles on the "servant problem" (Sutherland 1981:169–71).[7] . . .

---

[7]For current examples see "Service with a Sneer" (Lanpher 1988), "Getting Serious about Service" (Barron 1989), "Sure Ways to Annoy Consumers" (Wessel 1989), "Guerrilla Tactics for Shoppers" (Franzmeier 1987), and "Friendly Waiters and Other Annoyances" (Burros 1989). A common motif in service articles, and one which is commonly portrayed in the accompanying illustrations, is the service worker who eats, reads, or watches television while a long line of customers gathers cobwebs, grows old, or undergoes bodily decay while waiting to be served. In his examination of factors that contribute to the anxiety of waiting, David Maister (1985) suggests that the sight of service workers not serving while customers wait in line is irritating, because to the customer, the wait is "unexplained." He remarks that "the

The imagery of servitude is the most insidious and perhaps, therefore, 11 the most dangerous of hazards the waitress encounters. It pervades every aspect of her work, pressuring her to internalize a negative perception of self and assume a corresponding posture of submission; yet, because it is symbolically conveyed and not, for the most part, explicitly advocated, it cannot be directly confronted and may not even be consciously recognized. Nevertheless, the Route waitress successfully resists the symbolism of service, counterpoising company-supported understandings of her role as servant with her own images of self as a soldier confronting enemy forces, or alternatively, as an independent businessperson, working in her own interests, on her own territory. . . .

Perhaps the waitress's greatest victory is her success in insulating herself 12 against the psychological hazards of her work. Her methods of self-protection in this domain are not consciously developed or implemented, but grow out of and reflect the distinctive challenges of her work. Many of the pressures she faces are subtle and symbolic; so, too, are her methods of defense. She extricates herself from the coercive symbolism of service, countering company-backed and customer-supported images of servitude with her own metaphors of war and entrepreneurship. She inverts the symbolism of a bad tip, transforming it from a statement on her work skills or low status into evidence of the ignorance or cheapness of the customer. Customers do not treat her as an individual entitled to the courtesies of polite interaction; she in turn denies their personhood, treating them as inanimate material to be processed quickly and dispassionately in view of extracting a tip. They address her by first name, or hail her indecorously with a wave of the hand and a "Miss!"; she reciprocates the compliment, by referring to them as tables or numbers, which are *turned, coffeed, watered,* or *picked up* — not served. They regard her as a member of an incompetent and lazy class of servants; she sees them as part of an inherently hostile public and categorizes them within a customer typology according to their specific character deficiencies. The waitress's preference for silent resistance is not merely a reflection of the subtlety of the challenges she faces, nor is it a symptom of timidity. By cognitively repudiating the customer's status as master, while outwardly supporting the symbolic order, the waitress nurtures the pride and stimulates the generosity of those who provide the greater part of her income. She manipulates herself to manipulate the other to her financial advantage.

---

explanation that the 'idle' personnel are taking a break or performing other tasks is frequently less than acceptable," but does not indicate why this should be the case. In light of the argument presented here, it might be hypothesized that customers become anxious or angry at least partly because the server's behavior challenges their perception of service as an encounter between master and servant. By subordinating the customer's needs to her own need or right (if on break) to drink, eat, or rest, the server violates the customer's self-image as master whose needs are by definition paramount. Further, by openly engaging in such blatantly human acts as eating, the worker flaunts her personhood and her equality to those accustomed to looking upon those who serve as nonpersons or as beings of a lower order. [Au.]

References

Barron, Cheryll Aimee. 1989. "Getting Serious about Service." *New York Times Magazine,* June 11.

Burros, Marian. 1989. "Friendly Waiters and Other Annoyances." *New York Times,* May 24.

Federbush, Marsha. 1974. "The Sex Problems of School Math Books." In *And Jill Came Tumbling After: Sexism in American Education* pp. 178–84. Ed. J. Stacey, S. Bereaud, and J. Daniels. New York: Dell.

Franzmeier, Stephen. 1987. "Guerrilla Tactics for Shoppers." *Star* (Lantana, Fla.), August 25.

Goffman, Erving. 1971. "The Territories of the Self." In *Relations in Public: Microstudies of the Public Order.* New York: Basic Books.

Hochschild, Arlie. 1983. *The Managed Heart: Commercialization of Human Feeling.* Berkeley: University of California Press.

Hollander, Stanley. 1985. "A Historical Perspective on the Service Encounter." In *The Service Encounter: Managing Employee/Customer Interaction in Service Businesses* pp. 49–63. Ed. J. Czepiel, M. Solomon, and C. Suprenant. Lexington, Mass.: Lexington Books.

Jerome, Carl. N.d. "Tips on Tipping: Ten Commandments for All Food Servers." N.p. (from newspaper clipping posted on Route bulletin board).

Koepp, Stephen. 1987. "Pul-eeze! Will Somebody Help Me? Frustrated American Consumers Wonder Where the Service Went." *Time,* February 2.

Lanpher, Katherine. 1988. "Service with a Sneer." *Washington Post,* December 27.

Maister, David H. 1985. "The Psychology of Waiting Lines." In *The Service Encounter: Managing Employee/Customer Interaction in Service Business.* Ed. J. Czepiel, M. Solomon, and C. Suprenant. Lexington, Mass: D.C. Heath, Lexington Books, pp. 113–23.

Molloy, John T. 1977. *The Woman's Dress for Success Book.* New York: Warner Books.

Rothman, Robert A. 1987. "Direct-Service Work and Housework." In *Working: Sociological Perspectives.* Englewood Cliffs, N.J.: Prentice-Hall.

Simmel, George. 1950. "Types of Social Relationships by Degrees of Reciprocal Knowledge of Their Participants" and "Secrecy." In *The Sociology of Georg Simmel* pp. 317–44. Ed. and trans. K. Wolff. New York: Free Press.

Sutherland, Daniel E. 1981. *Americans and Their Servants: Domestic Service in the United States from 1800 to 1920.* Baton Rouge: Louisiana State University Press.

Wessel, David. 1989. "Sure Ways to Annoy Consumers." *Wall Street Journal.* November 6.

Wolfson, Nessa, and Joan Manes. 1980. "Don't 'Dear' Me!" In *Women and Language in Literature and Society* pp. 79–92. Ed. R. Borker, N. Furman, and S. McConnell-Ginet. New York: Praeger.

Analyzing This Selection

1. How do dress codes for servers differ from those for other workers? Do you agree with the author that executive styles are *uniforms*?

2. Paules explains and illustrates how waitresses defend against "the most dangerous of hazards" in their work. In your opinion, are their methods effective?

3. **THE WRITER'S METHOD** If conventions of servitude were eliminated, how would restaurants change? Does the author wish to eliminate these conventions? Does she convince you?

Analyzing Connections

4. Paules and Abigail Witherspoon (see "This Pen for Hire," p. 300) examine demoralizing kinds of work. In your opinion, which work is more entrapping and why?

Analyzing by Writing

5. Dress codes and name rules operate in all work situations, from casual, as in summer camp, to formal, as in the military. Examine the conventions of clothes and speech in a specific experience of gainful employment. How did the conventions regulate relations? How did they limit you? Analyze the codes and rules from the viewpoint of a sociologist wanting to understand how and for what purposes the system functions.

Gary Soto

BLACK HAIR

GARY SOTO (b. 1952) writes poetry, fiction, and essays about Mexican-American life. He grew up in Fresno, California, and received a B.A. from California State University (Fresno) and an M.F.A. from the University of California at Irvine. His work has appeared in the *Nation*, *Ploughshares*, the *Iowa Review*, and *Poetry*. Soto's most recent collection of essays and stories is *Jesse* (1994). "Black Hair" is from his volume of autobiographical pieces, *Living up the Street* (1985).

There are two kinds of work: One uses the mind and the other uses muscle. As a kid I found out about the latter. I'm thinking of the summer of 1969 when I was a seventeen-year-old runaway who ended up in Glendale, California, to work for Valley Tire Factory. To answer an ad in the newspaper I walked miles in the afternoon sun, my stomach slowly knotting on a doughnut that was breakfast, my teeth like bright candles gone yellow.

I walked in the door sweating and feeling ugly because my hair was still stiff from a swim at the Santa Monica beach the day before. Jules, the accountant and part owner, looked droopily through his bifocals at my application and then at me. He tipped his cigar in the ashtray, asked my age as if he didn't believe I was seventeen, but finally after a moment of silence, said, "Come back tomorrow. Eight-thirty."

I thanked him, left the office, and went around to the chain link fence to watch the workers heave tires into a bin; others carted uneven stacks of tires on hand trucks. Their faces were black from tire dust and when they talked — or cussed — their mouths showed a bright pink.

From there I walked up a commercial street, past a cleaners, a motorcycle shop, and a gas station where I washed my face and hands; before leaving I took a bottle that hung on the side of the Coke machine, filled it with water, and stopped it with a scrap of paper and a rubber band.

The next morning I arrived early at work. The assistant foreman, a pot-bellied Hungarian, showed me a timecard and how to punch in. He showed me the Coke machine, the locker room with its slimy shower, and also pointed out the places where I shouldn't go: The ovens where the tires were recapped and the customer service area, which had a slashed couch, a coffee table with greasy magazines, and an ashtray. He introduced me to

Tully, a fat man with one ear, who worked the buffers that resurfaced the white walls. I was handed an apron and a face mask and shown how to use the buffer: Lift the tire and center, inflate it with a footpedal, press the buffer against the white band until cleaned, and then deflate and blow off the tire with an air hose.

With a paint brush he stirred a can of industrial preserver. "Then slap this blue stuff on." While he was talking a co-worker came up quietly from behind him and goosed him with the air hose. Tully jumped as if he had been struck by a bullet and then turned around cussing and cupping his genitals in his hands as the other worker walked away calling out foul names. When Tully turned to me smiling his gray teeth, I lifted my mouth into a smile because I wanted to get along. He has to be on my side, I thought. He's the one who'll tell the foreman how I'm doing.

I worked carefully that day, setting the tires on the machine as if they were babies, since it was easy to catch a finger in the rim that expanded to inflate the tire. At the day's end we swept up the tire dust and emptied the trash into bins.

At five the workers scattered for their cars and motorcycles while I crossed the street to wash at a burger stand. My hair was stiff with dust and my mouth showed pink against the backdrop of my dirty face. I then ordered a hotdog and walked slowly in the direction of the abandoned house where I had stayed the night before. I lay under the trees and within minutes was asleep. When I woke my shoulders were sore and my eyes burned when I squeezed the lids together.

From the backyard I walked dully through a residential street, and as evening came on, the TV glare in the living rooms and the headlights of passing cars showed against the blue drift of dusk. I saw two children coming up the street with snow cones, their tongues darting at the packed ice. I saw a boy with a peach and wanted to stop him, but felt embarrassed by my hunger. I walked for an hour only to return and discover the house lit brightly. Behind the fence I heard voices and saw a flashlight poking at the garage door. A man on the back steps mumbled something about the refrigerator to the one with the flashlight.

I waited for them to leave, but had the feeling they wouldn't because there was the commotion of furniture being moved. Tired, even more desperate, I started walking again with a great urge to kick things and tear the day from my life. I felt weak and my mind kept drifting because of hunger. I crossed the street to a gas station where I sipped at the water fountain and searched the Coke machine for change. I started walking again, first up a commercial street, then into a residential area where I lay down on someone's lawn and replayed a scene at home — my mother crying at the kitchen table, my stepfather yelling with food in his mouth. They're cruel, I thought, and warned myself that I should never forgive them. How could they do this to me.

When I got up from the lawn it was late. I searched out a place to sleep and found an unlocked car that seemed safe. In the back seat, with my shoes off, I fell asleep but woke up startled about four in the morning when the owner, a nurse on her way to work, opened the door. She got in and was about to start the engine when I raised my head up from the backseat to explain my presence. She screamed so loudly when I said "I'm sorry" that I sprinted from the car with my shoes in hand. Her screams faded, then stopped altogether, as I ran down the block where I hid behind a trash bin and waited for a police siren to sound. Nothing. I crossed the street to a church where I slept stiffly on cardboard in the balcony.

I woke up feeling tired and greasy. It was early and a few street lights   12
were still lit, the east growing pink with dawn. I washed myself from a garden hose and returned to the church to break into what looked like a kitchen. Paper cups, plastic spoons, a coffee pot littered on a table. I found a box of Nabisco crackers which I ate until I was full.

At work I spent the morning at the buffer, but was then told to help Iggy,   13
an old Mexican, who was responsible for choosing tires that could be recapped without the risk of exploding at high speeds. Every morning a truck would deliver used tires, and after I unloaded them Iggy would step among the tires to inspect them for punctures and rips on the side walls.

With a yellow chalk he marked circles and Xs to indicate damage and   14
called out "junk." For those tires that could be recapped, he said "goody" and I placed them on my hand truck. When I had a stack of eight I kicked the truck at an angle and balanced them to another work area where Iggy again inspected the tires, scratching Xs and calling out "junk."

Iggy worked only until three in the afternoon, at which time he went to   15
the locker room to wash and shave and to dress in a two-piece suit. When he came out he glowed with a bracelet, watch, rings, and a shiny fountain pen in his breast pocket. His shoes sounded against the asphalt. He was the image of a banker stepping into sunlight with millions on his mind. He said a few low words to workers with whom he was friendly and none to people like me.

I was seventeen, stupid because I couldn't figure out the difference   16
between an F 78 14 and 750 14 at sight. Iggy shook his head when I brought him the wrong tires, especially since I had expressed interest in being his understudy. "Mexican, how can you be so stupid?" he would yell at me, slapping a tire from my hands. But within weeks I learned a lot about tires, from sizes and makes to how they are molded in iron forms to how Valley stole from other companies. Now and then we received a truckload of tires, most of them new or nearly new, and they were taken to our warehouse in the back where the serial numbers were ground off with a sander. On those days the foreman handed out Cokes and joked with us as we worked to get the numbers off.

Most of the workers were Mexican or black, though a few redneck   17
whites worked there. The base pay was a dollar sixty-five, but the average was three dollars. Of the black workers, I knew Sugar Daddy the best. His

body carried two hundred and fifty pounds, armfuls of scars, and a long knife that made me jump when he brought it out from his boot without warning. At one time he had been a singer, and had cut a record in 1967 called *Love's Chance*, which broke into the R and B charts. But nothing came of it. No big contract, no club dates, no tours. He made very little from the sales, only enough for an operation to pull a steering wheel from his gut when, drunk and mad at a lady friend, he slammed his Mustang into a row of parked cars.

"Touch it," he smiled at me one afternoon as he raised his shirt, his 18 black belly kinked with hair. Scared, I traced the scar that ran from his chest to the left of his belly button, and I was repelled but hid my disgust.

Among the Mexicans I had few friends because I was different, a *pocho* 19 who spoke bad Spanish. At lunch they sat in tires and laughed over burritos, looking up at me to laugh even harder. I also sat in tires while nursing a Coke and felt dirty and sticky because I was still living on the street and had not had a real bath in over a week. Nevertheless, when the border patrol came to round up the nationals, I ran with them as they scrambled for the fence or hid among the tires behind the warehouse. The foreman, who thought I was an undocumented worker, yelled at me to run, to get away. I did just that. At the time it seemed fun because there was no risk, only a goodhearted feeling of hide-and-seek, and besides it meant an hour away from work on company time. When the police left we came back and some of the nationals made up stories of how they were almost caught — how they out-raced the police. Some of the stories were so convoluted and unconvincing that everyone laughed *mentiras*, especially when one described how he overpowered a policeman, took his gun away, and sold the patrol car. We laughed and he laughed, happy to be there to make up a story.

If work was difficult, so were the nights. I still had not gathered enough 20 money to rent a room, so I spent the nights sleeping in parked cars or in the balcony of a church. After a week I found a newspaper ad for room for rent, phoned, and was given directions. Finished with work, I walked the five miles down Mission Road looking back into the traffic with my thumb out. No rides. After eight hours of handling tires I was frightening, I suppose, to drivers since they seldom looked at me; if they did, it was a quick glance. For the next six weeks I would try to hitchhike, but the only person to stop was a Mexican woman who gave me two dollars to take the bus. I told her it was too much and that no bus ran from Mission Road to where I lived, but she insisted that I keep the money and trotted back to her idling car. It must have hurt her to see me day after day walking in the heat and looking very much the dirty Mexican to the many minds that didn't know what it meant to work at hard labor. That woman knew. Her eyes met mine as she opened the car door, and there was a tenderness that was surprisingly true — one for which you wait for years but when it comes it doesn't help. Nothing changes. You continue on in rags, with the sun still above you.

I rented a room from a middle-aged couple whose lives were a mess.   21
She was a school teacher and he was a fireman. A perfect set up, I thought.
But during my stay there they would argue with one another for hours in
their bedroom.

When I rang at the front door both Mr. and Mrs. Van Deusen answered   22
and didn't bother to disguise their shock at how awful I looked. But they let
me in all the same. Mrs. Van Deusen showed me around the house, from
the kitchen and bathroom to the living room with its grand piano. On her
fingers she counted out the house rules as she walked me to my room. It
was a girl's room with lace curtains, scenic wallpaper of a Victorian couple
enjoying a stroll, canopied bed, and stuffed animals in a corner. Leaving,
she turned and asked if she could do laundry for me and, feeling shy and
hurt, I told her no; perhaps the next day. She left and I undressed to take a
bath, exhausted as I sat on the edge of the bed probing my aches and my
bruised places. With a towel around my waist I hurried down the hallway
to the bathroom where Mrs. Van Deusen had set out an additional towel
with a tube of shampoo. I ran the water in the tub and sat on the toilet, lid
down, watching the steam curl toward the ceiling. When I lowered myself
into the tub I felt my body sting. I soaped a wash cloth and scrubbed my
arms until they lightened, even glowed pink, but still I looked unwashed
around my neck and face no matter how hard I rubbed. Back in the room
I sat in bed reading a magazine, happy and thinking of no better luxury
than a girl's sheets, especially after nearly two weeks of sleeping on cardboard at the church.

I was too tired to sleep, so I sat at the window watching the neighbors   23
move about in pajamas, and, curious about the room, looked through the
bureau drawers to search out personal things — snapshots, a messy diary,
and a high school yearbook. I looked up the Van Deusen's daughter, Barbara, and studied her face as if I recognized her from my own school — a
face that said "promise," "college," "nice clothes in the closet." She was a
skater and a member of the German Club; her greatest ambition was to
sing at the Hollywood Bowl.

After awhile I got into bed and as I drifted toward sleep I thought about   24
her. In my mind I played a love scene again and again and altered it
slightly each time. She comes home from college and at first is indifferent
to my presence in her home, but finally I overwhelm her with deep pity
when I come home hurt from work, with blood on my shirt. Then there
was another version: Home from college she is immediately taken with me,
in spite of my work-darkened face, and invites me into the family car for a
milkshake across town. Later, back at the house, we sit in the living room
talking about school until we're so close I'm holding her hand. The truth
of the matter was that Barbara did come home for a week, but was bitter
toward her parents for taking in boarders (two others besides me). During
that time she spoke to me only twice: Once, while searching the refrigera-

tor, she asked if we had any mustard; the other time she asked if I had seen her car keys.

But it was a place to stay. Work had become more and more difficult. I   25 not only worked with Iggy, but also with the assistant foreman who was in charge of unloading trucks. After they backed in I hopped on top to pass the tires down by bouncing them on the tailgate to give them an extra spring so they would be less difficult to handle on the other end. Each truck was weighed down with more than two hundred tires, each averaging twenty pounds, so that by the time the truck was emptied and swept clean I glistened with sweat and my T-shirt stuck to my body. I blew snot threaded with tire dust onto the asphalt, indifferent to the customers who watched from the waiting room.

The days were dull. I did what there was to do from morning until the   26 bell sounded at five; I tugged, pulled, and cussed at tires until I was listless and my mind drifted and caught on small things, from cold sodas to shoes to stupid talk about what we would do with a million dollars. I remember unloading a truck with Hamp, a black man.

"What's better than a sharp lady?" he asked me as I stood sweaty on a   27 pile of junked tires. "Water. With ice," I said.

He laughed with his mouth open wide. With his fingers he pinched the   28 sweat from his chin and flicked at me. "You be too young, boy. A woman can make you a god."

As a kid I had chopped cotton and picked grapes, so I knew work. I   29 knew the fatigue and the boredom and the feeling that there was a good possibility you might have to do such work for years, if not for a lifetime. In fact, as a kid I imagined a dark fate: To marry Mexican poor, work Mexican hours, and in the end die a Mexican death, broke and in despair.

But this job at Valley Tire Company confirmed that there was some-   30 thing worse than field work, and I was doing it. We were all doing it, from foreman to the newcomers like me, and what I felt heaving tires for eight hours a day was felt by everyone — black, Mexican, redneck. We all despised those hours but didn't know what else to do. The workers were unskilled, some undocumented and fearful of deportation, and all struck with an uncertainty at what to do with their lives. Although everyone bitched about work, no one left. Some had worked there for as long as twelve years; some had sons working there. Few quit; no one was ever fired. It amazed me that no one gave up when the border patrol jumped from their vans, baton in hand, because I couldn't imagine any work that could be worse — or any life. What was out there, in the world, that made men run for the fence in fear?

Iggy was the only worker who seemed sure of himself. After five hours of   31 "junking," he brushed himself off, cleaned up in the washroom, and came out gleaming with an elegance that humbled the rest of us. Few would look him straight in the eye or talk to him in our usual stupid way because he was so much better. He carried himself as a man should — with that old world "dignity" — while the rest of us muffed our jobs and talked dully about dull things as we worked. From where he worked in his open shed he would now and then watch us with his hands on his hips. He would shake his head and click his tongue in disgust.

The rest of us lived dismally. I often wondered what the others' homes 32 were like; I couldn't imagine that they were much better than our work place. No one indicated that his outside life was interesting or intriguing. We all looked defeated and contemptible in our filth at the day's end. I imagined the average welcome at home: Rafael, a Mexican national who had worked at Valley for five years, returned to a beaten house of kids who were dressed in mismatched clothes and playing kick-the-can. As for Sugar Daddy, he returned home to a stuffy room where he would read and reread old magazines. He ate potato chips, drank beer, and watched TV. There was no grace in dipping socks into a wash basin where later he would wash his cup and plate.

There was no grace at work. It was all ridicule. The assistant foreman 33 drank Cokes in front of the newcomers as they laced tires in the afternoon sun. Knowing that I had a long walk home, Rudy, the college student, passed me waving and yelling "Hello," as I started down Mission Road on the way home to eat out of cans. Even our plump secretary got into the act by wearing short skirts and flaunting her milky legs. If there was love, it was ugly. I'm thinking of Tully and an older man whose name I can no longer recall fondling one another in the washroom. I had come in cradling a smashed finger to find them pressed together in the shower, their pants undone and partly pulled down. When they saw me they smiled their pink mouths but didn't bother to push away.

How we arrived at such a place is a mystery to me. Why anyone would 34 stay for years is even a deeper concern. You showed up, but from where? What broken life? What ugly past? The foreman showed you the Coke machine, the washroom, and the yard where you'd work. When you picked up a tire, you were amazed at the black it could give off.

Analyzing This Selection

1. **THE WRITER'S METHOD**   Soto presents abundant details about uninteresting places and routines. What makes the account itself interesting? How do the details serve the author's purpose?

2. Young Soto wasn't certain whether Iggy's "dignity" is false or genuine. What effects does Iggy have on his co-workers? Do you think Iggy should change or keep up his appearances?

3. Though it pays more, why is the tire job "worse than field work" (paragraph 30)?

4. The final paragraph states questions and uncertainties about the job. How do they weaken or strengthen the essay?

Analyzing Connections

5. Soto's job lasted only a summer, but he does not present the experience as a temporary summer job, like Dorris's unpleasant jobs in "Life Stories" (p. 45). How do the authors indicate different involvement or entrapment by their jobs? How do they send us different signals about the work?

Analyzing by Writing

6. Analyze Soto's views about the emotional and intellectual effects of poverty. Examine how he connects it to peoples' despair, illness, lawlessness, and breakdowns of civility. How does he illustrate poverty's lasting effects? You may wish to compare his assessment with Carver's account of hard physical labor in "My Father's Life" (p. 67).

John Updike

A & P

JOHN UPDIKE. See the earlier headnote about the author on page 38. This story appeared initially in the *New Yorker* in 1962.

In walks these three girls in nothing but bathing suits. I'm in the third 1 checkout slot, with my back to the door, so I don't see them until they're over by the bread. The one that caught my eye first was the one in the plaid green two-piece. She was a chunky kid, with a good tan and a sweet broad soft-looking can with those two crescents of white just under it, where the sun never seems to hit, at the top of the backs of her legs. I stood there with my hand on a box of HiHo crackers trying to remember if I rang it up or not. I ring it up again and the customer starts giving me hell. She's one of these cash-register-watchers, a witch about fifty with rouge on her cheekbones and no eyebrows, and I know it made her day to trip me up. She'd been watching cash registers for fifty years and probably never seen a mistake before.

By the time I got her feathers smoothed and her goodies into a bag — 2 she gives me a little snort in passing, if she'd been born at the right time they would have burned her over in Salem — by the time I get her on her way the girls had circled around the bread and were coming back, without a pushcart, back my way along the counters, in the aisle between the checkouts and the Special bins. They didn't even have shoes on. There was this chunky one, with the two-piece — it was bright green and the seams on the bra were still sharp and her belly was still pretty pale so I guessed she just got it (the suit) — there was this one, with one of those chubby berry-faces, the lips all bunched together under her nose, this one, and a tall one, with black hair that hadn't quite frizzed right, and one of these sunburns right across under the eyes, and a chin that was too long — you know, the kind of girl other girls think is very "striking" and "attractive" but never quite makes it, as they very well know, which is why they like her so much — and then the third one, that wasn't quite so tall. She was the queen. She kind of led them, the other two peeking around and making their shoulders round. She didn't look around, not this queen, she just walked straight on slowly, on these long white prima-donna legs. She came down a little hard on her heels, as if she didn't walk in her bare feet that much, putting down her heels and then letting the weight move along to her toes as if she was testing the floor with every step, putting a little deliberate extra action into it. You never know for sure how girls' minds work (do you really think it's a mind in there or just a little buzz like a bee in a glass jar?) but you got the idea she had talked the other two into coming in here with her, and now she was showing them how to do it, walk slow and hold yourself straight.

She had on a kind of dirty-pink — beige maybe, I don't know — bathing 3
suit with a little nubble all over it, and what got me, the straps were down. They were off her shoulders looped loose around the cool tops of her arms, and I guess as a result the suit had slipped a little on her, so all around the top of the cloth there was this shining rim. If it hadn't been there you wouldn't have known there could have been anything whiter than those shoulders. With the straps pushed off, there was nothing between the top of the suit and the top of her head except just *her*, this clean bare plane of the top of her chest down from the shoulder bones like a dented sheet of metal tilted in the light. I mean, it was more than pretty.

She had sort of oaky hair that the sun and salt had bleached, done up 4
in a bun that was unravelling, and a kind of prim face. Walking into the A & P with your straps down, I suppose it's the only kind of face you *can* have. She held her head so high her neck, coming up out of those white shoulders, looked kind of stretched, but I didn't mind. The longer her neck was, the more of her there was.

She must have felt in the corner of her eye me and over my shoulder 5
Stokesie in the second slot watching, but she didn't tip. Not this queen. She kept her eyes moving across the racks, and stopped, and turned so slow it made my stomach rub the inside of my apron, and buzzed to the other two, who kind of huddled against her for relief, and then they all three of them went up the cat-and-dog-food-breakfast-cereal-macaroni-rice-raisins-seasonings-spreads-spaghetti-soft-drinks-crackers-and-cookies aisle. From the third slot I look straight up this aisle to the meat counter, and I watched them all the way. The fat one with the tan sort of fumbled with the cookies, but on second thought she put the package back. The sheep pushing their carts down the aisle — the girls were walking against the usual traffic (not that we have one-way signs or anything) — were pretty hilarious. You could see them, when Queenie's white shoulders dawned on them, kind of jerk, or hop, or hiccup, but their eyes snapped back to their own baskets and on they pushed. I bet you could set off dynamite in an A & P and the people would by and large keep reaching and checking oatmeal off their lists and muttering "Let me see, there was a third thing, began with A, asparagus, no, ah, yes, applesauce!" or whatever it is they do mutter. But there was no doubt, this jiggled them. A few houseslaves in pin curlers even looked around after pushing their carts past to make sure what they had seen was correct.

You know, it's one thing to have a girl in a bathing suit down on the 6

beach, where what with the glare nobody can look at each other much anyway, and another thing in the cool of the A & P, under the fluorescent
lights, against all those stacked packages, with her feet paddling along
naked over our checkboard green-and-cream rubber-tile floor.

"Oh Daddy," Stokesie said beside me. "I feel so faint."   7

"Darling," I said. "Hold me tight." Stokesie's married, with two babies 8
chalked up on his fuselage already, but as far as I can tell that's the only difference. He's twenty-two, and I was nineteen this April.

"Is it done?" he asks, the responsible married man finding his voice. I 9
forgot to say he thinks he's going to be manager some sunny day, maybe in
1990 when it's called the Great Alexandrov and Petrooshki Tea Company
or something.

What he meant was, our town is five miles from a beach, with a big 10
summer colony out on the Point, but we're right in the middle of town, and
the women generally put on a shirt or shorts or something before they get
out of the car into the street. And anyway these are usually women with six
children and varicose veins mapping their legs and nobody, including
them, could care less. As I say, we're right in the middle of town, and if you
stand at our front doors you can see two banks and the Congregational
church and the newspaper store and three real-estate offices and about
twenty-seven old freeloaders tearing up Central Street because the sewer
broke again. It's not as if we're on the Cape; we're north of Boston and
there's people in this town haven't seen the ocean for twenty years.

The girls had reached the meat counter and were asking McMahon 11
something. He pointed, they pointed, and they shuffled out of sight behind
a pyramid of Diet Delight peaches. All that was left for us to see was old
McMahon patting his mouth and looking after them sizing up their joints.
Poor kids, I began to feel sorry for them, they couldn't help it.

Now here comes the sad part of the story, at least my family says it's sad, 12
but I don't think it's so sad myself. The store's pretty empty, it being Thursday afternoon, so there was nothing much to do except lean on the register
and wait for the girls to show up again. The whole store was like a pinball
machine and I didn't know which tunnel they'd come out of. After a while
they come around out of the far aisle, around the light bulbs, records at discount of the Caribbean Six or Tony Martin Sings or some such gunk you
wonder they waste the wax on, sixpacks of candy bars, and plastic toys done
up in cellophane that fall apart when a kid looks at them anyway. Around
they come, Queenie still leading the way, and holding a little gray jar in
her hand. Slots Three through Seven are unmanned and I could see her
wondering between Stokes and me, but Stokesie with his usual luck draws
an old party in baggy gray pants who stumbles up with four giant cans of
pineapple juice (what do these bums *do* with all that pineapple juice? I've
often asked myself) so the girls come to me. Queenie puts down the jar
and I take it into my fingers icy cold. Kingfish Fancy Herring Snacks in
Pure Sour Cream: 49¢. Now her hands are empty, not a ring or a bracelet,

bare as God made them, and I wonder where the money's coming from. Still with that prim look she lifts a folded dollar bill out of the hollow at the center of her nubbled pink top. The jar went heavy in my hand. Really, I thought that was so cute.

Then everybody's luck begins to run out. Lengel comes in from haggling with a truck full of cabbages on the lot and is about to scuttle into that door marked MANAGER behind which he hides all day when the girls touch his eye. Lengel's pretty dreary, teaches Sunday school and the rest, but he doesn't miss that much. He comes over and says, "Girls, this isn't the beach." 13

Queenie blushes, though maybe it's just a brush of sunburn I was notic- 14 ing for the first time, now that she was so close. "My mother asked me to pick up a jar of herring snacks." Her voice kind of startled me, the way voices do when you see the people first, coming out so flat and dumb yet kind of tony, too, the way it ticked over "pick up" and "snacks." All of a sudden I slid right down her voice into her living room. Her father and the other men were standing around in ice-cream coats and bow ties and the women were in sandals picking up herring snacks on toothpicks off a big glass plate and they were all holding drinks the color of water with olives and sprigs of mint in them. When my parents have somebody over they get lemonade and if it's a real racy affair Schlitz in tall glasses with "They'll Do It Every Time" cartoons stencilled on.

"That's all right," Lengel said. "But this isn't the beach." His repeating 15 this struck me as funny, as if it had just occurred to him, and he had been thinking all these years the A & P was a great big sand dune and he was the head lifeguard. He didn't like my smiling — as I say he doesn't miss much — but he concentrates on giving the girls that sad Sunday-school-superintendent stare.

Queenie's blush is no sunburn now, and the plump one in plaid, that I 16 liked better from the back — a really sweet can — pipes up, "We weren't doing any shopping. We just came in for the one thing."

"That makes no difference," Lengel tells her, and I could see from the 17 way his eyes went that he hadn't noticed she was wearing a two-piece before. "We want you decently dressed when you come in here."

"We *are* decent," Queenie says suddenly, her lower lip pushing, getting 18 sore now that she remembers her place, a place from which the crowd that runs the A & P must look pretty crummy. Fancy Herring Snacks flashed in her very blue eyes.

"Girls, I don't want to argue with you. After this come in here with your 19 shoulders covered. It's our policy." He turns his back. That's policy for you. Policy is what the kingpins want. What the others want is juvenile delinquency.

All this while, the customers had been showing up with their carts but, 20 you know, sheep, seeing a scene, they had all bunched up on Stokesie, who shook open a paper bag as gently as peeling a peach, not wanting to miss a word. I could feel in the silence everybody getting nervous, most of all Lengel, who asks me, "Sammy, have you rung up their purchase?"

I thought and said "No" but it wasn't about that I was thinking. I go 21 through the punches, 4, 9, GROC, TOT — it's more complicated than you think, and after you do it often enough, it begins to make a little song, that you hear words to, in my case "Hello (*bing*) there, you (*gung*) hap-py *pee*-pul (*splat*)!" — the *splat* being the drawer flying out. I uncrease the bill, tenderly as you may imagine, it just having come from between the two smoothest scoops of vanilla I had ever known were there, and pass a half and a penny into her narrow pink palm, and nestle the herrings in a bag and twist its neck and hand it over, all the time thinking.

The girls, and who'd blame them, are in a hurry to get out, so I say "I 22 quit" to Lengel enough for them to hear, hoping they'll stop and watch me, their unsuspected hero. They keep right on going, into the electric eye; the door flies open and they flicker across the lot to their car, Queenie and Plaid and Big Tall Goony-Goony (not that as raw material she was so bad), leaving me with Lengel and a kink in his eyebrow.

"Did you say something, Sammy?"   23

"I said I quit."   24

"I thought you did."   25

"You didn't have to embarrass them."   26

"It was they who were embarrassing us."   27

I started to say something that came out "Fiddle-de-doo." It's a saying of 28 my grandmother's, and I know she would have been pleased.

"I don't think you know what you're saying," Lengel said.   29

"I know you don't," I said. "But I do." I pull the bow at the back of my 30 apron and start shrugging it off my shoulders. A couple customers that had been heading for my slot begin to knock against each other, like scared pigs in a chute.

Lengel sighs and begins to look very patient and old and gray. He's been 31 a friend of my parents for years. "Sammy, you don't want to do this to your Mom and Dad," he tells me. It's true, I don't. But it seems to me that once you begin a gesture it's fatal not to go through with it. I fold the apron, "Sammy" stitched in red on the pocket, and put it on the counter, and drop the bow tie on top of it. The bow tie is theirs, if you've ever wondered. "You'll feel this for the rest of your life," Lengel says, and I know that's true, too, but remembering how he made that pretty girl blush makes me so scrunchy inside I punch the No Sale tab and the machine whirs "pee-pul" and the drawer splats out. One advantage to this scene taking place in summer, I can follow this up with a clean exit, there's no fumbling around getting your coat and galoshes, I just saunter into the electric eye in my white shirt that my mother ironed the night before, and the door heaves itself open, and outside the sunshine is skating around on the asphalt.

I look around for my girls, but they're gone, of course. There wasn't any- 32 body but some young married screaming with her children about some candy they didn't get by the door of a powder-blue Falcon station wagon. Looking back in the big windows, over the bags of peat moss and aluminum lawn furniture stacked on the pavement, I could see Lengel in my place in the slot, checking the sheep through. His face was dark gray and his back stiff, as if he'd just had an injection of iron, and my stomach kind of fell as I felt how hard the world was going to be to me hereafter.

Analyzing This Selection

1. Compare how Sammy looked at the girls with how the other three men looked at them. How do the looks reflect their characters?

2. **THE WRITER'S METHOD** Did the girls enter the store to buy herring snacks or for another reason? Find details to support your interpretation.

3. What has Sammy done that makes him fear the world will be hard on him? Do you think it will?

Analyzing Connections

4. Updike's essay on the male body (see "The Disposable Rocket," p. 38) suggests that men are somewhat detached from their bodies. Does Sammy show the detachment Updike attributes to men? Explain what, if anything, the essay contributes to our understanding of characters' responses in the story.

Analyzing by Writing

5. Sammy observes "Policy is what the kingpins want." Examine the widespread use of terms such as "our policy," "company policy," "school policy." What advantages are gained by using the term? What disadvantages arise for all parties? Explain its purpose and effects in interactive situations.

Peter Schwendener

REFLECTIONS OF
A BOOKSTORE TYPE

PETER SCHWENDENER (b. 1957) graduated from Northwestern University. He has worked as a jazz pianist and a staff writer for *Chicago Reader*. His essays and reviews have appeared in *TriQuarterly*, the *New Criterion*, and the *American Scholar*, where this essay was printed in 1997.

In 1936, George Orwell wrote an essay entitled "Bookshop Memories," which was a bitter account of a job he had held in a used bookstore. The thing he seems to have disliked the most was the clientele, who he arranged in a kind of hierarchy of loathsomeness. At the top are "unmistakable paranoiacs," also described as "not quite certifiable lunatics." Below are "the decayed person smelling of old breadcrusts," customers who order books without intending to purchase them, "the dear old lady who 'wants a book for an invalid,'" the customer who wants a certain book but knows nothing about it other than that it is red, and on and on, until one realizes that what Orwell hated was waiting on people, period. Anyone who has worked in a bookstore, new or used, large or small, will recognize the reality of what he is talking about.

I have been working for about nine months in a large bookstore in Evanston, Illinois, a Barnes & Noble superstore, to be exact. Although I have not researched the topic, I am aware that the superstore concept is still somewhat avant-garde, at least as far as traditionally small businesses such as bookstores are concerned. Our store is extremely large, easily as large as a supermarket, and it intimidated me the first time I laid eyes on it. It takes up two stories of a large building in the middle of downtown Evanston and is probably as much a microcosm of the town as a store could be. It is very far from the bookshop Orwell describes, yet much of what Orwell writes fits it exactly.

According to Orwell, "a bookseller lives on his windows"; my store is window-dominated, and looks like an oasis of leisure and enjoyment, especially at night. Orwell calls bookselling "a humane trade which is not capable of being vulgarized beyond a certain point." True: my store sells pornography, self-help books, books on how to "write that novel," stupid and possibly even degrading children's books, and yet these books, or rather these book-shaped objects ("things in book's clothing," as Charles Lamb calls them) do not give the store its tone. The tone is given by the unbought, rarely browsed complete set of Trollope's novels, the surprisingly large philosophy section, and other parts of the store that are bad economic risks, though perhaps less so than they would be in a non-college town. As long as only a few adult books, in the pre-1970s meaning of the word *adult*, are on the premises, the vulgarization to which Orwell refers cannot take hold.

The position I hold, along with several other people, is that of "book- 4 seller," which means "sales clerk." I walk around the store, making myself a moving target for customers with vague requests, take turns running one of the six cash registers (Orwell would be amazed at the size of our operation), station myself at the always-busy information desk, or engage in the activity known to all booksellers as "reshelve," as in (spoken by a supervisor), "There's a pile of reshelve over in Self-Help. Could you take care of it?" Easily the worst thing about the job is reshelving the books and magazines that customers have looked at and abandoned miles away from where they belong. Yet even with "reshelve" (the word is both a verb and a noun) one notices interesting things.

Savage browsing occurs in the Travel section, where customers, sick of 5 living where they live, rifle through seven or eight books on Colorado or Guam and leave them in piles. The one section I don't know much about is Children's, which is anachronistically taken care of by female booksellers, all of whom, even more anachronistically, seem to enjoy it, at least as much as anyone can enjoy a low-paying job. Some sections are never messed up by customers: Theater and Drama, consisting mostly of plays and books about acting and directing, attracts almost no one, probably because actors, in common with most performing artists, don't enjoy reading, and directing and acting are the last things one learns to do by reading books. Other sections that are chronically unvisited, kept on the premises merely to bolster our claim to have everything, are Linguistics and, I fear, Poetry, though we have a rather good poetry section.

The fact that "reshelve" is the worst thing about the job says 6 something — namely, that it is far from a bad job. The conventional wisdom, in fact, is that as far as retail work goes, working in a bookstore is as good as it gets. The job depresses me, when it does, simply because it pays barely enough to live on, but I can suffer that, for now at least.

There is a bookstore type, and I am afraid I am of that type. I like being 7 around books, even crappy ones, I'm not physically threatening, and waiting on customers doesn't upset me as much as it seems to have upset Orwell. The job asks almost nothing of me other than that I be there on time. What is more, the management does not mind if one browses as one works, as long as blatant loafing is avoided. One learns the difference between improving one's product knowledge and lounging at the information desk with a cup of coffee and a huge art book.

Our store has a problem with security. There is, I am told, a fair amount 8 of theft, or attempted theft, and yet the store has its hands tied as far as cracking down is concerned. A bookstore's primary association is with friendliness and leisure, and the presence of armed security guards, or security guards period, does not conduce to either. A small, I thought rather fierce-looking, man who didn't carry a gun was sent by one security agency, but he was eventually let go because the management didn't think he looked formidable enough. He was succeeded by two uniformed men with huge revolvers at their sides, as if they were prepared for Scorcese-like carnage in the Self-Help section. They are gone now, and a large individual without visible weaponry makes himself conspicuous among the shelves. Books are, unfortunately for us, not a bad thing to steal: a pile of fresh bestsellers, or new paperbacks, are apparently easy to unload. Many books are attractive, and I can see someone with no interest in reading stealing a pile just because of the way they look.

One thing taboo in bookselling is to let customers know what you think 9 of their purchases. The problem arises occasionally at the cash register. For the most part, maintaining impassive features in the face of curious (or worse) purchases is not hard. Once, someone materialized at the register with three self-help books and a magazine. The books all had gentle titles like *Managing Your Anger* or *Towards Serenity,* and the magazine was *Modern Handgun.* The sale went off without the hint of a grimace on my part. A well-known Chicago painter came in one evening with a female companion and bought her a book entitled *How to Write Erotica.* An older woman who seemed at, or near, the verge of mental collapse bought the complete, or near-complete works of the poet John Ashbery (did she know what she was doing?). There is a book among our stock entitled *Subway Art* that is basically a how-to for graffiti artists. Occasionally a distracted youth asks for it, but it is never on hand because, as soon as we order it, it is immediately stolen. One evening a worried-looking mother and her leather-jacketed teenage son came to the register with two or three books on punk rock, one I believe a biography of the singer Johnny Rotten. The weary mother, breaking out her checkbook, could not forbear to ask her son, "Are you *sure* this was approved as a project?" "I don't care if it was or not," the boy said with surprising hatred, or something near it. "You'll reimburse me when we get home," she said, handing me the check.

Books are not exactly luxuries, but neither are they necessities. They are 10 inveterately connected, as even Orwell seems to grasp, with pleasure. There is something gratuitous about them, even the ones that look drenched in boring or forbidding practicality such as electronics manuals and used-car price guides (we sell both). People are off their guard in a bookstore as they are not in a clothing or a toy store, which makes it unfair, if one is the typically overeducated bookstore employee, to make fun of what they buy.

Many of our customers take an undisguised pleasure in spending 11 money, as if the fact that books are involved sanctifies the lack of prudence. A bearded man came into the store one night and collected a huge pile of books on the theme of self-betterment: three or four oily self-help books, a couple of neo-pagan treatises from the New Age section, and (I'm not sure what his reasoning was) two or three books on how to write fiction. It was a huge tab, but he looked extremely happy, on the verge of some kind of transformation. The next evening he reappeared to return virtually all the books. Fortunately for him, our return policy is liberal in the extreme. Just buying the books had given him a lift, maybe saved him from doing something foolish.

Orwell comments on the different buying habits of men and women. 12 "Roughly speaking," he writes, "what one might call the *average* novel — the ordinary, good-bad, Galsworthy-and-water stuff which is the norm of the English novel — seems to exist only for women. Men read either the novels it is possible to respect, or detective stories." Today it can only safely be said that men buy magazines such as *Modern Handgun* and fishing magazines such as *Bassin'*, while women buy novels of all kinds. Bestsellers are all unisex in their audience. The real problem in updating Orwell's division of male and female purchases is the overwhelmingly large number of young people that increasingly seem to make up the book-buying public. The books, or in corporate terms the "product," has mutated, and is still mutating, to match the volatile tastes of the young.

There is a substantial category of books called "graphic novels," which 13 are, simply, comic books that feature Batman and Superman but cost around $12.95 apiece. Their entitlement to the honorific term "novel" is gravely in doubt, but some of them are attractive, and they are taken very seriously, and not just by adolescents. Many books in the Children's section contain, on their covers or elsewhere, buzzers, tiny music boxes, bells, and other encumbrances that make them amphibious, neither book nor toy but something indeterminate (there is a small, heavily picked over section in Children's called Classics, containing *Alice in Wonderland*, A. A. Milne, and the rest). Many of the titles in Self-Help are "workbooks," as in the *Depression Workbook*, a more or less graded series of exercises (I believe the pages tear out) designed to lead the reader, or purchaser, out of his or her despair.

According to a recent article in the *New York Times*, the physical iden- 14 tity of books is in deep flux, with publishers experimenting with various unconventional shapes: novels, for example, that are slightly larger than cigarette packs (Douglas Coupland's short-story collection *Life After God* is an example). A number of novels pitched to young people (the so-called members of Generation X, people in their twenties) are large colorful squares, eerily reminiscent of record albums. Only mysteries and detective stories are still issued in what might be called the traditional book shape, the quiet rectangle that looks as if it is made to be actually read as opposed to merely owned or looked at.

It is now obligatory for a bookstore to contain a café, and ours contains 15 a sizable one on the second floor. I have noticed that, while all kinds of people come into the store, not all kinds linger in the café, whose prices are fairly steep. The café is given over mostly to older people, students who seem to be actually studying, and quiet couples. The store's extreme permissiveness is apparent in its café policy. Cups of foaming coffee, donuts, butter-drenched scones, and muffins can be consumed anywhere in the store, among the opulent art books, while reading unpurchased novels, or dreaming over travel books. If I rack my brains I cannot really think of anything our customers are not, in principle, allowed to do. Generally, the policy of maintaining the store as a kind of moral free zone seems to pay off. Customers do not abuse the policy except in one area, that of the magazines. They swarm over the magazine racks on the first floor and leave their contents in shocking heaps, fashion magazines sprawling in V-shapes, computer magazines gutted for the free software they often contain, copies even of rational periodicals such as the *Economist* flipped through and thrown on the floor.

The bookstore is haunted, and even shaped, by some of the prevailing 16 issues of the day. Chief among these is the gap, which can be raged at or philosophized about but not wished away, between high and low culture. Anyone who thinks that this gap is frivolous should work in a bookstore. A rather accomplished artist has been retained by Barnes & Noble to furnish its stores with large caricatures of Shakespeare (the only writer with his own section, though Virginia Woolf commands something close to her own in fiction), George Bernard Shaw, and others, as well as popular deities such as John Grisham, James Michener, and Sue Grafton. From where I sit, John Grisham is the most powerfully popular writer in America, meaning that his fans seem the most intelligently devoted; the fans of other blockbuster novelists such as Tom Clancy seem to buy his huge dreary volumes out of something like duty. Grisham is regarded by the bookselling industry as a force of nature. I have been on the floor when shipments of bestsellers have arrived, and can testify to the almost numinous power that radiates from a V-cart (a rolling device used to move two or three dozen books) full of fresh copies of a Grisham novel.

Our store has a curiously large section entitled Literary Theory that 17 holds the works of deconstructionists, New Historicists, Reader Response Theorists, and other academic scrutinizers of texts. I don't think that this section is there simply for prestige; it is there because these books sell, and not just to academics. An utterly unpretentious woman asked me for a book on postmodernism, and she wasn't a student (I asked). It can now be said that deconstruction, though to a limited extent, is genuinely popular. We have, I think, the complete works of Paul de Man, and multiple copies of the complete works of Jacques Derrida, not to mention much of the latest scholarship connected with these and related writers. The increasingly mainstream profile of deconstruction came to mind as a possible paranoid hypothesis when I recently tried to order a book critical (though hardly dismissive) of the movement, David Lehmann's highly readable *Signs of the Times,* which offers a chronicle of the political misbehavior (among other things) of the late Paul de Man: it is unaccountably out of print.

As an ex-graduate student (surprise, surprise), I am both drawn to and depressed by the works of literary theory and I seek diversion in other sections. There is one book, in the section ambiguously designated Nature, that can always be counted on to brighten my mood after too much time in the theory section. It is a large collection of photographs entitled *Dangerous Aquatic Animals,* and it features not only pictures of killer whales, sharks, jellyfish, piranhas, and other bad actors of the sea, but photographs — not too gross, but gross enough — of the damage they have done to human beings (no decapitated scuba divers, just the anonymous swollen hands of someone who tried to embrace a toxic crustacean, etc.). The thing about the book is its dust jacket, which has been reduced to near tatters by, I like to think, myriads of ten-year-olds who have ritually gathered after school to gape at it ("Cool! Look at that guy!" "Come on, let me see it! Quit hogging it!"). Along with Woodworking perhaps, the Nature section is the most innocent in the store, a refuge from the rows of Tom Clancy novels and treatises of Derrida. I hope it doesn't sound like straining after paradox to observe how much Derrida and Clancy have in common: their books tend alike to strand the reader at some point infinitely removed from human thought and experience.

We have a very high turnover among the employees. I have been at the store longer than most of the other booksellers, and I have not been there that long. We hired a lot of part-timers to work over the Christmas holidays, and most of them were let go, some to their dismay, after the rush subsided. The store is fairly brusque in its hiring and, I fear, in its firing, policies. As with security, the matter of hiring and firing is interestingly complicated by the fact that books, meaning culture, meaning enlightenment, meaning humanism, are what we trade in. As a matter of fact, most of the employees do seem to have an unforced respect for books as more than saleable objects; otherwise they wouldn't work here. It is, however, a business, not a school or a church. The head office in New York recently sent out a Statement of Purpose that was posted in the employee lounges of Barnes & Noble stores around the country. It said that the company's ambition was to be the best retail store regardless of its product, but that because "our product happens to be books" we are obliged to make sure that our business practices "live up to the promise and idealism of the volumes that line our shelves."

Before one starts snickering at this, it is worth noting how indissoluble the tie between books and "idealism" (however understood) is. The Barnes & Noble CEO is, in his way, giving a bland rephrasing to the belief of Matthew Arnold, I. A. Richards, and others (here I draw triumphantly on my graduate school experience) that literature, or humanistic learning, is somehow capable of saving us. This is a belief that I do not share but nonetheless respect. Now for the snickering: our stock includes, besides *How to Write Erotica,* such idealism-soaked productions as *Transactional Analysis for Toddlers, The Dark Side of Your Inner Child,* and my nominee for the most pathos-drenched of our titles, *Seven Weeks to a Settled Stomach.* The proper response to the CEO's mandate that we live up to the books we sell was made by one of my co-workers: "I'm willing, as long as the company accepts legal responsibility."

It goes without saying that no one at the store, with the exception of the 21 boss and one or two of the assistant managers, regards it as a real job. I fell into conversation with an erudite customer one night, a retired history professor, and, without any obvious intention of offending me, he referred to working in a bookstore such as ours as a "McJob." If one presses further, into the dark heart of the average bookstore employee, one discovers that the only thing worthy of being called a job is something in, or vaguely related to, the arts. With its staggeringly large collection of art books, its substantial section devoted to Writing and Publishing, and the huge drawings of Oscar Wilde and Virginia Woolf staring down at everyone, the store itself is a kind of massive jibe at the fundamental unseriousness of everything that is not the arts. (I forgot to mention something that didn't bother me at all for the first few months but has now become maddening, the relentless twittering of classical music over the loudspeakers.) To subject oneself to such an art-saturated atmosphere once or twice a week is blissful, but to make it one's daily haunt is risking satiety. Marxist analysts of the corruption of culture under late capitalism would enjoy directing bitter commentary at the store, though they would have to step lightly around the fact that books by Marxists bitterly denouncing enterprises such as Barnes & Noble's make up the better part of our Sociology section.

Bookselling — at least at superstores such as ours that, like the gates of 22 hell, are open almost all the time (9:00 A.M. to 11:00 P.M. every day except Christmas) and accordingly need a large staff — is the ideal job for people who don't want to sleep in the streets but find most ways of earning money not to their liking. I fear that bookselling is for people who are somewhat work-shy. Let me revise that to people who are pathologically averse to exertion of most kinds. There is serious responsibility at our store, but it is monopolized by the managers, mostly by the general manager, a woman in our case, who has to answer to the district supervisor, and by the folks in Receiving, who undoubtedly, and justly, regard the booksellers as glorified wastrels.

Below the level of management there is not much to do. Books sell 23 themselves. In this, books differ from most merchandise. Nonetheless, I have noticed that, despite the extreme unstrenuousness of my job, not everyone can do it. One has to be courteous to customers without inducing in oneself overmastering feelings of servility. To grovel is not the way to ingratiate yourself, and to blow up at a customer, even if he insults you (it happens, it happens) is the only sure way to be fired immediately. When a putative book buyer whom I have never seen before abruptly calls me by my first name (we wear name tags), I begin, dangerously, wondering if sleeping on the streets is as bad as it seems.

What one observes in many booksellers, myself very much included, is an interest in, yes, the arts combined with a disinclination to align oneself with the forces of hard-core bohemia, the wearers of black clothing who swarm in cafés and have earned from an acquaintance of mine the name "art nuns." I have known many bohemians, and, contrary to what some may think, they often work, but not at bookstores, which are incurably square places, really: they earn whatever money they need at copy stores, as waiters and waitresses, or as bartenders. Orwell calls bookselling "an unhealthy life," but, as low-paying work goes, it is far from life-threatening. I do not find it impossible to leave work and read for a few hours, hang out with friends, and, in short, live. I don't love the job, but that is because I find the idea of work itself a kind of antidote to desire. The bouts of shame I endure at having to wear a tie and a name tag are not incapacitating. I cannot suppress the hope that I will one day leave the store, and I feel sure that if this hope is realized it will not occasion loud weeping on my employer's part.

Analyzing This Selection

1. How do book superstores differ in resources and atmosphere from other bookshops? What are Schwendener's views toward the differences?

2. Why do most employees and customers consider bookselling as not "a real job" (paragraph 21)? How does it differ from other retail sales jobs?

3. **THE WRITER'S METHOD**   Why, if at all, is Schwendener "afraid" that he is "a bookstore type" (paragraph 7)? What characteristics does he attribute to booksellers? Does he minimize or emphasize his typical characteristics?

Analyzing Connections

4. Compare bookselling and waitressing (see Paules's "Humble Pie," p. 312) as kinds of waiting on people. What aspects of Schwendener's job would Paules see differently from him?

Analyzing by Writing

5. You have probably held a McJob — perhaps as a McLifeguard, McCoach, or McWaiter. Write an essay of reflections or memories about your work experience. Examine matters such as the clientele, workplace, hierarchy, satisfactions, and dissatisfactions. Consider similarities and differences between you and others who work there. Write interesting reflections about matters that may or may not have been interesting at the time. In either case, as you think about them, they can gain significance.

Virginia Woolf

PROFESSIONS FOR WOMEN

VIRGINIA WOOLF (1882–1941) was an important British novelist noted for her emphasis on the subjective meaning of events rather than the outward circumstances of plot and appearance. Her novels include *Mrs. Dalloway* (1925) and *To the Lighthouse* (1927). Born into a distinguished literary family, she was educated at home and began her writing career as a book reviewer for the London *Times Literary Supplement*. With her husband she lived among a group of artists and intellectuals known as the Bloomsbury group — a group that included E. M. Forster, John Maynard Keynes, Bertrand Russell, and Lytton Strachey. She spoke out consistently for freedom and equality for women in works such as *A Room of One's Own* (1929) and the following address to the Women's Service League. Her essays are collected in four volumes of *Collected Essays* (1967).

When your secretary invited me to come here, she told me that your 1
Society is concerned with the employment of women and she suggested that I might tell you something about my own professional experiences. It is true I am a woman; it is true I am employed; but what professional experiences have I had? It is difficult to say. My profession is literature; and in that profession there are fewer experiences for women than in any other, with the exception of the stage — fewer, I mean, that are peculiar to women. For the road was cut many years ago — by Fanny Burney, by Aphra Behn, by Harriet Martineau, by Jane Austen, by George Eliot[1] — many famous women, and many more unknown and forgotten, have been before me, making the path smooth, and regulating my steps. Thus, when I came to write, there were very few material obstacles in my way. Writing was a reputable and harmless occupation. The family peace was not broken by the scratching of a pen. No demand was made upon the family purse. For ten and sixpence one can buy paper enough to write all the plays of Shakespeare — if one has a mind that way. Pianos and models, Paris, Vienna and Berlin, masters and mistresses, are not needed by a writer. The cheapness of writing paper is, of course, the reason why women have succeeded as writers before they succeeded in the other professions.

[1]*Fanny Burney . . . George Eliot* British women novelists of the eighteenth and nineteenth centuries.

But to tell you my story — it is a simple one. You have only got to figure 2 to yourselves a girl in a bedroom with a pen in her hand. She had only to move that pen from left to right — from ten o'clock to one. Then it occurred to her to do what is simple and cheap enough after all — to slip a few of those pages into an envelope, fix a penny stamp in the corner, and drop the envelope into the red box at the corner. It was thus that I became a journalist; and my effort was rewarded on the first day of the following month — a very glorious day it was for me — by a letter from an editor containing a check for one pound ten shillings and sixpence. But to show you how little I deserve to be called a professional woman, how little I know of the struggles and difficulties of such lives, I have to admit that instead of spending that sum upon bread and butter, rent, shoes and stockings, or butcher's bills, I went out and bought a cat — a beautiful cat, a Persian cat, which very soon involved me in bitter disputes with my neighbors.

What could be easier than to write articles and to buy Persian cats with 3 the profits? But wait a moment. Articles have to be about something. Mine, I seem to remember, was about a novel by a famous man. And while I was writing this review I discovered that if I were going to review books I should need to do battle with a certain phantom. And the phantom was a woman, and when I came to know her better I called her after the heroine of a famous poem, The Angel in the House. It was she who used to come between me and my paper when I was writing reviews. It was she who bothered me and wasted my time and so tormented me that at last I killed her. You who come of a younger and happier generation may not have heard of her — you may not know what I mean by the Angel in the House. I will describe her as shortly as I can. She was intensely sympathetic. She was immensely charming. She was utterly unselfish. She excelled in the difficult arts of family life. She sacrificed herself daily. If there was chicken, she took the leg; if there was a draught, she sat in it — in short she was so constituted that she never had a mind or a wish of her own, but preferred to sympathize always with the minds and wishes of others. Above all — I need not say it — she was pure. Her purity was supposed to be her chief beauty — her blushes, her great grace. In those days — the last of Queen Victoria — every house had its Angel. And when I came to write I encountered her with the very first words. The shadow of her wings fell on my page; I heard the rustling of her skirts in the room. Directly, that is to say, I took my pen in hand to review that novel by a famous man, she slipped behind me and whispered: "My dear, you are a young woman. You are writing about a book that has been written by a man. Be sympathetic; be tender; flatter; deceive; use all the arts and wiles of our sex. Never let anybody guess that you have a mind of your own. Above all, be pure." And she made as if to guide my pen. I now record the one act for which I take some credit to myself, though the credit rightly belongs to some excellent ancestors of mine who left me a certain sum of money — shall we say five hundred pounds a year? — so that it was not necessary for me to depend solely on charm for my living. I turned upon her and caught her by the throat. I did my best to kill her. My excuse, if I were to be had up in a court of law, would be that I acted in self-defense. Had I not killed her she would have killed me. She would have plucked the heart out of my writing. For, as I found, directly I put pen to paper, you cannot review even a novel without having a mind of your own, without expressing what you think to be the truth about human relations, morality, sex. And all these questions, according to the Angel in the House, cannot be dealt with freely and openly by women; they must charm, they must conciliate, they must — to put it bluntly — tell lies if they are to succeed. Thus, whenever I felt the shadow of her wing or the radiance of her halo upon my page, I took up the inkpot and flung it at her. She died hard. Her fictitious nature was of great assistance to her. It is far harder to kill a phantom than a reality. She was always creeping back when I thought I had despatched her. Though I flatter myself that I killed her in the end, the struggle was severe; it took much time that had better have been spent upon learning Greek grammar; or in roaming the world in search of adventures. But it was a real experience; it was an experience that was bound to befall all women writers at that time. Killing the Angel in the House was part of the occupation of a woman writer.

But to continue my story. The Angel was dead; what then remained? 4 You may say that what remained was a simple and common object — a young woman in a bedroom with an inkpot. In other words, now that she had rid herself of falsehood, that young woman had only to be herself. Ah, but what is "herself"? I mean, what is a woman? I assure you, I do not know. I do not believe that you know. I do not believe that anybody can know until she has expressed herself in all the arts and professions open to human skill. That indeed is one of the reasons why I have come here — out of respect for you, who are in process of showing us by your experiment what a woman is, who are in process of providing us, by your failures and successes, with that extremely important piece of information.

But to continue the story of my professional experiences. I made one 5 pound ten and six by my first review; and I bought a Persian cat with the proceeds. Then I grew ambitious. A Persian cat is all very well, I said; but a Persian cat is not enough. I must have a motor car. And it was thus that I became a novelist — for it is a very strange thing that people will give you a motor car if you will tell them a story. It is a still stranger thing that there is nothing so delightful in the world as telling stories. It is far pleasanter than writing reviews of famous novels. And yet, if I am to obey your secretary and tell you my professional experiences as a novelist, I must tell you about a very strange experience that befell me as a novelist. And to understand it you must try first to imagine a novelist's state of mind. I hope I am not giving away professional secrets if I say that a novelist's chief desire is to be as unconscious as possible. He has to induce in himself a state of perpetual lethargy. He wants life to proceed with the utmost quiet and regularity. He wants to see the same faces, to read the same books, to do the same things day after day, month after month, while he is writing, so that nothing may break the illusion in which he is living — so that nothing may disturb or disquiet the mysterious nosings about, feelings round, darts, dashes, and sudden discoveries of that very shy and illusive spirit, the imagination. I suspect that this state is the same both for men and women. Be that as it may, I want you to imagine me writing a novel in a state of trance. I want you to figure to yourselves a girl sitting with a pen in her hand, which for minutes, and indeed for hours, she never dips into the inkpot. The image that comes to my mind when I think of this girl is the image of a fisherman lying sunk in dreams on the verge of a deep lake with a rod held out over the water. She was letting her imagination sweep unchecked round every rock and cranny of the world that lies submerged in the depths of our unconscious being. Now came the experience, the experience that I believe to be far commoner with women writers than with men. The line raced through the girl's fingers. Her imagination had rushed away. It had sought the pools, the depths, the dark places where the largest fish slumber. And then there was a smash. There was an explosion. There was foam and confusion. The imagination had dashed itself against something hard. The girl was roused from her dream. She was indeed in a state of the most acute and difficult distress. To speak without figure she had thought of something, something about the body, about the passions which it was unfitting for her as a woman to say. Men, her reason told her, would be shocked. The consciousness of what men will say of a woman who speaks the truth about her passions had roused her from her artist's state of unconsciousness. She could write no more. The trance was over. Her imagination could work no longer. This I believe to be a very common experience with women writers — they are impeded by the extreme conventionality of the other sex. For though men sensibly allow themselves great freedom in these respects, I doubt that they realize or can control the extreme severity with which they condemn such freedom in women.

These then were two very genuine experiences of my own. These were 6 two of the adventures of my professional life. The first — killing the Angel in the House — I think I solved. She died. But the second, telling the truth about my own experiences as a body, I do not think I solved. I doubt that any woman has solved it yet. The obstacles against her are still immensely powerful — and yet they are very difficult to define. Outwardly, what is simpler than to write books? Outwardly, what obstacles are there for a woman rather than for a man? Inwardly, I think, the case is very different; she has still many ghosts to fight, many prejudices to overcome. Indeed it will be a long time still, I think, before a woman can sit down to write a book without finding a phantom to be slain, a rock to be dashed against. And if this is so in literature, the freest of all professions for women, how is it in the new professions which you are now for the first time entering?

Those are the questions that I should like, had I time, to ask you. And 7 indeed, if I have laid stress upon these professional experiences of mine, it is because I believe that they are, though in different forms, yours also. Even when the path is nominally open — when there is nothing to prevent a woman from being a doctor, a lawyer, a civil servant — there are many phantoms and obstacles, as I believe, looming in her way. To discuss and define them is I think of great value and importance; for thus only can the labor be shared, the difficulties be solved. But besides this, it is necessary also to discuss the ends and the aims for which we are fighting, for which we are doing battle with these formidable obstacles. Those aims cannot be taken for granted; they must be perpetually questioned and examined. The whole position, as I see it — here in this hall surrounded by women practicing for the first time in history I know not how many different professions — is one of extraordinary interest and importance. You have won rooms of your own in the house hitherto exclusively owned by men. You are able, though not without great labor and effort, to pay the rent. You are earning your five hundred pounds a year. But this freedom is only a beginning; the room is your own, but it is still bare. It has to be furnished; it has to be decorated; it has to be shared. How are you going to furnish it, how are you going to decorate it? With whom are you going to share it, and upon what terms? These, I think, are questions of the utmost importance and interest. For the first time in history you are able to ask them; for the first time you are able to decide for yourselves what the answers should be. Willingly would I stay and discuss those questions and answers — but not tonight. My time is up; and I must cease.

Analyzing This Selection

1. **THE WRITER'S METHOD**   In the first two paragraphs, what relation does Woolf establish with her audience? What details make her appear ingratiating? condescending? earnest?

2. Does the Angel in the House still exist? What has changed, and what remains the same, in current expectations of women?

3. Does Woolf assume that men writers encounter no difficulties or conflicts in thinking independently and expressing themselves? Is Woolf a female sexist in some of her observations?

4. What relationships between men and women are implied in Woolf's many references to women in a house and a room? What changes in the future are suggested by the metaphorical use of "house" in the final paragraph?

Analyzing Connections

5. How does Woolf's purpose as a lecturer differ from Steiner's (see "Books and the End of Literature," p. 274)? Whose tone do you think is more effective for the lecture's purpose?

Analyzing by Writing

6. Should young men and women ever be educated separately for part of their lives? At what age can it do the most good or the most harm to change or reinforce gender roles through separate schools or separate classes? Draw on any of your relevant experiences in single-sex associations such as scouting, sports, clubs, and being with just "the boys" or "the girls." Consider what it has meant to you to have these associations, and how they might have been more beneficial, or less limiting, than they were.

Laura L. Nash

THE VIRTUAL JOB

LAURA L. NASH is a writer and consultant on business ethics. She received her Ph.D. in classical philology from Harvard University. Nash writes textbooks and managers' handbooks on business practices and corporate culture. This selection is excerpted from an article in the *Wilson Quarterly* in 1994.

Something very odd is going on in the American corporate workplace. Employees are being told to prepare for a radical new condition of permanent insecurity, a future full of sporadic layoffs, endless efforts to upgrade job skills, and perpetually recombining work teams of insiders and "outsourcers." Continuous corporate "rightsizing" will dictate a "portfolio career" strategy: Since workers will no longer spend their careers with one or two employers, accumulating a portfolio of portable skills will be essential. Yet even as the corporation encourages "hard" qualities such as self-reliance and adaptability, it is also rushing headlong toward a supposedly kinder, gentler ethos. Large firms in particular are providing a growing variety of programs and social supports for those who remain under the corporate umbrella — however long that may be. The new formula might be described as a "love the one you're with" approach.

The turmoil in the workplace is being presented as stimulating and exciting, an opportunity for personal and professional growth. The modern corporation will supply precious training and experience, *Fortune* said recently in describing the "new deal" between employers and employees, and workers in turn will be expected to act like entrepreneurs (or "intrapreneurs") within the corporation: Find a way to "add value to the organization" and you get a new job. Fail and you look for a job elsewhere. But that is not so bad. "If the old arrangement sounded like binding nuptial vows," says *Fortune*, "the new one suggests a series of casual, thrilling — if often temporary — encounters."

One might almost be tempted to conclude that a new age of self-actualizing individualism is dawning. Released from the paternalistic and hierarchical strictures of the old corporation, the new employee will be free to blaze his or her own professional trail while the corporation stands by to help tend to personal needs that might impair performance, from child care to treatment for alcoholism. At the same time, it is also possible to see these developments as disturbing signs of an emerging form of corporatism in which areas of life once thought to be strictly private are increasingly regulated by a supposedly beneficent corporation. Those without ties to such a large institution will be spared such intrusions, of course, but may also be forced to go without many of the benefits accompanying it. Despite its simultaneous appeal to humanism and good economic sense, this new corporatism may not be kinder and gentler at all, and it may not even be all that good for business.

Even as it downsizes and rightsizes, the large American corporation is 4 increasingly assuming the role of a nanny. In 1992, benefits accounted for 32 percent of employee pay and were the fastest-growing element of compensation. Benefits include not only the traditional health insurance and pensions but a broad array of other goodies, ranging from those of the sensible-shoes variety (job training and tuition reimbursements at $35 billion annually) to more exotic offerings. Employer-provided legal services, for example, have increased sevenfold in the last decade. The corporate reach increasingly extends into what was once considered private life. Employer-sponsored health maintenance organizations, with their sometimes intrusive in-house "wellness" programs (Stop smoking! Lose weight!) are becoming part of the corporate way of life. Child-care programs of various kinds are proliferating, and among forward-looking people in the business world there is talk of the need to transform child care into "dependent care" programs providing various benefits to employees with elderly parents.

It is not unusual for today's large corporation to offer fitness programs, 5 marriage counseling, substance-abuse detection and treatment, AIDS counseling, diversity training, creative-thinking seminars, treatment of depression, diet and nutrition oversight, yoga instruction, interpersonal-relations counseling, and personal financial planning. One well-known company, EDS, even has on-site car care.

Many of these offerings involve things that were formerly considered 6 personal or domestic responsibilities, frequently managed by a wife who held no paying job. Now, as a demonstration of its newfound concern with employees' sense of well-being — and an undisguised desire to mitigate any condition that might detract from employee performance and the corporate bottom line — the corporation offers to take care of these matters. One might call this new, kinder and gentler approach to the employer-employee contract the "feminization" of the corporation.

Accompanying the trend is a growing emphasis on "softer" management 7 skills as the key to getting ahead in the managerial world. High on the list of qualities thought necessary for executive effectiveness in the 1990s are interpersonal skills, an ability to work with others in teams, and various kinds of "soft" abilities, such as intuitive reasoning, "people skills," and "creative thinking." Physical self-improvement is also in, and mental health is a major area of focus. Company-sponsored meditation programs and wilderness experiences designed to build trust and foster team spirit are becoming the vogue in corporate America. Now there are even humor consultants to help make fun and profit work together.

Despite its soft face and seemingly benign motivations, there is a distinctively hard edge to the new corporate humanism. Employees who are showered with benefits may pay a price in the loss of personal choice. Formerly private decisions about lifestyle and even personality may now be restricted by the company in the name of boosting personal performance and cutting costs. Today's well-bred manager may find, for example, that the powers that be in the personnel department regard his or her high cholesterol count as an indication of selfish disregard for the corporate team or a sign of insufficient self-discipline. The employee who insists on taking time off to care for a sick child despite the first-rate day-care services offered by the company may find his or her dedication to the job questioned a little more closely. . . .   8

Deep organizational changes are exacerbating instability. Business is moving inexorably toward a new model of operation, the "virtual corporation." As management specialists describe it, the virtual corporation will be a legal-financial entity whose physical plant is scattered across the globe and whose people-parts are almost as interchangeable as chips in a computer motherboard. Goods and services will be produced by a movable feast of temporary global teams. Geographically limited only by the reach of a telecommunications satellite, a team of "intrapreneurs" and outsiders will be patched together for a particular project and then disbanded when their work is through. Employees will then recombine into new teams for the next venture. A new product may be funded in Hong Kong, researched in Chicago and Japan, manufactured in Singapore, and marketed throughout the world. Economic factors being what they are (rotten and uncertain), the smart corporation will reduce its capital investment by farming out to smaller independent firms many of the functions it used to support in house, from manufacturing products to billing customers.   9

These trends contribute to individual uncertainty and promote a new individualism. In a flexible, unforgiving marketplace, people will need greater adaptive skills and self-confidence. The new training programs of the virtual corporation may offer a softer and more humane visage to its employees, but it will not offer any soft jobs. The successful future employee will be the person with transferable skills, high self-motivation — and no demands on the company pension plan. This is the "new deal."   10

The rise of nannyism, seemingly the antithesis of all that is implied by this trend toward a sink-or-swim workplace, is often justified as a rational response to the virtual corporation. Loyalty ("some degree of commitment   11 to company purpose and community for as long as the employee works there," as Robert Waterman describes it in a recent article with two co-authors) remains important to the virtual corporation, and indeed may be at a greater premium than before. Well-educated and well-trained employees are vital to its success, and training new employees is costlier than retraining old ones. The virtual corporation cannot offer job security, but it can offer another kind of security that comes from knowing that some of one's needs will be taken care of. This response, however, is more likely to foster *dependency* among employees than self-reliance. . . .

Company-subsidized programs may also carry hidden costs for the rest of 12 society. As corporations put more and more money into child-care programs for their employees, what will happen to the quality of the services available to others? Will the corporate programs sop up the best labor, for example, leaving second-rate child-care workers to tend the children of those outside the charmed corporate circle? Or consider an in-house fitness center, many of whose basic costs (such as space) can be easily and nearly invisibly subsidized through balance sheet complexities. Will the private health club that serves all comers be able to compete?

Most disturbing of all is the distant specter of a society in which many 13 people receive important social benefits from their companies and thus see no need to provide for the have-nots through publicly funded programs or voluntaristic means. Or perhaps people who have reoriented their private lives toward the corporation will find the duties and demands of citizenship in the larger community beside the point. Today's health-care debate suggests that such concerns are not completely far-fetched. Opinion polls consistently show broad but shallow support for change, in large part because those already insured (disproportionately employees of large organizations) are happy with their own arrangements. For better or worse, the expected groundswell of public support needed to push through reform has never materialized.

Discussion of such real and potential downsides of the new corporate 14 nannyism are generally considered taboo. But there are alternatives. All of the new benefits cost money — for example, money that comes directly out of salaries. Why not consider paying employees more, giving them the means (and the freedom) to decide on their own how to deal with their personal problems and challenges?

Every juncture of the new flexible work force and the new caring cor- 15 poration is a tension point of contradictory expectations. The first is the tension between job insecurity and stress relief. Many features of the new humanism in employee relations stem from a perception that stress is rising, not only among employees but in the institutions of public and private life. But a good deal of that stress is caused by the corporation itself, particularly in its inchoate vision of the temporary employee contract and its continued celebration of macho (male and female) workaholics who constantly sacrifice their personal and family lives to the demands of the job.

The ministrations of the nanny corporation can inadvertently worsen the   16
very problems they seek to address. The in-house child-care program, rationalized as a means to relieve stress, promote diversity, and retain employees, may provide an excuse to work managers even longer. After all, now there is no need to worry about the children. Meanwhile, with family life reduced to a few hours of private time a week, other forms of social stress begin to emerge. Where else but to the humane corporation would a dependent employee turn for help? Down the road, the parent of older children finds that he or she has made career decisions that require a commitment of time that leaves no room for attending to the many needs of, say, preteens who are too old for child-care but too young to drive themselves to music lessons or soccer practice. What is the corporation going to do now?

The second tension springs from the dismemberment of existing com-   17
munities inside (and outside) the corporation and the attempt to create a virtual corporation. Interchangeable gypsy job teams and portfolio careers will continue to undercut a sense of community in companies. The future corporation is said to depend on teamwork. The employer-employee contract, however, encourages self-aggrandizing career strategies. Nomadic managers, with no home in a single corporation, will have little motivation to compromise or sacrifice unless there is a negotiated, guaranteed payback in advance for Number One. Even their duties as citizens will have to be regulated by the corporation. Many communities today, for example, increasingly rely on help from public-private partnerships spearheaded by managers who "volunteer" their time for the public good only after the company guarantees in advance that their service will bring them later career benefits.

The third tension is the nearly utopian promotion of individualism, self-   18
actualization, and empowerment at the same time that teamwork, tolerance, and communication are emphasized. This tension will only be exacerbated if boundaries between private and corporate life continue to blur. As employees' personal identity, family life, and physical habits are increasingly "commodified" into performance issues, and as growing numbers of employees are regarded as permanently impermanent in the organization, calls for a new humaneness and self-actualization will ring more and more hollow. Widespread cynicism and disloyalty are likely results — a particularly volatile combination when mixed with the hyper-individualism of the virtual corporation.

Ultimately, the issues raised by the emergence of the new corporatism   19
are questions of personal and collective character. The danger is that what

seems a rational response to genuine problems in our society may in the end only raise those problems to a new pitch of urgency. New management doctrines that seek to make a virtue out of constant instability and insecurity will put the cynical, self-aggrandizing, hyper-individualistic character type that afflicts us today on a new footing and promote its spread. Meanwhile, the nanny corporation's protective cocoon for the chosen can only reduce our already diminished sense of citizenship and public responsibility. Historically, democratic capitalism has promoted a sense of mutuality, trust, and self-restraint among individuals, and it relies on these qualities for its continued survival. If the corporation now adds to the forces undermining them, these virtues may not hold.

Analyzing This Selection

1. **THE WRITER'S METHOD**   In paragraphs 1 to 8 does the author regard this "new deal" as a good one? How does her tone suggest her attitude toward these changes?

2. How does a "virtual job" reduce or increase nannyism?

3. Nash sees three tension points between new workers and companies. As an employee, how would each tension affect you?

4. According to Nash, how do the new conditions affect society? In your opinion, what additional or contrary effects are probable?

Analyzing Connections

5. In "The Value of Families" (p. 107), Etzioni is concerned about new conditions of employment affecting family life. What changes, if any, would Etzioni recommend on behalf of family in the "virtual job"? in the "nanny corporation"? Would Nash agree or disagree?

Analyzing by Writing

6. Attempts to stimulate excellence can result in the erosion of the quality of life and work, as Nash notes. Examine the effects of intense competitiveness in an athletic, musical, or artistic activity. Analyze some mixed results for you and others around you. Assess the gains and losses from your present perspective.

Ian Angell

WINNERS AND LOSERS
IN THE INFORMATION AGE

IAN ANGELL (b. 1947) is a leading British designer of computer graphics who writes about social issues in information technology. He earned undergraduate and doctoral degrees in mathematics from the University of London. He is a professor of information systems at the London School of Economics. Angell's research stresses the harsh consequences of advances in telecommunications. This selection is excerpted from a longer article in the *LSE Magazine* that appeared in 1996.

... "History," said Leon Trotsky, "is the natural selection of accidents," 1 and our world today is full of accidents just waiting to happen. The very natures of work, of institutions, of society, and even of capitalism itself are mutating. These mutations are confronting each other in the political power vacuum left by the fall of communism and the increasing impotence of liberal democracy, as the utopia promised by science and technology has turned into a nightmare for the "common man." Poverty, unemployment, pollution, overpopulation, mass migration, global plagues, and other catastrophes have left us with a world full of frightened people. For the masses will not win in the natural selection for dominance of an increasingly elitist world....

A new order (which many will call disorder) is being forced upon an 2 unsuspecting world by advances in telecommunications. The future is being born on the so-called information superhighways. Very soon these electronic telecommunication networks, covering the world via cable and satellite, will enable everyone in the world to "talk" to everyone else. We are entering a new elite cosmopolitan age. Global commerce will force the construction of multimedia highways, and anyone bypassed by these highways faces ruin. Information technology, together with speedy international travel, is changing the whole nature of political governance, its relationship to commerce, and commerce itself.

One major consequence emerging out of the new freedoms bestowed by 3 global telecommunications is the globalization — not merely the internationalization — of organizations. Individuals and companies are setting up large transnational networks that pay absolutely no heed to national boundaries and barriers. The commercial enterprise of the future will be truly global: it will relocate (physically or electronically) to where the profit is greatest and the regulation least. The umbilical cords have been cut; the global company no longer feels the need to support the national aspirations of the country of its birth. Recently this new business paradigm was expressed most forcibly by Akio Morita, who caused an uproar in Japan when he announced that Sony was a global company and not Japanese!

But, paradoxically, globalization is resulting in a trend toward localization or, as Morita calls it, "global localization." Global companies are setting themselves up within virtual enterprises at the hub of loosely knit alliances of local companies, all linked together by global networks, both electronic and human. These companies assemble to take advantage of any temporary business opportunity, and then they separate, searching for the next major deal. Apart from local products, local companies also deliver local expertise and access to home markets for other products created within the wider alliance. Companies and countries outside such networks have no future. 4

International trading now includes new forms of barter and exchange on these networks, particularly in superior scientific and technological expertise and knowledge. Money, which is merely a means of facilitating economic transactions, has itself become electronic information, and the ability to determine what constitutes money can no longer be monopolized by national governments. This inevitably lowers the transaction costs of money and makes taxation of profits and regulation of the process almost impossible — a real competitive advantage for any virtual enterprise with a movable center of gravity and for those individuals who are willing to trade their expertise in this electronic market. 5

Knowledge Workers versus Service Workers

The rise of teleworking/telecommuting/televillages has led Peter Drucker to a very interesting forecast. He says that humanity is polarizing into two employment categories: the intellectual, cultural, and business elite (the mobile and independent knowledge workers) and the rest (the immobile and dependent service workers). In a similar vein, Robert Reich believes that in the information age people will work in three categories: symbolic-analytic services (the knowledge workers who are problem identifiers, solvers, and brokers), in-person services, and routine production services. The latter two groups roughly correspond to Drucker's service workers. 6

Routine production services can either be performed by robots or exported anywhere on the globe. Wages in this sector are already beginning to converge worldwide to Third-World levels. British Polythene Industries

(BPI) is to close its factory at Telford, with the loss of 150 jobs, and switch to China. BPI's payroll bill will be cut by 90 percent. Even the British Home Office at one time was seriously considering subcontracting a large but straightforward data-entry job to the Philippines. Such "social dumping" is dragging down the wages of in-person service workers, a sector that is itself being increasingly automated. It is estimated that 150,000 UK bank jobs will eventually be lost because of automation. Millions of jobs will be lost if teleshopping takes off. Inevitably, the slow redistribution of wealth that has occurred over the last few centuries is being reversed, rapidly. Societies are stratifying; new elites are appearing. The future is inequality; at the very bottom of the heap, Western societies are already witnessing the emergence of a rapidly expanding underclass.

Now we can see that knowledge workers are the real generators of   7 wealth. The income of these owners of intellectual and financial wealth will increase substantially, and they will be made welcome anywhere in the world. As of October 1994, foreign "entrepreneurial investors" with £1 million at their disposal can bypass the usual entry rules into Britain. But Britain has been slow off the mark and suffers the added embarrassment that none of the migrant rich want to live there. In the United States, there is a fast-track immigration policy for businessmen and women who can offer $1 million and guarantee to employ ten people. Six hundred millionaires emigrated to the United States in 1993. It is only a matter of time before intellectual capital, such as scientific and technological expertise, will be included on the balance sheet.

On the other side of the coin, there is a growing realization that each   8 service worker is a net loss both to the state and to the company: They cost far more than they generate. Service workers will now be expected to add far more value to the company, unlike in the past, when service work meant just turning up. Companies will be reducing the wages and staffing levels of service workers, and it is no accident that most Western companies are presently instigating major downsizing programs.

This is all happening against a background of an exploding population   9 in the Third World (95 percent of the world's population increase is in developing countries). To combat the inevitable mass migrations, state barriers will be thrown up everywhere to keep out alien service workers; each state has a surplus of its own to support. This is already happening. Canada is to impose a $1,000 tax on people seeking landed immigration status, thus sending out a message that is likely to reduce applications from poor service workers but increase applications from richer knowledge workers. In California, Proposition 187 intends to bar the nearly two million illegal immigrants from schools, welfare services, and all but emergency health care. How long will it be before there are "differential rights" for "differentiated citizens," identified in a database and policed by smart cards? How long before the notion of "Human Rights" is as outdated as the "Divine Right of Kings"? . . .

We are rapidly approaching a situation in which, in order to attract the [10] elite who have the knowledge and money to enliven the economy, the elite group will be expected to pay less tax and not more. The great majority of governments are lowering top tax rates in line with declining global levels. Geoff Mulgan claims that "top income tax rates fell an average of 16.5% between 1975 and 1989." "The main producers and repositories of wealth — multinational companies — have increasingly been able to adjust their accounts and the prices of their internal international transactions so that their profits are declared in low tax countries, while they continue to operate in high tax ones." Very soon companies will be negotiating preferential tax deals not only for themselves but also for chosen elite employees. . . .

All the while, the disposable income for most of society will be drasti- [11] cally reduced. The power in global economic forces means that the tax burden is irrevocably moving onto the shoulders of the immobile as well as away from income and onto expenditure. When Leona Helmsley said, "Only the little people pay taxes," she was unwittingly making a prediction. This goes counter to every notion of social justice that has been prevalent over the past two hundred years. Inevitably in the transition we can expect massive civil unrest and disorder. . . .

A Future for Democracy?

Because of the need to employ the local masses, the major social prob- [12] lem for politicians in the coming decades is going to be how to attract global employers to partner local companies and how to keep them attracted. Governments will have no choice other than to acquiesce to the will of global enterprises. A new paradigm is upon us in which the nation-state has mutated into just another form of organization, a form of organization that will delegate market regulations — such as North American Free Trade Agreement or the European Union — to continent-wide bodies, which in turn will use their economic muscle to undermine each member state. Not only will state be pitted against state, but also area will compete against area, town against town, even suburb against suburb. Nation-states will inevitably fragment: rich areas will dump poor areas. Such shakeout trends can be interpreted as downsizing, a strategy that is being considered by most shrewd major corporations these days. As Daniel Bell so eloquently put it, "The nation-state is too small for the big things and too big for the small things." Some futurologists expect that early in the next century the number of states in the United Nations will increase from the present number of 184 to over a thousand. Each state will permit entry to holders of "UN style" company passports. Tax holidays and reduced regulation aimed at attracting employers will be the name of the game everywhere. . . .

One inevitable consequence of global trade will be the rise of the new [13] city-state at the hub of global electronic and transport networks. The non-democratic model of Hong Kong is an exemplar, even though the city itself doesn't yet realize that it has defined the future. Singapore under the enlightened leadership of Lee Kwan Yew is another. What European city will be the first to break ranks with the nation-state mentality holding back progress? A number of European cities can make the leap. Liechtenstein has already started; what about Monaco? And let us not forget Venice; perhaps it will rediscover former glories. What about Lisbon? They have the singular example of attracting the Gulbenkian wealth earlier this century. The Corporation of the City of London too has enormous potential and could be revitalized, although the dead hand of the "Mother of Parliaments" will make this far more difficult.

To protect their wealth, rich areas will also undertake a "rightsizing"   14
strategy, ensuring a high proportion of (wealth-generating) knowledge workers to (wealth-depleting) service workers. Rich areas have to maintain and expand a critical mass of scientific and technological expertise and have to use it to underpin an effective education system to regenerate the resource. These rich areas will reject the liberal attitudes of the present century as the expanding underclass being spawned by these liberal attitudes and the untrained migrants they welcomed previously are increasingly seen as economic liabilities. In Nietzsche's words, "Many too many are born. The state was devised for the superfluous ones." Mass-production methods needed an oversupply of humanity; in a sense, the machine age spawned the nation-state, but what is to be done with the glut as the machine age dies and we enter the information age?

As far as global enterprises are concerned, liberal democracy is an arti-   15
fact of the machine age, an ideology from a time when the masses were needed — but it will soon mutate into an irrelevancy. It will be merely the means of governing the immobile and dependent service workers. That citizens elect their slave masters makes democracy slavery none the less.

Analyzing This Selection

1. The author refers to the evolutionary process of natural selection (paragraph 1). Does natural selection apply to economics and politics? Do societies biologically evolve or change by other means? Explain your opinion.

2. Angell points out that telecommunication networks simultaneously globalize and localize companies. How do these changes affect knowledge workers? How do they affect service workers?

3. Assess Angell's evidence and arguments supporting his predictions about future states and citizenship. What is most convincing? Most disturbing?

4. **THE WRITER'S METHOD**   How do you feel at the end of the essay? Is that the intended effect of Angell's tone or a counterreaction to it?

Analyzing Connections

5. Angell and Nash (see "The Virtual Job," p. 348) both examine social consequences of new employment conditions. How do they agree or differ in their outlook on society?

Analyzing by Writing

6. Analyze positive and negative effects resulting from telecommunications in your work and life as a student. What evidence of winners and losers do you find in your segment of the information age? Do telecommunications place you in an elite cosmopolitan category? Examine how your access to the highway affects your relation to others who learn and teach. How does it affect your relation to those with whom you "talk" by network? Do inequities in telecommunications skills or access put deserving, intelligent people at a disadvantage?

PART 7

POSSESSIONS

INSIGHTS

It is easier for a camel to go through the eye of a needle, than for a rich man to enter into the kingdom of God.

— MATTHEW 19:24

A man is rich in proportion to the number of things which he can afford to let alone.

— HENRY DAVID THOREAU

There is something about holding on to things that I find therapeutic.

— EDNA O'BRIEN

I call people rich when they're able to meet the requirements of their imagination.

— HENRY JAMES

I instinctively like to acquire and store up what promises to outlast me.

— COLETTE

It is ironic that the very kind of thinking which produces all our riches also renders them unable to satisfy us. Our restless desire for more and more has been a major dynamic for economic growth, but it has made the achievement of that growth largely a hollow victory. Our sense of contentment and satisfaction is not a simple result of any absolute level of what we acquire or achieve. It depends upon our frame of reference, on how what we attain compares to what we expected. If we get farther than we expected we tend to feel good. If we expected to go farther than we have then even a rather high level of success can be experienced as disappointing. In America, we keep upping the ante. Our expectations keep accommodating to what we have attained. "Enough" is always just over the horizon, and like the horizon it recedes as we approach it.

We do not tend to think in terms of a particular set of conditions and amenities that we regard as sufficient and appropriate for a good life. Our calculations tend to be relative. It is not what we have that determines whether we think we are doing well; it is whether we have *more* — more than our parents, more than we had ten years ago, perhaps more than our neighbors. This latter source of relativity, keeping up with (or ahead of) the Joneses, is the most frequently commented upon. But it is probably less important, and less destructive, than our comparisons with our own previous levels and with the new expectations they generate. Wanting more remains a constant, regardless of what we have.

— PAUL WACHTEL

Private Property, the Law of Accumulation of Wealth, and the Law of Competition . . . these are the highest results of human experience, the soil in which society so far has produced the best fruit.

— ANDREW CARNEGIE

People who have lived for centuries in poverty in the relative isolation of the rural village have come to terms with this existence. It would be astonishing were it otherwise. People do not strive, generation after generation, century after century, against circumstances that are so constituted as to defeat them. They accept. Nor is such acceptance a sign of weakness of character. Rather, it is a profoundly rational response. Given the formidable hold of the . . . poverty within which they live, accommodation is the optimal solution. Poverty is cruel. A continuing struggle to escape that is continuously frustrated is more cruel. It is more civilized, more intelligent, as well as more plausible, that people, out of the experience of centuries, should reconcile themselves to what has for so long been the inevitable.

The deeply rational character of accommodation lies back, at least in part, of the central instruction of the principal world religions. All, without exception, urge acquiescence, some in remarkably specific form. The blessedness that Christianity accords to the meek is categorical. The pain of poverty is not denied, but its compensatory spiritual reward is very high. The poor pass through the eye of the needle into Paradise; the rich remain outside with the camels. Acquiescence is equally urged, or as in the case of Hinduism compelled, by the other ancient faiths. There has long been a suspicion, notably enhanced by Marx, that the contentment urged by religion is a design for diverting attention from the realities of class and exploitation — it is the opiate of the people. It is, more specifically, a formula for making the best of a usually hopeless situation.

— JOHN KENNETH GALBRAITH

A Summer Morning

Her young employers, having got in late
From seeing friends in town
And scraped the right front fender on the gate,
Will not, the cook expects, be coming down.

She makes a quiet breakfast for herself.
The coffee-pot is bright,
The jelly where it should be on the shelf.
She breaks an egg into the morning light,

Then, with the bread-knife lifted stands and hears
The sweet efficient sounds
Of thrush and catbird, and the snip of shears
Where, in the terraced backward of the grounds,

A gardener works before the heat of day.
He straightens for a view
Of the big house ascending stony-gray
Out of his beds mosaic with the dew.

His young employers having got in late,
He and the cook alone
Receive the morning on their old estate,
Possessing what the owners can but own.

— RICHARD WILBUR

FOCUSING BY WRITING

1. Our possessions can possess us, and they frequently do — sometimes delightfully, sometimes harmfully. Nearly everyone has felt that the essence of life was summed up for the moment by having a dog, a record collection, a pair of skis, or earrings, or special jeans. In a brief essay, define your past or present obsession with a special personal belonging that affects your life.

2. Do you prefer shopping at a department store, specialty boutique, discount store, superstore, or manufacturer's outlet? Examine the attractions of the ambience that make shopping more pleasurable in one kind of store, including the sales personnel, the sense of abundance, or other elements of the atmosphere.

3. In many households there is some treasured object that is associated with earlier generations or with an important period in the recent family past. Perhaps it is a vase or lamp, a Bible or jewelry, a piece of furniture or a rug. The object comes to be treated as something precious and irreplaceable — even though it may be fairly common — because it embodies certain ideals or meanings. Select any single object that holds special status in your household; explain its meanings and how they are kept alive by customs and habits.

4. Sometimes money is given as a gift instead of a present selected by the giver. Do you think it is a good way to avoid disappointments, or is it disappointing? On important occasions such as graduation, Christmas, a bar or bat mitzvah, or a wedding, significant amounts of money can accumulate instead of numerous presents. How, if at all, does the money increase or diminish the value of the traditional occasion?

Harry Crews

THE CAR

HARRY CREWS (b. 1935), who was raised in Georgia, joined the Marine Corps after high school and became a sergeant before he left the corps to go to college. He was educated at the University of Florida, where he now teaches writing. His novels include *CAR* (1972), *A Feast of Snakes* (1976), and *The Knockout Artist* (1988). He often writes for magazines such as *Playboy* and *Esquire,* in the latter of which this essay first appeared.

The other day, there arrived in the mail a clipping sent by a friend of 1
mine. It had been cut from a Long Beach, California, newspaper and dealt
with a young man who had eluded police for fifty-five minutes while he
raced over freeways and through city streets at speeds up to 130 miles per
hour. During the entire time, he ripped his clothes off and threw them out
the window bit by bit. It finally took twenty-five patrol cars and a helicopter
to catch him. When they did, he said that God had given him the car, and
that he had "found God."

I don't want to hit too hard on a young man who obviously has his own 2
troubles, maybe even is a little sick with it all, but when I read that he had
found God in the car, my response was: *So say we all.* We have found God
in cars, or if not the true God, one so satisfying, so powerful, and awe-
inspiring that the distinction is too fine to matter. Except perhaps ultimately, but pray we must not think too much on that.

The operative word in all this is *we.* It will not do for me to maintain 3
that I have been above it all, that somehow I've managed to remain aloof
from the national love affair with cars. It is true that I got a late start. I did
not learn to drive until I was twenty-one; my brother was twenty-five before
he learned. The reason is simple enough. In Bacon County, Georgia,
where I grew up, many families had nothing with a motor in it. Ours was
one such family. But starting as late as I did, I still had my share, and I've
remembered them all, the cars I've owned. I remember them in just the
concrete specific way you remember anything that changed your life. Especially I remember the early ones.

The first car I ever owned was a 1938 Ford coupe. It had no low gear 4
and the door on the passenger side wouldn't open. I eventually put a low
gear in it, but I never did get the door to work. One hot summer night on

a clay road a young lady whom I'll never forget had herself braced and ready with one foot on the rearview mirror and the other foot on the wind vent. In the first few lovely frantic moments, she pushed out the wing vent, broke off the rearview mirror, and left her little footprints all over the ceiling. The memory of it was so affecting that I could never bring myself to repair the vent or replace the headliner she had walked all over upside down.

Eight months later I lost the car on a rain-slick road between Folkston, Georgia, and Waycross. I'd just stopped to buy a stalk of bananas (to a boy raised in the hookworm and rickets belt of the South, bananas will always remain an incredibly exotic fruit, causing him to buy whole stalks at a time), and back on the road again I was only going about fifty in a misting rain when I looked over to say something to my buddy, whose nickname was Bonehead and who was half drunk in the seat beside me. For some reason I'll never understand, I felt the back end of the car get loose and start to come up on us in the other lane. Not having driven very long, I overcorrected and stepped on the brake. We turned over four times. Bonehead flew out of the car and shot down a muddy ditch about forty yards before he stopped, sober and unhurt. I ended up under the front seat, thinking I was covered with gouts of blood. As it turned out, I didn't have much wrong with me and what I was covered with was gouts of mashed banana.

The second car I had was a 1940 Buick, square, impossibly heavy, built like a Sherman tank, but it had a '52 engine in it. Even though it took about ten miles to get her open full bore, she'd do over a hundred miles an hour on flat ground. It was so big inside that in an emergency it could sleep six. I tended to live in that Buick for almost a year and no telling how long I would have kept it if a boy who was not a friend of mine and who owned an International Harvester pickup truck hadn't said in mixed company that he could make the run from New Lacy in Coffee County, Georgia, to Jacksonville, Florida, quicker than I could. He lost the bet, but I wrung the speedometer off the Buick, and also — since the run was made on a blistering day in July — melted four inner tubes, causing them to fuse with the tires, which were already slick when the run started. Four new tires and tubes cost more than I had or expected to have anytime soon, so I sadly put that old honey up on blocks until I could sell it to a boy who lived up toward Macon.

After the Buick, I owned a 1953 Mercury with three-inch lowering blocks, fender skirts, twin aerials, and custom upholstering made of rolled Naugahyde. Staring into the bathroom mirror for long periods of time I practiced expressions to drive it with. It was that kind of car. It looked mean, and it was mean. Consequently, it had to be handled with a certain style. One-handing it through a ninety-degree turn on city streets in a power slide where you were in danger of losing your ass as well as the car, you were obligated to have your left arm hanging half out the window and a very *bored* expression on your face. That kind of thing.

Those were the sweetest cars I was ever to know because they were my 8
first. I remember them like people — like long-ago lovers — their idiosyncrasies, what they liked and what they didn't. With my hands deep in crankcases, I was initiated into their warm greasy mysteries. Nothing in the world was more satisfying than winching the front end up under the shade of a chinaberry tree and sliding down the chassis on a burlap sack with a few tools to see if the car would not yield to me and my expert ways.

The only thing that approached working on a car was talking about one. 9
We'd stand about for hours, hustling our balls and spitting, telling stories about how it had been somewhere, sometime, with the car we were driving. It gave our lies a little focus and our talk a little credibility, if only because we could point to the evidence.

"But, hell, don't it rain in with that wing vent broke out like that?" 10

"Don't mean nothing to me. Soon's Shirley kicked it out, I known I was 11
in love. I ain't about to put it back."

Usually we met to talk at night behind the A&W Root Beer stand, with 12
the air heavy with the smell of grease and just a hint of burned French fries and burned hamburgers and burned hot dogs. It remains one of the most sensuous, erotic smells in my memory because through it, their tight little asses ticking like clocks, walked the sweetest softest short-skirted carhops in the world. I knew what it was to stand for hours with my buddies, leaning nonchalant as hell on a fender, pretending not to look at the carhops, and saying things like: "This little baby don't look like much, but she'll git rubber in three gears." And when I said it, it was somehow my own body I was talking about. It was *my* speed and *my* strength that got rubber in three gears. In the mystery of that love affair, the car and I merged.

But, like many another love affair, it has soured considerably. Maybe it 13
would have been different if I had known cars sooner. I was already out of the Marine Corps and twenty-two years old before I could stand behind the A&W Root Beer and lean on the fender of a 1938 coupe. That seems pretty old to me to be talking about getting rubber in three gears, and I'm certain it is *very* old to feel your own muscle tingle and flush with blood when you say it. As is obvious, I was what used to be charitably called a late bloomer. But at some point I did become just perceptive enough to recognize bullshit when I was neck deep in it.

The 1953 Mercury was responsible for my ultimate disenchantment 14
with cars. I had already bored and stroked the engine and contrived to place a six-speaker sound system in it when I finally started to paint it. I spent the better half of a year painting that car. A friend of mine owned a body shop and he let me use the shop on weekends. I sanded the Mercury down to raw metal, primed it, and painted it. Then I painted it again. And again. And then again. I went a little nuts, as I am prone to do, because I'm the kind of guy who if he can't have too much of a thing doesn't want any

at all. So one day I came out of the house (I was in college then) and saw it, the '53 Mercury, the car upon which I had heaped more attention and time and love than I had ever given a human being. It sat at the curb, its black surface a shimmering of the air, like hundreds of mirrors turned to catch the sun. It had twenty-seven coats of paint, each coat laboriously hand-rubbed. It seemed to glow, not with reflected light, but with some internal light of its own.

I stood staring, and it turned into one of those great scary rare moments when you are privileged to see into your own predicament. Clearly, there were two ways I could go. I could sell the car, or I could keep on painting it for the rest of my life. If twenty-seven coats of paint, why not a hundred and twenty-seven? The moment was brief and I understand it better now than I did then, but I did realize, if imperfectly, that something was dreadfully wrong, that the car owned me much more than I would ever own the car, no matter how long I kept it. The next day I drove to Jacksonville and left the Mercury on a used-car lot. It was an easy thing to do. 15

Since that day, I've never confused myself with a car, a confusion common everywhere about us — or so it seems to me. I have a car now, but I use it like a beast, the way I've used all cars since the Mercury, like a beast unlovely and unlikable but necessary. True as all that is, though, God knows I'm in the car's debt for that blistering winning July run to Jacksonville, and the pushed-out wing vent, and finally for that greasy air heavy with the odor of burned meat and potatoes there behind the A&W Root Beer. I'll never smell anything that good again. 16

Analyzing This Selection

1. What does Crews mean in saying, "We have found God in cars"? Why does the thought lead him to say, in almost the same breath, "pray we must not think too much on that"?

2. **THE WRITER'S METHOD**   Crews seems to be exaggerating some details in his descriptions of his cars and in his accounts of his experiences. What kinds of exaggerations does he lard into his essay, and what effects do they have on our response to him as a writer? What qualities of his might be objectionable? What qualities might be thought of as attractive?

3. At what point did Crews begin to realize that he was identifying himself too closely with his cars? What other realization is this one linked with?

4. In the final paragraph, Crews says that people around him seem to be confusing themselves with their cars. In what way do they do this? What features of common American life is he alluding to in that observation?

5. The tone of the essay includes some nostalgia. Over what does Crews feel nostalgic? What broader theme is included in his treatment of the main topic?

Analyzing Connections

6. Compare the ways that Crews and Simmons (see "Motorcycle Talk," p. 63) were changed by their vehicles. What aspects of themselves did they come to possess through their possessions?

Analyzing by Writing

7. Do young Americans currently idolize cars? What are contemporary teenage attitudes and expectations about cars? Discuss the role of the car in male or female rites of passage, new freedoms, and social relations, and consider its other symbolic and practical roles. If you think the thrill of cars has diminished for American youth (since Crews's generation), try to explain reasons for the decline.

E. M. Forster

MY WOOD

E. M. FORSTER (1879–1970) was a British novelist and essayist who was educated at Cambridge University. Except for periods of travel to India and the Mediterranean, where he was deeply affected by his contacts with ancient cultures, he continued to live at his college through most of his adulthood. His fiction is often about conventionally educated young English people discovering something unconventional in themselves in response to symbolic places, such as other countries or old houses. Even the titles of his novels suggest traveling to take up a fresh perspective on things: *Where Angels Fear to Tread* (1905), *The Longest Journey* (1907), *A Room with a View* (1908), *Howards End* (1910), and *A Passage to India* (1924), which is the book Forster mentions in the first sentence of this selection from his collection of essays *Abinger Harvest* (1936).

A few years ago I wrote a book which dealt in part with the difficulties 1 of the English in India. Feeling that they would have had no difficulties in India themselves, the Americans read the book freely. The more they read it the better it made them feel, and a check to the author was the result. I bought a wood with the check. It is not a large wood — it contains scarcely any trees, and it is intersected, blast it, by a public footpath. Still, it is the first property that I have owned, so it is right that other people should participate in my shame, and should ask themselves, in accents that will vary in horror, this very important question: What is the effect of property upon the character? Don't let's touch economics; the effect of private ownership upon the community as a whole is another question — a more important question, perhaps, but another one. Let's keep to psychology. If you own things, what's their effect on you? What's the effect on me of my wood?

In the first place, it makes me feel heavy. Property does have this effect. 2 Property produces men of weight, and it was a man of weight who failed to get into the Kingdom of Heaven. He was not wicked, that unfortunate millionaire in the parable, he was only stout; he stuck out in front, not to mention behind, and as he wedged himself this way and that in the crystalline entrance and bruised his well-fed flanks, he saw beneath him a comparatively slim camel passing through the eye of a needle and being woven into the robe of God. The Gospels all through couple stoutness and slowness. They point out what is perfectly obvious, yet seldom realized: that if you have a lot of things you cannot move about a lot, that furniture requires dusting, dusters require servants, servants require insurance stamps, and the whole tangle of them makes you think twice before you accept an invitation to dinner or go for a bathe in the Jordan. Sometimes the Gospels proceed further and say with Tolstoy that property is sinful; they approach the difficult ground of asceticism here, where I cannot follow them. But as to the immediate effects of property on people, they just show straightforward logic. It produces men of weight. Men of weight cannot, by definition, move like the lightning from the East unto the West, and the ascent of a fourteen-stone bishop into a pulpit is thus the exact antithesis of the coming of the Son of Man. My wood makes me feel heavy.

In the second place, it makes me feel it ought to be larger.   3

The other day I heard a twig snap in it. I was annoyed at first, for I   4 thought that someone was blackberrying, and depreciating the value of the undergrowth. On coming nearer, I saw it was not a man who had trodden on the twig and snapped it, but a bird, and I felt pleased. My bird. The bird was not equally pleased. Ignoring the relation between us, it took fright as soon as it saw the shape of my face, and flew straight over the boundary hedge into a field, the property of Mrs. Henessy, where it sat down with a loud squawk. It had become Mrs. Henessy's bird. Something seemed grossly amiss here, something that would not have occurred had the wood been larger. I could not afford to buy Mrs. Henessy out, I dared not murder her, and limitations of this sort beset me on every side. . . .

In the third place, property makes its owner feel that he ought to do   5 something to it. Yet he isn't sure what. A restlessness comes over him, a vague sense that he has a personality to express — the same sense which, without any vagueness, leads the artist to an act of creation. Sometimes I think I will cut down such trees as remain in the wood, at other times I want to fill up the gaps between them with new trees. Both impulses are pretentious and empty. They are not honest movements toward money-making or beauty. They sprang from a foolish desire to express myself and from an inability to enjoy what I have got. Creation, property, enjoyment form a sinister trinity in the human mind. Creation and enjoyment are both very, very good, yet they are often unattainable without a material basis, and at such moments property pushes itself in as a substitute, saying, "Accept me instead — I'm good enough for all three." It is not enough. It is, as Shakespeare said of lust, "The expense of spirit in a waste of shame": it is "Before, a joy proposed; behind, a dream." Yet we don't know how to shun it. It is forced on us by our economic system as the alternative to starvation. It is also forced on us by an internal defect in the soul, by the feeling that in property may lie the germs of self-development and of exquisite or heroic deeds. Our life on earth is, and ought to be, material and carnal. But we have not yet learned to manage our materialism and carnality properly; they are still entangled with the desire for ownership, where (in the words of Dante) "Possession is one with loss."

And this brings us to our fourth and final point: the blackberries.   6

Blackberries are not plentiful in this meagre grove, but they are easily   7 seen from the public footpath which traverses it, and all too easily gathered. Foxgloves, too — people will pull up the foxgloves, and ladies of an educational tendency even grub for toadstools to show them on the Monday in class. Other ladies, less educated, roll down the bracken in the arms of their gentlemen friends. There is paper, there are tins. Pray, does my wood belong to me or doesn't it? And, if it does, should I not own it best by allowing no one else to walk there? There is a wood near Lyme Regis, also cursed by a public footpath, where the owner has not hesitated on this point. He had built high stone walls each side of the path, and has spanned it by bridges, so that the public circulate like termites while he gorges on the blackberries unseen. He really does own his wood, this able chap. And perhaps I shall come to this in time. I shall wall in and fence out until I really taste the sweets of property. Enormously stout, endlessly avaricious, pseudo-creative, intensely selfish, I shall weave upon my forehead the quadruple crown of possession until those nasty Bolshies[1] come and take it off again and thrust me aside into the outer darkness.

[1]***Bolshies*** Bolsheviks.

Analyzing This Selection

1. In the second paragraph, the terms "heavy" and "weight" include nonliteral meanings. Give a literal explanation of this first effect of property on Forster's character. What is added by Forster's figurative presentation?

2. In paragraph 4, explain the effect of the short sentence "My bird."

3. Explain Forster's somewhat difficult point about property becoming a substitute for creativity and enjoyment. From his viewpoint, how is that to be avoided?

4. **THE WRITER'S METHOD** The essay includes an abundance of references to history, literature, and religion, and they occur without much introduction or clarification. What is their purpose? And what is the effect of their suddenness?

Analyzing Connections

5. In the Insights on page 362, Paul Wachtel offers an explanation of why riches fail to satisfy. Does Wachtel's theory about possessions explain Forster's reactions to his property? How much or how little does Forster's experience illustrate Wachtel's point?

Analyzing by Writing

6. If you were designing a better society, what would you allow individuals to own privately? Conversely, what should be owned publicly? Would you change the status of utilities, transportation systems, communication networks, hospitals, schools, shorelines, family housing, or any other major components of present society? Explain why your plan for ownership would be good for people.

Holly Brubach

MAIL-ORDER AMERICA

HOLLY BRUBACH (b. 1953) graduated from Duke University. In New York she wrote fashion articles for *Vogue* magazine and contributed dance criticism to the *Atlantic Monthly*. Joining the *New Yorker* as a fashion columnist, Brubach continued to write about dance, scripting television programs for *Dance in America*. Presently, she is the style editor of the *New York Times Magazine*, where this essay appeared in 1993.

Growing up in Pittsburgh, I had an uncle who never obtained a passport 1 because he had made up his mind that he was never going to need one: he had no intention of ever leaving the country. For that matter, he had never left the state of Pennsylvania, except for one brief foray into Ohio, which, he realized in retrospect, had been a mistake. For a soul so utterly lacking in wanderlust, however, he was full of curiosity. In the pages of *National Geographic*, he visited the steppes of Russia and the Pyramids and the Great Wall, and on those rare occasions when bona fide travelers happened to cross his path, he could converse with them about the average rainfall in the month of August or the mathematical basis of the architecture or the worsening condition of the mortar, as if he'd not only gone on a tour but guided it. I remember regarding this knowledge as somehow illegitimate, acquired rather than earned. And with all the superiority of youth, I viewed him as lazy and complacent for not having gone out and seen the world for himself.

Now, however, I confess that the older I get, the more I'm inclined 2 to follow his example, in my way. Late at night, when the stores are closed, or on a Saturday afternoon, while weary women with swollen feet and cranky children are competing for an overworked salesman's attention, I'm at home with a stack of mail-order catalogues, redecorating my apartment and browsing for Christmas presents and planning what I'll wear next season. With time, I find, the best catalogues come to seem familiar: you recognize their tone of voice, their quirks, the faces that appear over and over again in their pages. Leafing through one recent arrival, a friend shook his head at the sight of so many models who for years now have been turning up in his mailbox on a regular basis. "I feel like I know these people better than the people I know," he said.

374

For those of us who feel that our lives have been inundated with cata- 3
logues, there is corroboration in statistics: last year, according to the Direct
Marketing Association, more than 10,000 mail-order companies sent out
13.5 billion catalogues and some 55 percent of the adult population
bought $51.5 billion worth of goods by mail. These figures have been
steadily on the rise, climbing steeply during the 80's, when mail-order businesses grew at triple the rate of most retailers. Industry analysts say that this
boom has come about for a variety of reasons, including the introduction of
ZIP codes and toll-free telephone numbers, the spread of credit cards, the
use of computer networks that cross-check information about individual
spending habits and the sizable contingent of women in the work force.
Women no longer have the time for recreational shopping, it seems, and
men, who never had the time to shop, can no longer expect women to do
their shopping for them.

Somehow, over the course of the past 15 years or so, our collective atti- 4
tude toward shopping — or at least toward the idea of it — seems to have
shifted from delight to loathing. Those who once relished the chase, tracking down the perfect raincoat or duffel bag or fly-fishing rod or coffee
maker or scented candle, can no longer be bothered. The audience for the
department-store-as-theater has pretty much disappeared. In 1978, shoppers
flocked to Bloomingdale's India promotion, buying souvenirs and saving
themselves the trip (an idea that would have appealed to my uncle); now
they can save themselves the trip across town. Although (or maybe because) we still look on the things with which people surround themselves
as indicative of something deeply personal — as a form of self-expression —
the act of furnishing our lives now strikes us as a chore. Perhaps it's our
conscience, which we misplaced during the 80's, that is telling us not to set
foot in the temples of consumerism. Perhaps it's our sense of decorum:
we haven't stopped spending our money, but we're more reluctant to spend
it in public. Most likely, mail-order catalogues are about sheer convenience: the catalogues have done for stores what videos have done for
movie theaters.

Possibly due to the mistaken assumption that people who can afford 5
expensive clothes have more time to shop or that luxury goods would be
tainted by the stigma of catalogue shopping, the top of the retail market
has yet to be colonized by the mail-order business. Despite the occasional
exception . . . , mail order in many people's minds retains the down-market
connotations of the "wish books" that peddled dinette sets to the children
of immigrants. Within the past few years, however, fashion designers have
begun to view the success of catalogues like J. Crew with increasing envy,
and some — among them Calvin Klein and Carolyne Roehm — have
begun to make inroads into the field.

What industry analysts leave unsaid, but what millions of mail-order cus- 6
tomers know firsthand, is that the catalogues are beating not only the stores

but also the fashion magazines at their own game. Fashion magazines now find themselves preaching almost exclusively to the converted, reporting designers' runway proclamations as if they mattered (which they do, in a way). Mail-order catalogues, however, insinuate themselves into the homes of the indifferent and the disaffected, who couldn't care less what Karl Lagerfeld has to say. Where magazines have come to look more and more like catalogues, offering a little something for everyone (the advertisers, the designers, the multitudes of readers), catalogues have come to look more and more like magazines, with a distinct editorial point of view. While magazines have waxed prosaic, catalogues have turned poetic, portraying a world that, for all its resemblance to the one in which we live, is of their own creation — a place with its own landscape, its indigenous population, its native customs, its dialect. If our forays into this world are increasingly frequent, perhaps it's because they confirm a number of things we like to believe: that life is happy, harmonious and just and that people get what they deserve, which in our case is the best.

The territory staked out by J. Crew in the pages of its catalogue was,   7
until recently, easy to locate — just down the road from where the people in Ralph Lauren's ads lived. The real estate was a little more affordable, the local inhabitants — attractive, unfailingly stylish men and women — weren't quite so stuck-up and self-conscious. Clearly, we were somewhere in America, but in an America that was scenic and vaguely nostalgic, where there were no strip malls or nuclear power plants or fast-food restaurants. In this place, Coca-Cola still came in the old green glass bottles — no garish aluminum cans. The people who lived there drove Land Rovers and convertible two-seaters. They packed their picnics in antique wicker hampers. They painted an old table they bought at a yard sale and got the paint all over themselves. Shucking corn, eating watermelon, drinking iced tea and homemade lemonade, they were caught in the act by the camera, in pictures that could have been snapshots taken by a friend. These people's sailboats and their golden retrievers and their Alumni Day visit to a university that looked to be either Princeton or Yale situated them squarely in the upper middle class. The men were well groomed, clean shaven, with short hair and high cheekbones. The women wore little or no makeup, and an inordinate number of them were pale and blue-eyed and blond; one, a regular, bore a remarkable resemblance to Glenn Close. (The portfolio of dressier women's clothes modeled by Lauren Hutton, a regular feature every season, has always looked more like a fashion story from Mirabella than a weekday extension of the life depicted in the rest of the catalogue.)

Lately, however, there's been an influx of ethnicity into J. Crew's pages   8
(it's happening in Ralph Lauren's neighborhood, too). This fall, there are not one but four different editions of the J. Crew catalogue — one set in downtown Manhattan, the others in the usual picturesque country retreat, with small inset photographs from the urban version. Our old acquain-

tances have been moved aside to make room for an aspiring rock band and its assorted hangers-on. The split-rail fences, the stands of trees, the path along the crest of the dunes give way, in the downtown edition, to corrugated fencing, cracked windows held together with duct tape and graffiti. A pick-up basketball game in a city schoolyard includes three blacks, one Asian and a couple of white guys. There are men with long, unruly hair and women who appear to be of Mediterranean extraction, or part-Hispanic, or part-black. Blondes are rare.

But in one sense the demographics are still surprisingly narrow: there 9 are no old people. Here, as in the mythical place where J. Crew's catalogue used to reside, the population ranges in age from late teens to mid-30's, with a handful of children — none of them old enough to wear braces or need advice about birth control.

At first glance, the multiculturalism that has found its way into J. Crew's 10 catalogue looks like an injection of reality into what had been an airtight fantasy, but closer inspection reveals that only the trappings have changed; the fantasy remains the same. This is a world whose affable inhabitants live in harmony. Camaraderie prevails. No one is ever alone, unless it's to read a book, and even then we feel sure that there are friends somewhere close at hand, sleeping late or poring over the Sunday paper or planning dinner. All dark thoughts, all solitary bouts of melancholy and despair, have been banished. On page after page, the good times unfold. Life is a party to which we wish we'd been invited. The only difference is that this season, there are some new people on the guest list.

The voice in the copy that accompanies the photographs remains cor- 11 dial and sensible-sounding — no flowery odes to a shirt, no wheedling sales pitches about the role it will play in your wardrobe. No full sentences, either. The machine-gun rhythm gets to be a little irritating: "Buttons. Collar. Placket. Seams. A hefty cotton jersey." Every once in a while the polite reserve falls away and then J. Crew gives in to snobbery and name-dropping. "We can't say for sure, but we seem to remember old photos of Jackson Pollock in East Hampton wearing pants like these," one caption claims.

Nearly everything J. Crew sells — new editions of standard sportswear 12 that's in the public domain — seems calculated to be instantly familiar, to take its place beside those favorite items in our wardrobes that have earned the status of old friends. The "barn jackets" are "pre-aged" and appear slightly battered; the twill work shirts are dyed to look as if they've faded over the course of long years. Many of the items are just like something we already own, except for some small detail, some slight improvement that makes us suddenly feel that the version we have is inferior: the phys. ed. shorts are in vivid colors they never came in at school; the rope-soled espadrilles are gingham-checked; the denim jackets have a tartan lining. The appeal of these clothes is based on novelty rather than fashion. . . .

The guys in the J. Crew catalogue are the "new men" we've heard so 13 much about: they throw their arms around each other's shoulders; they know their way around a kitchen; they feed their baby children. Although in the past the men wearing wedding bands outnumbered the women who wore them, there was never the slightest suspicion that the men might be married to somebody else who wasn't pictured — that they'd left their wives at home and run off for an illicit weekend in the catalogue's pages. In fact, it seemed to go without saying that these women *were* the wives and that, while the new men may have relished a wedding ring as a token of commitment, the women were so secure and independent that they didn't need one.

This fall, however, there are fewer men and women wearing wedding 14 bands. What this means for marriage is anybody's guess. Maybe it's still going strong, but the signs of it aren't fashionable anymore. Maybe this crowd is younger and they're still waiting to meet their mates. Or maybe people who live in lofts in New York don't get married as much as people who live in places where Coke still comes in bottles. The old cast of characters had about it an air of satisfaction, of being settled; this new crowd projects a sense of possibilities.

Unlike J. Crew — the name of no one in particular, which conjures up 15 images of oarsmen on the Charles — L. L. Bean was a real person: Leon Leonwood Bean who, as faithful readers of his catalogues have learned over the years, loved to go fishing, hunting and camping, lived to be 94, sent his favorite dog tins of biscuits when he went away on trips and gave each newly married L. L. Bean employee a Hudson's Bay blanket as a wedding present. Though he is no longer the company's animating presence, there's a distinct personality that survives in the tone of the catalogue copy. Plain-spoken, chatty and respectful, the corporate voice of L. L. Bean keeps up a fairly steady monologue in a mature-sounding first-person plural, taking full responsibility for the products for sale, offering bits of arcane information (it takes 30 to 50 gallons of maple-sugar sap to produce a single gallon of syrup), creating the impression that on the other side of the image and the "800" number there's somebody home. "Our product testers found these versatile boots ideal for mountain biking and day hiking," the catalogue announces. At Christmas, L. L. Bean greets its customers with the fond good wishes of an old friend: "We hope to hear from you and hope you have a safe and memorable holiday season."

The people pictured in L. L. Bean's pages look like attractive customers 16 or friends of the employees or teachers at the local elementary school in Freeport, Me., the company's headquarters; they're simply too ordinary to qualify as models. All fantasy, all glamour, all aspirations to a better life than the one in which the readers might find themselves are absent here. The appeal rests entirely on reality — or, rather, on some approximation of reality, since the majority of L. L. Bean's customers probably don't live in log cabins or houses with stone hearths. Where several other, glossier catalogues with pretensions to elegance routinely offer certain items at discreet "marked-down" prices in order to avoid the stigma of discount retailing (in the Victoria's Secret catalogue, the Chancery Lace Bra has been on sale for at least four years now), L. L. Bean makes no bones about appealing to the reader's desire to save a dollar here, a dollar there; thrift is a Yankee virtue. A shirt is advertised as "priced at an exceptional value — $4 less than last year."

17   The houses are modest. The landscape is strictly local, off the circuit that the power brokers travel. The Christmas trees that appear in the background in the holiday edition are hung not with precious, glittering gold and cut-crystal ornaments, as they are in the Victoria's Secret catalogue, but with pretzels and cranberry strands and strung popcorn. If L. L. Bean is guilty of romanticizing anything, it's the continuous present of the American home, cozy and unbroken, as it exists for most people only in the imagination. Microwave ovens, Nintendo, 12-step programs — the world as we now know it has been held at bay, with no more than a few recent developments like step aerobics selectively admitted. The TV, VCR, stereo and CD player are housed in a cabinet designed to look like an old-fashioned icebox. Though the loving hands that stitch Bean's sampler quilts and crewel-embroidered sweaters are anonymous, their products are suffused with intimations of mythical grandmothers.

18   The people L. L. Bean depicts, one gathers, are mostly married, with car pools and mortgages and aging parents — the full weight of adult responsibility on their shoulders. They are pictured fetching a few logs from the woodpile, teaching their tow-headed children to read or curled up in their flannel pajamas, book in hand. Personality, 10. Sex appeal, 0. It's not so much the clothes they wear that make them look so dowdy, since many of the items aren't significantly different from their trendier counterparts (J. Crew's Barn Jacket is nearly indistinguishable from Bean's Canvas Field Coat). It's the way the clothes are worn — their tidy fit, their matching colors, their utter lack of any sense of adventure (paradoxical in people who profess to love exploring the outdoors). The cut is prudish at times: the caption for one cotton shirt assures the reader that the V-neck is "not too low." The catalogue repeatedly draws the line between "roomy" and "relaxed" (both desirable traits) and "oversized" (taboo in this context). Fashion is suspect, to be avoided at all costs. The people at L. L. Bean refer consistently to their "apparel designers," in a locution as quaint as a Norman Rockwell illustration. The free and loose style that dominates the pages of J. Crew would surely dismay these adherents to the rule book of convention. Shirts and turtleneck jerseys are worn close to the body and tucked in. Sweaters are ribbed at the cuffs and at the waistband. The effect is Republican.

19   In the world evoked by the L. L. Bean catalogue, there is no room for

the confusion about sex roles that currently besets the rest of our society. Androgyny is prohibited. Those garments that the Bean people countenance for both men and women are designated outright "For Men and Women," with separate sizes or, in a few cases, men's sizes followed by a list of women's equivalents; the word "unisex" is never spoken. Likewise, the people at L. L. Bean have their minds made up on the subject of color palettes and gender. Mock turtlenecks are available in, among other colors: "Maroon (Men's only). Honey (Women's only). Blue (Men's only)." When it comes to the Blanket Plaid Flannel Shirts, the men get brown; the women, red. There is, of course, nothing to prevent a woman from ordering the same shirt in brown, in a men's size, for a fit that's slightly funkier, but the distinctions here are so firmly drawn that so brash an act would be tantamount to cross-dressing.

This catalogue sure is talkative, with a lengthy caption for every item,   20 listing its attributes in scrupulous detail. "Buttons along left side for easy on/off," the catalogue says of a jumper. A jersey dress is "fun to wear — needs no special care." The longstanding Yankee suspicion of fashion is coupled here with the conviction that clothes are a lot of bother.

Ironically, plaid flannel shirts, along with Birkenstocks and several other   21 items L. L. Bean sells, are "hot" right now — a fact of which the Bean people seem oblivious. Where J. Crew takes essentially standard items and presents them in a manner that's glamorous and up to the minute — shirts tied around the waist, shorts two sizes too big, worn low on the hips of young models — L. L. Bean's approach is stolid and plain. The appeal of this is probably lost on people who buy into the heat of the moment, but for those who have opted out of the rat race, including (paradoxically) many full-time fashion types, L. L. Bean is a relief, a refuge from the onslaughts of trendiness.

Bean's style might be called New England provincial, and like all   22 provincial esthetics, it is ultimately corrupted by sentimentality. Ankle socks "patterned with cows and pigs grazing amid tulip rows." The "Warm Feelings Blanket." J. Crew has found a harmless enough outlet for its elegiac impulses in the names of colors, which ramble from the botanical (weed, thistle, yucca, aloe, glade, balsam) to the oceanographic (Pacific, surf, kelp, lake, lagoon) to the culinary (Dijon, cola, chili). But L. L. Bean refuses to get carried away in this respect: "yellow, orange, magenta, dark purple, white, turquoise, royal, navy," the catalogue states flatly. This penchant for simplicity is every so often overcome by some lyric impulse and then the hardheaded Yankee is revealed to be a sap, particularly when it comes to the local landscape: a sweater captures "the soft tones of a Maine seaside garden muted by fog" or a quilt evokes a wave of memories, including "the cry of loons in early morning." But these outbursts, rare and always brief, were outdone in the catalogue this spring by the emotionalism of one C. H. Gray, a customer from Hillsboro, Ore. His paean to his Maine Hunting Shoes, received in 1945 as a gift from his father, is written in iambic septameter, and the penultimate couplet reads: "These boots have kept my feet warm, comfortable and dry,/And the thought of simply discarding them can almost make me cry."

In the end, what saves L. L. Bean from bathos is the sense that the 23 people behind the catalogue actually live the life depicted in its pages. The outdoorsy, sports-loving attitude is not a pose. Though L. L. Bean's fishing vest may be worn by photographers and other people in need of lots of pockets, it is designed for someone who actually fishes. The context in which the clothes are presented confirms their authenticity. The Fly Fishing catalogue (a separate edition) is packed with fascinating lore, as well as flies called "Mickey Finn," "Fruit Cocktail" and — wonderful finds for the collector of affectionate nicknames — "Rat Face Irresistible" and "Gerbubble Bug." J. Crew may sell all the makings of an outfit that one could wear to go kayaking, but L. L. Bean sells the outfit *and* the kayak.

It is not at all clear whether the Victoria's Secret catalogue is intended 24 for the women who would wear the clothes featured in it or for the men who would like the women in their lives to wear the clothes featured in it — particularly the lingerie. In what is tantamount to an admission that the catalogue has acquired a considerable following among the kind of guys who maintain a small archive of *Sports Illustrated*'s swimsuit issues, the copy goes back and forth, addressing first the women, who are buying for themselves ("a great choice when dinner's at 8 and you're leaving straight from the office") and then the men, who are buying for the women ("a sumptuous gift so wonderful, you might let her have it just a little bit early"). The tone Victoria's Secret takes with men is hushed and conspiratorial, as if this were their girlfriend's best friend talking — steering them clear of all the pitfalls they would otherwise encounter in their search for the perfect gift. Even so, this catalogue is unquestionably a female enclave, like a beauty salon or a harem — a place to which women retreat to make themselves more attractive. And though men are seldom admitted, their presence and power in the world beyond its confines are implied in the women's diligent efforts to please them.

The Victoria's Secret cast revolves around a handful of recognizable 25 stars — "supermodels" who inhabit the pages of *Vogue*, ads for designer clothes and the runways of Europe. Linda Evangelista, Stephanie Seymour and Karen Mulder bring to the catalogue an aura of international glamour, or anyway that seems to be the intent. The truth is that it's always something of a shock to come upon them here, like finding movie stars playing the dinner theater on a cruise ship. Nearly all the women have long hair (long hair and sexy lingerie evidently go together). When it comes to clothing, models always wear the smallest size; when it comes to bras, the women in the Victoria's Secret catalogue look as if they take a medium at the very least.

To my mind, the better part of this catalogue's entertainment value 26 resides in watching the Victoria's Secret people walk the fine line between sexy and trashy. The trappings are endlessly amusing, intended to set a tone of thoroughbred elegance and high propriety by evoking the life of the English aristocracy. But a bona fide Mayfair drawing room would run the risk of being too subtle and musty to trigger in American readers the desired intimidation at the thought of a nation full of people supposedly more civilized than we are. Instead, the Victoria's Secret masterminds have constructed what is essentially a cartoon furnished with hoity-toity, English clichés: silver salvers, Battersea boxes, leather library sofas, paintings of horses. The models — clad in scant, lace-trimmed underwear, their bra straps slipping off their shoulders — look soulfully into the eye of the camera while lying on an Oriental rug or posing next to a tea table.

The catalogue copy is likewise strewn with Britishisms: "centre," "jew- 27 ellery," "colour," "favourite," "splendour.". . . An ongoing series of bathrobes has identified itself with a distinguished university (the Cambridge Robe), a country house open to tourists (the Chatsworth Robe), a legendary heroine harking back to the days of chivalry (the Guinevere Robe).

The merchandise itself, ranging from suits and dresses to sports clothes 28 and what the English call "frocks" for evening, isn't bad, despite a propensity for shiny synthetic fibers that give an impression of simulated satin with an almost adhesive cling. There's a good selection of bras and underpants: demi-cup underwires, halter-neck bras, strapless bustiers, merry widows, garter belts, flutter bikinis, high-cut briefs, G-strings. But over all, the clothing is strictly middle of the road — mall fashion that steers a safe and steady course, with an occasional detour to take in some recent trend. The catalogue would have us believe that its constituency is made up mostly of successful career women; an outfit is touted for its "executive finesse." But the only executives who dress like this are the ones in television miniseries. The colors are a little too bright for the corporate life; the cut calls too much attention to the shape of the body. Five years after fashion designers finally succeeded in abolishing shoulder pads, the people at Victoria's Secret seem either not to know or not to care; nor have they heard about the demotion of the "power suit," which has been discarded by the women it was intended for and taken up by the women who work for them. In fact, the likeliest candidate for the Victoria's Secret customer would appear to be not the *Business Week* subscriber but That Cosmopolitan Girl.

The catalogue speaks the language of romance novels, fraught with 29 histrionic verbs and overwrought adjectives. Bikinis "sizzle," skirts "sweep" and "cascade," necklines "plunge," dresses "bedazzle." The clothes are routinely described as "opulent," "lavish," "sophisticated." Why use a plain word when a fancy one will do? Some of the fabrics are "launderable."

Significantly, the famous models who might have been the obvious 30 choices — buxom blondes like Claudia Schiffer and Anna Nicole Smith, the Brigitte Bardot and Marilyn Monroe look-alikes — are absent here.

Victoria's Secret features good girls, well brought up, slightly nymphoma- niacal, but only behind closed doors and only when they're in love. Sey- mour — head back, back arched — writhes with longing. Mulder projects a certain reserve, even when she's reclining on a chaise longue, wearing a push-up bra and bikini briefs. The sex appeal is of the smoldering, read-my- mind variety, not kittenish or playful. Page after page, these contemporary odalisques offer themselves, like Manet's "Olympia," in repose: passive women, waiting for a man to come along and fulfill them — not just any man but the man of their dreams.

A generation that gleaned some of its earliest information about sex by   31 scrutinizing the pages of prosthetic-looking bras and briefs in the Sears cat- alogue (straightforward, almost clinical — like looking up dirty words in the dictionary) has finally come of age and now studies Victoria's Secret instead. The pleasure this experience holds for men is obvious. But what women get out of it — apart from the convenience of mail-order shopping — has been largely overlooked. There is perhaps an unspoken consensus that the subject is too loaded, that the less said these days about the pleasure women may take in projecting themselves into the role of a sex object, the better. But the fact remains that for many women, looking at pictures of other women is an incitement to fantasy — not because they want to know those women but because they want in some vague way to *be* those women, to evoke in men the feelings they imagine the women in the pictures do.

Lust, however, is only part of the equation. The eroticism is always sub- 32 ordinate to a higher goal: romance. Readers of novels about American girls adrift in international society or about 18th-century virgins ravished by pirates or about small-town daughters who conquer the hearts of lonesome millionaires will recognize in Victoria's Secret's lingerie pages a kindred sensibility. The hot-blooded lover rips the heroine's bodice and discovers . . . the lace-edged, demi-cup, underwire bra on page 14. I have an idea for a new marketing venture: a made-for-television movie subtitled with infor- mation about the clothes the characters are wearing (fabric content, sizes, price), along with a toll-free number the viewer can call to order them.

Year in and year out, this hunger for romance and passion — the sight of 33 all these women in heat — is like an obsessive drone so that, finally, what seems most remarkable about Victoria's Secret is a certain self-referential monotony. . . . Victoria's Secret recommends its Tapestry Keepsake Box as the perfect place to store love letters.

The heroine of the Victoria's Secret catalogue is, in many respects, the 34 ideal mail-order customer. House-bound in her lace-trimmed satin teddy, she lounges decoratively, leafing through the catalogues that get delivered to her door while she awaits the man who will transform her life. Every day brings a new harvest of things she never knew she needed: reproduction gargoyles (Design Toscano); copies of baseball uniforms from such historic teams as the Mexican Southwest League Tabasco Bananas and the Toledo Mud Hens (Ebbets Field Flannels); a lease on a lobster trap (Rent Mother Nature), and healing crystals and new-age cards dispensing sage advice: "Live Juicy. . . . Marry Yourself. . . . Be who you truly are and the money will follow" (Red Rose Collection). From "The Best Catalogues in the World" she orders other catalogues. In her Tapestry Keepsake Box she stashes a snack — a chocolate bar in the shape of a topographical map of Israel (The Source for Everything Jewish). . . .

The truth might ruin her illusion. She switches on the television, but 35 the Home Shopping Club, a cross between an auction and a telethon, strikes her as raucous and intrusive, to say nothing of the clinical way the merchandise is displayed, as if it were on exhibit in a courtroom. When information about . . . J. Crew's expanding retail empire makes its way into the papers, she instinctively avoids it. Too many facts would expose the stagecraft.

This is an alternative world she's living in, in which every catalogue 36 seizes on some facet of life and celebrates the hell out of it. J. Crew would have us believe that belonging to a community would fill the empty spaces in our souls. The people at L. L. Bean would turn our enthusiasm for the outdoors into a religion. . . . In Victoria's Secret, it's love. These are not misrepresentations, only exaggerations, and in many respects they are more comfortable than the ambiguities and compromises that permeate our everyday lives. If mail-order shopping is sweeping America, perhaps it's because we're such a willing audience for the fantasies that catalogues present: we've been led to believe that our circumstances can change overnight, that any day now we can get discovered, find true love, hit the jackpot.

So the woman reads the catalogues in solitude, in silence or while lis- 37 tening to "Classics by Request," Victoria's Secret's two-volume tape collection of classical music by Mozart, Vivaldi, Handel and others. In page after page, the catalogues lay out their merchandise for her perusal. They speak to her directly, flattering her vanity, courting her interest. "This is all for you," they say. "You are the only customer in the world."

Analyzing This Selection

1. **THE WRITER'S METHOD**   How do paragraphs 1 and 2 contribute to the rest of the essay? Since Brubach doesn't return to these personal details, do they continue to be relevant? Should paragraphs 1 and 2 be deleted?

2. Does the author condemn or enjoy each catalogue fantasy? What is the purpose of Brubach's analysis?

3. Examine Brubach's summaries of the pictorial content of each catalogue. How does her language describe the evocative pictures?

4. What does the author say about real, not mail-order, America?

Analyzing Connection

5. What is each catalogue's unspoken definition of middle class? Is the definition realistic, or is it a fantasy? Do the values resemble or differ from the middle-class values that are defined by Steele (see "On Being Black and Middle Class," p. 211)?

Analyzing by Writing

6. Examine connections between words and pictures in a catalogue or brochure. (You may still have a brochure you received as a prospective college student.) What elements of reality are missing? What attractive fantasy is suggested? Analyze the world it creates.

Richard Panek

SUPERSTORE INFLATION

RICHARD PANEK (b. 1958) graduated from Northwestern University and studied at the University of Iowa Writer's Workshop. His articles have appeared in *Elle, Mirabella,* and the *Village Voice.* Panek writes about the survival of small-town baseball in *Waterloo Diamonds* (1995). This article appeared in 1997 in the *New York Times Magazine.*

The superstore — that cropland-encroaching or square-city-block-swallowing shrine to seemingly limitless supply — is shaping up to be the defining shopping experience of the 1990's. It has established the scale that shoppers now demand and a strategy that retailers giddily emulate, and it has done both to an extent that would have been unimaginable only 10 years ago. Whatever bigger was, now it's *more.* 1

Superstores have gone from zero to $550 billion in annual sales, or fully one-third of the nation's retail revenue, in 10 years flat. In fiscal year 1996, Home Depot, the leading home-improvement superstore chain, showed a record $938 million profit on $19.5 billion in sales, a 28 percent improvement over the previous year's record profits; Staples, a $106 million profit on $4 billion in sales, or a 44 percent improvement. Borders, the No. 2 bookseller in the nation, has been opening new superstores at the rate of one every nine days; Barnes & Noble, the leading bookseller, one every four or five days; Staples, two a week. For Home Depot, nearly three a week. 2

That's three new-from-the-foundation-up pieces of real estate, each stocking 40,000 to 50,000 different kinds of building materials, home-improvement supplies and lawn and garden products, each with a garden center that by itself covers at least 20,000 square feet, each *week.* 3

Where only yesterday there was empty acreage, suddenly there are superstores selling books, sporting goods, home furnishings, athletic wear, baby products, bed and bath supplies, toys, consumer electronics, pet supplies, even off-the-rack bridal gowns. In some fields, the term no longer suffices; in the grocery trade the distinctions include conventional-format stores, warehouse stores, superstores, superwarehouse stores, combination food-and-drug stores and hypermarkets. As Richard S. Tedlow, a Harvard Business School professor and the author of "New and Improved: The Story of Mass Marketing in America," says, "I'm not sure what people *mean* when they use the term superstore." 4

Over the years in popular parlance it has applied to anything from an 5
ultra-inclusive Wal-Mart outside Madison, Wisc., to the ultra-exclusive
Emporio Armani on Madison Avenue. It definitely comes in a big box —
"big box" is a Wall Street synonym, in fact, for four walls that house a
wealth of consumer goods. But in recent months, thanks in part to the Federal Trade Commission's highly publicized resistance to the proposed
merger between the Staples and Office Depot superstore chains, its meaning has begun to settle on a specific breed of big-box retailer, one that lives
by a singular code.

Category killers, they are called. They sell one kind of merchandise, and 6
they sell it at deep discount. By buying from suppliers at high volumes,
they don't just give the local competition a run for its money — they eliminate it by design. As an enterprise with a responsibility to stockholders and
a board of directors, the superstore exists on the scale it does for one reason
only: not to sell the proverbial better mousetrap but to be the last mousetrap seller standing.

That's the theory, anyway. In practice, superstores often don't succeed in 7
killing all the competition. They eliminate the small and the weak, all
right, but in another way superstores *create* competition. After all, there's
nothing like a highly visible, phenomenally successful business venture to
invite rivalry. Ten years ago, Home Depot — "the quintessential category
killer," as *Forbes* magazine put it — had the home-improvement superstore
field to itself; by 1996, there were a dozen such chains. At the end of the
day (or decade), all that's left standing are other superstores.

What happened in the office-supply category is typical to the point of 8
being instructive — and for some observers, instructive to the point of
being cautionary. On May 1, 1986, in Brighton, Mass., Staples opened the
first office-supply superstore in the country. Six months later, in Fort Lau-
derdale, Fla., Office Depot followed suit. Within three years, 15 office-
supply superstore chains were competing, and already the battlefield had
claimed its first casualty, Office Station. Today, that competition has narrowed to three superstore chains, and if the Staples–Office Depot merger
that was first proposed last September goes through, there will be just
two — just like 10 years earlier, in the fall of 1986.

But what a difference a decade makes. The office-supply deal would cre- 9
ate a chain of more than 1,000 superstores in 47 states and 10 foreign
countries — big enough to attract the attention of an F.T.C. already suspicious of superstores. Last May the agency charged that Toys "R" Us was
using its 20 percent share of the toy market to pressure suppliers not to sell
products to competitors; now the F.T.C. has flagged a merger between the
No. 1 and No. 2 office suppliers for having all the makings of a monopoly.

Market share is an elusive concept, depending on who's doing the de- 10
fining. Staples maintains that at $10 billion in annual sales, even the
new company would account for only 5 percent of the $185 billion office-
supply industry. Less generous (and less advantageous) estimates might adjust

that market share to 8 percent of a $125 billion industry. The F.T.C. action, however, raises the question of which industry we are talking about here — the entire office-supply marketplace, including the corner pharmacy's half-aisle full of pushpins, protractors and, yes, staples, or the $23 billion superstore market, of which the newly merged giant would command a 44 percent share?

Clearly, the F.T.C. favors the latter interpretation. The press release   11
announcing the regulatory commission's complaint states that office-supply superstores "offer consumers the convenience of one-stop shopping for a wide variety of office supplies, computers and computer-related products, and office furniture at deep discount prices." They are "unlike any other retail stores in the United States."

In other words, the category killers have succeeded so well that they   12
have created a new category: themselves.

More, it turns out, was the easy part. More categories overall, more vari-   13
ety within each category, more inventory within each variety; 10,000 square feet of books; 50,000 square feet of CD's; 120,000 square feet of home furnishings. To enter a superstore is to know what the scale of Olympus or Eldorado must have looked like in the imaginations of mortals.

And then what? Achieving critical mass was a relatively simple matter: 14
raise money (Wall Street has been an early, ardent, unwavering advocate of the category-killer concept), buy real estate, build boxes, fill them with inventory; customers will show up if only to witness the spectacle, and they'll look around, and they'll buy. They'll even come back.

But will they *keep* coming back? Will a superstore be able to distinguish   15
itself from its competitors sufficiently so that it will become not just a novelty but a necessity? That's the tricky part, and that's where the superstores have had to get creative.

It's no longer enough to have the widest selection of CD's at the lowest   16
prices. That's why Wow!, a 60,000-square-foot West Coast combination of the Good Guys consumer-electronics store and Tower Records, features an $80,000 home stereo system on which classical connoisseurs can sample the latest releases at length and at leisure. That's why the 75,000-square-foot Virgin Megastore in Times Square offers 250 listening and viewing posts, in addition to live performances, a bookstore, a travel agency, a cafe and a movie theater. That's why no self-respecting video or audio retailer is complete without a giant video screen — or better yet, 25 video screens generating one gigantic image, which doesn't even have to match the soundtrack. Like the stores themselves, these screens are doing one thing while saying — or not saying — another.

"People are looking for a store that makes a statement," says Professor   17
Tedlow of Harvard Business School. Note that he says "makes a statement," not "has something to say." That's because what a superstore has to say for itself is pretty much what most any retail operation has to say: buy, buy,

buy. Its fundamental appeal might be the promise to save you time and money, but in fact, it depends for its survival on its ability to keep you on the premises and buying more than you came in for — in retail jargon, the "look around a while" factor and its "add-on item" impact. As one executive summarized his superstore's strategy: "Stay longer, sample more and visit more often."

Sometimes the distraction is sustenance. If a shopper is going to spend the two or three hours most superstores bank on, the retailer had better provide food and drink, or that customer is bound to wander off. Sometimes this distraction is seduction. An overwhelmed customer is a passive customer, and a passive customer is suggestable — turn here, go there, hold that, buy this. Either way, the distraction is what transforms the superstore into a destination.

Both Barnes & Noble and Borders have announced that their strategy through the end of the century is to focus on opening stand-alone superstores while cutting back on the older, smaller mall stores. And why not? These days, a bookstore is a bookstore, food court, music shop and newsstand rolled into one. Not only does it give the customer plenty of incentive to spend more time and more money on the premises, but it does so by keeping for itself the discretionary income that used to get spread around nearby stores in malls. During the superstore run-up in the early 1990's, according to one industry survey, mall traffic was down 14 percent, and a recent report estimated that 15 percent of conventional malls would go out of business by the end of the decade.

What happened to office-supply superstores will happen among other categories. After undergoing "a meaningful process of consolidation," as an analyst puts it, "the No. 1 and 2 players will remain, and maybe a third." But the specialty shop has not outlived its usefulness. For all their overwhelming inventory, superstores provoke a question of almost Zen-like clarity: What about consumers whose choice is not to have a choice? What if all a shopper wants is, as one retail analyst puts it, "to go on an errand instead of a shopping excursion?" In the cyclical nature of retail, the superstore is creating a demand for the very store it puts out of business — the small single-category specialty shop.

"Consumers like having an alternative," says Maureen McGrath, a vice president in the research department at Smith Barney. "They want to have the convenience of buying a screwdriver without having to cross a 300-foot parking lot and a 125,000-square-foot superstore. Superstores are great; that's a great way to spend an afternoon. But that's a lot of square feet to be covering if all you need is a box of nails." Still, even mall developers now are routinely including one or more category killers to serve the anchoring function that department stores once did, while keeping a handful of specialty shops to meet the traditional needs of customers.

The category killer has indeed become a distinct breed of retailer, as the F.T.C. suggests. It's a place to shop, yes, but a place to linger, too, to take a family on a Saturday afternoon, to meet a friend for breakfast, to steal a few minutes for yourself on the way home from work, to daydream, perhaps, over a magazine and a cup of coffee that's infinitely more aromatic than anything at the local coffee shop. In this respect, the superstore is no different from the suburban shopping center before it, or the downtown department store before that. In the midst of all the hyperbole — "super-," "mega-," "hyper-," "giga," "-max," — it has been easy to overlook a simple fact. Sure, a superstore is a stationery shop or hardware store writ huge. But far more to the point, it's also a mall writ small.

Most Americans of a certain sentimental bent still harbor a soft spot for   23 the mom-and-pop shop. Show them the shell of a department store in some middle American downtown, and they'll feel a pang for the distance between what a community must have imagined its future would be and what it has become. Even the once-unstoppable mall, as it exhibits signs of mortality, can evoke a fleeting nostalgia for a postwar period of economic expansion and optimism. But when the time comes to bid farewell to the heyday of the superstore — and come it will, one day deep in the next century — what will we be mourning?

Bigness, no doubt, but bigness of a type peculiar to the late 20th cen-   24 tury, an era when it was still easy to believe that more was more, not less.

Analyzing This Selection

1. What is the marketing concept that defines a superstore?
2. How do superstores compete with malls? Does the author think both can continue to expand?
3. **THE WRITER'S METHOD**   What tone and other details of style indicate Panek's attitude toward superstores?

Analyzing Connections

4. This article and Brubach's "Mail-Order America" (p. 374) were written for the weekly *New York Times Magazine*. Do they indicate a similar or different sense of their audience? Compare diction and sentences, the development of topics, and the authors' viewpoints.

Analyzing by Writing

5. Would you rather shop for records, books, or supplies in a mall or a stand-alone superstore? Examine the lures, satisfactions, and dissatisfactions of both shopping places. Develop your views into an opinion piece about consumers' responses to bigness.

William Ian Miller

GIFTS AND HONOR:
AN EXCHANGE[1]

WILLIAM IAN MILLER (b. 1946) is a professor of law at the University of
Michigan. He earned a Ph.D. in English at Yale University before turning to scholarship on ancient and modern law. His books include *Blood-
taking and Peacemaking: Feud, Law, and Society in Saga Iceland* (1990)
and *Humiliation and Other Essays on Honor, Social Discomfort, and Violence* (1993), from which the following selection is excerpted. In his most
recent book, *The Anatomy of Disgust* (1997), Miller continues his analyses of acute discomfort.

One Valentine's Day the doorbell rang around six in the evening. At the 1
door were the four-year-old boy who lived around the corner and his
mother. My wife answered the door, and seeing that they had a valentine
for Bess, my three-year-old daughter, got the valentine she had had Bess
make for the boy that afternoon. I marveled at my wife's skill in handling
this. How in the world did she know to be ready for this exchange? The
boy, a year older than our daughter, was not a very frequent playmate of
Bess's and we were only on cordial but standoffishly neighborly terms with
his parents. What luck, I thought, that she had thought to have something
ready for the boy. Then the glitch occurred. What Bobby handed over to
Bess was an expensive doll, some twenty dollars' worth, clearly bought for
this occasion. What Bess handed Bobby was some scribbling, representing
an attempt to draw a heart, and a cookie that my wife, with Bess's indispensable assistance, had baked that afternoon. The visit broke up quickly
after the exchange. We had been fixing dinner when they appeared, and
Bobby and his mother only got far enough beyond the threshold so that we
could close the storm door on the cold air outside. There was an undeni-
able look of disappointment on the boy's face when he left, and Bess,
though hardly disappointed, was mildly bewildered at having gotten such a
nice gift out of the blue. As soon as the door closed my wife expressed her
embarrassment and acute discomfort. What could we do? How could we
repay them? How could we rectify the situation? I too felt embarrassed

[1]Editor's title.

although not quite to the same extent as Kathy; for it was not me who was going to have to have future dealings with Bobby and his mother. It is also true that Kathy and I felt some amusement with our embarrassment. Discomfitures of this sort are funny even at the cost of your own pain. And of course, academic that I am, I started immediately wondering why we felt acutely embarrassed and maybe even shamed and Bobby's mother did not, because she did not manifest any sense that something had not been quite right in the exchange.

The structure of the valentine exchange can be described as a simple 2 game. The players each have one move and each must make that move (in this instance the move is giving a gift to the other) without knowledge of what the other has given. The object of the game is to match the value of the other's move. Both players lose if there is great discrepancy between their moves. Both win if there is a small increment between their moves. Normal social interaction presents various versions of this game fairly frequently. Christmas-gift exchanges and choosing how to dress for a party or other social function in which it is not totally clear that there is one correct way of attiring oneself follow this pattern. (Birthday-gift exchanges, however, follow a different structure unless the players celebrate their birthdays on the same day.) This game requires certain broad skills no matter what its particular setting may be. Adept players must understand the norms that govern the situation; they must also have the ability to judge the other party's understanding of those norms and his or her willingness to adhere to them even if understood, and they must make reasonably accurate assessments of the other party's assessments of themselves in these same matters.

Winning in the gift exchange does not mean getting the best present. 3 That is what Kathy and I understood to be a loss. Winning is guessing what the other will give and giving a gift adequate to requite it. Social norms do the work of coordinating people's behavior so that most of the time these interactions pass without glitch. We know what to give and how much to spend and we reasonably expect that others know what we know and that they will act accordingly. Small variations can be tolerated; they are even desired to some extent. If, for instance, you want to dress at a level of formality that will accord with that of everyone else, you might still want to wear something more tasteful or nicer than what others have on. If I give you a gift costing twelve dollars and you give me one costing ten dollars, no one is embarrassed, and I might even exact a very small amount of greater gratitude than the gratitude I have to give you to make up the difference. But when my gift to you cost a dime and your gift to me cost twenty dollars we should, if we are properly socialized, feel awkward and embarrassed. The embarrassment, however, will not be equally distributed. The person who spent the most will feel the least embarrassed, generally speaking. Why? We can even make the question a little harder by referring back to Bess's valentine. Why was it that my wife and I felt greater unpleasant feelings, when we followed the norms governing the situation, than I am supposing Bobby's mother did, who clearly broke the rules by vastly exceeding the appropriate amount of expenditure for little kids on Valentine's Day?

Just what are the sources of embarrassment, shame, humiliation, and 4 even guilt (perhaps) that were provoked by this situation? The lowrollers cannot feel embarrassed that they broke the rules of the Valentine game, because they did not. By one account the highrollers, if embarrassed, are embarrassed more because they caused the lowroller's embarrassment than because they exceeded the norms of propriety governing the game. No doubt there is a causal connection between the highrollers' embarrassment and their failure to adhere to the norms of the Valentine game inasmuch as that was what caused the lowrollers' embarrassment, but that would be getting the psychology of it wrong. Their experience is one of second-order embarrassment, the embarrassment of witnessing another's embarrassment, not the primary embarrassment of having done something embarrassing. It seems that what is going on here is that there is more than one game being played and that there are more than one set of norms governing the transaction. The true source of the lowrollers' embarrassment is that they have also been shamed by being bested in the much more primitive game of gift exchange. . . . The simple fact remains that a gift demands an adequate return even if that gift, by its size, breaks the rules governing the particular exchange. The norms of adequate reciprocity trumped the norms of Valentine's Day. Yet there is a cost here borne by the highrollers. Because the highrollers defied the normal expectation they do not acquire honor to the extent that they caused shame. Their action, in effect, has made the whole transaction less than zero-sum.

A somewhat difficult account also suggests itself. I have been supposing 5 the giver's lack of primary embarrassment. But it might be that Bobby's mother was more than embarrassed by embarrassing us, she might have felt humiliated, not by breaking the rules of the Valentine's Day game but by having to realize how much more greatly she valued us than we valued her. Her pain then, if pain she felt, was not really a function of misplaying the Valentine game in the same way ours was. To be sure, the game provided the setting for her humiliation but it needn't have. Her pain, in other words, was not caused because she violated the norms of Valentine's Day, but because she overvalued us. In contrast, our pain was solely a function of the Valentine's Day glitch. Yet I suspect that she felt no humiliation whatsoever, for the situation provided her with an adequate nondemeaning explanation for the smallness of our gift. Our gift, she would know, was exactly what the situation called for. The normal expectations of the situation thus shielded her from more painful knowledge.

The peculiar facts of Bess's gift show us also that who ends up bearing 6 the costs of norm transgression will depend on the makeup of the opposing sides. The discussion above assumed highroller and lowroller to be individual actors in a one-on-one game, but in our Valentine situation there were mother and son on one side and mother and daughter on the other. If we look now only at the emotions engendered by the exchange, Bobby's mother felt no shame and only a little embarrassment. Bess's mother felt much embarrassment. Bess felt quite pleased. But Bobby, alas poor Bobby. Here was the true bearer of the cost of his mother's indiscretion. Bobby, one can reasonably suppose, was deeply envious of the gift Bess was to receive and had been sick with desire for a similar gift. Recall, when you were little, the painful experience of being the guest watching the birthday child open the presents. But Bobby can console himself that this Valentine gift will lead to an immediate return and not be miserably deferred as with birthday gifts. And what has Bobby's mother led him to believe he will be receiving? I would guess it was a little more exciting than Bess's scribblings and one chocolate chip cookie (made according to a health-food recipe no less).

Our discomfort was utterly unassuaged by the knowledge that our gifts 7 involved our own efforts (or at least Bess's and Kathy's). Our personalized efforts did not match the larger money expenditure of the other party. The issue wasn't just the money, because if Bobby had handed Bess a twenty-dollar bill we would have refused the gift without much anxiety. Here a breach of norms governing the form of the gift (e.g., no money unless under very certain conditions) is not as capable of embarrassing the receiver, if at all, as are breaches of norms governing the value of the gift. But we need to be more specific. The failure to abide by the norms governing the value of a gift only embarrasses the receiver if it exceeds the value of a normal gift; embarrassment is the lot of the giver if the gift's value is less than the norm. It seems in the end that our judgments are also quite particularized, taking into account not only the money spent but time and energy expended, the uniqueness of the gift, the seriousness of it, how individualized it is, how much such things mean to the giver, how much they mean to the receiver, the state of relations between the parties, and so on. Our cookie and Bess's scribbling were not going to balance the money and the time Bobby's mother took in picking out a gift for Bess. Our cookies were promiscuous, meant to be eaten by us and by anyone who stumbled by when we were eating them. When it is not clear that the personalized effort of one party was significant, when the labors engaged in could also be interpreted as an attempt to avoid spending money or were not engaged in specifically for the recipient, then monetary value will probably trump mere expenditures of effort. Obviously these rankings can undergo readjustment. If Bess were a recognized art prodigy, if Kathy were a professional cook, then our gifts would carry other meanings, as they would, too, if Bobby were the Cookie Monster.

One of the immediate moves that the embarrassed recipient makes is 8 desperately to try to reconstruct a plausible account for the breach, to attempt to interpret it away by supposing legitimizing or justifying states of mind for the giver. Perhaps she was playing a different game. Could the value of the gift be partially excused because Bobby was a year older than Bess, or because Bobby was a boy, or because his mother had a warm spot for Kathy or a warm spot for Bess? Was this really a gift initiating a youthful courtship in which gifts do not demand returns in the same specie? Was it simply that Bobby's mother never stinted in buying Bobby anything and that the toy she bought Bess had a much lower value to her than it did to us? Was she known to be inept in these kinds of things and hence each subsequent ineptitude bore a diminishing power to humiliate and embarrass? Or was the embarrassment that we thought she might be making a pitiable attempt to buy our friendship, in which case our very palpable embarrassment at our own failings would be compounded with our embarrassment for her as well. Whatever, no amount of such explanation for her action made us feel any less embarrassed. And we had played by the rules! But, as it turns out, only by the rules of the Valentine game. This game, as we discovered, was nested within a larger game of honor that demanded that each gift be requited with an adequate return, and that game we had lost.

The cost of our losing was our minor humiliation and shame and our great embarrassment. In our culture in that particular setting it was a cost we could bear. In other settings we may have had to suffer the sanction of being reputed cheap and even ostracized on account of it. In other cultures humiliation and shame exact a greater toll. Reuters recently published the following story picked up by papers as column filler:

> *Monday June 10, 1991:* **Scorn over gift leads to double suicide.** Beijing: A couple from northern China committed suicide on their nephew's wedding day after relatives scoffed at the value of their gift to him, a Shanghai newspaper said.
>
> Following custom, the couple from the province of Shanxi wrote in a gift book that they were giving a total of $3.70 as a wedding gift, less than half the $8.50 other relatives gave, said the Xinmin Evening News.
>
> Unable to bear their relatives' scorn and worried about future wedding gifts for their other nephews and nieces, husband Yang Baosheng hanged himself after his wife, Qu Junmei, drowned herself in a vat, the newspaper said.

For Reuters and the newspapers that printed it, the story was clearly intended to be comical in a black way, an example of the strange behavior of people with strange names (note that giving the names of the suicides is part of the process of ridicule). The story is told as one of silly people who kill themselves for trifles. Any possibility of tragedy is skillfully prevented by several devices. There are the strange names already mentioned. There is the detail of drowning in a vat, which carries with it all the indignities of pure farce. Above all, there are the money amounts involved: these people committed suicide because of $4.80. And therein lies the real comedy of the presentation. Such levels of poverty and economic underdevelopment are so unthinkable for us to be a source of amusement and wonder. But anyone . . . should be able to discern the unfathomable shame and the desperate reassertion of dignity which these people tried to accomplish with their suicides. Suicide proved them anything but shameless and hence showed them to be people of honor. Reuters got their genre wrong. This is not comedy, but the stuff of epic and tragedy.

Analyzing This Selection

1. Explain the rules of gift exchange. Why did both parties lose in the Valentine episode? What constitutes "winning"?

2. **THE WRITER'S METHOD**   What is the author's use or purpose for the exhaustive abstract analysis of the episode? How does he win our patience for it?

3. Does the author approve of the suicide of the Chinese couple? What does their story illustrate to him? How does it affect you?

Analyzing Connections

4. Did the parting gifts between Zhou and Liang follow or break the rules of gift exchange (see Jin's "Ocean of Words," p. 281)? How does Miller's essay change our response to Zhou's loss?

Analyzing by Writing

5. Writing as an observer of the customs of high school seniors, explain the system of gift exchange that operated among your friends during your final year in high school. At Christmas, at graduation, or on birthdays, did you pay more than usual attention to expecting and giving gifts? How did you deal with problems involving esteem, embarrassment, and shame? Did some people receive gifts only because they were part of a group including other, more valued friends? How did you negotiate exchanges of adequate reciprocity among all your friends?

Toni Cade Bambara

THE LESSON

Toni Cade Bambara (1939–1995) grew up in the black districts of New York City, where she experienced racism and poverty set in sharp contrast to the opulence of white Manhattan, as the following story reflects. After graduating from Queens College, she studied dance and acting in Italy and France before returning to New York, where she took an M.A. degree at City College. Bambara worked as a welfare investigator and youth counselor as well as a college teacher of English while writing short stories. Her selected short fiction, essays, and interviews are collected in *Deep Sightings and Rescue Missions* (1996).

Back in the days when everyone was old and stupid or young and fool- 1
ish and me and Sugar were the only ones just right, this lady moved on our
block with nappy hair and proper speech and no makeup. And quite naturally we laughed at her, laughed the way we did at the junk man who went
about his business like he was some big-time president and his sorry-ass
horse his secretary. And we kinda hated her too, hated the way we did the
winos who cluttered up our parks and pissed on our handball walls and
stank up our hallways and stairs so you couldn't halfway play hide-and-seek
without a goddamn gas mask. Miss Moore was her name. The only woman
on the block with no first name. And she was black as hell, cept for her
feet, which were fish-white and spooky. And she was always planning these
boring-ass things for us to do, us being my cousin, mostly, who lived on the
block cause we all moved North the same time and to the same apartment
then spread out gradual to breathe. And our parents would yank our heads
into some kinda shape and crisp up our clothes so we'd be presentable for
travel with Miss Moore, who always looked like she was going to church,
though she never did. Which is just one of the things the grownups talked
about when they talked behind her back like a dog. But when she came
calling with some sachet she'd sewed up or some gingerbread she'd made
or some book, why then they'd all be too embarrassed to turn her down and
we'd get handed over all spruced up. She'd been to college and said it was
only right that she should take responsibility for the young ones' education,
and she not even related by marriage or blood. So they'd go for it. Specially
Aunt Gretchen. She was the main gofer in the family. You got some ole

dumb shit foolishness you want somebody to go for, you send for Aunt Gretchen. She been screwed into the go-along for so long, it's a blood-deep natural thing with her. Which is how she got saddled with me and Sugar and Junior in the first place while our mothers were in a la-de-da apartment up the block having a good ole time.

So this one day Miss Moore rounds us all up at the mailbox and it's   2 puredee hot and she's knockin herself out about arithmetic. And school suppose to let up in the summer I heard, but she don't never let up. And the starch in my pinafore scratching the shit outta me and I'm really hating this nappy-head bitch and her goddamn college degree. I'd much rather go to the pool or to the show where it's cool. So me and Sugar leaning on the mailbox being surly, which is a Miss Moore word. And Flyboy checking out what everybody brought for lunch. And Fat Butt already wasting his peanut-butter-and-jelly sandwich like the pig he is. And Junebug punchin on Q.T.'s arm for potato chips. And Rosie Giraffe shifting from one hip to the other waiting for somebody to step on her foot or ask if she from Georgia so she can kick ass, preferably Mercedes'. And Miss Moore asking us do we know what money is, like we a bunch of retards. I mean real money, she say, like it's only poker chips or monopoly papers we lay on the grocer. So right away I'm tired of this and say so. And would much rather snatch Sugar and go to the Sunset and terrorize the West Indian kids and take their hair ribbons and their money too. And Miss Moore files that remark away for next week's lesson on brotherhood, I can tell. And finally I say we oughta get to the subway cause it's cooler and besides we might meet some cute boys. Sugar done swiped her mama's lipstick, so we ready.

So we heading down the street and she's boring us silly about what   3 things cost and what our parents make and how much goes for rent and how money ain't divided up right in this country. And then she gets to the part about we all poor and live in the slums, which I don't feature. And I'm ready to speak on that, but she steps out in the street and hails two cabs just like that. Then she hustles half the crew in with her and hands me a five-dollar bill and tells me to calculate 10 percent tip for the driver. And we're off. Me and Sugar and Junebug and Flyboy hanging out the window and hollering to everybody, putting lipstick on each other cause Flyboy a faggot anyway, and making farts with our sweaty armpits. But I'm mostly trying to figure how to spend this money. But they all fascinated with the meter ticking and Junebug starts laying bets as to how much it'll read when Flyboy can't hold his breath no more. Then Sugar lay bets as to how much it'll be when we get there. So I'm stuck. Don't nobody want to go for my plan, which is to jump out at the next light and run off to the first bar-b-que we can find. Then the driver tells us to get the hell out cause we there already. And the meter reads eight-five cents. And I'm stalling to figure out the tip and Sugar say give him a dime. And I decide he don't need it bad as I do, so later for him. But then he tries to take off with Junebug foot still in the door so we talk about his mama something ferocious. Then we check out that we on Fifth Avenue and everybody dressed up in stockings. One lady in a fur coat, hot as it is. White folks crazy.

"This is the place," Miss Moore say, presenting it to us in the voice she 4 uses at the museum. "Let's look in the windows before we go in."

"Can we steal?" Sugar asks very serious like she's getting the ground 5 rules squared away before she plays. "I beg your pardon," say Miss Moore, and we fall out. So she leads us around the windows of the toy store and me and Sugar screamin, "This is mine, that's mine, I gotta have that, that was made for me, I was born for that," till Big Butt drowns us out.

"Hey, I'm goin to buy that there." 6

"That there? You don't even know what it is, stupid." 7

"I do so," he say punchin on Rosie Giraffe. "It's a microscope." 8

"Whatcha gonna do with a microscope, fool?" 9

"Look at things." 10

"Like what, Ronald?" ask Miss Moore. And Big Butt ain't got the first 11 notion. So here go Miss Moore gabbing about the thousands of bacteria in a drop of water and the somethinorother in a speck of blood and the million and one living things in the air around us is invisible to the naked eye. And what she say that for? Junebug go to town on that "naked" and we rolling. Then Miss Moore ask what it cost. So we all jam into the window smudgin it up and the price tag say $300. So then she ask how long'd take for Big Butt and Junebug to save up their allowances. "Too long," I say. "Yeh," adds Sugar, "outgrown it by that time." And Miss Moore say no, you never outgrow learning instruments. "Why, even medical students and interns and," blah, blah, blah. And we ready to choke Big Butt for bringing it up in the first damn place.

"This here costs four hundred eighty dollars," say Rosie Giraffe. So we 12 pile up all over her to see what she pointin out. My eyes tell me it's a chunk of glass cracked with something heavy, and different-color inks dripped into the splits, then the whole thing put into a oven or something. But for $480 it don't make sense.

"That's a paperweight made of semi-precious stones fused together under 13 tremendous pressure," she explains slowly, with her hands doing the mining and all the factory work.

"So what's a paperweight?" asks Rosie Giraffe. 14

"To weigh paper with, dumbbell," say Flyboy, the wise man from the 15 East.

"Not exactly," say Miss Moore, which is what she say when you warm or 16 way off too. "It's to weigh paper down so it won't scatter and make your desk untidy." So right away me and Sugar curtsy to each other and then to Mercedes who is more the tidy type.

"We don't keep paper on top of the desk in my class," say Junebug, fig- 17 uring Miss Moore crazy or lyin one.

"At home, then," she say. "Don't you have a calendar and a pencil case 18 and a blotter and a letter-opener on your desk at home where you do your homework?" And she know damn well what our homes look like cause she nosys around in them every chance she gets.

"I don't even have a desk," say Junebug. "Do we?" 19

"No. And I don't get no homework neither," says Big Butt. 20

"And I don't even have a home," say Flyboy like he do at school to keep 21 the white folks off his back and sorry for him. Send this poor kid to camp posters, is his specialty.

"I do," says Mercedes. "I have a box of stationery on my desk and a pic- 22 ture of my cat. My godmother bought the stationery and the desk. There's a big rose on each sheet and the envelopes smell like roses."

"Who wants to know about your smelly-ass stationery," say Rosie Giraffe 23 fore I can get my two cents in.

"It's important to have a work area all your own so that . . ." 24

"Will you look at this sailboat, please," say Flyboy, cuttin her off and 25 pointin to the thing like it was his. So once again we tumble all over each other to gaze at this magnificent thing in the toy store which is just big enough to maybe sail two kittens across the pond if you strap them to the posts tight. We all start reciting the price tag like we in assembly. "Hand-crafted sailboat of fiberglass at one thousand one hundred ninety-five dollars."

"Unbelievable," I hear myself say and am really stunned. I read it again 26 for myself just in case the group recitation put me in a trance. Same thing. For some reason this pisses me off. We look at Miss Moore and she lookin at us, waiting for I dunno what.

"Who'd pay all that when you can buy a sailboat set for a quarter at 27 Pop's, a tube of glue for a dime, and a ball of string for eight cents? It must have a motor and a whole lot besides," I say. "My sailboat cost me about fifty cents."

"But will it take water?" say Mercedes with her smart ass. 28

"Took mine to Alley Pond Park once," say Flyboy. "String broke. Lost it. 29 Pity."

"Sailed mine in Central Park and it keeled over and sank. Had to ask my 30 father for another dollar."

"And you got the strap," laugh Big Butt. "The jerk didn't even have a 31 string on it. My old man wailed on his behind."

Little Q.T. was staring hard at the sailboat and you could see he wanted 32 it bad. But he too little and somebody'd just take it from him. So what the hell. "This boat for kids, Miss Moore?"

"Parents silly to buy something like that just to get all broke up," say 33 Rosie Giraffe.

"That much money it should last forever," I figure. 34

"My father'd buy it for me if I wanted it." 35

"Your father, my ass," say Rosie Giraffe getting a chance to finally push 36 Mercedes.

"Must be rich people shop here," say Q.T. 37

"You are a very bright boy," say Flyboy. "What was your first clue?" And 38 he rap him on the head with the back of his knuckles, since Q.T. the only one he could get away with. Though Q.T. liable to come up behind you years later and get his licks in when you half expect it.

"What I want to know is," I says to Miss Moore though I never talk to 39 her, I wouldn't give the bitch that satisfaction, "is how much a real boat costs? I figure a thousand'd get you a yacht any day?"

"Why don't you check that out," she says, "and report back to the 40 group?" Which really pains my ass. If you gonna mess up a perfectly good swim day least you could do is have some answers. "Let's go in," she say like she got something up her sleeve. Only she don't lead the way. So me and Sugar turn the corner to where the entrance is, but when we get there I kinda hang back. Not that I'm scared, what's there to be afraid of, just a toy store. But I feel funny, shame. But what I got to be shamed about? Got as much right to go in as anybody. But somehow I can't seem to get hold of the door, so I step away for Sugar to lead. But she hangs back too. And I look at her and she looks at me and this is ridiculous. I mean, damn, I have never ever been shy about doing nothing or going nowhere. But then Mercedes steps up and then Rosie Giraffe and Big Butt crowd in behind and shove, and next thing we all stuffed into the doorway with only Mercedes squeezing past us, smoothing out her jumper and walking right down the aisle. Then the rest of us tumble in like a glued-together jigsaw done all wrong. And people lookin at us. And it's like the time me and Sugar crashed into the Catholic church on a dare. But once we got in there and everything so hushed and holy and the candles and the bowin and the handkerchiefs on all the drooping heads, I just couldn't go through with the plan. Which was for me to run up to the altar and do a tap dance while Sugar played the nose flute and messed around in the holy waters. And Sugar kept givin me the elbow. Then later teased me so bad I tied her up in the shower and turned it on and locked her in. And she'd be there till this day if Aunt Gretchen hadn't finally figured I was lyin about the boarder takin a shower.

Same thing in the store. We all walkin on tiptoe and hardly touchin the 41 games and puzzles and things. And I watched Miss Moore who is steady watchin us like she waiting for a sign. Like Mama Drewery watches the sky and sniffs the air and takes note of just how much slant is in the bird formation. Then me and Sugar bump smack into each other, so busy gazing at the toys, 'specially the sailboat. But we don't laugh and go into our fat-lady bump-stomach routine. We just stare at that price tag. Then Sugar run a finger over the whole boat. And I'm jealous and want to hit her. Maybe not her, but I sure want to punch somebody in the mouth.

"Watcha bring us here for, Miss Moore?" 42

"You sound angry, Sylvia. Are you mad about something?" Givin me 43 one of them grins like she tellin a grown-up joke that never turns out to be funny. And she's lookin very closely at me like maybe she plannin to do my portrait from memory. I'm mad, but I won't give her that satisfaction. So I slouch around the store bein very bored and say, "Let's go."

Me and Sugar at the back of the train watchin the tracks whizzin by large then small then gettin gobbled up in the dark. I'm thinkin about this tricky toy I saw in the store. A clown that somersaults on a bar then does chin-ups just cause you yank lightly at his leg. Cost $35. I could see me askin my mother for a $35 birthday clown. "You wanna who that costs what?" she'd say, cocking her head to the side to get a better view of the hole in my head. Thirty-five dollars and the whole household could go visit Grandaddy Nelson in the country. Thirty-five dollars would pay for the rent and the piano bill too. Who are these people that spend that much for performing clowns and $1000 for toy sailboats? What kinda work they do and how they live and how come we ain't in on it? Where we are is who we are, Miss Moore always pointin out. But it don't necessarily have to be that way, she always adds then waits for somebody to say that poor people have to wake up and demand their share of the pie and don't none of us know what kind of pie she talkin about in the first damn place. But she ain't so smart cause I still got her four dollars from the taxi and she sure ain't gettin it. Messin up my day with this shit. Sugar nudges me in my pocket and winks.

Miss Moore lines us up in front of the mailbox where we started from, seem like years ago, and I got a headache for thinkin so hard. And we lean all over each other so we can hold up under the draggy-ass lecture she always finishes us off with at the end before we thank her for borin us to tears. But she just looks at us like she readin tea leaves. Finally she say, "Well, what did you think of F.A.O. Schwartz?"

Rosie Giraffe mumbles, "White folks crazy."

"I'd like to go there again when I get my birthday money," says Mercedes, and we shove her out the pack so she has to lean on the mailbox by herself.

"I'd like a shower. Tiring day," say Flyboy.

Then Sugar surprises me by saying, "You know, Miss Moore, I don't think all of us here put together eat in a year what that sailboat costs." And Miss Moore lights up like something goosed her. "And?" she say, urging Sugar on. Only I'm standin on her foot so she don't continue.

"Imagine for a minute what kind of society it is in which some people can spend on a toy what it would cost to feed a family of six or seven. What do you think?"

"I think," say Sugar pushing me off her feet like she never done before, cause I whip her ass in a minute, "that this is not much of a democracy if you ask me. Equal chance to pursue happiness means an equal crack at the dough, don't it?" Miss Moore is besides herself and I am disgusted with Sugar's treachery. So I stand on her foot one more time to see if she'll shove me. She shuts up, and Miss Moore looks at me, sorrowfully I'm thinkin. And somethin weird is goin on. I can feel it in my chest.

"Anybody else learn anything today?" lookin dead at me. I walk away 52
and Sugar has to run to catch up and don't even seem to notice when I
shrug her arm off my shoulder.

"Well, we got four dollars anyway," she says. 53

"Uh hunh." 54

"We could go to Hascombs and get half a chocolate layer and then to 55
the Sunset and still have plenty of money for potato chips and ice cream
sodas."

"Uh hunh." 56

"Race you to Hascombs," she say. 57

We start down the block and she gets ahead which is O.K. by me cause 58
I'm goin to the West End and then over to the Drive to think this day
through. She can run if she want to and even run faster. But ain't nobody
gonna beat me at nuthin.

Analyzing This Selection

1. Based on details in the first paragraph, about how old is the narrator? What
   particular characteristics lead you to this informed guess?

2. Why does Sylvia continue to resist Miss Moore's efforts to teach the children?

3. **THE WRITER'S METHOD**   What tone do the slang and obscenities add to
   the story? What attitudes do you think the author has toward the kids?

Analyzing Connections

4. Bambara and Updike (see "A & P," p. 328) use young, naive speakers to tell
   the story. How do the authors get us to grasp more than the narrators do?

Analyzing by Writing

5. Going to look at the trappings of great wealth — for instance, the elegant
   houses of the very rich, royalty's crown jewels, or a magnificent yacht — can
   be sometimes enjoyable and sometimes disturbing. Think of an example of
   evidence of wealth that you admired or criticized. What lesson, if any, did
   you take from your exposure? Do you feel differently about it today?

Maguelonne Toussaint-Samat

CHOCOLATE AND DIVINITY

Maguelonne Toussaint-Samat is a French journalist and writer. She has published many books on the history of food and French regional culture. This essay is from her book titled A *History of Food* (1992) translated by Anthea Bell.

That witty letter-writer the Marquise de Sévigné had strong feelings 1 about the exotic foodstuff chocolate. On 11 February 1671 she was obviously madly in love with it. She writes to her daughter, Mme de Grignan: "If you are not feeling well, if you have not slept, chocolate will revive you. But you have no chocolate pot! I think of that again and again. How will you manage?" By 15th April disillusion has set in: "I can tell you, my dear child, chocolate is not what it was to me. I was carried away by the fashion, as usual. All who used to praise chocolate to me now condemn it. It is scorned. It is accused of causing every evil under the sun." On 13th May she is in a state of great anxiety, for her daughter is pregnant. "My dear, my beautiful child, I do beg you not to drink chocolate. In your present condition it would prove fatal to you." By 23rd October she is quite paranoid on the subject: "The Marquise de Coëtlogon drank so much chocolate when she was expecting last year that she was brought to bed of a little boy as black as the devil, who died." (There were rumors at court that, the year before that birth, Mme de Coëtlogon's chocolate had been brought to her every morning and evening by a young and very affectionate African slave.)

At the end of the nineteenth century a chocolate maker of Royat who 2 had literary leanings took the outspoken Marquise as the emblem of his brand, and made a fortune.

But long before the good lady ever raised a cup of chocolate to her lips 3 cocoa had existed — or rather *cacahuaquchtl*, a tree four to ten meters tall growing in the virgin forests of Yucatan and Guatemala. *Cacahuaquchtl* means not only cocoa tree but simply, and principally, just "tree." It was *the* Tree, the tree of the Mayan gods.

The gods, whoever they are and wherever they come from, do not eat 4 the food of ordinary mortals. In Greece, they fed on ambrosia. In Mexico and Guatemala they favored a decoction of the seeds of the fruit of the Tree, and it was not made like any ordinary tisane. You took the seeds (later

404

described by the unimaginative Spanish as "beans") of the cocoa pods, called *cabosses* in French, from Spanish *cabeza,* "head," a word perhaps suggested by the long, narrow heads of the Amerindians. You roasted them in an earthenware pot. You crushed them between two stones. You then mixed the powder you had obtained with boiling water and whisked it with little twigs — chac-chac, choc-choc, went the twigs as they whisked up little bubbles. You could add other things to this boiling liquid (*tchaca-houa,* as it was called in Mayan, or *tchocoatl,* in Aztec): either chilli, musk and honey, or ground maize when you were going to war and needed additional calories. Then you drank it.

You drank it because the gods were good and in certain very specific cir-   5
cumstances allowed mortals to taste their sacred food. This is one of the usual features of a sacrifice; there can be no question of the actual physical matter of the foods involved being lost to human consumption, it is the religious intention that counts. The Mayas, like other peoples, took that attitude.

Who exactly were the Mayas? Towards the beginning of the fourth cen-   6
tury A.D. the Maya people, who had come down from Alaska in the course of the millennia, occupied Yucatan, an enormous peninsula situated between Mexico and Guatemala. Around the year 900 their remarkable but bloodthirsty civilization was suddenly extinguished. We still do not know why. Their cities, some still being built, were abandoned, with temples, pyramids, paved roads and all. The Mayas went into the all-concealing virgin forest and never came out again. It was in this forest that the Tree grew. When the Spanish penetrated Central America for the first time in 1523 there was nothing left of the Mayas but a few primitive tribes, as if they had forgotten everything they once knew.

Meanwhile first the Toltecs and then the Aztecs of Mexico, who had   7
come down from North America in their turn, had occupied the territory, sending expeditions not always of a peaceful nature into the forest to get various provisions which included stocks of the beans of the Tree. The Aztecs loved *tchocoatl* as much as the Mayas had liked *tchacahoua.*

Now Quetzalcoatl, the great bearded god of the forest, was also the gar-   8
dener of Paradise. It was to him that mankind owed the Tree, *cacahua-quchtl,* giving both fortune and strength, for he even allowed the seeds of his tree to be used as money. However, in time the Aztecs found them-selves in great and lasting distress, and it was all his fault.

One day, no one knew just when — perhaps at the time of the decline   9
of the Mayas? — the god had boarded a raft and gone east across the ocean, towards the rising of the sun. Ever since then his people had been impa-tiently awaiting his return. It would be a day of great rejoicing. Everyone would whisk *tchocoatl* to a froth and drink it till they could drink no more.

Accordingly when the conquistador Cortez, bearded and clad in iron,   10
arrived on a strange creature which was also iron-clad, coming from the east across the sea, the Emperor Moctezuma and his subjects, delirious

with joy, hailed him as the god. Cortez took advantage of this warm welcome to ask at once where the treasures were kept. The treasures? "Come,
great god!" was the reply — as if the god did not know! Still, they led him
to the royal plantation of Maniapeltec where the Tree had been greatly
improved over the years, and offered him mountains of cocoa. After a fit of
rather discourteous mirth, the bearded newcomer managed to explain that
he had come for gold, not cocoa beans. He wanted mountains of gold.
Eventually, he realized that possession of the cocoa was the way to get possession of the precious yellow metal.

The ceremonial attending the growing and harvesting of cocoa   11
impressed the visitors, who were less world-weary than they liked to appear:
it included human sacrifice, masked dancing, propitiatory rites (13 days of
abstinence by the workers, followed by orgiastic erotic games on the day of
the harvest itself). This final ritual particularly interested the soldiers, and
they no longer felt like laughing during the community cocoa-parties when
the Emperor, behind a screen, and the court dressed in their best and
seated on the palace esplanade, religiously enjoyed the frothing drink
served in 2000 fine golden cups by delightfully unclad virgins.

When the Emperor explained, therefore, that he never entered his   12
harem without drinking this dark brown brew first, the Spanish held out
their cups with one accord. Whether because of the chilli, ambergris and
musk added to it or not, no one liked his first mouthful of chocolate. Then
they became used to the drink, either for its aphrodisiac virtues or as a substitute for the wine they missed. After Cortez had gone home in 1527 he
always kept a full chocolate-pot on his desk.

The first concern of the missionary nuns in Central America was to use   13
their culinary gifts to convert chocolate to Christianity. They thought, correctly, that it was diabolical only because of the spices and flavorings added
to it. They replaced them with vanilla, sugar and cream, and the result was
delicious.

In 1585 the fame of Moctezuma's brew had spread so far through   14
Europe that the first cargo to reach land from Vera Cruz was snapped up
at once, despite the high price.

Although he had been among the first to be informed of the discovery,   15
Pope Clement VII, formerly Giulio de Medici, could not actually drink
chocolate at his coronation in 1523, for all he had was the enthusiastic
description in Latin of Father Petrus de Angleria, who said it made the
mouth water and soothed the soul: "It is not only a delicious drink, but a
useful form of money which permits no speculation, since it cannot be
kept very long."

Pope Clement VIII did drink a cup of cocoa in 1594; it was given him   16
by the Florentine Father Francesco Carlati, just back from America, but he
was the eleventh Pope in line from Giulio de Medici, and it was his task to
resolve the grave question of whether or not drinking chocolate broke the
fast. Not only did Spanish ladies of both the colonies and the mother coun-

try have such a passion for cocoa flavored with cinnamon that they drank it all day long, they even had it served to them in church. The Jesuit Father Escobar, renowned for his casuistry, and Cardinal François-Marie Brancacio could hardly suppress the fashion unless they wanted to see the Communion table deserted, so they appeared to go along with it and reiterated, on behalf of their lady penitents, the old adage *liquidum non frangit jejunum*, "liquid does not break the fast" — in this case chocolate made with water. The Sorbonne fulminated; Pius V, who had not drunk chocolate any more than Clement VII, expressed his own doubts and let it be known that he differed from the cardinal and the reverend father.

In the year 1636 the problem loomed large. A priest of Madrid discussed 17 it at length in a quarto entitled *Question moral si el chocolate quebrante el ayuno ecclesiastico*. Was it mortal sin for a priest to drink chocolate before celebrating Mass? Mme de Sévigné, still an enthusiast at this point, wrote to her daughter that she drank chocolate before going to bed to nourish her at night, and on getting up in the morning so that she could fast better. "The agreeable part of it all is that what counts is the intention." (She was referring to the opinion held by such priests as Escobar that purity of intention justifies otherwise immoral actions.)

A certain Bachot, in a medical thesis published on 20 March 1685, 18 maintained that cocoa and not ambrosia must have been the food of the gods. This opinion aroused a certain amount of interest, and 50 years later, when Carl von Linné published his *Systema Naturae* in 1737, he classed the cocoa tree in "the eighteenth polyadelphy of Candire" as the genus *Theobroma*, meaning "divine food." Theobromine, a medicament extracted from cocoa, is an alkaloid similar to caffeine, and its diuretic qualities also make it a cardiovascular analeptic.

During the first half of the seventeenth century exorbitant taxes pre- 19 vented ordinary mortals from serving the drink of the gods on their own tables. The scientist Johann Georg Volkmer brought it from Naples to Germany in 1641 and then to the Netherlands, where it was a huge success in high society. England, perhaps for economic or political (anti-Spanish) reasons, politely turned its nose up at cocoa in 1657. It is true that the Londoners tried making it with Madeira.

France had received chocolate in two stages, with the successive mar- 20 riages of two of its kings to Spanish Infantas: Louis XIII to Anne of Austria, Louis XIV to Maria Theresa of Spain. The maid who brewed Maria Theresa's chocolate must have been better at it than her mother-in-law's maid, for "the Queen's one passion" ("after the King," the modest wife used to remind people, eyes cast down) soon spread spontaneously to the whole court. However, Fagon, the Queen's doctor, was accused of making a brew of it which hastened her demise at the eleventh hour, much to the satisfaction of Mme de Maintenon.

Louis XIV, with his habitual distrust, did not develop a taste for choco- 21 late until he developed one for Mme de Maintenon, another enthusiastic lover of chocolate who made her favorite drink for herself. It was the safer course. However, in 1682 the *Mercure de France* published an account of a party at Versailles where the popular drink of cocoa was served.

A former page of the queen mother Anne of Austria, one David Chail- 22 lon (or possibly Chalion), obtained from the Sun King, who still preferred Burgundy wine to the Aztec brew, the "sole privilege for 23 years of making, retailing and selling in all towns of the Kingdom a certain composition known as chocolate, in liquid form or as pastilles or in any other form that he may please." By now a way of evaporating the liquid chocolate and moulding it into solid shapes had been discovered.

David Chaillon (or Chalion) therefore set up shop at the sign of "La 23 Croix du Tiroir" (or "Trahoir") at the corner of the rue Saint-Honoré and the rue de l'Arbre-Sec, in the confectioners' quarter. His establishment was opened on 20 May 1659. In 1690 chocolate reached the Left Bank when the Sieur Rère and the Sieur Renaud, new license-holders, both occupied premises in the rue Dauphine. Then the great grocer François Dumaine extended his catalogue, which already listed coffee beans at four francs the pound and tea at 100 francs, to include cocoa at four francs and chocolate at six francs the pound.

You could drink a cup of cocoa for eight sous, expensive in view of the 24 fact that even in the most fashionable establishments tea or coffee cost three sous six deniers at the most. But the cocoa prices were of the black market variety, because of the license held by Chaillon and his successors. Finally, in 1693, the sale of cocoa and chocolate was thrown open to all, much to the annoyance of the religious communities, who had been dreaming for years of obtaining a monopoly of the drink of the gods.

In 1770 the first industrial chocolate-manufacturing firm was set up: 25 Chocolats et Thés Pelletier & Compagnie. Van Houten & Bvloker opened in Amsterdam in 1815. Cailler was set up at Vevey in Switzerland in 1819, and Suchard occupied Neuchâtel. The first true chocolate factories, however, were those of Menier in the Paris region, first opened in 1824.

In 1826, Brillat-Savarin, the pundit of gastronomy, was still advocating 26 "ambered chocolate," which he described as "the chocolate of the afflicted." He recommended it to "any man who has drunk too deeply of the cup of pleasure . . . who finds his wit temporarily losing its edge, the atmosphere humid, time dragging . . . or who is tortured by a fixed idea." Alexandre Dumas mentions Brillat-Savarin's endorsement of "chocolate with ambergris as a sovereign remedy for those fatigued by any sort of labour," which obviously means a great many people.

Le confiseur royal ou art du confiseur, published in Paris in 1818, how- 27 ever, mentions only confectionery or chocolate such as pistachios with *chocolat de santé, diablotins au chocolat*, and a pastille or dragée stuffed with chocolate paste "identical to that so greatly liked by the unfortunate Queen Marie-Antoinette."

Finally, in 1875, a Swiss from Vevey called Daniel Peter had the dis- 28
tinction of inventing milk chocolate. He then went into partnership with
his competitors Cailler and Kohler. The three brands merged with Nestlé
in 1929, and thereafter Switzerland was one of the world's great shrines to
chocolate.

Analyzing This Selection

1. **THE WRITER'S METHOD**   This selection is a chapter in A *History of Food*. Is the essay written principally for historians or eaters?

2. New information can change your view of something familiar. How, if at all, did this expository essay serve that purpose?

Analyzing Connections

3. This essay and Forster's "My Wood" (see p. 371) contain many allusions to knowledge not every reader has. Examine how the authors give informative contexts to knowledge they seem to take for granted. Which selection is written for a wider audience?

Analyzing by Writing

4. The tomato and potato have had colorful histories following their discovery by European colonizers. Using research sources, write a brief history of either one or a similar New World edible. Synthesize the available information, and come to a unified point about the food's effects on society.

PART 8

MEDIA IMAGES

INSIGHTS

Everybody watches it, but no one really likes it. This is the open secret of TV today. Its only champions are its own executives, the advertisers who exploit it, and a compromised network of academic boosters. Otherwise, TV has no spontaneous defenders, because there is almost nothing in it to defend. In many ways at once, TV negates the very "choices" that it now promotes with rising desperation. It promises an unimpeded vision of the whole known universe, and yet it shows us nothing but the laughable reflection of our own unhappy faces. It seems to offer us a fresh, "irreverent" view of the oppressive past, and yet that very gesture of rebelliousness turns out to be a ploy by those in power. Night after night, TV displays a bright infinitude of goods, employs a multitude of shocks and teases; and the only purpose of that spectacle is to promote the habit of spectatorship. It celebrates unending "choice" while trying to keep a jeering audience all strung out. TV begins by offering us a beautiful hallucination of diversity, but it is finally like a drug whose high is only the conviction that its user is too cool to be addicted.

— MARK CRISPIN MILLER

It should not be surprising that all sorts of Americans — not only the bed- and house-ridden — find solace in the mythically stable communities of soap operas. Some soap communities, after all, have lasted over thirty years. All potential viewers are members of a society that has been in constant transformation through geographic mobility and the loss of extended families. Loneliness, we are repeatedly told, has become pandemic in America, and the longing for community is a palpable need. Whether through religion, clubs, associations, or support groups — or through daily immersion in a favorite soap — many Americans search for some kind of communal life to counter varying degrees of social isolation and alienation.

— RUTH ROSEN

The Miss America pageant is the worst sort of "Americanism," the soft smile of sex and the hard sell of toothpaste and hair dye ads wrapped in the dreamy ideological gauze of "making it through one's own effort." In a perverse way, I like the show; it is the only live television left other than sports, news broadcasts, performing arts awards programs, and speeches by the president. I miss live TV. It was the closest thing to theater for the masses. And the Miss America contest is, as it has been for some time, the most perfectly rendered theater in our culture, for it so perfectly captures what we yearn for: a low-class ritual, a polished restatement of vulgarity, that wants to open the door to high-class respectability by way of plain middle-class anxiety and ambition. "Am I doing all right?" the contestants seem to ask in a kind of reassuring, if numbed, way. The contest brings together all the American classes in a show-biz spectacle of classlessness and tastelessness.

— GERALD EARLY

The movies are an encyclopedia of gestures. They fix indelibly the look of things — a woman throwing her drink in a man's face, someone being shot through the head, a swimmer wrestling a crocodile, a police car flying off the side of the road and executing a slow half twist before landing on its roof — that, if you are halfway lucky, you can pass a lifetime without seeing anywhere except in the movies. But the movies make these things familiar. They can even, through endless repetition, make them boring. If you have seen a swimmer wrestling a crocodile twice, you may choose the third occasion to go out for popcorn.

Some movie-made gestures never become boring, of course. They're returned to again and again, and are even incorporated into your own repertoire. One of the important social services the movies have performed over the years, for example, is the instruction of generations of interested pre-adolescents in the mechanics of kissing — from the early-movie manner, in which the man rather suddenly and violently mashes his face onto the woman's and grinds slowly against it (are both mouths wide open, or only his?), to more recent representations, in which sheer face-swallowing is less emphasized and a good deal of nibbling and tongue work are indicated. It's not that you would never have figured out how to kiss (or to perform related activities, since kissing in the movies is usually a synecdoche for intimacies that cannot be shown: as above, so below) if you hadn't had Gary Cooper or Ellen Barkin to help you out. It's that it is impossible to say what in your knowledge of kissing comes from kissing and what comes from movies of people kissing.

— LOUIS MENAND

Dear John Wayne

August and the drive-in picture is packed.
We lounge on the hood of the Pontiac

surrounded by the slow-burning spirals they sell
at the window, to vanquish the hordes of mosquitoes.
Nothing works. They break through the smoke-screen for blood.

Always the look-out spots the Indians first,
spread north to south, barring progress.
The Sioux, or Cheyenne, or some bunch
in spectacular columns, arranged like SAC missiles,
their feathers bristling in the meaningful sunset.

The drum breaks. There will be no parlance.
Only the arrows whining, a death-cloud of nerves
swarming down on the settlers
who die beautifully, tumbling like dust weeds
into the history that brought us all here
together: this wide screen beneath the sign of the bear.

The sky fills, acres of blue squint and eye
that the crowd cheers. His face moves over us,
a thick cloud of vengeance, pitted
like the land that was once flesh. Each rut,
each scar makes a promise: *It is*
not over, this fight, not as long as you resist.

Everything we see belongs to us.
A few laughing Indians fall over the hood
slipping in the hot spilled butter.
The eye sees a lot, John, but the heart is so blind.
How will you know what you own?

He smiles, a horizon of teeth
the credits reel over, and then the white fields
again blowing in the true-to-life dark.
The dark films over everything.
We get into the car
scratching our mosquito bites, speechless and small
as people are when the movie is done.
We are back in ourselves.

How can we help but keep hearing his voice,
the flip side of the sound-track, still playing:
Come on, boys, we've got them
where we want them, drunk, running.
They will give us what we want, what we need:
The heart is a strange wood inside of everything
we see, burning, doubling, splitting out of its skin.

                                                    — LOUISE ERDRICH

FOCUSING BY WRITING

1. Talk shows on television and radio offer a public forum for discussing controversial personal and national issues. They air diverse opinions from hosts, studio guests, and call-in listeners, and sometimes heated discussions get out of control. Are talk shows valuable as democratic forums of debate, or do they trivialize opinions into statements that shock but have no social or moral consequences? Consider a recent talk show that you have seen or heard. How did the program affect you? Did you become more or less concerned to form an opinion on the issues that were discussed?

2. What was the dominant impression you received during your visit to a Disney park or other entertainment park? Consider what details of the place created the atmosphere. (It is possible that the atmosphere you felt was not the one intended by the park.) Is your present memory of the park significantly different from your response to it at the time?

3. Examine the effects of telephone technology on your life. Consider the positive and negative ways that answering machines, cordless phones, cell phones, or other telecommunication devices play a part in your social and family relations. Consider your gains and losses in matters affecting your freedom, vulnerability to others, and social status.

4. Explain the appeal of two dissimilar television or radio celebrities. Mix your selection among entertainers, advertising images, and news reporters, and possibly include a cartoon or puppet personality. What personal qualities appear in their aura? What, if any, similarities underlie their different appeal?

Louise Erdrich

Z: THE MOVIE
THAT CHANGED MY LIFE

Louise Erdrich (b. 1954) grew up in Wahpeton, North Dakota, the eldest child of a Chippewa Indian mother and a German-American teacher at the Bureau of Indian Affairs school. Erdrich entered Dartmouth College in 1972, the year women were first admitted and the year the Native American Studies department was established. She earned a master's degree in the writing program at the Johns Hopkins University. Her first novel, *Love Medicine* (1984), won a National Book Critics Circle award and other prizes. Erdrich received a Guggenheim Fellowship in 1985. Her fiction often deals with contemporary Indian life in tribal communities and in urban settings. Her most recent novel is *Tales of Burning Love* (1996). The following essay was commissioned for the collection *The Movie That Changed My Life* (1991), in which writers reflect on the unexpected personal impact of a film they saw.

Next to writing full-time, the best job I ever had combined two passions — popcorn and narrative. At fourteen, I was hired as a concessioner at the Gilles Theater in Wahpeton, North Dakota. Behind a counter of black marbleized glass, I sold Dots, Red Hot Tamales, Jujubes, Orange Crush, and, of course, hot buttered popcorn. My little stand was surrounded by art deco mirrors, and my post, next to the machine itself, was bathed in an aura of salt and butter. All of my sophomore year, I exuded a light nutty fragrance that turned, on my coats and dresses, to the stale odor of mouse nests. The best thing about the job was that, once I had wiped the counters, dismantled the machines, washed the stainless steel parts, totaled up the take and refilled the syrup canisters and wiped off the soft drink machine, I could watch the show, free. 1

I saw everything that came to Wahpeton in 1969 — watched every movie seven times, in fact, since each one played a full week. I saw Zeffirelli's *Romeo and Juliet,* and did not weep. I sighed over Charlton Heston in *Planet of the Apes,* and ground my teeth at the irony of the ending shot. But the one that really got to me was Costa-Gavras's Z. 2

Nobody in Wahpeton walked into the Gilles knowing that the film was about the assassination in Greece of a leftist peace leader by a secret right-wing organization and the subsequent investigation that ended in a bloody 3 coup. The ad in the paper said only "Love Thriller" and listed Yves Montand and Irene Papas as the stars.

"Dear Diary," I wrote the morning after I'd seen Z for the first time. 4
"The hypocrites are exposed. He is alive! Just saw the best movie of my life.
Must remember to dye my bra and underwear to match my cheerleading
outfit."

I forgot to rinse out the extra color, so during the week that Z was play- 5
ing, I had purple breasts. The school color of my schizophrenic adolescence. My parents strictly opposed my career as a wrestling cheerleader, on
the grounds that it would change me into someone they wouldn't recognize. Now, they were right, though of course I had never let anyone know
my secret.

I had changed in other ways, too. Until I was fourteen, my dad and I 6
would go hunting on weekends or skating in the winter. Now I practiced
screaming S-U-C-C-E-S-S and K-I-L-L for hours, and then, of course, had
to run to work during the matinee. Not that I was utterly socialized. Over
my cheerleading outfit I wore Dad's army jacket, and on my ankle, a
bracelet made of twisted blasting-wire given to me by a guitar-playing Teen
Corps volunteer, Kurt, who hailed from The Valley of the Jolly Green
Giant, a real town in eastern Minnesota.

No, I was not yet completely subsumed into small-town femalehood. I 7
knew there was more to life than the stag leap, or the flying T, but it wasn't
until I saw Z that I learned language for what that "more" was.

After the third viewing, phrases began to whirl in my head. "The forces 8
of greed and hatred cannot tolerate us"; "There are not enough hospitals,
not enough doctors, yet one half of the budget goes to the military"; "Peace
at all costs"; and, of course, the final words, "He is alive!" But there was
more to it than the language. It was the first *real* movie I had ever seen —
one with a cynical, unromantic, deflating ending.

At the fourth viewing of the movie, I had a terrible argument with Vin- 9
cent, the Gilles's pale, sad ticket taker, who was also responsible for changing the wooden letters on the marquee. At the beginning of the week, he
had been pleased. It was he who thought of the ad copy, "Love Thriller."
By the middle of the run, he was unhappy, for he sided with the generals,
just as he sided with our boss.

Vincent always wore a suit and stood erect. He was officious, a tiger with 10
gatecrashers and tough with those who had misplaced their stubs while
going to the bathroom. I, on the other hand, waved people in free when I
was left in charge, and regarded our boss with absolute and burning hatred,
for he was a piddling authority, a man who enjoyed setting meaningless
tasks. I hated being made to rewash the butter dispenser. Vincent liked
being scolded for not tearing the tickets exactly in half. Ours was an argument of more than foreign ideologies.

Vincent insisted that the boss was a fair man who made lots of money. I 11
maintained that we were exploited. Vincent said the film was lies, while I

insisted it was based on fact. Neither of us checked for the truth in the library. Neither of us knew the first thing about modern Greece, yet I began comparing the generals to our boss. Their pompous egotism, the way they bumbled and puffed when they were accused of duplicity, their self-righteous hatred of "long-haired hippies and dope addicts of indefinite sex."

When I talked behind the boss's back, Vincent was worse than horrified; 12 he was incensed.

"Put what's-his-name in a uniform and he'd be the head of the security 13 police," I told Vincent, who looked like he wanted to pound my head.

But I knew what he knew. I had my reasons. Afraid that I might eat him 14 out of Junior Mints, the boss kept a running tab of how many boxes of each type of candy reposed in the bright glass case. Every day, I had to count the boxes and officially request more to fill the spaces. I couldn't be off by so much as a nickel at closing.

One night, made bold by Z, I opened each candy box and ate one 15 Jujube, one Jordan Almond, one Black Crow, and so on, out of each box, just to accomplish something subversive. When I bragged, Vincent cruelly pointed out that I had just cheated all my proletarian customers. I allowed that he was right, and stuck to popcorn after that, eating handfuls directly out of the machine. I had to count the boxes, and the buckets, too, and empty out the ones unsold and fold them flat again and mark them. There was an awful lot of paperwork involved in being a concessioner.

As I watched Z again and again, the generals took on aspects of other 16 authorities. I memorized the beginning, where the military officers, in a secret meeting, speak of the left as "political mildew" and deplored "the dry rot of subversive ideologies." It sounded just like the morning farm report on our local radio, with all the dire warnings of cow brucellosis and exhortations to mobilize against the invasion of wild oats. I knew nothing about metaphor, nothing, in fact, of communism or what a dictatorship was, but the language grabbed me and would not let go. Without consciously intending it, I had taken sides.

Then, halfway into Christmas vacation, Vincent told on me. The boss 17 took me down into his neat little office in the basement and confronted me with the denouncement that I had eaten one piece of candy from every box in the glass case. I denied it.

"Vincent does it all the time," I lied with a clear conscience. 18

So there we were, a nest of informers and counterinformers, each wait- 19 ing to betray the other over a Red Hot Tamale. It was sad. I accused Vincent of snitching; he accused me of the same. We no longer had any pretense of solidarity. He didn't help me when I had a line of customers, and I didn't give him free pop.

Before watching Z again the other night, I took a straw poll of people I 20 knew to have been conscientious in 1969, asking them what they remembered about the movie. It was almost unanimous. People running, darkness, a little blue truck, and Irene Papas. Michael and I sat down and put the rented tape of Z into the video recorder. Between us we shared a bowl of air-popped corn. No salt. No butter anymore. Back in 1969, Michael had purchased the soundtrack to the movie and reviewed it for his school newspaper. It had obviously had an effect on both of us, and yet we recalled no more about it than the viewers in our poll. My memories were more intense because of the argument that almost got me fired from my first indoor job, but all was very blurred except for Irene Papas. As the credits rolled I looked forward to seeing the star. Moment after moment went by, and she did not appear. The leftist organizer went to the airport to pick up the peace leader, and somehow I expected Irene to get off the plane and stun everyone with her tragic, moral gaze.

Of course, Yves was the big star, the peace leader. We watched. I waited   21 for Irene, and then, when it became clear she was only a prop for Yves, I began to watch for *any* woman with a speaking role.

The first one who appeared spoke into a phone. The second woman was   22 a maid, the third a secretary, then a stewardess, then finally, briefly, Irene, looking grim, and then a woman in a pink suit handing out leaflets. Finally, a woman appeared in a demonstration, only to get kicked in the rear end.

Not only that, the man who kicked her was gay, and much was made of   23 his seduction of a pinball-playing boy, his evil fey grin, his monstrosity. To the Costa-Gavras of 1969, at least, the lone gay man was a vicious goon, immoral and perverted.

Once Yves was killed, Irene was called in to mourn, on cue. Her main   24 contribution to the rest of the movie was to stare inscrutably, to weep uncomfortably, and to smell her deceased husband's after-shave. How had I gotten the movie so wrong?

By the end, I knew I hadn't gotten it so wrong after all. In spite of all   25 that is lacking from the perspective of twenty years, Z is still a good political film. It still holds evil to the light and makes hypocrisy transparent. The witnesses who come forward to expose the assassination are bravely credible, and their loss at the end is terrible and stunning. Z remains a moral tale, a story of justice done and vengeance sought. It deals with stupidity and avarice, with hidden motives and the impact that one human being can have on others' lives. I still got a thrill when the last line was spoken, telling us that Z, in the language of the ancient Greeks, means "He is alive." I remember feeling that the first time I saw the movie, and now I recalled one other thing. The second evening the movie showed, I watched Vincent, who hadn't even waited for the end, unhook the red velvet rope from its silver post.

Our argument was just starting in earnest. Normally, after everyone was   26 gone and the outside lights were doused, he spent an hour, maybe two if a Disney had played, cleaning up after the crowd. He took his time. After eleven o'clock, the place was his. He had the keys and the boss was gone.

Those nights, Vincent walked down each aisle with a bag, a mop, and a bucket filled with the same pink soapy solution I used on the butter machine. He went after the spilled Coke, the mashed chocolate, the Jujubes pressed flat. He scraped the gum off the chairs before it hardened. And there were things people left, things so inconsequential that the movie goers rarely bothered to claim them — handkerchiefs, lipsticks, buttons, pens, and small change. One of the things I knew Vincent liked best about his job was that he always got to keep what he found.

There was nothing to find that night, however, not a chewed pencil or a   27
hairpin. No one had come. We'd have only a few stragglers the next few nights, then the boss canceled the film. Vincent and I locked the theater and stood for a moment beneath the dark marquee, arguing. Dumb as it was, it was the first time I'd disagreed with anyone over anything but hurt feelings and boyfriends. It was intoxicating. It seemed like we were the only people in the town.

There have been many revolutions, but never one that so thoroughly   28
changed the way women are perceived and depicted as the movement of the last twenty years. In Costa-Gavras's *Missing, Betrayed,* and *Music Box,* strong women are the protagonists, the jugglers of complicated moral dilemmas. These are not women who dye their underwear to lead cheers, and neither am I anymore, metaphorically I mean, but it is hard to escape from expectations. The impulse never stops. Watching *Z* in an empty North Dakota theater was one of those small, incremental experiences that fed into personal doubt, the necessary seed of any change or growth. The country in *Z* seemed terribly foreign, exotic, a large and threatened place — deceptive, dangerous, passionate. As it turned out, it was my first view of the world.

Analyzing This Selection

1. How did *Z* stimulate Erdrich at age fourteen? Why did she immediately think that it was the best movie she had seen?

2. Twenty years later, did Erdrich's view of the movie change or remain the same? How has Erdrich personally changed or remained the same?

3. **THE WRITER'S METHOD** Readers don't learn until paragraph 27 that almost nobody else in Wahpeton saw the movie. What are the effects of delaying this unexpected information?

Analyzing Connections

4. How does Erdrich's response to a John Wayne movie in the Insights on page 413 indicate a larger personal and social context for her excitement about *Z?* What do her contrasting responses imply about the messages conveyed by movies?

Analyzing by Writing

5. Consider a movie that illuminated or jolted you into a larger, truer "view of the world." Examine the way it entered your life during a period of specific changes. Explain how it encouraged new attitudes, challenged old expectations, or supplied fresh perceptions. Following Erdrich's example, do not summarize the movie. Include, as she does, enough synopsis to help your reader grasp the story line. But analyze your experience, not the movie.

Kurt Andersen

ANIMATION NATION

KURT ANDERSEN (b. 1954) graduated from Harvard University and began writing for magazines as a reporter for *Time*. His articles have appeared also in *Rolling Stone, Vanity Fair,* and *New York,* where Andersen became the editor-in-chief. He is currently a staff columnist for the *New Yorker,* where this commentary appeared in 1997.

Are you by any chance hoping that the millennium will usher in some 1 sort of cleansing cultural flood tide — a next big thing that's not just a half-ironic recycling of a previous big thing, like miniskirts or Corinthian columns? Well, it may have happened already. The new era, which is about to ripen into its golden age, was born eight and a half years ago. It was then, over a brief period in 1988 and 1989, that *Who Framed Roger Rabbit?* posited a world cohabited by human beings and cartoon characters, *The Little Mermaid* inaugurated a new Disney animation hegemony, and — the key event — *The Simpsons* went on the air.

What will be the big musical of 1997? *Hercules,* the Disney cartoon that 2 opens in New York this weekend. What is the only successful new television series of the year so far? *King of the Hill,* a cartoon. What is the only genre of TV program to which Steven Spielberg attaches his name? Cartoon shows — four of them, including *Freakazoid* and *Pinky and the Brain.* Which is the most successful new cable channel? The Cartoon Network. What cable network is insanely profitable? Nickelodeon, thanks partly to its cartoon shows *Ren & Stimpy* and *Rugrats.* Who are the most deeply resonant, compellingly humane people on the tube? Cartoon characters.

There are now entire genres and character types that audiences will 3 wholeheartedly embrace only in cartoon form. The live-action movie musical has been a fading form since the time of *Mary Poppins,* but put old-fashioned tunes and drippy sentiment in the mouths of animated lions and princesses and toy cowboys, and audiences will buy them (plus all licensed gewgaws). Even small children aren't innocent enough nowadays to put up with actual human beings who profess love, perform heroic deeds, and then break into song about it. But animated characters can still plausibly portray purity and nobility. Cartoons — and, pretty much, only cartoons — allow us our corn.

Satire, too, has been rather suddenly yet thoroughly colonized by the   4 cartoons. There's *Duckman* (USA Network), *Dr. Katz, Professional Therapist* (Comedy Central), and *Beavis and Butt-head* and *Daria* (MTV). Not only is *The Simpsons* smarter, sharper, and more allusive than any other show on television; it's also TV's oasis of commedia dell'arte (a flesh-and-blood Homer Simpson would be bathetically repellent), and of believable warmth as well.

If cartoons on TV have become the form in which we permit ourselves   5 to enjoy poignancy and sass and human weirdness, in movies the distinction between cartoons and live action is blurry, on the way to moot. Digitally animated special effects transmute reality into cartoons and cartoons into reality. In Spielberg's new megahit, *The Lost World: Jurassic Park*, the animated dinosaurs seem in every way more genuine and less mechanical than the people. In *The Fifth Element*, Bruce Willis zooms through a real-looking twenty-third-century New York designed by the legendary French cartoonist Jean (Moebius) Giraud. The fourth in the current series of Batman movies will open against *Hercules* next week. A live-action *George of the Jungle* is to come out next month; two different Casper movies are on the way; and Philip Kaufman, who made *The Unbearable Lightness of Being*, is developing a movie about the Marvel Comics character Sub-Mariner.

It cannot be coincidental that millions of people now achieve their most   6 intimate and satisfying human connections electronically, by going on-line behind cartoony noms de net and exchanging pixels with other, uh, characters. Flirting with someone in an Internet chat room, making love to Jessica Rabbit — what's the difference? The plot of *Roger Rabbit*, remember, concerned a development scheme by a money-mad evil genius to destroy the cartoon characters and their funky L.A. quarter, and replace them with human beings: justice triumphs, Toontown survives. We are now living in a sequel, *Toontown Strikes Back*, in which the animated creatures (thanks to certain money-mad L.A. geniuses) have left their old ghetto and moved en masse into our human neighborhoods.

Welcome, Toons! A recent *Simpsons* episode lampooned, with perfect   7 contempt, various live-action TV genres. Its parody of a sitcom included, of course, plenty of robotically hysterical canned laughter. It was a joke that only an animated show could do perfectly, and it highlighted another virtue of *The Simpsons*: almost alone among TV comedies, it doesn't have a laugh track. *King of the Hill*, which follows it on Sunday nights, doesn't have one, either. If we find these shows funny, we have the luxury of grinning or chuckling or guffawing without electronic encouragement — by ourselves, at home, in real life. Thanks to cartoons, we can respond like human beings.

Analyzing This Selection

1. **THE WRITER'S METHOD**   In paragraphs 1 to 2, how do the rhetorical questions change? What is their cumulative effect? What risks does the author take in using this tactic?

2. How does Andersen imply regrets and reservations along with his endorsement of cartoons?

Analyzing Connections

3. In Erdrich's "Z: The Movie That Changed My Life" (see p. 416), would a cartoon movie have changed Erdrich's life? How does adding animated special effects or animated characters to a dramatic movie like Z affect its realism? Do you agree with Andersen that the distinction between cartoons and human acting is blurry? Would Erdrich agree?

Analyzing by Writing

4. Review a cartoon show Andersen mentions, and analyze its popular appeal. How does it differ from nonanimated situation comedies? Do cartoons broaden or narrow our range of empathy? If you select one of the satires, clarify its type of wit. Do cartoons strengthen or weaken the power of ridicule?

James B. Twitchell

"BUT FIRST, A WORD FROM OUR SPONSOR"

JAMES B. TWITCHELL (b. 1943) writes cultural studies about literature and about commercial society. He graduated from the University of Vermont and received a Ph.D. in English from the University of North Carolina at Chapel Hill. Twitchell teaches at the University of Florida. His books include *The Living Dead: A Study of the Vampire in Romantic Literature* (1981) and *Adcult USA: The Triumph of Advertising in America* (1995). This selection is excerpted from an essay in his collection *Dumbing Down: Essays in the Strip Mining of American Culture* (1996).

Whenever a member of my paunchy fiftysomething set pulls me aside 1 and complains of the dumbing down of American culture, I tell him that if he doesn't like it, he should quit moaning and go buy a lot of Fast-Moving Consumer Goods. And every time he buys soap, toothpaste, beer, gasoline, bread, aspirin, and the like, he should make it a point to buy a different brand. He should implore his friends to do likewise. At the same time, he should quit giving so much money to his kids. That, I'm sorry to say, is his only hope.

Here's why. The culture we live in is carried on the back of advertising. 2 Now I mean that literally. If you cannot find commercial support for what you have to say, it will not be transported. Much of what we share, and what we know, and even what we treasure, is carried to us each second in a plasma of electrons, pixels, and ink, underwritten by multinational advertising agencies dedicated to attracting our attention for entirely nonaltruistic reasons. These agencies, gathered up inside worldwide conglomerates with weird, sci-fi names like WPP, Omnicom, Saatchi & Saatchi, Dentsu, and Euro RSCG, are usually collections of established shops linked together to provide "full service" to their global clients. Their service is not moving information or creating entertainment, but buying space and inserting advertising. They essentially rent our concentration to other companies — sponsors — for the dubious purpose of informing us of something that we've longed for all our lives even though we've never heard of it before. Modern selling is not about trading information, as it was in the

19th century, as much as about creating an infotainment culture with sufficient allure to enable other messages — commercials — to get through. In the spirit of the enterprise, I call this new culture Adcult.

Adcult is there when we blink, it's there when we listen, it's there when we touch, it's even there to be smelled in scent strips when we open a magazine. There is barely a space in our culture not already carrying commercial messages. Look anywhere: in schools there is Channel One; in movies there is product placement; ads are in urinals, played on telephone hold, in alphanumeric displays in taxis, sent unannounced to fax machines, inside catalogs, on the video in front of the Stairmaster at the gym, on T-shirts, at the doctor's office, on grocery carts, on parking meters, on tees at golf holes, on inner-city basketball backboards, piped in along with Muzak . . . ad nauseam (and yes, even on airline vomit bags). We have to shake magazines like rag dolls to free up their pages from the "blow-in" inserts and then wrestle out the stapled- or glued-in ones before reading can begin. We now have to fast-forward through some five minutes of advertising that opens rental videotapes. President Bill Clinton's inaugural parade featured a Budweiser float. At the Smithsonian, the Orkin Pest Control Company sponsored an exhibit on exactly what it advertises it kills: insects. No venue is safe. Is there a blockbuster museum show not decorated with corporate logos? The Public Broadcasting Service is littered with "underwriting announcements" that look and sound almost exactly like what PBS claims they are not: commercials.

Okay, you get the point. Commercial speech is so powerful that it drowns out all other sounds. But sounds are always conveyed in a medium. The media of modern culture are these: print, sound, pictures, or some combination of each. Invariably, conversations about dumbing down focus on the supposed corruption of these media, as demonstrated by the sophomoric quality of most movies, the fall from the golden age of television, the mindlessness of most best-sellers, and the tarting-up of the news, be it in or on *USA Today, Time,* ABC, or *Inside Edition.* The media make especially convenient whipping boys because they are now all conglomerated into huge worldwide organizations such as Time Warner, General Electric, Viacom, Bertelsmann, and Sony. But, alas, as much fun as it is to blame the media, they have very little to do with the explanation for whatever dumbing down has occurred.

The explanation is, I think, more fundamental, more economic in nature. These media are delivered for a price. We have to pay for them, either by spending money or by spending time. Given a choice, we prefer to spend time. We spend our time paying attention to ads, and in exchange we are given infotainment. This trade is central to Adcult. Economists call this "cost externalization." If you want to see it at work, go to McDonald's. You order. You carry your food to the table. You clean up. You pay less. Want to see it elsewhere? Buy gas. Just as the "work" you do at the self-service gas station lowers the price of gas, so consuming ads is the "work" you do that lowers the price of delivering the infotainment. In Adcult, the trade is more complex. True, you are entertained at lower cost, but you are also encultured in the process.

So far, so good. The quid pro quo of modern infotainment culture is that if you want it, you'll get it — no matter what it is — as long as there are enough of you who (1) are willing to spend some energy along the way hearing "a word from our sponsor" and (2) have sufficient disposable income possibly to buy some of the advertised goods. In Adcult you pay twice: once with the ad and once with the product. So let's look back a step to examine these products because — strange as it may seem — they are at the center of the dumbing down of American culture.

Before all else, we must realize that modern advertising is tied primarily to things, and only secondarily to services. Manufacturing both things *and* their meanings is what American culture is all about. If Greece gave the world philosophy, Britain drama, Austria music, Germany politics, and Italy art, then America gave mass-produced objects. "We bring good things to life" is no offhand claim. Most of these "good things" are machine made and hence interchangeable. Such objects, called parity items, constitute most of the stuff that surrounds us, from bottled water to toothpaste to beer to cars. There is really no great difference between Evian and Mountain Spring, Colgate and Crest, Miller and Budweiser, Ford and Chevrolet. Often, the only difference is in the advertising. Advertising is how we talk about these fungible things, how we know their supposed differences, how we recognize them. We don't consume the products as much as we consume the advertising.

For some reason, we like it this way. Logically, we should all read *Consumer Reports* and then all buy the most sensible product. But we don't. So why do we waste our energy (and billions of dollars) entertaining fraudulent choice? I don't know. Perhaps just as we drink the advertising, not the beer, we prefer the illusion of choice to the reality of decision. How else to explain the appearance of so much superfluous choice? A decade ago, grocery stores carried about 9,000 items; they now stock about 24,000. Revlon makes 158 shades of lipstick. Crest toothpaste comes in 36 sizes and shapes and flavors. We are even eager to be offered choice where there is none to speak of. AT&T offers "the right choice"; Wendy's asserts that "there is no better choice"; Pepsi is "the choice of a new generation"; Taster's Choice is "the choice for taste." Even advertisers don't understand the phenomenon. Is there a relationship between the number of soft drinks and television channels — about 27? What's going to happen when the information pipe carries 500?

I have no idea. But I do know this: human beings like things. We buy things. We like to exchange things. We steal things. We donate things. We live through things. We call these things "goods," as in "goods and services." We do not call them "bads." This sounds simplistic, but it is crucial to understanding the power of Adcult. The still-going-strong Industrial Revolution produces more and more things, not because production is what machines do, and not because nasty capitalists twist their handlebar mustaches and mutter, "More slop for the pigs," but because we are powerfully attracted to the world of things. Advertising, when it's lucky, supercharges some of this attraction.

This attraction to the inanimate happens all over the world. Berlin Walls   10
fall because people want things, and they want the culture created by things. China opens its doors not so much because it wants to get out, but because it wants to get things in. We were not suddenly transformed from customers to consumers by wily manufacturers eager to unload a surplus of products. We have created a surfeit of things because we enjoy the process of "getting and spending." The consumption ethic may have started in the early 1900s, but the desire is ancient. Kings and princes once thought they could solve problems by amassing things. We now join them.

The Marxist balderdash of cloistered academics aside, human beings did   11
not suddenly become materialistic. We have always been desirous of things. We have just not had many of them until quite recently, and, in a few generations, we may return to having fewer and fewer. Still, while they last, we enjoy shopping for things and see both the humor and the truth reflected in the aphoristic "born to shop," "shop 'til you drop," and "when the going gets tough, the tough go shopping." Department store windows, whether on the city street or inside a mall, did not appear by magic. We enjoy looking through them to another world. It is voyeurism for capitalists. Our love of things is the *cause* of the Industrial Revolution, not the consequence. We are not only *homo sapiens,* or *homo ludens,* or *homo faber,* but also *homo emptor.*[1]

Mid-20th-century American culture is often criticized for being too   12
materialistic. Ironically, we are not too materialistic. We are not materialistic enough. If we craved objects *and* knew what they meant, there would be no need to add meaning through advertising. We would gather, use, toss out, or hoard based on some *inner* sense of value. But we don't. We don't know what to gather, we like to trade what we have gathered, and we need to know how to evaluate objects of little practical use. What is clear is that most things in and of themselves simply do not mean enough. In fact, what we crave may not be objects at all but their meaning. For whatever else advertising "does," one thing is certain: by adding value to material, by adding meaning to objects, by branding things, advertising performs a role historically associated with religion. The Great Chain of

---

[1]*homo sapiens, homo ludens, homo faber, homo emptor* Genus and species terms for "knowing man," "playing man," "making man," and "buying man."

Being, which for centuries located value above the horizon in the world Beyond, has been reforged to settle value into the objects of the Here and Now.

Analyzing This Selection

1. **THE WRITER'S METHOD**   How do modern sales techniques differ from earlier selling? Since the essay does not include examples of earlier selling, is the author's point in paragraph 2 fully acceptable or not? Explain your reasons either way.

2. Clarify Twitchell's statement, "We are not materialistic enough" (para. 12). What does he think should change?

Analyzing Connections

3. Which of Twitchell's causes and explanations of Adcult infotainment are suggested by Brubach in "Mail-Order America" (see p. 374)? In your opinion, which author's view of human nature is more accurate?

Analyzing by Writing

4. Examine the audio and visual techniques that advertisers use to promote superfluous choices. Brands of gasoline, jeans, sneakers, wash detergents, or phone services may offer examples. Since not all ads are successful, what attracts consumers to specific products?

Ellen Ullman

GETTING CLOSE
TO THE MACHINE

ELLEN ULLMAN (b. 1948) is a software engineer who writes about her profession. She graduated from Cornell University. This essay appeared in *Harper's* magazine in 1995.

People imagine that computer programming is logical, a process like fixing a clock. Nothing could be further from the truth. Programming is more like an illness, a fever, an obsession. It's like riding a train and never being able to get off.

The problem with programming is not that the computer is illogical — the computer is terribly logical, relentlessly literal. It demands that the programmer explain the world on its terms; that is, as an algorithm that must be written down in order, in a specific syntax, in a strange language that is only partially readable by regular human beings. To program is to translate between the chaos of human life and the rational, line-by-line world of computer language.

When you program, reality presents itself as thousands of details, millions of bits of knowledge. This knowledge comes at you from one perspective and then another, then comes a random thought, then you remember something else important, then you reconsider that idea with a what-if attached. For example, try to think of everything you know about something as simple as an invoice. Now try to tell an idiot how to prepare one. That is programming.

I used to have dreams in which I was overhearing conversations I had to program. Once I dreamed I had to program two people making love. In my dream they sweated and tumbled while I sat looking for the algorithm. The couple went from gentle caresses to ever-deepening passion, and I tried desperately to find a way to express the act of love in the C computer language.

When you are programming, you must not let your mind wander. As the human-world knowledge tumbles about in your head, you must keep typing, typing. You must not be interrupted. Any break in your concentration causes you to lose a line here or there. Some bit comes, then — oh no, it's

430

leaving, please come back. But it may not come back. You may lose it. You will create a bug and there's nothing you can do about it.

People imagine that programmers don't like to talk because they prefer 6 machines to people. This is not completely true. Programmers don't talk because they must not be interrupted.

This need to be uninterrupted leads to a life that is strangely asynchro- 7 nous to the one lived by other human beings. It's better to send e-mail to a programmer than to call. It's better to leave a note on the chair than to expect the programmer to come to a meeting. This is because the programmer must work in mind time while the phone rings and the meetings happen in real time. It's not just ego that prevents programmers from working in groups — it's the synchronicity problem. Synchronizing with other people (or their representations in telephones, buzzers, and doorbells) can only mean interrupting the thought train. Interruptions mean bugs. You must not get off the train.

I once had a job in which I didn't talk to anyone for two years. Here was 8 the arrangement: I was the first engineer to be hired by a start-up software company. In exchange for large quantities of stock that might be worth something someday, I was supposed to give up my life.

I sat in a large room with two other engineers and three workstations. 9 The fans in the machines whirred, the keys on the keyboards clicked. Occasionally one of us would grunt or mutter. Otherwise we did not speak. Now and then I would have an outburst in which I pounded the keyboard with my fists, setting off a barrage of beeps. My colleagues might have looked up, but they never said anything.

Real time was no longer compelling to me. Days, weeks, months, and 10 years came and went without much change in my surroundings. Surely I was aging. My hair must have grown, I must have cut it, it must have slowly become grayer. Gravity must have been working on my late-thirties body, but I didn't pay attention.

What was compelling was the software. I was making something out of 11 nothing, I thought, and I admit that the software had more life for me during those years than a brief love affair, my friends, my cat, my house, or my neighbor who was stabbed and nearly killed by her husband. One day I sat in a room by myself, surrounded by computer monitors. I remember looking at the screens and saying, "Speak to me."

I was creating something called a device-independent interface library. 12 ("Creating" — that is the word we used, each of us a genius in the attic.) I completed the library in two years and left the company. Five years later, the company's stock went public, and the original arrangement was made good: the engineers who stayed — the ones who had given seven years of their lives to the machine — became very, very wealthy.

If you want money and prestige, you need to write code that only   13
machines or other programmers understand. Such code is called "low." In
regular life, "low" usually signifies something bad. In programming, "low"
is good. Low means that you are close to the machine.

If the code creates programs that do useful work for regular human   14
beings, it is called "high." Higher-level programs are called "applications."
Applications are things that people use. Although it would seem that usefulness is a good thing, direct people-use is bad from a programmer's point
of view. If regular people, called "users," can understand the task accomplished by your program, you will be paid less and held in lower esteem.

A real programmer wants to stay close to the machine. The machine   15
means midnight dinners of Diet Coke. It means unwashed clothes and
bare feet on the desk. It means anxious rides through mind time that have
nothing to do with the clock. To work on things used only by machines or
other programmers — that's the key. Programmers and machines don't care
how you live. They don't care when you live. You can stay, come, go,
sleep — or not. At the end of the project looms a deadline, the terrible
place where you must get off the train. But in between, for years at a
stretch, you are free: free from the obligations of time.

I once designed a graphical user interface with a man who wouldn't   16
speak to me. My boss hired him without letting anyone else sit in on the
interview. My boss lived to regret it.

I was asked to brief my new colleague with the help of the third mem-   17
ber of our team. We went into a conference room, where my co-worker
and I filled two white boards with lines, boxes, circles, and arrows while the
new hire watched. After about a half hour, I noticed that he had become
very agitated.

"Are we going too fast?" I asked him.   18

"Too much for the first day?" asked my colleague.   19

"No," said our new man, "I just can't do it like this."   20

"Do what?" I asked. "Like what?"   21

His hands were deep in his pockets. He gestured with his elbows. "Like   22
this," he said.

"You mean design?" I asked.   23

"You mean in a meeting?" asked my colleague.   24

No answer from the new guy. A shrug. Another elbow motion.   25

Something terrible was beginning to occur to me. "You mean talking?"   26
I asked.

"Yeah, talking," he said. "I can't do it by talking."   27

By this time in my career, I had met many strange software engineers.   28
But here was the first one who wouldn't talk at all. We had a lot of design
work to do. No talking was certainly going to make things difficult.

"So how *can* you do it?" I asked.   29

"Mail," he said. "Send me e-mail."   30

Given no choice, we designed a graphical user interface by e-mail. Cor- 31 porations across North America and Europe are still using a system designed by three people in the same office who communicated via computer, one of whom barely spoke at all.

Pretty graphical interfaces are commonly called "user-friendly." But they 32 are not really your friends. Underlying every user-friendly interface is terrific contempt for the humans who will use it.

The basic idea of a graphical interface is that it will not allow anything 33 alarming to happen. You can pound on the mouse button, your cat can run across it, your baby can punch it, but the system should not crash.

To build a crash-proof system, the designer must be able to imagine — 34 and disallow — the dumbest action possible. He or she has to think of every single stupid thing a human being could do. Gradually, over months and years, the designer's mind creates a construct of the user as an imbecile. This image is necessary. No crash-proof system can be built unless it is made for an idiot.

The designer's contempt for your intelligence is mostly hidden deep in 35 the code. But now and then the disdain surfaces. Here's a small example: You're trying to do something simple such as copying files onto a diskette on your Mac. The program proceeds for a while, then encounters an error. Your disk is defective, says a message, and below the message is a single button. You absolutely must click this button. If you don't click it, the program will hang there indefinitely. Your disk is defective, your files may be bollixed up, but the designer leaves you only one possible reply. You must say, "OK."

The prettier the user interface, and the fewer replies the system allows 36 you to make, the dumber you once appeared in the mind of the designer. Soon, everywhere we look, we will see pretty, idiot-proof interfaces designed to make us say, "OK." Telephones, televisions, sales kiosks will all be wired for "interactive," on-demand services. What power — demand! See a movie, order seats to a basketball game, make hotel reservations, send a card to mother — all of these services will be waiting for us on our televisions or computers whenever we want them, midnight, dawn, or day. Sleep or order a pizza: it no longer matters exactly what we do when. We don't need to involve anyone else in the satisfaction of our needs. We don't even have to talk. We get our services when we want them, free from the obligations of regularly scheduled time. We can all live, like programmers, close to the machine. "Interactivity" is misnamed. It should be called "asynchrony": the engineering culture come to everyday life.

The very word "interactivity" implies something good and wonderful. 37 Surely a response, a reply, an answer is a positive thing. Surely it signifies an advance over something else, something bad, something that doesn't respond. There is only one problem: what we will be interacting with is a machine. We will be "talking" to programs that are beginning to look surprisingly alike; each has little animated pictures we are supposed to choose from, like push buttons on a toddler's toy. The toy is meant to please us. Somehow it is supposed to replace the rewards of fumbling for meaning with a mature human being, in the confusion of a natural language, together, in a room, within touching distance.

As the computer's pretty, helpful face (and contemptuous underlying code) penetrates deeper into daily life, the cult of the engineer comes with it. The engineer's assumptions and presumptions are in the code. That's the purpose of the program, after all: to sum up the intelligence and intentions of all the engineers who worked on the system over time — tens and hundreds of people who have learned an odd and highly specific way of doing things. The system reproduces and re-enacts life as engineers know it: alone, out of time, disdainful of anyone far from the machine.

Analyzing This Selection

1. What did Ullman like and what did she dislike in her work? What do you think led her to be a specialist at programming?

2. **THE WRITER'S METHOD** How is the term "interactive" misleading? Why is the "OK" reply demeaning? Do you agree or disagree with Ullman's assessments?

Analyzing Connections

3. How do programming and waitressing (see Paules's "Humble Pie," p. 312) affect normal functioning of thoughts and feelings? Explain why you would prefer either kind of work.

Analyzing by Writing

4. Examine the attractions and distresses of using personal computer and network terminals. How do they enhance or distort mental functions? Why do users get lost in cyberspace? Should users and society be concerned about how computers may cause the deterioration of certain ways of thinking and living?

Wendy Lesser

THE CONVERSION

WENDY LESSER (b. 1952) writes about painting and literature in relation to society. She graduated from Harvard University and received a Ph.D. in English from the University of California at Berkeley. Her essays have appeared in the *New Republic,* the *Yale Review,* the *Hudson Review,* and *Southwest Review,* and she is the founding editor of a similar magazine, *The Threepenny Review.* Lesser's books include *His Other Half: Men Looking at Women Through Art* (1991) and *Pictures at an Execution: An Inquiry into the Subject of Murder* (1994), which examines the moral issues surrounding a televised gas chamber execution. Lesser has received a Guggenheim Fellowship and other major awards. The following essay appeared in *Greywolf Forum* in an issue devoted to technology and the arts.

I resisted e-mail for at least two or three years. Many of my Berkeley friends are academics, so they got it automatically as part of their jobs and then annoyingly sang its praises. "It replaces long-distance phone calls!" "You can dig up old recipes from libraries across the Midwest!" "It allows you to communicate instantaneously with colleagues from South Africa!" None of these seemed like things I particularly wanted to do. Moreover, I had strong if somewhat irrational reasons for resisting. I did not want my computer talking on the phone to anyone else's computer, because who knew what could happen once you opened up those lines? I wasn't just worried about viruses, though those were indeed a concern; but how could you be sure that someone wouldn't sneak through the e-mail door and thereby penetrate your hard disk, stealing or at any rate messing up your closely held documents? I preferred to keep my computer chaste and self-contained, aloof from all potential communicants. And then, I didn't see the point of getting those unreadable little messages that seemed to go on forever, with little or no punctuation. To judge by the e-mail I had read in newspapers and magazines (the kind that was always reproduced to show how fun and liberating this new mode of communication was), these emissions were somewhere below the level of the worst unsolicited manuscripts I habitually receive in the course of editing a literary magazine. Why should I want to read *more* of the stuff, especially on a barely legible computer screen? What was the good of a technological form that erased the boundary between intimate friends and total strangers, reducing everyone

435

to a digital printout? Where was *handwriting* in all this? Where was *personal style?*

I should interrupt my screed to say that I am not a complete antitech- 2
nologist. I watch more television than just about anyone I know, and
believe that *Hill Street Blues* and *NYPD Blue* are among the major artistic
achievements of late twentieth-century America. I use the latest (well, the
second-latest) desktop publishing equipment to put out my magazine, and
rely on a rather complex database software to organize its subscriber list. I
adore the fax machine and have long considered it the single greatest
invention since the telephone — the fax machine, after all, respects and
transmits handwriting, just as the telephone conveys the nuances of the
individual voice. I am not, that is, a hermit. I constantly employ and enjoy
electronic transmissions of all sorts, and I do not feel that they in any way
sap my capacity to be an Emersonian individual. On the contrary, they
enhance it: without all my little machines, I could not make a living as a
self-employed, self-designated arbiter of cultural taste. In Emerson's time,
you had to inherit a comfortable income if you wished to subsist as a man
of letters; in our day, technology can substitute for and even generate the
freeing effects of wealth.

But for some reason this dashing perspective, this resolutely cheerful opti- 3
mism about mechanical progress, did not make a dent in my fear of e-mail.
From the perspective of one who has now crossed the great divide, I can see
that my phobia stemmed in part from a category error. That is, I thought
that "e-mail" and "the Internet" were identical: I believed that in order to
communicate with my friends and colleagues, I would have to place myself
squarely in front of all the oncoming lanes of traffic in the Information
Superhighway. Worse: I was persuaded that those snippets of generic e-mail
clipped from the bulletin boards of the Internet represented what my own
friends would sound like if I had to talk to them by computer. I wrongly
supposed that the machine controlled its own content, that the medium (as
we used to say, *pace* McLuhan, in the '60s) would be the message.

Why I should have believed Marshall McLuhan in this respect when I 4
had long since discarded his views on television is a question that perhaps
requires a cultural psychotherapist to answer. (I don't know that there *is*
such a thing as a cultural psychotherapist, but since I have recently learned
of something called "ecopsychology" — which is designed to help us bond
with Mother Earth — I assume there are no limits.) For some reason, fear
makes us believe in false prophets, the more apocalyptic the better. Clinging to the printed pages of my old-fashioned literary quarterly and my
beloved cloth- and paperbound books, I thought that e-mail spelt the end
of reading as I knew it. After all, you couldn't do it in the bathtub.

Well, there are lots of things you can't do in the bathtub and even I have 5
to admit that doesn't make them useless or unacceptable. I wouldn't want
to read a novel or even a ten-page story on e-mail, and faced with that little message screen, I probably couldn't compose an essay worth printing.
But for daily correspondence, electronic mail has become my essential

instrument. And like all tools, it is more than just a simple replacement of the previous technology — it acts on you as well as you on it, and it acts in ways you can't always predict. In effect, e-mail has restored the personal letter to my life.

If you are like me, you went through a phase when personal letters occu- 6 pied a central place in your existence. You were probably in your late teens or early twenties. Possibly you were living away from home for the first time, or perhaps you had just embarked on your first long-term (and long-distance) love affair, or maybe you were traveling alone through Europe, or all of the above. The mail became your lifeline, and you honored it accordingly. You poured everything into your letters — the engaging details of daily existence, the special sights, the serious emotions, the witty observations — to such an extent that even journal-keeping, by comparison, seemed onerous and redundant. You tailored each letter to the personality of the recipient, delightedly imagining the eventual response to the in-jokes of a shared history. You received as good as you gave, and each day's mail delivery marked an emotional high or low point. And then, at some point, you grew out of all this, and household bills, business letters, magazines, and fund-raising pleas came to fill your mailbox instead.

Just as personal letters define a phase in an individual's life, so do they 7 also define a period in Western history. I didn't realize this until I read P. N. Furbank's review of the *Oxford Book of Letters*, wherein he remarks

> . . . how deprived the ancient world was, not having discovered the secret of personal letters — long, spontaneous, chatty letters, as funny as they can be made but not always just funny, and coming nice and often — the sort of letters you might have got if you had known Henry James or Bernard Shaw or Philip Larkin. You would have been expected to answer them, and that would have been marvelous too, at least for oneself. It would be like enjoying a second life.

Exactly. And, as Furbank goes on to say, "The ancients knew nothing of this. With what leaden spirits one would have received a letter from Cicero! One may hazard that this best kind of letter-writing began in the eighteenth century and really came into its own in the nineteenth." Not coincidentally, this was just when the postal system was reaching a pinnacle of service, in terms of frequency and reliability.

For one of the keys to the pleasure of letters lies in that half-buried little 8 phrase, "and coming nice and often." In London, where P. N. Furbank lives, mail is still delivered twice a day, and a letter posted first-class will reach its destination anywhere in the United Kingdom by the next day. It is still possible to keep up a satisfying personal correspondence under such circumstances. For the rest of the world, however, mail is generally too slow to gratify the needs of the moment. You might choose to rely on the stamp and envelope on special occasions, or for particularly delicate communications, or if (like a young person in her teens or twenties) you live on a very limited budget; but when you have something important to say, you're much more likely to pick up the telephone.

The crisis in my attitude toward e-mail occurred when I realized that I   9
would no longer be able to afford the telephone. I was about to leave
America for four months, and to indulge in long-distance calling from
Europe would be ruinously expensive. Nor could I tolerate waiting the
two weeks it would take for the round-trip communication by post. It was
e-mail or nothing.

One problem with e-mail, though, is that it takes two actively willing   10
participants. Anyone in the modern world can receive a postal letter, but
only those with an e-mail hookup can receive e-mail. So I had to get my
near and dear to join up at the same time I did. Among those I had to persuade was a writer in New York, a friend of twenty years' standing on whom
I normally lavish at least one long-distance phone call a day. As he is even
more of a Luddite than I am, this was no easy task.

"I feel very resistant to the idea," he explained.   11

"I know, I know," I said. "I've already been resistant for three years, so   12
can't we take it as done?"

Finally, I just cheated. I ordered *his* CompuServe introductory package   13
when I ordered my own, knowing that when the user-friendly software
slipped through his mail slot, he would be unable to resist trying it on. (Or,
to put it more truthfully: I planned to make life miserable for him via telephone until he got around to applying his e-mail diskettes.)

It was slow to catch on. At first my friend and I used e-mail mainly as a   14
toy, in between the more substantial communication of our transcontinen-
tal phone calls, and most of our electronic conversation was metaconversa-
tion, in that it dealt with the ins and outs of using e-mail. But when I left
California on a Wednesday night, arrived in London on a Thursday morning, hooked up my computer, received my New York friend's welcoming
message, and instantly e-mailed back — well, that was a revelation for both
of us. Soon we were up to three or even four exchanges a day. The five-
hour time difference meant nothing: he could post a note before he went
to sleep, and I would receive it when I woke up the next day. And what I
discovered, to my enormous pleasure, was that the electronic mode did not
wash out his characteristic tones. On the contrary, he sounded in his virtual
incarnation exactly as he did in real life: wry, observant, dryly affectionate,
subtle, and sharp. Personal style, it turned out, did not get blotted out by
the machine. In some ways it was even enhanced, with new opportunities
for humorous self-expression and literary allusion afforded by the title
spaces in our messages. "Internettled," his title bar announced when he
had been fiddling all day to make the machine do something new. "Later
the Same Day," I called one of my frequent messages, echoing Grace
Paley.[1] And it was inevitable, given the technology, that we would soon feel
inspired to use E. M. Forster's "Only connect."[2]

---

[1]**Paley** An American fiction writer.
[2]**"Only connect"** The epigraph to Forster's novel *Howards End*.

Even in our differing responses to the availability of e-mail, my friend 15
and I were faithful to our respective personalities. Something of a self-styled
loner, he built up a tiny, highly selective list of e-mail addresses and mailed
only to those two or three people. (His willful resistance to technological
self-education may have had something to do with this. "How do you communicate with those outside our parish?" he once complained, stumped
by the difficulty of crossing over from CompuServe to America Online or
Prodigy.)

I, on the other hand, verged on epistolary promiscuity. Within my first 16
week on-line, I had mailed to a number of my Berkeley pals, a long-lost
classmate in Tasmania, three Londoners, my husband at his work address,
my stepson at college, my father, my sister, a good friend who had temporarily moved to St. Louis, and my exercise teacher. I became an e-mail
maniac, checking in every hour or so and collapsing with disappointment
if I got the empty-mailbox beep. I found myself waxing expansive on-
screen, chatting on about virtually nothing. I was responding, I now think,
to the special enticements of the form's mixed nature — at once private
and public, solitary and communal, so that it seems to combine the two
oldest types of American writing, the diary and the sermon. With e-mail, you
begin with the former, alone at your desk, and end (if you use your "multiple send" button) with the latter, broadcasting to the whole congregation.

One of the first responses I got from old e-mail hands, when I contacted 17
them with my newly acquired address, was scorn at the impersonal nature
of my mailing moniker. Everybody else, it appeared, had managed to craft
idiosyncratic, sometimes poetic, always memorable labels for themselves.
Using the loose conventions set up by most e-mail providers, they had
come up with word combinations that were nearly as distinctive as their
own names (and that often incorporated those names into the address). But
CompuServe allowed for no such creativity: we were simply allocated a
number. "Your address sounds like something from the Planet Zog," one of
my correspondents wrote. Another mocked me for my long resistance to
e-mail. "This is just the kind of address I would expect a confirmed Luddite
to get," he noted. "Those who resist the machine are doomed to be punished by it."

Whatever form it takes, your e-mail address becomes a part of your per- 18
manent identity in a way that no mere phone number can. For one thing,
you can't hide it. You can make an obscene phone call from an anonymous number or mail a poison pen letter without giving a return address,
but your e-mail message carries its provenance in its heading. This necessary mutuality is both e-mail's virtue and its curse. That is, you have to consider before engaging in any communication whether you want to hear
from someone as well as speak *to* him, because he will thereafter possess
your address. There are no one-way assaults in the world of e-mail: if you
launch a missive, you automatically open yourself up to a counterattack.

And unlike a phone number, which can be as temporary as your present 19 whereabouts, your e-mail address travels with you. I had exactly the same CompuServe number during my European stay as during my normal Berkeley life. People seeking to contact me didn't have to know I was out of the country or even out of the office. Sometimes I would amuse myself by trying to imagine where my virtual mailbox was located. Did it float somewhere in the fourth dimension, rushing into my computer only when it was actually consulted? Or did it hover somewhere over the Atlantic, relaying messages between my temporarily European self and my North American correspondents? I had been told it was in cyberspace — but what kind of space *was* that, exactly? Thinking such thoughts is a bit like trying to imagine how one's voice gets through those little telephone wires into the other person's receiver, only more so. You regress to your childhood self, for whom all such concepts are made concrete and miniature: the little person inside the telephone receiver, the tiny mailbox inside the computer. And the fact that my computer was itself a laptop (a ridiculously compact mechanism which, the dealer told me, was more powerful than the huge computer that had flown the first man to the moon) made the miniaturization imagery even more credible.

I discovered just how portable my e-mail was when a thief crept into my   20
house and walked off with my computer. One day I had been happily communicating with the entire world, the next I was reduced to virtual silence. My anxiety at the loss of my equipment was exacerbated by my sense of all the messages I was missing. I had become dependent on my daily fix, and the burglar, as if guessing at this aspect of my psychology, had even cut the phone wire that led into the computer — a symbolic act, easily remedied by the purchase of a new wire, but one that drove home for me my feeling of violent interruption. "I feel as if I'm hemorrhaging information," I told my husband. But information was only the half of it. All the little pieces of *me* that I had been feeding into cyberspace were loosed into the world, never to return.

Yet when I got a new computer, hooked myself back up to CompuServe,   21
and checked my old mailbox, there it still was, just as if no interruption had ever occurred. My e-mail had been patiently waiting for me out there in Nowhere Land, the messages accumulating until I was once again able to pick them up. The beauty of the system, it turns out, is precisely that it's *not* connected to any physical object. They can steal the transmitting device from you, but the mail service continues unabated in its ideal Platonic form — temporarily inaccessible, maybe, but always ready to be picked up. I had my answer to Bishop Berkeley's question:[3] if the tree had fallen in cyberspace, the sound could simply have waited decades or generations or millennia until someone came along to hear it, and *then* it

---

[3]***Bishop Berkeley's question*** "If a tree falls where no creature hears it, does it make a sound?" The English philosopher's attempt to answer this question led him to a philosophical proof of God's existence.

would have existed. In this respect, as in so much else, e-mail's qualities are strangely mixed. It is both speedy to the point of instantaneousness, and arrested in a state of timelessness.

So have I lost my soul to e-mail? I think not. Of course, proper use of it requires some mastery, and particularly self-mastery. One's initial sub-servience to the medium's surprising delights is inevitably a bit enslaving. (But this must have been true of all new media, even the cave paint at Las-caux.) Still, once it has been brought under control and made to function in the life you have already constructed for yourself, e-mail can be a great gift. If you keep all those strangers and business connections and mass-directory people off your screen, it can be, as Furbank put it, "like enjoying a second life." You will be rewarded with all the old-fashioned pleasures of the intimate personal letter. You will be offered, in other words, the chance to *gain* a soul rather than lose one. As an agnostic, I'm not even sure I believe in the very idea of a soul; but if I had to say where it resides, I would point to the thing in us that allows us to be and have intimate friends. And e-mail, by bringing back personal correspondence, reintro-duces us to the form of writing that best enables us to know and acknowl-edge friendship.

Analyzing This Selection

1. What role did letters once have for the author? What, if anything, plays this role in your life?

2. **THE WRITER'S METHOD**   In paragraph 22, does Lesser mock or believe in the significance of her conversion? What details throughout the essay indicate her attitude toward e-mail's effects?

Analyzing Connections

3. Do friendships through mail and e-mail avoid or intensify the sexual com-plexities that Goodheart observes in other kinds of friendships (see "Fast Friends," p. 131)?

Analyzing by Writing

4. Compare the telephone, letters, and e-mail for personal communications. Teenagers, many of whom appear to talk on the phone endlessly and tire-lessly, may be dealing with important interactive situations. Letters, as Lesser points out, are "like enjoying a second life." What are the positive and negative effects of e-mail on personal life?

Robert Goodman

THE LUCK BUSINESS[1]

ROBERT GOODMAN (b. 1936) is an urban planner and economic development consultant. He currently teaches at Hampshire College and is the executive director of the United States Gambling Research Institute in Northampton, Massachusetts. His books include *After the Planners* (1971) and *The Last Entrepreneurs* (1979). This selection is excerpted from *The Luck Business* (1995).

This could be your ticket out.

— AN ILLINOIS STATE LOTTERY BILLBOARD
IN A LOW-INCOME CHICAGO NEIGHBORHOOD[2]

The proliferation of legalized gambling in America is probably the only 1 example of a situation where government is not simply legalizing a potentially harmful activity, but is actually promoting it. . . . Governments did not decide to allow new gambling ventures in response to rising popular demands for more gambling. This is not, for example, like the repeal of Prohibition, where government found itself responding to a popular political movement to legalize the business of producing and selling liquor.

In the case of gambling, it is the government which is explicitly trying to 2 get people to participate more, through advertisements, media promotions, and public relations campaigns. It is the government which is expanding the availability of more addictive forms of gambling like electronic gambling machines. The result is a dangerous shift in the fundamental role of government — from regulator of gambling to promoter of gambling. Governments are gutting regulations designed to protect the public, spending millions on promotions and advertisements, and in some cases even subsidizing private gambling enterprises. In the process, they are also recruiting millions of people into gambling who have never gambled before.

This stands in stark contrast to the role of government, especially since 3 the 1930s, as a protector of citizens through a host of laws and regulations

---

[1]Editor's title.
[2]Taylor Branch, "What's Wrong with the Lottery," *New England Monthly* January 1990: 41.

designed to protect workplace conditions, health and safety, environment, civil rights, and so forth. In sponsoring more gambling, governments do not even require accurate social and economic impact statements about their expansion plans, the way they do in the case of potential environmental impacts of an expanding industry or the construction of a new highway.

In this new promotional role, government finds itself in a strange and   4 contradictory position which makes it difficult to carry out its role of protecting the public. While it once regulated gambling in order to guard against gambling operators who might take advantage of its citizens, the government's own growing dependence on gambling revenues puts pressure on state officials to increase advertising and relax regulations. A 1988 New Jersey Governor's Advisory Commission observing what happened in Atlantic City put it simply: "The more entrenched is gambling in the budget process, then the more successful the industry may be in causing the relaxation of regulatory policies and procedures with which they do not agree."[3]

As far back as the 1950s, politicians argued that by legalizing gambling,   5 governments would capture money that was already being bet illegally, eliminate the role of organized crime, and ensure that players weren't being cheated.[4] Yet criminals never promoted their gambling operations the way governments now do with multi-million dollar advertising campaigns, public relations efforts, focus group research, and penetration studies. "No matter what you do for a living," says a Massachusetts Lottery advertisement, "there's an easier way to make money."[5] And in contrast to the ventures of organized crime, government-supported gambling is given extensive free publicity through newspaper and TV stories about incredible jackpots, happy winners, and transformed lives.

From a psychological perspective, people's ability to dream and to hope   6 for a better life can be a very healthy and useful human attribute. It helps them persevere under difficult circumstances, and it can motivate people to change and improve their lives. But by enticing people to spend their money on fantasies, governments are preying on people's ability to dream and hope. Rather than providing real hope for economic improvement, public officials are promoting the illusion of economic improvement — becoming deeply involved in finding new ways of manipulating people's desire for a more secure future. They are enticing people into taking part in what should properly be called the "pathology of hope." When a government agency, like the New York State Lottery, says its players' "whimsical

---

[3] *Report and Recommendations of The Governor's Advisory Commission on Gambling*, Trenton, N.J. June 30, 1988: 12.

[4] See, for example, "Communication by Mayor William O'Dwyer to the New York State Legislature, January 10, 1950," in "Gambling," *Annals of the American Academy of Political and Social Science* 266 (1950): 35, 36.

[5] Paul Della Valle and Scott Farmelant, "A Bad Bet: Who Really Pays for the Massachusetts Lottery's Success?" *Worcester Magazine* January 27, 1993: 16.

fantasies" are being given "the hope of fulfillment" or that its gambling products offer people a chance to dream of paying off their debts or to dream about paying for their children's education, then governments have gotten themselves into playing a new and very dangerous role.[6]

By 1994, state lotteries were spending over $350 million a year to adver-   7 tise their products.[7] In 1991, the California Lottery had become the largest purchaser of advertising in Los Angeles County.[8] Gregory Ziemak, Director of the Kansas Lottery and the former director of the Connecticut State Lottery, reflected on government's schizophrenia of trying to both regulate and promote gambling. In his Connecticut job, Ziemak says, he was criticized by some legislators and community leaders for his advertisements. "They said just the fact that you're advertising the lottery is wrong." But the bottom line of keeping his job ultimately depended on pleasing politicians who were judging him by the revenues he generated. "My success or failure," he said "was how sales were. Were sales better than last year, or were they worse?"[9]

One of the most effective publicity techniques to promote more lottery   8 play, according to Ziemak, was getting the media to produce stories about the winners. "People see a picture of a Lotto winner in the paper," said Ziemak. "You know he's a guy like you; he works in the shop, he has kids, he's going to use the money to put the kids through college. You say, 'You know maybe I could win'." When some winners shun this publicity, lottery officials find ways of persuading them. According to Ziemak:

> What we tell the winners is, look you won $5 million, that's news. It's public information whether you agree to talk to the press, or allow us to release it to the press, we're still going to have to release your name, your town, and the amount won. And if we do that the press might call you because you're not saying anything. Sometimes they get more interested. What we suggest you do, is go downstairs and talk to them.[10]

Government promotion of its gambling products not only persuades people to gamble at legal operations, but, according to William Jahoda, a former gambling operator for organized crime in Chicago, also benefits illegal ventures. "[Public] agency marketing and media advertising blitzes promoting gambling," he told the Chicago Gaming Commission, give people the perception that gambling is "healthy entertainment." Jahoda characterized the

---

[6]See New York State Lottery, *Annual Report 1988–89.*

[7]Information provided by Bill Hennessey, Media and Advertising Specialist, State of Connecticut, Department of Revenue Services, Division of Special Revenue. See Robert Goodman, "Legalized Gambling . . . ," *Strategy for Economic Development* (Northampton, Mass.: United States Gambling Study, 1994).

[8]"Lottery Leads List of L.A. Radio Advertisers," *L.A. Business Journal* (June 4, 1990). Cited in I. Nelson Rose, "Gambling and the Law: Update 1993," *COMM/ENT,* Hastings Communications and Entertainment Law Journal, Hastings College of Law, University of California (Fall 1992).

[9]Personal Interview with Gregory A. Ziemak (July 8, 1992).

[10]Ibid.

public officials involved in promoting government gambling ventures as "our unwitting front men and silent partner."[11]

In finding new ways to stimulate more demand for their gambling products, government officials have become increasingly adept at manipulating player behavior through the use of sophisticated market research analysis, consumer surveys, penetration studies, and focus groups.[12] They continuously monitor player attitudes and behaviors in order to design new sales pitches which are closely attuned to people's psychological needs and fears. One Massachusetts Lottery television ad focused on a real fear of many hard-core players — that they won't play their number on the day that it finally comes up. In the staged commercial, a newsman attempts to interview a number of distraught players who would have won on the day they forgot to play. Lance Dodes, the operator of a Massachusetts treatment center for problem gamblers, described such government-promoted ads as ones which lead to more problem gambling. "[Players] are terrified not to play their number," he explained, "and the Lottery preys on those fears."[13]   9

Despite this obvious manipulation, in 1991 Jim Hosker, Kentucky's lottery director, said that lottery players tend to absolve government of responsibility for their losses. Since people know they are playing against enormous odds, he said, they tend to blame themselves and not the state when they lose. Their psychological reaction, according to Hosker, is "I didn't pick the right numbers."[14]   10

The goal of lottery advertising is not only to increase the amount of money that people gamble, but also to increase the number of people who gamble — what those who market gambling call "expanding the player base." To accomplish this, lottery managers are constantly trying to find new ways of getting people to shift their spending away from other consumer products and services and into gambling at lotteries. As the marketing director of a Canadian lottery said, "We believe any promotion that can alter the regular purchasing habits of the consumer is viewed as significantly benefiting our long-term success."[15]   11

According to Jim Davey, a former Oregon State Lottery director, "We're a market-driven organization and I mean we're going to go out and expand this business."[16] The way to increase sales, according to Davey and other lottery managers, is to constantly change games. "Offer something that   12

[11]Better Government Association, *Staff White Paper: Casino Gambling in Chicago*, Chicago (October 1992).

[12]Erik Calonius, "The Big Payoff from Lotteries," *Fortune* March 25, 1991; Jeffrey L. Katz, "Waking Up the Lottery," *Governing* September 1991.

[13]Mitchell Zuckoff, "State-Run Games Flout Ad Standards," *Boston Globe* September 27, 1993: 9.

[14]Katz, "Waking Up the Lottery."

[15]According to J. Jourdain, Marketing Director of the Western Canada Lottery, in "Quote of the Month," *Gaming and Wagering Business* July 15–August 14, 1992: 4.

[16]Interview with Jim Davey (September 17, 1992).

looks new," said Davey, who later became president of Automated Wagering International, an electronic gambling machine manufacturer. "At Christmas we do Holiday Cash. With Lucky Stars we play on people's astrological signs. We find that if you run two or three, four or five games at the same time, you'll sell more tickets."[17] . . .

To gain public support, gambling revenues are often used for highly visible and popular social programs — what one gambling executive called "the three big E's — education, environment and economic development."[18] He could have added a fourth "E," for the elderly. The arts have sometimes also received similar treatment. But when a specific program or a city's budget gets tied to gambling proceeds, it is relying on an unstable source of funds, since it is dependent on how much people can be persuaded to gamble. This gambling-for-good-things approach also hampers the ability of those who receive the revenues to lobby state legislators and voters for any additional funds they might need for their programs.   13

Most often, revenues from gambling simply replace, rather than supplement, the funds for programs whose budgets get tied to gambling revenues. By 1991, thirteen states, including rural ones, like Idaho and Montana, and urban ones, like New York and California, had earmarked all or part of their lottery proceeds for education.[19] According to Bill Honig, California's Public School Superintendent, "For every $5 the lottery gives to the schools, the state takes away $4."[20] Honig complained that lottery funds earmarked for education made it difficult to raise educational funds from other places. "The public is more reluctant to pass education bond issues because they think we're floating in lottery money."[21] In California, lottery funds for education depended on the fortunes of the state's lottery, which declined from about $1 billion in 1988 to $500 million in 1991.[22] . . .   14

While the actual chance of winning a big lottery jackpot is virtually zero, people play on the fantastic chance that their lives will somehow be dramatically transformed. Lottery advertising campaigns capitalize on such remote hope. Impossible dreams have been substituted for ones that once seemed real.   15

In May 1994, Peter Lynch, Director of the New York State Lottery, appeared before an international gathering of lottery directors at the exhi-   16

---

[17]James Cook, "Lottomania," *Forbes* March 6, 1989: 94.

[18]Bruce W. Wentforth, General Manager of Dubuque Greyhound Park, in Edward Walsh, "Despite Revenue Drop, States Continue to Bet on Gambling to Cure Economies," *Washington Post* October 3, 1991.

[19]Chris Pipho, "Watching the Legislatures," *Phi Delta Kappan* January 1990: 342.

[20]Peter Passell, "Lotto Is Financed by the Poor and Won by the States," *New York Times* May 21, 1989: E6.

[21]Erik Calonius, "The Big Pay-Off from Lotteries," *Fortune* March 25, 1991.

[22]Laurel Shaper Walters, "Taking a Chance on Education," *Christian Science Monitor* August 16, 1993: 9.

bition hall at the Louvre in Paris to illustrate the methods his state agency used to get people to gamble more money. Of primary importance, said Lynch, was conducting ongoing research to constantly monitor "what's going on in the minds of your customer." This included gathering information not only about their attitudes toward lottery games, but also about "their lives and their general outlook." This is done with the help of a yearly "Attitude and Usage Benchmark Study."

Such information allowed his agency to continually revise games in order not only to entice its steady players to gamble more, but also to encourage those nonplayers who, Lynch said, demonstrated "apathy" to the state's games to begin to play. Although the lottery has sometimes been enormously successful in persuading state residents to increase their gambling, it has had difficulty maintaining a constant high level of play. Lynch complained of "lapsed players," those who became "disenchanted" and "jaded," and of people who suffered from "high-odds burnout."   17

According to Lynch, the government's "all you need is a dollar and a dream campaign" was aimed at getting infrequent players to gamble more through what he called "anticipatory dreaming."   18

> We had to make Lotto a more socially acceptable thing to do. . . . we needed to remind occasional customers of the fun of anticipation and that it's okay to enjoy the experience because lots of people just like them share these emotions. We needed, therefore, to have our occasional players empathize with both the dream and dreamer. . . . the most critical move we made was to shift from advertising focused on winners to the anticipation of winning. . . . the theory was while only one person wins, everyone who plays enjoys the anticipatory dreaming.[23]

Describing the psychological backdrop to the success of its games, the Lottery agency's 1988–1989 Annual Report explained, "from the moment of a ticket's purchase to the conclusion of the drawing, the 'dream' that is impossible when seen in the cold, hard light of reality has the means of coming true — moments to be savored and enjoyed no matter what the ultimate outcome."[24] In planning their "dream" ads, the lottery relied on using real people instead of actors. According to Lynch, this involved the "casting of warm, lively, regular people." The goal, he said, was to create "a genuine empathy between the target audience and infrequent players with encouragement of infrequent players to play more frequently."[25] . . .   19

While people have always dreamed of a lucky break in a card game or perhaps picking a winning number, never before have they been so   20

---

[23]Peter Lynch, "Matching Advertising to Products," Talk at the Twentieth Congress of l'Association Internationale des Loteries d'Etat (AILE), Paris (May 1994), reprinted in *Gaming and Wagering Business* August 5, 1994: 45.

[24]New York State Lottery, *Annual Report 1988–89.*

[25]Lynch.

blatantly urged by their political leaders to risk their money in order to transform the declining situation of their lives. What began perhaps as a reasonable effort to capture, for the public coffers, dollars already being bet illegally has mushroomed into an enterprise that is radically transforming the role of government. In their attempt to solve economic problems with gambling, government leaders are further undermining their already precarious credibility with their constituents. They are encouraging a public perception that governments can do little to support a healthier economic climate for all citizens, and that the best they can do is to provide enormous windfalls for gambling companies and the limited possibility of jobs for those fortunate enough to work for these companies. That we have also arrived at a point in time where state government agencies are studying demographics and psychological behavior of state residents in order to encourage them to gamble more, not only raises serious moral questions, but calls for a more fundamental reassessment of the nature of government's role in the business of gambling.

Analyzing This Selection

1. What draws state governments into the gambling business? What are Goodman's criticisms of the purposes?

2. According to the author, why is gambling not good for people? Why are lotteries not good for governments? Which effect do you think is more harmful?

3. **THE WRITER'S METHOD** Find examples of Goodman's tactfulness. In opposing a popular activity, is his approach persuasive or weak?

Analyzing Connections

4. Fantasizing is an intended effect of all contemporary advertising, as Brubach observes about catalogues (see "Mail-Order America," p. 374). What differences, if any, make lottery ads more harmful than other sales pitches?

Analyzing by Writing

5. Analyze one government-sponsored media campaign such as advertising against drunk or reckless driving, against smoking, against forest fires, against pollution, or favoring health measures such as testing for cancer, reducing cholesterol, or other public policies. Examine the tactics used to scare and lure people into changing their behavior. Assess the ads by comparing their effectiveness with other media campaigns, including commercials and government ads for lotteries.

Oscar Hijuelos

THE MAMBO KINGS
PLAY SONGS OF LOVE

Oscar Hijuelos (b. 1951) was born of Cuban parents in New York City.
He graduated from City College, where he also earned a master's degree.
He has won several fiction awards, including a National Endowment for
the Arts fellowship and a Pulitzer Prize for his second novel, *The Mambo
Kings Play Songs of Love* (1989), from which this story was excerpted. His
most recent novel is *Mr. Ives' Christmas* (1995).

It was a Saturday afternoon on La Salle Street, years and years ago when 1
I was a little kid, and around three o'clock Mrs. Shannon, the heavy Irish
woman in her perpetually soup-stained dress, opened her back window and
shouted out into the courtyard, "Hey, Cesar, yoo-hoo, I think you're on
television, I swear it's you!" When I heard the opening strains of the *I Love
Lucy* show I got excited because I knew she was referring to an item of eternity, that episode in which my dead father and my Uncle Cesar had
appeared, playing Ricky Ricardo's singing cousins fresh off the farm in Oriente Province, Cuba, and north in New York for an engagement at Ricky's
nightclub, the Tropicana.

This was close enough to the truth about their real lives — they were 2
musicians and songwriters who had left Havana for New York in 1949, the
year they formed the Mambo Kings, an orchestra that packed clubs, dance
halls, and theaters around the East Coast — and, excitement of excite-
ments, they even made a fabled journey in a flamingo-pink bus out to
Sweet's Ballroom in San Francisco, playing on an all-star mambo night, a
beautiful night of glory, beyond death, beyond pain, beyond all stillness.

Desi Arnaz had caught their act one night in a supper club on the West 3
Side, and because they had perhaps already known each other from Havana
or Oriente Province, where Arnaz, like the brothers, was born, it was natural
that he ask them to sing on his show. He liked one of their songs in particular, a romantic bolero written by them, "Beautiful María of My Soul."

Some months later (I don't know how many, I wasn't five years old yet) 4
they began to rehearse for the immortal appearance of my father on this
show. For me, my father's gentle rapping on Ricky Ricardo's door has
always been a call from the beyond, as in Dracula films, or films of the

449

walking dead, in which spirits ooze out from behind tombstones and through the cracked windows and rotted floors of gloomy antique halls: Lucille Ball, the lovely red-headed actress and comedienne who played Ricky's wife, was housecleaning when she heard the rapping of my father's knuckles against that door.

"I'm commmmmming," in her singsong voice.   5

Standing in her entrance, two men in white silk suits and butterfly-   6
looking lace bow ties, black instrument cases by their side and black-brimmed white hats in their hands — my father, Nestor Castillo, thin and broad-shouldered, and Uncle Cesar, thickset and immense.

My uncle: "Mrs. Ricardo? My name is Alfonso and this is my brother   7
Manny . . ."

And her face lights up and she says, "Oh, yes, the fellows from Cuba.   8
Ricky told me all about you."

Then, just like that, they're sitting on the couch when Ricky Ricardo   9
walks in and says something like, "Manny, Alfonso! Gee, it's really swell that you fellas could make it up here from Havana for the show."

That's when my father smiled. The first time I saw a rerun of this, I   10
could remember other things about him — his lifting me up, his smell of cologne, his patting my head, his handing me a dime, his touching my face, his whistling, his taking me and my little sister, Leticia, for a walk in the park, and so many other moments happening in my thoughts simultaneously that it was like watching something momentous, say the Resurrection, as if Christ had stepped out of his sepulcher, flooding the world with light — what we were taught in the local church with the big red doors — because my father was now newly alive and could take off his hat and sit down on the couch in Ricky's living room, resting his black instrument case on his lap. He could play the trumpet, move his head, blink his eyes, nod, walk across the room, and say "Thank you" when offered a cup of coffee. For me, the room was suddenly bursting with a silvery radiance. And now I knew that we could see it again. Mrs. Shannon had called out into the courtyard alerting my uncle: I was already in his apartment.

With my heart racing, I turned on the big black-and-white television set   11
in his living room and tried to wake him. My uncle had fallen asleep in the kitchen — having worked really late the night before, some job in a Bronx social club, singing and playing the horn with a pickup group of musicians. He was snoring, his shirt was open, a few buttons had popped out on his belly. Between the delicate-looking index and forefingers of his right hand, a Chesterfield cigarette burning down to the filter, that hand still holding a half glass of rye whiskey, which he used to drink like crazy because in recent years he had been suffering from bad dreams, saw apparitions, felt cursed, and, despite all the women he took to bed, found his life of bachelorhood solitary and wearisome. But I didn't know this at the time, I thought he was sleeping because he had worked so hard the night before, singing and playing the trumpet for seven or eight hours. I'm talking about a wedding party in a crowded, smoke-filled room (with bolted-shut fire

doors), lasting from nine at night to four, five o'clock in the morning, the band playing one-, two-hour sets. I thought he just needed the rest. How could I have known that he would come home and, in the name of unwinding, throw back a glass of rye, then a second, and then a third, and so on, until he'd plant his elbow on the table and use it to steady his chin, as he couldn't hold his head up otherwise. But that day I ran into the kitchen to wake him up so that he could see the episode, too, shaking him gently and tugging at his elbow, which was a mistake, because it was as if I had pulled loose the support columns of a five-hundred-year-old church: He simply fell over and crashed to the floor.

A commercial was running on the television, and so, as I knew I wouldn't 12 have much time, I began to slap his face, pull on his burning red-hot ears, tugging on them until he finally opened one eye. In the act of focusing he apparently did not recognize me, because he asked, "Nestor, what are you doing here?"

"It's me, Uncle, it's Eugenio." 13

I said this in a really earnest tone of voice, just like the kid who hangs out 14 with Spencer Tracy in the movie of *The Old Man and the Sea*, really believing in my uncle and clinging on to his every word in life, his every touch like nourishment from a realm of great beauty, far beyond me, his heart. I tugged at him again, and he opened his eyes. This time he recognized me.

He said, "You?" 15

"Yes, Uncle, get up! Please get up! You're on television again. Come on." 16

One thing I have to say about my Uncle Cesar, there was very little he 17 wouldn't do for me in those days, and so he nodded, tried to push himself off the floor, got to his knees, had trouble balancing, and then fell backwards. His head must have hurt: His face was a wince of pain. Then he seemed to be sleeping again. From the living room came the voice of Ricky's wife, plotting as usual with her neighbor Ethel Mertz about how to get a part on Ricky's show at the Tropicana, and I knew that the brothers had already been to the apartment — that's when Mrs. Shannon had called out into the courtyard — that in about five more minutes my father and uncle would be standing on the stage of the Tropicana, ready to perform that song again. Ricky would take hold of the microphone and say, "Well, folks, now I have a real treat for you. Ladies and gentlemen, Alfonso and Manny Reyes, let's hear it!" And soon my father and uncle would be standing side by side, living, breathing beings, for all the world to see, harmonizing in a duet of that *canción*.

As I shook my uncle, he opened his eyes and gave me his hand, hard 18 and callused from his other job in those days, as superintendent, and he said, "Eugenio, help me. Help me."

I tugged with all my strength, but it was hopeless. Still he tried: With 19 great effort he made it to one knee, and then, with his hand braced on the floor, he started to push himself up again. As I gave him another tug, he began miraculously to rise. Then he pushed my hand away and said, "I'll be okay, kid."

With one hand on the table and the other on the steam pipe, he pulled   20
himself to his feet. For a moment he towered over me, wobbling as if powerful winds were rushing through the apartment. Happily I led him down
the hallway and into the living room, but he fell over again by the door —
not fell over, but rushed forward as if the floor had abruptly tilted, as if he
had been shot out of a cannon, and, wham, he hit the bookcase in the hall.
He kept piles of records there, among them a number of the black and
brittle 78s he had recorded with my father and their group, the Mambo
Kings. These came crashing down, the bookcase's glass doors jerking open,
the records shooting out and spinning like flying saucers in the movies and
splintering into pieces. Then the bookcase followed, slamming into the
floor beside him: The songs "Bésame Mucho," "Acérate Más," "Juventud,"
"Twilight in Havana," "Mambo Nine," "Mambo Number Eight," "Mambo
for a Hot Night," and their fine version of "Beautiful María of My Soul" —
all these were smashed up. This crash had a sobering effect on my uncle.
Suddenly he got to one knee by himself, and then the other, stood, leaned
against the wall, and shook his head.

"Bueno," he said.   21

He followed me into the living room and plopped down on the couch   22
behind me. I sat on a big stuffed chair that we'd hauled up out of the basement. He squinted at the screen, watching himself and his younger
brother, whom, despite their troubles, he loved very much. He seemed to
be dreaming.

"Well, folks," Ricky Ricardo said, "and now I have a real treat for you . . ."   23

The two musicians in white silk suits and big butterfly-looking lace bow   24
ties, marching toward the microphone, my uncle holding a guitar, my
father a trumpet.

"Thank you, thank you. And now a little number that we composed . . ."   25
And Cesar started to strum the guitar and my father lifted his trumpet to
his lips, playing the opening of "Beautiful María of My Soul," a lovely,
soaring melody line filling the room.

They were singing the song as it had been written — in Spanish. With   26
the Ricky Ricardo Orchestra behind them, they came into a turnaround
and began harmonizing a line that translates roughly into English as:
"What delicious pain love has brought to me in the form of a woman."

My father . . . He looked so alive!   27

"Uncle!"   28

Uncle Cesar had lit a cigarette and fallen asleep. His cigarette had slid   29
out of his fingers and now was burning into the starched cuff of his white
shirt. I put the cigarette out, and then my uncle, opening his eyes again,
smiled. "Eugenio, do me a favor. Get me a drink."

"But, Uncle, don't you want to watch the show?"   30

He tried really hard to pay attention, to focus on it.   31

"Look, it's you and Poppy."   32

"Coño, si . . ."   33

My father's face with his horsey grin, arching eyebrows, big fleshy   34 ears — a family trait — that slight look of pain, his quivering vocal cords, how beautiful it all seemed to me then . . .

And so I rushed into the kitchen and came back with a glass of rye   35 whiskey, charging as fast as I could without spilling it. Ricky had joined the brothers onstage. He was definitely pleased with their performance and showed it, because as the last note sounded he whipped up his hand and shouted "Olé!" a big lock of his thick black hair falling over his brows. Then they bowed and the audience applauded.

The show continued on its course. A few gags followed: A costumed bull   36 with flowers wrapped around its horns came out dancing an Irish jig, its horns poking into Ricky's bottom and so exasperating him that his eyes bugged out, he slapped his forehead and started speaking a-thousand-words-a-second Spanish. But at that point it made no difference to me, the miracle had passed, the resurrection of a man, Our Lord's promise which I then believed, with its release from pain, release from the troubles of this world.

Analyzing This Selection

1. Based on your impression of the story as a whole, what sort of boy is Eugenio? Find details in the first four paragraphs that support your view of his personality. What did these details first lead you to expect from the character and the story?

2. **THE WRITER'S METHOD** What is the significance of the falling bookcase? Explain the uncle's reaction. What tone of voice would you give his remark?

3. For the boy, what is the connection between television and his religion? What attitude does the story express about this connection? Find details that support your interpretation.

Analyzing Connections

4. Compare the influence of movies and television in Eugenio's life and in Erdrich's (see "Z: The Movie That Changed My Life," p. 416). What truths and illusions conflict in their responses to films?

Analyzing by Writing

5. Much of our sense of history comes from movie and television dramas. For instance, the Civil War, World War II, and the Holocaust are imprinted in public memory by films and miniseries. Consequently, our beliefs about their substance comes from the entertainment industry. By contrast, in school, our knowledge of history comes for the most part from reading and lectures, not screening. What is contributed by each medium of presentation? Choose one historical topic (you are not limited to the examples given), and consider its presentation in both books and film. How have film versions enhanced or distorted the views of the past that you formed through reading? How did your reading knowledge affect your response to the screened version?

Andrea Dworkin

LETTER FROM A WAR ZONE

ANDREA DWORKIN (b. 1946) was raised in Camden, New Jersey, and attended Bennington College. She lived in Crete and Amsterdam. Returning to New York, Dworkin worked as a free-lance writer and began her career of activism against pornography. Her first feminist book, *Woman Hating* (1974), won her a nationwide audience. In 1978 Dworkin participated in the first Take Back the Night March to protest urban districts that harbor prostitution and pornography. In *Intercourse* (1987), Dworkin attacks possessive and contemptuous attitudes in the way ordinary men write and speak about sexual intercourse. She has also published two novels, *Ice and Fire* (1987) and *Mercy* (1991). Dworkin's essays and speeches have been collected in *Letters from a War Zone* (1989).

It is late 1986 now, and we are losing. The war is men against women; the country is the United States. Here, a woman is beaten every eighteen seconds: by her husband or the man she lives with, not by a psychotic stranger in an alley. Understand: Women are also beaten by strangers in alleys but that is counted in a different category — gender-neutral assault, crime in the streets, big-city violence. Woman-beating, the intimate kind, is the most commonly committed violent crime in the country, according to the FBI, not feminists. A woman is raped every three minutes, nearly half the rapes committed by someone the woman knows. Forty-four percent of the adult women in the United States have been raped at least once. Forty-one percent (in some studies seventy-one percent) of all rapes are committed by two or more men; so the question is not how many rapes there are, but how many rapists. There are an estimated 16,000 new cases of father-daughter incest each year; and in the current generation of children, thirty-eight percent of girls are sexually molested. Here, now, less than eight percent of women have not had some form of unwanted sex (from assault to obscene harassment) forced on them.

We keep calling this war normal life. Everyone's ignorant; no one knows; the men don't mean it. In this war, the pimps who make pornography are the SS, an élite, sadistic, military, organized vanguard. They run an efficient and expanding system of exploitation and abuse in which women and children, as lower life forms, are brutalized. This year they will gross $10 billion.

We have been slow to understand. For fun they gag us and tie us up as 3
if we were dead meat and hang us from trees and ceilings and door frames
and meat hooks; but many say the lynched women probably like it and we
don't have any right to interfere with them (the women) having a good
time. For fun they rape us or have other men, or sometimes animals, rape
us and film the rapes and show the rapes in movie theaters or publish them
in magazines, and the normal men who are not pimps (who don't know,
don't mean it) pay money to watch; and we are told that the pimps and the
normal men are free citizens in a free society exercising rights and that we
are prudes because this is sex and real women don't mind a little force and
the women get paid anyway so what's the big deal? The pimps and the normal men have a constitution that says the filmed rapes are "protected
speech" or "free speech." Well, it doesn't actually *say* that — cameras, after
all, hadn't been invented yet; but they interpret their constitution to protect
their fun. They have laws and judges that call the women hanging from the
trees "free speech." There are films in which women are urinated on, defe-
cated on, cut, maimed, and scholars and politicians call them "free
speech." The politicians, of course, deplore them. There are photographs
in which women's breasts are slammed in rat traps — in which things
(including knives, guns, glass) are stuffed in our vaginas — in which we are
gang-banged, beaten, tortured — and journalists and intellectuals say: Well,
there is a lot of violence against women *but* . . . But what, prick? But we
run this country, cunt.

If you are going to hurt a woman in the United States, be sure to take a 4
photograph. This will confirm that the injury you did to her expressed a
point-of-view, sacrosanct in a free society. Hey, you have a right not to like
women in a democracy, man. In the very unlikely event that the victim can
nail you for committing a crime of violence against her, your photograph is
still constitutionally protected, since it communicates so eloquently. The
woman, her brutalization, the pain, the humiliation, her smile — because
you did force her to smile, didn't you? — can be sold forever to millions of
normal men (them again) who — so the happy theory goes — are having a
"cathartic" experience all over her. It's the same with snuff films, by the
way. You can torture and disembowel a woman, ejaculate on her dismembered uterus, and even if they do put you away someday for murder (a
rather simple-minded euphemism), the film is legally *speech. Speech.*

In the early days, feminism was primitive. If something hurt women, 5
feminists were against it, not for it. In 1970, radical feminists forcibly occupied the offices of the ostensibly radical Grove Press because Grove published pornography marketed as sexual liberation and exploited its female
employees. Grove's publisher, an eminent boy-revolutionary, considered
the hostile demonstration CIA-inspired. His pristine radicalism did not stop
him from calling the very brutal New York City police and having the
women physically dragged out and locked up for trespassing on his private
property. Also in 1970, radical feminists seized *Rat,* an underground rag

that devoted itself, in the name of revolution, to pornography and male chauvinism equally, the only attention gender got on the radical left. The pornographers, who think strategically, and actually do know what they are doing, were quick to react. "These chicks are our natural enemy," wrote Hugh Hefner in a secret memo leaked to feminists by secretaries at *Playboy*. "It is time we do battle with them. . . . What I want is a devastating piece that takes the militant feminists apart." What he got were huge, raucous demonstrations at Playboy Clubs in big cities.

Activism against pornography continued, organized locally, ignored by the media but an intrinsic part of the feminist resistance to rape. Groups called Women Against Violence Against Women formed independently in many cities. Pornography was understood by feminists (without any known exception) as woman-hating, violent, rapist. Robin Morgan pinpointed pornography as the theory, rape as the practice. Susan Brownmiller, later a founder of the immensely influential Women Against Pornography, saw pornography as woman-hating propaganda that promoted rape. These insights were not banal to feminists who were beginning to comprehend the gynocidal and terrorist implications of rape for all women. These were *emerging* political insights, not learned-by-rote slogans.

Sometime in 1975, newspapers in Chicago and New York City revealed the existence of snuff films. Police detectives, trying to track down distribution networks, said that prostitutes, probably in Central America, were being tortured, slowly dismembered, then killed, for the camera. Prints of the films were being sold by organized crime to private pornography collectors in the United States.

In February 1976, a day or two before Susan B. Anthony's birthday, a snazzy, first-run movie house in Times Square showed what purported to be a real snuff film. The marquee towered above the vast Times Square area, the word *Snuff* several feet high in neon, next to the title the words "made in South America where life is cheap." In the ads that blanketed the subways, a woman's body was cut in half.

We felt despair, rage, pain, grief. We picketed every night. It rained every night. We marched round and round in small circles. We watched men take women in on dates. We watched the women come out, physically sick, and still go home with the men. We leafleted. We screamed out of control on street corners. There was some vandalism: not enough to close it down. We tried to get the police to close it down. We tried to get the District Attorney to close it down. You have no idea what respect those guys have for free speech.

The pimp who distributed the film would come to watch the picket line and laugh at us. Men who went in laughed at us. Men who walked by laughed at us. Columnists in newspapers laughed at us. The American Civil Liberties Union ridiculed us through various spokesmen (in those days, they used men). The police did more than laugh at us. They formed a barricade with their bodies, guns, and nightsticks — to protect the film from women. One threw me in front of an oncoming car. Three protestors were arrested and *locked up* for using obscene language to the theater manager. Under the United States Constitution, obscene language is not speech. Understand: It is not that obscene language is unprotected speech; it is not considered speech at all. The protestors, talking, used obscene language that was not speech; the maiming in the snuff film, the knife eviscerating the woman, was speech. All this we had to learn.

We learned a lot, of course. Life may be cheap, but knowledge never is.   11
We learned that the police protect property and that pornography is property. We learned that the civil liberties people didn't give a damn, my dear: A woman's murder, filmed to bring on orgasm, was speech, and they didn't even *mind* (these were the days before they learned that they had to say it was bad to hurt women). The ACLU did not have a crisis of conscience. The District Attorney went so far as to find a woman he claimed was "the actress" in the film to show she was alive. He held a press conference. He said that the only law the film broke was the law against fraud. He virtually challenged us to try to get the pimps on fraud, while making clear that if the film had been real, no United States law would have been broken because the murder would have occurred elsewhere. So we learned that. During the time *Snuff* showed in New York City, the bodies of several women, hacked to pieces, were found in the East River and several prostitutes were decapitated. We also learned that.

When we started protesting *Snuff*, so-called feminist lawyers, many still   12
leftists at heart, were on our side: No woman could sit this one out. We watched the radical boy lawyers pressure, threaten, ridicule, insult, and intimidate them; and they did abandon us. They went home. They never came back. We saw them learn to love free speech above women. Having hardened their radical little hearts to *Snuff*, what could ever make them put women first again?

There were great events. In November 1978, the first feminist confer-   13
ence on pornography was held in San Francisco. It culminated in the country's first Take Back the Night March: Well over 3,000 women shut down San Francisco's pornography district for one night. In October 1978, over 5,000 women and men marched on Times Square. One documentary of the march shows a man who had come to Times Square to buy sex looking at the sea of women extending twenty city blocks and saying, bewildered and dismayed: "I can't find one fucking woman." In 1980, Linda Marchiano published *Ordeal*. World-famous as Linda Lovelace, the pornqueen extraordinaire of *Deep Throat*, Marchiano revealed that she had been forced into prostitution and pornography by brute terrorism. Gangraped, beaten, kept in sexual slavery by her pimp/husband (who had legal rights over her as her husband), forced to have intercourse with a dog for a film, subjected to sustained sadism rarely found by Amnesty International with regard to political prisoners, she dared to survive, escape, and expose the men who had sexually used her (including *Playboy*'s Hugh Hefner and

Screw's Al Goldstein). The world of normal men (the consumers) did not believe her; they believed *Deep Throat*. Feminists did believe her. Today Marchiano is a strong feminist fighting pornography.

In 1980, when I read *Ordeal*, I understood from it that every civil right   14 protected by law in this country had been broken on Linda's prostituted body. I began to see gang rape, marital rape and battery, prostitution, and other forms of sexual abuse as civil rights violations which, in pornography, were systemic and intrinsic (the pornography could not exist without them). The pornographers, it was clear, violated the civil rights of women much as the Ku Klux Klan in this country had violated the civil rights of blacks. The pornographers were domestic terrorists determined to enforce, through violence, an inferior status on people born female. The second-class status of women itself was constructed through sexual abuse; and the name of the whole system of female subordination was *pornography* — men's orgasm and sexual pleasure synonymous with women's sexually explicit inequality. Either we were human, equal, citizens, in which case the pornographers could do to us what they did with impunity and, frankly, constitutional protection; or we were inferior, not protected as equal persons by law, and so the pimps could brutalize us, the normal men could have a good time, the pimps and their lawyers and the normal men could call it free speech, and we could live in hell. Either the pornographers and the pornography did violate the civil rights of women, or women had no rights of equality.

I asked Catharine A. MacKinnon, who had pioneered sexual harassment   15 litigation, if we could mount a civil rights suit in Linda's behalf. Kitty worked with me, Gloria Steinem (an early and brave champion of Linda), and several lawyers for well over a year to construct a civil rights suit. It could not, finally, be brought, because the statute of limitations on every atrocity committed against Linda had expired; and there was no law against showing or profiting from the films she was coerced into making. Kitty and I were despondent; Gloria said our day would come. It did — in Minneapolis on December 30, 1983, when the City Council passed the first human rights legislation ever to recognize pornography as a violation of the civil rights of all women. In Minneapolis, a politically progressive city, pornography had been attacked as a *class* issue for many years. Politicians cynically zoned adult bookstores into poor and black areas of the city. Violence against the already disenfranchised women and children increased massively; and the neighborhoods experienced economic devastation as legitimate businesses moved elsewhere. The civil rights legislation was passed in Minneapolis because poor people, people of color (especially Native Americans and blacks), and feminists demanded justice.

But first, understand this. Since 1970, but especially after *Snuff*, feminist   16 confrontations with pornographers had been head-on: militant, aggressive, dangerous, defiant. We had thousands of demonstrations. Some were inside theaters where, for instance, feminists in the audience would scream like hell when a woman was being hurt on the screen. Feminists were physically dragged from the theaters by police who found the celluloid screams to be *speech* and the feminist screams to be *disturbing the peace*. Banners were unfurled in front of ongoing films. Blood was poured on magazines and sex paraphernalia designed to hurt women. Civil disobedience, sit-ins, destruction of magazines and property, photographing consumers, as well as picketing, leafleting, letter-writing, and debating in public forums, have all been engaged in over all these years without respite. Women have been arrested repeatedly: the police protecting, always, the pornographers. In one jury trial, three women, charged with two felonies and one misdemeanor for pouring blood over pornography, said that they were acting to prevent a greater harm — rape; they also said that the blood was already there, they were just making it visible. They were acquitted when the jury heard testimony about the actual use of pornography in rape and incest *from the victims:* a raped woman; an incestuously abused teenager.

So understand this too: *Feminism works*; at least primitive feminism ¹⁷ works. We used militant activism to defy and to try to destroy the men who exist to hurt women, that is, the pimps who make pornography. We wanted to destroy — not just put some polite limits on but *destroy* — their power to hurt us; and millions of women, each alone at first, one at a time, began to remember, or understand, or find words for how she herself had been hurt by pornography, what had happened to her because of it. Before feminists took on the pornographers, each woman, as always, had thought that only she had been abused in, with, or because of pornography. Each woman lived in isolation, fear, shame. Terror creates silence. Each woman had lived in unbreachable silence. Each woman had been deeply hurt by rape, the incest, the battery; but something more had happened too, and there was no name for it and no description of it. Once the role of pornography in *creating* sexual abuse was exposed — rape by rape, beating by beating, victim by victim — our understanding of the nature of sexual abuse itself changed. To talk about rape alone, or battery alone, or incest alone, was not to talk about the totality of how the women had been violated. Rape or wife-beating or prostitution or incest were not discrete or free-standing phenomena. We had thought: Some men rape; some men batter; some men fuck little girls. We had accepted an inert model of male sexuality: Men have fetishes; the women must always be blond, for instance; the act that brings on orgasm must always be the same. But abuse created by pornography was different: The abuse was multifaceted, complex, the violations of each individual woman were many and interconnected; the sadism was exceptionally dynamic. We found that when pornography created sexual abuse, men learned any new tricks the pornographers had to teach. We learned that anything that hurt or humiliated women could be sex for men who used pornography; and male sexual practice would change dramatically to accommodate violations and degradations promoted by pornography. We found that sexual abuses in a woman's life were intricately and complexly connected when pornography was a factor: Pornography was used to accomplish incest and then the child would be used to make pornography; the pornography-consuming husband would not just beat his wife but would tie her, hang her, torture her, force her into prostitution, and film her for pornography; pornography used in gang rape meant that the gang rape was enacted according to an already existing script, the sadism of the gang rape enhanced by the contributions of the pornographers. The forced filming of forced sex became a new sexual violation of women. In sexual terms, pornography created for women and children concentration camp conditions. This is not hyperbole.

One psychologist told the Minneapolis City Council about three cases   18 involving pornography used as "recipe books": "Presently or recently I have worked with clients who have been sodomized by broom handles, forced to have sex with over twenty dogs in the back seat of their car, tied up and then electrocuted on their genitals. These are children [all] in the ages of fourteen to eighteen . . . where the perpetrator has read the manuals and manuscripts at night and used these as recipe books by day or had the pornography present at the time of the sexual violence."

A social worker who works exclusively with adolescent female prostitutes   19 testified: "I can say almost categorically never have I had a client who has not been exposed to prostitution through pornography. . . . For some young women that means that they are shown pornography, either films, videotapes, or pictures as this is how you do it, almost as a training manual in how to perform acts of prostitution. . . . In addition, out on the street when a young woman is [working], many of her tricks or customers will come up to her with little pieces of paper, pictures that were torn from a magazine and say, I want this . . . it is like a mail order catalogue of sex acts, and that is what she is expected to perform. . . . Another aspect that plays a bit part in my work . . . is that on many occasions my clients are multi, many rape victims. These rapes are often either taped or have photographs taken of the event. The young woman when she tries to escape [is blackmailed]."

A former prostitute, testifying on behalf of a group of former prostitutes   20 afraid of exposure, confirmed: "[W]e were all introduced to prostitution through pornography, there were no exceptions in our group, and we were all under eighteen." Everything done to women in pornography was done to these young prostitutes by the normal men. To them the prostitutes were synonymous with the pornography but so were all women, including wives and daughters. The abuses of prostitutes were not qualitatively different from the abuses of other women. Out of a compendium of pain, this is one incident: "[A] woman met a man in a hotel room in the 5th Ward. When he got there she was tied up while sitting on a chair nude. She was gagged and left alone in the dark for what she believed to be an hour. The man returned with two other men. They burned her with cigarettes and attached nipple clips to her breasts. They had many S and M magazines with them and showed her many pictures of women appearing to consent, enjoy, and encourage this abuse. She was held for twelve hours, continuously raped and beaten. She was paid $50 or about $2.33 per hour."

Racist violation is actively promoted in pornography; and the abuse has 21 pornography's distinctive dynamic — an annihilating sadism, the brutality and concept taken wholesale from the pornography itself. The pornographic video game "Custer's Revenge" generated many gang rapes of Native American women. In the game, men try to capture a "squaw," tie her to a tree, and rape her. In the sexually explicit game, the penis goes in and out, in and out. One victim of the "game" said: "When I was first asked to testify I resisted some because the memories are so painful and so recent. I am here because of my four-year-old daughter and other Indian children. . . . I was attacked by two white men and from the beginning they let me know they hated my people. . . . And they let me know that the rape of a 'squaw' by white men was practically honored by white society. In fact, it had been made into a video game called 'Custer's Last Stand' [*sic*]. They held me down and as one was running the tip of his knife across my face and throat he said, 'Do you want to play Custer's Last Stand? It's great, you lose but you don't care, do you? You like a little pain, don't you, squaw?' They both laughed and then he said, 'There is a lot of cock in Custer's Last Stand. You should be grateful, squaw, that all-American boys like us want you. Maybe we will tie you to a tree and start a fire around you.'"

The same sadistic intensity and arrogance is evident in this pornography- 22 generated gang rape of a thirteen-year-old girl. Three deer hunters, in the woods, looking at pornography magazines, looked up and saw the blond child. "There's a live one," one said. The three hunters chased the child, gang-raped her, pistol-whipped her breasts, all the while calling her names from the pornography magazines scattered at their campsite — Golden Girl, Little Godiva, and so on. "All three of them had hunting rifles. They, two men held their guns at my head and the first man hit my breast with his rifle and they continued to laugh. And then the first man raped me and when he was finished they started making jokes about how I was a virgin. . . . The second man then raped me. . . . The third man forced his penis into my mouth and told me to do it and I didn't know how to do it. I did not know what I was supposed to be doing . . . one of the men pulled the trigger on his gun so I tried harder. Then when he had an erection, he raped me. They continued to make jokes about how lucky they were to have found me when they did and they made jokes about being a virgin. They started . . . kicking me and told me that if I wanted more, I could come back the next day. . . . I didn't tell anyone that I was raped until I was twenty years old." These men, like the men who gang-raped the Native American woman, had fun; they were playing a game.

I am quoting from some representative but still relatively *simple* cases. 23 Once the role of pornography in the abuse is exposed, we no longer have just rape or gang rape or child abuse or prostitution. We have, instead, sustained an intricate sadism with no inherent or predictable limits on the kinds of degrees of brutality that will be used on women or girls. We have torture; we have killer-hostility.

Pornography-saturated abuse is specific and recognizable because it is   24
Nazism on women's bodies: The hostility and sadism it generates are car-
nivorous. Interviewing 200 working prostitutes in San Francisco, Mimi H.
Silbert and Ayala M. Pines discovered astonishing patterns of hostility
related to pornography. No questions were asked about pornography. But so
much information was given casually by the women about the role of
pornography in assaults on them that Silbert and Pines published the data
they had stumbled on. Of the 200 women, 193 had been raped as adults
and 178 had been sexually assaulted as children. That is 371 cases of sexual assault on a population of 200 women. Twenty-four percent of those
who had been raped mentioned that the rapist made specific references to
pornography during the rape: "The assailant referred to pornographic materials he had seen or read and then insisted that the victims not only
enjoyed the rape but also the extreme violence." When a victim, in some
cases, told the rapist that she was a prostitute and would perform whatever
sex act he wanted (to dissuade him from using violence), *in all cases* the
rapists responded in these ways: "(1) their language became more abusive,
(2) they became significantly more violent, beating and punching the
women excessively, often using weapons they had shown the women, (3)
they mentioned having seen prostitutes in pornographic films, the majority
of them mentioning specific pornographic literature, and (4) after completing the forced vaginal penetration, they continued to assault the women
sexually in ways they claimed they had seen prostitutes enjoy in the pornographic literature they cited." Examples include forced and anal penetration with a gun, beatings all over the body with a gun, breaking bones,
holding a loaded pistol at the woman's vagina "insisting this was the way
she had died in the film he had seen."

Studies show that between sixty-five and seventy-five percent of women   25
in pornography were sexually abused as children, often incestuously, many
put into pornography as children. One woman, for instance, endured this:
"I'm an incest survivor, ex-pornography model, and ex-prostitute. My incest
story begins before pre-school and ends many years later — this was with
my father. I was also molested by an uncle and a minister . . . my father
forced me to perform sexual acts with men at a stag party when I was a
teenager. I am from a 'nice' middle-class family. . . . My father is an
$80,000 a year corporate executive, lay minister, and alcoholic. . . . My
father was my pimp in pornography. There were three occasions from ages
nine to sixteen when he forced me to be a pornography model . . . in
Nebraska, so, yes, it does happen here." This woman is now a feminist
fighting pornography. She listens to men mostly debate whether or not
there is any social harm connected to pornography. People want experts.
We have experts. Society says we have to prove harm. We have proved

harm. What we have to prove is that women are human enough for harm to matter. As one liberal so-called feminist said recently: "What's the harm of pornography? A paper cut?" This woman was a Commissioner on the so-called Meese commission.[1] She had spent a year of her life looking at the brutalization of women in pornography and hearing the life-stories of pornography-abused women. Women were not very human to her.

In pain and in privacy, women began to face, then to tell, the truth, first to themselves, then to others. Now, women have testified before governmental bodies, in public meetings, on radio, on television, in workshops at conventions of liberal feminists who find all this so messy, so declassé, *so unfortunate*. Especially, the liberal feminists hate it that this mess of pornography — having to do something about these abuses of women — might interfere with their quite comfortable political alliances with all those normal men, the consumers — who also happen to be, well, friends. They don't want the stink of this kind of sexual abuse — the down-and-dirty kind for fun and profit — to rub off on them. Feminism to them means getting success, not fighting oppression.

Here we are: Weep for us. Society, with the acquiescence of too many liberal-left feminists, says that pornographers must *not* be stopped because the freedom of everyone depends on the freedom of the pornographers to exercise speech. The woman gagged and hanging remains the speech they exercise. In liberal-left lingo, stopping them is called *censorship*.

The civil rights law — a modest approach, since it is not the barrel of a gun — was passed twice in Minneapolis, vetoed twice there by the mayor. In Indianapolis, a more conservative city (where even liberal feminists are registered Republicans), a narrower version was adopted: *Narrower* means that only very violent pornography was covered by the law. In Indianapolis, pornography was defined as the graphic, sexually explicit subordination of women in pictures and/or words that also included rape, humiliation, penetration by objects or animals, or dismemberment. Men, children, and transsexuals used in these ways could also use this law. The law made pornographers legally and economically responsible for the harm they did to women. Makers of pornography, exhibitors, sellers, and distributors could be sued for trafficking in pornography. Anyone coerced into pornography could hold the makers, sellers, distributors, or exhibitors liable for profiting from the coercion and could have the coerced product removed from the marketplace. Anyone forced to watch pornography in their home, place of work or education, or in public, could sue whoever forces them and any institution that sanctions the force (for instance, a university or an employer). Anyone physically assaulted or injured because of a specific

26

27

28

---

[1]Named by the pornographers and their friends after their very right-wing Edwin Meese, the Commission was actually set up by the moderate former Attorney General William French Smith. [Au.]

piece of pornography could sue the pornographer for money damages and get the pornography off the shelves. Under this law, pornography is correctly understood and recognized as a practice of sex discrimination. Pornography's impact on the status of women is to keep all women second-class: targets of aggression and civilly inferior.

The United States courts have declared the Indianapolis civil rights law   29 unconstitutional. A Federal Appeals Court said that pornography did all the harm to women we said it did — causing us both physical injury and civil inferiority — but its success in hurting us only proved its power as speech. Therefore, it is protected speech. Compared with the pimps, women have no rights.

The good news is that the pornographers are in real trouble and that   30 we made the trouble. *Playboy* and *Penthouse* are both in deep financial trouble. *Playboy* has been losing subscribers, and thus its advertising base, for years; both *Playboy* and *Penthouse* have lost thousands of retail outlets for their wares in the last few years. We have cost them their legitimacy.

The bad news is that we are in trouble. There is much violence against   31 us, pornography-inspired. They make us, our bodies, pornography in their magazines and tell the normal men to get us good. We are followed, attacked, threatened. Bullets were shot into one feminist antipornography center. Feminists have been harassed out of their homes, forced to move. And the pornographers have found a bunch of girls (as the women call themselves) to work for them: not the chickenshit liberals, but real collaborators who have organized specifically to oppose the civil rights legislation and to protect the pornographers from our political activism — pornography should not be a feminist issue, these so-called feminists say. They say: Pornography is misogynist *but* . . . The *but* in this case is that it derepresses us. The victims of pornography can testify, and have, that when men get derepressed, women get hurt. These women say they are feminists. Some have worked for the defeated Equal Rights Amendment or for abortion rights or for equal pay or for lesbian and gay rights. But these days, they organize to stop us from stopping the pornographers.

Most of the women who say they are feminists but work to protect   32 pornography are lawyers or academics: lawyers like the ones who walked away from *Snuff*; academics who think prostitution is romantic, an unrepressed female sexuality. But whoever they are, whatever they think they are doing, the outstanding fact about them is that they are ignoring the women who have been hurt in order to help the pimps who do the hurting. They are collaborators, not feminists.

The pornographers may well destroy us. The violence against us — in   33 the pornography, in the general media, among men — is escalating rapidly and dangerously. Sometimes our despair is horrible. We haven't given in yet. There is a resistance here, a real one. I can't tell you how brave and brilliant the resisters are. Or how powerless and hurt. Surely it is clear: The most powerless women, the most exploited women, are the women fighting the pornographers. Our more privileged sisters prefer not to take sides. It's a nasty fight, all right. Feminism is dying here because so many women who say they are feminists are collaborators or cowards. Feminism is magnificent and militant here because the most powerless women are putting their lives on the line to confront the most powerful men for the sake of all women. Be proud of us for fighting. Be proud of us for getting so far. Help us if you can. The pornographers will have to stop us. We will not give in. They know that and now so do you.

Love,
Andrea Dworkin

Analyzing This Selection

1. Describe the tone and explain the effect on you of Dworkin's letter. What did you find disturbing?

2. What is the effect of the statistics cited in the first paragraph? According to the author, why aren't these facts better known?

3. **THE WRITER'S METHOD** In the essay as a whole, how does Dworkin show that reading and viewing pornography affect men's actual behavior? Which kinds of evidence are more convincing, and why?

4. What does Dworkin imply by the terms "radical" and "liberal"? What do these terms mean to you? Does either term apply to you?

5. What is the author's recommendation for dealing legally with pornography? What has frustrated such attempts?

Analyzing Connections

6. Dworkin and Goodman (see "The Luck Business," p. 442) strongly oppose accepted practices and legal businesses, but they address audiences differently. How is the sense of an audience reflected in each writer's approach? Compare their tones and methods of persuasion. Keep in mind the difference in issues.

Analyzing by Writing

7. Examine mixed attitudes about sex in a recent issue of *Playboy* or *Cosmopolitan* magazine (or another glossy magazine that has an erotic but socially acceptable appeal). Take into consideration not only the articles and the photographs but also the advertising. Analyze the tone and other connotations as well as what is explicitly said and pictured. You will probably find a wide range of attitudes, from pleasing to offensive and from exalting to degrading, that will require careful differentiation. Try to identify and define different kinds and levels of erotic appeal to the audience.

PART 9

DILEMMAS

INSIGHTS

If I had to choose between betraying my country and betraying my friend, I hope I should have the guts to betray my country.

— E. M. FORSTER

It is not difficult to make peace with friends. It is difficult to make peace with your enemy.

— A SAYING OFTEN REPEATED BY YITZHAK RABIN

In our age there is no such thing as "keeping out of politics." All issues are political issues, and politics itself is a mass of lies, evasions, folly, hatred, and schizophrenia. When the general atmosphere is bad, language must suffer. . . . Political language — and with variations this is true of all political parties, from Conservatives to Anarchists — is designed to make lies sound truthful and murder respectable, and to give an appearance of solidity to pure wind.

— GEORGE ORWELL

It is hard for a free fish to understand what is happening to a hooked one.

— KARL MENNINGER

Our treatment of both older people and children reflects the value we place on independence and autonomy. We do our best to make our children independent from birth. We leave them all alone in rooms with the lights out and tell them, "Go to sleep by yourselves." And the old people we respect most are the ones who will fight for their independence, who would sooner starve to death than ask for help.

— MARGARET MEAD

The Road Not Taken

Two roads diverged in a yellow wood,
And sorry I could not travel both
And be one traveller, long I stood
And looked down one as far as I could
To where it bent in the undergrowth;

Then took the other, as just as fair,
And having perhaps the better claim,
Because it was grassy and wanted wear;
Though as for that the passing there
Had worn them really about the same,

And both that morning equally lay
In leaves no step had trodden black.
Oh, I kept the first for another day!
Yet knowing how way leads on to way,
I doubted if I should ever come back.

I shall be telling this with a sigh
Somewhere ages and ages hence:
Two roads diverged in a wood, and I —
I took the one less travelled by,
And that has made all the difference.

— ROBERT FROST

No trumpets sound when the important decisions of our life are made. Destiny is made known silently.

— AGNES DE MILLE

FOCUSING BY WRITING

1. Consider the pros and cons of offering payment for body parts to increase their supply. As medical technology develops better ways to transplant organs and tissues, their monetary value to sellers as well as buyers could soar. Legal commerce and illegal markets could swell the supply to meet demands. We offer payment for human blood, why not for skin? for an eye, a kidney, a lung, a liver, or a heart? Argue for the principle of prohibiting or regulating payment for body parts.

2. Where did you go right or wrong in life? Develop your second thoughts about a choice, a direction, or an action you once took that you now see from a different perspective. What was the strongest factor in your decision at the time? What other factor would gain importance now? As you look back on the decision or action, do you now feel mainly regret, pride, embarrassment, relief, resentment, nostalgia, resignation, or some other emotion?

3. We are asked to support, endorse, or contribute to many more good causes than we actually join in. How do you usually decide? Does your response depend mainly on the issue involved, the people involved, or the possible misinterpretations of your support or refusal? Examine all the elements that entered your recent decision to participate or not to participate in a cause.

4. Should restrictions on alcohol advertisements be removed? Or should restrictions be broadened to include beer? Consider that among college students drinking is often connected to accidental deaths, serious injuries, and sexual assaults. What, if anything, should be done to increase, modify, or deregulate the advertising of alcohol?

Sallie Tisdale

WE DO ABORTIONS HERE

SALLIE TISDALE (b. 1957) received her degree in nursing at the University of Portland in Oregon. She has written two books about health care and the nursing profession: *The Sorcerer's Apprentice* (1986) and *Harvest Moon* (1987). Her writings about the impact of nature on history, and the impact of humanity on nature, include *Lot's Wife: Salt and the Human Condition* (1988) and *Stepping Westward: The Long Search for Home in the Pacific Northwest* (1991). Her most recent book is *Talk Dirty to Me: An Intimate Philosophy of Sex* (1994). Tisdale was a registered nurse in an abortion clinic when she wrote the following reflections about the tasks, the suffering, and the moral issues involved in that work.

We do abortions here; that is all we do. There are weary, grim moments 1 when I think I cannot bear another basin of bloody remains, utter another kind phrase of reassurance. So I leave the procedure room in the back and reach for a new chart. Soon I am talking to an eighteen-year-old woman pregnant for the fourth time. I push up her sleeve to check her blood pressure and find row upon row of needle marks, neat and parallel and discolored. She has been so hungry for her drug for so long that she has taken to using the loose skin of her upper arms; her elbows are already a permanent ruin of bruises. She is surprised to find herself nearly four months pregnant. I suspect she is often surprised, in a mild way, by the blows she is dealt. I prepare myself for another basin, another brief and chafing loss.

"How can you stand it?" Even the clients ask. They see the machine, 2 the strange instruments, the blood, the final stroke that wipes away the promise of pregnancy. Sometimes I see that too: I watch a woman's swollen abdomen sink to softness in a few stuttering moments and my own belly flip-flops with sorrow. But all it takes for me to catch my breath is another interview, one more story that sounds so much like the last one. There is a numbing sameness lurking in this job: the same questions, the same answers, even the same trembling tone in the voices. The worst is the sameness of human failure, of inadequacy in the face of each day's dull demands.

In describing this work, I find it difficult to explain how much I enjoy it 3 most of the time. We laugh a lot here, as friends and as professional peers. It's nice to be with women all day. I like the sudden, transient bonds I forge

471

with some clients: moments when I am in my strength, remembering weakness, and a woman in weakness reaches out for my strength. What I offer is not power, but solidness, offered almost eagerly. Certain clients waken in me every tender urge I have — others make me wince and bite my tongue. Both challenge me to find a balance. It is a sweet brutality we practice here, a stark and loving dispassion.

I look at abortion as if I am standing on a cliff with a telescope, gazing 4 at some great vista. I can sweep the horizon with both eyes, survey the scene in all its distance and size. Or I can put my eye to the lens and focus on the small details, suddenly so close. In abortion the absolute must always be tempered by the contextual, because both are real, both valid, both hard. How can we do this? How can we refuse? Each abortion is a measure of our failure to protect, to nourish our own. Each basin I empty is a promise — but a promise broken a long time ago.

I grew up on the great promise of birth control. Like many women my 5 age, I took the pill as soon as I was sexually active. To risk pregnancy when it was so easy to avoid seemed stupid, and my contraceptive success, as it were, was part of the promise of social enlightenment. But birth control fails, far more frequently than laboratory trials predict. Many of our clients take the pill; its failure to protect them is a shocking realization. We have clients who have been sterilized, whose husbands have had vasectomies; each one is a statistical misfit, fine print come to life. The anger and shame of these women I hold in one hand, and the basin in the other. The distance between the two, the length I pace and try to measure, is the size of an abortion.

The procedure is disarmingly simple. Women are surprised, as though 6 the mystery of conception, a dark and hidden genesis, requires an elaborate finale. In the first trimester of pregnancy, it's a mere few minutes of vacuuming, a neat tidying up. I give a woman a small yellow Valium, and when it has begun to relax her, I lead her into the back, into bareness, the stirrups. The doctor reaches in her, opening the narrow tunnel to the uterus with a succession of slim, smooth bars of steel. He inserts a plastic tube and hooks it to a hose on the machine. The woman is framed against white paper that crackles as she moves, the light bright in her eyes. Then the machine rumbles low and loud in the small windowless room; the doctor moves the tube back and forth with an efficient rhythm, and the long tail of it fills with blood that spurts and stumbles along into a jar. He is usually finished in a few minutes. They are long minutes for the woman; her uterus frequently reacts to its abrupt emptying with a powerful, unceasing cramp, which cuts off the blood vessels and enfolds the irritated, bleeding tissue.

I am learning to recognize the shadows that cross the faces of the 7 women I hold. While the doctor works between her spread legs, the paper drape hiding his intent expression, I stand beside the table. I hold the woman's hands in mine, resting them just below her ribs. I watch her eyes, finger her necklace, stroke her hair. I ask about her job, her family; in a haze she answers me; we chatter, faces close, eyes meeting and sliding apart.

I watch the shadows that creep up unnoticed and suddenly darken her 8 face as she screws up her features and pushes a tear out each side to slide down her cheeks. I have learned to anticipate the quiver of chin, the rapid intake of breath, and the surprising sobs that rise soon after the machine starts to drum. I know this is when the cramp deepens, and the tears are partly the tears that follow pain — the sharp, childish crying when one bumps one's head on a cabinet door. But a well of woe seems to open beneath many women when they hear that thumping sound. The anticipation of the moment has finally come to fruit; the moment has arrived when the loss is no longer an imagined one. It has come true.

I am struck by the sameness and I am struck every day by the variety 9 here — how this commonplace dilemma can so display the differences of women. A twenty-one-year-old woman, unemployed, uneducated, without family, in the fifth month of her pregnancy. A forty-two-year-old mother of teenagers, shocked by her condition, refusing to tell her husband. A twenty-three-year-old mother of two having her seventh abortion, and many women in their thirties having their first. Some are stoic, some hysterical, a few giggle uncontrollably, many cry.

I talk to a sixteen-year-old uneducated girl who was raped. She has gon- 10 orrhea. She describes blinding headaches, attacks of breathlessness, nausea. "Sometimes I feel like two different people," she tells me with a calm smile, "and I talk to myself."

I pull out my plastic models. She listens patiently for a time, and then 11 holds out her hands wide in front of her stomach.

"When's the baby going to go up into my stomach?" she asks. 12

I blink. "What do you mean?" 13

"Well," she says, still smiling, "when women get so big, isn't the baby in 14 your stomach? Doesn't it hatch out of an egg there?"

My first question in an interview is always the same. As I walk down the 15 hall with the woman, as we get settled in chairs and I glance through her files, I am trying to gauge her, to get a sense of the words, and the tone, I should use. With some I joke, and others I chat, sometimes I fall into a brisk, business-like patter. But I ask every woman, "Are you sure you want to have an abortion?" Most nod with grim knowing smiles. "Oh, yes," they sigh. Some seek forgiveness, offer excuses. Occasionally a woman will flinch and say, "Please don't use that word."

Later I describe the procedure to come, using care with my language. I 16 don't say "pain" any more than I would say "baby." So many are afraid to ask how much it will hurt. "My sister told me —" I hear. "A friend of mine said —" and the dire expectations unravel. I prick the index finger of a woman for a drop of blood to test, and as the tiny lancet approaches the skin she averts her eyes, holding her trembling hand out to me and jumping at my touch.

It is when I am holding a plastic uterus in one hand, a suction tube in 17 the other, moving them together in imitation of the scrubbing to come, that women ask the most secret question. I am speaking in a matter-of-fact voice about "the tissue" and "the contents" when the woman suddenly catches my eye and asks, "How big is the baby now?" These words suggest a quiet need for a definition of the boundaries being drawn. It isn't so odd, after all, that she feels relief when I describe the growing bud's bulbous shape, its miniature nature. Again I gauge, and sometimes lie a little, weaseling around its infantile features until its clinging power slackens.

But when I look in the basin, among the curdlike blood clots, I see an   18
elfin thorax, attenuated, its pencilline ribs all in parallel rows with tiny knobs of spine rounding upwards. A translucent arm and hand swim beside.

A sleepy-eyed girl, just fourteen, watched me with a slight and goofy   19
smile all through her abortion. "Does it have little feet and little fingers and all?" she'd asked earlier. When the suction was over she sat up woozily at the end of the table and murmured, "Can I see it?" I shook my head firmly.

"It's not allowed," I told her sternly, because I knew she didn't really   20
want to see what was left. She accepted this statement of authority, and a shadow of confused relief crossed her plain, pale face.

Privately, even grudgingly, my colleagues might admit the power of   21
abortion to provoke emotion. But they seem to prefer the broad view and disdain the telescope. Abortion is a matter of choice, privacy, control. Its uncertainty lies in specific cases: retarded women and girls too young to give consent for surgery, women who are ill or hostile or psychotic. Such common dilemmas are met with both compassion and impatience; they slow things down. We are too busy to chew over ethics. One person might discuss certain concerns, behind closed doors, or describe a particularly disturbing dream. But generally there is to be no ambivalence.

Every day I take calls from women who are annoyed that we cannot see   22
them, cannot do their abortion today, this morning, now. They argue the price, demand that we stay after hours to accommodate their job or class schedule. Abortion is so routine that one expects it to be like a manicure; quick, cheap, and painless.

Still, I've cultivated a certain disregard. It isn't negligence, but I don't   23
always pay attention. I couldn't be here if I tried to judge each case on its merits; after all, we do over a hundred abortions a week. At some point each individual in this line of work draws a boundary and adheres to it. For one physician the boundary is a particular week of gestation; for another, it is a certain number of repeated abortions. But these boundaries can be fluid too: One physician overruled his own limit to abort a mature but severely malformed fetus. For me, the limit is allowing my clients to carry their own burden, shoulder the responsibility themselves. I shoulder the burden of trying not to judge them.

This city has several "crisis pregnancy centers" advertised in the Yellow   24
Pages. They are small offices staffed by volunteers, and they offer free preg-

nancy testing, glossy photos of dead fetuses, and movies. I had a client recently whose mother is active in the antiabortion movement. The young woman went to the local crisis center and was told that the doctor would make her touch her dismembered baby, that the pain would be the most horrible she could imagine, and that she might, after an abortion, never be able to have children. All lies. They called her at home and at work, over and over and over, but she had been wise enough to give a false name. She came to us a fugitive. We who do abortions are marked, by some, as impure. It's dirty work.

When a deliveryman comes to the sliding glass window by the reception   25 desk and tilts a box toward me, I hesitate. I read the packing slips, assess the shape and weight of the box in the light of its supposed contents. We request familiar faces. The doors are carefully locked; I have learned to half glance around at bags and boxes, looking for a telltale sign. I register with security when I arrive, and I am careful not to bang a door. We are a little on edge here.

Concern about size and shape seem to be natural, and so is the relief   26 that follows. We make the powerful assumption that the fetus is different from us, and even when we admit the similarities, it is too simplistic to be seduced by form alone. But the form is enormously potent — humanoid, powerless, palm-sized, and pure, it evokes an almost fierce tenderness when viewed simply as what it appears to be. But appearance, and even potential, aren't enough. The fetus, in becoming itself, can ruin others; its utter dependence has a sinister side. When I am struck in the moment by the contents in the basin, I am careful to remember the context, to note the tearful teenager and the woman sighing with something more than relief. One kind of question, though, I find considerably trickier.

"Can you tell what it is?" I am asked, and this means gender. This ques-   27 tion is asked by couples, not women alone. Always couples would abort a girl and keep a boy. I have been asked about twins, and even if I could tell what race the father was.

An eighteen-year-old woman with three daughters brought her husband   28 to the interview. He glared first at me, then at his wife, as he sank lower and lower in the chair, picking his teeth with a toothpick. He interrupted a conversation with his wife to ask if I could tell whether the baby would be a boy or a girl. I told him I could not.

"Good," he replied in a slow and strangely malevolent voice, "'cause if   29 it was a boy I'd wring her neck."

In a literal sense, abortion exists because we are able to ask such ques-   30 tions, able to assign a value to the fetus which can shift with changing circumstances. If the human bond to a child were as primitive and unflinchingly narrow as that of other animals, there would be no abortion. There would be no abortion because there would be nothing more impor- tant than caring for the young and perpetuating the species, no reason for sex but to make babies. I sense this sometimes, this wordless organic duty, when I do ultrasounds.

We do ultrasound, a sound-wave test that paints a faint, gray picture of   31 the fetus, whenever we're uncertain of gestation. Age is measured by the width of the skull and confirmed by the length of the femur or thighbone; we speak of a pregnancy as being a certain "femur length" in weeks. The usual concern is whether a pregnancy is within the legal limit for an abortion. Women this far along have bellies which swell out round and tight like trim muscles. When they lie flat, the mound rises softly above the hips, pressing the umbilicus upward.

It takes practice to read an ultrasound picture, which is grainy and   32 etched as though in strokes of charcoal. But suddenly a rapid rhythmic motion appears — the beating heart. Nearby is a soft oval, scratched with lines — the skull. The leg is harder to find, and then suddenly the fetus moves, bobbing in the surf. The skull turns away, an arm slides across the screen, the torso rolls. I know the weight of a baby's head on my shoulder, the whisper of lips on ears, the delicate curve of a fragile spine in my hand. I know how heavy and correct a newborn cradled feels. The creature I watch in secret requires nothing from me but to be left alone, and that is precisely what won't be done.

These inadvertently made beings are caught in a twisting web of motive   33 and desire. They are at least inconvenient, sometimes quite literally dangerous in the womb, but most often they fall somewhere in between — consequences never quite believed in come to roost. Their virtue rises and falls outside their own nature: They become only what we make them. A fetus created by accident is the most absolute kind of surprise. Whether the blame lies in a failed IUD, a slipped condom, or a false impression of safety, that fetus is a thing whose creation has been actively worked against. Its existence is an error. I think this is why so few women, even late in a pregnancy, will consider giving a baby up for adoption. To do so means making the fetus real — imagining it as something whole and outside oneself. The decision to terminate a pregnancy is sometimes so difficult and confounding that it creates an enormous demand for immediate action. The decision is a rejection; the pregnancy has become something to be rid of, a condition to be ended. It is a burden, a weight, a thing separate.

Women have abortions because they are too old, and too young, too   34 poor, and too rich, too stupid, and too smart. I see women who berate themselves with violent emotions for their first and only abortion, and others who return three times, five times, hauling two or three children, who cannot remember to take a pill or where they put the diaphragm. We talk glibly about choice. But the choice for what? I see all the broken promises in lives lived like a series of impromptu obstacles. There are the sweet, light promises of love and intimacy, the glittering promise of education and progress, the warm promise of safe families, long years of innocence and community. And there is the promise of freedom: freedom from failure, from faithlessness. Freedom from biology. The early feminist defense of abortion asked many questions, but the one I remember is this: Is biology destiny? And the answer is yes, sometimes it is. Women who have the fewest choices of all exercise their right to abortion the most.

Oh, the ignorance. I take a woman to the back room and ask her to 35 undress; a few minutes later I return and find her positioned discreetly behind a drape, still wearing underpants. "Do I have to take these off too?" she asks, a little shocked. Some swear they have not had sex, many do not know what a uterus is, how sperm and egg meet, how sex makes babies. Some late seekers do not believe themselves pregnant; they believe themselves *impregnable.* I was chastised when I began this job for referring to some clients as girls: It is a feminist heresy. They come so young, snapping gum, sockless and sneakered, and their shakily applied eyeliner smears when they cry. I call them girls with maternal benignity. I cannot imagine them as mothers.

The doctor seats himself between the woman's thighs and reaches into 36 the dilated opening of a five-month pregnant uterus. Quickly he grabs and crushes the fetus in several places, and the room is filled with a low clatter and snap of forceps, the click of the tanaculum, and a pulling, sucking sound. The paper crinkles as the drugged and sleepy woman shifts, the nurse's low, honey-brown voice explains each step in delicate words.

I have fetus dreams, we all do here: dreams of abortions one after the 37 other; of buckets of blood splashed on the walls; trees full of crawling fetuses. I dreamed that two men grabbed me and began to drag me away: "Let's do an abortion," they said with a sickening leer, and I began to scream, plunged into a vision of sucking, scraping pain, of being spread and torn by impartial instruments that do only what they are bidden. I woke from this dream barely able to breathe and thought of kitchen tables and coat hangers, knitting needles striped with blood, and women all alone clutching a pillow in their teeth to keep the screams from piercing the apartment-house walls. Abortion is the narrowest edge between kindness and cruelty. Done as well as it can be, it is still violence — merciful violence, like putting a suffering animal to death.

Maggie, one of the nurses, received a call at midnight not long ago. It 38 was a woman in her twentieth week of pregnancy; the necessarily gradual process of cervical dilation begun the day before had stimulated labor, as it sometimes does. Maggie and one of the doctors met the woman at the office in the night. Maggie helped her onto the table, and as she lay down the fetus was delivered into Maggie's hands. When Maggie told me about it the next day, she cupped her hands into a small bowl — "It was just like a small kitten," she said softly, wonderingly. "Everything was still attached."

At the end of the day I clean out the suction jars, pouring blood into the 39 sink, splashing the sides with flecks of tissue. From the sink rises a rich and humid smell, hot, earthy, and moldering; it is the smell of something recently alive beginning to decay. I take care of the plastic tub on the floor, filled with pieces too big to be trusted to the trash. The law defines the contents of the bucket I hold protectively against my chest as "tissue." Some would say my complicity in filling that bucket gives me no right to call it anything else. I slip the tissue gently into a bag and place it in the freezer, to be burned at another time. Abortion requires of me an entirely new set of assumptions. It requires a willingness to live with conflict, fearlessness, and grief. As I close the freezer door, I imagine a world where this won't be necessary, and then return to the world where it is.

Analyzing This Selection

1. **THE WRITER'S METHOD**   In the detailed description of an abortion, what does the author want the reader to recognize? How does her description affect you?

2. What attitude toward her clients does Tisdale reject? What attitude does she uphold? What problems does she have in controlling her attitudes? How do your responses to her clients differ from hers?

3. Explain Tisdale's stance on the public controversy over abortion. What is her attitude toward antiabortionists?

4. What is the author's outlook on humanity? What generalizations does Tisdale assert or imply about the human race?

Analyzing Connections

5. Should Tisdale quit her job? Compare her work problems with Ullman's reasons to quit programming (see "Getting Close to the Machine," p. 430). Whose job would you find more distressing?

Analyzing by Writing

6. Examine a controversy over abortion within a community, group, or family you know. What issues became important? How were disagreements handled? Present views on both sides fairly. If possible, include details from Tisdale's essay to illustrate how she regards these issues. Explain your own perspective.

Peter Marin

THE PREJUDICE AGAINST MEN

PETER MARIN (b. 1936) is an essayist and novelist living in Santa Barbara, California. He took his undergraduate degree from Swarthmore
College and his M.A. from Columbia University, both in literature. His
books include an autobiographical novel *In a Man's Time* (1972), *The
Limits of Schooling* (1975), and *The World of the Homeless* (1986). Marin
has received a Guggenheim Fellowship and other major awards. His articles appear in a wide range of national periodicals, and since 1982 he has
been a contributing editor to *Harper's*. The following essay appeared in
the *Nation* in 1991.

For the past several years advocates for the homeless have sought public 1
support and sympathy by drawing attention to the large number of homeless families on our streets. That is an understandable tactic. Americans
usually respond to social issues on the basis of sympathy for "innocent" victims — those whose blamelessness touches our hearts and whom we deem
unable to care for themselves. Families, and especially children, obviously
fill the bill.

But the fact remains, despite the claims of advocates, that the problem 2
of chronic homelessness is essentially a problem of *single adult men*. Far
more single adults than families, and far more men than women, end up
homeless on our streets. Until we understand how and why that happens,
nothing we do about homelessness will have much of an impact.

Most figures pertaining to the homeless come from limited studies or 3
educated guesses that tend, when examined, to dissolve in one's hand. The
most convincing figures I know can be found in James Wright's book
Address Unknown: The Homeless in America. According to Wright's data, out
of every 1,000 homeless people in America, 120 or so will be adults with
children, another hundred will be children, and the rest will be single
adults. Out of that total, 156 will be single women and 580 will be
single men. Now break that down into percentages. Out of all single homeless adults, 78 percent are men; out of all homeless adults, more than 64
percent are single men; and out of all homeless people — adults or children — 58 percent are single men.

But even those figures do not give the full story. Our federal welfare sys- 4
tem has been designed, primarily, to aid women with children or whole

families. That means that most of the families and children on the streets have either fallen through the cracks of the welfare system or have not yet entered it. They will, in the end, have access to enough aid to get them off the streets and into some form of shelter, while most men will be left permanently on their own.

I do not mean to diminish here the suffering of families or children, nor 5
to suggest that welfare provides much more than the meanest alternative to homelessness. It is a form of indentured pauperism so grim it shames the nation. But it does in fact eventually get most families off the streets, and that leaves behind, as the chronically homeless, single adults, of whom four-fifths are men. Seen that way, homelessness emerges as a problem involving what happens to men without money, or men in trouble.

Why do so many more men than women end up on the streets? Let me 6
begin with the simplest answers.

First, life on the streets, as dangerous as it is for men, is even more 7
dangerous for women, who are far more vulnerable. While many men in trouble drift almost naturally onto the streets, women do almost anything to avoid it.

Second, there are far better private and public shelters and services avail- 8
able to women.

Third, women are accustomed to asking for help while men are not; 9
women therefore make better use of available resources.

Fourth, poor families *in extremis* seem to practice a form of informal 10
triage. Young men are released into the streets more readily, while young women are kept at home even in the worst circumstances.

Fifth, there are cultural and perhaps even genetic factors at work. There 11
is some evidence that men — especially in adolescence — are more aggressive and openly rebellious than women and therefore harder to socialize. Or it may simply be that men are allowed to live out the impulses women are taught to suppress, and that they therefore end up more often in marginal roles.

More important, still, may be the question of work. Historically, the 12
kinds of work associated with transient or marginal life have been reserved for men. They brought in crops, worked on ships and docks, built roads and railroads, logged and mined. Such labor granted them a place in the economy while allowing them to remain on society's edges — an option rarely available to women save through prostitution.

And society has always seemed, by design, to produce the men who did 13
such work. Obviously, poverty and joblessness forced men into marginality. But there was more to it than that. Schools produced failures, dropouts, and rebels; family life and its cruelties produced runaways and throwaways; wars rendered men incapable of settled or domestic life; small-town boredom and provinciality led them to look elsewhere for larger worlds.

Now, of course, the work such men did is gone. But like a mad engine 14 that cannot be shut down, society goes right on producing them. Its institutions function as they always did: The schools hum, the families implode or collapse, the wars churn out their victims. But what is there for them to do? The low-paying service-sector jobs that have replaced manual labor in the economy go mainly to women or high school kids, not the men who once did the nation's roughest work.

Remember, too, in terms of work, that women, especially when young, 15 have one final option denied to men. They can take on the "labor" of being wives and companions to men or of bearing children, and in return they will often be supported or "taken care of" by someone else. Yes, I know: Such roles can often constitute a form of oppression, especially when assumed out of necessity. But nonetheless, the possibility is there. It is permissible (as well as often necessary) for women to become financially, if precariously, dependent on others, while such dependence is more or less forbidden to men.

Finally, there is the federal welfare system. I do not think most Ameri- 16 cans understand how the system works, or how for decades it has actually sent men into the streets, creating at least some male homelessness while aiding women and children. Let me explain. There are two main programs that provide care for Americans in trouble. One is Social Security Disability Insurance. It goes to men or women who are unable, because of physical or mental problems, to work or take care of themselves. The other is Aid to Families with Dependent Children (AFDC). It is what we ordinarily call "welfare." With its roots early in this century, it was established more or less in its present form during the Depression. Refined and expanded again in the 1960s, AFDC had always been a program meant mainly for women and children and limited to households headed by women. As long as an adult man remained in the household as mate, companion, or father, *no aid was forthcoming.* Changes have recently been made in the system, and men may remain in the household if they have a work history satisfying certain federal guidelines. But in poor areas and for certain ethnic groups, where unemployment runs high and few men have a qualifying work history, these changes have not yet had much of an impact and men remain functionally outside the welfare system.

When it comes to single and "able-bodied," or employable, adults, there 17 is no federal aid whatsoever. Individual states and localities sometimes provide their own aid through "general assistance" and "relief." But this is usually granted only on a temporary basis or in emergencies. And in those few places where it is available for longer periods to large numbers of single adults — California, for instance, or New York — it is often so grudging, so ringed round with capricious requirements and red tape, that it is of little use to those in need.

This combination of approaches not only systematically denies men aid 18 as family members or single adults. It means that the aid given to women has sometimes actually deprived men of homes, even as it has provided for women and children. Given the choice between receiving aid for themselves and their children and living with men, what do you think most women do? The regulations as they stand actually force men to compete with the state for women; as a woman in New Orleans once told me: "Welfare changes even love. If a man can't make more at a job than I get from welfare, I ain't even gonna look at him. I can't afford it."

Everywhere in America poor men have been forced to become ghost- 19 lovers and ghost-fathers, one step ahead of welfare workers ready to disqualify families for having a man around. In many ghettos throughout the country you find women and children in their deteriorating welfare apartments, and their male companions and fathers in even worse conditions: homeless in gutted apartments and abandoned cars, denied even the minimal help granted the opposite sex.

Is it surprising, in this context, that many African Americans see welfare 20 as an extension of slavery that destroys families, isolates women, and humiliates men according to white bureaucratic whim? Or is it accidental that in poor communities family structure has collapsed and more and more children are born outside marriage at precisely the same time that disfranchised men are flooding the streets? Welfare is not the only influence at work in all of this, of course. But before judging men and their failures and difficulties, one must understand that their social roles are in no way supported or made easier by the social policies that in small ways make female roles sustainable.

Is this merely an accidental glitch in the system, something that has hap- 21 pened unnoticed? Or does it merely have something to do with a sort of lifeboat ethic, where our scarce resources for helping people are applied according to the ethics of a sinking ship — women and children first, men into the sea?

I do not think so. Something else is at work: deep-seated prejudices and 22 attitudes toward men that are so pervasive, so pandemic, that we have ceased to notice or examine them.

To put it simply: Men are neither supposed nor allowed to be depen- 23 dent. They are expected to take care of both others *and* themselves. And when they cannot do it, or "will not" do it, the built-in assumption at the heart of the culture is that they are *less than men* and therefore unworthy of help. An irony asserts itself: Simply by being in need of help, men forfeit the right to it.

Think here of how we say "helpless as a woman." This demeans women. 24 But it also does violence to men. It implies that a man cannot be helpless and still be a man, or that helplessness is not a male attribute, or that a woman can be helpless through no fault of her own, but that if a man is helpless it is or must be his own fault.

Try something here. Imagine walking down a street and passing a group 25 of homeless women. Do we not spontaneously see them as victims and wonder what has befallen them, how destiny has injured them? Do we not see them as unfortunate and deserving of help and *want* to help them?

Now imagine a group of homeless men. Is our reaction the same? Is it 26 as sympathetic? Or is it subtly different? Do we have the very same impulse to help and protect? Or do we not wonder, instead of what befell them, how they have got themselves where they are?

And remember, too, our fear. When most of us see homeless or idle 27 men we sense or imagine danger; they make us afraid, as if, being beyond the pale, they are also beyond all social control — and therefore people to be avoided and suppressed rather than helped.

Here too work plays a crucial role. In his memoirs Hamlin Garland 28 describes the transient farm workers who passed through the countryside each year at harvest time. In good years, when there were crops to bring in, they were tolerated: fed, housed, and hired. But when the crops were bad and men weren't needed, then they were forced to stay outside of town or pass on unaided, having become merely threats to peace and order, barbarians at the gates.

The same attitude is with us still. When men work (or when they go to 29 war — work's most brutal form), we grant them a right to exist. But when work is scarce, or when men are of little economic use, then they become in our eyes not only superfluous but a danger. We feel compelled to exile them from our midst, banish them from view, drive them away to shift for themselves in more or less the same way that our Puritan forebears, in their shining city on its hill, treated sinners and rebels.

One wonders just how far back such attitudes go. One thinks of the 30 Bible and the myth of the Garden and the first disobedience, when women were cursed with childbirth and men with the sorrows of labor — destinies still, as if by intention, maintained by our welfare system and private attitudes.

And one thinks too of the Victorian era, when the idealized vision of 31 women and children had its modern beginnings. They were set outside the industrial nexus and freed from heavy labor while being rendered more than ever dependent on and subservient to men. It was a process that obviously diminished women, but it had a parallel effect on men. It defined them as laborers and little else, especially if they came from the lower classes. The yoke of labor lifted from the shoulders of women settled even more heavily on the backs of certain men, confining them in roles as narrow and as oppressive as those to which women were assigned.

We are so used to thinking of ours as a male-dominated society that we 32 tend to lose track of the ways in which some men are as oppressed, or perhaps even more oppressed, than most women. But race and class, as well as gender, play roles in oppression. And while it is true, in general, that men dominate society and women, in practice it is only *certain* men who are dominant; others, usually those from the working class and often darker skinned (at least 50 percent of homeless men are black or Latino), suffer endlessly from forms of isolation and contempt that often exceed what many women experience.

The irony at work in all of this is that what you often find among home- 33 less men, and what seems at the heart of their troubles, is precisely what our cultural myths deny them: a helplessness they cannot overcome on their own. You find vulnerability, a sense of injury and betrayal and, in their isolation, a despair equal to what we accept without question in women.

Often this goes unadmitted. Even when in deep trouble men under- 34 stand, sometimes unconsciously, that they are not to complain or ask for help. I remember several men I knew in the local hobo jungle. Most of them were vets. They had constructed a tiny village of half-caves and shelters among the trees and brush, and when stove smoke filled the clearing and they stood bare to the waist, knives at their hips, you would swear you were in an army jungle camp. They drank throughout the day, and at dusk there always came a moment when they wandered off individually to sit staring out at the mountains or sea. And you could see on their faces at such moments, if you caught them unawares, a particular and unforgettable look: pensive, troubled, somehow innocent — the look of lost children or abandoned men.

I have seen the same look multiplied hundreds of times on winter nights 35 in huge shelters in great cities, where a thousand men at a time will sometimes gather, each encapsulated in solitude on a bare cot, coughing and turning or sometimes crying all night, lost in nightmares as terrible as a child's or as life on the street. In the mornings they returned to their masked public personas, to the styles of behavior and appearance that often frightened passers-by. But while they slept you could see past all that, and you found yourself thinking: These are still, even grown, *somebody's* children, and many fare no better on their own, as adults, than they would have as children.

I remember, too, a young man in my town who was always in trouble for 36 beating up older drunken men. No one understood his brutality until he explained it one day to a woman he trusted: "When I was a kid my daddy ran off and my mother's drunken brothers disciplined me. Whenever I made a mistake they punished me by slicing my legs with a straight razor." And he pulled up his pant-legs to reveal on each shin a ladder of scars marking each childhood error or flaw.

This can stand for countless stories I've heard. The feeling you get, over 37 and over, is that most men on the street have been "orphaned" in some way, deprived somewhere along the line of the kinds of connection, support, and sustenance that enable people to find and keep places in the social order. Of course economics plays a part in this — I do not mean to suggest it does not. But more often than not, something else is also at work, something that cuts close to the bone of social and psychological as well as economic issues: the dissolution of family structures and the vitiation of community; subtle and overt forms of discrimination and racism; and institutions — schools, for instance — that harm or marginalize almost as many people as they help.

For decades now, sociologists have called our attention to rents in our 38 private social fabric as well as our public "safety nets," and to the victims they produce: abused kids, battered women, isolated adults, alcoholics, addicts. Why, I wonder, is it so hard to see homeless men in this context? Why is it so hard to understand that the machinery of our institutions can injure men as permanently as it does women? We know, for instance, that both male and female children are permanently injured by familial abuse and violence and "normal" cruelties of family life. Why, then, do we find it hard to see that grown men, as well as women, can be crippled by childhood, or that they often end up on the edges of society, unable to play expected roles in a world that has betrayed them?

And do not forget here the greatest violence done to men, the tyrannous 39 demand made upon them when young by older and more powerful males: that they kill and die in war. We take that demand for granted in our society and for some reason fail to see it as a form of oppression. But why? Long before the war in Vietnam had crowded our streets with vets — as far back as the Civil War — the male victims of organized state violence wandered across America unable to find or make places in the social world. The fact is that many men never fully recover from the damage done by war, having seen too much of death to ever again do much with life.

Nor is war the only form in which death and disaster have altered the 40 lives of troubled men. They appear repeatedly in the stories men tell. Listening to these tales one thinks of Oedipus and Lear, of tragedy in its classical sense, of the furies and fates that the Greeks believed stalk all human lives and that are still at work among us, no matter how much we deny them.

Gene, a homeless man I know, was conceived when his mother slept 41 with his father's best friend. Neither of his parents wanted him, so he was raised reluctantly by his mother's parents, who saw him only as the living evidence of her disgrace. As an adult he married and divorced twice, had two children he rarely saw later in life, and spent two years in jail for beating nearly to death a friend he found in bed with his second wife. When I first met him he was living in a cave he had dug by hand out of a hillside, and he spent the money he earned on dope or his friends. But then he met a woman on the streets and they moved together to a cheap hotel. He got her pregnant; they planned to marry; but then they argued and she ran off and either had an abortion or spontaneously miscarried — it was never clear which. When Gene heard about it he took to his bed for days and would not sleep, eat, or speak. When I later asked him why, he said: "I couldn't stand it. I wanted to die. I was the baby she killed. It was happening to me all over again, that bad stuff back when I was a kid."

Not everything you hear on the street is so dramatic. There are a thou- 42
sand quiet and gradual ways American lives can fall apart or come to nothing. Often it is simply "normal" life that proves too much for some men.
Some have merely failed at or fled their assigned roles: worker, husband,
father. Others lacked whatever it takes to please a boss or a woman or else
decided it wasn't worth the trouble to learn how to do it. Not all of them
are "good" men. Some have brutalized women or left families in the lurch
or fled lives in which the responsibility and stress were more than they
could handle. "Couldn't hack it," they'll say with a shrug, or "I had to get
out." And others have been so cruel to women or proved so unreliable or
sometimes so unsuccessful that women fled them, leaving notes on the
table or refrigerator such as the one a man in Seattle once repeated to me:
"Gone. Took the kids. So long."

Are such men irresponsible? Perhaps. But in working with homeless 43
men over the years, I've seen how many of them are genuinely unable to
handle the stress others can tolerate. Many manage, for instance, to steer
clear of alcohol or drugs for a certain period of time and then return to them
automatically as soon as they are subject again to the kinds of stress they
once fled. It is as if their defenses and even their skins are so much thinner
than those of the rest of us that they give way as soon as trouble or too
much responsibility appears.

The fact is that most such men seem to have tried to make a go of 44
things, and many are willing to try again. But if others have given up and
said, inside, *the hell with it* or *fuck it,* is that really astonishing? The curious world we've compounded in America of equal parts of freedom and
isolation and individualism and demands for obedience and submission is
a strange and wearing mix, and no one can be startled at the number of
victims or recalcitrants it produces or at those who can't succeed at it.

Finally, I must add one more thing. Whatever particular griefs men 45
may have experienced on their way to homelessness, there is one final and
crippling sorrow all of them share: a sense of betrayal at society's refusal to
recognize their needs. Most of us — men and women — grow up expecting that when things go terribly wrong someone, from somewhere, will step
forward to help us. That this does not happen, and that all watch from the
shore as each of us, in isolation, struggles to swim and then begins to sink,
is perhaps the most terrible discovery that anyone in any society can make.
When troubled men make that discovery, as all homeless men do sooner or
later, then hope vanishes completely; despair rings them round; they have
become what they need not have become: the homeless men we see everywhere around us.

What can be done about this? What will set it right? One can talk, of 46
course, about confronting the root causes of marginalization: the failure
of families, schools, and communities; the stupidities of war, racism, and

discrimination; social and economic injustice; the disappearance of generosity and reciprocity among us. But what good will that do? America is what it is; culture has a tenacity of its own; and though it is easy to call for major kinds of renewal, nothing of the sort is likely to occur.

That leaves us with ameliorative and practical measures, and it will do 47 no harm to mention them, though they too are not likely to be tried: a further reformation of the welfare system; the federalization of assistance to single adults; increases in the amount and duration of unemployment insurance; further raises in the minimum wage; expanded benefits for vets; detox centers and vocational education for those who want them; the construction of the kinds of low-cost hotels and boarding houses where men in trouble once stayed.

And remember that back in the Depression when the welfare system was 48 established, it was paralleled by programs providing work for men: the Civilian Conservation Corps and the Works Progress Administration. The idea seems to have been welfare for women, work for men. We still have the welfare for women, but where is the work for those men, or women, who want it? Why no one is currently lobbying for contemporary forms of those old programs remains a mystery. Given the deterioration of the American infrastructure — roads, bridges, public buildings — such programs would make sense from any point of view.

But beyond all this, and behind and beneath it, there remains the prob- 49 lem with which we began: the prejudices at work in society that prevent even the attempt to provide solutions. Suggestions such as those I have made will remain merely utopian notions without an examination and renovation of our attitudes toward men. During the past several decades we have slowly, laboriously, begun to confront our prejudices and oppressive practices in relation to women. Unless we now undertake the same kind of project in relation to men in general and homeless men in particular, nothing whatever is going to change. That's as sure as death and taxes and the endless, hidden sorrows of men.

Analyzing This Selection

1. What historical changes in America's work force have increased male homelessness? According to Marin, what are society's "deep-seated prejudices" (paragraph 22) against homeless men?

2. **THE WRITER'S METHOD** What are Marin's criticisms of the welfare program? Why does he believe that welfare improvements "are not likely to be tried" (paragraph 47)? Have recent welfare changes reflected his hopes or doubts?

3. What do self-sustaining men gain and lose from the prejudice against homeless males?

Analyzing Connections

4. How does Marin's social analysis hold up when applied to Carver's father (see "My Father's Life," p. 67)? Did Carver's father have a "marginal" life? Was he affected by "the prejudice against men"?

Analyzing by Writing

5. Whose responsibility is it to provide care for the homeless? Should funds and programs come from cities where the homeless live? From state governments? From the federal government? From churches and philanthropic organizations? Consider the issues of race and gender Marin discusses. Persuasively explain your reasons for recommending one approach, without getting bogged down with details.

Jonathan Swift

A MODEST PROPOSAL

JONATHAN SWIFT (1667–1745) has been called "the greatest satirist in the English language." Born in Ireland to English parents, he was educated at Kilkenny School and Trinity College, Dublin, and later spent much of his time in England. An active participant in the political and literary life of London, Swift became a brilliant political pamphleteer. In 1713, he obtained the deanery of St. Patrick's Cathedral in Dublin and later published several books, including his masterpiece, *Gulliver's Travels* (1726). "A Modest Proposal," published in 1729, was Swift's response to extreme poverty in Ireland, brought on by drought and exploitation by the English, who controlled a large proportion of Irish farm land.

1   It is a melancholy object to those who walk through this great town or travel in the country, when they see the streets, the roads, and cabin doors, crowded with beggars of the female sex, followed by three, four, or six children, all in rags and importuning every passenger for an alms. These mothers, instead of being able to work for their honest livelihood, are forced to employ all their time in strolling to beg sustenance for their helpless infants, who, as they grow up, either turn thieves for want of work, or leave their dear native country to fight for the Pretender[1] in Spain, or sell themselves to the Barbados.[2]

2   I think it is agreed by all parties that this prodigious number of children in the arms, or on the backs, or at the heels of their mothers, and frequently of their fathers, is in the present deplorable state of the kingdom a very great additional grievance; and therefore whoever could find out a fair, cheap, or easy method of making these children sound, useful members of the commonwealth would deserve so well of the public as to have his statue set up for a preserver of the nation.

3   But my intention is very far from being confined to provide only for the children of professed beggars; it is of a much greater extent, and shall take in the whole number of infants at a certain age who are born of parents in

---

[1]*Pretender* James Edward Stuart (1688–1766), "the Old Pretender," a Catholic who claimed the British throne from exile in France.

[2]*Barbados* In Swift's time, many Irish sailed to Barbados, exchanging labor there for their passage.

effect as little able to support them as those who demand our charity in the streets.

As to my own part, having turned my thoughts for many years upon this 4 important subject, and maturely weighed the several schemes of other projectors, I have always found them grossly mistaken in their computation. It is true, a child just dropped from its dam may be supported by her milk for a solar year, with little other nourishment; at most not above the value of two shillings, which the mother may certainly get, or the value in scraps, by her lawful occupation of begging; and it is exactly at one year that I propose to provide for them in such a manner as instead of being a charge upon their parents or the parish, or wanting food and raiment for the rest of their lives, they shall on the contrary contribute to the feeding, and partly to the clothing, of many thousands.

There is likewise another great advantage in my scheme, that it will pre- 5 vent those voluntary abortions, and that horrid practice of women murdering their bastard children, alas, too frequent among us, sacrificing the poor innocent babes, I doubt, more to avoid the expense than the shame, which would move tears and pity in the most savage and inhuman breast.

The number of souls in this kingdom being usually reckoned one mil- 6 lion and a half, of these I calculate there may be about two hundred thousand couples whose wives are breeders; from which number I subtract thirty thousand couples who are able to maintain their own children, although I apprehend there cannot be so many under the present distress of the kingdom; but this being granted, there will remain an hundred and seventy thousand breeders. I again subtract fifty thousand of those women who miscarry, or whose children die by accident or disease within the year. There only remain an hundred and twenty thousand children of poor parents annually born. The question therefore is, how this number shall be reared and provided for, which, as I have already said, under the present situation of affairs, is utterly impossible by all the methods hitherto proposed. For we can neither employ them in handicraft or agriculture; we neither build houses (I mean in the country) nor cultivate land. They can very seldom pick up a livelihood by stealing till they arrive at six years old, except where they are of towardly parts; although I confess they learn the rudiments much earlier, during which time they can however be looked upon only as probationers, as I have been informed by a principal gentleman in the country of Cavan, who protested to me that he never knew above one or two instances under the age of six, even in a part of the kingdom so renowned for the quickest proficiency in that art.

I am assured by our merchants that a boy or a girl before twelve years 7 old is no salable commodity; and even when they come to this age they will not yield above three pounds; or three pounds and half a crown at most on the Exchange; which cannot turn to account either to the parents or the kingdom, the charge of nutriment and rags having been at least four times that value.

I shall now therefore humbly propose my own thoughts, which I hope   8
will not be liable to the least objection.

I have been assured by a very knowing American of my acquaintance in   9
London, that a young healthy child well nursed is at a year old a most delicious, nourishing, and wholesome food, whether stewed, roasted, baked, or
boiled; and I make no doubt that it will equally serve in a fricasee or a
ragout.

I do therefore humbly offer it to public consideration that of the hun-   10
dred and twenty thousand children, already computed, twenty thousand
may be reserved for breed, whereof only one fourth part to be males, which
is more than we allow to sheep, black cattle, or swine; and my reason is
that these children are seldom the fruits of marriage, a circumstance not
much regarded by our savages, therefore one male will be sufficient to
serve four females. That the remaining hundred thousand may at a year old
be offered in sale to the persons of quality and fortune through the kingdom, always advising the mother to let them suck plentifully in the last
month, so as to render them plump and fat for a good table. The child will
make two dishes at an entertainment for friends; and when the family dines
alone, the fore or hind quarter will make a reasonable dish, and seasoned
with a little pepper or salt will be very good boiled on the fourth day, especially in winter.

I have reckoned upon a medium that a child just born will weigh twelve   11
pounds, and in a solar year if tolerably nursed increaseth to twenty-eight
pounds.

I grant this food will be somewhat dear, and therefore very proper for   12
landlords, who, as they have already devoured most of the parents, seem to
have the best title to the children.

Infant's flesh will be in season throughout the year, but more plentiful in   13
March, and a little before and after. For we are told by a grave author, an
eminent French physician, that fish being a prolific diet, there are more
children born in Roman Catholic countries about nine months after Lent
than at any other season; therefore, reckoning a year after Lent, the market
will be more glutted than usual, because the number of popish infants is at
least three to one in this kingdom; and therefore it will have one other col-
lateral advantage, by lessening the number of Papists among us.

I have already computed the charge of nursing a beggar's child (in   14
which list I reckon all cottagers, laborers, and four-fifths of the farmers) to
be about two shillings per annum, rags included; and I believe no gentleman would repine to give ten shillings for the carcass of a good fat child,
which, as I have said, will make four dishes of excellent nutritive meat,
when he hath only some particular friend or his own family to dine with
him. Thus the squire will learn to be a good landlord, and grow popular
among the tenants; the mother will have eight shillings net profit, and be
fit for work till she produces another child.

Those who are more thrifty (as I must confess the times require) may   15 flay the carcass; the skin of which artificially dressed will make admirable gloves for ladies, and summer boots for fine gentlemen.

As to our city of Dublin, shambles[3] may be appointed for this purpose in   16
the most convenient parts of it, and butchers we may be assured will not be wanting; although I rather recommend buying the children live, and dressing them hot from the knife as we do roasting pigs.

A very worthy person, a true lover of his country, and whose virtues I   17
highly esteem, was lately pleased in discoursing on this matter to offer a refinement upon my scheme. He said that many gentlemen of his kingdom, having of late destroyed their deer, he conceived that the want of venison might well be supplied by the bodies of young lads and maidens, not exceeding fourteen years of age nor under twelve, so great a number of both sexes in every county being now ready to starve for want of work and service; and these to be disposed of by their parents, if alive, or otherwise by their nearest relations. But with due deference to so excellent a friend and so deserving a patriot, I cannot be altogether in his sentiments; for as to the males, my American acquaintance assured me from frequent experience that their flesh was generally tough and lean, like that of our schoolboys, by continual exercise, and their taste disagreeable; and to fatten them would not answer the charge. Then as to the females, it would, I think with humble submission, be a loss to the public, because they soon would become breeders themselves; and besides, it is not improbable that some scrupulous people might be apt to censure such a practice (although indeed very unjustly) as a little bordering upon cruelty; which, I confess, hath always been with me the strongest objection against any project, how well soever intended.

But in order to justify my friend, he confessed that this expedient was   18
put into his head by the famous Psalmanazar, a native of the island of Formosa, who came from thence to London above twenty years ago, and in conversation told my friend that in his country when any young person happened to be put to death, the executioner sold the carcass to persons of quality as a prime dainty; and that in his time the body of a plump girl of fifteen, who was crucified for an attempt to poison the emperor, was sold to his Imperial Majesty's prime minister of state, and other great mandarins of the court, in joints from the gibbet, at four hundred crowns. Neither indeed can I deny that if the same use were made of several plump young girls in this town, who without one single groat to their fortunes cannot stir abroad without a chair,[4] and appear at the playhouse and assemblies in foreign fineries which they never will pay for, the kingdom would not be the worse.

Some persons of a desponding spirit are in great concern about the vast   19
number of poor people who are aged, diseased, or maimed, and I have

---

[3]*shambles* Slaughterhouses.
[4]*chair* A portable chair in which the passenger is carried by two people on foot.

been desired to employ my thoughts what course may be taken to ease the nation of so grievous an encumbrance. But I am not in the least pain upon the matter, because it is very well known that they are every day dying and rotting by cold and famine, and filth and vermin, as fast as can be reasonably expected. And as to the younger laborers, they are now in almost as hopeful a condition. They cannot get work, and consequently pine away for want of nourishment to a degree that if any time they are accidentally hired to common labor, they have not strength to perform it; and thus the country and themselves are happily delivered from the evils to come.

I have too long digressed, and therefore shall return to my subject. I 20 think the advantages by the proposal which I have made are obvious and many, as well as of the highest importance.

For first, as I have already observed, it would greatly lessen the number 21 of Papists, with whom we are yearly overrun, being the principal breeders of the nation as well as our most dangerous enemies; and who stay at home on purpose to deliver the kingdom to the Pretender, hoping to take their advantage by the absence of so many good Protestants, who have chosen rather to leave their country than to stay at home and pay tithes against their conscience to an Episcopal curate.

Secondly, the poorer tenants will have something valuable of their own, 22 which by law may be made liable to distress, and help to pay their landlord's rent, their corn and cattle being already seized and money a thing unknown.

Thirdly, whereas the maintenance of an hundred thousand children, 23 from two years old and upwards, cannot be computed at less than ten shillings per annum, the nation's stock will be thereby increased fifty thousand pounds per annum, besides the profit of a new dish introduced to the tables of all gentlemen of fortune in the kingdom who have any refinement in taste. And the money will circulate among ourselves, the goods being entirely of our own growth and manufacture.

Fourthly, the constant breeders, besides the gain of eight shillings ster- 24 ling per annum by the sale of their children, will be rid of the charge of maintaining them after the first year.

Fifthly, this food would likewise bring great custom to taverns, where the 25 vintners will certainly be so prudent as to procure the best receipts for dressing it to perfection, and consequently have their houses frequented by all the fine gentlemen, who justly value themselves upon their knowledge in good eating; and a skillful cook, who understands how to oblige his guests, will contrive to make it as expensive as they please.

Sixthly, this would be a great inducement to marriage, which all wise 26 nations have either encouraged by rewards or enforced by laws and penalties. It would increase the care and tenderness of mothers toward their children, when they were sure of a settlement for life to the poor babes, provided in some sort by the public, to their annual profit instead of expense. We should see an honest emulation among the married women, which of them could bring the fattest child to the market. Men would become as fond of their wives during the time of their pregnancy as they are now of their mares in foal, their cows in calf, or sows when they are ready to farrow; nor offer to beat or kick them (as is too frequent a practice) for fear of a miscarriage.

Many other advantages might be enumerated. For instance, the addition 27 of some thousand carcasses in our exportation of barreled beef, the propagation of swine's flesh, and improvements in the art of making good bacon, so much wanted among us by the great destruction of pigs, too frequent at our tables, which are no way comparable in taste or magnificence to a well-grown, fat, yearling child, which roasted whole will make a considerable figure at a lord mayor's feast or any other public entertainment. But this and many others I omit, being studious of brevity.

Supposing that one thousand families in this city would be constant cus- 28 tomers for infants' flesh, besides others who might have it at merry meetings, particularly weddings and christenings, I compute that Dublin would take off annually about twenty thousand carcasses, and the rest of the kingdom (where probably they will be sold somewhat cheaper) the remaining eighty thousand.

I can think of no one objection that will possibly be raised against this 29 proposal, unless it should be urged that the number of people will be thereby much lessened in the kingdom. This I freely own, and it was indeed one principal design in offering it to the world. I desire the reader will observe, that I calculate my remedy for this one individual kingdom of Ireland and for no other that ever was, is, or I think ever can be upon earth. Therefore let no man talk to me of other expedients: of taxing our absentees at five shillings a pound: of using neither clothes nor household furniture except what is of our own growth and manufacture: of utterly rejecting the materials and instruments that promote foreign luxury: of curing the expensiveness of pride, vanity, idleness, and gaming in our women: of introducing a vein of parsimony, prudence, and temperance: of learning to love our country, in the want of which we differ even from Laplanders and the inhabitants of Topinamboo: of quitting our animosities and factions, nor acting any longer like Jews, who were murdering one another at the very moment their city was taken: of being a little cautious not to sell our country and conscience for nothing: of teaching landlords to have at least one degree of mercy toward their tenants: lastly, of putting a spirit of honesty, industry, and skill into our shopkeepers; who, if a resolution could not be taken to buy only our native goods, would immediately unite to cheat and exact upon us in the price, the measure, and the goodness, nor could ever yet be brought to make one fair proposal of just dealing, though often and earnestly invited to it.

Therefore I repeat, let no man talk to me of these and the like expedi- 30 ents, till he hath at least some glimpse of hope that there will be some hearty and sincere attempt to put them in practice.

But as to myself, having been wearied out for many years with offering 31 vain, idle, visionary thoughts, and at length utterly despairing of success, I fortunately fell upon this proposal, which, as it is wholly new, so it hath something solid and real, and of expense and little trouble, full in our own power, and whereby we can incur no danger in disobliging England. For this kind of commodity will not bear exportation, the flesh being of too tender a consistence to admit a long continuance in salt, although perhaps I could name a country which would be glad to eat up our whole nation without it.

After all, I am not so violently bent upon my own opinion as to reject 32 any offer proposed by wise men, which shall be found equally innocent, cheap, easy, and effectual. But before something of that kind shall be advanced in contradiction to my scheme, and offering a better, I desire the author or authors will be pleased maturely to consider two points. First, as things now stand, how they will be able to find food and raiment for an hundred thousand useless mouths and backs. And secondly, there being a round million of creatures in human figure throughout this kingdom, whose sole subsistence put into a common stock would leave them in debt two millions of pounds sterling, adding those who are beggars by profession to the bulk of farmers, cottagers, and laborers, with their wives and children who are beggars in effect; I desire those politicians who dislike my overture, and may perhaps be so bold to attempt an answer, that they will first ask the parents of these mortals whether they would not at this day think it a great happiness to have been sold for food at a year old in this manner I prescribe, and thereby have avoided such a perpetual scene of misfortunes as they have since gone through by the oppression of landlords, the impossibility of paying rent without money or trade, the want of common sustenance, with neither house nor clothes to cover them from the inclemencies of the weather, and the most inevitable prospect of entailing the like or greater miseries upon their breed forever.

I profess, in the sincerity of my heart, that I have not the least personal 33 interest in endeavoring to promote this necessary work, having no other motive than the public good of my country, by advancing our trade, providing for infants, relieving the poor, and giving some pleasure to the rich. I have no children by which I can propose to get a single penny; the youngest being nine years old, and my wife past childbearing.

Analyzing This Selection

1. **THE WRITER'S METHOD** The first three paragraphs straightforwardly express concern for the poor. What details in paragraph 4 begin to raise our suspicions about the speaker's concern for poor people?

2. What abilities and traits comprise the speaker's view of himself? What is our view of him? At what point in the essay are we fully shocked by his discussion of the problem?

3. Why is the idea of cannibalism first suggested to him by an American? Why would his references to Americans be amusing to Swift's contemporaries?

4. What are the causes of poverty in Swift's Ireland?

Analyzing Connections

5. Swift and Marin (see "The Prejudice Against Men," p. 479) rouse concern over the large numbers of destitute people in their countries. What reaction to the problem does each writer stimulate? Without his ironic mask, would Swift agree with Marin's attitude toward the problem?

Analyzing by Writing

6. In addition to attacking the problem of poverty, Swift satirizes the kind of reasoning that is rational without being moral, and logical without being ethical. Point out some absurdities of the so-called objective reasonableness that you find in current controversy over a public issue such as pornography (see Dworkin's "Letter from a War Zone," p. 454), gun control, welfare reform, capital punishment, drug legalization, doctor-assisted suicide, or perhaps a campus issue. (You may wish to take an ironic stance as an advocate of a "reasonable" position that you find absurd.)

George Johnson

DARK MATTER LIGHTS THE VOID

GEORGE JOHNSON (b. 1952) writes about contemporary science. He graduated from the University of New Mexico and studied journalism at
American University. He has served as staff editor of The Week in Review
in the *New York Times,* where the following selection and other articles
appeared. His books include *In the Palaces of Memory: How We Build the
Worlds Inside Our Heads* (1991) and *Fire in the Mind: Science, Faith,
and the Search for Order* (1995).

Many moons from now, when extraterrestrial archeologists sift through 1
the records of our brief civilization, they might be amused to stumble
across the proceedings of an annual convention of stargazers called the
American Astronomical Society. They would be right in concluding that
1996 was, in one way or another, a landmark year.

Last week, at this cosmological jamboree in San Antonio, astronomers 2
unveiled photographs from the Hubble Space Telescope that were so
jammed with stars that the estimated number of galaxies in the universe
quintupled overnight, to 50 billion. Before we earthlings had time to
absorb this stunning revelation, we were hit with still more.

By analyzing the wobble of distant stars, astronomers found deviations 3
that could be caused by large, orbiting planets. Scrutinizing the wiggles
within the wobbles, they even dared speculate that the two unseen planets
would be close enough to their suns to soak up the rays needed for life.

But perhaps the single revelation that the aliens would find most amus- 4
ing involves a strange hypothetical substance called dark matter, which by
its very nature cannot be seen. Over the years it has become clear that if
the prevailing cosmological theories are right, some 90 percent of the universe must be made up of dark matter. Last week, astronomers said they
may have identified half of this unseen stuff. But the implications remain
as mysterious as ever.

And the aliens might wonder: How was it that this ancient race was 5
forced to conclude that almost all of the universe is invisible?

The earthlings, the anthropologists might report, kept track of time by 6
counting the trips their planet had taken around its sun since the time of a

highly regarded prophet named Jesus. It was after about 1,930 of these revolutions that the planet's stargazers began to notice something seriously
wrong with the galaxies. Even their own Milky Way was violating what
earthlings, with characteristic lack of humility, called a Law of the Universe. This particular law had been laid down by another prophet called
Newton. Newton's law did such a fine job describing how apples fell from
trees and arrows flew through the air that the earthlings were sure that the
stars themselves must obey it.

How shocking then that the Milky Way seemed to be spinning much   7
faster than Newton decreed — so fast, in fact, that it should have flown
apart long before. Could it be that the great prophet was wrong, that his
laws were no more universal than such earthly concoctions as British common law and the Internal Revenue Code?

But these stargazers were far more clever than that. Perhaps, they pro-   8
posed, some kind of unseen cosmic glue is holding the Milky Way
together. If 90 percent of the galaxy consists of this invisible stuff, then
Newton's laws would again reign supreme.

In the annals of astronomy, this was duly recorded as the "discovery" of   9
dark matter.

This dark matter — whatever it was — turned out to be quite useful.   10
Later on, when Earth's inhabitants were having problems with their creation myth, the Big Bang, all it took was a hefty dose of dark matter to set
it straight.

The elders had taught that the universe began 10 billion earth orbits ear-   11
lier with a great explosion that still reverberated. Just one problem. The
debris from the explosion — all this hurtling star stuff — would have been
flying too fast to clump together to form galaxies and clusters of galaxies.
The prophet Newton's gravity just wasn't strong enough.

Then dark matter came to the rescue. If most of the universe had simply   12
escaped the astronomers' notice, then there would be enough mass — and
therefore enough gravity — to cause the congealing.

Before long, nearly every stargazer on earth had joined the cult of dark   13
matter. But then there came a schism. Two factions, called the Wimps and
the Machos, went to war over the true nature of the invisible cosmic glue.

"Wimp" stood for Weakly Interacting Massive Particles. No one had ever   14
seen such things. But the believers in Wimps took the radical view that
these exotic particles, which would neither emit nor absorb light,
accounted for most of the dark matter. According to this daring heresy,
everything made from "normal" matter, including the earthlings themselves, was a mere aberration.

Against this disheartening view arose a more orthodox faith: the believers   15
in Machos, or Massive Compact Halo Objects. This faction insisted that
the dark matter needed to preserve the laws of the universe was simply ordinary matter — dead stars called white dwarfs that emitted too little light to
be detected.

In decree after decree, the Wimps and the Machos fought to a stand- 16
still. Then the Machos suddenly gained the upper hand. On the 16th
earthly spin of the first lunar cycle in trip No. 1,996 around the sun, some
stargazers announced that they had "found" the dead stars the Machos so
coveted.

Gazing at a nearby stellar cluster — called the Magellanic Clouds, after 17
a dead explorer who never even left the planet — the astronomers saw that
some stars would suddenly become brighter, only to dim again.

What if, the Machos proposed, this brightening was caused by great 18
lenses, magnifying the light? No, they weren't crazy enough to think there
were big pieces of polished glass floating around in the sky, like those in
their telescopes. These were gravitational lenses. Starlight was bent and
magnified by the gravity of invisible dead stars hiding in the halo of their
own Milky Way.

If you did the numbers right, you could show that maybe half the galaxy 19
was made of this stuff. And if this were true of all the galaxies (what confidence these people had!), then half the dark matter would be found.

What about the other half? Did the Machos eventually explain it away? 20
Or did the Wimps lay claim to it?

That is not yet clear. There were apparently some interesting revelations 21
in the next great meeting, during the cycle they called 1997.

Analyzing This Selection

1. Does the author regard Newton's law as valid? Since Johnson doesn't state
   his own views, how do we know?

2. What assumptions about the universe do the Wimps and Machos share?

Analyzing Connections

3. **THE WRITER'S METHOD**   Johnson and Swift (see "A Modest Proposal,"
   p. 489) use ridicule for different purposes. What details illustrate their contrasting tones and effects?

Analyzing by Writing

4. Examine the implications of an explanation such as "computer virus" or
   "missing link" or "imaginary number" or "the netherworld." Try to identify
   the underlying assumptions, or accepted law, that the term upholds. You
   may wish to spoof the idea.

Bel Kaufman

SUNDAY IN THE PARK

Bel Kaufman, granddaughter of the Yiddish humorist Sholem Aleichem, was born in Berlin, and she spent her childhood in Russia before coming to the United States at the age of twelve. She graduated magna cum laude from Hunter College and earned a master's degree from Columbia University. From 1949 Kaufman taught English in New York City high schools, an experience that led to her best-selling novel, *Up the Down Staircase* (1964), which was later made into a popular film. Kaufman has written another novel, *Love, etc.* (1979), and many essays and short stories. She has taught writing at the City University of New York.

1   It was still warm in the late-afternoon sun, and the city noises came muffled through the trees in the park. She put her book down on the bench, removed her sunglasses, and sighed contentedly. Morton was reading the *Times Magazine* section, one arm flung around her shoulder; their three-year-old son, Larry, was playing in the sandbox: A faint breeze fanned her hair softly against her cheek. It was five-thirty on a Sunday afternoon, and the small playground, tucked away in a corner of the park, was all but deserted. The swings and seesaws stood motionless and abandoned, the slides were empty, and only in the sandbox two little boys squatted diligently side by side. *How good this is,* she thought, and almost smiled at her sense of well-being. They must go out in the sun more often; Morton was so city-pale, cooped up all week inside the gray factorylike university. She squeezed his arm affectionately and glanced at Larry, delighting in the pointed little face frowning in concentration over the tunnel he was digging. The other boy suddenly stood up and with a quick, deliberate swing of his chubby arm threw a spadeful of sand at Larry. It just missed his head. Larry continued digging; the boy remained standing, shovel raised, stolid and impassive.

2   "No, no, little boy." She shook her finger at him, her eyes searching for the child's mother or nurse. "We mustn't throw sand. It may get in someone's eyes and hurt. We must play nicely in the nice sandbox." The boy looked at her in unblinking expectancy. He was about Larry's age but perhaps ten pounds heavier, a husky little boy with none of Larry's quickness and sensitivity in his face. Where was his mother? The only other people left in the playground were two women and a little girl on roller skates leav-

ing now through the gate, and a man on a bench a few feet away. He was a big man, and he seemed to be taking up the whole bench as he held the Sunday comics close to his face. She supposed he was the child's father. He did not look up from his comics, but spat once deftly out of the corner of his mouth. She turned her eyes away.

At that moment, as swiftly as before, the fat little boy threw another 3 spadeful of sand at Larry. This time some of it landed on his hair and fore-head. Larry looked up at his mother, his mouth tentative; her expression would tell him whether to cry or not.

Her first instinct was to rush to her son, brush the sand out of his hair, 4 and punish the other child, but she controlled it. She always said that she wanted Larry to learn to fight his own battles.

"Don't *do* that, little boy," she said sharply, leaning forward on the 5 bench. "You mustn't throw sand!"

The man on the bench moved his mouth as if to spit again, but instead 6 he spoke. He did not look at her, but at the boy only.

"You go right ahead, Joe," he said loudly. "Throw all you want. This 7 here is a *public* sandbox."

She felt a sudden weakness in her knees as she glanced at Morton. He 8 had become aware of what was happening. He put his *Times* down care-fully on his lap and turned his fine, lean face toward the man, smiling the shy, apologetic smile he might have offered a student in pointing out an error in his thinking. When he spoke to the man, it was with his usual rea-sonableness.

"You're quite right," he said pleasantly, "but just because this is a public 9 place. . . ."

The man lowered his funnies and looked at Morton. He looked at him 10 from head to foot, slowly and deliberately. "Yeah?" His insolent voice was edged with menace. "My kid's got just as good a right here as yours, and if he feels like throwing sand, he'll throw it, and if you don't like it, you can take your kid the hell out of here."

The children were listening, their eyes and mouths wide open, their 11 spades forgotten in small fists. She noticed the muscle in Morton's jaw tighten. He was rarely angry; he seldom lost his temper. She was suffused with a tenderness for her husband and an impotent rage against the man for involving him in a situation so alien and so distasteful to him.

"Now, just a minute," Morton said courteously, "you must realize . . ." 12

"Aw, shut up," said the man. 13

Her heart began to pound. Morton half rose; the *Times* slid to the 14 ground. Slowly the other man stood up. He took a couple of steps toward Morton, then stopped. He flexed his great arms, waiting. She pressed her trembling knees together. Would there be violence, fighting? How dread-ful, how incredible. . . . She must do something, stop them, call for help. She wanted to put her hand on her husband's sleeve, to pull him down, but for some reason she didn't.

Morton adjusted his glasses. He was very pale. "This is ridiculous," he   15
said unevenly. "I must ask you . . ."

"Oh, yeah?" said the man. He stood with his legs spread apart, rocking a   16
little, looking at Morton with utter scorn. "You and who else?"

For a moment the two men looked at each other nakedly. Then Morton   17
turned his back on the man and said quietly, "Come on, let's get out of
here." He walked awkwardly, almost limping with self-consciousness, to the
sandbox. He stooped and lifted Larry and his shovel out.

At once Larry came to life, his face lost its rapt expression and he began   18
to kick and cry. "I don't *want* to go home, I want to play better, I don't *want*
any supper, I don't *like* supper. . . ." It became a chant as they walked,
pulling their child between them, his feet dragging on the ground. In order
to get to the exit gate they had to pass the bench where the man sat sprawling again. She was careful not to look at him. With all the dignity she
could summon, she pulled Larry's sandy, perspiring little hand, while Morton pulled the other. Slowly and with head high she walked with her husband and child out of the playground.

Her first feeling was one of relief that a fight had been avoided, that no   19
one was hurt. Yet beneath it there was a layer of something else, something
heavy and inescapable. She sensed that it was more than just an unpleasant incident, more than defeat of reason by force. She felt dimly it had
something to do with her and Morton, something acutely personal, familiar, and important.

Suddenly Morton spoke. "It wouldn't have proved anything."   20

"What?" she asked.   21

"A fight. It wouldn't have proved anything beyond the fact that he's big-   22
ger than I am."

"Of course," she said.   23

"The only possible outcome," he continued reasonably, "would have   24
been — what? My glasses broken, perhaps a tooth or two replaced, a couple
of days' work missed — and for what? For justice? For truth?"

"Of course," she repeated. She quickened her step. She wanted only to   25
get home and to busy herself with her familiar tasks; perhaps then the feeling, glued like heavy plaster on her heart, would be gone. *Of all the stupid,
despicable bullies,* she thought, pulling harder on Larry's hand. The child
was still crying. Always before she had felt a tender pity for his defenseless
little body, the frail arms, the narrow shoulders with sharp, winglike shoulder blades, the thin and unsure legs, but now her mouth tightened in
resentment.

"Stop crying," she said sharply. "I'm ashamed of you!" She felt as if all   26
three of them were tracking mud along the street. The child cried louder.

If there had been an issue involved, she thought, *if there had been some-*   27
*thing to fight for. . . . But what else could he possibly have done? Allow him-
self to be beaten? Attempt to educate the man? Call a policeman? "Officer,
there's a man in the park who won't stop his child from throwing sand on*

mine. . . ." The whole thing was as silly as that, and not worth thinking about.

"Can't you keep him quiet, for Pete's sake?" Morton asked irritably. 28

"What do you suppose I've been trying to do?" she said. 29

Larry pulled back, dragging his feet. 30

"If you can't discipline this child, I will," Morton snapped, making a 31 move toward the boy.

But her voice stopped him. She was shocked to hear it, thin and cold 32 and penetrating with contempt. "Indeed?" she heard herself say. "You and who else?"

Analyzing This Selection

1. Before the bully speaks, what are the positive and negative aspects of the woman's frame of mind?

2. Toward the end the woman wonders what there was to fight over. In your opinion, was anything really at stake?

3. **THE WRITER'S METHOD** At the end, what is your attitude toward Morton? toward the woman? What do you think is the author's viewpoint?

Analyzing Connections

4. Rabin, in the Insights on page 468, compares making peace to resolving hostility between individuals. But do political alternatives to violence apply to individuals, as in this story, or only to nations? How should individuals react when all "rules" are broken?

Analyzing by Writing

5. Violent force is widely accepted if the violence is used to preserve "the nation's honor" or a person's "manly honor." Also, violence confers honor in film and video entertainment. Less acceptable but equally pervasive uses of violence are linked with honor among members of neighborhood gangs and organized crime families. What, if any, positive human attributes are contained in the link between violence and honor? What honorable goals and ideals might be separable from the violence? Try to define a concept of honor that does not depend on violence for confirmation. For details to illustrate your points, use "Sunday in the Park," news stories, videos, or just your imagination.

George Orwell

SHOOTING AN ELEPHANT

GEORGE ORWELL (1903–1950) was the pen name of Eric Blair, who was born in India and sent by his English parents to England for his education at Eton. He returned to India as an officer in the Imperial Police, but he became bitterly disenchanted with service to the empire, and he soon abandoned his career in the government. His first book, *Down and Out in Paris and London* (1933), recounts his struggles to support himself while he learned to write. His lifelong subject, however, is not bohemian life as a writer but his personal encounters with totalitarianism, which he addressed in his novel *Burmese Days* (1935) and his book *Homage to Catalonia* (1938), a chronicle of his developing despair over all political parties after he participated in the Spanish Civil War. His feelings toward politics and government are also expressed in his fiction, *Animal Farm* (1945) and *1984* (1949). The following essay is a memoir of his early period of conflicting loyalties as a British magistrate in Burma.

In Moulmein, in lower Burma, I was hated by large numbers of 1 people — the only time in my life that I have been important enough for this to happen to me. I was subdivisional police officer of the town, and in an aimless, petty kind of way anti-European feeling was very bitter. No one had the guts to raise a riot, but if a European woman went through the bazaars alone somebody would probably spit betel juice over her dress. As a police officer I was an obvious target and was baited whenever it seemed safe to do so. When a nimble Burman tripped me up on the football field and the referee (another Burman) looked the other way, the crowd yelled with hideous laughter. This happened more than once. In the end the sneering yellow faces of young men that met me everywhere, the insults hooted after me when I was at a safe distance, got badly on my nerves. The young Buddhist priests were the worst of all. There were several thousands of them in the town and none of them seemed to have anything to do except stand on street corners and jeer at Europeans.

All this was perplexing and upsetting. For at that time I had already 2 made up my mind that imperialism was an evil thing and the sooner I chucked up my job and got out of it the better. Theoretically — and secretly, of course — I was all for the Burmese and all against their oppressors, the British. As for the job I was doing, I hated it more bitterly than I can perhaps make clear. In a job like that you see the dirty work of Empire at close quarters. The wretched prisoners huddling in the stinking cages of the lock-ups, the grey, cowed faces of the long-term convicts, the scarred buttocks of the men who had been flogged with bamboos — all these oppressed me with an intolerable sense of guilt. But I could get nothing into perspective. I was young and ill-educated and I had had to think out my problems in the utter silence that is imposed on every Englishman in the East. I did not even know that the British Empire is dying, still less did I know that it is a great deal better than the younger empires that are going to supplant it. All I knew was that I was stuck between my hatred of the empire I served and my rage against the evil-spirited little beasts who tried to make my job impossible. With one part of my mind I thought of the British Raj as an unbreakable tyranny, as something clamped down, in *saecula saeculorum,* upon the will of prostrate peoples; with another part I thought that the greatest joy in the world would be to drive a bayonet into a Buddhist priest's guts. Feelings like these are the normal by-products of imperialism; ask any Anglo-Indian official, if you can catch him off duty.

One day something happened which in a roundabout way was enlight- 3
ening. It was a tiny incident in itself, but it gave me a better glimpse than I had had before of the real nature of imperialism — the real motives for which despotic governments act. Early one morning the subinspector at a police station the other end of the town rang me up on the phone and said that an elephant was ravaging the bazaar. Would I please come and do something about it? I did not know what I could do, but I wanted to see what was happening and I got on to a pony and started out. I took my rifle, an old .44 Winchester and much too small to kill an elephant, but I thought the noise might be useful *in terrorem.* Various Burmans stopped me on the way and told me about the elephant's doings. It was not, of course, a wild elephant, but a tame one which had gone "must." It had been chained up, as tame elephants always are when their attack of "must" is due, but on the previous night it had broken its chain and escaped. Its mahout, the only person who could manage it when it was in that state, had set out in pursuit, but had taken the wrong direction and was now twelve hours' journey away, and in the morning the elephant had suddenly reappeared in the town. The Burmese population had no weapons and were quite helpless against it. It had already destroyed somebody's bamboo hut, killed a cow, and raided some fruit-stalls and devoured the stock; also it had met the municipal rubbish van and, when the driver jumped out and took to his heels, had turned the van over and inflicted violences upon it.

The Burmese subinspector and some Indian constables were waiting for 4
me in the quarter where the elephant had been seen. It was a very poor quarter, a labyrinth of squalid bamboo huts, thatched with palm-leaf, winding all over a steep hillside. I remember that it was a cloudy, stuffy morning at the beginning of the rains. We began questioning the people as to

where the elephant had gone and, as usual, failed to get any definite information. That is invariably the case in the East; a story always sounds clear enough at a distance, but the nearer you get to the scene of events the vaguer it becomes. Some of the people said that the elephant had gone in one direction, some said that he had gone in another, some professed not even to have heard of any elephant. I had almost made up my mind that the whole story was a pack of lies, when we heard yells a little distance away. There was a loud, scandalized cry of "Go away, child! Go away this instant!" and an old woman with a switch in her hand came round the corner of a hut, violently shooing away a crowd of naked children. Some more women followed, clicking their tongues and exclaiming; evidently there was something that the children ought not to have seen. I rounded the hut and saw a man's dead body sprawling in the mud. He was an Indian, a black Dravidian coolie, almost naked, and he could not have been dead many minutes. The people said that the elephant had come suddenly upon him round the corner of the hut, caught him with its trunk, put its foot on his back, and ground him into the earth. This was the rainy season and the ground was soft, and his face had scored a trench a foot deep and a couple of yards long. He was lying on his belly with arms crucified and head sharply twisted to one side. His face was coated with mud, the eyes wide open, the teeth bared and grinning with an expression of unendurable agony. (Never tell me, by the way, that the dead look peaceful. Most of the corpses I have seen looked devilish.) The friction of the great beast's foot had stripped the skin from his back as neatly as one skins a rabbit. As soon as I saw the dead man I sent an orderly to a friend's house nearby to borrow an elephant rifle. I had already sent back the pony, not wanting it to go mad with fright and throw me if it smelt the elephant.

The orderly came back in a few minutes with a rifle and five cartridges, 5 and meanwhile some Burmans had arrived and told us that the elephant was in the paddy fields below, only a few hundred yards away. As I started forward practically the whole population of the quarter flocked out of the houses and followed me. They had seen the rifle and were all shouting excitedly that I was going to shoot the elephant. They had not shown much interest in the elephant when he was merely ravaging their homes, but it was different now that he was going to be shot. It was a bit of fun to them, as it would be to an English crowd; besides they wanted the meat. It made me vaguely uneasy. I had no intention of shooting the elephant — I had merely sent for the rifle to defend myself if necessary — and it is always unnerving to have a crowd following you. I marched down the hill, looking and feeling a fool, with the rifle over my shoulder and an ever-growing army of people jostling at my heels. At the bottom, when you got away from the huts, there was a metalled road and beyond that a miry waste of paddy fields a thousand yards across, not yet ploughed but soggy from the first rains and dotted with coarse grass. The elephant was standing eight yards from the road, his left side towards us. He took not the slightest notice of the crowd's approach. He was tearing up bunches of grass, beating them against his knees to clean them and stuffing them into his mouth.

I had halted on the road. As soon as I saw the elephant I knew with perfect certainty that I ought not to shoot him. It is a serious matter to shoot a working elephant — it is comparable to destroying a huge and costly piece of machinery — and obviously one ought not to do it if it can possibly be avoided. And at that distance, peacefully eating, the elephant looked no more dangerous than a cow. I thought then and I think now that his attack of "must" was already passing off; in which case he would merely wander harmlessly about until the mahout came back and caught him. Moreover, I did not in the least want to shoot him. I decided that I would watch him for a little while to make sure that he did not turn savage again, and then go home.

But at that moment I glanced round at the crowd that had followed me. It was an immense crowd, two thousand at the least and growing every minute. It blocked the road for a long distance on either side. I looked at the sea of yellow faces above the garish clothes — faces all happy and excited over this bit of fun, all certain that the elephant was going to be shot. They were watching me as they would watch a conjurer about to perform a trick. They did not like me, but with the magical rifle in my hands I was momentarily worth watching. And suddenly I realized that I should have to shoot the elephant after all. The people expected it of me and I had got to do it; I could feel their two thousand wills pressing me forward, irresistibly. And it was at this moment, as I stood there with the rifle in my hands, that I first grasped the hollowness, the futility of the white man's dominion in the East. Here was I, the white man with his gun, standing in front of the unarmed native crowd — seemingly the leading actor of the piece; but in reality I was only an absurd puppet pushed to and fro by the will of those yellow faces behind. I perceived in this moment that when the white man turns tyrant it is his own freedom that he destroys. He becomes a sort of hollow, posing dummy, the conventionalized figure of a sahib. For it is the condition of his rule that he shall spend his life in trying to impress the "natives," and so in every crisis he has got to do what the "natives" expect of him. He wears a mask, and his face grows to fit in. I had got to shoot the elephant. I had committed myself to doing it when I sent for the rifle. A sahib has got to act like a sahib; he has got to appear resolute, to know his own mind and do definite things. To come all that way, rifle in hand, with two thousand people marching at my heels, and then to trail feebly away, having done nothing — no, that was impossible. The crowd would laugh at me. And my whole life, every white man's life in the East, was one long struggle not to be laughed at.

But I did not want to shoot the elephant. I watched him beating his bunch of grass against his knees, with that preoccupied grandmotherly air that elephants have. It seemed to me that it would be murder to shoot him. At that age I was not squeamish about killing animals, but I had never shot an elephant and never wanted to. (Somehow it always seems worse to kill a *large* animal.) Besides, there was the beast's owner to be considered. Alive, the elephant was worth at least a hundred pounds; dead, he would only be worth the value of his tusks, five pounds, possibly. But I had got to act quickly. I turned to some experienced-looking Burmans who had been there when we arrived, and asked them how the elephant had been behaving. They all said the same thing: He took no notice of you if you left him alone, but he might charge if you went too close to him.

It was perfectly clear to me what I ought to do. I ought to walk up to   9 within, say, twenty-five yards of the elephant and test his behavior. If he charged, I could shoot; if he took no notice of me, it would be safe to leave him until the mahout came back. But also I knew that I was going to do no such thing. I was a poor shot with a rifle and the ground was soft mud into which one would sink at every step. If the elephant charged and I missed him, I should have about as much chance as a toad under a steam-roller. But even then I was not thinking particularly of my own skin, only of the watchful yellow faces behind. For at that moment, with the crowd watching me, I was not afraid in the ordinary sense, as I would have been if I had been alone. A white man mustn't be frightened in front of "natives"; and so, in general, he isn't frightened. The sole thought in my mind was that if anything went wrong those two thousand Burmans would see me pursued, caught, trampled on, and reduced to a grinning corpse like that Indian up the hill. And if that happened it was quite probable that some of them would laugh. That would never do. There was only one alternative. I shoved the cartridges into the magazine and lay down on the road to get a better aim.

The crowd grew very still, and a deep, low, happy sigh, as of people who   10 see the theater curtain go up at last, breathed from innumerable throats. They were going to have their bit of fun after all. The rifle was a beautiful German thing with cross-hair sights. I did not then know that in shooting an elephant one would shoot to cut an imaginary bar running from ear-hole to ear-hole. I ought, therefore, as the elephant was sideways on, to have aimed straight at his ear-hole; actually I aimed several inches in front of this, thinking the brain would be further forward.

When I pulled the trigger I did not hear the bang or feel the kick — one   11 never does when a shot goes home — but I heard the devilish roar of glee that went up from the crowd. In that instant, in too short a time, one would have thought, even for the bullet to get there, a mysterious, terrible change had come over the elephant. He neither stirred nor fell, but every line of his body had altered. He looked suddenly stricken, shrunken, immensely old, as though the frightful impact of the bullet had paralysed him without knocking him down. At last, after what seemed a long time — it might have been five seconds, I dare say — he sagged flabbily to his knees. His mouth slobbered. An enormous senility seemed to have settled upon him.

One could have imagined him thousands of years old. I fired again into the same spot. At the second shot he did not collapse but climbed with desperate slowness to his feet and stood weakly upright, with legs sagging and head drooping. I fired a third time. That was the shot that did for him. You could see the agony of it jolt his whole body and knock the last remnant of strength from his legs. But in falling he seemed for a moment to rise, for as his hind legs collapsed beneath him he seemed to tower upward like a huge rock toppling, his trunk reaching skywards like a tree. He trumpeted, for the first and only time. And then down he came, his belly towards me, with a crash that seemed to shake the ground even where I lay.

I got up. The Burmans were already racing past me across the mud. It 12 was obvious that the elephant would never rise again, but he was not dead. He was breathing very rhythmically with long rattling gasps, his great mound of a side painfully rising and falling. His mouth was wide open — I could see far down into caverns of pale pink throat. I waited a long time for him to die, but his breathing did not weaken. Finally I fired my two remaining shots into the spot where I thought his heart must be. The thick blood welled out of him like red velvet, but still he did not die. His body did not even jerk when the shots hit him, the tortured breathing continued without a pause. He was dying, very slowly and in great agony, but in some world remote from me where not even a bullet could damage him further. I felt that I had got to put an end to that dreadful noise. It seemed dreadful to see the great beast lying there, powerless to move and yet powerless to die, and not even to be able to finish him. I sent back for my small rifle and poured shot after shot into his heart and down his throat. They seemed to make no impression. The tortured gasps continued as steadily as the ticking of a clock.

In the end I could not stand it any longer and went away. I heard later 13 that it took him half an hour to die. Burmans were bringing dahs[1] and baskets even before I left, and I was told they had stripped his body almost to the bones by the afternoon.

Afterwards, of course, there were endless discussions about the shooting 14 of the elephant. The owner was furious, but he was only an Indian and could do nothing. Besides, legally I had done the right thing, for a mad elephant has to be killed, like a mad dog, if its owner fails to control it. Among the Europeans opinion was divided. The older men said I was right, the younger men said it was a damn shame to shoot an elephant for killing a coolie, because an elephant was worth more than any damn Coringhee coolie. And afterwards I was very glad that the coolie had been killed; it put me legally in the right and it gave me a sufficient pretext for shooting the elephant. I often wondered whether any of the others grasped that I had done it solely to avoid looking a fool.

[1]**dahs** Large knives.

Analyzing This Selection

1. Why did Orwell hate his job even before this incident occurred? What effect was the job having on his feelings and attitudes? How would you describe his state of mind at the time?

2. **THE WRITER'S METHOD**   What details in the descriptions of the elephant connect it with human life? What details in the descriptions of the Burmans connect them with animals? What evokes Orwell's humane, sympathetic responses?

3. Orwell says that he acted "solely to avoid looking a fool." If he had believed in the goals and values of British imperialism, would his actions have had more integrity?

Analyzing Connections

4. In the Insights on page 468, Orwell says that "all issues are political." In this essay are there issues that are nonpolitical? any that go beyond the political? For what reasons, political or otherwise, are issues in this essay important to *you?*

Analyzing by Writing

5. You have probably openly or privately opposed something on the grounds of justice, power, equality, or rights. Perhaps it involved your parents or your school. Examine your role as a participant in or observer of a politicized confrontation. Be specific about the stages of your engagement with the issues, and be clear about your response to the outcome. How have your views changed or developed since that confrontation?

John Hoberman

STEROIDS AND SPORTS[1]

JOHN HOBERMAN (b. 1944), a professor of German at the University of Texas, writes about the cultural significance of sports. His books include *The Dehumanization of Sport: Sport and Political Ideology* (1984), *Mortal Engines: The Science of Performance* (1992), and most recently *Darwin's Athletes: How Sport Has Damaged Black America and Preserved the Myth of Race* (1997). Hoberman has published widely on the doping issue, and this selection on that topic is excerpted from a longer essay that appeared in the *Wilson Quarterly* in 1995.

The existence of powerful drugs forces us to think about human nature 1 itself and how it can or should be transformed. As modern science increases our power to transform minds and bodies, we will have to make momentous decisions about how the human beings of the future will look and function, how fast they will run, and (perhaps) how fast they will think. To what extent do we want to preserve — and to what extent do we want to alter — human traits? It is already clear that in an age of genetic engineering advocates of the medical transformation of human beings sound reasonable, while the proponents of preserving human traits (and, therefore, human limitations) are likely to sound naive and opposed to progress in principle. The unequal contest between those who favor experimentation upon human beings and those who oppose it will be the most profound drama of 21st-century postindustrial society. Yet few people are aware that its essential acts have already been rehearsed during the past century of scientific sport.

Drugs have been used to enhance sexual, military, intellectual, and 2 work performances as well as sportive ones. Yet sport is somehow different. Its exceptional status as a realm of inviolable performances becomes clear if we compare it with some other vocations. Consider, for example, another group of performers for whom mental and physical stress is a way of life. Their life expectancy is 22 percent below the national average. They suffer from tendinitis, muscle cramps, pinched nerves, a high incidence of mental health problems and heart attacks, and anxiety levels that threaten to cripple their performance as professionals. These people are not fire fighters

[1]Editor's title.

or police officers or athletes; they are orchestral musicians, and many use "beta-blocker" drugs to control their stage fright and thereby improve their performances. The use of these same anti-anxiety drugs has been banned by the Medical Commission of the International Olympic Committee as a form of doping.

What accounts for this discrepancy? What makes sport the one type of performance that can be "corrupted" by pharmacological intervention? One might argue that an orchestral performance, unlike a sporting event, is not a contest. Since the performers are not competing against one another, deceit is not an issue. Yet even if we leave aside the prominent international music competitions, this argument overlooks the fact that an entire field of equally doped runners who knew exactly which drugs their competitors had taken would still violate the ethics of sport, which require both fair competition and the integrity of the performance itself — an untainted, and therefore accurate, measure of human potential. But why is the same requirement not imposed on the orchestral musician? Indeed, one would expect "high" cultural performances to carry greater ethical and anthropological significance than sportive ones. Sport's role as a special index of human capacity makes drug use by athletes uniquely problematic.

The "doping" issue within pharmacology thus originates in a tension between the licit and the illicit, a conflict that is inevitable in a society that both legitimizes and distrusts pharmacological solutions to human problems. The enormous market for substances that are supposed to boost the human organism in various ways benefits from the universal presumption that almost any attempt to expand human capacities is worth trying. Technological civilization always tends to turn productive activities into measurable performances, catalyzing an endless search for performance-enhancing technologies, from psychotherapy to caffeine tablets.

The modern obsession with performance enhancement is reflected in the wide range of substances and techniques enlisted on behalf of improving the human organism and its capacities. Commercial "brain gyms" employ stress-reduction devices such as flotation tanks, biofeedback machines, and somatrons (which bombard the body with musical vibrations) in an attempt to affect the brain waves and thereby increase intelligence, boost memory, strengthen the immune system, and combat phobias. So-called "smart drugs," none of which have been proven effective in scientifically valid trials, are sold to promote "cognitive enhancement."

The never-ending contest between the performance principle and the cultural restraints that work against it blurs the line separating the licit and the illicit. Consider, for example, the response in 1993 to charges of steroid doping among Chinese swimmers. A Chinese newspaper responded that the swimmers' world-class performances had been made possible by a "multifunctional muscle-building machine" that sends electronically controlled bursts of electricity through the muscles. That is to say, an accusation of illicit performance boosting of one kind was met with earnest assurances that Chinese athletes had succeeded by employing an equally artificial (but still legal) procedure. Few anecdotes could better illustrate the prevailing opportunism in the field.

Doping in sport has been banned for the past 25 years, yet less than a century ago European scientists were discussing pharmacological aids to athletic performance without any qualms. The physiologists of that time understood that the pharmacologically active substances they worked with displayed a range of effects: they could be medicines, stimulants, depressants, intoxicants, antiseptics, narcotics, poisons, or antagonists of other drugs. But during this phase, physicians and others had little interest in using drugs to improve athletic performance. Sports simply did not have the social and political importance they have today. At the same time, the athletic world did not yet recognize drugs as a threat to the integrity of sport. The distinction between performance-enhancing and therapeutic medications — a prerequisite of the doping concept — was not yet established. 7

Condemnation of doping on ethical grounds appeared during the 1920s as sport became a genuine mass-cultural phenomenon. The growth of international sporting events after the first modern Olympics, held in Athens in 1896, created a new arena for nationalistic competition that served the interests of various governments. Larger financial investments and the prominence of sport in the emerging mass media gave elite athletes a new social and political significance, which helped foster new suspicions about the competitive practices of others. Having left its age of innocence behind, sports medicine was now embarked upon a new experimental phase involving the collaboration of athletes, trainers, physicians, and the pharmaceutical industry. At the same time, a new international sports establishment arose championing an ideal of sportsmanship that was threatened by the use of drugs. 8

Lacking a systematic definition of doping, biomedical conservatives adopted a position based on a kind of moral intuition. Dr. Otto Riesser, director of the Pharmacological Institute at the University of Breslau, was one of the few who understood the biochemical complexities of doping and its uncertain effects. In an address to the German Swimming Federation in 1933, he deplored widespread doping in German sport and blamed physicians for their collusion in these unethical practices. Riesser's response to the problem of defining doping was to say that in difficult cases "common sense and conscience must be the final judges." Such homespun wisdom, though it could not always prevail over the temptation to cheat, was an important statement of principle. . . . "All of us feel a healthy inner resistance to such experiments in artificially boosting athletic performance, and, perhaps, a not unjustified fear that any pharmacological intervention, no matter how small, may cause a disturbance in the healthy organism." 9

The history of doping tells us that our "healthy inner resistance" to such   10
temptations is constantly being subverted by the problem of distinguishing
between licit and illicit techniques.... The culturally conservative
response to performance-enhancing drugs, in society at large as well as in
sport, is today under siege as it has never been before. In *Listening to
Prozac*, Peter Kramer makes a point of undermining what he calls "pharmacological Calvinism," defined as "a general distrust of drugs used for
nontherapeutic purposes." Pharmacological Calvinism, he suggests, "may
be flimsy protection against the allure of medication. Do we feel secure in
counting on our irrationality — our antiscientific prejudice — to save us
from the ubiquitous cultural pressures for enhancement?" As Kramer (and
his critics) well know, we do not. Indeed, the transformation of Otto
Riesser's "healthy inner resistance" into "antiscientific prejudice" is one
more sign that . . . "cosmetic psychopharmacology" has benefited from (and
strengthened) an increasingly activist view of therapeutic intervention. . . .

Therapy aims at human improvement, not necessarily the curing of a   11
specific malady. Precisely because we now treat the legitimacy of "therapy"
as self-evident, we overlook its expanded role in modern life. Drugs in particular have a vast range of applications that extend far beyond the treatment of organic diseases. Drugs now in wide use help people cope with
such "normal" challenges of daily life as work performance and mood control. The elastic concept of therapy easily accommodates the physiological
conditions and psychological stresses experienced by high-performance
athletes, and the fusion of everyday stress and extreme athletic exertion
makes it difficult to condemn doping in sport on a priori grounds. We
simply do not . . . distinguish . . . on a deep enough level between the pressures of everyday life and sportive stress. The modern English (and now
internationalized) word "stress" homogenizes an entire spectrum of experiences and simultaneously implies the need for "therapies" to restore the
organism to its original healthy state.

The power of this therapeutic ideal is already transforming the status   12
of the male hormone testosterone and its anabolic-androgenic steroid deriv-
atives. These hormonal substances have been leading a double life as
(legitimate) medications and (illegitimate) doping agents for almost half
a century. Over the past three decades, steroid use by male and, more
recently, female elite athletes has become epidemic, covertly supported by
a prosteroid lobby among sports physicians that has received almost no
media coverage outside Germany.

The advent of mass testosterone therapy would represent a dramatic cul-   13
tural change. The use of sex hormones as a "popular nutritional supplement"
(as one German expert has put it) to strengthen aging muscles would be a
major step toward equating therapy with performance enhancement. And if
testosterone products proved to have a restorative effect on sexual function-

ing in the elderly, this would surely foster a new ideal of "normal" sexual capacity that many people would regard as a "health" entitlement. The certification of low doses as medically safe would transform the image of these drugs, "gentrifying" testosterone products and paving the way for wider use by athletes and body builders. . . .

The use of doping substances is driven by the ambiguous status of 14 drugs that have (or may have) legitimate medical applications as well as performance-boosting value for elite athletes. The "dual-uses" of such drugs make it difficult to argue that they should be banned from sport as medically hazardous. . . .

The gradual "gentrification" of such drugs will have diverse effects. 15 Testosterone products will be more available to the elderly and thus more acceptable to everyone, creating a market much larger than the estimated one million American males who now buy these drugs on the black market. Gentrification will also undermine the campaign against doping in sport. At the same time, destigmatizing these drugs will enable physicians to treat large groups of patients in new ways. Ironically, the criminalization of steroids has been an obstacle to their use for legitimate purposes. At the Ninth International Conference on AIDS, held in Berlin in 1993, physicians urged that anabolic steroids become a standard treatment for AIDS patients and people who are HIV-positive. The potential market represented by these patients already numbers in the tens of millions around the world. . . .

While drug use has been epidemic among elite athletes since the late 16 1960s, the new respectability of testosterone products will put international sports officials in an unprecedented bind. How will the Medical Commission of the International Olympic Committee maintain the official notoriety of steroids once these drugs have become a standard medical therapy for millions of ordinary people? In a word, the hard line against doping is not likely to survive the gentrification process. This outcome of the contest between our "healthy inner resistance" to doping and ambitions to "improve" the human organism will have fateful consequences. New roles for drugs will promote the medicalization of everyday life at the expense of our sense of human independence from scientific domination. It will certainly affect our thinking about licit and illicit applications of genetic engineering. . . .

The elastic concept of therapy will help to legitimize hormonal manip- 17 ulation as a mass therapy of the future. It is interesting to speculate about how the advertising experts will promote these products. It is hard to imagine that they will not turn to elite athletes, portraying them as pharmacologically improved examples of supercharged health. One can see the athletes now, lined up at the start of an Olympic final early in the next century, their drug-company logos gleaming in the sun.

Analyzing This Selection

1. How does drug use for improved athletic performance differ from other pursuits of excellence? Do you agree with the author that difficult issues arise only in sports?

2. **THE WRITER'S METHOD**   What is the purpose of Hoberman's historical review of medical attitudes? What does he suggest about the past and future?

3. How do steroids raise social problems beyond their use in sports?

Analyzing Connections

4. Sternberg cites new theories that athletic ability is a form of intelligence (see "What Should We Ask About Intelligence," p. 269). What would IQ testers say about drugs? How would drug enhancement affect scientific measures of human potentials?

Analyzing by Writing

5. Explain the cultural significance of a specific sport, and consider the possible national effects of drug enhancement. Select a sport popular for ordinary players and spectators that embodies values people want confirmed by their entertainment, such as baseball, football, basketball, hockey, or golf. Perhaps the sport expresses ideals of physical perfection, team cooperation, control of power, or similar qualities people may not find in their work or home life. Perhaps the sport includes impulses that are malign or destructive. How is the cultural meaning of that sport affected by legal or illegal drugs?

Leon R. Kass

THE MORAL REPUGNANCE
OF CLONING

LEON R. KASS (b. 1939) writes about biomedical ethics. He graduated from
the University of Chicago, where he earned an M.D. degree, and then
completed a Ph.D. in biochemistry at Harvard University. His books
include *Toward a More Natural Science: Biology and Human Affairs*
(1985) and *The Hungry Soul: Eating and the Perfecting of Our Nature*
(1994). This selection is excerpted from a longer article in the *New
Republic* in 1997.

Our habit of delighting in news of scientific and technological break- 1
throughs has been sorely challenged by the birth announcement of a sheep
named Dolly. Though Dolly shares with previous sheep the "softest clothing, woolly, bright," William Blake's question, "Little Lamb, who made
thee?" has for her a radically different answer: Dolly was, quite literally,
made. She is the work not of nature or nature's God but of man, an Englishman, Ian Wilmut, and his fellow scientists. What's more, Dolly came
into being not only asexually — ironically, just like "He [who] calls Himself a Lamb" — but also as the genetically identical copy (and the perfect
incarnation of the form or blueprint) of a mature ewe, of whom she is a
clone. This long-awaited yet not quite expected success in cloning a mam-
mal raised immediately the prospect — and the specter — of cloning
human beings: "I a child and Thou a lamb," despite our differences, have
always been equal candidates for creative making, only now, by means of
cloning, we may both spring from the hand of man playing at being God.

Cloning turns out to be the perfect embodiment of the ruling opinions 2
of our new age. Thanks to the sexual revolution, we are able to deny in
practice, and increasingly in thought, the inherent procreative teleology of
sexuality itself. But, if sex has no intrinsic connection to generating babies,
babies need have no necessary connection to sex. Thanks to feminism and
the gay rights movement, we are increasingly encouraged to treat the natural heterosexual difference and its preeminence as a matter of "cultural
construction." But if male and female are not normatively complementary
and generatively significant, babies need not come from male and female
complementarity. Thanks to the prominence and the acceptability of
divorce and out-of-wedlock births, stable, monogamous marriage as the

517

ideal home for procreation is no longer the agreed-upon cultural norm. For this new dispensation, the clone is the ideal emblem: the ultimate "single-parent child."

People are repelled by many aspects of human cloning. They recoil 3 from the prospect of mass production of human beings, with large clones of look-alikes, compromised in their individuality; the idea of father-son or mother-daughter twins; the bizarre prospects of a woman giving birth to and rearing a genetic copy of herself, her spouse or even her deceased father or mother; the grotesqueness of conceiving a child as an exact replacement for another who has died; the utilitarian creation of embryonic genetic duplicates of oneself, to be frozen away or created when necessary, in case of need for homologous tissues or organs for transplantation; the narcissism of those who would clone themselves and the arrogance of others who think they know who deserves to be cloned or which genotype any child-to-be should be thrilled to receive; the Frankensteinian hubris to create human life and increasingly to control its destiny; man playing God. Almost no one finds any of the suggested reasons for human cloning compelling; almost everyone anticipates its possible misuses and abuses. Moreover, many people feel oppressed by the sense that there is probably nothing we can do to prevent it from happening. This makes the prospect all the more revolting. . . .

We are repelled by the prospect of cloning human beings not because of 4 the strangeness or novelty of the undertaking, but because we intuit and feel, immediately and without argument, the violation of things that we rightfully hold dear. Repugnance, here as elsewhere, revolts against the excesses of human willfulness, warning us not to transgress what is unspeakably profound. Indeed, in this age in which everything is held to be permissible so long as it is freely done, in which our given human nature no longer commands respect, in which our bodies are regarded as mere instruments of our autonomous rational wills, repugnance may be the only voice left that speaks up to defend the central core of our humanity. Shallow are the souls that have forgotten how to shudder.

The goods protected by repugnance are generally overlooked by our cus- 5 tomary ways of approaching all new biomedical technologies. The way we evaluate cloning ethically will in fact be shaped by how we characterize it descriptively, by the context into which we place it, and by the perspective from which we view it. The first task for ethics is proper description. And here is where our failure begins.

Typically, cloning is discussed in one or more of three familiar contexts, 6 which one might call the technological, the liberal and the meliorist. Under the first, cloning will be seen as an extension of existing techniques for assisting reproduction and determining the genetic makeup of children. Like them, cloning is to be regarded as a neutral technique, with no inherent meaning or goodness, but subject to multiple uses, some good, some bad. The morality of cloning thus depends absolutely on the goodness or badness of the motives and intentions of the cloners: as one bioethicist defender of cloning puts it, "the ethics must be judged [only] by the way the parents nurture and rear their resulting child and whether they bestow the same love and affection on a child brought into existence by a technique of assisted reproduction as they would on a child born in the usual way."

The liberal (or libertarian or liberationist) perspective sets cloning in the   7 context of rights, freedoms and personal empowerment. Cloning is just a new option for exercising an individual's right to reproduce or to have the kind of child that he or she wants. Alternatively, cloning enhances our liberation (especially women's liberation) from the confines of nature, the vagaries of chance, or the necessity for sexual mating. Indeed, it liberates women from the need for men altogether, for the process requires only eggs, nuclei and (for the time being) uteri — plus, of course, a healthy dose of our (allegedly "masculine") manipulative science that likes to do all these things to mother nature and nature's mothers. For those who hold this outlook, the only moral restraints on cloning are adequately informed consent and the avoidance of bodily harm. If no one is cloned without her consent, and if the clonant is not physically damaged, then the liberal conditions for licit, hence moral, conduct are met. Worries that go beyond violating the will or maiming the body are dismissed as "symbolic" — which is to say, unreal.

The meliorist perspective . . . see[s] in cloning a new prospect for im-   8 proving human beings — minimally, by ensuring the perpetuation of healthy individuals by avoiding the risks of genetic disease inherent in the lottery of sex, and maximally, by producing "optimum babies," preserving outstanding genetic material, and (with the help of soon-to-come techniques for precise genetic engineering) enhancing inborn human capacities on many fronts. Here the morality of cloning as a means is justified solely by the excellence of the end, that is, by the outstanding traits or individuals cloned — beauty, or brawn, or brains.

These three approaches, all quintessentially American and all perfectly   9 fine in their places, are sorely wanting as approaches to human procreation. It is, to say the least, grossly distorting to view the wondrous mysteries of birth, renewal and individuality, and the deep meaning of parent-child relations, largely through the lens of our reductive science and its potent technologies. Similarly, considering reproduction (and the intimate relations of family life!) primarily under the political-legal, adversarial and individualistic notion of rights can only undermine the private yet fundamentally social, cooperative and duty-laden character of child-bearing, child-rearing and their bond to the covenant of marriage. Seeking to escape entirely from nature (in order to satisfy a natural desire or a natural right to reproduce!) is self-contradictory in theory and self-alienating in practice. For we are erotic beings only because we are embodied beings, and not merely intellects and wills unfortunately imprisoned in our bodies. And, though health and fitness are clearly great goods, there is something deeply disquieting in looking on our prospective children as artful products perfectible by genetic engineering, increasingly held to our willfully imposed designs, specifications and margins of tolerable error.

The technical, liberal and meliorist approaches all ignore the deeper   10
anthropological, social and, indeed, ontological meanings of bringing forth new life. To this more fitting and profound point of view, cloning shows itself to be a major alteration, indeed, a major violation, of our given nature as embodied, gendered and engendering beings — and of the social relations built on this natural ground. Once this perspective is recognized, the ethical judgment on cloning can no longer be reduced to a matter of motives and intentions, rights and freedoms, benefits and harms, or even means and ends. It must be regarded primarily as a matter of meaning: Is cloning a fulfillment of human begetting and belonging? Or is cloning rather, as I contend, their pollution and perversion? To pollution and perversion, the fitting response can only be horror and revulsion; and conversely, generalized horror and revulsion are prima facie evidence of foulness and violation. The burden of moral argument must fall entirely on those who want to declare the widespread repugnances of humankind to be mere timidity or superstition.

Asexual reproduction, which produces "single-parent" offspring, is a rad-   11
ical departure from the natural human way, confounding all normal understandings of father, mother, sibling, grandparent, etc., and all moral relations tied thereto. It becomes even more of a radical departure when the resulting offspring is a clone derived not from an embryo, but from a mature adult to whom the clone would be an identical twin; and when the process occurs not by natural accident (as in natural twinning), but by deliberate human design and manipulation; and when the child's (or children's) genetic constitution is preselected by the parent(s) (or scientists). Accordingly, as we will see, cloning is vulnerable to three kinds of concerns and objections, related to these three points: cloning threatens confusion of identity and individuality, even in small-scale cloning; cloning represents a giant step (though not the first one) toward transforming procreation into manufacture, that is, toward the increasing depersonalization of the process of generation and, increasingly, toward the "production" of human children as artifacts, products of human will and design (what others have called the problem of "commodification" of new life); and cloning — like other forms of eugenic engineering of the next generation — represents a form of despotism of the cloners over the cloned, and thus (even in benevolent cases) represents a blatant violation of the inner meaning of parent-child relations, of what it means to have a child, of what it means to say "yes" to our own demise and "replacement."

Much harm is already done by parents who try to live vicariously   12 through their children. Children are sometimes compelled to fulfill the broken dreams of unhappy parents; John Doe Jr. or the III is under the burden of having to live up to his forebear's name. Still, if most parents have hopes for their children, cloning parents will have expectations. In cloning, such overbearing parents take at the start a decisive step which contradicts the entire meaning of the open and forward-looking nature of parent-child relations. The child is given a genotype that has already lived, with full expectation that this blueprint of a past life ought to be controlling of the life that is to come. Cloning is inherently despotic, for it seeks to make one's children (or someone else's children) after one's own image (or an image of one's choosing) and their future according to one's will. In some cases, the despotism may be mild and benevolent. In other cases, it will be mischievous and downright tyrannical. But despotism — the control of another through one's will — it inevitably will be. . . .

The defenders of cloning, of course, are not wittingly friends of despo- 13 tism. Indeed, they regard themselves mainly as friends of freedom: the freedom of individuals to reproduce, the freedom of scientists and inventors to discover and devise and to foster "progress" in genetic knowledge and technique. They want large-scale cloning only for animals, but they wish to preserve cloning as a human option for exercising our "right to reproduce" — our right to have children, and children with "desirable genes." As law professor John Robertson points out, under our "right to reproduce" we already practice early forms of unnatural, artificial and extramarital reproduction, and we already practice early forms of eugenic choice. For this reason, he argues, cloning is no big deal.

We do indeed already practice negative eugenic selection, through 14 genetic screening and prenatal diagnosis. Yet our practices are governed by a norm of health. We seek to prevent the birth of children who suffer from known (serious) genetic diseases. When and if gene therapy becomes possible, such diseases could then be treated, in utero or even before implantation — I have no ethical objection in principle to such a practice (though I have some practical worries), precisely because it serves the medical goal of healing existing individuals. But therapy, to be therapy, implies not only an existing "patient." It also implies a norm of health. In this respect, even germline gene "therapy," though practiced not on a human being but on egg and sperm, is less radical than cloning, which is in no way therapeutic. But once one blurs the distinction between health promotion and genetic enhancement, between so-called negative and positive eugenics, one opens the door to all future eugenic designs. "To make sure that a child will be healthy and have good chances in life": this is Robertson's principle, and owing to its latter clause it is an utterly elastic principle, with no boundaries. Being over eight feet tall will likely produce some very good chances in life, and so will having the looks of Marilyn Monroe, and so will a genius-level intelligence.

Proponents want us to believe that there are legitimate uses of cloning   15
that can be distinguished from illegitimate uses, but by their own principles
no such limits can be found. (Nor could any such limits be enforced in
practice.) Reproductive freedom, as they understand it, is governed solely
by the subjective wishes of the parents-to-be (plus the avoidance of bodily
harm to the child). The sentimentally appealing case of the childless married couple is, on these grounds, indistinguishable from the case of an individual (married or not) who would like to clone someone famous or
talented, living or dead. Further, the principle here endorsed justifies not
only cloning but, indeed, all future artificial attempts to create (manufacture) "perfect" babies.

The "perfect baby," of course, is the project not of the infertility doctors,   16
but of the eugenic scientists and their supporters. For them, the paramount
right is not the so-called right to reproduce but what biologist Bentley Glass
called, a quarter of a century ago, "the right of every child to be born with
a sound physical and mental constitution, based on a sound genotype . . .
the inalienable right to a sound heritage." But to secure this right, and to
achieve the requisite quality control over new human life, human conception and gestation will need to be brought fully into the bright light of the
laboratory, beneath which it can be fertilized, nourished, pruned, weeded,
watched, inspected, prodded, pinched, cajoled, injected, tested, rated,
graded, approved, stamped, wrapped, sealed and delivered. There is no
other way to produce the perfect baby.

Analyzing This Selection

1. **THE WRITER'S METHOD** Explain the conflicting attitudes that the
   cloned lamb and poetic lamb symbolize in paragraphs 1 to 2. Does the use
   of symbols contribute to Kass's continuing point, or do you think his opening technique is merely a clever introduction?

2. In paragraphs 9 to 10 Kass opposes the three perspectives favoring cloning.
   Does the full essay persuade you against all three points, some, or none?

Analyzing Connections

3. Kass and Hoberman (see "Steroids and Sports," p. 511) resist engineering
   human perfection. Which author indicates more concern about social problems? about moral problems? Which author sounds more insistent about
   averting bad consequences?

Analyzing by Writing

4. In your opinion, which perspective favoring human cloning offers the best
   reasons to develop further technology? Take up that argument, and respond
   to Kass's objections. Even if you personally oppose cloning, the perspectives
   raise issues that can be partially supported. Develop your best case, and clarify your own position.

Henry Louis Gates, Jr., "In the Kitchen." From *Colored People* by Henry Louis Gates, Jr. Copyright © 1994 by Henry Louis Gates, Jr. Reprinted by permission of Alfred A. Knopf, Inc.

Eugene Goodheart, "Fast Friends," *Sewanee Review*, Fall 1996. Copyright © 1996 by Eugene Goodheart. Reprinted by permission of the author.

Robert Goodman, "The Luck Business." Reprinted with the permission of The Free Press, a Division of Simon & Schuster, from *The Luck Business: The Devastating Consequences and Broken Promises of America's Gambling Explosion* by Robert Goodman. Copyright © 1995 by Robert Goodman.

Ha Jin, "Ocean of Words." Copyright 1996 by Ha Jin. From *Ocean of Words*, Zoland Books, Cambridge, Massachusetts. Reprinted by permission of the publisher.

Robert Hayden, "Those Winter Sundays," copyright © 1966 by Robert Hayden, from *Angle of Ascent: New and Selected Poems* by Robert Hayden. Reprinted by permission of Liveright Publishing Corporation.

Oscar Hijuelos, "The Mambo Kings Play Songs of Love," excerpt from *The Mambo Kings Play Songs of Love* by Oscar Hijuelos. Copyright © 1989 by Oscar Hijuelos. Reprinted by permission of Farrar, Straus & Giroux, Inc.

John Hoberman, "Steroids and Sports." Excerpted from "Listening to Steroids," *Wilson Quarterly*, Winter 1995. Copyright © 1995 by John Hoberman. Reprinted by permission of the author.

Anndee Hochman, "Extending Family" from *Everyday Acts and Small Subversions: Women Reinventing Family, Community and Home*. Copyright © 1994 by Anndee Hochman. Reprinted by permission of Eighth Mountain Press, Portland, OR.

Pico Iyer, "In Praise of the Humble Comma," *Time*, June 13, 1988. © 1988 Time Inc. Reprinted by permission.

George Johnson, "Dark Matter Lights the Void," *The New York Times*, January 21, 1996. Copyright © 1996 by The New York Times Co. Reprinted by Permission.

Leon R. Kass, "The Moral Repugnance of Cloning," *The New Republic*, June 2, 1997. Reprinted by permission of *The New Republic*, © 1997, The New Republic, Inc.

Bel Kaufman, "Sunday in the Park." Reprinted by permission of the author.

Jamaica Kincaid, "Girl" from *At the Bottom of the River* by Jamaica Kincaid. Copyright © 1983 by Jamaica Kincaid. Reprinted by permission of Farrar, Straus & Giroux, Inc.

Maxine Hong Kingston, "The Misery of Silence." From *The Woman Warrior* by Maxine Hong Kingston. Copyright © 1975, 1976 by Maxine Hong Kingston. Reprinted by permission of Alfred A. Knopf, Inc.

Susanne K. Langer, "Language and Thought." Reprinted by permission of Leonard Langer, on behalf of the author's literary estate. Originally published in *Ms*.

Wendy Lesser, "The Conversion." Copyright © 1996 by Wendy Lesser. From *Tolstoy's Dictaphone*, edited by Sven Birkerts (Graywolf, 1996). Reprinted by permission of the author.

Philip Levine, "M. Degas Teaches Art and Science at Durfee Elementary School." From *What Work Is* by Philip Levine. Copyright © 1991 by Philip Levine. Reprinted by permission of Alfred A. Knopf, Inc.

Peter Marin, "The Prejudice Against Men," copyright © 1991 by Peter Marin. Originally appeared in *The Nation*. Reprinted by permission of the author.

William Ian Miller, "Gifts and Honor: An Exchange." Reprinted from William Ian Miller, *Humiliation: And Other Essays on Honor, Social Discomfort, and Violence*. Copyright © 1993 by Cornell University. Used by permission of the publisher, Cornell University Press.

N. Scott Momaday, "The Eagle Feather Fan" from *The Gourd Dancer*, copyright © 1976 by N. Scott Momaday. Reprinted by permission of the author.

Laura Nash, "The Virtual Job." Excerpted from *Wilson Quarterly*, Autumn 1994. Copyright © 1994 by Laura Nash. Reprinted by permission of the author.

Sharon Olds, "Sex Without Love." From *The Dead and the Living* by Sharon Olds. Copyright © 1983 by Sharon Olds. Reprinted by permission of Alfred A. Knopf, Inc.

Tillie Olsen, "I Stand Here Ironing," copyright © 1956, 1957, 1960, 1961 by Tillie Olsen, from *Tell Me a Riddle* by Tillie Olsen. Introduction by John Leonard. Used by permission of Delacorte Press/Seymour Lawrence, a division of Bantam Doubleday Dell Publishing Group, Inc.

George Orwell, "Shooting an Elephant" from *Shooting an Elephant and Other Essays* by George Orwell, copyright 1950 by Sonia Brownell Orwell and renewed 1978 by Sonia Pitt-Rivers, reprinted by permission of Harcourt Brace & Company, Mark Hamilton as the Literary Executor of the Estate of the Late Sonia Brownell Orwell, and Martin Secker and Warburg Ltd.

Richard Panek, "Superstore Inflation," *The New York Times*, April 6, 1997. Copyright © 1997 by The New York Times Co. Reprinted by Permission.

Greta Foff Paules, "Humble Pie." Excerpted from *Dishing It Out: Power and Resistance in a New Jersey Restaurant* by Greta Foff Paules, © 1983 by Temple University. Reprinted by permission of Temple University Press.

Jonathan Rauch, "For Better or Worse?" *The New Republic*, May 6, 1996. Copyright © 1996 by Jonathan Rauch. Reprinted by permission of the author.

Richard Rodriguez, "Public and Private Language." From "Aria: Memory of a Bilingual Childhood," copyright © 1980 by Richard Rodriguez. Reprinted by permission of Georges Borchardt, Inc. for the author. Originally published in *The American Scholar*.

Leo Rosten, "Home Is Where to Learn How to Hate," *World Magazine*, August 29, 1972. Copyright © 1972 by Leo Rosten. Reprinted by permission of the author.

Scott Russell Sanders, "Voyageurs," copyright © 1995 by Scott Russell Sanders; excerpted from *Writing from the Center* (Indiana University Press, 1995); reprinted by permission of the author.

Peter Schwendener. "Reflections of a Bookstore Type," *The American Scholar*, Autumn 1995. Copyright © 1995 by Peter Schwendener. Reprinted by permission of the author.

Thomas Simmons, "Motorcycle Talk." From *The Unseen Shore* by Thomas Simmons. © 1991 by Thomas Simmons. Used by permission of Beacon Press, Boston.

Gary Soto, "Black Hair" is from *Living Up the Street* (Dell, 1992). Copyright © 1985 by Gary Soto. Used by permission of the author.

Brent Staples, "Black Men and Public Space." Copyright © 1986 by Brent Staples. Reprinted by permission of the author.

Shelby Steele, "On Being Black and Middle Class," *Commentary*, January 1988. Copyright © 1988 by Shelby Steele. Reprinted by permission of the author.

George Steiner, "Books and the End of Literature" from *New Perspectives Quarterly*, Fall 1996. Reprinted by permission of Blackwell Publishers.

Robert J. Sternberg, "What Should We Ask About Intelligence?" Reprinted from *The American Scholar*, Volume 65, No. 2, Spring 1996. Copyright © 1996 by the author. By permission of the publisher.

Andrew Sullivan, "What Is a Homosexual?" From *Virtually Normal* by Andrew Sullivan. Copyright © 1995 by Andrew Sullivan. Reprinted by permission of Alfred A. Knopf, Inc.

Amy Tan, "Mother Tongue." First appeared in *The Threepenny Review*. Copyright © 1989 by Amy Tan. Reprinted by permission of the author and the Sandra Dijkstra Literary Agency.

Deborah Tannen, "Talking Up Close," text from pp. 236–41 of *Talking from 9 to 5* by

Deborah Tannen. Copyright © 1994 by Deborah Tannen. By permission of William Morrow & Company, Inc.

Sallie Tisdale, "We Do Abortions Here," first published in *Harper's Magazine*, October 1987. Reprinted by permission of the author.

Alexis de Tocqueville, excerpt from *Democracy in America*. Edited by J. P. Mayer and Max Lerner. Translated by George Lawrence. English translation copyright © 1965 by Harper & Row, Publisher, Inc. Copyright Renewed. Reprinted by permission of HarperCollins Publishers, Inc.

Susan Allen Toth, "Boyfriends." From *Blooming: A Small-Town Girlhood* by Susan Allen Toth. Copyright © 1978, 1981 by Susan Allen Toth. Reprinted by permission of The Aaron M. Priest Literary Agency, Inc.

Maguelonne Toussaint-Samat, "Chocolate and Divinity" from *A History of Food* by Maguelonne Toussaint-Samat, translated by Anthea Bell. English translation © Blackwell Publishers Ltd., 1992, 1994. Reprinted by permission of the publisher.

Calvin Trillin, "It's Just Too Late." From *Killings*, published by Ticknor and Fields. Copyright © 1984 by Calvin Trillin. This usage granted by permission.

James B. Twitchell, "But First, A Word from Our Sponsor," *Wilson Quarterly*, Summer 1996. Copyright © 1996 by James B. Twitchell. Reprinted by permission of the author.

Ellen Ullman, "Getting Close to the Machine," *Harper's Magazine*, June 1995. Copyright © 1995 by Ellen Ullman. Reprinted by permission of the author.

John Updike, "The Disposable Rocket," copyright © 1993 by John Updike. Published in *Michigan Quarterly Review*, Vol. 32, No. 4, 1993. Reprinted by permission of the author. "A & P." From *Pigeon Feathers and Other Stories* by John Updike. Copyright © 1962 by John Updike. Reprinted by permission of Alfred A. Knopf, Inc. Originally appeared in *The New Yorker*.

Lindsy Van Gelder, "Marriage As a Restricted Club." Copyright © 1984 by Lindsy Van Gelder. Originally appeared in *Ms.* Magazine. Reprinted by permission of the author.

Helen Vendler, "Knowing Poems." Excerpted from "Psalms and John" by Helen Vendler in David Rosenberg, ed., *Communion: Contemporary Writers Reveal the Bible in Their Lives*. Copyright © 1996 by Helen Vendler. Reprinted by permission of the author.

Alice Walker, "Everyday Use" from *In Love & Trouble: Stories of Black Women*, copyright © 1973 by Alice Walker, reprinted by permission of Harcourt Brace & Company.

Barbara Dafoe Whitehead, "Women and the Future of Fatherhood," *Wilson Quarterly*, Spring 1996. Copyright © 1996 by Barbara Dafoe Whitehead. Reprinted by permission of the author.

Richard Wilbur, "A Summer Morning" from *Advice to a Prophet and Other Poems*, copyright © 1960 and renewed 1988 by Richard Wilbur, reprinted by permission of Harcourt Brace & Company.

Patricia J. Williams, "My Best White Friend: Cinderella Revisited," originally appeared in *The New Yorker*, February 26/March 4, 1996. Copyright © 1996 by Patricia Williams. Reprinted by permission of Brandt & Brandt Literary Agents, Inc. All rights reserved.

Abigail Witherspoon (pseud.), "This Pen for Hire." Copyright © 1995 by *Harper's Magazine*. All rights reserved. Reproduced from the June issue by special permission.

Virginia Woolf, "Professions for Women" from *The Death of the Moth and Other Essays* by Virginia Woolf, copyright 1942 by Harcourt Brace & Company and renewed 1970 by Marjorie T. Parsons, Executrix, reprinted by permission of the publisher.

RHETORICAL INDEX

Analogy

Argument and Persuasion

Cause and Effect

Comparison and Contrast

*Fiction

Definition

Description

*Fiction

Division and Classification

Example

*Fiction

*Fiction

INDEX OF
AUTHORS AND TITLES

David Cavitch

Life Studies

An Analytic Reader

SIXTH EDITION

Prepared by **David Cavitch** and **Debra Spark**

Resources for Teaching

LIFE STUDIES

An Analytic Reader

Sixth Edition

Prepared by

David Cavitch, *Tufts University*

Debra Spark, *Colby College*

BEDFORD BOOKS   Boston

For information, write: Bedford Books, 75 Arlington Street, Boston, MA 02116
(617-426-7440)

ISBN: 0–312–18286–4

Instructors who have adopted *Life Studies: An Analytic Reader,* Sixth Edition, as a textbook for a course are authorized to duplicate portions of this manual for their students.

PREFACE

Life Studies is organized with the goal of taking students from writing personal pieces — probably unlike anything they were asked to do in high school — to writing critical, argumentative, and research essays. Students start with the material they have on hand — their lives — and then branch out to consider material that needs more effort, whether that means carefully reading an essay to discover an author's thoughts or exploring an unfamiliar issue through library research.

Close examination of the structure of the *Life Studies* essays should help students see how to expand on what they've learned about writing in the past — that a strong essay has a thesis sentence, that paragraphs have topic sentences that support the thesis, that sentences have examples and ideas that support the topic sentence. These essays demonstrate how ideas are developed (not merely repeated), how transitions are made from subject to subject, and how ideas are supported. They illustrate the importance of the particular especially well: the smaller the subject, the deeper the possible point; the more specific the example, the tighter and more effective the argument.

It may be helpful to prepare students for class discussion and assignments by using in-class writing exercises. The Insights that precede each section or the questions that follow each selection can be used to prompt directed automatic writing during which students write as quickly as possible for a set period of time, never lifting pen from paper, even if it means scribbling nonsense words. Students may then begin discussion by reading out loud what they've written or by asking more in-depth questions based on their immediate responses.

This manual presents brief comments to supplement the questions following each selection in Life Studies, Sixth Edition. The comments are meant to provide additional topics for class discussion, rather than "answers" to the questions in the reader. Issues and ideas we expect the class will notice and discuss are included, as well as connections between readings that may help you use one selection to illuminate others. We also offer alternative writing suggestions for each selection and advice about how to deal with difficult subjects. We hope you find this practical information useful as you teach the essays and stories in *Life Studies*.

CONTENTS

Contents

Part 3   SIGNIFICANT OTHERS   24

Part 4   GROUP PICTURES   34

Part 5   WORD POWER   46

Contents

PART 1

SELF-IMAGES

Starting the Course

The essays in Part 1 are first and foremost pieces of personal reflection, though they touch on large issues of sexuality, race, identity, and physical appearance. When students mimic these pieces, they will already have their "material" with them, so they can postpone the learning of some of the more intimidating skills needed to write a college paper (such as textual analysis and research). Students can concentrate instead on self-reflection and the requirements of the personal essay form.

While some students may enjoy the opportunity to write creative nonfiction, others may be uneasy — and not only because they are being asked to consider themselves as subjects. They may feel locked into the five-paragraph essay structure that they learned in high school (that is, introduce your topic and thesis in one paragraph, present three points in three subsequent paragraphs, and repeat your thesis in the final paragraph). In encouraging students to go beyond this structure, you may find the personal essay a useful starting point, since it seems unnatural to talk about one's life in three clear-cut paragraphs.

This raises the question, of course, about what a personal essay *is*. Students' reading will help the class shape its own definition. Before they get started, you might offer a provisional definition that describes a personal essay as an emotionally and intellectually significant piece of prose in which the author discloses aspects of the self to the reader. In the best essays, the disclosure represents a genuine discovery for the reader and the writer — that is, while writing the author learns something about himself or herself. As Flannery O'Connor expressed, "I write because I don't know what I think till I read what I say."

Often personal essays are narratives — stories (frequently, but not always, chronological) that have a specific point. Since later you will ask students to produce other kinds of nonfiction, you might emphasize now how the strengths of the personal essay — good, clear writing; honesty and intelligence — are the strengths of the analytic piece and of the argumentative essay as well. You might note too that, like statistics or results in a scientific paper or evidence in an argumentative work, anecdote and observation in a personal essay often have a cumulative effect, moving the reader to the central insight that, more often than not, was the writer's impetus for producing the piece in the first place.

Insights

In his paean to self-reflection, D. H. Lawrence's words seem to be enjoining us to take advantage of what Rollo May considers the distinguishing characteristic of human beings — the blessing of self-consciousness. But who is the self that thinks and reflects? Mark Twain essentially reverses Lawrence's (and possibly

René Descartes') notion and says the self consists of the influences on the self. Certainly the weight given to names, nicknames, and totemic objects in the quotes from N. Scott Momaday, Fay Weldon, and Rom Harré suggests this is, at least, partially true.

Interestingly enough, for Weldon and Harré, the word virtually creates the reality of the thing. The Romans spoke of this phenomenon in an aphorism, *nomen omen*, which means that a name is a prediction of what will be. Although the absolute truth of the aphorism may be questionable, it does seem that names, nicknames, and totems convey a powerful wish. To prove this point, you might ask students to jot down the reasons they were given their names. You might ask, too, whether they like their names — a question essentially about how they feel about the "wish" a name implies. (What, after all, does it mean when someone named after a deceased aunt says, "I just don't feel like an Alice"?)

For those who don't like their names, you might ask if they'd be willing to take Weldon's suggestion and pick a new name. If not, ask why. Choosing, it's true, isn't the same as receiving, and there is, as Twain says, something powerful about that which is received from without. In traditional societies and formal religions, the giving of a name is a ritual. In some societies people are renamed or given additional names at different stages of their development, as they acquire new attributes that need to be acknowledged. Even children confer powers by nicknaming, as Harré points out. The deepest power of the self is actively propitiated in the totem, as Momaday's poem illustrates. In the end, people usually feel that a name is more than a changeable label.

Nora Ephron

SHAPING UP ABSURD (p. 20)

Nora Ephron's "Shaping Up Absurd," like John Updike's "The Disposable Rocket" (p. 38), focuses on the body as wellspring of identity. But Ephron's essay is both less and more revelatory than Updike's.

In "Shaping Up Absurd," the style is informal, and the content is quite personal. Ephron doesn't shy away from giving private details about herself. Indeed, she almost eagerly confesses her adolescent fears and dissimulations, as well as her adult experiences and neuroses. Given her direct disclosures, this essay has the potential to make some students uncomfortable, but everything about Ephron's approach to her subject — her tact, humor, sensitivity, and candor — encourages a similarly open, easy response on the part of her readers. That said, you may have students who are embarrassed to discuss the body, no matter how buried in humor such discussion is.

If students write personal essays for class, they'll have to decide where to place their narrator — their remembering self — in relationship to the remembered self. Beginning writers often choose one of two obvious extremes. Either they write as if they are still the person of the memory (using, for instance, a child's voice if they are remembering something from their early years), or they write as a reminiscent narrator, looking back on times past. Both points of view have advantages and pitfalls. The child's voice may seem more direct, as if it can access, more honestly, the emotions of the memory, but such a voice can seem boring or cloying to the adult reader. The adult voice can be used to summarize and reflect and to arrive at fairly sophisticated conclusions, but it may lose some sense of immediacy or authenticity in the process.

Ephron resolves the point-of-view problem in an interesting way. At intervals, she uses the language of an early adolescent, re-creating the exaggerations, language, and abruptness of response that characterized her young self. She is frightened that she might "gum" things up, she has an "utterly-hateful-about bras mother," and she uses phrases like "That was the killer." But one never forgets that it is the adult Ephron, not the adolescent, who is writing this piece, and it is the adult's humor, shrewdness, and maturity, rather than the adolescent's embarrassment, that decide what to tell and what to omit.

Ephron's opening sentence nicely mimics adolescent self-absorption. It also suggests a degree of self-consciousness regarding the act of writing. This self-consciousness continues throughout the essay with lines like "That is a true story." Given her subject, this self-referential quality seems appropriate. But point out to students that she avoids potentially wooden constructions (like "as you can see" or "for these three reasons") as she supports her general observations with anecdotes and details.

In considering the structure of this essay, you might note how Ephron develops her theme as well as her narrative. She tells a story, *and* she develops an argument. In the end, it is the shape of the story and the shape of the argument that determine the shape of the essay. Her narrative moves forward in time (telling us about how her concerns with flat-chestedness played out over the years), and the discussion progresses from fear of androgyny to fear of rejection by men. Given this latter concern, why are men dispensed with so quickly in paragraphs 29 and 30? What does the brevity of those paragraphs reveal about the nature of her concern about breast size? How does the stylistic choice of constructing a paragraph that isn't even a sentence long help make her point?

Since the author presents her views primarily by telling her story, you might ask students why certain details are included. For instance, in paragraph 10, what purpose does the lengthy list of food serve? Also, why does she shift to present tense in paragraph 11? (Here Ephron breaks a "rule," since verb tenses should be consistent.) Why does she shift to italics in paragraphs 21 to 27? Finally, look at the amusing concluding paragraph, where Ephron purposefully undercuts her claim that she's grown past her adolescent obsession with her chest. Note that she doesn't use her essay's closing to sum up her argument or story. Instead, she keeps things moving and changing till the very last minute. The humor of the final line comes from its brevity and informality after the reasoned, careful lines prior to it. Ephron nicely lets the contradictions in her own thoughts emerge as (admitted) contradictions in her essay.

Ephron was a teenager in the 1950s. Is her experience relevant for adolescents of the 1990s? Are the opening lines of paragraph 3 still true? Has the vogue of androgyny changed things?

To consider these questions, students might be interested in Tracy Young's "A Few (More) Words About Breasts" (*Esquire*, September 1992). Young starts out by reminding us that Ephron's essay was originally published in 1972 under the title "A Few Words About Breasts." Young goes on to write, "If you read the piece today, what strikes you is how well it works both as a nostalgic artifact and as an uncanny prediction of where we've ended up: In 1992, a smart, successful, flat-chested feminist of sorts feels exactly the way Ephron did twenty years ago — only by now she's had implants."

3

Another option for considering the contemporary relevance of Ephron's piece would be to read the essay against James Baldwin's complicated thoughts on androgyny in "Here Be Dragons," first published in 1985 in Baldwin's collection *The Price of the Ticket*.

Since Ephron's essay was originally published in *Esquire* ("The Magazine for Men"), one might use "Shaping Up Absurd" to address the question of audience. Is there anything about the piece that suggests it was written for male, rather than female, readers? If so, how might the piece change if its original home had been *Glamour* or *Elle*?

Finally, assumed connections between physical traits and character traits may lead to classroom consideration of stereotypes (and provide a transition into the Terry Galloway and Brent Staples essays). When we stereotype one another, we are guilty of prejudice. What, you might ask the class, are we guilty of when we stereotype ourselves?

WRITING SUGGESTION   Nora Ephron says of big breasts, "If I had had them, I would have been a completely different person. I honestly believe that." Is there any attribute, physical or otherwise, that you feel the same way about? Explain, describing what it would mean to suddenly acquire that attribute.

Terry Galloway

I'M LISTENING AS HARD AS I CAN (p. 28)

Terry Galloway's description of her gradual loss of hearing provides a convincing picture of the "particular hell" her handicap became to her. She feels less than human with her hearing aid buckled to her body "like a dog halter." She believes she is "trapped in a monster's body." Part of Galloway's early difficulties have to do with the fact that she is fitted for a hearing aid during the precarious period in her life between childhood and adulthood. As a result, she feels inhuman: "a monster I would be." (In Nora Ephron's essays, feelings of being "nongendered" come at the same period of development.)

Galloway uses clichés ("blind as a bat" and "deaf as a doornail") in a crucial moment of self-definition in the essay. As a writer she is certainly aware that these are clichés; her other descriptions are decidedly more imaginative. Why then does she choose clichés? In one sense they function as shorthand in the way most clichés do: her readers think they know what she means; the clichés make her condition easier to identify with. But they also point out the absurdity of her condition (comparing herself to a bat and a doornail); such light treatment resists self-pity, as well as other more self-reflective emotions.

Throughout high school and college, Galloway denies that she suffers from a handicap. This denial requires that she fight hard to keep up with her contemporaries, and it eventually leads to a breakdown in her senior year when she finally faces her handicap and can acknowledge it to others. Ironically, when she finally accepts that she is not like everyone else, she can acknowledge who she *is* — a feisty, talented human being who understands both the limitations deafness imposes on her and its rewards. How does the language she uses to describe herself change once she can acknowledge her handicap and individuality?

Though readers might be inclined to pity Galloway's condition, her tone prohibits such an attitude, much as her humor undercuts the "knee-deep hysteria of the preacher." Galloway is no sentimentalist; she rejects her grandmother's efforts to soften her fate: no god could have singled her out for some mysterious special plan. Honesty, toughness, and acceptance are the author's best defenses. The final sentence fits the no-nonsense, straight-talking tone of the entire essay. Ask students to examine how Galloway uses language to resist her grandmother's palliative.

WRITING SUGGESTION Analyze why both Galloway and Nora Ephron ("Shaping Up Absurd," p. 20) feel, at points, as if they are something other than "human." Why does being apart from the group (developed girls in the case of Ephron, hearing people in the case of Galloway) make them feel that they are apart from the species?

Brent Staples

BLACK MEN AND PUBLIC SPACE (p. 34)

In the opening lines of paragraph 1, readers are led to believe that they are witnessing a crime to which the writer is confessing. There is no clue that we should take the words "my first victim" and "I came upon her" as sarcastic or ironic. Instead, Staples lets these words create a kind of suspense; we feel we're going to get insight into the criminal mind at the moment of violence. What we discover, of course, is that the tall, broad African American man, not the skittish white woman, is the victim in this brief, tense drama. The author's strategy is to have us make the same fearful assumptions about the black man on the street that the white woman does. He convinces us our assumptions are wrong, at least initially, by letting our preconceptions about young graduate students at the University of Chicago replace our preconceptions about large, bearded African Americans in military jackets. Or, perhaps, students realize even sooner — with the phrase "discreet, uninflammatory distance"— that the author is not who he first appears to be.

Structuring his piece around a central incident, Staples reckons with his "unwieldy inheritance"—"the ability to alter public space in ugly ways"— and tries to understand why it took him so long to recognize that he had this problematic power. Racism has given him the power, but it is a complicated form of racism, one that both blacks and whites share in, since blacks as well as whites lock their cars when they see a young African American man on the street, since both races find black men "ever the suspect." And Staples concedes that there is some reason for the young woman's fear in the opening scene. After all, "women are particularly vulnerable to street violence, and young black males are drastically overrepresented among the perpetrators of that violence." This admission, however, does little to comfort Staples. He's still alienated by the terrified woman's reaction. She has still made him "an accomplice in tyranny." What's more, her reaction — considered in light of the anecdotes in paragraphs 8, 9, and 10 — is on a continuum with the more obviously racist behavior of the jewelry store proprietor and the Waukegan police officers. Nor are these responses merely unpleasant for Staples and other black men, for, as Staples notes, "being perceived as dangerous is a hazard in itself." It invites the very sort of violence that Staples, from an early age, has tried to avoid.

Despite his analysis, Staples refrains from explicitly chastising the white woman in the opening scene or from openly characterizing her behavior as racist. You might ask students if this essay nonetheless implies reproach? If so, where? If not, why?

In this essay, instead of offering a solution to a large sociological problem, the author's goal is to identify the problem and then to describe his response to it. Anger, though Staples has felt it, doesn't help — not if self-preservation is his goal. It is better to find ways to keep himself safe from others' fear. He closes his essay by returning to his opening anecdote and describing how, during his night-time strolls, he whistles classical music, the "equivalent of the cowbell that hikers wear when they know they are in bear country." With this final metaphor, Staples reminds us again that white fear is dangerous for African American men: it is the bear, not the hiker, who attacks when bear and hiker meet.

The author's "tension-reducing measure[s]"— his willingness to alter his movements or whistle classical melodies at night — may be a conformist ploy or even an abdication of self. They may also be a reflection of his education, taste, humor, and savvy. Students should note that Staples closes with an image of himself whistling in the dark. Their evaluation of his behavior will, no doubt, rest on whether they view the closing irony as intended or not.

WRITING SUGGESTIONS   (a) In the second paragraph of this essay, Staples describes himself as "surprised, embarrassed, and dismayed all at once." Later, it becomes clear that he also has reason to fear those who fear him. Why? What is the danger of being perceived as hazardous? What is the danger of trying to compensate for the way in which one is perceived?

(b) Tell a story about a time when you were, for some reason, misperceived by others. How did you respond to the misperception, and what do you now think of your behavior?

John Updike

THE DISPOSABLE ROCKET (p. 38)

As a piece to discuss early in the semester, John Updike's "The Disposable Rocket" is tricky. The author's subject is quite intimate — at times, embarrassingly so — and his meaning — on the first reading, at least — isn't completely transparent. Both of these problems can easily be turned into opportunities — first, for a discussion of the value of careful reading; and second, for a discussion of the various levels on which nonfiction can be written.

Students may accuse Updike of saying something here that he is, in fact, not saying, and they should be asked to articulate his points carefully before launching into discussion. Ostensibly, Updike's subject is a man's relationship with his body — and the different relationship a woman has with her body. Quickly, however, he makes it clear that he means to make this comparison "from the standpoint of reproduction." You may need to help students sort out when Updike is talking about reproduction, when he's looking at the larger issue of male-female differences, or, indeed, when he is using biology to make claims about general differences between the sexes.

If looked at without considering the rhetorical strategies, some of Updike's points will probably strike the reader as infuriating or outrageous. What his figurative language, occasional hedging, and hyperbole indicate, however, is that his meaning is somewhat subtler than is initially apparent.

Updike's central metaphor is of the male body as a disposable rocket. "Once the delivery is made," he writes, "men feel a faint but distinct falling-off of interest." The metaphor here is both about the sexual act — desire falls away soon after — and about reproduction in general — after the delivery of sperm, a man is more or less uninvolved in the creation process. Women, then, are the heroes of the story of birth, a fact Updike wants to oppose with his own sense of male bravery. There's purposeful self-deprecation alongside the bravado, exaggeration coupled with crudeness — all meant, one suspects, to be taken at least partially as self-mockery. You might ask your students whether such mockery strikes them as particularly modest and whether the comparison that Updike sets up — for all its elevated language about pregnancy — slights women's active participation in the mating game.

Updike continues the elevated language as he develops his rocket metaphor, writing about "the release from gravity" that men seek. He uses personal anecdotes to equate falling with flying and then claims that males have a "superior recklessness" and that the male sense of space is outer while the female sense of space in inner.

Ask your students to translate Updike's claims into less elegant language; at heart, his views can be seen as mundane and old-fashioned. Have students consider the difference language makes — the great rush of the penultimate sentence in paragraph 3, a line that seems to mimic the very activity it describes, or the grand, detailed elaboration of examples of "outer" space in paragraph 4. Students who dislike this essay may concede that Updike's skill enables him to get away with what may be a reductive view of the sexes, just as it is the relative formality of his language that allows him to talk about his penis. (Some students may, however, be embarrassed by talking too closely about his claims, no matter how elegant the vehicle.) Metaphors and similes allow him to approach subjects that might otherwise seem inappropriate.

You might move from discussing the essay's central metaphor to a discussion of figurative language in general. Updike twice writes of being a tenant in his body. He also opens by comparing the healthy body to a bank account and closes by comparing a man and his body to a boy and his buddy out for a car ride. Ask why Updike uses these comparisons — all examples of figurative language. Writers use figurative language to illustrate the unseen in terms of the seen. "A parsnip looks like a large, white carrot" assumes that the person who has never seen a parsnip will be familiar with a carrot. Metaphors and similes compare in order to explain. With more inchoate experiences or perceptions, figurative language works in much the same way, helping the writer communicate an otherwise private moment or vision through shared experiences or perceptions. In his essay, Updike doesn't shy away from a direct discussion of genitals and sex, but his figurative language may help him convey what is, for reasons other than propriety, hard to communicate more directly.

That said, Updike's verbal skills end up, ironically enough, clothing — perhaps cloaking — the author. Despite the personal subject, "The Disposable Rocket" doesn't reveal that much about the author even as it touches on penises, vaginas, erection, and ejaculation. The most naked moment of the essay is when Updike talks about his ankles. This detail — so much better than the equivalent abstraction "I'm surprised I'm growing old" — is given with real emotion and without the rhetorical flights one sees earlier in the essay.

In the final two paragraphs, Updike shifts his topic from sex to aging. Ask students to identify two transitions — one in paragraph 6, about time, and one in paragraph 7, about the different ways the sexes age. You may want to point out that this shift is anticipated in the essay's opening simile, since we associate aging with declining health. But in making the shift, Updike hasn't left his central point behind: the self-possessed, hidden, wholeness of a woman is what man lacks. Man's anatomy leaves him in a vulnerable position: his desires are exposed, and his body is split in two. This split is a result of both the sex act, which splits the sperm from the man, and the placement of the genitals outside the body. Man's experience of his body is similarly divided; even in relative health, he feels not himself but "like a boy and the buddy who has a driver's license and the use of his father's car for the evening; one goes along, gratefully, for the ride." Given the broad reaches of the male's sense of space, according to paragraph 4, and the "superior recklessness" described in paragraph 3, the boy's gratefulness here reminds one that this essay is as much about falling as flying — as much as about failure, exposure, and death — as it is about being a man.

WRITING SUGGESTION   Think of a time when your sense of your physical self was sharpened, changed, or enhanced. It might be a memory of a sports success, a physical difficulty, an illness, or a growth spurt. How did (or does) that memory affect your sense of self?

Scott Russell Sanders

VOYAGEURS (p. 42)

This short piece opens with a literal leap — the otters jumping into the water — and a metaphorical leap (the otters are stones, no, they're beavers, no, finally, they are what they are — otters). Both jumps presage the later discussion about crossing boundaries, from human to animal, from human to human. The opening image itself crosses the boundary from mineral to animal. Though the essay's subject is ultimately large and metaphysical, its starting point is a small, quite ordinary moment — that of a man watching animals in the Boundary Waters Wilderness. (The place name might be coincidental, but, more likely, the name brought Sanders to his thoughts, much as he hopes — in paragraph 1 — that the naming of the "otter" will have magic power, will bring the "shapeshifter" before him and "hold it still.")

In the essay's opening description, the author's visual perceptions precede, by a beat, his awareness of what he's looking at, and this allows him, in a manner, to animate the inanimate. Similarly, the simile — they are "like tireless children taking turns on a playground slide"— gives Sanders a way to dissolve lines between animals and humans. His daughter helps him in this project with her funny appraisal of the otters' activity: "The technical term for it is goofing around." The joke confirms the father's belief that "science had complicated her vision without lessening her delight in other creatures." Here, too, boundaries are flexible.

The daughter, like the father, wants some relationship with these otters — to swim with them, to be noticed by them. Ask students how this desire differs from the father's. In the conversation with the daughter, why does the father say he doesn't want to swim with the otters? They will probably see how participation in the otters' lives differs from the complete, if fleeting, identification the father wants.

Without access to shamanistic powers, Sanders comes as close as he can to knowing the otter. Though he can't do it through direct identification, he does do it through careful observation, imagination, and love — all skills Sanders employs when it comes time to depict the otters. Have students examine the descriptions of otter movement. Sanders uses a variety of verbs, but he never shows off by using an inappropriately elaborate word in order to sound erudite or sensitive. He prefers a single strong adjective or adverb — like "mercury" or "buoyantly" in paragraph 2 — over numerous modifiers.

When Sanders wonders, explicitly, what it is he and his fellow canoers want from the otters, he makes it clear he can answer only for himself. Why does he feel this way? Why can't he answer for others? Is he admitting the impossibility of the very identification he desires?

As far as Sanders is concerned, it doesn't matter that boundaries don't dissolve or that slabs of stone don't, after all, turn into otters. The impulse to cross boundaries has its own value. "It is," Sanders concludes, "the same impulse that moves us to reach out to one another across differences of race or gender, age or class." Is it? Ask students what they think, and ask, too, if it strikes them as equally impossible to cross boundaries that are culturally constructed. Does Sanders, within the space of the essay, successfully "leap across the distance" of age to his daughter?

With the closing lines, Sanders returns to the question he posed and answered in paragraph 14. He says that he wants from otters what he wants from "neighbors and strangers." He wants "their blessing." He wants to "dwell alongside them with understanding and grace." What does this mean? What are the clues (particularly in the choice of language) that the desire has a spiritual dimension? Ostensibly, Sanders is still talking about otters, using humans to clarify his feelings for the animals, but his narrative purpose runs counter to his stated purpose. He closes by using otters to clarify how he feels about humans, an appropriate enough strategy given his essay's content.

WRITING SUGGESTIONS   (a) Read Robert Olen Butler's short story "Jealous Husband Returns in Form of Parrot" (in *Best American Short Stories 1996*, edited by John Edgar Wideman) or Julio Córtazar's "Axolotl" (in *Blow-Up and Other Stories*). Both stories are about men who "become" animals. What do the men learn? How is their experience different from or similar to Sanders's fantasy of what might happen if he could enter the otter's skin?

(b) Toward the end of his essay, Sanders writes that his impulse to cross the species boundary, to reach out to a "fellow creature," is similar to the impulse to cross cultural boundaries that have to do with race, gender, age, and class. Is it a similar impulse? Why or why not?

Michael Dorris

LIFE STORIES (p. 45)

Personal essays tend to start with autobiography and then move outward to conclusions about the self, culture, society, or nature. Michael Dorris inverts the traditional structure, opening his piece with an argument about how different cultures handle maturation. Contemporary American culture, he maintains, delays adulthood, while nineteenth-century Plains Indian culture anticipated a quicker transition. On a solitary wilderness trip, a teenage Plains Indian was expected to have an experience — intense and visionary — that offered him a sense of the meaning not just of life but of *his* life, *his* purpose.

As described by Dorris, the journey of a nineteenth-century Cheyenne or Lakota teenager is similar to the shamanistic voyages that Scott Russell Sanders refers to in "Voyageurs" (p. 42). There is the same retreat from the known world and the same expectation that the experience in the alien milieu will transform. And there is the promise of return. One doesn't stay in the wilderness or stay metamorphosed but comes home with knowledge. In paragraph 3, Dorris speaks of the Native American adolescent returning with a "foresight of both his adult persona and of his vocation." The word *vocation* provides a link to Dorris's unmystical conclusion (in paragraph 4) that the closest "many of us" come to this sort of foreknowledge is through our summer jobs.

Ask students about Dorris's audience. When he uses the third person plural, who is he including? What assumptions is he making about his readers?

Dorris opens paragraph 5 with a transition that both introduces the personal part of his essay and limits the scope of his initial claim. Limiting his claim *after* articulating it, Dorris manages to authoritatively present his theory while protecting himself from having to prove it for anyone but himself.

Since the sentence that starts paragraph 5 marks a major shift in the essay — from the analytic and possibly argumentative to the personal — students might evaluate the value of the essay's opening four paragraphs. What would the piece gain, and what would it lose, if those paragraphs were omitted? (Answers should lead to the essay's final sentences. Would those sentences have less weight — or make as much sense — if the essay began later?)

And what about paragraph 5 itself? What is Dorris's purpose in situating his stories about his summer jobs in the context of his family life?

Dorris devotes the majority of the essay to elaborating the list in paragraph 6 — to detailing the peculiar, difficult, ridiculous, or tedious aspects of his past employment. Despite the focus, Dorris emphasizes the positive. He relates his troubles with plucky, good cheer. Sure, he was cheated, swindled, and hassled, but the point of each anecdote is the experience's value, how Dorris always found something to enjoy or appreciate.

Have students consider how concisely Dorris conveys his experiences. Rather than say a position is frustrating or boring, he gives details — he tells the story of what happened — and he doesn't try to push the reader into feeling that something was outrageous by embellishing each anecdote with hyperbole or by insisting on his own reactions. On the occasions when Dorris does indulge in hyperbole — for example, when he describes his job at the Tribal Youth Programs in paragraph 9 — he's clever, speaking of the kids' "preternatural allegiance to sloth." But Dorris's critical eye isn't turned primarily outward. He confesses his mail route errors and depicts his youthful self in Paris as something of a Buster Keaton, stumbling just at his moment of greatest resolve. How does Dorris's willingness to mock himself affect the reader?

Dorris concludes with a story that focuses less on his finding the virtue in a difficult experience than on his persevering against the odds and receiving an unexpected gift. Why end here? Have students look back at paragraphs 17 to 24. Is there something, beyond chronology, that accounts for their arrangement? Does the arrangement contribute to the reader's sense of how the summer experiences ultimately influenced Dorris? What does Dorris mean when he writes that his jobs unfolded a "pattern at once haphazard and inevitable"? Ask students to articulate the emotion of the final line. Is it the same emotion that governs the body of the essay?

WRITING SUGGESTION   Interview four or five people you admire to ascertain when they felt they reached adulthood. What, for them, were the defining experiences? Use your notes to argue for or against Dorris's thoughts about how, and when, Americans achieve adulthood.

Jamaica Kincaid

GIRL (p. 51)

This unusual short story consists of a single (very long) sentence in which a series of commands and bits of advice stream from a mother to her daughter. Twice in the space of the monologue, the daughter speaks up — once to protest an accusation and once to ask a question. Students may disagree about what is going on. Are we listening to the actual voice of a mother badgering the girl, or are we listening to the often-heard phrases that now play in the more grownup girl's head as she recalls her upbringing?

The nature of the mother's instructions varies as the story proceeds. At first, the advice concerns domestic chores such as washing clothes, cooking, sewing, gardening, and housecleaning, but the mother soon incorporates advice about manners, giving the reader a bit of a shock when she says, "On Sundays try to walk like a lady and not like the slut you are so bent on becoming." This warning quickly becomes the refrain of the piece.

The refrain is surprising, in part, because the daughter seems, at first, quite young and rather well-behaved; but the girl may not be the same age at the beginning and end of the story. You may want to have the class find the clues "Girl" provides about the daughter's age. Such a discussion will probably note the nature of the mother's fears. Explore possible inconsistencies in her advice, such as when the mother tells the daughter how "to make a good medicine to throw away a child before it even becomes a child," and when she tells her "how to love a man." Earlier the mother warned the daughter about singing benna in Sunday school, but now she is telling her daughter "how to spit up in the air" when she feels like it. Both pieces of advice are delivered in the same way — using either the command form or beginning with the words "this is how." Why? What, for instance, is the effect of using the same construction for talking about how to make a pepper pot and how to give yourself an abortion? What is the mother telling the daughter about women's lives? Where does the mother's knowledge come from?

WRITING SUGGESTION   The daughter in "Girl" constantly hears her mother's advice about how to act appropriately. How is this advice specific to a girl? What might a father's advice to a boy sound like? Write a monologue entitled "Boy" in the same style as Kincaid's story. How does the impact of your monologue differ from that of "Girl"?

Andrew Sullivan

WHAT IS A HOMOSEXUAL? (p. 53)

This selection from Sullivan's book *Virtually Normal* is not a personal essay, per se, but an example of a writer using his experiences to further a point. Here, the argument has to do with Sullivan's sense of the relationship between a gay teenager's development and his later character. The formative experience is the gay male's concealment of sexual desire in order to survive the harsh world of adolescence. This concealment — necessary, Sullivan maintains, in even the most liberal of atmospheres, for the homosexual will always be in the minority and conformity is the rule in adolescence — requires some skills. And these skills — "the rituals of deceit, impersonation and appearance"— carry forward into later life. No surprise, then, that you find so many gays in the worlds of art or fashion. And, no surprise, that you find gays distinguishing between sexual desire and emotional longing; they've had to do so since they were boys.

Sullivan knows, as he claims all this, that he's furthering a stereotype, and he tries to hedge against it. Later in the essay, he criticizes advocates of diversity who are reluctant to make group generalizations. Earlier he simply argues that it's not the stereotype that's wrong, but the understanding of the psychological underpinnings of the stereotype. Thus, he argues, gays are promiscuous because they've been damaged by early concealment and by the trauma of exclusion. The splitting of the sexual and emotional becomes a habit reinforced by a relatively limited pool of potential partners. (Have students consider the logic of this claim. Why would a limited pool of partners or a higher chance of rejection change the nature of an attachment? Might the same premises result in the opposite conclusion — that the gay male ventures out less and forms permanent attachments in order to avoid rejection?)

To explain the presence of gays in "professions of appearance," Sullivan states that a gay man learns early to be attuned to surfaces and to decipher the relationship of the surface to the interior. These skills, developed under painful circumstances, have their virtues, marketable and otherwise, in later life.

Like Michael Dorris in "Life Stories" (p. 45), Sullivan has found the worthwhile aspects of a trying experience. And, like Dorris, Sullivan knows that he must anticipate and respond to potential objections to his ideas. Sullivan tries to protect himself from attack by saying essentially what Dorris actually says in his essay: "At least that's how it seem[s] to me."

In paragraph 9, when asked to give evidence for why he thinks homosexuality is a predilection not a choice, Sullivan says his only evidence is himself. This might be an admission of the weakness of his argument, but he has set up the discussion by acknowledging that plenty of gay people have had relatively comfortable adolescences. This admission isn't presented as a counterargument but as an opportunity for Sullivan to consider his emotions about contradictory evidence. Opposing experiences "rebuke" his own, make him "marvel at the naturalness of their self-confidence," but they don't alter his sense that his experience is common.

Sullivan is not interested in having his reader make a decision on the issue of how or why someone is homosexual or even what homosexuality is. Instead, he wants the reader to have a sense of "what the homosexual experience is actually like." Though Sullivan doesn't insist on the universal validity of his interpretation of gay experience, he *is* prepared to make claims that aren't merely personal. His generalizations about homosexual and lesbian character aren't true, he says, but "have the ring of truth." His evidence, beyond his own experience, is simply his familiarity with the gay community. Point out to students that this is one way in which an argumentative paper can persuade — by presenting the writer's qualifications to address the matter at hand.

Paragraph 14 presents Sullivan's group characterization. He holds that, along with an eye for surfaces, the homosexual male is liable to be "more wary and distant . . . more self-conscious and perhaps more reflective" than others. He is likely to be arch and to have found outlets for expression in the arts. And just in case the reader is offended by all this, Sullivan limits his claim in his final paragraph: "My point is simply that the universal experience of self-conscious difference in childhood and adolescence — common, but not exclusive, to homosexuals — develops identifiable skills."

Ask students to analyze this final claim. If it's true, do all people who experience themselves as outsiders end up with the "skills of mimesis"? Up to this point, Sullivan had been arguing that it's the specific nature of the homosexual's "self-conscious difference" that is crucial. Is he changing his mind? Ask students to account for Sullivan's strategy in the selection's closing paragraphs. You might also ask students to go through the essay and see where else he modifies his thoughts. What is the purpose and effect of his qualifying language?

WRITING SUGGESTIONS   (a) Sullivan fears he'll be accused of homophobia when he offers his description of homosexual character. Would it be fair to accuse him of propagating a stereotype? Explain why or why not.

(b) Both Sullivan and Michael Dorris ("Life Stories," p. 45) understand their adult characters in light of early, possibly formative, experiences. Identify two or three experiences in your life that seem similarly significant. Describe the experiences and how they came to affect you. Instead of trying to give a full picture of yourself, concentrate on two or three linked memories and one related aspect of your current character.

FAMILY TIES

Recognizing Knots in the Ties

Family relationships, always complicated, seem even more so in a time when families have changed but definitions and expectations haven't. Part 2's early selections ask us to look past outmoded notions and into some actual homes — the households described in Thomas Simmons's, Raymond Carver's, and Calvin Trillin's essays and in Tillie Olsen's short story. Later selections analyze what we see, arguing for improvements in parenting, better definitions of family, and a more honest handling of emotion.

To help students make the transition from the writing of personal essays to analytic, argumentative, and research papers, you may want to use the selections in this part to assign *analytic* personal response essays in which students use their experiences to refute or further the arguments of Leo Rosten, Anndee Hochman, Barbara Dafoe Whitehead, or Amitai Etzioni.

Students may need reminding that papers that relate experience to reading require different skills than personal essays. Instead of using the reading solely as a jumping off point for their own memories and ideas, students should analyze the essays for truth value, and they should compare and contrast the ideas and experiences of the authors with their own. They should find a way to focus on the similarities and differences between the reading and their experiences and not simply respond to the essay, point by point, with observations and personal anecdotes. To do this they'll have to read the essays carefully, distill the essence of each, identify key ideas, summarize relevant points, and evaluate argumentative strategy.

Now is probably the time to talk to students about how to integrate references to and discussions of other sources into their work. This requires a discussion of how to summarize, paraphrase, and quote. (It might be a good time, too, to talk about plagiarism — unintentional and otherwise — since plagiarism is, essentially, about a failure to appropriately attribute paraphrases and quotations.)

Insights

Is the family unit the bulwark of society, as Robert Nisbet states, or is it, as Ferdinand Mount claims, the principal refuge of the individual against the pressures of society? Or is it increasingly irrelevant, as J. H. Plumb suggests? Students can be led to see that these contrasting views of family life probably pertain to different social circumstances and that each observation correctly assesses the role of the family in a particular social context. Ask them for examples to support Nisbet's and Mount's claims.

Plumb's assertion might be considered in light of the economic function of the family. When large families became an economic liability rather than an asset, the shape of the family changed. Changes in the family's social function followed. But does a change in the shape of the family mean that the institution itself is weak? Ask students what social functions the family still serves and, as a transition into the Robert Weiss quote, what functions, outside the social, the family serves.

Weiss clearly sees a psychological role for the family, and he suggests the attachment of children to parents is fated. This perspective links human family structure to more primitive imprinting among animals.

Robert Hayden's poem provides a nice transition from Part 1 to Part 2, since the son in "Those Winter Sundays" has to examine his own life before he can discover his father. In the essays that follow about fathers, Carver and Simmons also look back, with a certain regret, at their complicated fathers and the idiosyncratic ways in which they revealed their affection for their sons.

Thomas Simmons

MOTORCYCLE TALK (p. 63)

Thomas Simmons opens by telling us that his father was an unhappy and difficult man with one significant virtue — his devotion to machines. While another writer might indulge in parental analysis, considering the source of his father's depression or what made him so hard to get along with, Simmons chooses instead to focus on his father's skill with machines. This talent was a medium of affection that allowed father and son to communicate.

From what is left unsaid, we can see this essay as an attempt to look past the problems in the author's relationship with his father. You might ask students to characterize these difficulties. What has Simmons left out? Do students feel the omissions detract from the essay? Why or why not?

Our sense of the father is expanded by scattered details about him and by the story of "the go-kart he built from scrap parts in his father's basement in the Depression"— the story he frequently tells about himself despite its disastrous ending. Why then does he tell it? An important ingredient in the story is the harsh scolding that Simmons's father receives when he makes an understandable — if financially devastating — mistake as a result of boyhood exuberance. Might the father, in repeating the story, be trying to apologize for or explain his own behavior as a father? Is he saying that he still feels "stupid" and "irresponsible"?

We quickly learn that the father is tender with machines. Later Simmons concludes that his father cares for him the way a flat-truck mechanic cares for his driver. Ask students what they make of this metaphor. Is it a positive or a negative one, in the context of the essay?

When speaking the language of machines, Simmons connects with his father, but this connection is eventually not enough. First, as he writes, "What we shared through the motorcycle contradicted most of our other encounters in the family." Second, Simmons "began to leave him behind": he's learning other ways of connecting, and he doesn't want to be limited to his father's often inadequate forms of communication.

In the essay's final paragraph, however, Simmons seems to accept his father's limited communication by adapting to it. Like an immigrant, or a child who has grown up and out of the ghetto, he has learned the language that will help him get by in the larger world, while still appreciating what he left behind.

You may want to raise for the class the significance of Simmons's occupation: he is a writer, a man of words. Indeed, it is wordplay, in paragraph 10 and again in the final metaphor, that allows Simmons to discover the truth of his relationship with his father.

WRITING SUGGESTION   Consider current cultural norms for what a good father is. How do they resonate with your own beliefs about what makes a good father? How does the father in "Motorcycle Talk" meet or fail your standards?

Raymond Carver

MY FATHER'S LIFE (p. 67)

Raymond Carver's first paragraph focuses on names and nicknames, suggesting comparisons with Rom Harré's quote in Part 1's Insights. Carver's many names indicate the special ambiguities of identity for both father and son, and they indicate how the lives of father and son will blur at points.

The true identity of the father is an ambiguity that the essay resolves in part. Many of the mother's references to her husband are tinged with criticism of his unreliability. She criticizes herself as well for throwing her life away on him. Still, her emotions are complicated by her attachment, and her criticisms are followed up with statements such as: "He was my first and last. I never had another man. But I didn't miss anything."

The son understands the father as an ordinary man of his type, fairly steady in his early life, committed to family relationships, and generous in sharing his small gains. The son sees the father in a historical and social context that the mother may not perceive, for she is embedded in the same context, and she is sharing (or victim to) many of the father's struggles. Carver allows us to see the mother as a suspicious, insistent, but entirely dependable person.

In Carver's account, the rugged but boyish good nature of the father — who becomes a more helpless boy after the son grows to manhood — seems too soft to bear up under the harsh working experiences of his life. Carver shows us this by combining his own early memories with a direct narrative of events in his father's life. Alcohol plays a role in all of this — in the early memories of poverty, in the stories of the father's hard luck, and, eventually, in the author's own life.

Although the essay doesn't let us know where the author's life leads him, we do see the final outcome of the father's struggles. He has a psychological breakdown that is not recognized by his family until his sickness is so severe that shame and remorse accompany the memory for Carver.

In one of the more affecting moments of the essay, Carver goes to tell his father about his child's birth. Point out to students that in this scene, as elsewhere, Carver doesn't tell us that the moment was moving. He doesn't say, "I felt my heart would break." Rather he shows us the moment, and we are, necessarily, moved by it. (In their own writing, students should take care not to narrate their own emotions but to present the events that give rise to their emotions. By communicating the source of their feelings to their readers, they may elicit similar feelings in their audience.)

It is not evident that the father wanted to be bold, as Carver's poem asserts; it is more apparent that Carver wished his father was bolder, tougher, and more durable. The gentleness of the father is hard for Carver to acknowledge, for it leads him to the pain that the essay has deferred until the conclusion. The repetition of the name *Raymond* expresses both a deep sense of loss and the extent to which the son identifies with his father. Not only do they share the same name, but they possess the same vulnerabilities and, possibly, the same future.

WRITING SUGGESTION   In several pieces in Part 2 — the poem by Robert Hayden ("Those Winter Sundays" in the Insights on p. 61) and the essays by Carver and Thomas Simmons ("Motorcycle Talk," p. 63) — the male author needs to learn something about himself before he can understand his father. Pick two of these works, and analyze the lessons the sons learned and the ways those lessons helped them to appreciate their fathers.

Calvin Trillin

IT'S JUST TOO LATE (p. 75)

In the first paragraph, Calvin Trillin observes that the Coopers, FaNee's parents, "were the sort of people who might have been expected to have an ideal child." You might ask the class to interpret Trillin's ironic statement. His implicit criticism invites consideration of how the parents' own values contributed to their daughter's rebellion. As an ideal child, FaNee embodied the conventional and impersonal standard of goodness by which the Coopers live. Trillin allows us to see that the parents are childish, defining themselves by adolescent concepts of adulthood. Leo overrates his high-school athletic achievement, hanging on to his boyhood laurels long after they should have been superseded by a different sense of worth. His ponderously elaborate style of talking suggests an immature and awkward assumption of adult dignity. He has chosen to work as a coach, preserving his preeminence among young athletes; and as a junior high school principal, he is disingenuous and dogmatic toward his easily dominated students. His wife, JoAnn, "created" the daughter's fanciful name, indicating that her child is a doll-like possession whose name and other attributes should satisfy a parent's whim. In the second paragraph, Trillin gives the impression that the parents minimized FaNee's genuine devotion to her grandmother, prizing only the display of FaNee's talent as a poet in her conventional expression of pieties. They failed to allow her to retain any of her grandmother's trinkets that would acknowledge her love and loss. When FaNee enters junior high school they anticipate only cosmetic problems — her "double affliction of glasses and braces"— and show concern over her social role as their daughter.

Trillin places the Coopers in a social context that might increase our sympathy for them as parents trying to construct a respectable life for their family. The distinction the Coopers are trying to make, however, might be read as a class distinction rather than a moral one. They differentiate themselves from the disreputable mountain people of Union County by choosing to live in Knox County, a uniform and featureless place. In such bleak and precarious circumstances, where people are classified as the right or wrong sort, any genuine desire for individuality is likely to be seen as freakish by society. Ironically, it is Leo Cooper who describes the log cabin that his family is building as "just a little bit different," like FaNee's name (paragraph 3), while FaNee is the one who becomes entangled with a group of friends who call themselves "Freaks."

17

Trillin's viewpoint suggests that the Coopers and FaNee's friends are driven into their crazy, unreasonable actions by the narrowness of the choices they see. They seem compelled to react in rigid patterns. FaNee's sense that nothing can be done to improve her situation at home, that "it's just too late," indicates her intuition that people around her are governed by unalterable modes of behavior. They live by fantasy roles and empty standards. The wild car chase comes to exemplify their blindness to any alternatives. You might ask your students at what point it really is "too late" for FaNee, and why.

In an interview in the *Journal of Basic Writing* (Fall/Winter 1981), Calvin Trillin says that the story of a violent death contains its "own narrative line," since it has a natural beginning, middle, and end. Given that, Trillin tries to make his own methodical reporting invisible to the reader. He says, "What I try to do when I write is get out of the way and just let the story tell itself. I try to get as many details as cleanly as possible into the story and try to get all the marks of writing off of the story." Ask students how "It's Just Too Late" reflects this methodology. You might note, in particular, how and when Trillin uses dialogue (including bits of FaNee's writing) to narrate parts of the story.

WRITING SUGGESTION   Tell the story of a rebellious act that was committed in your hometown or your current place of residence. Do some research to uncover different responses to the act, and then discuss where you think responsibility for the act lies.

Leo Rosten

HOME IS WHERE TO LEARN HOW TO HATE (p. 84)

Leo Rosten's essay acknowledges the existence of hate and even trumpets its virtues. He contends that people are suspicious of hate because it's so often been used in the service of evil, which doesn't mean that *it* is evil. Hate can have a constructive, even moral, purpose. People need to learn how to hate properly because, for Rosten, correct hate is relevant, fitting, controlled, and justifiable. But that's not how most people hate. Instead "they hate what they fear, and kill what they hate."

As proof of his point, Leo Rosten describes a woman's response to his lecture about the human *"capacity* to hate and the will to slaughter." Ask students how her unintentionally ironic words in paragraph 3 prove Rosten's point. How do students feel about Rosten's description of his attacker as a "pink-cheeked, beaming little dowager"? Is this funny? condescending? a result of Rosten's own anger? Do students agree that the woman was angry because she was frightened, as Rosten's claim that people "hate what they fear" suggests?

The origins of hate are, for Rosten, mysterious and irrelevant. All that matters is that hate exists. You might ask students to evaluate Rosten's evidence of hate. Is it all equally persuasive? (A baby's furious crying doesn't necessarily indicate fury. What about a toddler's kicks and punches?) In paragraphs 9 and 10 Rosten seems to conflate any distinction between anger and hate. Do students? How might this hurt or help Rosten's argument?

If hate starts young, then instructions in the proper use of hate should start early, too. Rosten argues that we should neither deny children's hate nor ask them to repress their emotions. Instead, we should recognize that hate denied is hate intensified. Children shouldn't be asked to understand that which is truly repellent or to suppose that turning the other cheek is an invariably moral response.

In paragraphs 17 to 26, Rosten argues by using the second person, setting up an imaginary opponent and defeating that naysayer's points, one by one. This device allows Rosten to respond quickly to obvious objections to his argument then move on to a refinement of his thought — to claim that it is irrational, unloving, and indecent to fail to hate. Though Rosten uses humor in the early part of the essay, his tone becomes progressively more inflamed. How does the writing style — the brevity of the paragraphs, the use of repetition, the abundance of parentheticals and italics — suggest his mood? Does Rosten's essay seem angry?

If so, Rosten would probably argue that his anger is proper. After all, the stakes are high. If good men don't hate, evil will triumph. We have history as evidence. Lines of the Bible may contradict Rosten's beliefs, but other lines confirm them. Rosten mimics the Eighty-ninth Psalm when he lists, in paragraphs 33 to 36, objects of his hatred. What's the purpose of this stylistic device?

Rosten concludes by continuing the argument of paragraphs 17 to 26. The points echo what Rosten's already said, while adding a final idea: "Home is where it is *safe* to hate — first." Before students consider this claim, have them examine paragraphs 9 to 16. How do these paragraphs work within the context of the larger essay? Do they seem to be apiece — in terms of tone, argumentative strategy, and writing style? How do they contribute or detract from Rosten's overall case for a morally justifiable anger? Do these paragraphs describe safe anger? How do they do so? If not, what is safe anger? Can a home make anger safe? Should it?

WRITING SUGGESTION   Recall a time when you felt and expressed anger. Describe the situation that gave rise to the emotion, and then critique or justify your behavior. Would Rosten have considered your anger proper? Why or why not?

Tillie Olsen

I STAND HERE IRONING (p. 90)

This story abruptly plunges us into a mother's internal monologue, stimulated by a phone call from someone who thinks her daughter Emily needs counseling. The mother's first response to the phone call is to do what she says she doesn't have time to do — "to remember, to sift, to weigh, to estimate, to total." Twice the mother tells us that Emily was "a beautiful baby." She finally proceeds, as we sense she will, to "but." Instead of following with a list of Emily's shortcomings, the mother gives us a list of the failures of the outside world, the limitations of the "seeing eyes" and the mother's own difficult circumstances.

Ask students whether they have sympathy for the mother. On the surface, the narrator's detailing of her own situation might seem to include a great deal of self-justifying and special pleading, as she recounts a long string of unmanageable circumstances — "of depression, of war, of fear"— that prevented her from being a better mother. What emerges from her monologue, however, is not self-pity but understated compassion for Emily, insight into the girl's growing autonomy and trust in her strengths. The mother's love and sympathy for her child increase as a result of the misfortunes they both suffered. The mother was also ridden down by harsh forces — like the dress flattened by the iron — but both women steadily exercised sufficient power to resist the flattening of their spirits. They "bloom" at least partially with pride and wisdom, qualities that arrive late in both their lives — in the mother's second marriage and in the daughter's early adulthood.

Neither of them blooms as a result of the "help" they received along the way, and this explains, in part, the mother's resistance to the caller. After all, the help Emily got at the nursery school and convalescent home only seemed to hurt her. In the end, the mother says, "I will never total it all." But then she does total it all — for the reader, if not the phone caller. By the end we know that Emily has been shaped by her unhappy circumstances — her unpopularity, her illness, her fatherlessness, her poverty, her mother's exhaustion, and her rivalry with her siblings. But she also has a gift and is loved and supported by many.

Ask students to discuss the significance of the ironing and its relation to the story's theme. Is the iron a positive or a negative force, smoothing or crushing?

WRITING SUGGESTION   Consider the social background of this piece (as opposed to the personal background that includes the mother's struggles). What does the specter of nuclear war have to do with Emily's personality? Where do social circumstances reinforce Emily's hardships?

Anndee Hochman

EXTENDING FAMILY (p. 98)

Anndee Hochman's essay starts by noting the popular (heterosexual) culture's habit of portraying ex-lovers as vengeful enemies. (You might ask students for some representative examples.) Of course, the truth of contemporary relationships is usually more complex than what one sees in the movies or on television: certain ex-lovers do maintain friendships. Hochman offers the common occurrence of friendships among former lesbian couples and her experience with her former boyfriend Barry as evidence. While she acknowledges that continuing such relationships may be difficult, requiring "emotional endurance" and a readiness "to paddle through jealousy, possessiveness, grief, guilt, and anger," she goes on to say that difficulty doesn't rule out the possibility of a new kind of friendship.

And yet these friendships are not acknowledged — not in popular culture and not in our dictionaries. This is, in part, because such friendships are not easy to depict or define. They challenge long-standing myths, and they confuse convention — from gift-giving etiquette to loyalty issues. Hochman emphasizes the need for representation, in particular for "semantic ingenuity" that will give postrelationship friendships a name. Ask students why this is so important to Hochman. What does she think a word can do? The answer should lead to the final paragraphs of the essay, where Hochman uses the Yiddish word *mishpokhe* to consider what a redefinition of family requires.

Hochman's vision is an expansive one: she's willing to conceive of kinship broadly, partially because she doesn't feel that affection is limited. How do students interpret this generosity? Does it seem convincing? realistic? admirable? In the end, who is included and who excluded from Hochman's family?

WRITING SUGGESTION   Hochman redefines family so it includes more than blood relatives. Do you define your family similarly? Why or why not? When you think of your family, who do you include and who do you exclude? Explain, using your reasons to support or contradict Hochman's argument.

Barbara Dafoe Whitehead

WOMEN AND THE FUTURE OF FATHERHOOD (p. 101)

One way to start discussion of this essay is to have the class do some brief research on the "contemporary debate over fatherhood" to which Barbara Dafoe Whitehead refers in her opening sentence. You might split the class into groups and assign different topics — such as the men's movement and the Million Man March — and then have students report in class on the rhetoric that surrounds current discussions of fatherhood. This will give students a better sense of the debate Whitehead joins with this essay.

Whitehead's criticism of the so-called fatherhood movement isn't thorough-going. She admires the "cultural" goal of making responsible, loving parenting a masculine attribute, and she has no difficulty with the movement's political goal of acquiring a voice for men. What she objects to is the exclusion of women from the fatherhood debate. As Whitehead sees it, "marital disruption" is the source of "the fatherhood problem." Before you ask students to tackle this premise, ask them exactly what Whitehead means by "the fatherhood problem" and why she chooses not to define it. Only after the class has reached a consensus should they try to explain her conclusion about marital disruption. Her argument is that men need marriage for fatherhood in a way that women *don't* need marriage for motherhood. Since marriage is presumably what keeps men in close proximity to their children, the absence of marriage means men don't have a chance to make the contributions (emotional and instrumental) that are necessary for effective parenting. What is more, they don't have "access to the social and emotional intelligence of women in building relationships," and the father who doesn't live at home may be denigrated by the mother who does.

Whitehead finds her conclusion about the central role of marriage troubling, since women aren't particularly willing to solve the fatherhood problem by reinstating marriage to its former incarnation. Indeed, now that women are no longer economically dependent on marriage, they are no longer willing to stay in unhappy relationships, especially since they can meet many of their emotional and personal goals without marriage. Whitehead says that women have not lost interest in satisfying marriages but that they have grown cynical and despairing of men — in particular, the demands of the male ego.

According to Whitehead, the fact that women can have motherhood without marriage — and that men can't have fatherhood similarly — results in a "virtue gap" (see paragraph 11) between the sexes. Popular culture reflects our sense of the single mother as hard-working and the absent father as selfish, perhaps even a "deadbeat dad." (She cites *Waiting to Exhale* as an instance of this. You might ask students for other examples.)

So what's to be done? Women aren't going to give up the achievements of the last few decades and return to outmoded arrangements. Nor does Whitehead think they should, for though she holds the solution to the fatherhood problem will have to include women, she finds men primarily to blame for the situation: they have to understand what *they* need to do to find a solution that involves an effective arrangement between the sexes. Should it be a new kind of marriage? Perhaps. Whitehead doesn't say what the arrangement will be but only what it will have to consider, notably "some mutual understanding and commitment to an equitable division of tasks" and a discussion of expectations for marriage. In paragraph 15, Whitehead concludes that women want fidelity and emotional intimacy (which presumably men aren't as interested in), while men want sexual intimacy (which presumably women don't value as highly). You might ask students about these conclusions. Are these stereotypes or accurate portrayals?

Whitehead also reminds us that to be fair, the roles of mother and father don't need to be the same. Like Anndee Hochman in "Extending Family" (p. 98), she proposes "another kind of language" to talk about relationships. Right now, our understanding focuses on individual needs — which may make some sense for a childless marriage but makes less sense when the needs of children must be considered. When marriage is seen as an arrangement for raising children, the language of relationships, Whitehead suggests, needs to recognize "differences, mutuality, complementarity, and, more than anything else, altruism."

While Whitehead's arguments may seem reasonably persuasive, students may be irked by her assumptions about the sexes. Ask them to identify and examine them. Also, Whitehead gives ample evidence that divorce is a detriment to fatherhood, since it often leaves the father at a physical distance from the child. Does this mean, necessarily, that marriage improves fatherhood?

WRITING SUGGESTION   Consider Whitehead's claims about the role of women in successful fatherhood. Further or disprove her points using your personal experience or your observations about families. Alternatively, analyze Whitehead's argument by comparing it with one of the following: Tobias Wolff's memoir, *This Boy's Life*; Mary Karr's memoir, *The Liars' Club*; or Raymond Carver's essay "My Father's Life" (p. 67).

Amitai Etzioni

THE VALUE OF FAMILIES (p. 107)

Sociologist Amitai Etzioni's point in this excerpt is fairly straightforward: parents need to spend more time, a lot more time, with their children. The stand-ins for parental attention — notably child-care facilities — are woefully inadequate. Though Etzioni offers short-term suggestions for avoiding the worst of their damage, his idea for long-term improvement is simply not to rely on them — that is, to get parents back in the home and caring for their children.

Since Etzioni's argument isn't overly complex, it might be interesting to use this essay to talk about how outside sources can bolster an argument. Many of the writers in this section have relied heavily on personal experience to make their points, or they've used their familiarity with a certain community to establish their authority to speak on a matter. Etzioni does a bit of this in paragraph 14, but, in general, he uses written sources to prove, illustrate, authenticate, or support his points. In many ways, his essay looks like the kind of papers students will be asked to write throughout their college years.

Have students highlight places in the article where Etzioni refers to an outside source. Aside from the footnoted material, they should note the reference to *The Good Society* in paragraph 4 and the public service commercial in paragraph 5. Then ask them to consider Etzioni's purpose in citing all this material. They should quickly see that Etzioni uses the research material for different effects. Sometimes (as with footnotes, 1, 3, and 9) he presents a statistic as evidence for a claim that needs proof. At other times (as in paragraph 4 and with footnotes 2, 4, and 7), Etzioni quotes an authority (a family expert, a Yale professor) who echoes his ideas. In paragraph 6, for example, he uses Barbara Dafoe Whitehead to confirm his notion that "quality time occurs within quantity time." Without the Whitehead quote, Etzioni's argument makes sense, and Whitehead is only offering another opinion. She's not offering evidence, but she's been introduced as an authority, and, as such, her words are meant to carry weight with the reader.

In footnotes 6 and 8, Etzioni offers the conclusions of various child psychology studies to prove his point. And in footnote 5 and paragraph 5, Etzioni uses a shocking fact (from a popular magazine) and a disturbing image (from a commercial). The commercial is essentially a piece of fiction, and the story about children strapped into car seats (para. 10) is an extreme example. Etzioni knows this, so he uses the commercial or the car-seat story not to prove anything but only to demonstrate how dire the parenting and child-care situation can become.

Point out for students that Etzioni never uses his sources to argue for him. He has his own ideas, and he doesn't rely on long quotes of outside material in lieu of articulating his own thoughts.

Ask students to consider the advantage of using different types of sources. How might Etzioni's essay have differed if he relied exclusively on expert opinion or solely on statistics?

Finally, should Etzioni have offered more supporting evidence at any point? If so, where? One possibility occurs in paragraph 16, where Etzioni writes, "Over the last twenty-five years we have seen the future, and it is not a wholesome one." Should he have elaborated?

Amitai Etzioni's argument, for all its documentation, may sound scholarly and still not convince. Students will need to trace his thoughts carefully to evaluate his conclusion that "we have made a mistake in assuming that strangers can be entrusted with the effective personality formation of infants and toddlers."

WRITING SUGGESTION   What, in your opinion, is the ideal child-care arrangement? Is your ideal a practical one? Explain why or why not, making reference, when appropriate, to your personal experience, your observations of other families, or your *Life Studies* reading.

PART 3

SIGNIFICANT OTHERS

Comparing Experiences

In considering love, friendship, and marriage, the selections in this chapter touch on race, gender, and sexual preference, while addressing issues of morality, basic rights, and propriety. The topics here remain personal. Several of the pieces include the kind of reflection that students have encountered in Parts 1 and 2, while others consider personal issues from a scientific or social policy perspective.

You may want to continue to have students compare and contrast their experiences with those of the authors, or you may want to assign more critical analysis of the essays. Either way, students should be encouraged to examine rhetorical strategies, as well as the author's role and voice. Even Diane Ackerman — who doesn't talk about her personal experience — is present in her article.

Insights

Simone de Beauvoir's skepticism can provide a good approach to this topic because she doubts that men and women have the same concepts of love. The other Insights raise questions about the *origin* of love. Is its source divine or personal? They also question the *goal* of love. Is love an escape, an egotistic foray, or a transcendent endeavor? The statement by Walker Percy exalts love as the supreme spiritual experience. The statements by Selma Fraiberg and Francesco Alberoni will probably provoke students' refutations or resistance because by relating love to infancy and to depression, these statements appear to challenge the authenticity of the emotion itself.

The poem by Sharon Olds develops an ironic perspective that students may fail to grasp on their own. The poet's opening tone of naive curiosity, even envy, may remain unmodified for them, despite the details that introduce repugnance, revulsion, criticism, and foreknowledge of abandonment for the unloving sexual athletes. The sense of absolute isolation at the end is eerie and frightening — maybe fascinating, too.

Susan Allen Toth

BOYFRIENDS (p. 118)

This essay may seem archaic to some students. It is important, therefore, to locate the similarities between dating rituals of the 1950s and those of today. Some things Toth discusses still hold true — early uncertainty, networks of girlfriends and boyfriends, the importance of secrets, and the search for privacy.

You might ask students to discuss their high school and college dating rituals. While some students may engage on this topic, others may insist that they belong to an era of people who never date. What, then, are the steps by which people today move to romance?

Certainly, current dating practices aren't codified for young adults as they once were. Toth is aware of this, and her essay reflects her sense that she is writing of a time that has passed.

Toth speaks of Peter Stone with great affection, but it is always clear that she never loved him. Still, Peter Stone fulfilled the youthful Toth's need for a boyfriend. Much as Nora Ephron in "Shaping Up Absurd" (p. 20) felt she needed big breasts to assure herself of her female identity, Toth needed a boyfriend to assure herself of her desirability and, more important (and with some irony), her place in the female community.

In Toth's memory of her girlhood, Peter Stone fulfills a need as well, for the adult writer partially misses the unthreatening (meaning nonsexual) physical affection and tenderness of the 1950s. She calls her piece "Boyfriends," not "Boyfriend," to indicate that this piece is as much a tribute to that passing phenomenon as it is about Peter Stone. Here, affection without love seems sweet, but in Sharon Olds's poem (see the Insights on p. 115), sex without love is devastating. It is the difference between the two pieces that explains Toth's nostalgia. Toth feels that for all the naiveté of the 1950s, there was something touching about the slow, safe wooing. You might ask students whether they agree or whether they feel Toth is romanticizing the period.

WRITING SUGGESTION   Toth's essay was written about dating rituals in the 1950s. Sharon Olds's poem "Sex Without Love" (see the Insights on p. 115) was published in the early 1980s. Use the claims that Olds's poem seems to be making and your own observations about current wooing rituals to discuss what has been gained and what has been lost since Toth's time.

Stephen Dunn

LOCKER ROOM TALK (p. 124)

Students are so often told that a thesis should be in a first paragraph that you might start discussion by noting that Stephen Dunn ends with his thesis. Instead of starting by presenting his central point, Dunn uses the initial paragraphs of "Locker Room Talk" to detail the experiences that led him to his conclusion about sexual braggadocio.

The occasion for the essay, introduced in paragraph 4, is an overheard conversation, but Dunn's familiarity with locker room talk predates that event. In paragraphs 1 to 3, Dunn gives a quick rundown of his past feelings about locker room talk (and his reluctance, through the years, to engage in it). As a teenager and young man, he feels "wonderment and then embarrassment" when others tell their stories, and he experiences some awkwardness at his failure to contribute. Later, he's simply embarrassed, though he recognizes the impulse to talk about sexual experience.

Dunn never gives us the sense, however, that he once wanted to brag about his sexual exploits, as the young man in the college locker room does. Still, Dunn feels complicitous. He is discomfited by how he and the other men in the locker room gave their "quiet sanctions" of the young man's talk. That said, he's less interested in exploring his discomfort than in speculating on why men engage in such talk. In paragraph 6, he considers several possibilities but rejects them. Ask students why Dunn doesn't just tell us what he's concluded. What does he achieve by revealing his thought process?

Do students agree with Dunn's eventual interpretation — that the young man brags in order to protect himself from feeling? When Dunn confesses (in paragraph 3) that he would have liked to tell his friend Alan about his sexual life, was he trying to protect himself similarly? Does Dunn's memory of feeling "excessively private, cut off" suggest another explanation for sexual confession?

Dunn's thesis is in paragraph 6, but he refines and elaborates on his idea in paragraph 7. What are the purposes of paragraph 8? In shifting the focus of the essay, what is Dunn able to say about mature love?

Have students consider the words "prophylactic" and "immunity" in paragraphs 7 and 8. Using these words, Dunn suggests to us the rhetoric of AIDS and safe sex. What is his purpose in doing so?

Finally, ask students to look at the closing line and articulate what they felt on finishing the essay. Dunn might have judged or mocked the young man in the locker room. Instead, he leaves the reader where he couldn't leave the young man — with an emotion.

WRITING SUGGESTION   At the close of his essay, Dunn expresses sorrow for the young man in the locker room. Why? Do you share his feelings? Explain why or why not.

Diane Ackerman

THE CHEMISTRY OF LOVE (p. 127)

In "The Chemistry of Love," Diane Ackerman examines the role of three chemicals — oxytocin, PEA, and endorphins — in mother love, romantic love, infatuation, and long-term attachment. Though her information is undeniably fascinating, people may resist her approach, which seems to reduce our complex subjective selves — our personalities and desires — to chemical compounds. Ackerman's purpose is primarily informational, though she does allow herself to hazard some guesses about the implications of her information. Students should note how often Ackerman uses qualifying words here. Things "might" or "may" help explain a phenomenon. A chemical "seems" to have certain effects. Can your students find places where she fails to examine her conclusions or assumptions? Her facts are often so pleasingly wild that it's easy to accept her speculations enthusiastically, especially since much of what Ackerman presents *is* factual.

Science writing is often considered dry or dull, so students should look at how Ackerman manages to keep things lively here. Her descriptions are at times infused with awe. Where do students get a sense of the writer's personal voice in her essay? How would they describe her attitudes toward nature and the human body? How does this affect their reading of her essay? An analysis of any one paragraph will show her skill at playfully packing a wealth of technical material into readable, entertaining prose. It might be a good idea to do this as a class. In paragraph 4, for example, Ackerman makes interesting information more so, by prefacing it with a quotation from Carl Jung and then using highly charged language to describe the highly charged effects of PEA. After describing PEA's effect, she cites two fascinating studies that elaborate on the chemical's effect. She summarizes what the studies might imply and ends with a funny (but, she encourages us to think, accurate) quip. Love just might be "a sweet fix."

WRITING SUGGESTION   How might Ackerman's essay help account for the various loves described in Raymond Carver's story "What We Talk About When We Talk About Love" (p. 160)? Does a purely physiological explanation ever feel insufficient? If so, explain why.

Eugene Goodheart

FAST FRIENDS (p. 131)

Organizing his essay around sweeping statements, Eugene Goodheart nonetheless avoids easy generalizations and sentimentality as he considers the nature of friendship. Rather than qualify his thoughts, he explores their contradictory nature, as when he writes (para. 13), "Friendship has no rules of deference. Yet equality is impossible."

Goodheart's essay is more expository than persuasive, offering an extended definition of friendship. He elaborates on his subject by comparing friendship to marriage, by considering friendship's quirks and qualities, and by delineating the phases of friendship. Some of Goodheart's thoughts go entirely unsupported, while others are fleshed out with literary references or personal anecdotes. Ask students for their reaction to Goodheart's use of D. H. Lawrence. Does it matter that Goodheart uses fiction to establish his point? (Would a reference to a lesser book be acceptable? What about a movie?)

"Fast Friends" doesn't have a thesis exactly, though it does leave the reader with a strong sense of the overall value of friendships. Still, almost every paragraph has a strong topic sentence. Indeed, the individual paragraphs read like mini-essays, with the central point introduced in the first or second sentence and elaborated in subsequent lines. The flow from paragraph to paragraph, while not awkward, isn't as natural as the movement in an essay like Dunn's "Locker Room Talk" (p. 124). Goodheart avoids Dunn's explicit transitional phrases, relying instead on the essay's internal logic to provide unity. The logic is most apparent in paragraphs 1 to 3, where Goodheart considers past writers on friendship (by way of introducing his subject and distinguishing his approach), and in paragraphs 14 to 30, where Goodheart details the stages of friendship, allowing himself two brief detours — for the Alyosha anecdote and for a discussion of those with a "talent for friendship" (in paragraph 24). You might have students describe the rationale behind the arrangement of paragraphs 4 to 13. Can they suggest an alternative order?

Ask students what prevents Goodheart from idealizing friendship. Their answer should center on Goodheart's perceptions about power. Friendship, as Goodheart writes (para. 13), "is ideally the relationship of democracy," but it is not democratic, and inequalities in power result in jealousy, hurt feelings, fear, and irritation. How does the anecdote in paragraph 9 or the Alyosha anecdote illustrate this? After many years have passed, Alyosha avoids the narrator. Why? What changes in Alyosha make him unwilling to renew the friendship? Are they the same changes that make "disembodiment" (para. 27) a characteristic of the friendships between the elderly?

Goodheart refuses to idealize friendship, but he certainly values it. For him, what are the virtues of friendship? Where does he make the most powerful case for the bond?

WRITING SUGGESTION   Consider the nature of friendship among your peers. Use your experience, as well as references to contemporary literature and film, to detail three or four characteristics of friendship in the college years. (If you are an older or returning student, alter the assignment to fit your present circumstances.)

Patricia J. Williams

MY BEST WHITE FRIEND (p. 140)

This is, in many ways, a complicated essay. On the face of it, two friends are getting ready for a party. The preparations, however, are a setting for exploration of the much weightier issues of gender, class, and race. In fact, the essay is subtitled "Cinderella Revisited" as a way of both setting the preparty scene and introducing cultural notions of class and gender, which Williams recasts in the context of race as well. Revisiting a fairy tale is no small matter either. Part of the subject of Williams's essay is how history and myth have come to shape the friends' psyches (their dreams and desires) and their potential for relationships beyond their differences (both with men and with each other). Students may indeed be wondering why, or if, these two women are friends at all, and closely examining the fairy-tale elements of the essay may be one way into a discussion of whether this is a real friendship or not.

How does setting the essay in the context of the Cinderella story shape your students' expectation for the essay? What elements of fairy tale (or storytelling) does Williams incorporate into her essay? From the opening line (even before that, in the title) the women are defined, however ironically, by type rather than name: terms like "my best white friend" and "trophy-wife-in-waiting" seem to cast the friends as characters rather than real people. In fact by paragraph 13, the name "my best white friend" has shifted into an acronym. What is the effect of the acronym for your students? Oddly, it is both intimate and distant. What does this suggest about the friendship? Is the author respecting her friend by protecting her identity or hurting her by exposing her in some way?

Williams achieves a sense of immediacy and intimacy through extensive dialogue and highly detailed scenes. Students probably associate these elements with fiction rather than essays, and you could point out how much of the subject's complexity lies in what is played out in dialogue and scene rather than explanation. Like the characters themselves, the readers are left to puzzle out how the friendship between these two women has survived their differences. They want different things out of their lives. They have completely different approaches to their appearances. They see race in completely different ways. And yet there are connections between them: there is a playful tenderness in the way they attend to one another, even though their dialogue is relentlessly flip. As they address each other, both women seem always to be conscious of their race and class and of how those identities define them. To a degree, both women are trying to thwart the expectations of their respective class and race with irony. So, for instance, M.B.W.F. purposefully says rather appalling things. In paragraph 30, she characterizes Williams as a would-be "ethnic woman warrior, always on that midnight train to someplace else, intent on becoming the highest-paid Aunt Jemima in history." Although Williams doesn't seem particularly offended at this, she does choke on her possible response. Part of Williams's willingness to let comments slide has to do with M.B.W.F.'s personality, her apparent relish for hyperbolic, outrageous statements. (Of herself, she says that she has "actively aspired . . . to be 'a cunning little meringue of a male prize.'")

In turn, Williams says rather unflattering things about her friend, too, using the essay to paint M.B.W.F. as funny, quick, and generous but also narcissistic and somewhat oblivious in her privilege. What, for instance, is the point of disclosing the discussion about aging, particularly the anecdote about M.B.W.F. looking at Princess Diana and exclaiming, "God! Bulimia must work!"? Does Williams connect this discussion to the women's racial difference? How?

In paragraph 45, Williams and M.B.W.F.'s final appraisal of one another reflects the "deep disapproval of one gazing into a mirror." The moment captures both their seemingly irreconcilable differences as well as the sense that they are somehow connected by difference itself. When Williams describes herself as "a rude construction of mud and twigs, bright glass beads, and flashy bits of tinfoil" and M.B.W.F. as a "high-tech product of many hours of steam rollers, shine enhancers, body spritzers, perms, and about eighteen hundred watts of blow-dried effort," what is she comparing? What points of view do the different descriptions represent? In the end the women are left wondering (as readers must) how they have remained friends. A slightly campy shake of the head and a sigh signal mutual recognition: they're *so* different. What, then, is the source of their sympathy for one another? According to your students, why have they remained friends?

Williams closes her essay by placing herself literally in her white friend's shoes and then rejecting those shoes. Ask your students what they make of the shoe detail given the essay's Cinderella motif? Remind them that Cinderella gets the man when her foot fits the shoe, but the shoe doesn't fit Williams. Are we meant to read Williams as an evil stepsister who tries shoving her foot into overly dainty shoes?

Presumably, the white friend's attentions to Williams have a fairy godmother quality, but Williams insists these efforts are wasted on her, because "white knights just don't play the same part in my mythical landscape of desire." What part do white knights play, given what we learn about the author? What does it mean to compare a self-described "over-thirty black professional with an attitude" to Cinderella?

In the context of the party Williams is about to attend, what is the import of the mother's stories in paragraph 7? Williams may be saying to her friend that she doesn't want what her friend wants for her — that she wants to be a woman who invents her own ending. But her desires are not all that easily untangled, given the unhappy dreams she relates, in which she's unsuitably placed for love, safety, or power. Interestingly, M.B.W.F. doesn't take her friend's fears seriously until Williams's dramatic "queen" speech in paragraph 43. While it may not be clear how the queen analysis accounts for the dreams, the rhetoric does speak directly to Williams's sense of herself as burdened by cultural images and, as a result, "a wee bit tense." M.B.W.F. is surprised by the weakness that is implied in Williams's fears, and readers see why the prospect of being the belle of the ball seems impossible to Williams — no matter how much primping her fairy godmother helps her do. What does M.B.W.F.'s exclamation in paragraph 44 say about the kind of connections that might be possible (or impossible) in their friendship?

The final paragraph is intriguing and puzzling. "I do not envy her. I do not resent her," Williams writes. Do readers ever suspect her of having either of these emotions about M.B.W.F.? And then: "I do not hold my breath." What does this mean? Is Williams saying she's not going to hold her breath against M.B.W.F.'s husband's cigar, that she's not going to resist *that* world? Is she saying she's not going to hold her breath for the man for whom, supposedly, she has been preparing all evening? What are the other possibilities?

WRITING SUGGESTION   Explain Williams's complicated responses to being made up by her "Best White Friend." We know Williams both resists the makeover and is looking forward to it. Why?

Lindsy Van Gelder

MARRIAGE AS A RESTRICTED CLUB (p. 146)

Lindsy Van Gelder argues for the right of gay and lesbian couples to marry legally and be recognized by society. Until society extends that right, she will not celebrate anyone else's engagement, wedding, or anniversary. She knows others may regard this kind of boycott as "mean-spirited, eccentric, and/or politically rigid," but she believes it necessary for her own integrity.

Though there are practical financial reasons for wanting to marry her lesbian lover, her major reason is that she wants the *choice* to stand up and "show the world that we've made a *genuine* commitment"— the same option that members of the heterosexual community have. At the same time, as long as she's excluded from the "restricted club," she has more sympathy for people who marry because a partner needs health insurance than for those who marry for love.

Van Gelder's approach to the issue of gay and lesbian marriage excludes any extended consideration or refutation of the reasons some people think gays and lesbians should not have the right to marry legally. If asked, students are likely to come up with some reasons that could initiate useful class discussion and debate. Why does Van Gelder choose to ignore these potential objections to her argument?

Examine other aspects of Van Gelder's argumentative strategy. Why does she argue by analogy? Why does she speak of the "dollar-and-cents benefits" of marriage before she talks about more sentimental reasons for marrying?

WRITING SUGGESTION   Should Van Gelder's heterosexual friends grant her wish and avoid the institution of marriage? Why or why not? If you were interested in marrying, would you be willing to accede to a similar request?

Jonathan Rauch

FOR BETTER OR WORSE? (p. 151)

Jonathan Rauch's tightly argued essay recasts the same-sex marriage debate in light of marriage's *social* purpose. In this context, love, which is the basis of the private, emotional meaning of marriage, is irrelevant. As Rauch writes, "Love is a desirable element of marriage. In society's eyes, however, it cannot be the defining element. You may or may not love your husband, but the two of you are just as married either way. You may love your mistress, but that certainly doesn't make her your spouse."

So what is the defining element of "society's most fundamental institution" (para. 12)? The common understanding is that marriage is a consensual relationship between two heterosexual adults. After that, Rauch says, things get fuzzy; neither gays nor traditionalists have offered a definition that might further the debate.

In arguing for same-sex unions, Rauch starts by considering his opponents' don't-tamper-with-it stance. Outlining the libertarian underpinnings of such a view, Rauch might seem, however briefly, to be on the side of the Hayekians, but by paragraph 12, he states his position unequivocally: the ban on gay marriage is "scaldingly inhumane," essentially immoral. He imagines the contradictory argument — "gay marriage might lead to bad things"— and points out why this is invalid, and then he anticipates the "social traditions shouldn't be tampered with . . . lightly" argument and responds to it. Ask students why Rauch ping-pongs back and forth between conservative claims and his own views in paragraphs 8 through 14. Why doesn't he jump straight ahead to paragraph 15, where he asks what he first asked in paragraph 3: What is the purpose of marriage?

Students will probably see that Rauch uses paragraphs 8 through 14 to disarm his opponents, just as he does in paragraphs 15 through 25, when he invalidates the "child-centered" view of marriage and the "anatomical possibility" position. In anticipating and responding to possible objections to his argument, Rauch employs classic argumentative strategy. But Rauch addresses opposing views *before* he's fully presented his own. As a result, he appears to persuade on his opponents' terms. In paragraphs 26 to 36, when Rauch finally describes the social purpose of marriage, he seems, in certain ways, more traditional than the traditionalists. He even uses an arguably clichéd view of male behavior and gay promiscuity to further his point.

Marriage, Rauch holds, is for "domesticating men and providing reliable caregivers." From society's point of view, these virtues have profound legal, economic, and social consequences. As Rauch details these consequences, he suggests he values marriage and understands its virtues more than his opponents do. But his conclusions about same-sex marriage are hardly traditional, and his sense that gays should marry isn't even traditionally liberal. This raises the question of audience. To whom is this piece addressed? Is Rauch preaching to the converted or genuinely hoping to persuade?

In analyzing Rauch's argument, have students identify his premise (para. 2). Do they find it acceptable? Also have them notice how his thesis (in its undeveloped form) is incorporated into his summary of the same-sex marriage debate: notions about love and children "misunderstand and impoverish the social meaning of marriage." Note, too, how he limits the parameters of his discussion by carefully distinguishing between the public and private meaning of marriage. You might ask students to characterize Rauch's tone. He doesn't belittle his opponent; at the same time, he doesn't refrain from strong statements about morality, or even humor, as his essay proceeds.

In the end, are students persuaded by Rauch's argument? Why or why not? You might try to ascertain if anyone's views changed as a result of reading the essay. Finally, ask students if they agree with Rauch's final claim that gays should be not only permitted but expected to marry.

WRITING SUGGESTION   Use Rauch's and Lindsy Van Gelder's ("Marriage as a Restricted Club," p. 146) arguments about same-sex marriage to present your own views on the subject. Do you think same-sex marriage should be permitted or expected? Explain why or why not.

Raymond Carver

WHAT WE TALK ABOUT
WHEN WE TALK ABOUT LOVE (p. 160)

This story explicitly borrows from Plato's *Symposium* and James Joyce's "The Dead," but because your students may not have read either, a short summary of the *Symposium*, at least, might make the discussion more interesting. Like Carver's story, Plato's famous dialogue takes place at a drinking party. The gathered Greeks are still hung over from the previous night's debauchery, so they agree to keep their drinking to a minimum and debate a relatively light subject — love. Each person present is asked to define it. As with the Carver story, the individual definitions are as revealing as the manner of delivery.

In "What We Talk About When We Talk About Love," Mel is a cardiologist, an expert, supposedly, in the heart, but we also know that he's a man who is interested in absolutes. (Why do we think he left the seminary? Why did he join in the first place?) More intensely than any of the other characters, Mel believes in traditional definitions of love, yet he comes to recognize that even his love is not as pure as he wishes. All his life he has been inclined to serve an ideal of pure love — he would like to be a courtly knight — but his experience has shown him so many examples of weird, mixed, irrational love that he is increasingly desperate to redefine true love, fearing that no such thing exists. His use of profanity and the details he chooses in describing the elderly couple he treated in the accident show his paradoxical feelings. He is moved by what love has done for the couple and yet repelled by that love's power to persist despite pain and misfortune. Mel's story of the lifelong devotion of the elderly man reawakens Mel's feelings of attachment to his ex-wife, a woman whom he insists he hates and would like to kill. Ironically, he reveals himself as similar to Terri's ex-husband, who was driven by the pain of love to want to kill someone. As the evening goes on, Mel loses his certainty about love and finally ends up feeling the urge to phone his children, as if he does not realize that the call will, for a moment, reconnect him with their mother. The powerful upsurge of buried and illogical ties to former loves frightens all four friends, who find themselves pulling away from or worrying about losing one another. The confident conviviality of the late afternoon vanishes as each character sinks into a somber, anxious recognition of the mixed, intractable nature of love.

The passage of the day — from sunlight to dusk to dark — parallels the stages of love and of life and of the couples' relative degrees of drunkenness. The one constant in the story is the beating of their hearts. The story's closing words — "when the room went dark"— links the progress of light in this story with the progress of emotions and time. The final words also evoke the ending of a play: the curtain is down, the room has darkened, the drama is over.

In this story, the stages of love are demonstrated by three different couples. Laura and the narrator are like a young couple, still dewy with the fresh bloom of love. Mel and Terri are a middle-stage couple, struggling with their relationship and striving, despite what they say, against each other. The elderly man and woman seem to be an example of mature affection; their love persists despite pain and despite the impossibility of a physical component to the love. Mel doesn't really differentiate between husband and wife as he tells their story, perhaps indicating how much the elderly lovers have become one.

Point out to the students that the narrator does not offer explicit interpretations of the evening's events as he touches on many different kinds of love. Even though the narrative presents a continuous discussion and unbroken flow of time, Carver leaves breaks after paragraphs 31, 42, 54, 66, 88, 101, and 121. Ask students what these seven spaces emphasize or suggest about each preceding event. What narrative exposition could be inserted at each place? Why does the author omit that exposition?

WRITING SUGGESTIONS   (a) Like Plato in his *Symposium*, Carver demonstrates love while he has his characters discuss definitions of love. Sometimes what he shows contradicts what his characters say. Conduct your own symposium, and gather definitions of love from those you know well. Is there any discrepancy between how these people talk about love and how they conduct themselves in affairs of the heart? What similarities or differences do you find between the people you know and Carver's characters? Given your observations, how do you define love? Try to be as specific as possible.

(b) In "What We Talk About When We Talk About Love," Carver's narrator pays special attention to the quality of light in the room. Why? What do these details have to do with the characters' conversation? How is the subject of love influenced by observations about the passage of time and even death?

PART 4

GROUP PICTURES

Representing and Responding to the Ideas of Others

The material in Part 4 deals with the complications of group identity. We often define ourselves in relation to a community, whether as insider or outsider. Many people inhabit more than one world, while others feel they don't have a true community, even if they have a group — racial, class-based, religious, or cultural — to which they belong. Although it's common to lament this lack of a sense of belonging, the pulls within a community can be confusing and painful, as well as joyful, as the Insights in the beginning of this section attest.

In this part, content and methodology dovetail, since students will be asked to move beyond their own identities and respond to the ideas of others in the context of the authors' communities. Rather than personal reflection, students' papers should contain more straightforward critical analysis. Asking students to refrain from using the first-person in their papers will help them shift the focus away from themselves as subjects and instead emphasize their interpretations of the readings.

Insights

Theodor Reik uses the memorable phrase "the community of fate" to refer to the sense of fundamental association with others. Often *fate* has negative connotations of powerlessness and defeat, but Reik considers fate to be a limitation that gives form and moral meaning to human experience. Using Reik's Insight as a touchstone, ask students what ideas about society's effect on the individual are implied in the other Insights. What kinds of personal fulfillment and social order are suggested in the different passages? If each of the other writers could create a new world, what values would be emphasized, and what present social forms might be preserved or superseded?

Maya Angelou

GRADUATION (p. 178)

At the beginning of this essay, Maya Angelou conveys the sense of dignity and even grandeur that she and her classmates felt on the morning of their graduation. You might start by asking students whether they anticipated that disappointment would follow. What do they think explains the children's enthusiasm, given the community's awareness of limited opportunities for African Americans at the time? The answer to these questions might center around the nature of this community — economically depressed but hard working and self-respecting.

The threat to the community's self-respect comes from white society. The initial contrast in paragraph 2 between the schools for white and black children introduces the reality of racism, which will undermine the graduates' dreams. The youthful narrator is clearly responding to the atmosphere of both her immediate and larger worlds when she describes everything as simultaneously significant and portentous in paragraph 9.

You might want to ask students what the young Angelou expects from the world, using the text as evidence. They should note that Angelou lets details do double or triple work. When she describes herself reciting the preamble to the Constitution with Bailey, she's showing the reader that she's a top student and that she has a close, intellectual relationship with her brother. She's also deftly placing information that will be referred to later. By the end of the essay, the reader will see that Angelou expected the promise of her country to hold true for her, too. Ask students to find other early details that Angelou continues to develop later. You might steer them to, among other things, information about Henry Reed's character and the Negro National Anthem.

The direct threat finally arrives in the form of Edward Donleavy and his colleague. The latter is present, presumably, because Donleavy feels he cannot walk among African Americans without another white man for protection. As Donleavy insults the entire graduating class and audience in numerous ways, the pride Angelou had been feeling turns abruptly to self-loathing and sardonic contempt for black delusions. Donleavy's speech and behavior is "educational" in that it tells the listeners what their opportunities are in a racist white world. Angelou is crushed. But after Henry Reed speaks, yet another emotional change will open Angelou's heart, perhaps for the first time, to the heroism of her people's struggle for dignity.

It is significant that Henry Reed is able to restore the community's dignity by returning to the moment when the graduation celebrants were "interrupted" in paragraph 29. The community's earlier failure to sing the Negro National Anthem was, no doubt, a result of Donleavy's presence backstage. Denied the opportunity to express self-respect, the graduates are discombobulated, and the way has been prepared for Angelou's self-loathing. In singing the anthem, Henry Reed turns back the clock on the graduation to the moment when things started to go wrong. By doing this, he recalls the community to the words of the anthem, recaptures the optimism that ruled earlier in the day, and transforms their naive enthusiasm into a pride in what they truly have to celebrate.

On graduation day, the wide swing of Angelou's response — from exultation to degradation to sympathy and solidarity — organizes the memory, which also includes many light touches of humorous characterization and satire. In the end, her graduation *has* been as important as she thought it would be.

WRITING SUGGESTION   If Angelou had ended her essay with paragraph 60, it would have seemed complete. Why does she add paragraphs 61 and 62? How have poets helped the African American community survive? Be specific. You might want to address the question of whether contemporary black musicians and poets continue to serve this function for the African American community.

Amy Tan

MOTHER TONGUE (p. 189)

Like Virginia Woolf in "Professions for Women" (see Part 6), Amy Tan starts out with an apparent disclaimer. She emphasizes her professional viewpoint as a writer, almost apologizing, as if the viewpoint is a limitation. By the end of the essay, however, she has suggested the opposite: the language of the scholar is insufficiently textured for the richness of the world.

Tan's goal is not so much to critique scholarly language as to express the inestimable value of other underappreciated "Englishes." Although her mother's use of English may not be grammatically or syntactically correct, it is "vivid, direct, full of observation and imagery" and constitutes a language in and of itself for Tan, who describes it as "my mother's tongue," a pun that cleverly gives her mother's English official status while acknowledging its intimate source. Its importance to Tan as a writer should not go underestimated; as a language that "helped shape the way [she] saw things, expressed things, made sense of the world," it could not help but inform her fiction as well. Because the way Tan's mother speaks English doesn't resemble standard written English, people incorrectly assume she isn't bright, and, in the case of the rude doctor, that assumption results in substandard treatment. What's more, Tan's perception of her mother was once limited by her difficulties with the language. "I believed," Tan writes, "that her English reflected the quality of what she had to say. That is, because she expressed them imperfectly her thoughts were imperfect." You might ask students how this compares to Richard Rodriguez's perceptions about his parents' imperfect English in his essay "Public and Private Language" (p. 200).

Tan feels that she, too, was once limited by her mother's English, a limitation reflected in her performance on standardized tests. While efforts have been made, in recent years, to create culturally neutral standardized tests, Tan's examples of the kinds of questions that were problematic for her indicate how difficult a task that is. Technically, for instance, her example about analogies does not relate to language; instead it suggests that imaginative people have more trouble on standardized tests than literal-minded people do. Do students think that the example undercuts her argument?

Tan, like Stephen Dunn in his essay "Locker Room Talk," makes the occasion for her thoughts to become part of her essay. Paragraphs 3, 4, 8, and 18 all refer to something that happened "recently," "just last week" or "lately." Why does Tan include these references to time?

The central question, as opposed to the central event, that prompts Tan's considerations is in paragraph 18: Why aren't "more Asian Americans represented in American literature"? What do students think of Tan's (admittedly incomplete) answer to the question? (Note that this device of getting away with an incomplete answer by simply acknowledging the incompleteness is something students can, when appropriate, do in their own papers.) Why does Tan feel she was able to defeat the odds — and apparent early criticism — to become a writer?

Students should be made aware of the kind of popularity Amy Tan's fiction has had. It's significant that the language she pieces together — an English that is a combination of all the Englishes she knows and that tries to reflect her experience of her mother, her language, and her world — is well received by many readers. Her mother's final compliment is one given by many non-Chinese-American readers. Ask students why this is important. Alternatively, bring in some sample pages from one of her novels, and see whether students agree with Tan's assessment of her own work.

WRITING SUGGESTION   Compare and contrast the language in brief sections of two novels by contemporary, female Asian-American authors. You might consider Tan's *The Joy Luck Club*, Maxine Hong Kingston's *Women Warrior*, or Gish Jen's *Typical American*. Does Tan's analysis of her own Englishes shed light on the language in these novels? Explain.

Maxine Hong Kingston

THE MISERY OF SILENCE (p. 195)

As a child Kingston is expected to bridge the two cultures that neither her Chinese parents nor her American teachers could bring together. She withdraws into a silence where she observes the incohesiveness of her world while waiting for someone to help her emerge from behind the curtain symbolized in her elementary-school paintings.

Her confused sense of identity makes her especially sensitive to personality traits that appear contrived or histrionic. The mannerisms of African American children, adult Chinese women, and American girls all seem interesting but curious; the author describes them as if they are acting out masked roles. Some of what is at issue for the young Kingston is individuation. After all, what she finds most problematic is speaking with "one voice" and not "together." You might ask students to find points in the essay where she begins to make connections as an individual and what those connections are based on.

For Kingston, different personality types are defined chiefly by people's voices. Her style reflects this observation, and the aural imagery in this piece is particularly striking. In "The Coming Book," an essay in Janet Sternburg's *The Writer on Her Work*, Kingston writes, "I heard somewhere that aural hallucinations are a more severe symptom of psychosis than visual ones. But in healthy people, auricular images may be only a more advanced form of imagination than pictures."

In this selection, note how aural imagery *always* precedes the visual and how that imagery is rather ingeniously captured in English *words* — the very things that, in their spoken form, cause Kingston so much pain.

WRITING SUGGESTION   Read "No-Name Woman," the first chapter of Kingston's memoir *The Woman Warrior*. How do you understand Kingston's childhood silence in the context of the prohibition against speech that runs throughout "No-Name Woman"? Alternatively, how do you perceive Kingston's silence after you've read Amy Tan's essay "Mother Tongue" (p. 189)?

Richard Rodriguez

PUBLIC AND PRIVATE LANGUAGE (p. 200)

Like Shelby Steele in "On Being Black and Middle Class" (p. 211), Richard Rodriguez writes as an insider here, and his qualifications in the subject of bilingual education come from his own experience. He plays his argument out by comparing what he gained and lost as a child who had to learn English in school.

For Rodriguez, supporters of bilingual education, who imply that children "miss a great deal" by not being educated in their family's language, need to look at what these children gain from being forced to learn the dominant language — "a public identity." Without denying that his education entailed some personal losses, Rodriguez argues in favor of assimilation (at least on the level of language). He concludes that children should not avoid learning the language of public society, no matter how comforting it may be to stick to the private language of home. He uses his father to illustrate the consequences of not mastering the public language: diminished by his inability to speak English, his father's private identity suffers. Even his family comes to think of him as withdrawn, though his shyness is less a character trait than a result of his uncertainty with English.

Rodriguez notes that public language demands words in meaningful order; communicating to a wide audience is as important as self-expression. The audience at home — being an intimate one — does not require the same precision. Before he learns English, Rodriguez is relatively silent in public. After, he trades his public silence for a private quiet and some loss of the intimacy in his "special feeling of closeness at home." Part of the loss is a result of the way the family defined its identity (at least initially) in opposition to the *gringo* majority. Why are his parents willing to give up "in an instant" speaking Spanish at home? (You might refer students to Shelby Steele's argument to note the similarities and differences between the two writers' definitions of ethnic identity.)

Rodriguez feels fortunate that his teachers were "unsentimental" about educating him. Though such sentimentality would have comforted him, he believes it would have hurt him in the long run. The implication here might be that resisting the dominant language is somewhat childish, like the wish for continual pampering, but the grief Rodriguez describes in paragraph 8 seems profound. What do students make of the tradeoff? How might Rodriguez's life have been different had he not been forced to speak English in school?

Once Rodriguez starts to learn English, the literal quiet at home is matched by a new kind of "public silence." Students might find the discussion in paragraph 10 a bit confusing, but Rodriguez means that when he attended to the content of the English language, he became less conscious of the sounds, the form, of that language. If language is a window, he began looking through it instead of at it.

Rodriguez closes by repeating his thesis, saying that a person is individualized both publicly and privately and that assimilation therefore is both valuable and necessary. Ultimately, he explains his point more than he proves it. In his opening line, Rodriguez oversimplifies his opponents' position and goes on to present his thoughts without considering the complexities of the bilingualists' argument. Not until his closing paragraph does he expand on the opposing view. What's more, he makes some jumps that the reader might not be willing to make with him. In paragraph 18, he speaks of the necessity of assimilation in general, as opposed to the importance of learning the country's dominant language. Does he mean to imply that there are other things a first- or second-generation immigrant needs to do in order to have a public identity?

This piece is an excerpt from Rodriguez's book *Hunger of Memory*, which was both vilified and praised when it originally appeared in the early 1980s. To his critics, Rodriguez betrayed his blood by buying into white, middle-class myths about what is necessary to participate in public culture. According to Marcelo Rodriguez's article on Richard Rodriguez's subsequent book, *Days of Obligation,* for the *San Francisco Weekly* (Sept. 30, 1992), Rodriguez now says he wrote *Hunger of Memory* in "the heat of youthful anger" and that he would not write the same book today. Though he is viewed otherwise by his critics and some of his supporters, Richard Rodriguez does not think of himself as political.

WRITING SUGGESTION   Do some brief research into the arguments of bilingualists — first to see if Rodriguez has characterized their position fairly, and second, to see if his analysis convincingly refutes their arguments. Then, argue your own position, taking care to address the concerns of the opposing point of view.

Arthur Ashe and Arnold Rampersad

THE BURDEN OF RACE (p. 206)

If Arthur Ashe is correct, white students should be surprised by this essay, while black students should find it less surprising. By placing race above AIDS in his hierarchy of woes, Ashe suggests what he later says explicitly: "being an African American . . . may be one of those fates that are worse than death." Ashe emphasizes that he is proud to be both American and African American. Ask students how his conclusions about AIDS square with this claim. Their answer should lead them to Ashe's analysis of segregation's after-effects, the "shadow of contempt that lays across [his] identity and [his] sense of self-esteem." The "shadow" does its work "subtly," and yet it is omnipresent. To illustrate how he's been damaged by racism, Ashe tells the story about his daughter and the blonde doll.

In setting up the doll story, Ashe emphasizes the general good-will around him, as well as the fond intentions of his friends. There is no enemy in the scene. No one actually speaks the words in paragraphs 15 to 18. And yet Ashe's certainty that the words will be spoken causes him to act in a manner that he feels is both ungracious and unjust. Having acted, he remains unsettled, aware that his behavior, while expedient, was not moral.

What do students think of Ashe's analysis of the doll story? In his reading of the experience, the imagined voices (and his response to them) are products of racism. Where does responsibility for the racism lie? How does the scene clarify why professional and material successes offer Ashe no protection from racism? Make sure students consider Ashe's emotions in the scene. Is he making too much of the matter? Why or why not?

Ashe says he's an optimist, but he feels that "only death will free [him from racism's] pall." (Have students look up the word *pall* to see if the definition adds any shades of meaning to Ashe's words.) The racism of segregation can be legislated out of existence, but can the racism revealed in the doll story be eliminated as easily? Ask students what, if anything, can be done about it. Does Ashe think this sort of racism has a solution?

In examining the essay's strategy, students should note that Ashe argues by example, using a single, relevant story to support his generalization. Because Ashe relies on the one example, he describes the incident in great detail, paying particular attention to emotional nuances. Do students feel the single example suffices to make Ashe's point?

Ashe's essay is developed through narration and description. The doll anecdote is placed within the framework of the *People* magazine interview, and direct analysis is kept to a minimum. In both stories, Ashe is surrounded by kind people. He doesn't portray the *People* magazine reporter as a crass gossip-hound but as a genuinely concerned, caring woman. He describes his friends as loving and generous. Ask students why. How does Ashe strengthen his point about the insidious effects of racism by making condemnation (of the reporter or friends) impossible?

WRITING SUGGESTIONS (a) After reading Shelby Steele's essay (p. 211), decide whether Ashe responds to race according to Steel's paradigm of a victim attacked by a victimizer (in paragraph 23 of "On Being Black and Middle Class"). Explain your conclusions by imagining what Steele might have to say about Ashe's description of racism's effects on him or by imagining what Ashe might have to say about Steele's views of race and class in America.

(b) Use Ashe's and Brent Staples's "Black Men and Public Space" (p. 34) essay to consider contemporary racism. Describe the nature of the racism depicted in each essay. What sort of solutions do the authors propose for the racism they experience? Can you offer additional alternatives?

Shelby Steele

ON BEING BLACK AND MIDDLE CLASS (p. 211)

Shelby Steele builds his argument by using his own experience. First, he establishes his authority and suitability for addressing the matter at hand by immediately disclosing his skin color. Second, instead of presenting and systematically critiquing the opposing argument, Steele simply lets us know that he once held the view he now rejects — that race completely defined his identity, that "most aspects of [his] life found their explanation, their justification, and their motivation in race."

Steele doesn't feel that his old position was accurate for its time and inappropriate for the present. Rather, he claims, the old position was *always* insufficient to explain the situation of African Americans in the United States; race never completely defined identity, for *class* had and has a significant role. In examining why he feels so uncomfortable confessing his beliefs, he concludes that his discomfort is a result of how class and race are defined in this country. You might begin discussion of this essay by asking students who defines such terms. Are the definitions immutable?

When Steele sets out to articulate the separate definitions, he gives examples of middle-class values, and he characterizes these values as raceless and assimilationist. When he goes on to define race, Steele turns his attention to a consideration of racial identity. He notes that the definition of racial identity that emerged in the 1960s still holds sway today. It is a definition of the self as victim, as "embattled minority," and as such it encourages an adversarial stance toward the majority and an ethnic consciousness rather than an individual one.

Given these definitions, Steele continues, African American members of the middle class are in a position that requires them to feel two opposing things at once: they are to embrace middle-class individualism while giving their ethnic identity primacy.

Steele says that the images required to identify with race are in conflict with those required to identify with class and vice versa. As a result, African American members of the middle class are in "a very specific double bind." "There is," Steele writes, "no forward movement on either plane that does not constitute backward movement on the other." By asserting a middle-class identity a person's ethnic identity suffers. African Americans who define themselves as middle class first seem bound, as a result, to feel the guilt that Steele experiences in the opening scene, a guilt that suggests betrayal of the group. Alternatively, asserting an ethnic identity hurts a person's middle-class identity. (This seems to be Steele's point in including the scene with the debate coach, where Steele's need to identify with his race cuts him off from the "resources [his] class values might have offered" and provides him only with the fury of the victim.)

As the essay proceeds to discuss values, Steele enters difficult territory. In paragraph 11, he writes that a sense of identity within a collective (whether of class or race) comes from "embracing a polarity of positive and negative images." He explains, "To identify as middle class, for example, I must have both positive and negative images of what being middle class entails; then I will know what I should and should not be doing in order to be middle class. The same goes for racial identity." Steele lists middle-class values in paragraph 6, but he never gives us the positive and negative images of what being black entails. Or he never gives us anything beyond the victim identity of which he disapproves. Instead he writes about "negative images of lower-class blacks" and uses the character of Sam to let us know what those are. As a result, he doesn't offer positive images associated with racial identity — only the positive values of middle-class life, which leaves him in the very place "the sharp tug of guilt" he expresses in paragraph 4 would suggest he doesn't want to be.

Steele's closing anecdote reinforces his association of negative values with his race and positive ones with his class, since he identifies his rage at the debate coach as a result of his racial identity, his victim status. He concludes that the more dignified approach of victim to victimizer belongs to him not as an African American man but as a middle-class man. You may want to ask about the implications of this statement. Is Steele suggesting that a lower-class black doesn't have the power of the measured, dispassionate response?

How do students interpret the debate-team anecdote? The middle-class "propriety" that is referred to in paragraph 20 is indisputably racist, so the anecdote appears to demonstrate that class itself is necessarily racist. (Students might be asked if they can think of another example of class and race, according to Steele's paradigm, coming into conflict.)

Since Steele says that race and class are largely a matter of definition, his sense of the "problem" here has, in the end, mostly to do with the ways African Americans define themselves as victims. If there were another definition, then perhaps Steele would have some positive values to associate with his racial identity. Are there reasons, historical or otherwise, that victim identity might have been necessary? Is it still necessary? Can students propose alternate definitions?

In an essay titled "The New Sovereignty," Steele has written about the "narcissism of victims" who hold on to their grievances because grievances are a way to have an identity and — in an age of affirmative action and identity politics — power. Philip Roth, in his essay "Writing About Jews," leveled this same criticism against Jews with persecution complexes. Roth took the insistence on claiming wounds where none necessarily existed to be a way of claiming identity that was an insult to the memory of those who *had* been wounded. Sharing this fact with your class may be a good way to open up discussion from African Americans as a social group to other groups that claim victim status in our society.

Another possible way to open discussion of this essay is with the following quotation from the *New York Times* (May 30, 1990): "To many whites and conservative blacks, Mr. Steele has given eloquent voice to painful truths that are almost always left unspoken in the nation's circumscribed public discourse on race. To many black politicians and civil rights figures, he is a turncoat, a privileged black man whose visibility and success stem from his ability to say precisely what white America most wants to hear." The first sentence of this quotation, without the introductory phrase, is used as a blurb on the back of Shelby Steele's book *The Content of Our Character*.

WRITING SUGGESTION   In making his argument about the double bind of African Americans in the middle class, Steele offers definitions of race and class in the United States. Explain what his definitions are, and then analyze the definitions for completeness. Do the results of your analysis affect your perception of his argument? Do they lend support to or contradict his conclusions? Explain.

Barbara Ehrenreich

CULTURAL BAGGAGE (p. 218)

Barbara Ehrenreich's conclusions about her ethnic identity are clear enough. She doesn't have an obvious cultural heritage, and her attempts to latch onto one have been forced, even ridiculous. If she looks honestly at her past, at what links her to her forebears, it's a rejection of the past, an insistence instead on the new. Her true heritage is her mother's "militant ecumenicism" and her father's insistence on independent thinking: her tradition isn't cultural or religious but a broadly conceived humanism that encourages self-reliance, skepticism, curiosity, and tolerance.

That said, ask students what Ehrenreich's attitude is toward those who identify themselves according to ethnicity or religion. In justifying her own inheritance of "none," is she suggesting something about others? Before they answer, have students describe Ehrenreich's tone in this piece. Where is she sarcastic or funny? Where does she use hyperbole? Ehrenreich makes obvious fun of her acquaintance in paragraph 1, just as she makes fun of the language of identity politics in paragraph 2. Ask students to identify additional places where she mocks others (or herself). What seems to be the object of her scorn? Presumably her issue isn't with those who have a true relationship to their cultural or religious traditions, but with those who fabricate such a relationship (the "newly enthusiastic celebrants of Purim and Kwanzaa and Solstice"). What are her own reasons for trying to claim "more" of an ethnic identity or a different ethnic identity? Part of the answer is her awareness (detailed in paragraph 3) of having descended from those who oppressed the very people who made ethnic and cultural identity fashionable. The other part is the truth of her experience (para. 4), her impression of her forebearers (para. 6), and her sense of maternal obligation (para. 7). In the end, what are her motives for holding an updated Passover service?

The concluding paragraph is delivered in the same light tone as the rest of the essay. The children's conclusion — that they have no sense of ethnic identity and that's all for the good — pleases the mother. How are we to read their statement that "the world would be a better place if nobody else did either"? And what do we make of the mother's final pride? Why does Ehrenreich use clichés at the close, letting her chest "swell with pride" "to know that the race of 'none' marches on"? What are the dangers of ethnic identity? (Ehrenreich recalls us subtly to them by using "Serbian" and "Croatian" in an unrelated context in the penultimate paragraph.)

WRITING SUGGESTION   In Part 4, members of minority groups feel momentary shame about their ethnic identity. Compare this embarrassment to the complex feelings Ehrenreich has about her own heritage. Do the emotions have similar or different sources? Explain.

Alice Walker

EVERYDAY USE (p. 221)

"Everyday Use" looks at both group identity and family relationships. Your students will most likely focus on racial identity, and you should remind them that there are a variety of ways in which that identity might be defined. In this story, Dee's racial identity (in a historical sense) seems inauthentic within the context of her immediate family. The details that suggest she has embraced the Nation of Islam (changing her name to an African one; dating another adherent, a man who doesn't eat pork or collards) are lightly mocked here. Dee has decided to return to her people, but that return has nothing to do with who her people, in a more intimate sense, are.

Indeed, the details we are given characterize Dee's life by a desire to distance herself from the past. Instead of being literally scarred, as Maggie is, by the loss of her original home, Dee is pleased to see the place burn down. Apparently, Dee moves on from that loss in a way that Maggie and their mother do not. "I have," the mother says of the new place, "deliberately turned my back on the house." When she decides her past is fashionable, Dee doesn't make a distinction between the original house and the house her mother and sister now occupy. When she takes snapshots, she's sure to place this "authentic" detail in every frame.

Given Dee's previous relationship to her past, her current behavior seems false and self-conscious, part of the same slight arrogance and determination that characterized her desire to get away from her family in the first place. The mother's fantasy of herself as the light-skinned, slim woman who Dee would want her to be is meant to show us that Dee is afflicted by racial self-hatred, not racial pride. Dee's new enthusiasm for the very things she once scorned is meant to seem mannered and selfish, particularly when opposed to the appallingly selfless, shuffle-footed generosity of the darker-skinned, burned Maggie. Maggie is somehow the "true" member of her people. She uses the butter churn for butter making and a quilt for covering. She doesn't abstract her experience. And Dee, now that it has become fashionable to "be" black, is willing to claim her race and its artifacts, but only if both can be used for display.

The mother has limited sympathy for her more glamorous daughter's struggle for identity. When the mother gives the quilts to Maggie, her decision is hardly surprising: her sympathies have been with Maggie all along. Even as she praises Dee's determination, we sense her anger.

Ask students to analyze the mother's character. What are her strengths and weaknesses as Maggie's mother? as Dee's? In both cases, the answer is more complicated than it might seem. For example, the mother tells us that Dee once hated Maggie, but there's also evidence that Maggie might hate Dee. Maggie sees Dee as friendless at the end of paragraph 14 (though the observation is presented as if it were entirely innocent). And while Dee may be impossibly critical, her mother's pleasure in Jimmy T's flight from Dee's "faultfinding power" to marry "a cheap city girl from a family of ignorant flashy people" should be considered.

On first reading, it's clear that Maggie is favored. But ask students what they make of the demeaning language that describes Maggie as a lame dog and, in Maggie's final triumph, as having "a kind of dopey, hangdog look . . . with her scarred hands hidden in the folds of her skirt."

Dee is certainly hard on her family. She calls Maggie "backward" and speaks of the family's difficult circumstances as if they were chosen. At the same time, Dee, despite her outbursts of frustration and anger, does seem to struggle with the way the family perceives her. During the discussion of her new name, she finally says, "You don't have to call me by it if you don't want to," and in this moment of abdication, her mother is willing to abdicate, too, saying she'll use the name her daughter wants.

The story doesn't end on this moment of reconciliation, however, but with both sides retreating back to their "positions" on their heritage. The positions are nicely encapsulated when Asalamalakim says, "Well, there you are," and the mother responds, "There I was not."

WRITING SUGGESTION   Evaluate Dee's apparent relationship to class and race. Consider who Dee appears to be before she comes home for her visit (before her mother learns of the changes she's made) and after her visit. How might Shelby Steele's essay ("On Being Black and Middle Class," p. 211) help explain her character and the changes she decides to make in herself?

Henry Louis Gates, Jr.

IN THE KITCHEN (p. 229)

Henry Louis Gates once disapproved of the way his mother used to examine his daughters' "kitchens" when he visited home. He writes, "I didn't like the politics it suggested — the notion of 'good' and 'bad' hair. 'Good' hair was 'straight,' 'bad' hair kinky." And yet, Gates confesses, when no one was looking, he'd peek at his daughters' hair, too.

Gates's peeking and his own recollected emotion at Nat King Cole's hair may seem surprising, since clearly the whole effort to straighten hair is a matter of denying one's self. When the light-skinned Mr. Charlie Carroll shows up with his white Stetson hat and has Gates's mother straighten his hair, it is clear that he is trying to eliminate evidence of his race. In *The Autobiography of Malcolm X*, dictated to Alex Haley, Malcolm X described the physically painful experience of getting his "first conk," concluding:

That was my first really big step toward self-degradation: when I endured all of that pain, literally burning my flesh to have it look like white

44

man's hair. I had joined that multitude of Negro men and women in America who are brainwashed into believing that the black people are "inferior" and white people "superior"— that they will even violate and mutilate their God-created bodies to try to look "pretty" by white standards.

In Gates's essay, all the examples of straightening and processing hair are undeniably related to a societal (and subsequently a personal) failure to value the race. But the matter isn't as simple as that, for the efforts at erasing or straightening natural features *are* a part of Gates's ancestry, both his family's ancestry and his community's. Gates finds his community's efforts disturbing, no doubt, but also funny, and there is real affection when he remembers the details of his own efforts.

When Gates writes "From Murray's to Duke to Afro Sheen: that was my progression in black consciousness," he's saying there was no real progression, just a change of styles. He's implicitly underlying Malcolm X's words to "any black man who conks today, or any white-wigged black woman." Malcolm X said that if all those people "gave the brains in their heads just half as much attention as they do their hair, they would be a thousand times better off."

Still, Gates notes, "It's not an accident that some of the biggest black-owned companies in the fifties and sixties made hair products." Here he's emphasizing, once again, that despite the "politics," hair straightening was a community experience that even meant financial success and power for some members of the community.

There are, of course, contradictions in trying so hard for a natural look that isn't natural, in having an ideal for a community that denies the beauty inherent in that community. But, as Gates points out, straight hair was an ideal only if it was done right. A bad process seemed to carry all the negative implications of what the process was; a good process was another thing altogether. Ask students to explain Gates's feelings for Nat King Cole's process. Why did he and he alone have the right to wear it? The answer may center on a successful struggle for identity. Nat King Cole was something no one else could be; even if his self was a fictitious construct, he had created that self out of his community's desires.

At the essay's close, a much older Gates is moved, once again, by the image of Nat King Cole's hair. Gates takes care to mention that when he lovingly recalled Cole's hair, he was in an unfamiliar culture. The image moved him because it restored him to his own community for a moment. Ironically, of course, Gates was restored to the community by an image that may seem like an indication of how much self-hate there was within his community. Still, by struggling against their hair together, the community's efforts may have been transformed into a struggle — if not for the natural self then at least for something that was all their own.

WRITING SUGGESTION   Read James Baldwin's essay "If Black Language Isn't English, Then Tell Me What Is" in *The Price of the Ticket*. Then analyze Gates's essay for examples of black language. What rhetorical purposes do these various phrases serve?

PART 5

WORD POWER

Developing a Critical Point of View

Leaving identity issues behind, Part 5 focuses on language and learning, examining links between thought and expression. These authors have distinctive slants on their subject, viewpoints determined by their current jobs, professional allegiances, and personal responses.

The readings lend themselves to assignments that emphasize analysis, interpretation, evaluation, and criticism — skills that encourage students to develop a critical viewpoint. Students can begin by identifying what most interests them in their reading and then using that concern to develop a principle of analysis. The principle, in turn, will help lead them to a thesis, as well as a structure by which they can examine their subject. What's more, by making their principles of analysis clear to their readers, students will show why their analyses are valuable, different, interesting, or meaningful.

Insights

Life's lessons, as the essays in this section make clear, aren't necessarily the lessons of the classroom. What, then, are people doing when they seek out education in a formal setting or from a formal source? Maybe nothing at all, the D. H. Lawrence quote suggests. For Lawrence, questions about education raise questions about the self. But Lawrence slips into something like an either-or fallacy when he considers the matter. An institution, he feels, offers instruction only in how to conform. The man of passion will have to look elsewhere for true knowledge. In the days when Yale and Harvard were gentlemen's schools, Lawrence's sense of the institution as *necessarily* close-minded may have had more basis in fact. Today one might reasonably hope for more out of Harvard and other institutions of higher learning.

Though Lawrence's protest may seem adolescent, it does touch on the obvious limits of, as Ralph Waldo Emerson says, "the book, the college, the school of art, the institution of any kind." Emerson's test for valuable books (and, by extension, worthwhile institutions) has to do with whether they prompt individuals to become active, creative thinkers. In this emphasis on the soul in its *creative* aspect, Emerson extends William Cory's notion of the function of a "great school" as a place where skills of analysis, expression, and judgment are taught.

What might Emerson or Cory think of M. Degas in Philip Levine's poem? What is M. Degas teaching when he draws a line across his blackboard and solicits interpretations? What do the responses reveal about M. Degas's students? What exactly does the narrator think "could go on forever"?

Instructors may want to put Richard Wright's quote into a sociohistorical context. Unlike Helen Vendler ("Knowing Poems," p. 250), whose early encounters with the Psalms left her with the sense that literature could articulate her own inchoate emotions, Wright saw literature as a way to understand a world that eluded him. Growing up in the Jim Crow South, Richard Wright's view of the world was limited by race. He could adopt the prevailing white perspective and thus accept his own denigration, or he could identify with the African American point of view. As represented by his family, the black point of view was religious: *suffer here; the next world will be better.* Outside his family, the black point of view was hypocritical: *play the white man's game; become who the white man thinks you are, so you can get by.* Either option stunted Richard Wright, made him a black "boy" who could never hope to be a man. Wright's sense that the world could be different from the world he experienced came directly from books. It's not too much to say that Wright had the strength to resist a brutal, wholly hostile environment because books allowed him to imagine an alternative for himself.

While many essays in this section suggest language's expressive power, Sheila Rowbotham's Insight focuses on its political power, how language can be used to dominate. Ask students to explain her quote by thinking of instances in which language ensures "supremacy."

Joan Didion

ON KEEPING A NOTEBOOK (p. 243)

Though she denies it vehemently, Joan Didion does keep a notebook to provide herself with material for writing. As Didion explores her subject, she gives readers a sense of both what it is to be a writer and what kind of world she inhabits.

Didion's notebook is neither a diary nor a simple recording of events and thoughts. Instead, it is a repository for scattered observations that have meaning for her, "bits of the mind's string too short to use, an indiscriminate and erratic assemblage with meaning only for its maker." These "bits of the mind's string" are hardly useless. The vivid moments she shares reveal a good deal in themselves and more when Didion plays them out. They are also linked thematically. The oxymoronic opening image is a "dirty crepe-de-Chine wrapper," an image of dissipation and wealth. Have students think about the world for such an object — by turns, glamorous, fashionable, and depressing — and the circumstances surrounding Didion's details. Even the sauerkraut recipe is really a story of existential panic, where the trappings of existence include money (a stay on Fire Island, a resort community for fashionable New Yorkers) and alcohol ("we drank a lot of bourbon").

Didion's notebook helps her remember what something *was* to her, how she felt in certain past moments. Though Didion claims in paragraph 17 that remembering such detail serves no one but herself, her very essay — with its wonderful elaboration of the notebook quotes — belies her. As she plays out each detail — describing things such as "the ground hardening and summer already dead"— she does what every writer most wants to do; she transfers her feelings to her readers. Indeed, by writing "On Keeping a Notebook," she creates a public audience for the words that, she insists, have an audience of only one: Didion herself. What do students think is her purpose in writing this essay, as opposed to keeping a notebook?

Didion says her notebook serves a personal purpose; she writes, "I think we are well advised to keep on nodding terms with the people we used to be whether we find them attractive company or not." Keeping a notebook, then, is a form of self-education. That said, as Didion points out, notebook writing is an undeniably narcissistic activity, for we write to put our own opinions, perceptions, and thoughts into the world. What other kinds of writing might be considered narcissistic? (Is, for example, this essay?) Is that necessarily a bad thing? What does Didion leave unsaid about herself, and her former selves, in the essay? Why?

In another often anthologized essay, "Why I Write," Joan Didion explains what she likes about the phrase "Why I Write" (a title that she borrows from Orwell's essay by the same name):

> I like the sound of the words . . . three short unambiguous words that share a sound, and the sound they share is this:
>
> I
>
> I
>
> I.
>
> In many ways writing is the act of saying *I*, of imposing oneself upon other people, of saying, *listen to me, see it my way, change your mind.*

WRITING SUGGESTION   Keep two records of a week of your life — a conventional diary and a journal along the lines of Didion's notebook. Analyze the results, with an eye to uncovering the purpose of these different records.

Helen Vendler

KNOWING POEMS (p. 250)

You might begin discussion by asking students to describe Helen Vendler as an adolescent. What clues does the author give about her early personality? How does she suggest her deep unhappiness without offering specifics about her home life or school days? (Why might this be a useful technique for a writer?)

Vendler feels her adolescent self "needed" the Psalms because they articulated emotions she couldn't yet express. Ask students to describe the nature of the quotes in paragraphs 5 and 6. The author speaks of these as "the wild psalms." Why? What emotions are expressed in lines such as "I am poured out like water; and all my bones are scattered"? If students have trouble answering, it may be because such despair eludes expression, save for in the vaguely fanatical, lyrical hyperbole of the Psalms.

Vendler suggests that there is something soothing in having one's emotions articulated, that language can act like a poultice. Of the Psalms, she writes, "They drew off the worst of the poison . . . , and they filled my mouth with language." Words give Vendler a sense of connection and make her feel less alone with her emotions. Given all this, it's no surprise that the adult Vendler is less drawn to narrative than meditative work, which she describes as "the ripples of intensification extending out from a center of thought."

Vendler's closing paragraph implies that contemporary adolescents are capable of connecting with the "wild verities" of the Psalms. Ask students what they think of Vendler's final suggestion. While many will agree with Vendler's perceptions of adolescent emotions, they may question her faith in teenagers' interest in literature. How do they think Vendler would define *literacy*?

Another possible approach to this essay would be to start discussion by asking students to write about a book, song, or poem that affected them as the Psalms affected Vendler. Then have one person collect the assignments and read them out loud. (Anonymity might be appropriate for this exercise.) Have students characterize the results. What work did the class once respond to? What do the answers reveal about where adolescents look for connection? For instance, what does it mean if the class writes more about song lyrics than books?

WRITING SUGGESTION   What books should be assigned reading in American middle schools? Draw up a list, and make an argument for your choices, considering your sense of what is most important for adolescent readers. How do your choices reflect or counter Helen Vendler's interests?

Deborah Tannen

TALKING UP CLOSE (p. 255)

Deborah Tannen's essay may be somewhat confusing to students because the excerpt is so loosely developed along the lines of scientific inquiry: she asks a question ('what does it mean to say that males fight more than females?"), looks at specific examples (what arguing might mean in different contexts, not necessarily ones that hinge on gender), and then, rather than directly addressing the question she posed earlier, concludes by discussing the importance of the question. Tannen isn't interested in resolving an argument but in understanding how arguing itself functions and in asserting that its different meanings in different contexts may actually lead to far more hurtful misunderstandings (and arguments) between individuals of different genders or cultural backgrounds.

Throughout the essay, Tannen's strategy is to follow a generalization with several examples and then conclude with a summary statement. Paragraph 6 starts with a sentence that summarizes the examples in paragraphs 2 through 5. The first lines of paragraphs 9 and 11 work similarly. You might have students compare Tannen's strategy to Stephen Dunn's use of a similar strategy in "Locker Room Talk" (p. 124). Dunn doesn't draw a conclusion until near the end of his essay either. Have your students compare how the same strategy yields different effects in the different essays. What kind of essay might better lend itself to this strategy?

Ask students to mark lines in Tannen's essay that are hard to understand because they appear to be especially vague or overly general. For instance, the terms in the third sentence of paragraph 2, particularly the phrase "because status and connection are mutually evocative," will probably need to be defined. Paragraph 11 may also present some questions, since Tannen refers to her research as a "discussion of fighting, silence, and interrupting," and the examples in this essay don't include a discussion of silence. Tannen uses the passive voice in her summary statements and even starts her essay with the weak construction. Ask students what the effect of this is. How might they rewrite the opening sentence? Is the result stronger or weaker? Why?

Because Tannen's essay relies heavily on outside sources, this selection could be used to discuss sources. Tannen bolsters her argument by referring to expert opinion, linguistic research, personal experience, and folklore. How relevant is all this material to her point? What if instead of commenting on the importance of her question she limited her discussion to fighting and bonding and how certain cultures consider arguing a sign of intimacy? What examples could she then leave out? (Is bonding in war truly about arguing? Do fellow soldiers even argue in war? Or is their "argument" with the enemy? Might there be other features of life-and-death experiences that account for wartime friendships?)

When Tannen summarizes her thoughts (as in paragraphs 11, 13, and 14), do students feel her examples have been sufficient to prove her point? Though she has offered material to support her notion about arguing, has she convinced her reader of her larger point — that "the same way of speaking can create either status differences or connection, or both at the same time"?

WRITING SUGGESTION   Use a tape recorder to capture a conversation between a group of male friends and a group of female friends. Then analyze the results with the goal of furthering or challenging Tannen's notions about how the genders differ in their use of argument to bond.

Pico Iyer

IN PRAISE OF THE HUMBLE COMMA (p. 260)

Pico Iyer's clever essay proves its point in the conventional way — by providing examples — and in an unconventional way — by having form mimic content, so individual sentences self-consciously illustrate their own meaning, as in paragraph 8 or the second sentence of paragraph 1. The result is amusing and instructive, reminding readers that language relies on silences for meaning. Because Iyer conceives of silence as "breath," he's able to link punctuation to a life-giving force — to God, eventually. Before he does this, he has other, lesser (but still significant) claims for punctuation marks: they're language's policemen, keeping law and order; they establish the relationship between words and thus people; they are a "civic prop" and a "signature of cultures"; they refine meaning. You might proceed through the essay by asking students to elaborate on each of these claims, providing additional examples, while noting how Iyer's punctuation contributes to his meaning.

Iyer concludes that punctuation is "a matter of care." What, then, is misused punctuation? Why, in Iyer's mind, do errors make a difference? Ask students if they think Iyer is making too much of the matter. Why or why not?

Iyer ends with a famous line from Isaac Babel's story "Guy de Maupassant": "No iron can pierce the heart with such force as a period put just at the right place." Ask students how this can be true by having them articulate the difference between the three "Jane whom I adore" sentences. How does punctuation change the meaning of those lines? Have students consider the difference between optional and required punctuation. Does required punctuation — like a serial comma — strike them as having as much potential meaning as the stylistic comma in the V. S. Naipaul sentence in paragraph 7?

WRITING SUGGESTIONS   (a) Write an essay in which you try to convince recalcitrant, unmotivated secondary school students that grammar and punctuation matter. Alternatively, write an essay in which you try to convince a taskmaster of a teacher that grammar and punctuation aren't that important.

(b) Find a piece of short fiction — such as one of the stories in Carolyn Ferrell's *Don't Erase Me* — that purposefully uses unconventional punctuation, grammar, and spelling. What shades of meaning do the "errors" give to the story? Be specific, using close analysis of the story's sentences to describe effects.

Susanne K. Langer

LANGUAGE AND THOUGHT (p. 263)

Susanne K. Langer's essay is sufficiently difficult that it might make sense to start discussion by having students restate her thoughts. Langer's most basic point is not so hard to grasp: what distinguishes humans from animals is an ability to symbolize. A symbol, Langer makes clear, is similar to a sign, but it "does not announce the presence of the object, the being, condition, or whatnot." Signs always announce the presence (or existence or imminence) of something. As such, signs are "closely bound up with something to be noted or expected in experience." (Ask students to elaborate by explaining how a stop sign or sign of inclement weather is related to the physical world.) Signs are "embedded in reality." A symbol is not necessarily. It may even be divorced from reality, referring to ideas or dreams. Signs are "in face" of the thing signified. Symbols are "about" the thing symbolized.

The distinction between signs and symbols is important, Langer emphasizes, because symbols free human thought from the physical world and from the present moment. Without the ability to symbolize, man might be a sophisticated user of signs, but he would not live in a world of "rights and property, social position, special talents and virtues, and . . . ideas."

Having defined signs and symbols and made her claim about human's capacity to symbolize, Langer complicates her argument by talking about "the process of conception" (para. 12), whereby direct experience or the things of the world are transformed into symbols like words, pictures, and "memory images."

What makes the human mind special is the way in which the activity of conception has evolved. (Langer distinguishes this from an evolution of signifying, or animal, intelligence.) The whole process depicted above — the process of conception or of transforming things into symbols — is an ability humans have. It is also a need. Humans have to do this thing they *can* do. In fact, the process of conception underlies all behavior. Before humans act, they think, and thinking is one of the activities of "the process of conception."

And how *has* the process of conception evolved? It has evolved into language. In paragraph 17, Langer notes that some psychologists think language is essentially sign making, a more sophisticated version of what animals do. Langer disagrees, holding that language's essence is in the process of conception, in symbol making. As an evolution of the process of conception, we use language "to formulate and hold ideas in our own minds." Language does this through names that abstract conception from fact. Names let us have ideas of things without having the thing in front of us. Without language, we can't have ideas or thought.

This final point is a difficult one to grasp. One way to elaborate on it might be to remind students of Helen Keller's famous description of the moment when she first understood language. Prior to that day, Keller — who was both deaf and blind — considered herself to be existing in a thoughtless fog. The decisive moment came when Keller realized "w-a-t-e-r" (her teacher tapped the word into her hand) was related to the cold, wet stuff running over her fingers:

> Suddenly, I felt a misty consciousness as of something forgotten — a thrill of returning thought; and somehow the mystery of language was revealed to me. . . . Everything had a name, and each name gave birth to a new thought. As we returned to the house every object which I touched seemed to quiver with life. That was because I saw everything with the strange, new sight that had come to me. On entering the door I remembered the doll I had broken. I felt my way to the hearth and picked up the pieces. I tried vainly to put them together. Then my eyes filled with tears; for I realized what I had done, and for the first time I felt repentance and sorrow.

Helen Keller was obviously human before that day when (at the age of seven) she connected water with "w-a-t-e-r." But she wasn't fully human. It was not until she acquired (in Langer's words) a "symbolistic human mind" that she had the ability to think, feel, and know.

WRITING SUGGESTIONS   (a) Consider the virtue of vocabulary building. There are whole books devoted simply to adding to one's personal lexicon. Is this a mindless exercise? What can people learn from such books?

(b) Read Helen Keller's autobiography *The Story of My Life* (New York: Doubleday, 1902, 1904), and then use Langer's theories to explain what happened to Helen Keller on the day she discovered language. Account for Keller's feelings about the broken doll as well as her sense that objects "seemed to quiver with life."

Robert J. Sternberg

WHAT SHOULD WE ASK ABOUT INTELLIGENCE? (p. 269)

Robert Sternberg's essay evokes Amy Tan's complaints about standardized tests in "Mother Tongue" (p. 189). Here, though, Sternberg writes as a professional — a psychologist — frustrated with the narrow way in which intelligence has been traditionally defined. Sternberg lays the groundwork for his discussion of the "battle" between theories of intelligence by giving an overview of the players in the argument — the traditionalists and the revolutionaries. Even before we know what both sides think, we have a sense of Sternberg's impatience with the old guard and its members' willingness to defend outmoded concepts in order to protect their personal power. (Have students consider the efficacy of embroiling the reader in the politics of a matter before its substantive issues. Is this an interesting or persuasive approach?)

The issue, Sternberg finally explains, isn't about answers but questions. The old guard gets the "right" answers to the "wrong" questions. Instead of wondering what should be asked about intelligence, they define the notion based on tests that measure it. In other words, the means of measurement determines the nature of the thing measured. This is an arbitrary way of defining intelligence, at best, Sternberg argues; ideally, tests would have a strong base in *theories* about intelligence. Sternberg says the tests don't, but he also makes it clear that the traditional notion of intelligence is analytic. (Ask students if this is a contradiction.) For Sternberg, the traditionalists' definition is overly narrow. As an alternative, he offers his own "triarchic theory of human intelligence" and Howard Gardner's theory of multiple intelligences. Together, Sternberg and Gardner add a number of kinds of intelligence — creative, practical, musical, interpersonal, and so on — to the linguistic, logical-mathematical, and spatial intelligences that conventional tests measure.

Sternberg suggests a possible objection to his ideas in paragraphs 12 and 13, noting that conventional tests do appear to be a good predictor of academic success. Might this mean that the tests do, in fact, measure intelligence? Not necessarily, Sternberg claims, since schools have the same flaws as standardized tests; they emphasize analytic over creative and practical skills.

In paragraph 14, Sternberg asks what, presumably, readers might be wondering: What difference do definitions of intelligence make? If tests do a decent job of measuring one kind of intelligence and predicting academic success, why bother with new ideas about intelligence? Sternberg's answer is that tests and schools ill-serve students by emphasizing one kind of intelligence and failing to value others. As a result, schools produce a "cognitive elite," who have easy access to educational and professional opportunities, even though they aren't truly smarter than those who are denied such access. Indeed, the cognitive elite's intelligence is entirely manufactured by the educational system.

Ask students to respond to Sternberg's suggestion, in paragraph 16, that if we were "to admit students to competitive colleges and graduate programs on the basis of their height, eventually we would find that individuals who are in highly regarded occupations are tall." Does this claim make sense? Is the analytic notion of intelligence as arbitrary as a fanciful notion of intelligence based on height? If so, revising notions of intelligence and rewriting tests isn't an academic exercise; it's a crucial matter of politics and social policy.

WRITING SUGGESTION   Should college and universities use standardized tests as part of the admission process? Explain your answer, making reference, where appropriate, to Sternberg's article and your own experience.

George Steiner

BOOKS AND THE END OF LITERATURE (p. 274)

You might begin discussing George Steiner's lecture by looking at how its details hold together. An essay is unified when its parts work together to support a single idea or purpose and there are no stray details to mislead or confuse the reader. At first, Steiner's essay appears to be organized somewhat randomly. If his argument were a river, Steiner would be leaping from tributary to tributary — not making apparent (until the end) how or why he moved from one waterway to the next or whether the tributaries were eventually going to lead to the same river.

But Steiner's piece does have its own logic. Ask students what unifies the work. Their answer should center on Steiner's initial question about how current technology and trends in talent will influence literature. Steiner doesn't completely answer his question, but he seems unworried by this failure, since concerns about literature's future date back to the fifth century. Literary genres have fallen in and out of favor, the shape and sense of literature has changed, but literature has not — not yet, anyway — disappeared.

Current technology will affect literature. Steiner doesn't know how exactly but suspects books may come to be an "archive of remembrance" if electronic means of reproduction prevail. The number of talented individuals who choose careers in the sciences or media, instead of literature, also suggests significant changes. Do these changes mean the end of literature? Hard to say, Steiner acknowledges and then reviews current literary genres, to imagine how they'll weather the drain of talent and onslaught of technology. Some genres seem hardier than others. Steiner feels oral literature, particularly poetry, has "an immense future." Have students analyze Steiner's evidence for this claim. What qualities does he attribute to poetry that seem distinct from other kinds of literature? What does Steiner mean in paragraph 16 when he says, "Poetry means every form of drama"? If this paragraph seems unclear to students, ask them how Steiner might have clarified his thoughts. For example, he could have defined his terms. (What is "the art of the human body"?) And he could have linked his point more clearly to the overall discussion.

In paragraph 17, Steiner starts to talk about novels. His notion (borrowed from Hegel) that novels thrive in a "large, rich, stable, social context" (even if the novels are about chaos and instability) is clear enough. Is George Lukacs saying the same thing when he wrote that the possibility of rereading means that "no novel ends unhappily"? When Steiner writes, in paragraph 18, that novels flourish during revolutions, is he contradicting Hegel's notion? Or does he resolve the possible contradiction by conceiving of revolution as an "earlier stage of bourgeois culture"?

According to Steiner, even though novels thrived in the earlier stages of bourgeois culture, they're not thriving now; in fact, there's a market glut of fiction. What do students think this glut may reflect about middle-class culture and the development of technology? Steiner feels the best current literature, the most exciting forms, are hybrid, related to journalism; he calls the best journalists "masters of the immediate." Do students think this praise is related to the development of new technologies? Recently there has been a flurry of interest in memoir in the United States. Often memoirs, which are obviously nonfiction, borrow the narrative technique of fiction writers. You may want to bring in a list of examples from bestseller lists (such as Mary Karr's *The Liars' Club*, Caroline Knapp's *Drinking: A Love Story*, Frank McCourt's *Angela's Ashes*, and James McBride's *The Color of Water*) or an article from *Publishers' Weekly* (or even *Vanity Fair*) about the phenomenon. What do students make of the current popularity of this genre?

Steiner says thinking about literature means thinking about literacy and perhaps acknowledging other literacies, such as computer literacy. What's more, thinking about the future and literacy means acknowledging that literature may no longer be immortal but is aggressively temporal. This brings Steiner to an answer to his initial question about literature's future: literature will probably continue to exist. It will even continue to be inventive, but it may no longer be as stable or permanent as it once was.

WRITING SUGGESTION   What do computers mean for previous means of communication? How do you think e-mail and the Internet are altering our culture? Consider the effects of the computer on snail mail, libraries, books, and even direct (person-to-person) communication. A possible source for ideas — Sven Birkerts's book *The Gutenberg Elegies: The Fate of Reading in the Electronic Age* (Boston: Faber & Faber, 1994).

Ha Jin

OCEAN OF WORDS (p. 281)

The central character of Ha Jin's story, Zhou Wen, lives and works among those hostile to books and scholarship. Their intolerance alienates "bookworm" Zhou, leaving him uncomfortable and friendless until he encounters Liang Ming. Liang shares Zhou's sense of the value of books and gives him a place to continue his studies.

Zhou doesn't appear to consider learning as having a purpose per se. When Liang asks what motivates his enthusiasm for learning, Zhou says he doesn't know but adds that he comes from a family that emphasized learning and that he enjoys reading and writing.

Liang's reasons differ. Years earlier, Liang, unable to read an important message, condemned his comrades to death and lost his own arm. His youthful illiteracy functioned like a weapon, pointed at the wrong target. Liang now conceives of literacy as a weapon, pointed at the right target. He believes words and learning can defeat the enemy. The greatest gift he can give Zhou, when Zhou leaves the military, is a "Revolutionary Pen." Zhou accepts the instrument in the spirit in which it is given, imagining himself as "a socialist man of letters, fighting with the Revolutionary Pen for the rest of his life." (Ask students what these words mean.)

Party Secretary Si Ma also conceives of language's power in terms of its value. After he first browses through Zhou's exhaustive dictionary *Ocean of Words*, he exclaims, "I love this book. What a treasure. It's a gold mine, an armory!" What do students make of this list of metaphors? How does it fit with Si Ma's rather capitalist notion that Zhou should sell him the heirloom? Why does Si Ma want Zhou's book so badly? (Students might be interested to know that the Isaac Babel line, quoted in Pico Iyer's essay "In Praise of the Humble Comma" (p. 260), is preceded by the following: "I began to speak of style, of the army of words, of the army in which all kinds of weapons may come into play.")

At the end of the story, Zhou gives Liang the book he could not bring himself to sell to Si Ma, even though this failure threatened Zhou's future membership in the Party. When Zhou presents the book to Liang, he does so because he feels indebted to the man who "had helped him join the Party, which was an important event in everyone's life, like marriage or rebirth." Do students accept this explanation? The story suggests that Zhou's willingness to depart with the book is less about Party politics than Liang's feeling for words.

Liang must have learned to read sometime after the battle in which he lost his arm. (He can read the title of Zhou's book when he first meets him.) Even so, there are limits to his knowledge, as the operation-apparition conversation makes clear. And yet the character has a wisdom that Si Ma certainly doesn't have. Liang knows (in paragraph 23) that if his gift is to be accepted he'll have to order the recalcitrant Zhou to use his study. What kind of intelligence is this? Finally, Liang's eclectic reading list suggests Liang may understand the value of words even more deeply than Zhou, who is puzzled by Liang's choice of books for his son. Ask students why Zhou is puzzled. What might be Liang's reason for having his son read a book that isn't in political favor?

WRITING SUGGESTIONS   (a) Liang, Zhou, and Si Ma all value books for different reasons. Zhou's comrades don't value books at all. What is the purpose of literacy according to the characters in Ha Jin's story? Does the story suggest that all these purposes are equally valuable?

(b) Explain why Zhou gives *Ocean of Words* to Liang and not to Si Ma. Which man truly deserves the book? Explain why, making specific reference to Zhou's sense of family obligation, his political notions, and his love of words.

PART 6

WORK RULES

Arguing Audibly

The injunction to "make something of yourself" is invariably about work, a command to find worthy employment. From early childhood, we're encouraged to imagine the possibilities. We ask, and are asked, "What do you want to be when you grow up?" The question suggests the options are limited only by our desires, but, as Part 6's selections make clear, satisfying employment can be hard to come by. Indeed, work is often corrupting, exhausting, and demoralizing. Most students find themselves at some point worrying about a discrepancy between the work they want, their ambitions, and the demands of the marketplace. Over time we all define and redefine what we value in a job.

One of the ways students learn to do this is by articulating their thoughts and values. The pieces in this section give students the opportunity to write argumentative essays that challenge the *Life Studies* authors and themselves. While reading, students should ask, "What is the author trying to prove?" They should look at the ways in which the author tries to support points. Is the evidence sufficient, relevant, reasonable, and representative? How does the author apply it to the needs and values of the reader? What assumptions underlie the argument?

To argue effectively, students need to state their own opinions clearly, to support their claims fully, and to anticipate and respond to possible objections to their positions. As they prepare to do this, you might want to give them the advice that E. B. White received from his teacher Will Strunk. When you write, Strunk said, "Make definite assertions." Avoid, as White himself later wrote, "the vague, the tame, the colorless, the irresolute."

Will Strunk also told E. B. White's college composition class, "If you don't know how to pronounce a word, say it loud!" Ask students why a teacher would give such advice. White's own conclusion was that Strunk thought, "Why compound ignorance with inaudibility? Why run and hide?"

Insights

Men and women need to work, and they need to take pride in what they do, as Nikki Giovanni makes clear, but how are we to value our efforts? Society's messages about worth are bound to confuse. For instance, what are we to make of a college that subsidizes athletes through scholarships but not the editor-in-chief of the campus newspaper? Wilfrid Sheed answers that such a school subverts its own noblest intentions, but this subversion is certainly of a piece with a society "in which money determines value," as Margaret Lowe Benston puts it, and where "winning," as Vince Lombardi says, is "the only thing."

Those outside the money economy, including parents who stay at home, need to find ways to value their efforts. Those who lose in a money economy — people with minimal salaries or financial resources — also need to find ways of valuing their work. W. B. Yeats suggests an alternative when he comforts, and implicitly honors, his "friend whose work has come to nothing," reminding him that the hardest, most difficult thing isn't success but unacknowledged struggle.

The quotation by Vincent van Gogh touches on the important question of how the artist should handle internal rejection. Don't, van Gogh says, look to your friends for support. Don't, one might add, look to your teachers for a sense of your own writing. Ultimately, the external approval you seek has to come from within. This advice, as van Gogh's quotation should make clear, is not ultimately for the self but for the good of the work.

Abigail Witherspoon (Pseud.)

THIS PEN FOR HIRE (p. 300)

Students ought to have strong feelings about this essay, with its cynical conclusions about the quality of contemporary education and the ultimate value of learning. Rather than address the obvious moral issues that surround cheating, the pseudonymous Abigail Witherspoon brings readers back, again and again, to economics. In the first line of the essay, she says she is an "academic call girl," and her essay bears this out. She feels a sense of shame about her job. Her clients feel shame, too, but within the context of the intimate relationship, they are often arrogant and selfish. What's more, their relative stupidity or laziness or incompetence hasn't harmed them in the world of commerce; they're donned in fashionable clothes, while Witherspoon — clearly educated and knowledgeable — shivers in her apartment. In Witherspoon's world, money is power, and education counts for little. Indeed, Tailormade's writers are failures; down and out in Canada, they're smart, but that doesn't make much difference. Their hard work barely sustains them financially; it certainly compromises them morally. The work even harms its beneficiaries, robbing them of an education (although Tailormade's clients are happy to be robbed).

Ask students how Witherspoon understands her clients' motivation. Why does she think people buy academic papers? Can students provide additional reasons? Why is Witherspoon more sympathetic to certain clients than others? How do her sympathies suggest what she most values in others?

Witherspoon's essay intrigues because it presents information about an essentially clandestine organization. It tells secrets. Here, details that might seem workaday in another context — such as financial arrangements or workplace procedure — are bound to fascinate. Witherspoon offers her descriptions with weary disdain. She's disgusted — with herself, with her employers, with her clients. But she does have a measure of feeling for her fellow writers, as described in paragraph 7. Ask students why. It's not, of course, that she admires them, exactly. Like her, they have reason to be ashamed. But like her they're struggling. And they're smart.

They're hostile, too, and arrogant in their own way, eager to make clients feel dumb or frustrate their desires or make fools of them. While the hostility is often funny — as when the writers unsimplify "Simple English," handing in papers with "the mega-watt vocabulary and tortured syntax of the Frankfurt School" — it also suggests how employment with Tailormade corrupts. Ask students for other examples of hostility. How is Witherspoon, for instance, debased by her treatment of the client in paragraph 31?

After paragraph 8, Witherspoon begins the sections of her essay with dates, so that they resemble diary entries. Ask students why. Is the nature of the later information substantially different from the earlier material? Although in paragraph 5 she says, "This afternoon, October 10, I'm here to hand in a paper," the introduction does not begin with a date the way the rest of the essay's sections do. How does the format help Witherspoon organize her thoughts?

As she works, how does Witherspoon both criticize contemporary education and suggest its worth? Do students value Witherspoon's criticism? Some of her perceptions (paras. 20 and 22) may register with their own academic experiences. Then again, Witherspoon's perceptions about education may be compromised by her character. Ask students how they view the author. Do they feel sorry for her? Does she ever seem mean or self-pitying? Does the humor and intelligence of her writing redeem — or further condemn — her in students' minds?

Witherspoon never makes it entirely clear why she's doing what she's doing. She has her reasons, of course; she's an illegal immigrant in a town with a 10 percent unemployment rate. But does this suffice? Students may wonder why she's in Canada in the first place or why, given her talents, she's not capable of writing (long distance) for a reputable American business. It may be that Witherspoon has pardoned her own behavior for reasons that owe more to her clients' excuses than she's willing to admit. The essay suggests some basic flaws in society and the educational system. Without these flaws, Tailormade wouldn't flourish. Even if students acknowledge this, they may wonder how the expedient course became the chosen course for Witherspoon and her clients.

Finally, it might be interesting to ask students whether Witherspoon is a good writer. What in the essay suggests her talents? How do her skills affect students' sense of her situation? What does it make them feel about their own academic efforts?

WRITING SUGGESTION   Interview members of your school's administration to determine the prevalence of cheating on your campus. How does your school handle cases of academic dishonesty? Do you think the school's response is appropriate? Why or why not?

Greta Foff Paules

HUMBLE PIE (p. 312)

To begin discussion of this excerpt, you might ask students to examine Paules's opening sentence, the premise for her subsequent analysis. Do students agree that employees in service jobs "are encouraged to treat customers with unflinching reverence and solicitude"? If students concur, ask them why such behavior is encouraged. Paules offers her own reasons, but students may be able to add additional ones.

In "Humble Pie," Paules's argues that the "customer is king" rule perpetuates a symbolism that denigrates service employees. Related conventions — of behavior, dress, and language — only worsen matters, encouraging "customer and worker alike to approach service as an encounter between beings of vastly different social standing, with unequal claims to courtesy, consideration, and respect."

Paragraphs 2 to 9 detail these conventions. Paragraph 10 seems to prove these conventions work to make service employees unequal in customers' eyes, since they often subject employees to rude and insulting behavior, as well as constant criticism. What's especially pernicious about this behavior is the suggestion that the server isn't an employee but actually in servitude. The symbolism has a historic basis, since service employees have inherited the duties previously performed by domestic servants. "It seems likely," Paules writes, "that the symbolism of service was simply transported along with the physical and social functions of the domestic from private home to private enterprise." But that doesn't mean the source of the negative symbolism is entirely historical. Contemporary businesses insist on conventions that suggest servitude and even come up with new conventions that emphasize ties with the past.

Writing about Route, the New Jersey restaurant where she did her field work, Paules concludes, "In promoting an image of server as servant to the public, the restaurant encourages customers to treat, or mistreat, the waitress as they would a member of a historically degraded class." But servers at Route manage to protect themselves, to "resist[ ] the symbolism of service." Rather than feel undervalued or denigrated by insulting interchanges, they protect themselves with alternative symbolic systems. They view themselves as embattled soldiers or shrewd, independent businesspeople, and they type customers accordingly, sometimes "treating them as inanimate material to be processed quickly and dispassionately in view of extracting a tip." However, the symbolic inversion is purely cognitive. It isn't enacted in the customer-server relationship: a waitperson may think one way but still give outward assent to "the symbolism of service" because apparent assent to such imagery is a financial necessity.

"Humble Pie" is a selection from a chapter titled "Resisting the Symbolism of Service." As an excerpt, it doesn't detail all the forms of resistance Paules acknowledges. Can students suggest other forms of resistance — such as humor, bonding with fellow workers, wearing a required uniform but also wearing a nose ring? Neither the resistance Paules describes nor customers' behavior fits with humanistic ideals about how people should treat one another. What might be a better symbolic system for a restaurant? In the current business climate, would a guest-host relationship be possible? (A bed-and-breakfast operates under such a symbolic rubric.) How would guest-host symbolism serve to respect customer and server? What sorts of behavior would such symbolism encourage?

WRITING SUGGESTION   Paules's chapter "Resisting the Symbolism of Service" in her book *Dishing It Out* starts with the following epigraph from Arlie Hochschild's *The Managed Heart*:

> In the public world of work, it is often part of an individual's job to accept uneven exchanges, to be treated with disrespect or anger by a client, all the while closeting into fantasy the anger one would like to respond with. Where the customer is king, unequal exchanges are normal, and from the beginning customer and client assume different rights to feeling and display.

Examine the truth of Hochschild's claim by observing the interchanges at three of the following — a diner, restaurant, convenience store, coffee house, gas station, department store, or hardware store. Does the truth of Hochschild's claim seem to fluctuate with the nature of the establishment? Interpret your findings, using, when appropriate, material from Paules's excerpt.

Gary Soto

BLACK HAIR (p. 320)

A possible way to start discussion of this essay is to have students describe their worst jobs and then consider their experiences against those of Gary Soto, Abigail Witherspoon ("This Pen for Hire," p. 300), and Michael Dorris ("Life Stories," p. 45). Dorris finds something to value in his summer jobs, and Witherspoon, distraught as she is, finds humor (at times) in her experience. But Soto's essay is unrelentingly sorrowful. Even a situation that another writer might have played for laughs — like the startled nurse (of paragraph 11) or the unfriendly Barbara (of paragraph 24) — is viewed darkly.

Soto persuades readers of the bleakness of his job — and of his situation in the summer of 1969 — by keeping abstract language to a minimum. Between the opening and closing abstractions, the narrative is primarily descriptive. The accumulation of details, though, implies an argument about how work can corrupt.

Soto's job at Valley Tire Factory is dirty, exhausting, and boring. Everything about the physical place is unattractive. The showers are slimy, and even the magazines in the off-limits waiting room are greasy. Though the tire enterprise isn't as thoroughly steeped in dishonesty as Tailormade (see "This Pen for Hire"), the business is crooked. The men who work at Valley Tire are similarly sordid or grotesque. They look repulsive — Tully is a fat man with one ear and gray teeth — and their behavior isn't much better. A rare light moment comes when the Mexicans share stories after scrambling away from Immigration officers. But what Soto emphasizes is the darkness of work, a darkness that is not alleviated by his after-hours situation, since he's hungry and homeless. Eventually Soto earns enough money to rent a room, but the "luxury" of "a girl's sheets" quickly diminishes, until he only acknowledges, "It was a place to stay."

Ask students about Soto's character. Despite his youth, he seems to know, right away, how to handle the politics of work, smiling at Tully both because he wants to get along and keep his job. He's quick to apologize to the nurse he startles, and he doesn't want his landlady to wash his clothes because he feels "shy and hurt" by her offer. In paragraph 20, he's reluctant to accept money from the Mexican woman. When he does, he honors the woman's motives, and his essay departs, for a moment, from the concrete and offers an abstraction: "Her eyes met mine as she opened the car door, and there was a tenderness that was surprisingly true — one for which you wait for years but when it comes it doesn't help. Nothing changes. You continue on in rags, with the sun still above you." As a single abstraction after 25 paragraphs of concrete material, the sentences have a force they might not otherwise have. In another context, these lines might seem self-pitying, but the author has given ample reason for despair. Ask students why it's a moment of affection, rather than one of the essay's disturbing moments, that occasions Soto's observation about the relentless nature of poverty.

Soto's job at Valley Tire isn't his first exposure to hard manual labor. He makes this clear in paragraph 29, but even before, the reader senses Soto's no stranger to hard work. Soto says that the work at Valley Tire is worse than the field work he's known. Why is this so? After all, field work is fatiguing and boring. Field workers feel as trapped as tire workers in their jobs. The answer has to do with dignity, which is why Iggy is such an important part of Soto's essay. Because there is nothing in the tire work to value, Soto's associates no longer value themselves. At the end of the day, each man (with the exception of Iggy) looks "defeated and contemptible in our filth," unable even to imagine a better life. "There was," Soto repeats, "no grace" in the work, or in the lives that included the work. In Insights, Nikki Giovanni claims, "The ability to take pride in your own work is one of the hallmarks of sanity. Take away the ability to both work and be proud of it and you can drive anyone insane." Soto's coworkers may not be insane, but Soto suggests they're ruined. In the essay's final line, what might the black tire dust be a metaphor for?

WRITING SUGGESTION   Soto, in his essay "Black Hair," rarely interacts with customers, yet his job suggests a symbolic system that denigrates as much as the imagery of servitude described in Greta Foff Paules's "Humble Pie" (p. 312). How would you describe the culture of Valley Tire? What symbolism does working in a tire factory hold? How does it contribute to the feelings Soto and his fellow employees have about themselves?

John Updike

A & P (p. 328)

The narrator of John Updike's often anthologized short story "A & P" bears out many of Greta Foff Paules's conclusions about how service workers resist the symbolism of their jobs. Sammy stereotypes customers — speaking of one disgruntled woman as a witch, another as "an old party in baggy gray pants," and thinking of still others as "sheep," "houseslaves in pin curlers," or "scared pigs in a chute." Part of this quick dismissal of others has to do with the narrator's personality; as an adolescent he's more comfortable with reducing people — even Stokesie and Lengel — than imagining them in their full complexity. But part of the stereotyping has to do with the supermarket atmosphere, which encourages conformity. This changes — not dramatically, but somewhat — when three girls enter the store, wearing their bathing suits. The story — reflective of the mores of the 1950s — makes it clear that the girls' behavior is shocking. Even if it weren't, the girls are unusual, because they resist supermarket conventions: they walk "against the usual traffic," they neglect to use a shopping cart, they go barefoot, they don't appear to need the item they're buying. Indeed, Sammy suggests they intend to shock, and their power as a group, and Queenie's power as ringleader, is in their ability to act as if their behavior is entirely natural — for them.

The adolescent narrator's initial interest in the girls is surely sexual, as his focus on their physical attributes makes clear. While hardly an enlightened young man — he's quite sexist about the girls, wondering if their skulls contain minds or "just a little buzz like a bee in a glass jar"— Sammy sees the girls more fully than he sees others. His ability to elaborate for several paragraphs on the girls' looks and manner makes this clear. Ask students what makes the group worthy of Sammy's careful attention. They will probably agree that the girls' flaunting of convention is as suggestive as their sexuality. They seem — in their subtle defiance — to offer an alternative to the life that otherwise awaits Sammy, a life he disparages in paragraph 14 (when he imagines Queenie's family, as compared to his own) and as he describes Lengel and Stokesie. How is the narrator distinguishing himself from his family when he says in paragraph 12, "Now here comes the sad part of the story, at least my family says it's sad, but I don't think it's so sad myself"? What part of the story is he talking about exactly?

Lengel — in asking the girls to dress "decently" when they next come to the market — doesn't seem mean. Nor does he appear to want to embarrass the girls — though Queenie blushes at his words. Both at the beginning and end of paragraph 21, Sammy tells us that he is "thinking." What is he thinking about? Is it significant that his thoughts take place while he's performing his cashier duties? Why exactly does Sammy quit? Perhaps he resigns over the issue of embarrassing the girls. More likely, Sammy (however unconsciously) recognizes Lengel's request — that the girls dress "decently" for the store — as an insistence that the girls conform to the ethic of the market. Certainly, what Sammy most prizes in the girls is their refusal to conform. In quitting, he wants to align himself with the forces that go against the grain rather than with sheep who always go in the same direction.

Do students feel Sammy's action is less heroic because he wants to be recognized for it? How do they understand his use of the possessive in the first line of paragraph 32 ("my girls")?

Lengel's reaction to Sammy's quitting isn't anger but weariness. How come? Why does he tell Sammy, "You'll feel this for the rest of your life"? The statement seems almost inappropriately grand, given what has just happened, which suggests Lengel is talking less about Sammy's quitting than about what it means to reject (or simply want to reject) convention. Sammy gets a taste for what it means in the story's final line. Ask students how they understand the closing sentence and the final image of Lengel.

In rejecting one convention, Sammy does briefly fantasize of embracing another. He's going to be a hero. He's trapped, briefly, by this new convention: "once you begin a gesture," he realizes, "it's fatal not to go through with it." But the girls' quick departure means the hero scenario doesn't pan out. Which means, Sammy is left without a job or the rewards he hoped for or a clear sense of what's next.

WRITING SUGGESTION   Consider Lengel's, Stokesie's, and Sammy's attitudes toward work. How do their respective feelings about their jobs reflect their personalities and thus shape their reactions to the girls in Updike's "A & P"?

Peter Schwendener

REFLECTIONS OF A BOOKSTORE TYPE (p. 334)

Peter Schwendener's essay is exactly what its title promises — random reflections of a Barnes & Noble clerk, who also happens to be a well-educated, underemployed lover of books. Schwendener describes his job and his place of employ, touching on issues such as security, clerks' attitudes toward customers, gender patterns in book purchases, pleasure versus luxury, literary theory, and valorization of the arts among store employees.

George Orwell's 1936 essay "Bookshop Memories" provides some structure for Schwendener's thoughts, but for the most part, the author's observations wander. Individual paragraphs are not always connected in an obvious way to the preceding paragraphs, and there isn't a strong sense of an overall point. Students may have been criticized for just such loose organization in their own papers, so you might ask how Schwendener gets away with what others don't. Part of the answer has to do with how Schwendener uses several thematically related subpoints. In the end, he produces a descriptive collage that emphasizes personal reflection. The intelligence of the reflection is part of the piece's appeal, as is the promise of insider knowledge.

Most students probably haven't thought a great deal about books as consumer products or commodities, and Schwendener's essay provides an opportunity to talk about the commodification of ideas. Why does the author feel compelled to state that the bookstore is "a business, not a school or a church"? What do books symbolize in our culture, and how does the meaning get exploited? Although Schwendener says he does not share in the belief that books can "save us," he and his coworkers possess an "unforced respect" for books that make selling books a lesser form of evil than other kinds of work. Why? What value does he attribute to reading? How does this compare to students' experience of reading for pleasure or reading for work?

In paragraph 21 Schwendener says that the bookstore employees associate real jobs with "the arts," a point that seems to underscore the tension between what the employees must do (sell books in a McJob) and what they might want to do. How is this tension related to the drawings of Wilde and Woolf and the presence of Marx on the sociology shelves?

Unlike many of the authors in this section, Schwendener likes his job — well enough. And he doesn't feel diminished by his position's service nature, by his employer's failure to value him, or by the limited use his job makes of his creative and intellectual talents. Ask students what accounts for Schwendener's relative happiness. What about the position, management policy, or Schwendener's nature prevents him from being demoralized as Witherspoon and Soto are by their jobs?

Long-term employment at the store is, Schwendener clearly hopes, not in his future. Why not? Why does he call himself a bookstore "type" in the title of the essay and then express reservations about it in paragraph 7 with "I am afraid I am of that type"? When do students think it is helpful to be a "type"? When is it demeaning?

You might use questions about Schwendener's attitude toward his job to ask students what they hope to get out of their future employment. What is their ideal job?

WRITING SUGGESTION   Almost all the pieces in Part 6 suggest that management behavior affects employee performance and sense of self. What is the effect of Barnes & Noble's management policy (fairly relaxed but brusque about hiring and firing) on Schwendener? Would Barnes & Noble's management policy work for the businesses described in the essays by Witherspoon, Paules, Soto, and Nash or in the market described by Updike? Explain why or why not, arguing for the ideal management policy for one or two of these businesses.

Virginia Woolf

PROFESSIONS FOR WOMEN (p. 342)

The original circumstances of this talk — it was delivered to the Women's Service League in London in 1931 and only later published in *The Death of the Moth and Other Essays* — influence Woolf's opening. Her rather ordinary title suggests we'll get a dry, straightforward listing of what the opportunities are —

something like a 1930s version of what students may have experienced at their school's career-services office. Instead, we get a powerful image of what keeps the (supposedly) emancipated woman from true freedom — "the Angel in the House."

Cleverly, Woolf takes the Society's request and uses it for her own purposes. She fulfills the assignment but talks about what really concerns her. (Something, you might point out, students should also try to do.) Woolf uses the practical concern about the economics of writing to discuss her larger concern about the personal economics of writing. How can one afford to do this? What are the costs to the self, particularly the self that has been told to take care of others' needs?

Woolf's audience may have known that "The Angel in the House" is the title of a poem by Coventry Patmore (1823–1896). The heroine of that poem was a self-sacrificing individual, and, as such, she represented an ideal for nineteenth-century British women. But even for contemporary readers who have not read the poem, Woolf's image should seem apt. Why?

Ask students if the male writer has to deal with the Angel in the House. Why or why not? Then ask if the angel is still in the house for women writers. The second problem Woolf cites is more peculiar to female novelists than female book reviewers: Can today's women express the truth of their sensual experiences? Can men? (Students might be encouraged to look back to Stephen Dunn's "Locker Room Talk," p. 124, as they consider this matter.)

Another way to approach this essay is to discuss the directions and progress of feminism since the days of Woolf. Ask the class what changes in the 1920s were affecting society's attitudes toward professional women. (The most notable was suffrage.) Are Woolf's views consistent with the more contemporary issues of feminism? Or do they seem outdated? How have attitudes toward women who seek careers changed since this address was delivered?

In paragraph 5, Virginia Woolf uses the masculine pronoun, even though she is speaking about female writers. Why? (This might be a good time to broach the topic of nonsexist language.)

In the final paragraph of her essay, Woolf tells the members of her audience that her problems as a writer are their problems. Ask your students if they think these problems exist for working women today. What professions require the same degree of interior and exterior accommodation? What does Woolf seem to be exhorting women to do in the essay's final paragraph?

WRITING SUGGESTION   Update Woolf's essay for your gender. What professional opportunities do you have and what constrictions do you feel as a man or woman? Examine externally and internally imposed restrictions.

Laura L. Nash

THE VIRTUAL JOB (p. 348)

In the first three paragraphs, Laura L. Nash identifies two trends in American corporations. First, individual employees are increasingly expected to operate like freestanding businesses, offering themselves as the best deal — the most qualified and talented person for a job — and thereby sacrificing job security, as employers select contractors on an as-needed basis. (While Nash notes businesses have presented this development as an exciting opportunity for the individual employee, it's clear why Nash considers this trend "hard.") The second trend, the "soft" trend, paradoxically, offers employees better (and increasingly unusual) benefits for the length of their employ. This soft trend might seem rather benign, even advantageous since it fulfills employee needs, but Nash reads it as a form of corporate nannyism that limits personal choice. Having identified the two trends, Nash uses the rest of her opening to present the conventional wisdom on these trends, to suggest alternative readings, and then to offer her thesis (in the final sentence of paragraph 3).

The body of Nash's essay expands on the initial thesis by essentially repeating the information of the first three paragraphs, offering considerably more detail as it proceeds. This allows Nash to conclude with a more refined notion about what corporate trends mean for workers and society. She starts her discussion with the second trend: paragraphs 4 to 8 elaborate on corporate nannyism while linking it to corporations' emphasis on interpersonal skills, team work, and "soft" abilities. Returning to the first trend, Nash describes the organizational changes she introduced in paragraph 1 as "a new model of operation, the 'virtual corporation.'" It might be useful to have students compare Nash's definition of the virtual corporation in paragraph 9 to Ian Angell's parallel definition in paragraph 4 of "Winner and Losers in the Information Age" (p. 354). Which author does a better job of describing the phenomenon?

In paragraph 10, Nash reminds us that the virtual corporation contributes to job insecurity, while requiring a greater need for "individualism," as well as "adaptive skills and self-confidence." Here Nash is returning to her opening criticism of corporate trends. Does her essay seem repetitive, ill-organized, or insufficiently developed for that reason? Ask students why or why not.

The soft trend of corporate nannyism is supposed to alleviate some of the pressures of the hard trend toward a "flexible work force." But, Nash argues, the soft trend fosters dependency and may have "hidden costs for the rest of society," since nannyism may absorb resources that should be generally available. Nannyism may also encourage corporate hard-heartedness about social benefits for those outside the corporate system. Do Nash's concerns, as presented in paragraphs 12 and 13, seem reasonable to students? What about her suggested alternative in paragraph 14? Even if they agree with Nash, have students imagine possible objections to her argument. (Ask students whether Nash should have considered these objections in her essay.)

As described by Nash, there are some inherent contradictions in corporate trends: "Every juncture of the new flexible work force and the new caring corporation is a tension point of contradictory expectations." She lists three of these "tension points" (an arguably awkward term) in paragraphs 15 to 18. First, soft trends may exacerbate the stresses they are meant to alleviate, and hard trends make for more stress. Paragraph 16 offers an example. Can students think of others? The second paradox has to do with how a virtual corporation destroys communities — both inside and outside the business — at the same time it requires teamwork (within the corporation) and volunteerism as a form of community relations (outside the corporation). The third ambiguity has to do with the paradoxical emphasis on individualism and teamwork. Nash quickly details the likely outcome of these three "tension points": employees will be increasingly stressed, self-aggrandizing, cynical, and disloyal. Such an employee is, of course, bad for business and, Nash adds in her final paragraph, bad for society. Nash concludes, "Historically, democratic capitalism has promoted a sense of mutuality, trust, and self-restraint among individuals, and it relies on these qualities for its continued survival. If the corporation now adds to the forces undermining them, these virtues may not hold."

You may want to help students see how Nash uses her final paragraph to repeat her thesis but move past it to an even stronger, and more detailed, claim about the potential damage of current corporate trends. Have students note that this is Nash's strategy throughout her essay — to return to her initial points, each time deepening her argument, so that she's clarified, developed, and even expanded her argument by the time she's finished.

WRITING SUGGESTION   Use Nash's and Amitai Etzioni's ("The Value of Families," p. 107) essays to argue for or against on-site corporate daycare. Supplement your argument with library research on corporate daycare. Alternatively, interview corporate workers who use an existing facility, and parents who don't have an on-site option.

Ian Angell

WINNERS AND LOSERS
IN THE INFORMATION AGE (p. 354)

Ian Angell's vision borders on the apocalyptic as he details how the real possibility of global communication, commerce, and travel will make the rich richer, the poor poorer, government irrelevant, and social unrest inevitable. In paragraph 2, he writes that anyone bypassed by the information superhighways "faces ruin," and he doesn't choose that word lightly. Oft-heralded, information technology has a disturbing talent — the ability to transcend national borders and thereby ignore government curbs on business's rapacious nature. In the new globalized world, it will be easier to be greedy — to manipulate or avoid tax laws, to hire people at criminally low wages, to use money (and soon enough) knowledge to buy power.

In paragraph 3, Angell distinguishes globalization from internationalization. Ask students to clarify the difference. Then Angell describes "global localization," in much the way that Laura L. Nash ("The Virtual Job," p. 348) describes the virtual corporation. Angell, however, emphasizes the way in which local companies hook up to the global network to provide a market for local products and expertise and offer global businesses access to local consumers. While such a system might sound advantageous, Angell notes that the system makes it easier to exclude government from commerce and even from continuing to determine what money is.

All this may be good for business, but it will be terrible for most people, who will be polarized into two classes — "the mobile and independent knowledge workers" and "the immobile and dependent service workers." Service workers who aren't replaced by an electronic device will be paid terribly. Meanwhile, knowledge workers will get richer and richer by continuing to elude national stipulations for taxes and to work immigration laws to their advantage. Human rights, Angell suggests, will become an outdated notion, replaced by knowledge workers' privilege and service workers' right to little beyond the right to pay the taxes that they can ill afford. "Inevitably . . . ," Angell writes of the transition to the information age, "we can expect massive civil unrest and disorder."

Where does this leave government? It won't be scrambling to control global corporations, but because citizens need to be employed, it will try to entice global companies into a partnership with local concerns. Angell concludes, "Tax holidays and reduced regulation aimed at attracting employers will be the name of the game everywhere." Government, he holds, will just be another organization, which "will delegate market regulations — such as North American Free Trade Agreement or the European Union — to continent-wide bodies, which in turn will use their economic muscle to undermine each member state."

All of this, Angell argues, will contribute to the rise of "the new city-state at the hub of global electronic and transport networks." Angell opposes this new city-state to the old nation-state, which he defines (in a paragraph omitted from this excerpt) as requiring individuals to submit "to the legitimate violence of the state in return for protection and security." But the masses, in the information age, won't be needed, as they were in the machine age for production, so they will be disregarded and allowed to slip into the equivalent of slavery.

Angell's view is sobering, and students may find themselves trying to resist his ideas as they read. Because he writes with authority, his conclusions seem inevitable. Are they? Ask students to identify Angell's premises about corporate ethics and his overall evidence. Have them distinguish between predictions that are based on other predictions and predictions that are based on current trends. Are any of his claims too broad? If so, which ones and why? Is his voice consistently measured, reliable, and convincing, or does he seem, at points, extreme? What possible forces might resist the essentially immoral forces Angell describes?

WRITING SUGGESTION   Evaluate Ian Angell's analysis of the fate of government and human rights in the information age. Are Angell's predictions reasonable, fair, and convincing? Explain why or why not, paying close attention to the virtues and flaws of Angell's argument.

PART 7

POSSESSIONS

Seeking Out Substance

Our possessions reflect our taste, and as such, their value extends beyond function. We speak of objects as having monetary value, to be sure, but also of having sentimental value or of making us feel secure or well cared for. That said, we may be diminished by ownership, as Harry Crews and E. M. Foster ultimately are. Or we may be manipulated into desiring what we don't truly want. Current marketing trends — mail-order shopping and superstores — embroil us in complicated fantasies (or clever marketing strategies) that encourage consumption. Our passion for what we have can be almost as intense (as Maguelonne Toussaint-Samat notes) as our feelings about what we don't possess.

Of course, objects aren't the only thing we value. "I call people rich," Henry James says in the Insights, "when they're able to meet the requirements of their imagination." For the purposes of Part 7, *intellect* might be added to James's *imagination*, since students should be increasingly comfortable writing argumentative pieces that require them to challenge the *Life Studies* authors and themselves. To prepare students to write research papers in the final weeks of the semester, you might assign argumentative papers that require outside research. If students are using the Internet as a resource, you should spend some class time talking about how to judge the reliability and quality of its information and how to cite and document sources on it. Two helpful books in this regard are *Online! A Reference Guide to Using Internet Sources* by Andrew Harnack and Eugene Kleppinger (New York: St. Martin's Press, 1997) and *Research and Documentation in the Electronic Age* by Diana Hacker and Barbara Fister (Bedford Books, 1998), also available at http://www.bedfordbooks.com.

Insights

The words of Jesus quoted by Matthew imply that private property corrupts the soul, expressing the traditional religious view that all wealth is God's. John Kenneth Galbraith interprets the sanctification of poverty as a necessary accommodation to specific hopeless conditions. Most people, Jesus and Galbraith notwithstanding, remain conflicted over the meaning and value of possessions, as the other Insight writers illustrate. We do not know what we own and what is given to us; we scarcely can determine under what material conditions we are rich or poor. Our attachment to personal possessions may be illogical from a utilitarian viewpoint, but it serves an emotional function, as Edna O'Brien and Colette make clear.

Richard Wilbur's poem makes a tidy distinction between what can be owned and what can be experienced. The careless "young employers" spend the morning in bed, probably hung over, while the cook and gardener go about their business and "receive the morning" almost as one would receive a sacrament. The charm of the delicately described morning is lost on the owners, who, ironically, possess nothing of value. The cook and gardener possess the estate imaginatively. Henry David Thoreau and Henry James suggest that such imaginative possession is the only measure of wealth. Andrew Carnegie is poor by these standards, as are the Americans Paul Wachtel describes.

Harry Crews

THE CAR (p. 366)

Crews's "love affair" with his car has a meaning beyond the obvious one, since the affair *was* sexual and may have actually replaced sexual experience. There is only one point in his essay where Crews explicitly says that he remembers his cars like old lovers, but his metaphoric language tells us a great deal about the function cars served for him. It's no accident that one of his happiest memories is when the metaphoric and actual content of a car merged — when he made love with Shirley in the front seat of his car. Crews says of that night when Shirley kicked his wing vent out, "Soon's Shirley kicked it out, I known I was in love" (para. 11). And this doesn't mean he's claiming affection for the spirited Shirley.

Crews's cars are always female. He refers to them with a feminine pronoun and says, "I remember them like people — like long-ago lovers." Crews remembers the cars' moves and recalls having his hand deep in them, being initiated into "their warm greasy mysteries" and eventually getting under them and trying to see if they would "yield to me and my expert ways." When he brags about his car, he sounds like a boy bragging about a sexual conquest. One car makes him study his face in the mirror, the way another man might study himself before a date. Indeed, he feels his "muscle tingle and flush with blood" when he talks "about getting rubber in three gears." His pride in his possession is much like the pride of a man who has an attractive woman on his arm; her looks elevate him. When he talks about the car, he allows, "it was somehow my own body I was talking about" (para. 12).

In the end, Crews realizes he could fritter away his life on his car and that the car's requirements enable him to avoid life. When he abandons his car, we have the feeling that he finds other things — actual lovers, for one, and (perhaps) adulthood. Ask students what they make of the final line. Does it contradict the message of the piece? There is, clearly, some disappointment about settling down into a real life.

WRITING SUGGESTION   Apply E. M. Forster's analysis of his woods ("My Wood," p. 371) to Crews's essay about his car. Are the two men affected the same way by their possessions? What are the similarities, and what are the differences?

E. M. Forster

MY WOOD (p. 371)

Forster's response to his coming into ownership of private property is close to Henry David Thoreau's attitude in the Insights. Like Thoreau, Forster finds that ownership impoverishes the self. In paragraph 2, his ironic but sympathetic reconsideration of the saying of Jesus, also included in the Insights, freshens a point of Christian doctrine that Forster rediscovers experientially. That is the basic strategy of the essay — to validate a generalization by examining particulars. Behind the pretense of modestly reporting his personal experience, Forster alludes to Jesus, Tolstoy, Shakespeare, Dante, and the Bolsheviks, establishing a broad cultural context for his response to property. He brings the full weight of Western culture into his gentle but unequivocal condemnation of natural greed.

WRITING SUGGESTION   Forster isn't an ascetic. He says "Our life on earth is, and ought to be, material and carnal" (para. 5). And yet "we have not learned how to manage our materialism and carnality properly; they are still entangled with the desire for ownership." What, implicitly, is he suggesting here and elsewhere in the essay? Without lapsing into insupportable generalizations, describe an ethics that shows us how appropriately to manage our materialism and carnality. Use examples to make your theory clear.

Holly Brubach

MAIL-ORDER AMERICA (p. 374)

Holly Brubach's long article is dominated by her interpretation of the catalogues of three companies — J. Crew, L. L. Bean, and Victoria's Secret. Her analysis amounts to cultural criticism, an approach possible because Brubach views mail-order catalogues as magazines with "a distinct editorial point of view" (para. 6). As such, catalogues present a well-considered, relatively consistent fantasy of a world related to our own but distinctly different. In each case, the fantasy provides "a place with its own landscape, its indigenous population, its native customs, its dialect." If we want to visit that world — if we are habitual perusers of mail-order catalogues — it may be because we don't like shopping (para. 3 and 4), because we're at a distance from stores, or because we find shopping by mail convenient. But it's also possible, as Brubach emphasizes in paragraph 6 and at the close of her article, that we like the fantasies in the catalogue. The fantasies are less confusing than everyday life, and they offer something better than reality — myths about self-transformation, community, home, and love. Brubach suggests we *believe* these myths — which may be a somewhat reductive conclusion, since we don't need to believe them to enjoy them or escape to them or (as Brubach does) have some fun with them.

You could use class time to rehash Brubach's reading of the various catalogues, but it might be more instructive to bring in fairly well-known catalogues and ask students to do their own cultural critiques. Then have them compare their written critiques to Brubach's article, paying close attention to one or two of her paragraphs. What makes Brubach's analysis so strong is how she weaves in numerous examples — all evidence for her interpretation — without seeming to do so. Her initial construct in paragraph 6 — that catalogues depict a world that can be interpreted — frees her when it comes time to write. Instead of offering a generalization and then providing an example introduced by the phrase "for example," she acts like a travel writer and allows her description of the catalogue's world to support her points. She lets herself forget that she's looking at a catalogue, until it comes time to do her analysis of catalogue copy. (This approach explains, in part, her opening paragraph.)

Brubach's readings are entertaining and insightful. They will probably seem fair enough to those familiar with J. Crew, L. L. Bean, and Victoria's Secret catalogues. But what is Brubach's purpose in engaging in such readings? Her article structures itself around the question of why we read mail-order catalogues. As noted above, paragraph 4 offers practical reasons for our interest, and paragraphs 6 and 35 offer more ineffable reasons. There is another implied reason in the opening paragraph about the uncle who is an armchair traveler. But Brubach's essay wants to decipher the cultural underpinnings of the boom in mail-order catalogues (well documented in paragraph 3) and to read our collective character.

Presumably, our collective fantasies mean something about our collective nature. A mail-order catalogue may appeal to existing fantasies, or it may actually create consumer fantasies. Either way, an interpretation of those fantasies amounts to an interpretation of an aspect of our culture. So what *do* these catalogues suggest? Ask students to answer this question without resorting to easy generalizations about what Americans want. In responding, students may be tempted to speak of the general population's desires in a broad and somewhat condescending fashion. To steer them away from this, you might have students acknowledge their own desires first. What mail-order catalogues do they like and why?

WRITING SUGGESTION   Brubach looks at mail-order catalogues from the point of view of a style editor and a cultural critic. Consider the relatively recent increase in catalogue shopping from the point of view of an urban planner. What does mail-order shopping mean for the health of our cities? Compare the phenomenon to the widespread use of VCRs and the subsequent fate of movie theaters. Do library research to answer this question authoritatively.

Richard Panek

SUPERSTORE INFLATION (p. 386)

If readers doubt Richard Panek's sweeping opening claim about superstores — "the defining shopping experience of the 1990's"— they're sure to be convinced by the startling facts in paragraph 2. Superstores are overwhelming, and their profits and swift popularity are even more so. Panek cleverly conveys this success in terms of the number of superstores built *each week*, giving readers another way to comprehend the enormous sales figures of paragraph 2.

In defining superstores, Panek first has recourse to what even a casual observer might be able to conclude: a superstore is a "big box" with a lot of stuff in it. But he quickly refines his definition, so the reader understands not only what superstores are but what they do (in the market). Superstores, Panek explains, are "category killers": they succeed not by competing but by eliminating competition. Thus, superstores might be accused of operating like virtual monopolies, and indeed the FTC has been suspicious of certain superstore practices (para. 9) and of planned superstore mergers (para. 10).

Category killers aren't true monopolies, however, for while they wipe out smaller competitors, they create competition in the form of more superstores. Paragraphs 8 to 12 use "the office-supply category" to illustrate how category killers work, concluding that superstores eliminate the little guy while cloning themselves. In the end, superstores dramatically affect independent retailers and even malls. Students may have stories that bear this out — tales of the local bookstore that closed when a Barnes & Noble opened in the next town or of half-empty malls where former retail space is being used for community organizations.

What's distinctive, beyond scale, about superstores is a retail strategy that requires the store to be "a mall writ small" (para. 22), offering extras to attract customers and keep them in the store. Ask students why stores need to offer these extras. Why aren't bargain prices and a wide selection enough? Will people buy more if their furniture store has a cafe or if their record store has listening booths? Why?

"Most Americans of a certain sentimental bent still harbor a soft spot for the mom-and-pop shop," Panek writes. Are these shops doomed? If a store is a form of specialty shop, perhaps not, since customers don't always want to be subjected to the rigors of a superstore excursion when they have to run an errand. Of course, enough people have to feel this way — and be willing to pay higher prices — for such stores to stay afloat.

You might ask students to imagine the sort of research Panek did for this article. Where might Panek have gone for the statistics in paragraphs 2 and 3, the quote in paragraph 4, the definitions in paragraphs 5 and 6, the information in paragraph 7, the retail history in paragraphs 8 to 12, the retail strategy in paragraphs 13 to 19? What about the quotes in paragraphs 20 and 21? Answering these questions will show students how much work Panek did — numerous interviews, inquiries into books and periodicals, and visits to superstores.

Students may also note that paragraphs 22 and 23 don't seem to depend on outside sources. Instead, in these concluding paragraphs, Panek offers his interpretation of the superstore phenomenon. By delaying judgment, Panek encourages the reader to trust his views, since they seem to be based on such a solid understanding of the stores — what they are and how they work. What, in the end, appears to be Panek's attitude toward superstores? How does the arrangement of the material in the first 21 paragraphs, as well as Panek's language, foreshadow his conclusions?

In the end, you might ask students if an analysis of retail strategy makes them more resistant to that strategy. If students visit a superstore after they read this essay, are their spending habits likely to change? The same question might be asked of Greta Foff Paules's "Humble Pie" (p. 312). Did Paules's essay make students more polite to service workers? Did Holly Brubach's "Mail-Order America" (p. 374) change their attitudes toward the fantasy world of catalogues? If we understand how retailers are manipulating us — or how we're participants in an insulting symbolic system as Paules's essay claims — are we likely to change our behavior? Why or why not?

WRITING SUGGESTION   Conservation and consumption do not — it would seem — go hand in hand. But while Americans are being encouraged to recycle and reuse, superstores encourage us to "buy buy buy" (para. 17). Who or what then encourages us not to buy? Which message should (or do) we listen to? Does a conservationist ethic hurt the economy? Explain why or why not.

William Ian Miller

GIFTS AND HONOR: AN EXCHANGE (p. 391)

Why is an unequal gift exchange embarrassing? This might seem like a slight topic for discussion, but William Ian Miller places a specific instance of unequal exchange within a larger context, ultimately providing an analysis for an otherwise puzzling suicide.

To understand the source of his Valentine Day's emotion, Miller uses the analogy of a game. Like any other game, the Valentine Day's exchange has a goal. Skills are required to make moves to meet that goal. Miller explains what it means to win and lose this game. Ultimately, the Valentine's Day game is nestled within the game of gift exchange, which is nestled within the game of honor. Valentine's Day may seem silly to us, but honor doesn't, and by taking the time to analyze what breaches in norms mean to respective "players," Miller tries to make sense of the Japanese couple who, losing the game of gift exchange, won the game of honor.

WRITING SUGGESTION   Typically, at the close of high school, people inscribe each other's yearbooks. Analyze the exchange of messages at this time. What are the implicit rules of exchange? What codes determine how a high school senior values or fails to value an inscription? Alternatively, consider the rules of exchange at a gift-giving occasion, such as a bridal shower, baby shower, birthday party, or graduation party. Use a combination of your own experience and interviews with others to determine what gifts (and reactions to gifts) mean in the context of a celebratory gathering.

Toni Cade Bambara

THE LESSON (p. 397)

Sylvia, like many of the young girls in Toni Cade Bambara's short fiction, is appealingly mouthy, self-confident, honest, funny, vulnerable, and street-wise. "The Lesson" opens with Sylvia doing what she does best — dismissing everyone. Save for "me and Sugar," who "were the only ones just right," she tells us, her world is cluttered with people who are "old and stupid or young and foolish." Given a different narrator in different circumstances, this sort of pride would be hubris. Here, it seems a wonderful sign of Sylvia's strength, a clue that her circumstances will not defeat her. Even her initial lack of interest in Miss Moore and her lessons has its virtue, for Sylvia's ability to doubt and to resist authority is going to serve her well in a society that is economically and racially unjust. And yet part of her resistance to authority is a resistance to the very idea of education, and that, of course, is something she needs to outgrow.

Ask students exactly what Miss Moore's lesson for the day is and whether she successfully imparts it. At first, it seems Miss Moore simply wants to teach the children about the value of money, but none of the children are unaware of money's importance. (Witness Sylvia's feelings about getting the taxi change and the way in which Mercedes makes it clear that she has more than the others.) Nor are the children completely unaware of their own financial situation: they know they're poor. (Flyboy's skilled, Sylvia tells us, at keeping "the white folks off his back and sorry for him. Send this poor kid to camp poster, is his specialty.") But

Miss Moore isn't concerned, of course, about who gets the pocket change or how the children might "work" their economic situation. Rather, she wants to make the children aware of the injustice of great luxury in the midst of widespread poverty. Her goal seems to be to make them angry. Ask students what Miss Moore thinks the children's anger will do for them.

At first, the children find the sights of Fifth Avenue merely funny. The turning point comes when Flyboy notices the expensive toy sailboat. This stuns Sylvia and attracts the attention of all the children, for a sailboat is something they might want — it is a toy, after all — and it is also something they can weigh the value of; they know what their toy boats cost and how easily they can be destroyed.

The emotions they feel about the toy boat continue in the toy store. A general loss of confidence makes them all uneasy. Sugar and Sylvia hang back, too, and then, in paragraph 41, there is a split in the unity between the two friends. When Sugar touches the boat, Sylvia says, "I'm jealous and want to hit her." This isn't so surprising given the unity between the friends has always been about a shared self-confidence. Once the self-regard drops away, Sylvia's confused by, and alone with, her emotions.

Though Sylvia articulates Miss Moore's lesson for the reader in paragraph 44, she doesn't do the same for Miss Moore and the other children. Why? Instead, it is Sugar who gives Miss Moore what she wants, and Sylvia immediately views her explanation as the betrayal of a goody-goody ("I am disgusted with Sugar's treachery"). Have students explain why Sylvia views Sugar's behavior this way.

Immediately, the betrayal results in a further split between the friends. Sylvia walks away from Sugar, while Sugar tries to recement their bond by suggesting a trip to Hascombs. Sylvia agrees, but the small satisfactions of her life aren't going to mitigate the larger problems anymore. Instead of racing Sugar to the store, Sylvia splits off, but not before she concludes that she isn't going to let anyone beat her at any competition. In the moment, Sylvia is talking about the new rivalry she has with her best friend, but, unconsciously, she is referring to a larger socioeconomic competition — the one that, as Miss Moore has already shown Sylvia, she *is* losing.

As readers, we feel that Sylvia's attitude will save her. After the trip, she is roused by anger, shame, and envy to begin to consider the causes and remedies of the inequalities she scarcely recognized earlier. Has Sugar learned the same lesson? Perhaps not — or not in the same way as Sylvia — as Sugar's reconciliatory behavior (and attitude toward money) at the end suggests. It may be Sugar's final actions, as much as her betrayal, that create the distance between the girls at the story's close. And though the friends' split might be inevitable, it feels like a loss, one that presages future losses, for the wonderful buoyancy and shrewdness of childhood itself has been threatened by the economic and racial injustice of the adult world. If the losses will be met with concomitant gains, it will be a result of Sylvia's strength and her ability to resist the messages of adult society.

After discussing the story, students might be interested in hearing Bambara's thoughts on her own work, from Claudia Tate's *Black Women Writers at Work* (New York: Continuum, 1983):

> I do not think that literature is *the* primary instrument for social transformation, but I do think it has potency. So I work to tell the truth about people's lives; I work to celebrate struggle, to applaud the tradition of struggle in our community, to bring to center stage all those characters, just ordinary folks on the block, who've been waiting in the wings, char-

acters we thought we had to ignore because they weren't pimp-flashy or hustler-slick or because they didn't fit easily into previously acceptable modes or stock types.

WRITING SUGGESTION   Evaluate Miss Moore as a teacher. What do you think of the way she goes about imparting her lesson? What does she mean to teach the children? What do they learn?

Maguelonne Toussaint-Samat

CHOCOLATE AND DIVINITY (p. 404)

Maguelonne Toussaint-Samat's selection, a chapter from her *A History of Food*, is a chronicle — a list, however elaborated, of important dates and events in chocolate's history.

The opening is entertaining, potentially provocative, and one might expect the author to circle back to the fevered emotions of Marquise de Sévigné. Instead, she suggests that fevered emotions and chocolate have always gone hand in hand, especially since cocoa was, for the Mayans and then the Aztecs, intimately connected with the gods. Colonizing Europeans grew to like and value the brew, bringing it home to "ladies" who had such a passion for the drink that the Pope had to consider "the grave question of whether or not drinking chocolate broke the fast" (para. 16). The emphasis, through paragraphs 2 and 17, is on how cultures came to know and value chocolate. From paragraph 18 on, the history changes. The author offers various facts, but the thematic connection between the material isn't as strong as it was in the earlier paragraphs. The ending itself feels somewhat arbitrary, and within the context of the selection it's not clear why Toussaint-Samat stopped here, instead of continuing on through the twentieth century.

Students may feel the piece bogs down some. If so, ask them to identify where and why they felt impatient with the excerpt. How does the author's voice affect their reading of the essay? (You might ask students how they picture the author and why.) At the same time, the author's facts are not uninteresting, and she is somewhat playful in her language. Note her use of the second person in paragraphs 4 and 5, her chatty transitions into paragraphs 8 and 9, and her humor in paragraphs 1 and 11. While Toussaint-Samat's history is clear, her purpose in presenting it is more elusive. What seems to draw Toussaint-Samat to this subject or to the details she chooses to elaborate? What organizing principle, other than chronological order, might she have used?

Have students consider what sort of research Toussaint-Samat might have done for this selection. Does it bother them that none of the information is footnoted? Should it be? (This might be a chance to talk about the types of material that require source notes.)

WRITING SUGGESTION   Complete Toussaint-Samat's history of chocolate by researching the food's fate in the twentieth century. Complicate her approach by focusing on one aspect of chocolate. You might consider chocolate's physiological effects (and how that accounts for people's fondness for the sweet). Or you could read articles about Hershey, Pennsylvania, examining the town's transformation in the twentieth century. You could also look at the business of chocolate, identifying the top companies and their marketing strategies.

PART 8

MEDIA IMAGES

Questioning Received Ideas

Though none of the essays in Part 8 mentions it, one of the things the media loves most is to analyze itself. This self-analysis has become so widespread that a news story often is accompanied by a story about the coverage of that story. Stories about the O. J. Simpson case were followed by stories about the media's handling of the case. Ted Koppel apologized for hopping on the media bandwagon with the Michael Jackson child abuse scandal, just before he began a segment on that scandal. One might fault the media for being hypocritical — you can't both cover and not cover an issue — but for the purposes of this part, the true problem with the media's self-reflection is that it is, so often, shallow. When it comes to talk about media — the entertainment world, as well as the new electronic forms of communication — the appeal of, as Gustave Flaubert would have it, "received ideas" is particularly strong. Intelligence and the appearance of intelligence are easily conflated. Students have to be steered away from the easy conclusions and simple analyses to which they've been exposed. One way to do this is to insist that students use several outside sources to help them reconsider their own thoughts on a matter.

Insights

Television and movies are more real to some young people than the real world. At least, that's the loosely tossed about claim. Louis Menand takes the notion one step further and analyzes what is real to us about media images. It's not that we can't distinguish between truth and fiction or life and depictions of life but that depictions of life have influenced life in complicated ways. As Menand says, we learn a whole "encyclopedia of gestures" from the movies, and later it's hard to remember the gestures' origins. This is especially true for physical intimacy, since real life doesn't offer instructions in how to touch others. Real life also doesn't, as Ruth Rosen notes, offer us stable communities. But the entertainment world does, even if it bores us in the process, as Mark Crispin Miller suggests. We "know" who celebrities are, though we've never met them. Our knowledge extends to details about their lives. Indeed, when we think of gossip these days, we often don't think of talk about people we know but of talk about people we don't know.

Louise Erdrich's poem points to another way art influences life. The Native Americans watching the John Wayne movie cheer and laugh at what they see, but it's clear that the images break through the movie screen, just as the mosquitoes break through the smoke-screen, and both come for the viewers' blood. It's no surprise Erdrich leaves hearing the movie's unspoken message — updated for contemporary viewers but no less devastating.

Louise Erdrich

Z: THE MOVIE THAT CHANGED MY LIFE (p. 416)

Louise Erdrich breaks her essay into two parts, and it is only when we get to the second part, with its deceptively simple analysis of the first part, that we see the full force of what this essay has to say.

As a teenager, Erdrich's attraction to Z is somewhat Manichaean. The movie teaches her to make distinctions between good and evil and to consider issues of justice, equality, and freedom. Still, as these issues play out in her own life — or at least her life at the movie theater — they seem humorous. She doesn't yet have the skills to judge what she sees on screen in terms of accuracy. She knows nothing of Greek history, but she recognizes the types she sees in Z, and she implicitly trusts the way in which the movie exposes hypocrisy and evil.

Z gives Erdrich her first sense of a political world and her first sense, as she will say later, of the "real" world. Still, when, as a girl, she finds parallels in her own life to what she sees on screen, the parallels are funny. She doesn't give evidence to suggest her boss is truly oppressive or that she is oppressed. Her "subversive" action, in the form of snacking, is amusing. Vincent may represent a conservative voice, but he is without the power to be a true oppressor. He seems more like a conformist who is unwilling to question the simple set of rules by which he lives.

Notably, Louise Erdrich does not discuss her Native American heritage. Ask students why. After all, if she had, we'd have a reason to understand her automatic connection with the oppressed class. The answer is in the information she gives about the kind of person she used to be — a small-town girl, not completely subsumed into small-town girlhood; a wrestling cheerleader, who could write in her diary about exposing hypocrites in the same paragraph that she reminded herself "to dye my bra and underwear to match my cheerleading outfit." Although in retrospect she sees herself as oppressed by cultural stereotypes of women, when she was working at the movie theater, she was so unconscious of this repression that she didn't even notice how Z portrayed women.

As an adult, Erdrich concedes that, despite its flaws, Z is still a good political film. Even though sexual politics aren't the subject of the film, for Erdrich the political subject influenced her feminist consciousness. When she argues with Vincent about the movie, she begins her intellectual life. When she watches the film, she has a sense that she isn't living her life right. Z, ironically, is the beginning of Erdrich's personal feminist revolution.

WRITING SUGGESTION   Why doesn't Erdrich mention her Native American heritage in this essay? How would information about her ethnicity add and how would it detract from this piece?

Kurt Andersen

ANIMATION NATION (p. 422)

Kurt Andersen's sarcastic opening question suggests that he's not going to be completely serious as he details cartoons' hegemony in the entertainment (and maybe the real) world. This is an opinion piece — with a point but with no intention of persuading with evidence or even of describing in great detail. More outrageous statements aren't qualified, and cartoon shows aren't described. But the essay's point isn't complicated: cartoons, particularly in the past decade, have been enormously successful. They function in ways that other forms of entertainment don't: they "allow us our corn" and provide us with satire. Cartoons have also infiltrated live-action movies, which use animation techniques but ignore other aspects of a successful script, so animation is often the most interesting part of a film. (Of course, this says less about animation's success per se than the weakness of other elements of films.)

Have students consider the concluding sentences of paragraph 2 and the opening sentence of paragraph 6. Do these conclusions seem fair, or is Andersen overstating his case? Is the essay's final line reasonable? reductive? Students' answers will surely affect their response to the overall essay. Do they think Andersen is praising cartoons, complaining about current entertainment, or analyzing contemporary culture?

One possible weakness of this essay is that, for readers unfamiliar with current cartoons, it's hard to weigh the author's claims. Have students consider how other writers — like Holly Brubach in "Mail-Order America" (p. 374) or Andrea Dworkin in "Letter from a War Zone" (p. 454) — offer their readers the information they need to consider the authors' arguments. This raises the issue of what sort of knowledge writers can expect from their readers. When students write an English paper, should they assume their reader has read the novel they're discussing? What should they expect from readers of papers in other subjects? Brubach and Dworkin may be helpful, since they assume their readers have looked at catalogues and pornography but also provide descriptions in order to give readers a common point of reference, in addition to their interpretations of the details.

WRITING SUGGESTION   What is the effect of addressing a serious subject or issue, such as racism or homophobia, in the form of an animated cartoon? Use details from a show that you have seen to support your discussion. What can a cartoon accomplish that other genres cannot? What problems arise when animation is used for social commentary?

James B. Twitchell

"BUT FIRST, A WORD FROM OUR SPONSOR" (p. 425)

Advertising underwrites culture. This means that culture in its various forms reaches us only because advertising carries it to us. In the case of television, we see shows because commercials fund them. Even public television is paid for by corporate sponsors. But entertainment is only one aspect of culture. If students read *culture* as "the arts," James B. Twitchell's article may confuse, but if *culture* is read more broadly, as "civilization," his thoughts make sense. As Twitchell uses the word, *culture* includes our fashions and habits, the look of our cities, the content of our magazines, as well as literature and art. Almost everything is an aspect of culture, which makes Twitchell's claim about advertising-as-underwriter even more disturbing.

Advertising's goal is to sell products. It no longer does this by informing consumers about products but by immersing society in an infotainment culture, which Twitchell nicknames "Adcult" (para. 5). What is Adcult or "infotainment"?

Twitchell doesn't define the term so much as describe its goal — to make the public receptive to commercial messages by offering "something sufficiently alluring" to look at or hear or read. Paragraph 3 offers plenty of examples of Adcult in action. Students can surely add their own, proving that Adcult is, indeed, ubiquitous.

When people complain about our culture and media, Twitchell says, they speak of the "dumbing down" of America and often "focus on the corruption of these media." Twitchell offers an economic explanation instead. Twitchell's argument depends on a premise buried in paragraph 7: "Manufacturing both things *and* their meanings is what American culture is all about." If students keep this premise in mind, then Twitchell's argument will be easier to follow. His claim is essentially that Adcult — in addition to making us pay both in time and money for products — encultures us. That is, it tells us the meaning of the things we buy. Our culture is shallow because we've let advertisers (whose only interest is money) determine meaning. Why don't we object? Why don't we, as Twitchell suggests, simply read *Consumer Reports* and buy on a purely utilitarian basis? Twitchell doesn't know but speculates that Americans prefer choice, even its mere illusion, to no choice. And he notes Americans like buying, owning, and trading things. Advertising feeds into this preference and desire, and, in the process, it suggests a value system for objects that have no such inherent system. It may be, Twitchell concludes, that what we desire is meaning. Ironically, what we get is "dumbness," since advertising offers such shallow meanings. Twitchell ends by suggesting that the limited role that religion plays in our lives leaves a vacuum that advertising is only too happy to fill.

Twitchell's article turns on his premise in paragraph 7. Do students accept this premise? Can they offer alternative definitions for American culture? Do they agree that advertising defines the meaning of things? If not, how is meaning determined in American culture? If consumers took a universally utilitarian approach to objects, what would happen to American culture?

How do Twitchell's neologisms — "infotainment," "Adcult"— help students understand his essay? Do they ever confuse? What about his phrase "dumbing down of America"? It's a commonly used phrase, but what exactly does it mean?

WRITING SUGGESTION   Advertising has been subject to a fair amount of cultural criticism concerning depictions of women and minorities such as African Americans and Native Americans. Consider a self-consciously politically correct ad campaign. Does the campaign redress problems or create new ones? Explain your answer, using specific examples.

Ellen Ullman

GETTING CLOSE TO THE MACHINE (p. 430)

Ellen Ullman's essay confirms and explodes the "computer geek" stereotype by reading the computer-centered behavior of programmers in light of their complicated relationship to computers, a relationship determined by the nature of programming itself. Essentially, the activity requires a person "to translate between the chaos of human life and the rational, line-by-line world of computer language"; to write an algorithm "in order, in a specific syntax, in a strange language that is only partially readable by regular human beings." As Ullman details this process, she focuses not on the complexities of the algorithm, but on the way in which "knowledge comes at you from one perspective and then another, then comes a random thought, then you remember something else important, then you reconsider that idea with a what-if attached."

Understandably, this process requires absolute concentration. "Synchronizing with other people . . . ," Ullman says, "can only mean interrupting the thought train." An interruption is tantamount to getting off the train: you can't get back on, and the next train might not take you to the place you want to go. Programmers don't talk or accommodate others because "any break in concentration causes you to lose a line here or there."

Programming takes place in "mind time, while the phone rings and the meetings happen in real time." Ask students for a definition of both kinds of time. Do other activities — in addition to programming — take place in mind time? Do students feel they've ever worked in mind time? How does mind time differ from the semitrance of creative artists or the concentration of writers?

After the break between paragraphs 7 and 8, Ullman describes a job where she didn't talk to anyone for two years. Ullman's already used her introductory paragraphs to suggest practical reasons for her silence, but paragraphs 8 through 12 describe something more extreme, a situation in which "real time" and even real people receded to be replaced by "mind time" and the thrill of "the software . . . , of making something out of nothing." What does Ullman reveal in the final line of paragraph 11? How does she differ from the man described in paragraphs 15 to 29? Presumably she does differ, since her discovery about the man strikes her as "something terrible." This isn't to say she valorizes herself in paragraphs 8 to 12, but she conveys the thrill of obsession, even as she mocks it.

As a programmer, Ullman's world differs from our own, and not just in terms of how it encourages her to think. In her world, money and prestige depend on communication with machines. "A real programmer wants to stay close to the machine," she writes. What does this mean? What does closeness to the machine offer, beyond prestige? In paragraph 15, she answers, suggesting that a relationship with a machine frees programmers from social obligations and even "the obligations of time." (Ask students to define "the obligations of time" so that the attractions of such freedom will be apparent.)

In the programmers' world, prestige is also related to the ability "to write code that only machines or other programmers understand." The need to design a "crash-proof system" translates into a "terrific contempt" for users. And though the programmers' disdain is often hidden, occasionally it surfaces, as Ullman demonstrates in paragraph 35.

Ullman maintains that widespread dependence on computers will eventually make the general public more like computer designers. Users are going to get "close to the machine" instead of other humans since they won't need "to involve anyone else in the satisfaction of [their] needs." By way of example, Ullman presents situations in which computers eliminate service encounters. (This is partially what Ian Angell predicts in his "Winners and Losers in the Information Age," p. 354.) However, her conclusion — in the last line of paragraph 37 — seems to include other sorts of encounters (just as Kurt Andersen mentions in paragraph 6 of "Animation Nation," p. 422). Is this a flaw in her argument?

When they get to the end, are students surprised by the depth of Ullman's criticism? Even though her final judgment is amply foreshadowed, Ullman is a programmer herself and, as such, well acquainted with the thrills and financial rewards of the activity. If we look back to her opening paragraph, it's clear she never thinks the thrills are healthy. It's also clear she's embroiled in her work, though the very fact of the article suggests her resistance. As frightening as Ullman's conclusion is, it doesn't make her want to quit her job. How do students judge her as a writer? The answer seems significant for the content of the essay, since if they find her prose compelling, well crafted, and intelligent, they will judge her quite capable of communicating with humans and doing so at the expense of machines.

You might use this essay to discuss the organization of paragraphs. How are human-interest anecdotes interspersed with more technical material? How do the paragraphs build to an argument that isn't about programmers but users? Why are paragraphs 13, 14, and 15 placed before paragraph 16 instead of after paragraph 31?

WRITING SUGGESTION   Consider the communications technology you use in a typical week. Include automatic teller machines, automated telephone directories, e-mail, the World Wide Web, and faxes. What kind of personal interactions do you avoid by using these technologies? Use your answer to argue for or against Ullman's conclusion about the pernicious nature of electronic communication.

Wendy Lesser

THE CONVERSION (p. 435)

The *OED* definition of a Luddite is "a member of an organized band of English mechanics and their friends, who (1811–1816) set themselves to destroying manufacturing machinery in the midlands and north of England." The term, if Pellew's *Life of Lord Sidmouth* (1847) is to be trusted, derives from Ned Lud, "a person of weak intellect . . . who in a fit of insane rage rushed into a 'stockinger's' house, and destroyed two frames so completely that the saying, 'Lud must have been here' came to be used throughout the hosiery districts when a stocking-frame had undergone damage."

Typically, we first learn of the English Luddites in conjunction with the Industrial Revolution; the Luddites, we are told, were frightened about what the new machines meant for their livelihood. We see some of that same fear today with regard to computers. Witness Ian Angell's concern that robots will replace service workers in the information age (see "Winners and Losers in the Information Age," p. 354). Or Laura L. Nash's sense of how the new communications technology undermines job security ("The Virtual Job," p. 348). Or Ellen Ullman's worries about how "interactivity" alters character ("Getting Close to the Machine," p. 430).

In paragraph 17, when Wendy Lesser's friend calls her a "confirmed Luddite," he's calling her a technophobe. But she's "not a complete antitechnologist," as paragraph 2 makes clear. Not only does she use a great deal of technology, she sings its praises, writing "in our day, technology can substitute for and even generate the freeing effects of wealth." That said, her resistance to, and subsequent appreciation of, e-mail centers on what she see as the virtues of the personal letter. There are other reasons for her resistance — paranoia about damaging her hard disk, an early conflation of e-mail and the Internet, a belief that e-mail is connected to the death of the book — but her essay centers on comparison to the letter.

What does she initially feel a personal letter can do that e-mail can't? Though personal letters were once "central" to her life, Lesser says she "grew out of" them. Ask students why, especially given how much she treasures "the second life" that letters offer (para. 22). The e-mail helps "restore" the personal letter to Lesser's life, and what she discovers, as she uses the technology, is that her earlier fears were ungrounded. Personal style is not obliterated by the computer. Rather, the technology offers a new means of expression. Indeed, even her eventual response to the device reflects her personality, as much as it reflects her New York friend's quirks. Though she once feared that the medium would be the message, now she sees how the medium offers interesting possibilities for the message. She notes "the special enticements of the form's mixed nature . . . so that it seems to combine the two oldest types of American writing, the diary and the sermon."

Once she's been convinced of e-mail's virtues for daily communication, Lesser notes that e-mail, unlike so-called snail mail, is portable — you can take your mailbox with you — and e-mail is unconnected to a transmitting device. Her mailbox is still "there," even after her computer is stolen. What's more, e-mail is never anonymous (which is, of course, a mixed blessing).

Lesser concludes with something like an ontology of e-mail, defining e-mail's nature as paradoxically instantaneous and timeless. Rather than losing something by using this technology — and the most common complaint about contemporary technology is that it makes us less human and less able to connect in normal ways — Lesser argues that e-mail gives us something we once had — the personal letter, a childlike curiosity about the magic mailbox (unlocatable but still "there"), and "the chance to *gain* a soul rather than lose one." E-mail doesn't further estrange us from others but "reintroduces" the personal message, through which we maintain and develop friendships, while exercising our most important human capacity, the ability to care for others.

Among the topics Lesser doesn't take up is e-mail's temporary nature. You might ask students how impermanence influences communication. Though Lesser uses e-mail to connect, do students suppose she pours everything into her e-mail messages as she once did with letters?

Ask students to describe Lesser's writing style and voice. You might have them compare her wit to Kurt Andersen's ("Animation Nation," p. 422) or to the satiric essays by Jonathan Swift and George Johnson in Part 9. In which of the pieces does the humor seem the most intelligent, fresh, and amusing?

WRITING SUGGESTION   Do you use the Internet? Why or why not? If you don't have access to the technology, do you feel you're missing something? Explain.

Robert Goodman

THE LUCK BUSINESS (p. 442)

Robert Goodman's excerpt looks at how involvement in legalized gambling compromises the government's role as protector. While the government's original rationale for legalizing gambling may make sense (para. 5), the legalization has added something new to gambling — advertising. Government pursues publicity — and encourages people to gamble more — because essential social programs depend on gambling revenue. As a result, the government is in a paradoxical position: in order to help citizens, it needs to prey on people's dreams, relax its own regulations, and manipulate desires. Such a government may, oddly enough, remind us of gambling's illegal operators. After all, in its promotional role, government considers money the bottom line, it pressures winners (for free advertising), and it actually aids illegal ventures by making the entire enterprise seem healthy.

Of course, Goodman's premise is that gambling *isn't* healthy. Ask students if Goodman should have persuaded readers of gambling's fundamental dangers. What do students think his assumption is based on — moral or economic grounds? or both? Goodman finds government's manipulation of "people's psychological needs and fears" reprehensible, and he's disturbed by the amount spent on researching potential players' psyches. (Certainly, this money, he implies, might be better used for the social programs that gambling supports.)

Goodman says that "people have always dreamed of a lucky break," but "never before have they been so blatantly urged by their political leaders to risk their money in order to transform the declining situation of their lives." Directly hurting its citizens with gambling, government also hurts itself, for how can citizens have respect for or faith in an institution that acts immorally and that substitutes fantasies for an economic climate in which dreams might become reality?

Have students consider the overall structure of this piece. Does the author develop, or simply repeat, his thesis as the chapter proceeds? If they were to revise Goodman's excerpt, which sections would students cut and which would they expand?

WRITING SUGGESTION   Goodman notes that social programs depend on gambling revenue. Though such funding may have its drawbacks (para. 17), what would happen to social programs if the government ceased to heavily promote gambling? Address Goodman's concerns and this question, as you make a case for government's involvement, limited involvement, or retreat from gambling operations.

Oscar Hijuelos

THE MAMBO KINGS PLAY SONGS OF LOVE (p. 449)

Eugenio, the appealing narrator of the opening chapter of Oscar Hijuelos's novel *The Mambo Kings Play Songs of Love*, is a romantic. For him, television is a link to the dead because it offers him an image of his deceased father (in a rerun of an episode of *I Love Lucy*). Because Eugenio is an adult when he tells his story, he knows the promise of the TV image will eventually disappoint. But the young Eugenio doesn't know this yet. He is steeped in the magic of the movies, just as the generation before him was steeped in illusions about the promise of the United States. As a boy, Eugenio's image of Cesar is somewhat at odds with the Cesar he sees before him.

Movies are part of what clouds Eugenio's vision. When Eugenio wakes his uncle from what is probably a despairing dream about Nestor, Eugenio's father, he uses a voice that is borrowed from the movies. (As Louis Menand says in the Insights, "the movies are an encyclopedia of gestures.") For Eugenio, the line between movies and real life is complicated by the way in which the fiction of the *I Love Lucy* television episode resembles the truth of his father's life and by the way TV gives him the father that life has denied him. It's no surprise, then, that even the records that fall on top of Cesar seem, to Eugenio, like "flying saucers in the movies" (para. 20).

Seeing his father on television, Eugenio thinks, "My father . . . He looked so alive!" Presumably, a still image wouldn't make Eugenio feel this way. The television episode, in fact, helps him reconstruct memories of his father. What does the flood of details in the beginning of paragraph 10 suggest about the relationship between memory and the media? In young Eugenio's case, memories of his father gave meaning to the Mambo Kings' image, but the older narrator is remembering the experience of remembering his father, and the television image seems to take on a different meaning. How might the older Eugenio see the episode differently now? Why does he say in paragraph 34 that his father's face seemed beautiful "then . . ."? What is he leaving unsaid with the ellipsis?

What does the story seem to be saying about how television or the movies shape an individual, perhaps even collective, unconscious? You might have students compare their own memories of what they saw on television and then talk about whether there is a shared sense of identity based on those memories. If so, is it meaningful? How?

WRITING SUGGESTION   Find a short story (like James Joyce's "The Dead" or Joyce Carol Oates's "Where Are You Going? Where Have You Been?") that has been made into a movie. (Joyce's story was made into a movie of the same name; Oates's story was made into a movie called *Smooth Talk*.) What was gained and what was lost in the transition to film?

Andrea Dworkin

LETTER FROM A WAR ZONE (p. 454)

Andrea Dworkin's outspoken indictment of pornography focuses on sadism as the defining element in pornography. Does she think all erotica is sadistic? The examples she gives of pornography are inarguably sadistic. But she does say, "We wanted to destroy — not just put some polite limits on but *destroy* — their power to hurt us" (para. 17). Though one probably wouldn't argue with the goal of destroying someone's power to hurt women, the first part of her sentence suggests an impatience with people who want to make distinctions between violent and nonviolent pornography. Is all pornography violent, even if it doesn't depict violence? This is the thorny question that Dworkin doesn't answer. (Students who are interested in the value of suppressing pornography while preserving the freedom to produce and enjoy other sexually explicit material may want to read D. H. Lawrence's essays, written in the late 1920s, against the "censor morons" who banned *Lady Chatterley's Lover*.)

Dworkin's outrage over the pornographic exploitation of women raises all the liberal issues — maddening to her — concerning constitutional restraints that result in protection for manifestly evil behavior. Ask students about the effect of her outrage. Does her fury whip the reader into a similar state of horror and indignation? Does it ever make her seem unreliable?

Consider other details of her argumentative strategy. What parts of her argument are the strongest? (Students will probably find her use of examples effective.) What parts are the weakest? At times, she argues by analogy, comparing her fight to a war and comparing the situation of women to the situation of African Americans during segregation. The former analogy may be more problematic than the latter. Why? Is her statement at the end of paragraph 14 an either-or fallacy? Are there any points where she gives thinkers two options, neither of which seem right?

WRITING SUGGESTIONS (a) Find and read Sallie Tisdale's essay "Talk Dirty to Me," in her book *Talk Dirty to Me: An Intimate Philosophy of Sex* (New York: Doubleday, 1994). Can a feminist be supportive of pornography? Explain.

(b) Analyze Andrea Dworkin's response to those who consider pornography a matter of freedom of speech. Present Dworkin and her opponent's positions, while making your own views clear.

DILEMMAS

Recasting the Problem

Part 9 includes two classic essays — Jonathan Swift's "A Modest Proposal" and George Orwell's "Shooting an Elephant"— as well as recent pieces on troubling issues. The works all share a similar strength in that they recast the terms of a much-debated problem in order to advance discussion. Swift's irony casts light on the subject and tone of the parliamentary proposals and "social solution" papers that he satirizes. Orwell's decision to consider the colonizer-colonized relationship in terms of personal emotions was, for its time, also new. Perhaps Peter Marin and Sallie Tisdale's essays will be most striking for students, since they'll be familiar with other ways in which homelessness and abortion have been presented.

In their final work for class, encourage students to recast a hotly debated dilemma in order to add a new voice to the existing arguments. This will require students to familiarize themselves with the positions of a current debate (that is, to do significant outside research). It will also require students to look intelligently at the *form* of a debate, so they can advance the discussion by helpfully altering it.

Insights

Given that the semester is drawing to a close, you might use George Orwell's quote (from "Politics and the English Language") to discuss how bad writing can be, as Orwell claims elsewhere, "morally bad." Students have been warned away from abstractions, passive expressions, and jargon. So why do politicians use all three? Did they fail freshman English? Perhaps they learned their lessons too well, realizing that because bad writing obscures, it prevents an audience from forming a picture and, thus, from having a clear sense of what's being said. From the politician's point of view, confusion may be a virtue. How else would the populace accept the unacceptable unless it is disguised with vague phrases? Political language aims to do away with opposition simply by disguising politicians' intentions.

Ordinarily, to settle conflicts, we must imagine our opponents' point of view, but this may be hard to do. If we're not suffering, we may not be able to understand the suffering of others, as Karl Menninger suggests. And as Yitzhak Rabin's words — and indeed his life and death — make clear: peace with friends is natural, while peace with enemies may be a contradiction in terms.

Life is a dilemma in its own right. How will we choose what to do with it? Robert Frost's poem and Agnes De Mille's answers seem to contradict one another. Frost suggests that our lives will offer us a clear moment to decide the course of things; De Mille suggests we're never granted such a moment, and yet we make our choices.

Sallie Tisdale

WE DO ABORTIONS HERE (p. 471)

Sallie Tisdale's perspective as insider governs the content of this essay. "We Do Abortions Here" consists of a description of Tisdale's work, its paradoxical character (monotonous, varied, grim, enjoyable), and the way in which it affects both Tisdale and her clients. But the essay is as striking for its approach as its content. In paragraph 4, Tisdale introduces the telescope metaphor that guides her views of abortion, and she concludes, "In abortion the absolute must always be tempered by the contextual, because both are real, both valid, both hard."

Tisdale lets her essay mimic her approach to abortion and thus the movement of the telescope; she sweeps the horizon and then focuses on small details. The paragraphs that focus on the small details take the reader through the upsetting abortion procedure from start to finish. Here, Tisdale presents the grimness of abortion — the actual basin contents — and the ways in which an abortion is a "failure to protect." The surveying paragraphs examine the abortion issue in the context of specific women's lives and specific societal concerns, like the failure of "the great promise of birth control." Taken together, all these paragraphs are Tisdale's position on abortion. Most people in the abortion debate take only one side or another — to admit the validity of the contextual position might damage the absolute position and vice versa. As Tisdale writes, "Privately, even grudgingly, my colleagues might admit the power of abortion to provoke emotion. But they seem to prefer the broad view and disdain the telescope."

At times Tisdale herself has to put the telescope aside, to not even look, to distance herself from the actual abortions, to cultivate "a certain disregard." Still Tisdale points out that those involved with abortions need to draw a boundary for themselves, a boundary between the "up close" and "pulled back" views of abortion. This boundary recognizes the other side of the abortion issue, for if no other side existed, no boundary would be needed. Since Tisdale's position already encompasses the contextual and absolute, she needs boundaries on both sides. She needs to decide where she is going to place herself given her sympathies with the contextual (she is going to allow her "clients to carry their own burden") and where she is going to place herself given her sympathies with the absolute (she is not going to "judge" her clients).

Tisdale holds clear beliefs about abortion that she doesn't present as open to debate. She writes, in paragraph 21, "Abortion is a matter of choice, privacy, control." Despite her convictions, her essay isn't about persuasion as much as it is about sympathy, and as such, it doesn't shy from contradiction. Tisdale describes her own slight dissimulation as nurse along with the fabrications of the antiabortion people who staff "crisis pregnancy centers." In paragraph 17, she admits that in response to the question, "How big is the baby now?" she "sometimes lie[s] a little, weaseling around [the fetus's] infantile features until its clinging power slackens." But she doesn't, then, choose to lie to the reader, for she gives us, in paragraph 18, the very image she withholds from the client. How do we feel about her decision as nurse here? about her decision as writer?

Though Tisdale finds much of her clients' behavior natural — their fear, their relief, their questions about size and shape — she does stumble on the clients' interest in the fetus's gender. Why? Is it surprising that the question comes only from couples? Tisdale tells an anecdote in paragraphs 28 to 29 about a rather unattractive husband who asks the sex of the baby. She then follows it up by using even his ugliness to make her point. What is the effect of this shift from paragraph 29 to 30? Have students explain what Tisdale means when she writes, "In a literal sense, abortion exists because we are able to ask such questions, able to assign a value to the fetus which can shift with changing circumstances."

Have them look at Tisdale's final paragraph. As she closes the narrative of the day that loosely structures her essay, she also closes her argument. Her last line — with its concrete detail ("the freezer door") and abstract hope (imagining "a world where this won't be necessary") — ends with a phrase that is literal and metaphoric and, on both levels, precise and powerful.

WRITING SUGGESTION   Both a pro-choice activist and an antiabortion activist might feel disturbed by Tisdale's essay. Why? In what way does Tisdale's article change the traditional form of the abortion debate?

Peter Marin

THE PREJUDICE AGAINST MEN (p. 479)

Peter Marin looks at prejudice against men in light of his long-standing interest in how society views — and creates and treats — the homeless. Though advocates for the homeless have focused attention on women and children — in order to gain public sympathy — Marin argues that homelessness is "essentially a problem of *single adult men*." Statistics (para. 2) bear him out, as does the nature of our welfare system, which provides, however poorly, for women and children who have bouts with homelessness but are not as chronically homeless as men. "Homelessness," Peter Marin concludes, "is a problem involving what happens to men without money, or men in trouble." As we know from Robert J. Sternberg ("What Should We Ask About Intelligence?," p. 269), to solve a problem, you need to ask the right question. Ask students if, by paragraph 6, Marin has convinced them that the right question about homelessness is "Why do so many more men than women end up on the streets?" If students say yes, ask how Marin managed to persuade them in so short a space. They may refer to the statistics in paragraph 2. They may also note that Marin's qualifying statement, in paragraph 5, prevents him from overstating his case, while making him appear reasonable and caring. (Later, in paragraph 15, Marin qualifies a claim by self-consciously answering a voice — his own? the reader's? — with a "Yes, I know." Who is Marin's ideal reader? What are the clues that he's writing for a liberal, intelligent, compassionate, skeptical person?)

Marin answers the question he poses in paragraph 6 by initially resorting to several short paragraphs, each starting with a "first," "second," and so on. Ask students why Marin does this. They should see that Marin wants to dispatch quickly with the simplest of answers, the ones that need little explanation, so he can move on to other matters. He stops numbering reasons when he needs to elaborate on his points, even though he continues his "list" through paragraph 20, talking about work and then the federal welfare system.

According to Marin, the people who are now the homeless were once men doing "the kinds of work associated with transient or marginal life." The homeless have always been with us; they just once had jobs and, presumably, homes, however bleak. The homeless are society's marginalized citizens, and society has always produced people destined to live on the margins. Poverty and joblessness marginalize, but Marin doesn't expand on these factors because he suspects a focus on poverty and joblessness ignores who the marginalized *are* — men who've been failed by schools or families or years in war, men who can no longer cope. If they scraped by with labor jobs in the past, they now find these jobs gone or occupied by women and teens.

If they turn to the government for help, the homeless learn what Marin thinks too few of us know — that welfare consists of Social Security Disability Insurance (SSDI) and Aid for Families with Dependent Children (AFDC). In other words, the system has no way of providing for adult men without handicaps. Men are not only denied aid, but, through AFDC, they're denied homes. Ironically, the system designed to help women helps them only if men are absent.

Having provided seven reasons why men are more likely than women to end up on the street, Marin asks another question: "Is this merely an accidental glitch in the system"? The question is directed to the federal welfare system's limitations. Marin is asking why we don't have a system to help men. His answer has to do with society's attitudes, most of them unexamined, about men. Men, we believe, should not be helpless. If they are helpless, it is probably their own fault. To measure the truth of his conclusion, Marin asks readers to consider their own reaction to a group of homeless men and a group of homeless women. Our instinctual response — blame for men, sympathy for women — tells us a lot about what we might not even know we think. (Elsewhere, Marin has written about the matter alluded to in paragraph 26 — our fear of the homeless, our sense that they are dangerous, beyond social control, and thus to be hidden rather than helped.)

How deep-seated are our prejudices against men? They go back to the Bible and the Victorian age. But that doesn't mean they're based on truth. Indeed, they fly in the face of Marin's conviction — based on extensive observation — that the homeless feel a helplessness they can't overcome on their own. The homeless themselves may be sufficiently affected by society's cultural myths not to admit their own helplessness, but Marin provides examples (para. 34 to 36) of men who seem, as he later writes, "'orphaned' . . . deprived somewhere along the line of the kinds of connection, support, and sustenance that enable people to find and keep places in the social order." This is an economic problem, of course, but it is also a problem about psychological damage and social failure. Homeless men are victims, Marin says. Why is it hard to recognize this? War is "the greatest violence done to men," and yet we "fail to see it as a form of oppression." And men don't need to be veterans to be "legitimate" victims. Marin writes, "There are a thousand quiet and gradual ways American lives can fall apart or come to nothing." Some men, for whatever reason, are "genuinely unable to handle the stress others can tolerate."

And all of us, of course, experience stress. Marin views America as a country that is "equal parts of freedom and isolation and individualism and demands for obedience and submission." It's almost surprising there aren't more people who collapse under this "strange and wearing mix." Those who do are ironically the ones who despair the most when they realize no one will help them. Presumably, the additional psychological damage makes it that much harder for these men to help themselves.

A bleak picture. So what can we do to help? Paragraphs 46 and 47 list several necessary long-term social changes and short-term solutions, though Marin suggests none are likely to come about. Is he being defeatist? Realistic? If his essay has been a call to arms, these paragraphs may surprise students. Just when they're ready to do something, he seems to say nothing can be done. But the essay continues on for two more paragraphs. Why does Marin elaborate on only one possible solution in paragraph 48? Is this idea somehow better than the ones presented in paragraph 47? Its virtues may have to do with something Marin has written about elsewhere: you can't necessarily unmarginalize the marginal. Jobs of the sort first discussed in paragraph 12 allow men to remain marginal — if that's all they're capable of — while providing them with work, some money, and a home. But even this solution isn't liable to be implemented without a change in attitudes toward men. Marin makes clear that even attempts at solutions presuppose our willingness to revise our notions about men.

WRITING SUGGESTION   Marin argues that federal welfare policy has contributed to the problem of homelessness. Others have argued that public policy toward mental illness has flooded our streets with those who can't take care of themselves. Do research on present mental illness policies, and then argue for an ideal policy that considers the relevant economic, health, and human rights issues.

Jonathan Swift

A MODEST PROPOSAL (p. 489)

Some historical background will help students fully understand this piece. The Catholics of Ireland supported James Francis Edward Stuart, "the Pretender" (para. 1), in his war for the English throne. When he failed, the English confiscated his supporters' land and took away, among other things, their right to vote, bear arms, run schools, and own luxuries. The Irish Catholics also had to pay rent to those landowners who supported the king and lived in England to dodge taxes and avoid the payment of church duties. The result was widespread poverty in Ireland. In 1729, when this piece was written, the Irish farmlands had been subjected to three years of drought, and there were some 35,000 beggars wandering the country. Some Irish may, as the fictitious narrator suggests, have gone to fight for the exiled Pretender; others sold themselves as indentured servants.

This essay is probably the most famous satire in the English language, and it is widely used in writing courses to point out, among other things, the uses of irony, sarcasm, and satire. Some of Swift's contemporaries didn't understand that he had adopted a persona in writing this piece and were outraged. Ask your students when they realized Swift was being ironic.

Ask students to describe Swift's persona here. Clearly, this man is evil — unlike Swift, who is incensed at the English cruelty he has seen. Nonetheless, the speaker takes pains to appear all the things he is not — caring, thoughtful, selfless, rational, sincere, and humble. In his mind, his proposal is "modest," both because it is moderate in tone and because a reasonable man puts it forward. The irony comes when he details his plan, for it is malevolent and violent in the extreme. There's a similar irony in the way the narrator says he intends to present his argument — clearly and briefly — and the language he actually uses, which is full of official jargon, repetitions, and digressions.

Swift's real targets here are religious intolerance, the cruel English landlords who destroyed the Irish economy, and the moral bankruptcy that allows officials to sacrifice human life for a supposedly well-meaning social program. Swift also satirizes the very literary form he is using, making fun of the speeches and papers that offer solutions to horrendous problems. Swift does this by using a classic debate structure for his piece: he presents the need for a change, a specific suggestion, his proposal's advantages, and a refutation of possible objections. In doing this, Swift satirizes the conventional styles of address. Among other things, he points to how data can be used to support even the most outlandish of points.

When Swift speaks of landlords who "have already devoured most of the parents" (para. 12), his own voice shines through his fictional persona's. This happens, too, at the end of paragraphs 21 and 31. Ask students to identify other places where Swift himself seems to be speaking. Does paragraph 29 represent Swift's true proposal?

WRITING SUGGESTION   Find and analyze a recent proposal to deal with a current social problem. What is the writer's strategy for making the proposal acceptable to the reader? Does the strategy work? Why or why not?

George Johnson

DARK MATTER LIGHTS THE VOID (p. 497)

"Dark Matter Lights the Void" is an opinion piece but also an informational essay. Its success depends on its ability to persuade, inform, and entertain. Ask students to evaluate the essay's success on these three terms.

Like Swift, George Johnson uses a fanciful conceit to make his point. While Swift's satire was new for its time, the extraterrestrial-viewing-the-strange-earthling notion is a bit shopworn. You might ask students if Johnson's piece strikes them as genuinely funny or if it is straining for laughs. How, ideally, should humor work in an essay?

It's possible that the joke here obscures rather than clarifies Johnson's material. It's not that Johnson's argument isn't clear: he's making fun of scientists who say, essentially, "If the facts don't fit the theory, the facts must change." But Johnson's humor may obscure his facts. It's probably fair to say the general public doesn't really understand dark matter, ordinary matter, dead stars, white dwarfs, weakly interacting massive particles, or massive compact halo objects. Johnson assumes we're conversant with Newton's laws but offers a quick explanation of the other terms. Still, his humor may risk confusing the reader: for instance, are the terms *WIMP* and *MACHO* acronyms for real theories or part of the joke?

Johnson is responding to the same frustration Swift feels about the powers that be in "A Modest Proposal" (p. 489). As Johnson sees it, astronomers — or at least those who determine what is going on in the field — have consistently based their notions on an earlier mistake. Ask students to explain the mistake according to Johnson. Is he blaming Newton in particular? What larger forces seem to be at work in perpetuating the astronomers' misconception? Curiously, Johnson seems to think that astronomers believe humans are the center of the universe, even though they've proved otherwise.

WRITING SUGGESTION   Write a research paper in which you explore dark matter. Carefully explain ideas and theories about what it is, and then consider Johnson's views. Is dark matter simply a fashionable theory, or does it appear to explain some things about our universe?

Bel Kaufman

SUNDAY IN THE PARK (p. 500)

The brutishness of the bully in this story tears down the fabric that is civility, and reacting with force against him would also violate our code of decent behavior. But it seems that doing nothing about the bully also betrays some standard of conduct. At the conclusion of the story, all the characters have been demeaned by their behavior during the episode. In such a trivial confrontation, would it have been absurd for Morton to defend his honor? Morton would surely look better in our eyes if he had some higher reason — such as a doctrine of nonviolence — for turning away from the aggressor.

Ask students if the wife in this story doesn't, on some level, desire a fight. What does it mean that she uses, in the final line of the story, the childish retort of the man at the park?

How are class issues a part of this story?

WRITING SUGGESTION   Use the game theory of shame, honor, and dignity that William Ian Miller employs in his essay "Gifts and Honor: An Exchange" (p. 391) to explain why the couple in this story act the way they do when they leave the park.

George Orwell

SHOOTING AN ELEPHANT (p. 504)

Students will easily grasp George Orwell's main point that tyranny enslaves the tyrant as well as the oppressed. But they may decide that Orwell himself is a racist rather than a writer using irony to describe the way imperial power influences the mindset, as well as the behavior, of the imperialist. As a representative of European forces, Orwell is not able to prevent the Burmese from hating him or from requiring a certain sort of behavior from him in the scene with the elephant. Even worse, perhaps, is that he's not able to sustain his own humanistic views over the course of his tenure as a subdivisional police officer.

Orwell tells this story from a distance at a time when his political sympathies and emotions are in accord. While in Burma, Orwell, despite his political leanings, felt both contempt for and some fear of the Burmese. He begins his essay by writing, "In Moulmein, in Lower Burma, I was hated by large numbers of people — the only time in my life that I have been important enough for this to happen to me." Quickly, however, he establishes that "I had already made up my mind that imperialism was an evil thing and the sooner I chucked up my job and got out of it the better." In paragraph 2, Orwell clarifies his attitude toward imperialism: he is not one of the bad guys. And yet he acts like a bad guy. Orwell's use of derogatory language ("sneering yellow faces," "the evil-spirited little beasts") and his attitude toward the behavior of the Burmese show that he is not free of the dehumanizing effects of the imperialism he has to enforce.

In looking back at his younger self, Orwell self-critically reveals his apparent lack of emotional sympathy for the Burmese. He shows, too, that the emotions he withheld from human beings flowed intuitively toward the elephant. One of the piece's great ironies — an intended one — is the lengthy, loving description of the elephant's death. Here, Orwell personifies the elephant — its "preoccupied grandmotherly air," its grave and pitiful death in paragraph 11 — while he adopts the colonizer's dehumanizing language to talk about the Burmese. He sees them, as he has been instructed to, generically. They have "their bit of fun," he writes, over and over again, using an entirely patronizing phrase, and he speaks of their "devilish roar of glee" at the elephant's murder.

In the situation with the elephant, the real power belongs to the tyrannized Burmese and not the individual tyrannizer (that is, not to Orwell in his official role). Ultimately the source of tyranny is British imperialism, and the sarcastic close makes the full ugliness and inhumanity of that imperialism apparent.

Ask students to locate the essay's thesis sentence and explain why it is placed where it is. Also, ask them to consider why the essay was written by a reminiscent narrator, instead of in the voice of the young Orwell. Finally, you might have them consider why the piece doesn't begin with paragraph 3.

WRITING SUGGESTION   What is the historical context for this essay, written in 1936? What relevance does the essay have for contemporary society?

John Hoberman

STEROIDS AND SPORTS (p. 511)

Although this excerpt from a longer essay by Hoberman focuses on the difficulties of defining *doping*, students may be confused because there is no clear definition of the term at the outset. Of course, readers can guess that *doping* refers to an ethically questionable use of drugs to improve athletic performance, but that may not clarify some of Hoberman's more imprecise language, such as his references to "the doping concept" and "the 'doping' issue."

One of this excerpt's weaknesses is the overly broad claim in the fourth and fifth sentences of the opening paragraph. Ask students to identify places where Hoberman's language feels complex or where they don't understand what he's saying. Then have the class rewrite these sentences. Hoberman's language is, on occasion, needlessly complex. Consider the second sentence of paragraph 3. How might it be simplified? What about the final sentence of paragraph 4?

Hoberman is skilled at laying out the points of his argument and at giving examples. His overall analysis has to do with how and why drug use is reprehensible in one context and acceptable in another. He leaves aside the whole issue of the medical use of drugs and focuses on "performance-enhancing" and "therapeutic" uses. For most people, the distinction between them is irrelevant. For those involved in sports, it is not. Sports are "a special index of human capacity," and as such, the integrity of the activity is threatened by the improper use of drugs.

But what constitutes improper drug use? Hard to say, Hoberman argues. For years, people relied on "moral intuition" to make the distinction between illicit performance-enhancing drugs and licit therapeutic ones. But moral intuition may succumb, virtually unwittingly, to doping, especially since the cultural pressures for enhancement are so great.

Doping can't be easily condemned because it so resembles drug therapy, which as Hoberman points out, people have come to accept as a reasonable remedy for everyday conditions. Hoberman applies his general analysis to steroids in paragraphs 13 to 15. Steroids have a legal medical use and an illegal performance-enhancing use. The performance-enhancing use is widespread and even advocated by certain sports physicians. If the drug came to have a widely accepted therapeutic use, what would happen? What, Hoberman wonders, if people used the drug to strengthen aging muscles or improve sexual functioning in the elderly? He answers by saying there would no longer be a difference between the therapeutic and performance-enhancing uses of the drug. If low doses of the medicine were certified as safe, the drug would be gentrified.

Have students consider the claim of paragraph 14 in light of steroids. What has the author failed to acknowledge? The most notable failure is assuming that a drug that has medical and performance-enhancing uses isn't dangerous. People who take steroids for medical reasons take them only because the dangers of their medical condition are more serious than the dangers of the drug. Might the dangers — and the drastic consequences of misusing steroids by not correctly adjusting one's doses — argue as much as anything against the popularization of the drug? What about the drug's side effects, which are also considerable? To be fair, Hoberman imagines only that low doses of the drug might be considered safe at some point in the future.

Gentrification of drugs, Hoberman says, will make it harder and harder to protest doping in sports. Ask students why. In the end, Hoberman concludes that such ambiguities will "promote the medicalization of everyday life at the expense of our sense of human independence from scientific domination." Students might be asked to consider this conclusion against Leon R. Kass's fears in "The Moral Repugnance of Cloning" (p. 517) or to note how Hoberman's final image resonates with James B. Twitchell's claims about Adcult in "But First, A Word from Our Sponsor" (p. 425).

WRITING SUGGESTION   Write a research paper on the medical and performance-enhancing uses of steroids. Given your information, do you think that there are ethical issues involved in using steroids as a therapeutic drug? Why or why not?

Leon R. Kass

THE MORAL REPUGNANCE OF CLONING (p. 517)

If Leon R. Kass is right, people are universally repulsed by the idea of cloning. So why write an article objecting to it? Before students answer this question, you might point out that it's possible to agree with someone's conclusions but not with the way they reach their conclusions or even necessarily with their method of arguing. Ask students to consider how Kass's essay could be used to make a case against lesbian couples who want to be parents or infertile couples who choose in-vitro fertilization or an unmarried woman in her thirties who conceives through a sperm bank.

Exactly what is cloning? Kass assumes two things: cloning is asexual, and it produces a "genetically identical copy." Our repulsion about cloning is most likely due to the second feature; Kass uses this to make faulty emotional appeals to the reader. Such appeals — normally to a reader's fears or sympathies — often have the effect of concealing the real issue. And what is the real issue here? There does not, at present, seem to be a reason to think the monstrous scenarios of paragraphs 3 and 16 are technologically feasible (or desirable in anyone's mind). The real issue for Kass may be asexual reproduction. In other words, Kass's essay may be setting up a straw-man argument; Kass may be less interested in convincing readers of what (according to him) they already believe than of contesting "the ruling opinions of our new age," among them the notion that sexuality is a "cultural construction."

But Kass's argument is structured around cloning. He starts by explaining that there are three typical ways of looking at cloning — through a technological, liberal, or meliorist lens. Each of these suggests its own ethical evaluation. (Who, one might ask, holds these views?) And each fails to address the issue of human procreation. The correct view, Kass says, is an "anthropologic, social . . . , ontological perspective" from which cloning appears to be "a major violation, of our given nature as embodied, gendered and engendering beings — and of the social relations built on this natural ground." Ask students what kind of "social relations" Kass is referring to. Does homosexual parenting (through adoption or artificial insemination) violate these social relations? What about single-parenthood?

Of course, true asexual parenting, the technology of cloning, doesn't manipulate sperm and eggs, as does current reproductive technology. The asexual nature of cloning stems from the fact that it involves "duplication," a notion that "threatens confusion of identity and individuality" and reduces procreation to manufacturing. The "despotism" of cloning has to do with its clear relationship to eugenics, and even though we currently embrace the "negative eugenics" of prenatal and genetic testing, positive eugenics has nothing to do with "a norm of health" but rather with questionable notions of perfectibility.

WRITING SUGGESTION   Who benefits from current reproductive technology? Write a research paper on artificial insemination or in-vitro fertilization in which you answer this question as you examine related ethical issues.